Consumer**Behavior**

2e

Frank R. Kardes
University of Cincinnati

Maria L. Cronley
Miami University

Thomas W. Cline
Saint Vincent College

Australia • Brazil • Mexico • Singapore • United Kingdom • United States

***Consumer Behavior,* Second Edition**
**Frank R. Kardes, Maria L. Cronley,
Thomas W. Cline**

Senior Vice President, Global Product Manager,
Higher Education: Jack W. Calhoun

Vice President, General Manager, Social Science &
Qualitative Business: Erin Joyner

Product Director: Mike Schenk

Sr. Product Manager: Jason Fremder

Associate Content Developer: Josh Wells

Sr. Product Assistant: Megan Fischer

Sr. Content Project Manager: Martha Conway

Associate Media Developer: Elizabeth Beiting-Lipps

Manufacturing Planner: Ron Montgomery

Sr. Marketing Manager: Robin LeFevre

Production Service: diacriTech

Sr. Rights Acquisitions Specialist, Text and
Image: Deanna Ettinger

Sr. Art Director: Stacy Jenkins Shirley

Internal Designer: Mike Stratton

Cover Designer: Mike Stratton

Cover and Part Opener Image: © iStockphoto.
com/csm_web

Global Perspectives icon: © iStockphoto.com/
soberve

Ethics icon: © iStockphoto.com/DrAfter123

Marketing in Action icon: © iStockphoto.com/
DrAfter123

All tables, figures, and exhibits not sourced or
credited: © Cengage Learning.

For product information and technology assistance, contact us at
**Cengage Customer & Sales Support, 1-800-354-9706
or support.cengage.com.**

For permission to use material from this text or product, submit all
requests online at **www.cengage.com/permissions.**

Exam*View*® is a registered trademark of eInstruction Corp. Windows is
a registered trademark of the Microsoft Corporation used herein under
license. Macintosh and Power Macintosh are registered trademarks of
Apple Computer, Inc. used herein under license.
© 2008 Cengage Learning. All Rights Reserved.

Library of Congress Control Number: 2013950682

ISBN 13: 978-1-133-58767-5
ISBN 10: 1-133-58767-4

Cengage
20 Channel Street
Boston, MA 02210
USA

Cengage is a leading provider of customized learning solutions
with employees residing in nearly 40 different countries and sales in more
than 125 countries around the world. Find your local representative at:
www.cengage.com.

Cengage products are represented in Canada by Nelson Education, Ltd.

To learn more about Cengage platforms and services, register or access
your online learning solution, or purchase materials for your course,
visit **www.cengage.com.**

Printed in Mexico
Print Number: 06   Print Year: 2019

Brief Contents

*These two chapters are available on the book's companion website, accessible at www.cengage.com.

Contents

Contents |

Contents |

Contents |

*Chapters 18–19 are available on the companion website, accessible at www.cengage.com.

Preface

Businesses spend enormous amounts of time, money, and other resources on monitoring, predicting, understanding, and influencing the behavior of consumers. Success depends on convincing consumers to use their products and services rather than competitors' offerings. Toward this end, consumers are inundated by marketing communications in the traditional media (e.g., television, radio, print advertising, and direct mail), the new media (e.g., Internet), and in retail stores (e.g., packaging and point-of-purchase displays). However, effective marketing requires an in-depth understanding of the variables that capture the attention and interest of consumers; that influence how consumers acquire, retain, and update product knowledge; and that influence how consumers use product knowledge as a basis for judgment and choice.

Consumer behavior encompasses all consumer activities associated with the purchase, use, and disposal of goods and services, including the consumer's emotional, mental, and behavioral responses that precede, determine, or follow these activities. The unwavering focus on the consumer is the unique contribution of marketing that distinguishes this activity from the other business functions (e.g., accounting, finance, production, management). An in-depth understanding of consumers is needed to develop better products and services, to market these products and services more effectively, and to achieve a sustainable competitive advantage.

This book provides in-depth, scientifically grounded explanations of consumer behavior without sacrificing breadth. We discuss a variety of "classic" consumer behavior topics, including consumer information processing, consumer decision making, persuasion, and the role of culture and society on consumer behavior. In addition, we address some novel topics that enhance the usefulness and impact of the text, including an emphasis on international and ethical perspectives, an examination of "contemporary" or "state-of-the-art" media, and a discussion of online tactics and branding strategies. In summary, we aim to strike a balance among theoretical concepts, research findings, and applied marketing examples to achieve a strong, consumer-focused, strategy-oriented approach.

Organization of the Book

This book is organized in five main parts. Part One focuses on consumer behavior and marketing strategy. It explores what consumer behavior comprises, how it fits into the larger field of marketing, and how marketers study it. Part One also explains how marketing managers use their research-based knowledge about consumers to develop more effective segmentation, positioning, and branding strategies. Effective strategic decisions related to segmentation, positioning, and branding are essential for successful marketing practice.

Part Two focuses on consumer information processing, or the steps or stages of thinking and reasoning that influence how consumers acquire, retain, and revise product knowledge. Here, we take an internal view of the consumer to examine how these fickle, stubborn, passionate, and fascinating creatures interact with the marketing world by processing information and making decisions.

Part Three focuses on consumer decision making, or how consumers use their knowledge about products and services to choose the brands they buy. The chapters in Part Three break down consumer decision making and examine each step in detail.

Part Four focuses on consumer social influences and contemporary strategies for marketers. It looks at the influence of consumer self-concept and personality and how those interact with the more external influences of culture, values, and the influence of others on consumers and their behaviors. Part Four also explains how to reach consumers more effectively and how to develop more effective online tactics.

Part Five focuses on common biases and errors in managerial decision making and how to avoid them. Even experts are susceptible to a wide range of decision-making biases that can hurt business. A clearer understanding of managers' decision-making processes helps managers to avoid some common pitfalls. The chapters in Part Five (Chapters 18 and 19) can be found on the book companion site, accessible at www.cengage.com.

Finally, it should be noted that although the chapters are presented in separate sections in this book, all chapters, topics, and themes are related to all the others.

Pedagogical Enhancements

We believe that students work best when they can see phenomena from all angles—when they can understand what theories and concepts mean, see how they integrate with other concepts, and see how they are applied to smart business practice. To help students understand, apply, and integrate the concepts of consumer behavior in terms of real companies and marketing situations, this book is filled with a variety of features that heavily emphasize interesting examples, strong visuals, and applied exercises.

Part Features

Each of the first four parts of the book begins with an interview with one or two well-respected consumer researchers to stimulate student interest. This helps set the tone for each part, providing a "big picture" of its theme that helps students understand the relevance of the topics addressed in the part.

Chapter Features

Each chapter includes a variety of aids to enrich student interaction and learning, including:

- **Learning Objectives.** A list of key concepts and objectives for each chapter.
- **Opening Vignette.** A mini-case using a real company, product, or situation to bring the subject of the chapter alive.
- **Marketing in Action.** A feature that illustrates the use of various consumer behavior concepts in the practice of marketing for a real company, product, or situation.
- **Global Perspectives.** A feature that discusses the use of consumer behavior concepts in real companies, products, or situations in international contexts.
- **Ethics.** A feature to increase student sensitivity to ethical issues and to stimulate classroom discussion.
- **Advertisements, Websites, Photos, Charts, and Illustrations.** Specific examples show students how companies attempt to persuade and influence consumers. Numerous photographs and illustrations of products, package designs, and consumers in action increase student interest and involvement in the material.
- **Chapter Summary.** An overview of key topics and concepts addressed in the chapter. Students can check their comprehension of the material by reviewing the summary.
- **Key Terms.** A list of the key concepts presented in the chapter, which can be used to reinforce students' comprehension.
- **Review and Discussion.** Questions to encourage students to think critically about what they have just read.
- **Short Application Exercises.** Questions help students apply the knowledge they have gained from reading the chapter.
- **Managerial Application.** A mini-case problem requiring the use of multiple concepts discussed in the chapter.
- **Marketing Metrics.** At the end of selected chapters is a short marketing statistics problem with an accompanying data set

The *Consumer Behavior* Resource Package

Teaching consumer behavior is an exciting and challenging task. A comprehensive set of ancillary materials has been created to support instructors.

For the Instructor

Instructor's Manual This teaching tool provides suggestions and additional assignments designed to supplement the textbook and help enhance the classroom experience. Each chapter includes the following materials:

- Learning objectives and teaching tips
- Lecture outlines

- Answers to review and discussion questions
- Suggested classroom activities and assignments

The Instructor's Manual can be downloaded from the book companion site, accessible at www.cengage.com/login.

Test Bank Cengage Learning Testing Powered by Cognero is a flexible, online system that allows you to:

- Author, edit, and manage test bank content from multiple Cengage Learning solutions
- Create multiple test versions in an instant
- Deliver tests from your LMS, your classroom or wherever you want

Start right away!
Cengage Learning Testing Powered by Cognero works on any operating system or browser.

- No special installs or downloads needed
- Create tests from school, home, the coffee shop—anywhere with Internet access

What will you find?

- Simplicity at every step. A desktop-inspired interface features drop-down menus and familiar, intuitive tools that take you through content creation and management with ease.
- Full-featured test generator. Create ideal assessments with your choice of 15 question types (including true/false, multiple choice, opinion scale/Likert, and essay). Multi-language support, an equation editor, and unlimited metadata help ensure your tests are complete and compliant.
- Cross-compatible capability. Import and export content into other systems.

For *Consumer Behavior* 2e, the test bank contains more than 1,200 questions, including a mix of:

- Definitional questions that test knowledge of concepts
- Conceptual questions that test the ability to recognize concepts and relate to situations
- Applied questions that test the ability to integrate and apply concepts

Question formats include multiple-choice, true/false, and essay questions for each chapter.

Recent pressure on faculty and institutions to implement and report on learning outcome requirements by the AACSB and other accreditation bodies is a challenge in higher education. The development of *Consumer Behavior* has given us the opportunity to help faculty meet these needs. We have tagged test items with general business and marketing discipline outcomes that allow you to more easily produce learning outcome reports for accreditation purposes.

PowerPoint Presentation A comprehensive set of PowerPoint slides is available to adopters of the textbook. These chapter-by-chapter slides include important figures, tables, and graphs taken directly from the text, as well as an overview of the key concepts of each chapter. These user-friendly PowerPoint slides can be used "as is" or integrated with the instructor's own PowerPoint presentations. Instructors can modify or delete any slide or add their own slides to the existing set. In addition, instructors may choose to share the slides with students by uploading them to the school's network. The PowerPoint slides are available on the book companion site, accessible at www.cengage.com.

Additional Online Chapters Part 5 of the textbook (Chapters 18, "Biases in Managerial Decision Making" and Chapter 19, "Strategies for Improving Managerial Decision Making") can be found on the book companion site, accessible at www.cengage.com.

Acknowledgments

We would like to warmly acknowledge the many helpful comments and insights from David Ackerman, Ph.D. (California State University—Northridge), Ronald J. Adams, Ph.D. (University of North Florida), Jeri Mullins Beggs (Illinois State University), Nivein A. Behairy, Ph.D. (University of California—Irvine), Drew Boyd (Ethicon EndoSurgery), Deborah L. Cowles, Ph.D. (Virginia Commonwealth University), Susan Emens (Kent State University), Vicki Blakney Eveland, DBA, (Mercer University), Annette D. Forti, DBA (SUNY College at Old Westbury), Dorothy Harpool (Wichita State University), Curtis Haugtvedt, Ph.D. (Ohio State University), Dale F. Kehr (University of Memphis), Michael Lynn, Ph.D. (Cornell University), Susan Powell Mantel, Ph.D. (Ball State University), Havva J. Meric, Ph.D. (East Carolina University), Bruce E. Pfeiffer, Ph.D. (University of New Hampshire), Andrew J. Rohm, Ph.D. (Northeastern University), Joel Saegert, Ph.D. (The University of Texas at San Antonio), and Eric Yorkston, Ph.D. (Texas Christian University). Finally, we would like to acknowledge the many undergraduate and graduate students we have taught over the years who have helped shape our thinking for this textbook.

About the Authors

Frank R. Kardes

Frank R. Kardes is the Donald E. Weston Professor of Marketing at the College of Business at the University of Cincinnati. He is a recipient of the Distinguished Scientific Achievement Award of the Society for Consumer Psychology, and a Fellow of the American Psychological Association, the American Psychological Society, the Society for Consumer Psychology, the Society for Experimental Social Psychology, and the Society for Personality and Social Psychology. His research focuses on omission neglect, consumer judgment and inference processes, persuasion and advertising, and consumer and managerial decision making. He has published in many leading scientific journals and is frequently invited to present his research at leading universities throughout the world—including Wharton, Yale, Cornell, Chicago, Northwestern, Michigan, the Australian Graduate School of Management, the London Business School, the Hong Kong University of Science and Technology, and INSEAD (France). Dr. Kardes was an Editor of the *Journal of Consumer Psychology*, *Advances in Consumer Research*, and the *Handbook of Consumer Psychology*, and was an Associate Editor of the *Journal of Consumer Research* and the *Journal of Consumer Psychology*. He is currently Co-Editor of *Marketing Letters*.

Maria L. Cronley

Maria L. Cronley is Interim Associate Dean and Professor of Marketing at the Farmer School of Business at Miami University, in Oxford, Ohio, where she teaches undergraduate and graduate courses in Consumer Behavior, Marketing Research, and Marketing Strategy. She earned her Ph.D. in Marketing from the University of Cincinnati, and her undergraduate degree in business from Bowling Green State University, and brings several years of marketing industry experience to the field. Her primary research interests center on consumer judgment and decision processes, with specific emphasis in the areas of consumer inference, biased processing, persuasion, and healthcare marketing. She sits on the *Journal of Consumer Psychology* Editorial Review Board and has published numerous articles in scholarly journals, including the *Journal of Consumer Psychology*, *Journal of Consumer Research*, *Journal of Public Policy and Marketing*, *Journal of Business Research*, *Journal of Economic Psychology*, *Advances in Consumer Research*, *Health Communication*, and the *Journal of Experimental Psychology: Applied*. She has received over three dozen awards and grants for her scholarship and teaching.

Thomas W. Cline

Thomas W. Cline is Professor of Marketing at the Alex G. McKenna School at Saint Vincent College, where he teaches courses in consumer behavior, marketing research, advertising and promotion, strategic marketing, and statistical methods. He is a recipient of the International Teaching Excellence Award from the Association of College Business Schools and Programs. Dr. Cline has twenty years' experience as a marketing research consultant, specializing in surveys, experimental designs, and focus groups. He earned a Ph.D. at the University of Cincinnati and an MBA from the University of Virginia. Dr. Cline has published numerous articles in academic journals, including the *Journal of Advertising, Journal of Consumer Psychology, Journal of Economic Psychology, Psychology and Marketing,* and *Journal of Marketing Communications.* Dr. Cline is widely cited in the popular press, including *USA Today, Psychology Today, CBS News, The LA Times, MSNBC,* and *The Washington Times.* Dr. Cline also serves as head coach for the men's and women's golf teams for Saint Vincent College, hosted at Arnold Palmer's Latrobe Country Club in Latrobe, PA.

ConsumerBehavior

PART 1

CONSUMER BEHAVIOR AND MARKETING STRATEGY

SEGMENTATION

POSITIONING

© iStockphoto.com/csm_web

CHAPTERS

AN INTERVIEW WITH CHERYL STALLWORTH

Chief Executive Officer
Greenfield Consulting Group

Cheryl Stallworth is the Chief Executive Officer for the Greenfield Consulting Group, a global marketing research firm that specializes in qualitative research methodologies. The Greenfield Consulting Group is part of Millward Brown, one of the top ten global marketing research agencies. As a marketing generalist with expertise in qualitative research methodologies, Greenfield Consulting Group focuses on using insights to develop effective marketing strategies.

Q. Why is it important for companies to acquire a deep understanding of their consumers?

Without a deep understanding of consumers it is impossible to meet their expectations. Going beyond the fundamental "functional" needs, e.g., the need for food and shelter, it is important to understand deeper needs like the need for social acceptance. These are the higher order needs that only surface when marketers dig deeper into brand relationships and how these relationships allow consumers to express themselves. For example, a consumer can tell me that they are purchasing a car because they need transportation. A deeper exploratory of their *real* need is to convey a certain image … so this consumer doesn't need just a *car*, they need a Toyota Prius because they want to be accepted within the tribe of people that are environmentally conscious opinion leaders.

Q. What research techniques do you use to learn about your consumers?

Our company specializes in qualitative research, so these are tools that are not designed to be projectable to large populations. They are designed to allow us to probe deeply into motivations and desires. In addition to focus groups, we practice "qualographies" which are "ethnographic-like" tools that enable us to actively observe and interact with people in real-life environments like their kitchens, or in-store in order to:

- Understand how people interact with categories and brands in a socio-cultural context
- Understand people's rituals, artifacts, and folklore to help de-codify the role and meaning of brands

We also use a number of digital tools that enable us to speak to creative consumers across broad geographies to understand trends, social development, and differences in attitudes based on geographic influencers.

Basic focus groups are a terrific way of letting consumers "play off of" perceptions relative to categories and brands. In order to understand the strengths and weaknesses of a brand's equity, we can create a "consumer brawl" in a focus group with consumers taking opposing sides to "argue" the benefits or drawbacks of a brand and highlight issues and opportunities for positioning enhancement.

These are just examples of the many tools that can be employed to "dig deeply."

Q. How can knowledge about consumer behavior be used to develop more effective segmentation strategies?

Consumers can be clustered based on similar attitudes and behavior to determine which clusters are most similar. This then enables marketers to develop messages that appeal to specific clusters. The size of clusters is often quantified to determine if a viable business opportunity exists.

Q. How can knowledge about consumer behavior be used to develop more effective positioning strategies?

Understanding consumer motivations, attitudes, and ensuing behavior helps determine the role of a category or brand in the consumer's world. Uncovering the brand's role provides the context or language for talking about that brand in a way that makes sense and is useful for the consumer. So, for example, understanding that a consumer feels better about the world that they are living in when they are doing something active to care for the environment, taps into a basic need for well-being (for them and their family). Not saying that Toyota has done this, but a brand like Toyota Pruis can become part of the consumer's "personal toolkit" of products that help them to achieve a personal sense of well-being. Thus, this can then be a position for Prius to play in, based on an insight that well-being is an important attribute/feeling/state-of-mind for environmentally conscious consumers.

Q. How can knowledge about consumer behavior be used to help consumers make better choices?

This knowledge can help marketers develop products and shape messages that actually meet people's needs instead of creating products that "trick" consumers into buying them based on gimmickry. In other words, identifying and delivering against *real* needs allow marketers to develop sustainable long-term relationships with consumers, which is much more efficient and profitable in the long run.

UNDERSTANDING CONSUMER BEHAVIOR AND CONSUMER RESEARCH

OBJECTIVES *After studying this chapter, you will be able to…*

1 Define consumer behavior.

2 Explain why it is important to understand consumer behavior.

3 Describe how the study of consumer behavior has evolved as a scientific field of study.

4 Discuss how consumer behavior is specifically examined and measured through marketing research to develop consumer insights.

5 Examine the marketing research process and discuss various methods for designing and collecting consumer research data.

Reality Television Works for Consumers and Marketers

Reality programming had its humble beginnings in MTV's *The Real World*. Broadcast since 1992, the show is one of the longest running reality shows on television and is usually credited with sparking the reality genre. Today, blockbuster shows such as ABC's *Dancing with the Stars* and CBS's *Survivor* underscore reality programming as a legitimate and predominant genre of television entertainment. Indeed, the most popular reality TV programs, such as *The Voice* and *The Amazing Race*, have been among the top-rated shows over the last several seasons, according to the Nielsen Company's TV Ratings.[1] Every major American television network has produced at least one reality show, and 16% of all primetime television viewing is devoted to reality programming.[2] Furthermore, reality television isn't produced just for American viewers' tastes. *Bargain Hunt* (an antique purchasing contest) appears on UK television, and *Australian Idol* and *Big Brother Italy* (similar to their U.S. counterparts) are popular in those countries.

Reality TV programming is a product, just like t-shirts and coffee, and consumers can't seem to get enough of it. But why do consumers keep watching? This is one type of question that consumer behavior researchers are interested in answering. Why are consumers continually and passionately tuning in to watch a woman in search of Mr. Right, dating a group of eligible bachelors and weeding them out one by one? According to consumer behavior researchers, reality television offers several benefits to consumers, including satisfying their fundamental voyeuristic tendencies. "We all like to watch people in situations where we ourselves might be pressured or tense… It is a safe way of experiencing a socially traumatic event… We can vicariously feel what they are feeling but at a safe distance," says Professor Kip Williams of Macquarie University.[3] We also role-play with ourselves in the context of the show, imagining how we might react in a similar situation, which researchers say can teach us to be self-improving and also improve feelings of self-worth.[4]

Knowing that these shows satisfy consumers and keep them viewing is the biggest reason television producers keep churning them out. But there are also lots of reasons for marketing executives to love reality programming, the most obvious of which is that people are watching, and high ratings mean that the advertisements are also potentially viewed.

Another added benefit of reality programming is that marketers can place their products in the settings of the program, allowing consumers to view the products in the context of everyday living. These subtle product endorsements can't be tuned out like an advertisement; they appear to consumers unsolicited. The contestants on *The Amazing Race* drive around in Fords, while the chefs on *Top Chef* drink out of red Solo cups. In fact, *product placement* is so popular more than half of all broadcast TV product placements during primetime take place on reality shows.[5]

Finally, reality programs are often cheaper to produce than other forms of programming such as dramas or situation comedies, so an advertiser can afford to sponsor a show, place products in the show, run 30-second commercials during the breaks, and block competitors from running advertisements. Coca-Cola is reported to have paid $35 million in one season for its role on Fox's *American Idol*.[6] With the winning combination of consumer devotion and a surplus of revenue-generating opportunities, reality television is a phenomenon that shows how consumers' behaviors can influence an entire industry.

People engage in behaviors as consumers on a daily, even hourly, basis. What purchases have you made in the last few days? Maybe you bought a cup of coffee or something more expensive and long-lasting, like a new cell phone. What were you thinking when you made the purchase? What were you feeling? Even if you didn't actually buy something, you were probably exposed to marketing information in the form of advertisements, product information on packages, opinions from friends or family, and brand symbols on almost everything. Simply being exposed to marketing information is a form of consumer behavior. Consumers devote a great deal of effort, time, and material wealth to evaluating products and services and purchasing and using products of all kinds. Thus, people's behavior as consumers is a critical component of their everyday lives. In our role as consumers, we define our world and our place in it; we interact with the world and collectively, we even shape and change that world, creating phenomena like reality TV.

OBJECTIVE # What Is Consumer Behavior?

Not many years ago, when students opened a textbook on consumer behavior, they read that consumer behavior (usually called *buyer behavior*) involves the study of how consumers decide to buy products. While this definition is accurate, it is an inadequate description of the full scope of activities in which consumers engage prior to purchase and during and after consumption. Contemporary definitions are much broader and try to capture the full range of consumer activities. **Consumer behavior** entails all consumer activities associated with the purchase, use, and disposal of goods and services, including the consumer's emotional, mental,

FIGURE 1.1 | **What Is Consumer Behavior?**

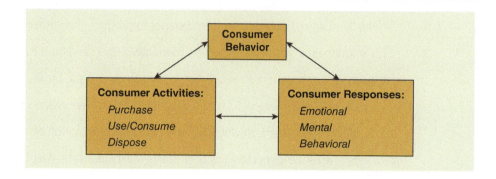

and behavioral responses that precede, determine, or follow these activities (see Figure 1.1).

This definition covers a lot of ground. Let's break down the definition and examine consumers, consumer activities, and consumer responses more closely.

Consumers: Individual versus Organizational

The term "consumer" can describe either individual or organizational consumers. **Individual consumers** purchase goods and services to satisfy their own personal needs and wants or to satisfy the needs and wants of others. Purchases for others can include satisfying household uses, such as filling the family car with gasoline or paying the home's electric bill; gift purchases, such as buying a birthday gift for a brother; or charitable contributions, such as buying cookies from a Girl Scout or a raffle ticket at a school fundraiser. Individual consumers come in all ages, life stages, and social backgrounds; they range from the six-year-old boy begging his mother for chocolate-flavored cereal in the grocery aisle to the 20-something college graduate renting her first apartment to the retired couple in their 70s browsing in antique shops while on vacation.

Organizational consumers purchase goods and services in order to:

- produce other goods or services
- resell them to other organizations or to individual consumers
- help manage and run their organization[7]

For example, Starbucks Coffee Company purchases coffee beans, brewing equipment, and paper cups in order to produce and offer its products. The company also purchases (and repackages) coffee beans to resell to individual consumers and other organizations, such as restaurants and grocery stores. Finally, Starbucks purchases office equipment, uniforms, and cleaning supplies, and may even hire a tax accounting firm—all to help keep the organization running smoothly.

Organizational consumers include for-profit firms, such as manufacturers, farmers, financial institutions, wholesalers, and retailers, and not-for-profit businesses, such as charities, political groups, and civic clubs. Local, state, and federal government agencies and other public institutions such as schools, hospitals, and libraries are also organizational consumers. Although organizational consumer behavior is an important area of study, this book concentrates on individual consumer behavior.

Now that we understand who consumers are, let's examine consumer activities as they relate to our definition of consumer behavior.

Consumer Activities

Consumer behavior is broken down into purchase, use, and disposal activities. Categorizing consumer behavior by type of activity is useful because consumers' responses to stimuli may differ depending on whether they are purchasing, using, or disposing of a single product or service. For example, when leading up to purchase, a long line outside a nightclub or bar is a positive factor in evaluating that club. Long lines imply that everyone wants to go there, and that the club is probably very good. But, after you have purchased your ticket, that long line is no longer a desirable factor, as you impatiently wait to get in. Furthermore, once you make it to the door, that long line ahead of you now means that the club is overly crowded, and therefore, a lot less appealing. So, from this example, categorizing activities by whether they occur prior to purchase versus during use shows how consumer responses can change significantly within a situation. Before we closely examine consumers' responses, let's first consider consumer purchase, use, and disposal activities in more detail.

Purchase activities are those through which consumers acquire goods and services. Purchase activities also include everything done leading up to the purchase, such as gathering and evaluating information about the product or service and choosing where to make the purchase. The purchase method, such as paying with cash or credit, and any additional services desired—home delivery and installation, and extended warranties, for instance—also influence purchase activities. So too are factors unique to the situation, such as the atmosphere of a store, the design of a website, the reason for the purchase, and the amount of time the consumer devotes to the buying decision.

Use activities describe where, when, and how consumption takes place. For example, do consumers immediately consume the product after purchase, like an ice cream cone or a haircut, or do they delay consumption, such as when they buy new clothing for a future occasion or an airline ticket? Is the product consumed as part of a special event, such as going on vacation or attending a wedding, or as part of a special occasion, such as a holiday or birthday, or is it a product used everyday, such as toothpaste? Is the entire product consumed before disposal, such as a movie theater ticket or a candy bar, or is some left unconsumed, such as a pack of chewing gum or ink remaining in a toner cartridge?

Finally, *disposal activities* are the ways consumers get rid of products and/or packaging after consumption, and these include discarding products, recycling, reuse, and resale. For example, sorting biodegradable trash, giving outgrown clothing to charity, and using plastic grocery bags as trash can liners are recycling and reuse behaviors. Reselling is hugely popular today, with opportunities both local and offline, such as garage sales, classified ads, and flea markets; and online, with websites like eBay and Craig's List.

Donating gently used products to charitable organizations is one type of disposal activity.

B Christopher/Alamy

Consumer Responses

Central to our definition of consumer behavior are consumers' emotional, mental, and behavioral responses to goods and their marketing.

Emotional or affective responses reflect a consumer's emotions, feelings, and moods. More specifically, moods are states of mind at a particular time; feelings are the expressions of our moods. Emotion is moods, plus feelings, plus some type of psychological and physical arousal. (We will discuss more about emotion in Chapter 7.) Combined, these elements capture consumers' affective responses. For example, when a consumer buys his first car, both excitement and uncertainty are probably among his affective responses.

Mental or cognitive responses include a consumer's thought processes, opinions, beliefs, attitudes, and intentions about products and services. Weighing the pros and cons of financing a new car, making a mental list of attributes the car should have, and imagining oneself driving that car are some of the cognitive processes a consumer might experience in purchasing a new automobile. Mental responses can be evaluative, involving making a judgment that assigns value to something. They can also be non-evaluative, involving thinking about something without making a value judgment. Cognitive responses can be very specific and refer to one brand or even one attribute of that brand; they can also be very broad and deal with entire categories of products.

Finally, *behavioral responses* include a consumer's overt decisions and actions during the purchase, use, and disposal activities identified earlier. To continue the car purchase example, a consumer is likely to pay close attention to various car advertisements, read online car reviews, read sales literature at the car dealership or on a manufacturer's website, test drive a car prior to purchase, discuss the decision with friends or family, and regularly maintain the car with oil changes after the purchase. Each of these actions exemplifies behavioral responses.

A consumer buying a new car will experience several affective, cognitive, and behavior responses.

OBJECTIVE

Why Study Consumer Behavior?

People study consumer behavior for a variety of reasons and in a variety of contexts, such as a student in a university class, a marketing executive working in an organization, an advertising designer working at a large agency, or a professor teaching and doing scholarly research. Let's examine a few of the benefits of studying consumer behavior, specifically, to improve business performance, to influence public policy, and to educate and help consumers make better decisions.

To Improve Business Performance

Organizations that market products and services often study consumer behavior—or use the results and recommendations of others' research—to improve business performance through customer-focused strategies. Marketers who understand their customers can create better products and services, promote their products and services more effectively, and develop marketing plans and strategies that foster sustainable competitive advantages. Their goal is to understand the general dynamics of consumer behavior that remain constant regardless of fads or trends. This understanding enables marketers to predict what motivates people to buy and then to deliver products that respond to those motivations, thereby successfully meeting and exceeding customer expectations over time.

For example, global consumer goods producer Procter & Gamble (P&G) recently introduced Crest 3D White Intensive Professional Effects Toothpaste and Whitestrips as additions to its hugely successful teeth-whitening dental product line. P&G conducted extensive consumer behavior studies and drew upon everything it knew about consumers when developing and marketing these products. As a result, P&G has gained a significant competitive advantage over its competitors in the home dental products market.

To Influence Public Policy

People working in government agencies or in nonprofit organizations often are called upon to influence public policy and improve society's well-being. *Public policy* is the establishment of laws and regulations that govern business practices in order to protect consumers. Those interested in shaping public policy study consumer behavior to understand the public needs and wants, and at the same time, to protect the public from unfair, unethical, or dangerous business practices. For example, in the packaged foods industry, the use of chemicals and preservatives has steadily increased as manufacturers have developed longer-lasting and more convenient forms of packaged food. In response, consumers have become increasingly concerned about the ingredients in processed food products because of their potential health risks and the nutritional consequences of synthetic additives. As a result, U.S. Food and Drug Administration (FDA) regulations now require marketers of food products to supply nutritional information on product packages in the form of "Nutritional Food Panels."

To Educate and Help Consumers Make Better Decisions

Many people study consumer behavior because they want to educate consumers or help them act responsibly. For example, in addition to enacting labeling laws to protect consumers, the FDA provides detailed advice to consumers on how to interpret dietary information. You can visit the FDA's website on food and nutrition to learn more at http://www.fda.gov. How consumers gather, process, and use information, as well as what motivates them, are important research topics for those interested in consumer education.

Finally, agencies and organizations involved in consumer education and assistance study consumer behaviors that are socially (or individually) destructive. These behaviors are often referred to as the "dark side of consumer behavior." This dark side includes consumer actions that are

US Food and Drug Administration FDA

Nutrition food panels are the result of consumer behavior research related to public policy.

unhealthy, unethical, illegal, and potentially dangerous to individuals or society, such as misusing or overusing products, compulsive purchasing, shoplifting, and product tampering. Governments, businesses, and consumer interest groups want to curb these undesirable behaviors. Accordingly, these groups often study consumer behavior to best formulate strategies to promote positive behaviors (e.g., getting regular mammograms) or aid in the cessation of negative behaviors (e.g., quitting smoking).

Understanding the definition of consumer behavior and examining some of the benefits of studying consumer behavior provide a foundation for how research measures consumer behavior. First, let's look at how consumer behavior became a scientific field of study. This subject is useful in understanding how the current scientific discipline of consumer behavior evolved and suggests future directions for consumer research. In the next few pages, we also discuss how this text approaches the study of consumer behavior.

OBJECTIVE ③ # Consumer Behavior as a Field of Study

Consumer behavior is an applied social science that draws on theories and concepts of psychology, sociology, anthropology, economics, history, and statistics. A fairly young science, the study of consumer behavior emerged in the late 1940s when many firms shifted from a *selling orientation* (the marketing philosophy of focusing on production and the company's capabilities and then selling consumers the excess inventory of what was produced) to producing goods that consumers actually needed and wanted. This change in focus was the beginning of the **marketing concept**, the idea that firms should discover and satisfy customer needs and wants in an efficient and profitable manner, while benefiting the long-term interests of the company's stakeholders.

Today, the marketing concept is a core philosophy for many successful organizations. As a result, these successful organizations focus on delivering customer perceived value and customer delight. **Customer perceived value** "is the consumer's overall assessment of the utility of a product based on perceptions of what is received and what is given."[8] In other words, it is the estimated net gain customers receive from their sacrifice of time, money, and effort expended to purchase, use, and dispose of a product or service (i.e., benefits versus costs). **Customer delight** goes a step beyond customer perceived value, suggesting customer benefits that not only meet, but also exceed expectations in unanticipated ways. P&G executives state that offering customers better value when they first encounter a product in the store and purchase the product, and then subsequently delighting customers during their usage experience with the product, represents fundamental "moments of truth" for the company.[9] In other words, generating value and delight for consumers is essential for long-term success. Likewise, L'Oréal, a French cosmetic company, attempts to create customer delight by offering consumers products in its line of *Nutricosmetics*, products that combines cosmetics and nutrition. The company markets a "beauty pill" that reportedly firms the skin. While both cosmetics and vitamins satisfy customer needs and wants, the interconnection of the two creates *unanticipated* benefits for the consumer, and hence, customer delight.

Global Perspectives

L'Oréal: Delighting Customers with Beauty Inside and Out

L'Oréal, the French cosmetic company known worldwide for its cosmetics and hair-care products, is at the forefront of a marketing concept designed to deliver customer delight. The concept, called *Nutricosmetics*, combines cosmetics and nutrition to offer consumers nutritional supplements with beauty benefits that work from the inside out. The company markets Innéov Firmness and Innéov Hair, oral nutritional supplements that firm the skin and energize and boost the growth of hair, according to laboratory research. Of course, L'Oréal claims the supplements are even more effective when used in conjunction with the company's line of topical anti-aging creams. L'Oréal teamed up with Nestlé, a Swiss multinational company with expertise in nutrition, to create the product. The "beauty pill" contains lacto-lycopene, which is similar to a natural molecule found in tomatoes and soy. The supplement is designed for women over 40 who are concerned about aging and want to improve skin tone and elasticity.[10]

Marketed in Europe, China, and South America, Innéov is a considered a leader in nutritional cosmetics. This is crucial to L'Oréal's success, since nutricosmetics is one of the fastest growing market segments in the global skin care market.[11] While not yet popular in the United States, this market is firmly established globally, especially in Asia, where government regulations for nutricosmetics are well defined. As manufacturers

like L'Oréal continue to invest in new products and educate consumers, nutricosmetics may become a regular part of many consumers' beauty regimes.

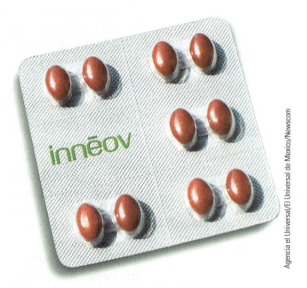

Agencia el Universal/El Universal de Mexico/Newscom

Products that create unanticipated benefits for consumers create customer delight.

Most competitors in a product category can satisfy customers' expectations about the functional benefits of a product or service, but firms gain competitive advantage by anticipating and providing benefits that customers are initially unaware of and/or will desire in the future. Identifying and satisfying consumers' latent demand is critical to providing customer delight.[12] Thus, the overarching goal of a consumer-centered firm is to maximize long-term customer value and delight, while also maximizing profits and doing so better than the competition.

As for the future, the field of consumer behavior will continue to focus on delighting customers, but it is also currently evolving toward a stronger values-based philosophy. This philosophy includes satisfying customer needs and wants and providing customer value and delight, while also supporting the growth of "spirit of humanity." Companies that follow this philosophy believe that in our technologically driven and interconnected global environment, consumers will increasingly demand that companies work toward positive societal change and benefit.[13] For example, Ben & Jerry's is a premium ice cream and novelty company that distinguishes itself with a corporate philosophy that stresses social responsibility and environmental sustainability, which is evidenced in the company's marketing and promotional efforts.

The Evolution of Consumer Behavior Research

How researchers study consumer behavior has also evolved over the past several decades. Three prominent approaches are examined here: motivation research, behavioral science, and Interpretivism.

Motivation Research One of the earliest approaches to studying consumer behavior, *motivation research* applied psychoanalytic therapy concepts from clinical psychology to consumer behavior research. The method was developed by Ernest Dichter, a Freudian psychoanalyst, shortly after World War II. He used in-depth interviewing techniques to uncover a person's hidden or unconscious motivations. In consumer research, an *in-depth interview* (IDI) is a lengthy (sometimes lasting several hours), probing interview, where a carefully trained interviewer extensively questions a subject about his or her purchase motivations. In-depth interviews are more formally described later in this chapter under specific research methods.

During the peak of motivation research's popularity, Dichter performed IDIs in more than 200 different product categories.[14] He applied Freudian interpretations to consumer actions and viewed consumers as largely immature, irrational, and driven by hidden subconscious desires. For example, Dichter believed that an underlying reason for the popularity of canned soup was that women unconsciously associated it with breast milk—nutritious and warm—and therefore didn't feel guilty about serving it in place of preparing a full meal.[15]

Over the years, many advertisers have embraced motivation research because of its seeming ability to tap into deep-rooted needs. For example, Dichter's contention that baking cakes fulfilled a woman's inner desire for children may have helped lead to the Pillsbury doughboy character and slogan, "Nothing says lovin' like something from the oven." Exxon's tiger mascot with the slogan, "Put a tiger in your tank!" was created in part based on the supposed masculine symbol of virility and strength conveyed by the animal.[16]

Motivation research fell out of fashion in the 1960s. However, motivation research left two important legacies to the field of consumer research: (1) a focus on consumer motivations, i.e., trying to answer the question of why people behave as they do, and (2) the technique of in-depth interviewing. Today, motivation research is still used occasionally, but usually in conjunction with other, more rigorous techniques.

A Behavioral Science Perspective Since the 1960s, a behavioral science perspective (also referred to as *Positivism* and *Social Science*) has dominated the field of consumer research. **Behavioral science** applies the scientific method, relying on systematic, rigorous procedures to explain, control, and predict consumer behavior. Thus, behavioral scientists study people and their behaviors in the same way that natural scientists study physical phenomena. Because behavioral scientists study people, however, research findings are more difficult to interpret. The primary methods of behavioral science include the *experimental approach*—conducting controlled experiments—and the *marketing science*

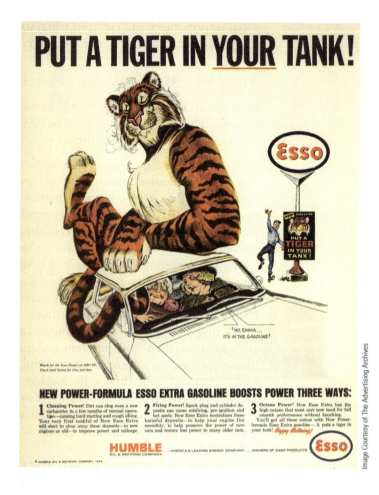

Motivation research helps advertisers create memorable brand images.

approach—employing computer-based simulations and mathematical models to explain and predict consumer behavior.

Behavioral scientists who study consumer behavior tend to view consumers as largely rational; they seek causes for behavior, conduct research to be used for strategic marketing decision making, and primarily use quantitative research methods. In **quantitative research methods**, *empirical data* are collected. Empirical data are numerical, based on observation, experiment, or experience, rather than on speculation or theory. These data are used to perform sophisticated statistical analyses. Because quantitative research methods typically use representative samples of a larger consumer group of interest (also called a *population* of interest), these results can typically be generalized from the study group to the larger group.

This textbook uses a predominantly behavioral science perspective for studying consumer behavior, although alternative approaches are also discussed. The scientific approach is advantageous for those interested in developing consumer-focused strategies and provides a foundation for critical thinking, creative problem solving, and decision making. This approach is based on the *scientific method*, a collection of systematic activities that enables researchers to study problems and find answers to questions.[17] Like a roadmap, the scientific method leads scientists in the right direction, but different researchers may take

FIGURE **1.2** | **The Scientific Method**

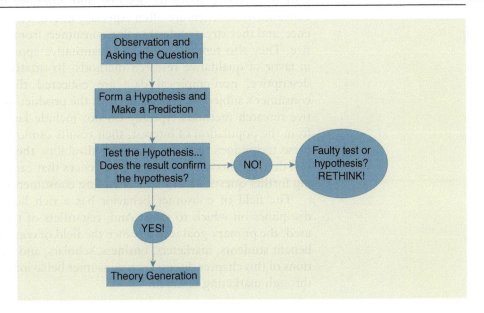

different routes to arrive at the same destination. But they always follow the rules of the road. (See Figure 1.2.) The steps of the scientific method include:

1. *Observe and ask the question*: Observations we make of the world around us are the basis for formulating questions or problems we want to solve.
2. *Form a hypothesis and make a prediction*: When a question or problem emerges from observation, we generate a potential explanation called a hypothesis that may provide the answer. A prediction is what we expect to happen if our hypothesis is correct.
3. *Test the hypothesis*: We test our hypotheses under controlled conditions, including testing only one hypothesis at a time and limiting the circumstances/ environment of the testing to see if our predictions are correct. Hypotheses that cannot be confirmed through testing must be rejected, and hypotheses must be tested and re-tested before they can be accepted as true. When behavioral scientists test a hypothesis, an *empirical confrontation* ensues; that is, empirical data are collected, and the results are compared to those suggested by the hypothesis.
4. *Theory generation*: If a hypothesis is confirmed via testing and re-testing, we generate a *theory*, which is a general answer to our original question. Once a theory is established, it also guides future research.

A scientific foundation should serve you well as a student and in your chosen career. Depth of understanding is key to success in today's complex marketplace. Marketers and business practitioners who possess in-depth, scientific understanding of their customers are more likely to succeed where others fail.

Interpretivism An alternative research approach to behavioral science that relies less on scientific and technological methodology is called **Interpretivism** (or *Postmodernism*). Researchers working from this perspective view consumers as non-rational beings and their reality as highly subjective. These researchers' goal is to collect data to describe and *interpret* this reality. Interpretivist consumer researchers are often especially interested in the consumption experience, and they stress understanding consumers from a broader societal perspective. They also tend to reject the quantitative approach of behavioral science in favor of qualitative research methods. In **qualitative research methods**, descriptive, non-empirical data are collected that describe an individual consumer's subjective experience with the product or service. Because qualitative research methods typically do not include large, representative samples from the population of interest, their results cannot be generalized. But while these techniques typically lack generalizability, they provide in-depth, detail-rich descriptions of consumers' experiences that can be very useful in developing further questions and understanding consumers on an abstract level.

The field of consumer behavior has a rich heritage of diverse scientific disciplines on which to draw. And, regardless of the perspective or methods used, the primary goal is to advance the field of consumer behavior in order to benefit students, marketers, business, scholars, and society. The following sections of this chapter discuss how consumer behavior is examined and measured through marketing research.

OBJECTIVE (4) # Developing Consumer Insights through Research

At the intersection of consumer behavior and marketing research is the synergy of consumer insight. **Consumer insight** is a deep, profound knowledge of the consumer that comes from integrating traditional marketing research tools with consumer behavior theories. These insights can then structure a company's thinking and decision making. In other words, it is an "ah-ha" moment of seeing what everyone else sees and understanding what no one else understands. Developing consumer insights is why understanding consumer behavior theory is so important in marketing research, and it is why we examine several of these theories and concepts in this textbook.

Consumer researchers study consumer responses and activities by using marketing research methods. **Marketing research** is a systematic process of planning, collecting, analyzing, and interpreting data and information relevant to marketing problems and consumer behavior. Marketing research also enables businesses to better understand the market(s) in which they compete and the broader environment in order to identify opportunities and threats. Finally, consumer researchers use marketing research to analyze the effectiveness of marketing strategies, programs, and tactics. Ultimately, effective marketing and consumer research should provide marketers with relevant information for making decisions, reducing uncertainty, improving profits, and developing consumer insights.

Unfortunately, sometimes marketers forego conducting marketing research. Instead, they often rely on their intuition. Intuition is simply common sense, a guess, or "gut feeling." Decisions based on intuition are often made with limited or incomplete information. Relying too heavily on intuition and "gut

Ethics

Tampering with research results is a serious ethical problem. A few years ago, The Coca-Cola Company and Burger King conducted an applied consumer research project in the form of a three-week promotional campaign in some Burger King restaurants in Richmond, Virginia. The objective of the project was to test the appeal of Frozen Coke, a slushy drink. Coke wanted Burger King to offer the frozen drinks as a kids' snack. If the tests were successful, Burger King would make Frozen Coke a regular offering on its menu.

Apparently the initial research results of the campaign weren't pleasing to some people at Coke, and they decided to inflate their test results—without Burger King's knowledge, of course. It was reported that this involved paying a man $9,000 to get hundreds of kids to go to Burger King restaurants and ask for the Frozen Coke value meal. With the "rigged" results of the test market sales appearing to be quite positive, Burger King ramped up the Frozen Coke program, investing an estimated $65 million in advertising and the equipment and syrup to make the frozen drinks.

Then a finance executive in Coke's fountain-drink division was let go. He filed a lawsuit, claiming that he had been unfairly fired for complaining about these, and other, unethical practices at Coke. In his lawsuit, he accused Coke of rigging the Frozen Coke research project. This led to investigations by the U.S. Securities and Exchange Commission (SEC) and the U.S. Justice Department. Coke was subpoenaed by a federal grand jury and eventually the company admitted that it had rigged the test. Needless to say, Coke's customer, Burger King, was not thrilled and threatened to discontinue the drink. Finally, Coke reached a monetary settlement with Burger King and its franchisees.

Wouldn't you hate to be in the shoes of the marketing managers who created this whole mess? Not surprisingly, the executive who approved the rigged project is no longer employed by Coke. Unfortunately, cases like this one have been too common in today's highly competitive business environment, with marketers on the front lines when it comes to producing positive results for their stakeholders. While finding the "right" results from the research may seem crucial, failing to maintain integrity and high ethical standards in research can be a serious mistake that everyone typically pays for in the end.[18]

feelings" rather than on sound research can lead to costly business mistakes. This is one reason why so many new products fail. For example, not long ago, Heinz introduced a new clam chowder made with the finest ingredients, including expensive, very tender clams, working under the assumption that consumers would prefer high-quality ingredients—a rather common sense assumption. The product was a failure. If the company had done systematic research on consumer preferences, it would have discovered that, counter to the common sense assumption, consumers actually prefer lower quality, rubbery clams in their chowder.

Now that we've broadly examined consumer behavior research, the remaining sections of this chapter examine marketing research in more depth. First, we will look at the major classifications of research: basic versus applied. Next, we will discuss the broad steps of the research process, and in particular, take a deeper dive into research design and data collection methods.

Basic versus Applied Research

Basic Research Consumer research is divided into two broad categories based on the goals of the research: basic research and applied research. **Basic research** looks for general relationships between variables, regardless of the specific situation. For example, basic research has shown that using celebrity endorsers in advertising can increase consumers' positive attitudes toward a brand, especially when the celebrity is well liked and fits well with the product or the product's image. Examples include David Beckham endorsing Adidas and Beyoncé endorsing Pepsi.[19]

The key benefit of basic research is that conclusions drawn from it generally apply across a variety of situations, and researchers can use these generalizations to guide strategic planning and develop marketing tactics. Thus, basic research findings apply not only to David Beckham wearing Adidas apparel but also to most celebrities and brands in general. This helps marketers make more informed decisions, such as whether to use a celebrity endorser in advertising a product.

Basic research variables studied can include those related to the consumer, such as personality or demographic variables; they can also relate to the *marketing mix* (product, price, place, and promotion). Examples include advertising tactics, concepts related to pricing, or the consumer's environment or personal situation, such as music played in a retail store, or shopping when pressed for time, e.g., 5:00 P.M. on Christmas Eve.

Applied Research **Applied research** examines many of the same variables as basic research, but within a specific context of interest to a marketer. Applied research is more common than basic research because consumer researchers want to solve particular business-related problems of immediate interest.

Let's revisit our celebrity endorser example. Given what researchers know about the influence of celebrity endorsers from basic research, a company, let's say Kraft, decides to use a celebrity endorser to advertise a new line of kids' yogurt. The company develops two or three advertisements, each with a different celebrity endorser. These celebrities are people who might fit with the product or convey an image desired by the company, such as Kelly Ripa, the famous talk-show host and mom, or Hillary Duff, a popular young actress (and also a mom). The company then conducts applied research to test which of the endorsers is most effective. In this case, the research is aimed at evaluating a specific brand and endorser combination, and the results would not apply to other situations.

OBJECTIVE **5** # The Marketing Research Process

Now we will discuss the broad steps of the research process, and in particular, take a deeper dive into research design and data collection. Whether a market researcher is engaged in applied or basic research, there is a sequence of steps that are followed when designing a research project. While this process may be customized to fit the unique circumstances of a particular research question, this process provides a roadmap for the market researcher (see Figure 1.3). The steps of the marketing research process include:

1. *Define the problem or opportunity:* The first step in the research process is to define the research issue. What is the problem to be solved or the opportunity to be explored? When this step is done accurately, the research can ultimately yield valuable insights. This step also includes clearly delineating the specific goals and objectives of the research project, which guide the execution of the research.

FIGURE **1.3** | **The Marketing Research Process**

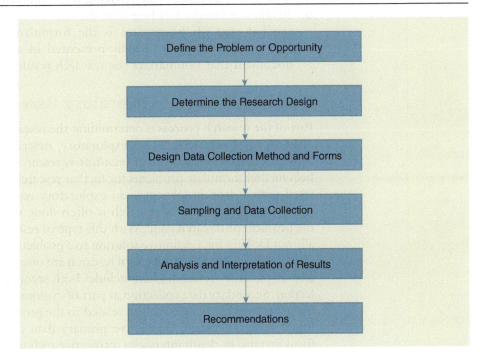

Define the Problem or Opportunity

Determine the Research Design

Design Data Collection Method and Forms

Sampling and Data Collection

Analysis and Interpretation of Results

Recommendations

2. *Determine the research design:* The design of the research depends on how much and what kind of information is already known and what information needs to be gathered. There are three main types of research design: exploratory, descriptive, and causal research. If very little is known about the research issue, exploratory research is likely needed. If the goal of the research is to obtain precise information, then descriptive or causal research may be warranted. These designs will be discussed in more depth later in the chapter.

3. *Design data collection methods and forms:* This step involves determining what type of data will be collected, secondary or primary. **Secondary data** are data that already exist and are readily accessible, whereas **primary data** are new data collected specifically for the research purpose at hand. If we have to collect primary data, we must decide what method will be used to collect the information and how specific instruments will be designed. These topics will also be expanded upon later in the chapter.

4. *Sampling and data collection:* In this step, the researcher must determine from whom the information will be solicited and how many people must be studied. Once this criteria is decided upon, the data can be collected.

5. *Analysis and interpretation of results:* A researcher may collect a large amount of data, but those data are useless without precise and accurate analysis and interpretation of the results. The data analysis method will depend on the type of data collected. It should be noted that numbers and analyses are simply inputs to decisions. Numbers don't make

decisions – people do, and a good marketing researcher will temper research results with judgment when making recommendations.

6. *Recommendations:* Leading from the analysis and interpretation of results, the last step of the process is the formulation of recommendations. Recommendations are usually presented in a *research report*, a formal document that summarizes the research results and recommendations.

Research Design: Exploratory Research

Part of the research process is determining the research design. There are three main types of research design: exploratory, descriptive, and causal research. **Exploratory research** is broad, *qualitative* research done to generate ideas or help further formulate problems for further research. For example, a magazine faced with a drop in sales may do exploratory research to generate possible explanations. This type of research is often done when little is known about the problem or research issue. With this type of research, the researcher is usually not looking for a definitive solution to a problem, but guidance for the next step. Key descriptors of this type of research are unstructured, flexible, and general. Exploratory research often includes both secondary and primary data collection. Secondary data collection as part of exploratory research might include literature searches of information related to the problem or the analysis of published business cases.[20] Qualitative primary data collection methods include focus groups, in-depth interviews, projective techniques, and observation.

Focus Groups An extremely popular tool in marketing research, a **focus group** consists of 8 to 12 participants run by a moderator who monitors and guides the group discussion of the research topic at hand. Participants are usually carefully screened so that the group members are relatively homogeneous and have the desired characteristics (age, gender, income, etc.) for the situation. The moderator usually follows a very detailed but flexible script of questions. Focus groups are conducted for a variety of reasons, including brainstorming for ideas, generating hypotheses that can be tested further, assessing new products, and evaluating promotional campaigns. With a skilled moderator, focus groups are opportunities to generate energy and group synergies that can result in new ideas or unique insights. On the downside, like interviews, focus groups *require* a skilled moderator or otherwise may yield unwieldy data. In addition, focus groups are vulnerable to problems associated with group dynamics. For example, *groupthink* is the tendency for groups to make poor quality decisions for the sake of unanimity.[21] Groupthink occurs when groups are highly cohesive, and when they are under considerable pressure to make a quality decision.

In-depth Interviews A form of direct questioning, an **in-depth interview (IDI)** is a one-on-one interview lasting at least one hour, but sometimes considerably longer. A highly trained interviewer establishes rapport with a respondent and then proceeds to lead him or her through a loosely structured discussion of the research topic. This method is particularly appropriate for sensitive or emotionally charged topics, or when the researcher is attempting to gather detailed information about very complicated behaviors. In an IDI, the interviewer can peel away layers of respondents' emotions, thoughts, or behaviors. The disadvantages of IDIs are that they tend to be time-consuming and costly because the interviewer must be highly trained. Furthermore, there

Marketing in Action

Twitter as a Focus Group

Twitter is a database of real-time opinions, where users send and read text posts of up to 140 characters known as tweets. This social networking site has become a rich source of information about consumers, the products they use and care about, how they live their lives, and what's important to them. According to the Twitter website, "Twitter connects businesses to customers in real time—and businesses use Twitter to quickly share information with people interested in their products and services, gather real-time market intelligence and feedback, and build relationships with customers, partners and influencers." The service has steadily gained in popularity, with over 140 million users and 340 million daily tweets.

More and more companies are finding that this database can become a form of focus group. Twitter can be used to ask marketing research questions and monitor feedback. While certainly not a traditional focus group, the advantage of using Twitter is that responses are posted in real-time at any time—day or night. Opinions can be generated on any topic. Participants offer opinions freely and come from everywhere.

For example, when Tropicana Pure Premium Orange Juice redesigned its popular picture on its package not long ago, the response from the social network community was passionate, immediate, and negative. Within weeks, the picture on the package was discontinued. Cases such as these are becoming increasingly common as digital technology allows consumers to rapidly engage with marketers.

According to Peter Shankman, a social media expert, "Twitter is the ultimate focus group. I can post something and

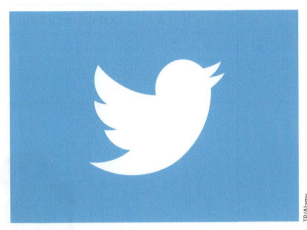

TP/Alamy

in a minute get feedback from 700 people around the world, giving me their real opinions."

While this unconventional type of focus group is unique for its affordability and accessibility, there are some downsides. First, traditional focus groups engage participants in a guided, controlled atmosphere. With Twitter, the researcher doesn't have much control over the conversation. Twitter and other social network sites are driven by an anything-goes type of community of commentators. Nor can the researcher control who engages in the conversation. Twitter users are not screened and therefore are not targeted or representative. Despite these obstacles, companies are looking more and more to the online environment for marketing research.[22]

---

are cost considerations (respondents are typically compensated for their time), and the data can be difficult to analyze and interpret.

Projective Techniques Borrowed from psychology, **projective techniques** are an "unstructured, indirect form of questioning that [encourage] respondents to project their underlying beliefs, attitudes, feelings, and motivations in an apparently unrelated or ambiguous scenario."[23] In other words, projective techniques use seemingly meaningless exercises to uncover consumers' unconscious points of view. Projective techniques consist of a variety of tests that fall under four broad categories:

1. *Word-association tests*, which ask subjects to respond to a list of words with one or more associated words that come to mind.
2. *Completion tests*, which ask subjects to fill in the blanks by finishing sentences or stories.

3. *Construction tests*, including cartoon construction, which ask subjects to fill in the word/thought "bubbles" in a cartoon; or picture construction, where subjects tell a story about a picture (see Figure 1.4).
4. *Expression tests*, including role-play activities and third-person techniques, which ask subjects to describe the actions of typical others.

FIGURE 1.4 | **Example of a Construction Projective Technique**

© Michael Greenlar/The Image Works

Projective techniques can often generate responses that participants would be unwilling or unable to give if questioned directly. For example, the makers of Old Spice High Endurance Antiperspirant-Deodorant use an expression-type projective technique, asking research participants to describe a "typical" user of their product and a "typical" user of a competing product. This technique helps paint a rich picture of how each brand is perceived and reveals subtle differences between brands that research participants are not able to articulate directly. On the negative side, projective techniques can be time-consuming and awkward to code (input as data) and analyze, and interpretations can be subjective.

Observation By using *observational techniques*, researchers can record people's behavior, either with or without their knowledge. When a person is aware of the observation, the research is referred to as *obtrusive observation*. For example, toy manufacturers routinely invite children in for "playtime." In a research facility made to resemble a classroom, playground, or family room, children are encouraged to play with toys while researchers record all their behaviors and comments.

When a person is unaware of being observed, the research is *unobtrusive observation*. For example, in addition to monitoring security, cameras in retail stores can track traffic patterns, examining path and pace as customers move through the store and see where traffic jams occur. P&G sends employees into grocery stores to casually observe consumers shopping for its products. These observations yield valuable information about how much time customers spend at the store shelf, how many products they examine, where customers' attention is focused, and whether they seem confused.

A specialized form of observation called *participant observation* occurs when a researcher joins a family or group for an extended period and observes members' behaviors. Adapted from cultural anthropology, it is also called *ethnographic research*. This type of research is growing in popularity, especially when the researcher needs an honest, behind-the-scenes peek into consumers' lives. For example, Innovations Focus, a firm that uses ethnographic research for new product development, was interested in understanding how women use lipstick. To that end, they observed Mary Kay in-home make-up parties run by a make-up consultant, participated in several in-home make-up application sessions, and even accompanied women while shopping for lipstick.[24]

Observational techniques are valuable because they can measure what consumers actually do, but observation alone cannot reveal a person's underlying motivations, attitudes, and preferences. In addition, observation may also raise ethical issues when it is used to collect data that consumers regard as private.

Descriptive Research

The second type of research design is **descriptive research**. More structured and rigid than exploratory research, a descriptive research study is done to describe the characteristics of some group or their behaviors, or to make predictions about trends or variables.[25] For example, a study that measures the sales trends of a product over time in relation to the economy would be a descriptive study. A study that attempts to characterize the members of a company's target customer group by characteristics such as age, income, and education would be considered descriptive research. Data related to descriptive research design are collected with longitudinal studies or cross-sectional studies.

Longitudinal Studies: Panels A *longitudinal study* is simply data that are collected at various points in time, over time. For example, measuring the high temperature every day for the month of April to determine the average temperature during that month is longitudinal data. In marketing research, a common form of longitudinal study is the consumer panel. Panels are typically made up of a sample of customers or potential customers. Panel members may provide the same repeated measurements of the same variables over time (called a *true panel*). For example, the consumer research company Nielsen collects panel members' weekly grocery purchases through its Homescan program. Purchases are recorded with a handheld scanner and sent to Nielsen. By aggregating this data, Nielson can track regional and national purchasing trends. Alternatively, panel members may also be asked to provide varied information over time (called an *omnibus panel*), depending on the researcher's questions. For example, marketing researcher NPD Group runs the National Eating Trends Panel. Members of this panel might be asked about their snacking behaviors at one time, and at another time, asked about what they eat for breakfast. Generally, panels can provide a comprehensive view of consumer attitudes, preferences, and behaviors as these views evolve over time.

Cross-sectional Studies: Surveys Cross-sectional studies are the most frequently used type of research in descriptive research, and involve taking a "snapshot" in time of some variables of interest from a specific sample group of interest.[26] Cross-sectional studies are usually conducted using surveys. Surveys are probably the most popular types of consumer data collection techniques because researchers can collect a wide variety of data, such as group versus individual data, brief answers versus long answers, and qualitative versus quantitative data. Surveys can take a number of forms, including written and oral surveys, which can be administered via mail, telephone, fax, email, the Internet, or face-to-face.

A **survey** is simply a set of structured questions to which a person is asked to respond. For example, The Harris Poll, run by Harris Interactive, is one the country's largest Internet survey providers, with an active multimillion participant database covering 40 countries.[27] Mail and email surveys are relatively inexpensive, but response rates are typically low—from 5 to 20 percent. Phone surveys achieve higher response rates but reduce the number of questions that can be asked because many answer options have to be repeated, and few people are willing to stay on the phone for more than 5 to 10 minutes. To talk to customers face-to-face, companies often recruit research participants in malls and shopping centers, a technique referred to as *mall-intercept*. Mall-intercepts are a convenient way to reach consumers, but respondents may be reluctant to discuss anything sensitive face-to-face with an interviewer.

Surveys are useful for collecting specific, often complex, information from a large number of individuals. They are typically easy to administer, and the general public is familiar and comfortable with this technique. However, as is true of all research techniques, surveys are vulnerable to bias. Wording questions correctly can be very difficult, and the language can influence a consumer's response. For example, consider the question, "In order to prevent terrorism, should airports be allowed to conduct passenger searches based on racial profiling and suspicious behavior?" This question has a number of potential problems. First, it is ambiguous. What behavior exactly is considered suspicious behavior in an airport? Second, the question is *double-barreled*, which means that it is really asking more than one question. What if the respondent approves of passenger searches on the basis of suspicious behavior but not on the basis of racial profiling—how should the respondent answer? Third, it is a leading question. Qualifying the question with, "In order to prevent terrorism …" clearly tips the respondent off to the fact that a "yes" answer is desired. This question may also suffer from what is referred to as *social desirability bias*. In this situation, respondents may not answer a question honestly or completely because they feel that the information is too personal or socially sensitive.

In face-to-face interviews, *interviewer bias* is an additional problem. Interviewer bias occurs when responses are influenced by variables such as the interviewer's age, gender, appearance, verbal or nonverbal reactions, or by an interviewee's desire to please the interviewer. For example, male respondents may hesitate to give personal information to a female interviewer. Or, a respondent may fabricate answers in an attempt to not appear ignorant to an interviewer.

Causal Research

The third type of research design is causal research. **Causal research** is concerned with identifying and understanding cause-and-effect relationships through experimentation. Consumer researchers are especially interested in uncovering two special types of relationships—correlations and causal (cause-and-effect). When a statistically testable and significant relationship exists between two variables, we say the variables are **correlated** (see Figure 1.5).[28] A *variable* is simply any factor that can potentially change. For example, if a researcher is studying the relationship between advertising and sales, those would be the variables of interest. There are three main types of correlations: positive, negative, and zero. In a positive correlation, the two variables increase or decrease together. A negative correlation means that as one variable increases, the related variable decreases. For example, research has shown that there is a positive correlation between advertising expenditures and level of sales.[29] As advertising increases, sales also increase. On the other hand, a negative correlation between product malfunctions and customer satisfaction exists—as product malfunctions increase, customer satisfaction tends to decrease.

FIGURE 1.5 | Graphs Showing Correlations between Advertising and Sales

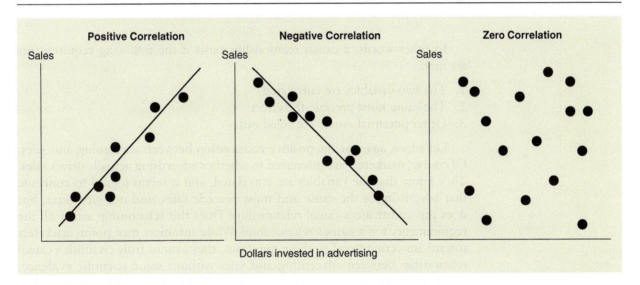

A *zero correlation* means that there is no predictable relationship between two variables. For example, there is zero correlation between the quality of nonfrozen, concentrated orange juice and the physical distance between the orange grove and the processing facility. This may surprise you, because many consumers believe (and many orange juice marketers imply) that the closer the processing plant is to the field, the fresher and higher quality the orange juice. Believing there is a correlational relationship between variables where none actually exists is called an *illusory correlation*.

One limitation in identifying correlations is that they tell us nothing about which variable influences the other. This means that even if we know that two variables (A and B) are correlated, we still do not know whether variable A influences variable B, B influences A, or A and B influence each other. Applying the advertising and sales example, even though we know that sales and advertising are positively correlated, advertising may influence sales, sales may influence advertising, or both variables may influence each other simultaneously.

In contrast, causal relationships capture both correlation and direction of the relationship. A **causal relationship** between two variables means that the variables are correlated and that one variable influences the other, but not vice versa (see Figure 1.6).

FIGURE 1.6 | **The Cause-and-Effect Relationship**

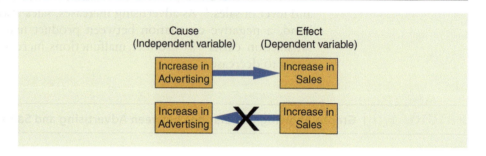

In other words, a causal relationship exists if the following requirements are met:

1. The two variables are correlated.
2. The cause must precede the effect.
3. Other potential causes are ruled out.

Let's look again at the positive relationship between advertising and sales. Of course, marketers are interested in whether advertising actually drives sales. They know that the variables are correlated, and it seems logical to conclude that advertising is the cause and must precede sales, and not vice versa, but does this constitute a causal relationship? Does this relationship satisfy all the requirements for a causal relationship? While intuition may point marketers toward answering "yes" to these questions, they cannot truly establish a causal relationship between advertising and sales without some scientific evidence. Can they obtain such evidence? Yes—by employing the scientific method, they can conduct experiments to test causality. In fact, there *is* a causal relationship between advertising and sales.

Interestingly, marketers suspected the causal relationship between advertising and sales for centuries, and anecdotal evidence suggests that this relationship was tested systematically as long ago as the early 1800s in Boston. As the story goes, there was a woman, Lydia Pinkerton, who invented and marketed a tonic to women for "medicinal needs." To promote his mother's product, Mrs. Pinkerton's son created large banners advertising the tonic and placed them in neighborhoods and on bridges and buildings. Much to his amazement, he discovered that every time he moved the banners into a new neighborhood, sales increased in that area. So, he decided to specifically test the relationship. He went into several neighborhoods where sales were very high, and he removed all the banners. Not surprisingly, sales dropped in the neighborhoods that had been stripped of the advertisements. Mr. Pinkerton concluded that advertising was related to sales and that the more he advertised in a given geographic area, the better were his sales. This is one of the first recorded marketing research studies examining the causal relationship.[30]

Systematic testing allows researchers to determine causal relationships with a high degree of certainty. However, whereas a scientific approach allows researchers to establish causality among variables in a controlled setting, variables seldom exist in isolation in the real world. Rather, confounding elements introduce uncertainty, making research difficult. Causal relationships also tend to overlap, with some effects—like increased sales—having many different causes that may work together or independently, such as amount of advertising, product quality, and price. Fortunately, although uncertainty can't be completely eliminated, scientific techniques (described in this book) allow consumer researchers to minimize it.

Experiments Causal research is conducted using experiments. **Experiments** manipulate variables in a controlled setting to determine their relationship to one another. Researchers use experiments to rule out all but one explanation for a particular observation. In designing an experiment, researchers first identify any variables that can possibly change. There are three broad types of variables:

- *Independent variables* are the factors that are changed or manipulated.
- *Dependent variables* are factors that change in response to researchers' manipulations of the independent variables.
- *Constants* are factors that researchers do not allow to change, but instead control.

Recall our discussion of the potential causal relationship between advertising and sales. Experiments are the best methods for determining causality. For instance, a marketer could manipulate advertising (the independent variable) by showing an advertisement for a product to one group of participants and not showing the advertisement to a second *control group*—a group that is not exposed to any independent variables and serves as a standard of comparison. The marketer could then examine the resulting influence of the advertisement on average sales (the dependent variable). If sales are significantly higher in the ad group than in the no-ad group, the marketer could conclude that changes in advertising are likely to cause changes in sales.

Participants in experiments should be *randomly assigned* to the conditions, which means the assignment is determined by chance, such as flipping a coin. Random assignment helps to rule out other possible causes for the results, such as different personalities among participants and varying levels of product knowledge and interest, among others. Random assignment forces these individual differences to cancel out. Ideally, researchers would replicate the experiment a number of times and in different settings to show additional support for their findings.

Experimentation is the most effective technique for determining causal relationships, but it does have a drawback in that consumers are removed from their natural surroundings. The contrived laboratory setting may prevent consumers from acting as they would in a real market setting.

Up to this point in our discussion of consumer behavior research, we have seen that researchers conduct different broad types of research, namely basic and applied research, and that when choosing research designs, marketing researchers may engage in exploratory, descriptive, or causal research. Finally, we turn our attention to the two broad types of data collection: secondary and primary data.

Secondary versus Primary Data

Where do marketers collect data? There are two broad sources of data: secondary data and primary data. As stated earlier, **secondary data** are data that already exist and are readily accessible. One source could be internal organizational sources, such as a company's sales history records, customer database, sales force observations, or even previous company research projects. Secondary data are also available from outside sources, including U.S. and foreign government agencies that offer a variety of reports, such as the *U.S. Census Population Report* and the *Vital Statistics Report;* academic and trade publications, such as *Moody's Manuals*, the *Journal of Consumer Psychology*, and *Advertising Age*, which often publish the results of both basic and applied research; and finally, commercial syndicated data sources, such as Nielsen TV Ratings Reports and InfoScan data from supermarket scanners. *Syndicated data* are data that are periodically collected using standardized procedures and analyzed by a commercial firm, which then makes the results available for purchase. For example, Nielson monitors people's television viewing habits. Research participants are asked to keep journal information on their viewing habits, and electronic monitors attached to their televisions record channel selection and viewing times. Table 1.1 lists some examples of secondary data sources.

The advantages of secondary data are that they are usually readily available, rich in detail, and may not cost any more than the time and effort it takes to search the Internet or go to the library. The disadvantages of secondary data are that they may lack currency and relevancy. For example, the U.S. Census is done every 10 years, and eight- or nine-year-old information may not be timely enough to address our current problems. Furthermore, secondary data are often *aggregated*, which means they are reported as a whole, rather than broken down in detail. So, these data may not be specific enough to directly relate to a marketer's situation.

Recall that **primary data** are new data collected specifically for the research purpose at hand. For example, prior to this textbook's availability for sale, the publisher collected primary data, in the form of surveys sent to potential users, to predict how students and instructors would like the book. Types of information that are collected using primary data collection techniques might include demographics, lifestyle information, personality testing, awareness, knowledge, attitudes, preference, motivations, intentions, and behaviors.

The advantages of primary data are that the information is specific and relevant to a specific project, is current, and data collection can be controlled. On the downside, primary data tend to be very expensive and may require considerable time to collect, organize, and analyze.

TABLE 1.1 | **Secondary Data Sources**

Internal Sources:

a. Company customer records and databases
b. Financial statements, such as annual reports, profit/loss statements, and balance sheets
c. Sales call sheets and records
d. Inventory records
e. Prior research study reports

External Sources:

a. Online Indexes and Databases
   - Business Source Complete
   - Business and Industry
   - Global Market Information Database
   - IBISWorld
   - Marketline (Datamonitor)
   - MRI 1 (Mediamark)
   - SRDS Media Solutions
   - Country Profiles and Country Commerce Online
   - Europa World Plus
   - Secondarydata.com
   - Sports Business Research Network
b. Specific Periodicals and Books
   - Standard and Poor's Industry
   - Moody's Manuals
   - *The Handbook of Consumer Psychology*
   - *The Advertising Age Encyclopedia of Advertising*
   - Marketing journals, such as *Journal of Consumer Research, Journal of Consumer Psychology, Journal of Marketing, Journal of Marketing Research, Journal of Retailing, Journal of Advertising*
   - Trade magazines such as *Advertising Age, Progressive Grocer, Sales and Marketing Management*
   - General business publications such as *Business Week, Forbes, The Wall Street Journal, Harvard Business Review, The Economist, Fortune*
c. Government Sources
   - U.S. Bureau of the Census (http://www.census.gov). The census includes reports not only on general population, but also on housing, the labor force, manufacturers, business, agriculture, and foreign aspects.
   - Integrated Public Use Microdata Series (http://www.ipums.umn.edu). This series of data includes samples of the U.S. census (gathered for over 100 years) and historical census files from other countries.
   - Bureau of Labor Statistics (http://stats.bls.gov). This source collects data on employment, industrial relations, prices, earnings, living conditions, occupational safety, technology, and productivity.

Chapter Summary

Welcome to the exciting world of consumer behavior research! Now you have an idea of what consumer behavior entails, how it fits into the larger field of marketing, and how we study it. Consumer behavior comprises all consumer activities associated with the purchase, use, and disposal of goods and services, including the consumer's emotional, mental, and behavioral responses that precede, determine, or follow these activities. One dominant approach to studying consumer behavior is the behavioral science perspective, which relies on rigorous quantitative research methods and procedures to describe, explain, control, and predict consumer behavior. An alternative approach, which relies less on scientific and technological methodology and more on the qualitative approach, is called Interpretivism.

Understanding, explaining, and predicting consumer behavior are complicated tasks. At the intersection of consumer behavior theory and marketing research are consumer insights. This textbook adopts a scientific approach to achieve a deeper understanding of consumer behavior and develop consumer insights. In this approach, researchers are especially interested in two special types of relationships between variables, namely, correlational and causal relationships. When a statistically testable and significant relationship exists between an event and a condition, we say that the event and the condition are correlated. A causal relationship between two variables means that the variables are correlated and that one variable influences the other, but not vice versa.

Consumer researchers conduct basic and applied research to identify important variables relevant to consumer behavior. Basic research aims to understand relative relationships between variables, whereas applied research examines variables within a specific context of interest to the marketer.

Researchers design research that is exploratory, descriptive, and causal. Exploratory research is broad, qualitative research done to generate ideas or help further formulate problems for further research. More structured and rigid than exploratory research, a descriptive research study is done to describe the characteristics of some group or their behaviors, or to make predictions about trends or variables. Causal research is concerned with identifying and understanding cause-and-effect relationships through experimentation. Exploratory qualitative methods include focus groups, in-depth interviews, projective techniques, and observation. Longitudinal and cross-sectional studies, including panels and surveys, are typical in descriptive research, and causal research is conducted using experimentation. Experiments manipulate variables in a controlled setting to determine their relationship to one another and are the most effective technique for determining causal relationships.

There are two broad sources of research data— secondary data and primary data. Secondary data are data that already exist and can be accessed within an organization or from external sources. Primary data are new data collected on a project-by-project basis.

Researchers analyze consumer behavior research data in order to discover customer needs and wants, deliver products and services that satisfy those needs and wants, and ensure that the customer remains satisfied over time. Ultimately, effective consumer behavior research provides marketers with relevant information for making better decisions, reducing uncertainty, and developing consumer insights.

Key Terms

applied research	customer perceived value	marketing research
basic research	descriptive research	organizational consumers
behavioral science	experiments	primary data
causal relationship	exploratory research	projective techniques
causal research	focus group	qualitative research methods
consumer behavior	in-depth interview (IDI)	quantitative research methods
consumer insight	individual consumers	secondary data
correlated	Interpretivism	survey
customer delight	marketing concept	

Review and Discussion

1. Based on the definition of consumer behavior, identify some of the consumer behavior-related activities you have engaged in today.

2. What is/are the key difference(s) between customer perceived value and customer delight?

3. How do public policy makers use the results of consumer research?

4. How might an Interpretivist researcher attempt to examine why more men (versus women) have an emotional attachment to their automobiles? How would a behavioral science researcher approach the same question?

5. What is consumer insight?

6. Define qualitative research and quantitative research and highlight the differences between them. Provide one example of each technique.

7. Discuss the differences between exploratory, descriptive, and causal research design.

8. Give an example of a correlational relationship and a causal relationship that you have observed in daily life. Explain how each example illustrates the relationship.

9. Why is random assignment important in any experiment that seeks to determine causality?

10. Describe the major differences between secondary and primary data collection, as well as the advantages and disadvantages of each.

Short Application Exercises

1. Find an advertisement that attempts to influence consumers' disposal activities and describe the disposal activity. In your opinion, is the advertisement effective? Why or why not?

2. Design an experiment that tests the effect of using a celebrity endorser on consumers' brand attitudes. In addition, identify the independent and dependent variables and state the hypothesis.

3. Conduct a library search and find one article that describes either a basic or applied marketing research project. What were the goals of the project, the research method employed, and the major results of the project?

4. Using the Internet, conduct a secondary data collection to investigate aging trends in the United States. Hint: you may want to start at the U.S. Census Bureau website.

Managerial Application

The truths and power of consumer analysis become real when you observe consumers in real shopping situations. This is a common technique (sometimes called mystery shopping) used by many companies to better understand their customers. Your challenge is to use observational research to answer a behavioral research question.

Procedure:

Step 1. Choose one of the observational research tasks shown here to complete or make up a question/task of your own.

Possible Research Tasks:

1. Compare the behaviors of men shopping alone for groceries with those of women shopping alone for groceries.

2. Compare the behaviors of preadolescent boys shopping with an adult with those of preadolescent girls shopping with an adult.

3. Compare the shopping behaviors of senior citizen couples with those of young couples.

4. Observe the behaviors of teenage boys and girls shopping without a parent.

5. Compare the purchase of a specific food or beverage item in a supermarket versus a restaurant/bar.

6. Observe the purchase of impulse items at the point of check-out.

Step 2. Plan to go on at least two data-gathering trips.

Step 3. Collect your observations. You should collect at least five observations of each type of subject (for example, five men and five women for a total of ten). You will definitely want to take notes on each observation and know what types of information you are looking for before you start. (And while you are observing, make sure that you do not distract or disrupt your subjects. You should make sure that you are as inconspicuous as possible.)

Step 4. Summarize the information you collected and see if there are differences among the groups you selected. What are your findings? What are the potential implications for a company that wants to market to those groups?

End Notes

1 Top 10 list for prime broadcast network TV—United States. (2013, May 6). [Company website]. Retrieved from: http://www.nielsen.com/us/en/insights/top10s/television.html.

2 TV dramas account for most primetime viewing, timeshifting and ad spend. (2012, April 19). [Company website]. Retrieved from: http://blog.nielsen.com/nielsenwire/media_entertainment/tv-dramas-account-for-most-primetime-viewing-timeshifting-and-ad-spend/.

3 There's no sign that reality TV is about to die. (2003, December 6). *Canberra Times (Federal Capital Press of Australia Pty. Limited)*, p. B3.

4 Johnson, A. (2004, April 4). Speakers reveal reality hooks. *Daily Illini*. Retrieved from: http://www.uwire.com.

5 TV dramas account for most primetime viewing, timeshifting and ad spend. (2012, April 19). [Company website]. Retrieved from: http://www.nielsen.com/us/en/newswire/2012/tv-dramas-account-for-most-primetime-viewing-timeshifting-and-ad-spend.html.

6 Gunelius, S. (2008, January 18). Ford, Coke & AT&T pay more to sponsor American Idol. *Brandcurve*. Retrieved from: http://www.bizzia.com/brandcurve/ford-coke-att-pay-more-to-sponsor-american-idol.

7 Definition adapted from, Kerin, R. A., Berkowitz, E. N., Hartley, S. W., and Rudelius, W. (2003). *Marketing* (3rd ed.). New York: McGraw-Hill, p. 150.

8 Zeithaml, V. A. (1988). Consumer perceptions of price, quality, and value: A means-end model and synthesis of evidence. *Journal of Marketing, 52 (July)*, 2–22, p. 14.

9 2012 Procter & Gamble Annual Report. (2013, May) [Company website]. Retrieved from: http://www.pg.com.

10 Inneov. (n.d.). [Company website]. Retrieved from: http://www.inneov.com.

11 Nutricosmetics—beauty goes deeper. (2011, March 3). Retrieved from: http://www.cosmeticsbusiness.com/technical/article_page/Nutricosmetics__beauty_goes_deeper/59562.

12 Keiningham, T., and Vavra, T. (2001). *The Customer Delight Principle*. New York: McGraw-Hill.

13 Kotler, K. and Keller, P. K. (2012). *Marketing Management* (14th ed.). Upper Saddle River, NJ: Prentice Hall.

14 Dichter, E. (1960). *A Strategy of Desire*. Garden City, NY: Doubleday. Dichter, E. (1964). *Handbook of Consumer Motivations*. New York: McGraw-Hill.

15 Durgee, J. F. (1991). Interpreting Dichter's interpretations: An analysis of consumption symbolism in the handbook of consumer motivations. In H. Hartvig-Larsen, D. G. Mick, and C. Alstead (Eds.), *Marketing and Semiotics: Selected Papers from the Copenhagen Symposium* (as cited in Solomon, M. R. (2002). *Consumer behavior* (5th ed.). Upper Saddle River, NJ: Prentice Hall).

16 Dichter, E. (1964). *Handbook of Consumer Motivations: The Psychology of the World of Objects*. New York: McGraw-Hill.

17 Kardes, F. R. (2002). *Consumer Behavior and Managerial Decision Making* (2nd ed.). Upper Saddle River, NJ: Pearson Education/Prentice Hall.

18 Jennings, M. (2009). *Business Ethics Case Studies and Selected Readings* (6th ed.). Mason, OH: South-Western Cengage Learning.

19 Cronley, M. L., Houghton, D. C., Goddard, P., and Kardes, F. R. (1998). Endorsing products for the money: The role of the correspondence bias in celebrity advertising. *Advances in Consumer Research*, 26, 627–631. McCracken, G. (1989). Who is the celebrity endorser? Cultural foundations of the endorsement process. *Journal of Consumer Research*, 16 (December), 310–321.

20 Iacobucci, D., and Churchill, G. A. (2010). *Marketing Research: Methodological Foundations* (10th ed.). Mason, OH: South-Western Cengage Learning.

21 Irving, J. (1972). *Victims of Groupthink.* Boston: Houghton Mifflin. Irving, J. (1982). *Groupthink: Psychological Studies of Policy Decisions and Fiascos.* (2nd ed.). Boston: Houghton Mifflin.

22 Sources for the article: http://www.Twitter.com. Twitter Team (2012, March 21). Twitter turns six [Twitter Blog]. Retrieved from: http://blog.twitter.com/2012/03/twitter-turns-six.html. Mikles, L. (2008, December 29). Using Twitter as your focus group. [New York Times website]. Retrieved from: http://www.nytimes.com/2009/02/23/business/media/23adcol.html?_r=3.

23 Malhotra, N. K., Peterson, M., and Kleiser, S.B. (1999). Marketing research: A state-of-the-art review and directions for the twenty-first century. *Journal of the Academy of Marketing Science, 27 (2)*, 160–184.

24 Mcfarland, J. (2001, September 24). The consumer anthropologist. *Harvard Business School: Working Knowledge* [Online]. Retrieved from: http://hbswk.hbs.edu/archive/2514.html. Wellner, A. S. (2002, October 1). The test drive—ethnographic research and marketing research. *Amercian Demographics* [Online]. Retrieved from: http://www.findarticles.com.

25 Iacobucci, D. and Churchill, G. A. (2010). *Marketing Research: Methodological Foundations* (10th ed.). Mason, OH: South-Western Cengage Learning.

26 Iacobucci, D., and Churchill, G. A. (2010). *Marketing Research Methodological Foundations* (10th ed.). Mason, OH: South-Western Cengage Learning.

27 For more information, visit the company website at http://www.harris.com.

28 Rosenthal, R. and Rosnow, R. L. (1991). *Essentials of Behavioral Research: Methods and Data Analysis* (2nd ed.). New York: McGraw-Hill.

29 Assmus, G., Farley, J. U., and Lehmann, D. R. (1984). How advertising affects sales: Meta-analyses of econometric results. *Journal of Marketing Research, 21*, 65–74.

30 Geary, S. P. (Producer). (1999). *Sell and Spin: A History of Advertising* [Film]. (Available from A&E Home Video, A&E Television Network, Cat. No AAE-17607.)

MARKETING METRICS

Descriptive Statistics

Imagine that you are a consultant who has been asked to provide some descriptive data to your client related to typical Twitter users. You have collected the data related to Twitter subscribers in the table shown below. The table provides data for 20 Twitter subscribers who have used Twitter for at least one year.

Column 1 shows the subscriber number. Column 2 indicates the subscriber's gender (1 = the subscriber is male; 2 = the subscriber is female). Column 3 indicates the number of other subscribers that each person follows. (On Twitter, subscribers "follow" each other, which means they track the text postings, or tweets, of those they follow.) Column 4 indicates the number of tweets the subscriber has posted in the last year.

Twitter Subscriber Data

Subscriber Number	Subscriber Gender	Number Following	Number of Tweets Made
1	1	7	2
2	2	14	13
3	1	20	38
4	1	52	67
5	1	87	70
6	2	71	34
7	2	90	119
8	1	26	56
9	2	56	48
10	1	9	1
11	2	18	27
12	2	11	9
13	2	121	76
14	1	66	34
15	1	5	19
16	1	27	39
17	1	89	60
18	1	43	21
19	2	89	59
20	2	56	40

Your Task:

Use the Excel file (DT1-1.XLSX) to execute the following analyses:

1. Calculate the frequency of men versus women.
2. Calculate the median number of followers and the median number of tweets made. (For a data set, the median is the numerical value that separates the sample in half.)
3. Calculate the overall mean number of tweets made and the mean number of followers. (For a data set, the mean is the sum of values divided by the total number of values.)
4. Calculate the number of tweets made and the mean number of followers by gender. (For this calculation, you will need to calculate a cross-tabulation. In a cross-tabulation, two or more variables are considered simultaneously, and the values are counted for each category.)
5. What conclusions can you draw from these analyses?

© Mike Flippo/Shutterstock.com

CHAPTER 2

CONSUMER FOCUSED STRATEGY: SEGMENTATION AND POSITIONING

OBJECTIVES   *After studying this chapter, you will be able to…*

1   Define segmentation, target markets, and positioning, and understand why the segmentation process is important to marketers.

2   Explain how society benefits from market segmentation.

3   Describe the factors that influence the determination of a segmentation strategy.

4   Discuss various bases of segmentation.

5   Provide examples of strategies marketers use to position brands after segmentation.

CafeMom Caters to Moms

Uniquely appealing to the female mom market segment, CafeMom.com is a social networking website targeted to mothers and moms-to-be. According to the website, "Moms come to CafeMom to connect, give and get advice, be entertained, and make friends." The social networking website has over nine million visitors each month and represents a large and profitable market segment. Through the website, registered users can interact in special groups focusing on pregnancy, military moms, and recipe sharing, and users can seek and post advice, share information, and interact. Through CafeMom's blog (called The Stir), users can access news articles on a wide range of topics.

While set up like typical social networking websites, such as Facebook or LinkedIn, one unique aspect of CafeMom is that the registered users are solely women. While anyone can access the "public" content on the site, dads are not allowed to join. If a man tries to join,

CafeMom is a targeted social network, composed of a community of mothers and powered by advertising revenue.

Jeff Morgan 10/Alamy

their accounts are deleted. CafeMom typically attracts women between the ages of 25 and 54 who have children under the age of 18.

CafeMom is an advertisement-supported social network, which means that the website uses advertisers to generate revenue. Some revenue comes from traditional ads placed on the website. However, CafeMom generates most of its revenue by allowing registered users to interact with a sponsor's products. For example, selected registered moms might be given a product to sample. These products are then marketed to other network members through the opinions and comments about the product posted on the website. This program allows marketers to reach a highly desirable target market in a unique and personal way.

By carving out a unique position in the social networking community and serving the specific needs of its users, CafeMom has become a popular destination for moms everywhere.[1]

OBJECTIVE (1)

A Divide-and-Conquer Strategy

A primary aim of organizations operating from a marketing perspective is anticipating and satisfying customer needs and wants. One of the most important ways in which marketers do this efficiently and profitably is through the strategic use of market segmentation and positioning.

Market segmentation is the process of dividing the large and diverse mass market into subsets of consumers who share common needs, characteristics, or behaviors, and then targeting one or more of those segments with a distinct marketing mix. By identifying groups of highly similar consumers, a marketer can develop products and services specifically tailored to that group's needs that also closely match the capabilities of the organization, thus maximizing the chances of profit and success. Specifically, market segmentation allows a company to efficiently focus resources and efforts by avoiding those parts of the market it cannot satisfy well, thereby avoiding unwieldy competition. Given the diverse preferences of consumers today and the myriad products and services available, it is difficult for most companies to be everything to everyone. In addition, when evaluating a market through the segmentation process, a company is able identify segments that are saturated with strong and powerful competitors, as well as underserved segments that may represent areas of opportunity.

Two key assumptions underlie market segmentation. First, consumer preferences vary. Some consumers prefer plain pizza with only tomato sauce and cheese, while others prefer their pizza "loaded." Some consumers prefer a car that gets good gas mileage, whereas others are more concerned about cargo space and towing features. Although this may seem obvious, if all consumer preferences were universal, there would be few advantages to market segmentation. Second, by tailoring a product or service to a segment's specific needs, marketers can make the offering so appealing that the members of the segment are willing to pay a price that offsets the costs associated with catering to the specialized needs of the segment. We will return to these assumptions when we examine the factors that influence whether a firm engages in market segmentation and to what extent.

Given the number of choices available coupled with the diverse preferences of customers, effective segmentation and positioning is crucial for marketers today.

Michael Blann/Getty Images

After a marketer has segmented its market, the firm can select appropriate segment(s) to target. Thus, a **target market** is simply the segment(s) toward which a firm's marketing efforts are directed. Selection of the target market(s) should be based on a thorough strategic analysis of the organization's external environments (the mass market, competitors, and general technical, political, and sociocultural environments) and internal situations (past performance analysis and determination of future options), ultimately matching organizational strengths with market opportunities (commonly referred to as *SWOT analysis*). Finally, a positioning strategy is developed. **Positioning** is the process of communicating with our target market(s) through the use of marketing mix variables—a specific product, price, distribution channel, and promotional appeal—in such a way as to help consumers differentiate a product from competitors and understand how a particular product best satisfies their needs.

Market segmentation and positioning are two of the most important concepts in the study of consumer behavior and in marketing, because consumers today have more product categories from which to choose and more choices within those categories. Marketers conduct a great deal of consumer research to identify appropriate bases for market segmentation, select appropriate target markets, and develop effective positioning and marketing mix execution strategies.

OBJECTIVE (2) # How Consumers and Society Benefit from Market Segmentation

Through market segmentation, a firm offers products and services specifically tailored to the needs and wants of consumers within a specific segment. While this implies an obvious benefit to consumers, namely having their specific needs catered to, other benefits to consumers and to society may not be so obvious.

First, with companies effectively engaging in market segmentation, consumers no longer have to receive and evaluate marketing information that is irrelevant or unwanted. This reduces consumers' time spent on search, evaluation, and purchase activities. For example, a married, suburban, stay-at-home mom doesn't need or desire to receive direct-mail containing an offer for an urban nightclub's rapid dating service any more than a young, urban, single woman living in an apartment, needs or wants a telemarketer calling and offering lawn and landscaping services. While these marketing misfires occasionally happen, in general, consumers benefit by the efficiency that market segmentation offers in terms of appropriately directing marketing information.

Imagine for a moment that marketers never discovered the efficiencies of dividing consumers into segments and targeting those segments. Most consumers are so accustomed to this marketing practice that such a scenario is hard to imagine. But, if the process of market segmentation did not exist, consumers' lives would probably be very different. For instance, if you're living in Savannah, Georgia, imagine getting pizza coupons in the mail from a pizza parlor in Rome, Italy. Or, imagine a telemarketer calling you and attempting to sell you industrial lubricant for your large industrial

Ethics

Can market segmentation create market *segregation*? Although segmentation offers several important benefits that we discuss in this chapter, it is not a panacea. Namely, segmentation may reinforce societal prejudice.

While market segmentation may seem far removed from the serious social problem of prejudice, some marketing researchers and sociologists argue that market segmentation reinforces separatism between groups and individual members of society, minimizing exposure to others and reinforcing a "me" orientation— "I own certain products, have particular interests and

activities, and belong in a group with others like me."

Formally, *prejudice* is defined as unfounded fear, hatred, or mistrust of a person or group of people, based on insufficient knowledge and typically centered on ethnicity, nationality, religion, or social class. If prejudice is based on insufficient knowledge and fear of others, it is possible that market segmentation reinforces societal prejudice. After all, market segmentation certainly does not encourage the coming together of the diverse marketplace. On the contrary, the explicit goal of market segmentation is to create homogenous subsets from the diverse marketplace. Once that is accomplished, marketers deliver—via the marketing mix and mass media—products, services, and promotional messages that feed consumers' most narcissistic tendencies. From personalized tennis shoes and

exclusive customer reward programs to advertisements that speak directly to the customer and the customer's peers (and to no one else), marketers do encourage people to develop personal and distinctive styles, stress the uniqueness and "special-ness" of a person's own in-group, and highlight differences between his or her group and others.

Although there are a number of ways that segmentation is beneficial to consumers, marketers, and society, consumers should also recognize the degree to which segmentation reinforces stereotypes and prejudice. We have yet to learn how harmful to society and its values this separatism or segregation is, but it is important for current and future marketers (that's you!) to consider potential hidden costs and ethical implications of marketing strategies.[2]

drill press—you don't have a large industrial drill press in your dorm room or apartment, do you? Beyond being buried in paper and flooded with irrelevant telemarketing and email, chances are you would also never learn about the new products and services that actually would benefit you and make your life better—products like low-cost cellular phones, ergonomically correct backpacks that don't hurt your spine, and vitamin-enriched bottled water. Many marketers would argue that the reason for our high standard of living is that marketers learned that for most products and services a single-product marketing strategy cannot efficiently or effectively reach and service everyone, and that markets must be broken into manageable segments. It is then that companies can tailor offerings and messages to their benefit and the benefit of consumers and society.

OBJECTIVE 3

Factors Influencing Market Segmentation Strategies

Market segmentation is a multi-product strategy: different products are developed for different subcategories. For example, in the United States, car manufacturer Jeep markets the Grand Cherokee, Compass, Liberty, Wrangler, and Patriot to different market segments. **Market aggregation** is the opposite of market segmentation—a single-product, one-size-fits-all strategy in which individual differences among consumers are ignored.

FIGURE **2.1** | **Market Segmentation Strategies**

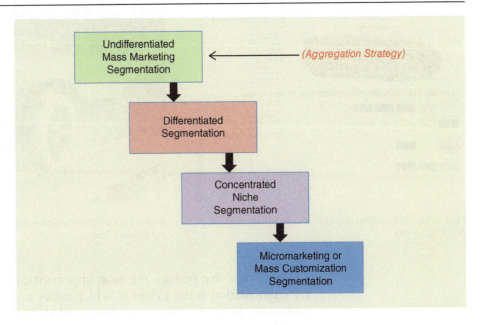

Figure 2.1 shows various market segmentation strategies. If a firm chooses not to target specific segments, but rather pursues an aggregation strategy offering the same product and marketing mix to all consumers, this is called *mass marketing*. The first generally recognized mass marketer in the United States was Henry Ford, founder of the Ford Motor Company, who offered the Model-T automobile to the market "in any color as long as it is black." Ford was also the first company to advertise on a national level.[3]

Traditional segmentation strategies like the Jeep strategy described above is called *differentiated segmentation*. A firm targets several market segments with the goal of having a strong position and share of the market in each segment. A special form of differentiated segmentation, called *niche segmentation*, is where a brand attempts to capture a large share of a smaller niche market segment. For example, Spike TV, a channel geared toward young men, and The Travel Channel, aimed at travel enthusiasts, are cable television channels that try to capture niche audiences.

Finally, opposite of mass marketing, a firm may choose to market one-to-one with a customer, a strategy also called *micromarketing*. A special form of one-to-one marketing, called *mass customization*, is the targeting of large segments, or traditionally mass markets, with highly customized products.[4] For example, BMW's Build-a-Car website feature allows BMW customers to design their own BMW 3-Series car, mixing and matching exterior and interior colors, options, and accessories.

When should a firm pursue a market segmentation strategy (instead of an aggregation strategy), and at what level of individual targeting? The best answer follows from four main considerations: consumer preference heterogeneity, the majority fallacy, the sales-cost trade-off, and the potential for cannibalization.

Courtesy of BMW of North America

Mass customization allows marketers to cater to individual needs and wants.

Keystone Features/Getty Images

The Ford Motor Company is generally recognized as the first "mass marketer" in the United States.

We've seen that perhaps the most important consideration related to market segmentation is the extent to which tastes and preferences differ among consumers. Formally, this assumption is called **consumer preference heterogeneity**. Some people prefer spicy food, whereas others prefer bland foods. As preference heterogeneity increases, the case for segmentation increases. Moreover, the greater the variability, the more potential profits provided by individual segments.

When consumers' preferences vary, it is important to analyze how these preferences are distributed. Let's return to our spicy food example. In terms of level of spiciness, the vast majority of consumers prefer foods that are average (not too bland and not too spicy), but there are also smaller segments of consumers who prefer very mild, bland tastes, and customers who prefer extremely hot and spicy foods. Because it is logical to assume that size of the potential market segment is positively correlated to profit, it is often easy for a company to focus exclusively on large average segments, where the majority of customer preferences lie, and neglect smaller, less typical segments. This tendency is called the **majority fallacy**; pursuing the majority segment is considered a "fallacy" because the largest segment, where competition tends to be most intense, is not always the most profitable. Smaller segments can actually be more profitable when there is less competition. (Figure 2.2 illustrates the majority fallacy.) For example, Ragu spaghetti sauce and many other sauces are average in terms of spiciness and are very popular, but competition in this segment is intense. There are at least 10 different brands that would be considered an average spicy sauce. On the other hand, Hunt's Zesty and Spicy Pasta Sauce is a fairly spicy spaghetti sauce that appeals to a much smaller market segment. Although this segment is small, it is quite profitable because there is little competition.

Another influence on segmentation strategy is the **sales-cost trade-off**. This trade-off recognizes that, as market segmentation increases, sales increase because a firm's offerings align more closely to consumers' preferences. But at the same time, costs also increase because a multi-product strategy costs more to implement than a one-product strategy. Why? Manufacturing and marketing

---

FIGURE 2.2 | **The Majority Fallacy**

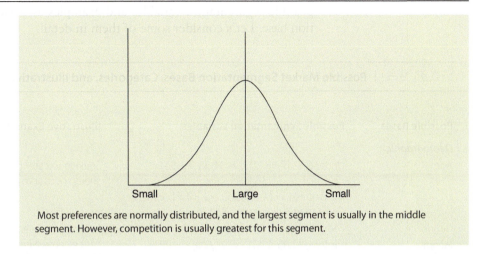

Small	Large	Small

Most preferences are normally distributed, and the largest segment is usually in the middle segment. However, competition is usually greatest for this segment.

costs increase as the number of products offered increases due to additional equipment, skills, and resources needed to make and market a variety of products. Hidden marketing costs associated with multi-product strategies also exist. For example, retail shelf space is limited, and retailers may be unwilling to carry many different varieties of a product or may force the decision back on the brand manufacturer. For example, when a company comes out with a new brand extension, the retailer may force the company to fit the new product into the existing shelf space already held by the brand. Thus, the brand doesn't gain any new shelf space but must crowd its current offerings together.

Finally, the risk of cannibalization influences market segmentation decisions. **Cannibalization** occurs when products offered by the same firm are so similar that they compete among themselves, thus creating a case of *over-segmentation*. For example, if a consumer drinks Pepsi, she might also drink Diet Pepsi; thus Pepsi competes against itself for her drink purchase. At one time, Quaker State offered 1,500 different brands of motor oil. The company cut its product line in half and profits increased dramatically because cannibalization and other types of costs decreased. Sharing manufacturing and marketing costs across product offerings is important when cannibalization is a potential issue. Thus, a company must strike a delicate balance between effective market coverage and too many offerings.

Now that we have discussed what market segmentation is and some of the influences related to market segmentation and targeting strategies, we turn our attention to the various bases of market segmentation.

OBJECTIVE **4** # Bases of Segmentation

There are many different ways to segment a market, and marketers should consider multiple approaches. Consumers differ on many dimensions, and each dimension suggests a potentially useful basis for dividing up the market. While we will discuss each base of segmentation as a single strategy, remember that firms almost always use multiple methods in combination to divide and group consumers. A number of segmentation bases are listed in Table 2.1, along with possible segmentation variables and examples associated with that segmentation base. Let's consider some of them in detail.

TABLE 2.1 | Possible Market Segmentation Bases, Categories, and Illustrative Examples

Possible Bases:	Possible Segmentation Variables:	Illustrative Examples:
Demographic		
Age	Under 6, 7–12, 13–21, 22–34, 35–50, 50+	Seeking to cater to the under-25 market, Vans shoes sponsors a concert tour
	Pre-depression, Depression era, Baby boomers, Generation X, Generation Y, Millennials	
Gender	Female, Male	In Japan, females are targeted as the main
Income	Under $25,000, $25,000–$75,000, $75,000+	coffee consumers by coffee companies like
Education	Some H.S., H.S. graduate, Some college, College graduate, Postgraduate	Starbucks, which operates over 900 outlets in that country.[5]
Occupation	Blue-collar, White-collar, Military, Craft	
Social Class	Lower, Middle, Upper	
Marital Status	Single, Married, Divorced, Co-habitating, Widowed	Carnival Cruises offers a line of special cruises
Family Life Cycle	Single, Young married, Full nester, Empty Nester, Single elderly	aimed at couples.
Culture/Ethnicity	White, African American, Hispanic, Asian, Pacific Islander, Middle Eastern, American Indian	Hallmark offers specialty card collections targeted to African Americans, the Latino culture, and the those of the Jewish faith.
Geographic		
Pop. Density	Urban, Suburb, Exurb, Penturbia, Rural	Rural King's home improvement chain targets smaller rural markets to avoid competing with large national home improvement stores (avoiding the majority fallacy).
Region	North, South, East, West Neighborhood, Town, City, State, Country Mountains, Plains, Deserts, Ocean, Jungle	Campbell's Soup markets a spicy nacho soup in Texas and California.
Climate	Temperate, Hot, Rainy, Dry	
Psychographic		
	VALS (see discussion) 4C's (see discussion)	Dyson vacuum cleaners, with their trendy and innovative design, appeal to Aspirers in the 4C's group.
Behavioral		
Attribute/Benefit	Price, Convenience, Ease-of-use, Status	Snackwell's products are aimed at people who want sweet snacks but are also conscious of their health and weight.
Occasion	Morning, Evening Leisure, Work, Rush Holiday, Special day	Campbell's markets Soup-On-The-Go for those times when people don't have time to sit down and eat lunch.
Product Usage	Current user, Potential user, Lapsed user Light, Medium, Heavy	Subway offers frequent users rewards of free food after a certain number of purchases.

Demographic Bases

Market segmentation is often based on customers' vital population statistics, called **demographic characteristics**. Popular demographic characteristics include age, gender, income, education, occupation, social class, marital status, household size, family life cycle, and culture or ethnicity. Demographics-based segmentation is the most popular segmentation base because demographic characteristics are visible, relatively easy and inexpensive to measure, and most secondary data, such as U.S. Census data, are described in terms of demographic characteristics.

Not surprisingly, our preferences, buying habits, and behaviors vary dramatically as a function of many different demographic characteristics. For example, males and females prefer different brands of clothes, health and beauty products, and many brands are targeted exclusively at a particular gender, such as Dove for women and Axe for men.

Geographic Bases

In **geographic based segmentation**, marketers split the market based on physical location of potential customers. An underlying assumption of this

Marketing in Action

Hallmark Reaches African Americans in a Culturally Relevant Way

African Americans account for approximately 13% of the population, according to the U.S. Census, and Hallmark, a leader in greeting cards since the early 1900s, has tapped into this market with their line of Mahogany greeting cards. The selection of seasonal and everyday cards is the largest, most extensive brand of cards centered on the African American demographic and culture. According to the company website (www.hallmark.com), "Mahogany features more than 800 everyday and seasonal cards to help African Americans honor their relationships in innovative, compelling, and culturally relevant ways."

Hallmark conducts extensive research to maintain its understanding of this unique market segment, including working with African American artists and writers in card design, seeking out culturally relevant African American artwork to incorporate into Mahogany cards, and talking to consumers about their lifestyles. The goal is to truly understand African-American culture and heritage and reflect that understanding in the product line.

The top two retail markets for Mahogany cards are Washington D.C. and New York City, which have high concentrations of African American populations. Other top markets include Chicago, Philadelphia, and Atlanta. In addition to

traditional retail stores, Mahogany has a presence on both Facebook and Twitter as a way to connect with African American consumers. By effectively employing demographic segmentation, Hallmark is meeting the needs of this ethnic community.[6]

Courtesy of Hallmark Cards, Inc.

market segmentation base is that consumers located in geographic proximity share similar needs and preferences for products and services. Boundaries defined by zip code districts, towns, cities, states, regions, countries, and continents might indeed be useful to a company. For example, Heineken markets a non-alcoholic beer in several countries in the Middle East, where the sale of alcoholic beverages is forbidden. Procter & Gamble markets different formulations of Tide detergent throughout the world, depending on regional water quality and washing machine type. Geographic segmentation also includes climate or topographical characteristics of an area. Snow blowers are marketed in cold areas of the country, and surfboards sell better along warm, coastal regions.

Community type is also a segmentation variable and includes urban environments, suburbs, *exurbs* (remote suburbs), and *penturbia* (small towns). In the United States throughout the twentieth century, people made an exodus out of the cities, which began in the 1920s, first to suburbs and then to the exurbs, and finally to small towns, called penturbia. This trend strongly influenced the growth of the suburban "strip" mall and large regional shopping malls. Only more recently have U.S. cities seen a resurgence in urban living, with younger generations moving to urban areas. Worldwide, the trend continues toward the urban, and by 2050 some estimates show that 70% of the world's population will be living in urban areas, with the number of mega cities, defined as urban areas of 10 million people or more, projected to continue to grow (there are currently 21 mega cities).[7]

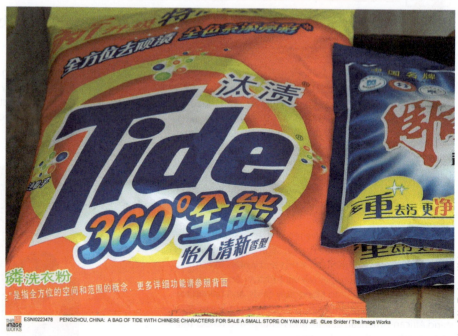

Tide is marketed worldwide and adapted to local markets.

ESNI0223478   PENGZHOU, CHINA: A BAG OF TIDE WITH CHINESE CHARACTERS FOR SALE A SMALL STORE ON YAN XIU JIE. ©Lee Snider / The Image Works

Lee Snider/The Image Works

Geo-demographic segmentation combines geography and demographic segmentation bases. Sometimes called *zip-code marketing,* this segmentation strategy relies on the common tendency for people who are similar along demographic dimensions to live in close proximity. In other words, we tend to live near people who are like us (i.e., "birds of a feather..."). For example, it is not surprising to drive into certain suburban neighborhoods in the United States and see swing-sets in almost every yard, minivans and SUVs in the garages, and bicycles in the driveways. Sometimes we may make a conscious choice to live near others who are similar to us on a certain dimension. For example, in San Francisco, there is a neighborhood called The Castro District, which is predominantly populated by gay and lesbian households. Alternatively, we may not consciously choose to live by those who are similar to us, but situational factors simply make a certain neighborhood or living situation a logical choice. Take our suburban neighborhood example. That neighborhood may attract young families more than other kinds of homebuyers or renters because it is near a school, or has houses in the price range of what a young family can afford, or simply because there are so many families with children already living there. Those who also have children find the presence of potential playmates for their kids an attractive social benefit of the neighborhood.

Another interesting aspect of this phenomenon is that people who live near each other may become even more alike over time. Neighbors observe one another and may compare their actions, opinions, activities, and possessions, which could translate to purchasing products in order to gain social acceptance and fit in—or they may simply see the benefits of owning a product their neighbors already enjoy. For example, suppose someone in a suburban neighborhood builds an outdoor patio. In order to fully enjoy the patio, the homeowner has frequent outdoor cookouts and parties, inviting friends and neighbors. It isn't long until one of the neighbors thinks, "This patio is great; I want one for myself." And, even better, the patio owner will probably recommend his own patio builder.

Nielsen markets a segmentation system called PRIZM® (originally developed by Claritas, Inc.) that incorporates geographic data down to the neighborhood and household levels, demographic data from the U.S. Census, and consumption and media usage information, resulting in segmentation of the U.S. market into 66 distinct segments, combined into 14 broad social groups. Each of the 66 segments includes a corresponding illustration to depict the individuals within that group. Any household or neighborhood in the United States can be profiled. Here is a sampling of some of the 66 segments.

#3 Movers and Shakers is the nation's group of upwardly mobile executives, who are highly educated, wealthy, and live in dual-income suburban households. Members of this group are the most likely to own a small business and/or have a home office.

#4 Young Digerati is an affluent, well-educated, ethnically diverse group that is comfortable in this high-tech era. They are singles and couples living in high-end condos and apartments in trendy urban neighborhoods.

#13 Upward Bound represents the legendary soccer moms and dads and are a key market for child-centered products. Households in this group consist of dual-income earners with college degrees and white-collar jobs. These upper-class families live in newer suburban subdivisions.

#39 Domestic Duos is a group that consists of middle-class empty-nesters living in older suburban neighborhoods. With homes paid off and fixed-pension incomes, living is stable and enjoyable, although not extravagant.

#51 Shotguns and Pickups tend to be young, working-class couples with large families, and not surprisingly, are the most likely of all the segments to own a hunting rifle and a pickup truck. One third of this group also lives in mobile homes.

#61 City Roots is a segment of lower-income retirees living low-key lifestyles on fixed incomes. These individuals—made up largely of African Americans and Hispanics—live in urban neighborhoods in condos and townhouses that they have owned for many years.[8]

Companies can use the PRIZM® system to identify clusters in their markets and custom design marketing campaigns to penetrate into specific segments. For example, Cox Communications, a large cable provider, was able to identify segments nationwide that used its products. Armed with this information, the firm could target non-users in these segments in various markets, thus increasing sales and market penetration.

Psychographic Bases

Marketers also segment markets based on **psychographics**, which is a general term variously used to describe the measurement of lifestyle, attitudes, beliefs, and social values. Lifestyle, which is simply how we live, is traditionally defined in terms of a person's activities (how they spend their time doing things such as volunteer work, vacationing, and exercising), interests (what they consider important or value in life such as home, recreation, and family), and opinions (how they feel about the world around them such political, religious, and social beliefs). Researchers use large batteries of questions (called *AIO Inventories*) to measure activities, interests, and opinions to develop consumer profiles, usually called *psychographic profiles* or *AIO's*. Psychographic information is more comprehensive than demographic information. Whereas demographic analysis focuses on who buys products, AIO research can provide context and robust consumer profiles but do not explain why consumers buy because these measures are not included.

VALS™ VALS is a widely used psychographic segmentation. The Framework described is for the United States and Canada only. VALS was originally developed by SRI International and is currently owned by Strategic Business Insights (SBI; a spinoff from SRI). VALS originally stood for "values and lifestyles," and when it was first introduced in 1978, it segmented consumers based on social values and lifestyle variables. VALS was completely revised and validated in a two-year research effort and was re-launched in 1989; values and lifestyles were replaced with enduring measures that explain and predict underlying drivers of consumer choice. An individual's VALS type is determined by their answers to 35 attitude and 4 demographic questions; a proprietary algorithm classifies each respondent into one of eight consumer groups on the basis of their answers.

VALS classifies adults age 18 years of age and older into eight distinct consumer segments, as shown in Figure 2.3 and Table 2.2. The segments are

FIGURE 2.3 | **The VALS Segments***

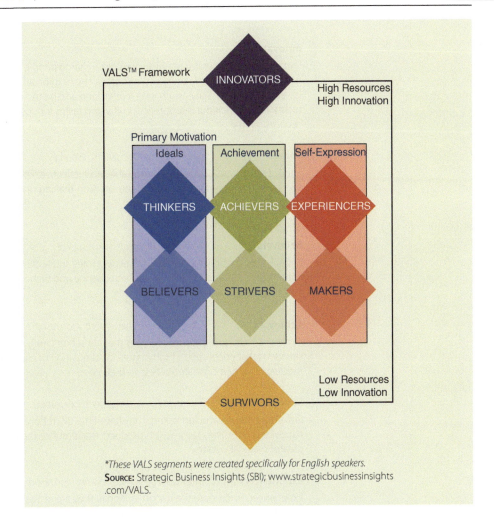

*These VALS segments were created specifically for English speakers.
Source: Strategic Business Insights (SBI); www.strategicbusinessinsights
.com/VALS.

grouped along two dimensions: (1) primary motivation and (2) resources. An individual's *primary motivation* expresses his or her self-perception or mindset. Consumers are driven by one of three primary motivations—ideals, achievement, or self-expression. Consumers motivated by ideals are guided by strongly held ethical codes, beliefs or personal philosophies, and a general quest for life knowledge and understanding. Those motivated by achievement seek social approval from society and base their behaviors on the reactions of their peer or group to which they aspires to belong. Consumers motivated by self-expression seek individuality, action, and direct experience.

Resources comprise a range of physical, emotional, and psychological attributes, such as self-confidence, energy, vanity, and intellectualism. Coupled with demographic characteristics such as education and income, resources influence one's ability to act on his or her primary motivation. Table 2.2 provides a description of each of the VALS segments.[9]

TABLE 2.2 | **Description of the VALS Segments**

Innovators

Innovators are successful, sophisticated, take-charge people with high self-esteem. Because they have such abundant resources, they exhibit all three primary motivations in varying degrees. They are change leaders and are the most receptive to new ideas and technologies. Their purchases reflect cultivated tastes for upscale, niche products and services.

Thinkers   *Motivated by ideals; high resources*

Thinkers are mature, satisfied, comfortable, and reflective. They tend to be well educated and actively seek out information in the decision-making process. They favor durability, functionality, and value in products.

Believers   *Motivated by ideals; low resources*

Believers are strongly traditional and respect rules and authority. Because they are fundamentally conservative, they are slow to change and technology averse. They choose familiar products and established brands.

Achievers   *Motivated by achievement; high resources*

Achievers have goal-oriented lifestyles that center on family and career. They avoid situations that encourage a high degree of stimulation or change. They prefer premium products that demonstrate success to their peers.

Strivers   *Motivated by achievement; low resources*

Strivers are trendy and fun loving. They have little discretionary income and tend to have narrow interests. They favor stylish products that emulate the purchases of people with greater material wealth.

Experiencers   *Motivated by self-expression; high resources*

Experiencers appreciate the unconventional. They are active and impulsive, seeking stimulation from the new, offbeat, and risky. They spend a comparatively high proportion of their income on fashion, socializing, and entertainment.

Makers   *Motivated by self-expression; low resources*

Makers value practicality and self-sufficiency. They choose hands-on constructive activities and spend leisure time with family and close friends. Because they prefer value to luxury, they buy basic products.

Survivors

Survivors lead narrowly focused lives. Because they have the fewest resources, they are not active consumers and therefore do not exhibit a primary motivation. They tend to be brand loyal and buy discounted merchandise. While they make do with limited material goods they are often satisfied with their lives.

Source: http://www.strategicbusinessinsights.com/vals/ustypes.shtml

National U.S. data about VALS segment preferences for products, services, leisure activities, and media is provided through GfK/Mediamark Research Intelligence's *Survey of the American Consumer* in which the VALS survey is embedded. Proprietary surveys are conducted regularly for specific client projects. To develop a VALS Framework for another country, the survey used to measure motivations and resources must be sensitive to both language and culture. To date VALS Frameworks exist for Japan, the United Kingdom, Venezuela, the Dominican Republic, Nigeria, and China. The three primary motivations are found to be consistent across cultures; segment sizes differ by country and resulting groups express their primary motivation differently because of resources.

Behavioral Bases

Behavioral-based segmentation groups consumers based on their preference for a particular product attribute or benefit, usage occasion, user status, rate of product usage, and loyalty status.

Product Attributes or Benefits Important product attributes like taste are useful segmentation tools because they are easy to identify. When segmenting the market for digital cameras, for example, companies have relied on product attributes such as resolution quality to define market segments and develop appropriate products. Canon U.S.A. offers cameras with a wide range of megapixels for the non-professional camera buyer.

Which is among the most common product attributes used to segment consumers? *Price.* Consumers can be segmented based on price in many ways. One price segmentation model is presented here (see Figure 2.4). It divides segments based along two dimensions. One dimension, referred to as *perceived pain*, is the amount of anxiety and negative feelings a consumer experiences when paying what he or she believes is a high price for a product. The other dimension is called *perceived value*, the amount of product differentiation a consumer perceives among products, or the degree to which a consumer views brands within a product category as unique based on price. A consumer rated high on perceived value tends to view large differences among brands in terms of quality and other product benefits. A consumer rated low on perceived value tends to view brands as commodities with little brand differentiation.

Will a consumer always fall into one category for all products purchased? Of course not—the segment will depend on the product category and is influenced by situational variables.

These two dimensions form four price segments. Consumers who possess high levels of perceived pain and low levels of perceived value represent the *price segment*. These consumers reside in the upper-left quadrant of Figure 2.4. In other words, consumers in this segment feel that most brands are pretty much alike and don't want to pay a high price for a particular brand. These consumers tend to be the ultimate price shoppers and may sacrifice extra benefits and services in order to achieve the lowest price. For example, stores that

Global Perspectives

Segmentation Across Cultures is Gaining Importance

While several market segmentation models are available for the U.S. market, they don't necessarily translate into foreign markets. To address this need, market researchers have attempted to create more global segments based on psychographics. One example of a cross-cultural lifestyle market segmentation system is called the *Cross-Cultural Consumer Characterization*, or the 4Cs for short. This model was developed by leading advertising agency Young and Rubicam. It is considered cross-cultural because its developers believe that the target values upon which the segments are based are universal and found in all cultures. The model was developed based on data from seven European countries: the United Kingdom, France, Italy, Spain, Germany, Switzerland, and the Netherlands, but it now includes a worldwide database. Using a method that adapts values to local cultural norms, 4Cs has been constructed in over 50 countries including places as various as Iceland, Lithuania, Thailand, El Salvador, and Kazakhstan.

The model is based on seven *enduring human values*, a set of accepted personal principles and standards that emerged in the data, namely the need for status, security, control, discovery, enlightenment, survival, and escape. 4Cs is constructed using only value statements; nonetheless, values do connect with demographic circumstances. Based on these core values and data, seven relatively stable lifestyle segments were constructed:

Resigned: Tends to be older; is rigid, strict, authoritarian, and oriented to the past and to the value of survival. Brand choices stress economy, familiarity, and communication with the segment is best centered on expert opinion and simple messages. (About 10% of the population.)

Struggler: Limited resources and capabilities; disorganized and alienated from mainstream society. Brand choices are centered on sensation and escape. (About 8% of the population.)

Mainstreamer: The largest segment; members are conventional, conforming, passive, and above all avoid risk; represents the majority view. Focus is on well-known brands and value-oriented brands, and communication with the segment should be emotionally warm and reassuring. (About 30% of the population.)

Aspirer: Tends to be younger; may be in entry-level white-collar profession; oriented to status value and the external—material possessions, appearance, image, and fashion. Brand choices are trendy, fun, and unique. (About 13% of the population.)

Succeeder: Confident and accomplished but is all about control; may be an executive or in top management; oriented to confidence, work ethic, goals, and leadership. Brand choices are based on prestige, reward, and caring for oneself, and communication with the segment should focus on evidence of claims. (About 16% of the population.)

Explorer: Based in discovery, explorers are adrenaline junkies who love breaking rules, seeking out the unconventional, and being impulsive. Brands for this segment are innovative and daring. (About 9% of the population.)

Reformer: Focused on enlightenment, freedom, and personal growth; typically higher education and higher income; oriented to healthy debate and is not impressed by status. Brand choices tend to innovative and practical. (About 14% of the population.)[10]

carry discontinued or slightly damaged items (called *off-price discounters*) have become very popular and appeal to the price segment. Also, generic brands and store brands tend to appeal to this segment.

Those consumers with low levels of perceived pain and low levels of perceived value fall into the *convenience segment*. They reside in the lower-left quadrant of Figure 2.4. While these consumers also view brands as having little differentiation, unlike the price segment, these consumers are not particularly

FIGURE 2.4 | Market Segmentation Based on Price

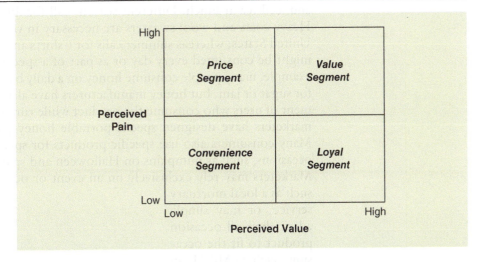

sensitive to price. These consumers are most sensitive to the time they have to spend shopping and want to minimize search and evaluation, and thus, they are willing to pay a higher price for the convenience of easy brand selection. Internet and catalog shopping appeal to these consumers. Although shipping costs associated with buying on the Internet or from a catalog tend to drive up product prices, the consumer can conveniently shop and compare several brands very quickly from the comfort of home.

Consumers residing in the lower-right quadrant of Figure 2.4 represent the *loyal segment*, a combination of low perceived pain and high perceived value. This segment is highly desirable to marketers who have invested to build meaning into their brand name and offer a premium product. This is the "choosy mom" who chooses Jif (whether she has a coupon for it or not), and she *always* buys Jif. If the brand is not available, then she won't purchase peanut butter that week because she is so brand loyal that substitutes are unacceptable.

The last segment is called the *value segment*. Consumers who reside in the upper-right quadrant of Figure 2.4 demonstrate a combination of high perceived pain and high perceived values. While these consumers view brands as highly differentiated, they also do not want to pay for that differentiation. In other words, these consumers want it all: the best brand names at the very lowest price. In many ways, this is the most difficult segment to satisfy. For example, outlet malls that carry overstocks of premium brands—Coach bags, Calvin Klein clothing, and Wedgwood china, for instance—are very popular and appeal to the value segment. Coupon usage is also high among this group because coupons allow shoppers to feel like they are getting a special, exclusive deal on a quality brand.

Usage Occasions and Product Usage Usage occasion segmentation describes purchasing and consuming products at different times of day, different times of year, and at different events or on different occasions. For example, people prefer to eat toast and drink hot tea at breakfast but prefer sandwiches and iced tea at lunch. Different seasons call for different types of products. Heavy coats and wool sweaters are necessary in winter in many parts of the United States, whereas summer calls for t-shirts and shorts. Finally, products might be consumed every day or as part of a special event or occasion. For example, many people consume honey on a daily basis, using it as a substitute for sugar or jam, but honey manufacturers have also identified a specific segment of users who consume the product while running or exercising. Clever marketers have designed special portable honey packets for this purpose. Many consumers also use specific products for specific events or on special occasions, such as pumpkins on Halloween and sparklers on the 4th of July. Marketers may rely exclusively on an event or occasion for product usage, such as a local mortuary service, or may simply adapt their all-occasion product to fit the occasion, such as M&Ms in holiday themes.

Carolyn Jenkins/Alamy Limited

Product usage segmentation is based on identifying light, medium, or heavy users of a product or identifying current, potential, or lapsed users. Different marketing tactics are required for different groups of consumers. For example, potential users may be unaware of the product category or unaware of the benefits of the product. Thus, marketing efforts targeted toward this group should work to increase awareness and educate potential consumers about the specific product benefits. Heavy users, on the other hand, already know about and like the product. Therefore, marketing efforts targeted toward this group should remind them to keep purchasing and maintaining their loyalty. For example, many firms now practice *customer loyalty programs*, marketing tactics and programs designed to reward and retain a company's most loyal customers. For years, airlines and hotels have offered special reward programs for frequent travelers. Frequent airline flyers can earn free tickets, class upgrades, and faster check-in service, while hotels offer free rooms or room upgrades to frequent guests. Nowadays, a wide variety of firms offer customer loyalty programs, including bookstores, restaurants, movie theatres, and gas stations, just to name a few. The more purchases the customer makes, the more rewards and benefits he or she earns.

OBJECTIVE ⑤ # Positioning

The previous sections have detailed the various segmentation bases by which consumers can be divided, clustered, and targeted. So far, we've explained why it's important for marketers to identify individual customer segments, i.e., the "divide" portion of the divide-and-conquer strategy. Next, we describe the "conquer" portion of the strategy, namely positioning. We've already seen that positioning is the process of communicating with target market(s) in such a way as to help consumers differentiate the firm's product from other products and understand how the product can specifically satisfy their needs and wants. Sometimes marketers use terms like *value proposition* or "*The Big Idea!*" to describe a brand, product, or company's specific positioning strategy within the market. For example, Dove's big idea is The Campaign for Real Beauty and is reflected in the brand's promotional efforts. Based on this campaign, Dove has expanded its social mission to include the Dove Mission for Self-Esteem and Make Girls Unstoppable, programs of community-based outreach and online tools to mentor young women.

According to positioning experts Al Reis and Jack Trout, the "position" of a product is the place the product occupies in the customers' minds, relative to the competitor's products.[11] What's important about this definition is: (1) a firm must always position in terms of the competition, and (2) positioning is not something a marketer *does* to a product, it's actually something that happens in the mind of the prospect as a result of the brand messages and communication that the marketer provides. Thus, marketers can't definitively position a product, although they talk about positioning strategy as if that is what they do. All marketers can do, however, is communicate the marketing mix to the target market in such a way that the consumer accurately positions the product in his or her own mind, hopefully in line with the intentions of the marketer.

All marketing activities influence positioning and vice versa. For example, Armani does not allow Walmart to carry its men's clothing line because this low-cost retailer would undermine Armani's high-end positioning strategy. Likewise, Walmart does not want to carry Armani suits because this would be inconsistent with its image as a low-cost retailer. Such inconsistent channel decisions would confuse customers of both firms.

Companies use several strategies to position their products, depending on the product's characteristics, market segmentation bases used, the competitive environment, and the goals of the company. We'll review some of them here.

Positioning a Leader

Some brands have the distinction of being the first brand to enter and define a market. These brands are referred to as *pioneering brands*. Research has shown that pioneering brands have an advantage in the market for a number of reasons. First, they are novel and interesting so consumers pay attention to them.[12] Also, when a new product category is created, consumers are typically unsure of their preferences. When this is the case, the combination of features and benefits associated with the pioneering brand seems especially useful, so much so that the pioneer actually sets the ideal standards for the category against which other follower brands' product attributes, features, and benefits are judged.[13] (You will learn more about the advantage of pioneer brands in Chapter 3.)

These advantages lead to greater strategic opportunities for pioneering brands because they enable the pioneer to clearly position itself as the leader of a category, and positioning as a leader means setting a *standard of comparison*, which means being the brand against which all the other brands in the category are judged. Consider the following classic positioning statements (communicated via Coke's advertising): "It's the real thing," "Coke is it!", "Always Coca-Cola," "Coca-Cola… Real." All these messages imply that everything else is a pale imitation. Coca-Cola invented the cola category and much of its marketing emphasizes this point. Similarly, advertising for many pioneering brands argues, "we invented the product," implying that the brand knows more about the product category than any other competitor. Some examples are Jeep—"There's Only One," and Xerox—"The Document Company" and "The Knowledge Company."

Positioning a Follower

How do firms market a product that isn't the pioneering or leader brand? One strategy for positioning a follower brand is to separate the brand from the leader by creating what appears to the customer as a new product category. For example, Pepsi has been very successful competing against Coca-Cola by positioning itself as a hipper, trendier brand for a younger generation. Several years ago, Anheuser-Busch held the domestic beer market. When Heineken entered the U.S. market, it was positioned under a new category—*premium imported beer*—and is still the leader in this category. Anheuser-Busch also wanted to expand in the premium category so it invented the *premium domestic beer* category with Michelob. Anheuser-Busch quickly followed with Michelob Ultra to serve the *diet beer category*.[14]

Pursuing a "doing the opposite" positioning strategy is also an option for a follower brand.[15] When taking this approach, a brand positions itself opposite the leader. Take, for example, the battle between Mercedes-Benz and BMW. For many years, Mercedes-Benz was the most famous luxury car in the world. BMW decided to take an opposite strategy. While Mercedes was known for comfort and luxuriant roominess, BMW focused on nimble performance. Its value proposition was "The Ultimate Driving Machine." Today, BMW outsells Mercedes in many markets around the world, including in the United States.[16]

Another classic example of doing the opposite is the famous 7-Up "uncola" campaign, which began in the 1960s. A cola is dark, sweet, and strong in after-taste, and the opposite of a cola is uncola. Television advertising for 7-Up used a highly successful comparative theme in which dried-up, shriveled cola nuts (actually cocoa beans) were compared with juicy, colorful, lively "uncola nuts" (fresh lemons and limes). The company also created uncola drinking glasses, which had an upside-down Coca-Cola hourglass design. During the campaign in the late 1960s, sales rose a whopping 20% per year. Prior to the campaign, consumers did not think of 7-Up when they purchased soft drinks. 7-Up was used primarily as a headache remedy and alcoholic mixer (it was promoted "for home and hospital use" when first introduced in 1929). Interestingly, despite 7-Up's growth in the soft drink market, its old reputation has persisted. Many older U.S. consumers still keep it in their liquor cabinet, and some people still drink it when they are sick, although there is no medicinal benefit to the beverage.

Finally, turning disadvantages into advantages is a useful strategy for follower brands. In another classic and very successful advertising campaign, Avis car rental, a clear follower brand, said "we try harder." Often, smaller companies will also use the phrase "not the biggest, just the best" to convey that smaller can mean higher quality and more individualized service.

Positioning Linked to Segmentation Bases

Beyond broad strategies for positioning leaders and followers, some specific strategies apply to all types of brands. These strategies parallel bases of segmentation discussed earlier in the chapter.

Positioning by Core Benefit One popular strategy employs a **core benefit proposition**, which relies on a single attribute or benefit that differentiates the brand from competitors' offerings. When positioning with a core benefit, the proposition should be short and easy to remember and should *sharply* differentiate the product from competing brands. In others words, the benefit should be exclusively associated with the brand and strongly held in the consumers' minds.[17] Volvo is safety; Federal Express is overnight; Brawny Paper Towels are strong; and Subway is fresh.

When positioning with a core benefit, the proposition should sharply differentiate the product from competing brands.

Positioning by Price Sometimes it is difficult to focus on a core benefit. Perhaps a competitor already is known for a key benefit; or perhaps a firm's core benefit is complicated and difficult to communicate to the consumer. Price is an alternative attribute. It is easy to understand and communicate, and it is important to most consumers because they consistently use price as a gauge of quality with the notion, "You get what you pay for."[18] The assumption that there is a strong relationship between price and quality leads consumers to infer that high price signals high quality. This is called the *price-quality heuristic*. Communicating price differences among brands to consumers translates into perceived quality differences. (You will hear more about this concept later.)

Positioning by price typically takes the form of using premium pricing or pricing below competitor brands. **Premium pricing**, sometimes called prestige pricing, is pricing the brand at the high end of product category's price range. It can be applied to any type of product, such as Piaget watches for $15,000; S. T. DuPont lighters for $7,000; Clive Christian #1 Perfume for $1,900 per ounce; and Ben & Jerry's Ice Cream for $5.00 a cone.

Pricing lower than competitors' brands is a strategy often used by store brands, such as Walmart brands, Kroger brands, and so on. These brands typically promote the store brand as being the same as the name brand, but simply lower in price. Moreover, retailers can highlight price differences easily by placing store brands next to name brands on the store shelf. Walmart is the most well-known low-price positioned company in history. It sets prices up to 10% less than competitors in many areas.

Positioning by Product Usage Situation   Product usage strategy focuses on when or how a product is purchased and consumed. Promotion that builds a strong association between a particular brand and a particular usage situation leads consumers to think of that brand whenever the situation arises. For example, LinkedIn is predominantly positioned for use by business professionals. Gatorade is positioned as good for replacing bodily fluids lost during vigorous exercise and participation in sporting activities. Finally, Peeps candies are a must-have at Easter, although the marshmallow treats are now sold during most holidays throughout the year.

Positioning by Product User   Sometimes it is useful for marketers to identify their brand with the user of the product. As you read at the beginning of the chapter, CafeMom.com is positioned exclusively toward women. When positioning by user, marketers may use either "real-life" representations—Secret Deodorant is "strong enough for a man but made for a woman," for instance—or through characters that are *archetypes* (typical, ideal, or classic examples) of the user, such as the fictitious Betty Crocker or the Marlboro Man. Interestingly, Marlboro cigarettes were originally targeted toward women; they had red-tipped filters to hide lipstick stains and were packaged in a pink box. When the brand failed to do well, the rugged Marlboro man helped reposition the brand toward men. We will discuss repositioning next.

Repositioning

Repositioning attempts to change the way consumers perceive a brand, either a firm's own brand or a competitor's. For example, the soda brand Sunkist recently began a campaign to reposition itself as a more fun, quirky, and cool brand aimed at trend-savvy teens and young adults. To do so, the company revamped its promotional messages and utilized YouTube, Facebook, and Twitter to engage its target audience.[19]

In a classic example of repositioning a competition's brand, Tylenol ran advertisements that stated, "For the millions who should not take aspirin, if your stomach is easily upset, or if you have an ulcer, or if you suffer from asthma, allergies, or iron-deficiency anemia, it would make sense to check with your doctor before you take aspirin. Aspirin can irritate the stomach lining, trigger asthmatic or allergic reactions, and cause small amounts of gastrointestinal bleeding. Fortunately, there's Tylenol." Aspirin, especially the Bayer brand, was up to that point known as the "miracle drug," but Tylenol's campaign repositioned aspirin as potentially harmful to health. Today, aspirin is once again the miracle drug, through Bayer's and other brands' repositioning based on its core benefit of heart health.

In another famous campaign, Scope mouthwash used repositioning to combat the competition, Listerine, quite effectively. Scope's advertising campaign stated that Listerine "gives you medicine breath," but Scope delivers "fresh minty breath." This campaign was even more effective because Listerine's slogan at the time was, "The taste you hate twice a day."

In summary, there are many different positioning strategies. The best depends on the characteristics of the product, the competition, and the type of mental associations marketers want consumers to form about their brands. If a brand is the pioneer, the firm should emphasize this in their promotion, i.e., take credit for being first. If a brand is markedly different on a single easy-to-communicate and important dimension, a single core benefit proposition can succeed. If a brand is highly similar to competitors' offerings or difficult to differentiate, a firm may be able to differentiate via price, usage situation, or user. Finally, if competing brands have an exploitable weakness, repositioning is a tenable strategy.

Perceptual Mapping

Measuring consumer perceptions is an important part of positioning. **Perceptual mapping** measures the way products are positioned in the minds of consumers and show these perceptions on a graph whose axes are formed by product attributes. They are appealing because they provide pictorial representations of how consumers envision a brand. The maps provide a research tool to assess how multiple products in a category are positioned, how the attributes relating to the product are seen in the customers' eyes, and whether there are any product "gaps" in the market.

Researchers create perceptual maps by surveying members of the target market, asking people to rate products across multiple product attributes. For example, if researchers were interested in cars, likely attributes used in the analysis would include perceived price, sportiness, fuel efficiency, performance, reliability, etc. Attribute ratings are then subjected to various statistical techniques and a perceptual map can be extracted. On the map, similar brands are plotted close together, and dissimilar brands are plotted far apart. Thus, one thing a perceptual map tells marketers is who their direct competitors are (those plotted near to one another) and what brands represent less vigorous competition. Blank spaces on perceptual maps indicate *gaps* in the market. Gaps typically indicate:

- a true opportunity in the market that marketers might be able to pursue
- a combination of attributes that nobody actually needs or wants, which is why there is not a competitor there

- a combination of attributes that is impossible to deliver to the consumer without the development of new technology (here are many examples of products invented to fill these types of gaps, such as athletic shoes with shocks, lightweight cell phones, and mouse pads on laptop computers)

FIGURE 2.5 | **Perceptual Map**

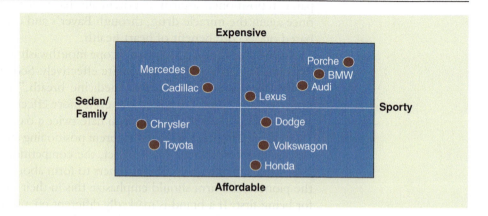

Figure 2.5 shows a hypothetical map for our car example. This map is based on two dimensions: (1) perceived price and (2) sportiness. (Perceptual maps can have more than two dimensions but then they become more difficult to interpret.) What does this map show if we work for the Cadillac brand? It shows that our closest direct competitor is Mercedes-Benz; the brand is perceived as a fairly expensive sedan; and there appears to be a gap in the market in the lower right quadrant. Additional research is required to determine the nature of the gap.

Finally, *ideal vectors* can also be plotted on perceptual maps, which show ideal combinations of attributes. The slope of the ideal vector indicates the ratio of the two dimensions preferred by consumers. We can generate ideal vectors for all consumers or by specific market segments.

Chapter Summary

One of the most important ways in which marketers discover and satisfy customer needs and wants efficiently is through the divide-and-conquer process of market segmentation and positioning.

Market segmentation is the process of dividing the large and diverse mass market into subsets of consumers who share common needs, characteristics, or behaviors, and targeting one or more of those segments with a distinct marketing mix. By identifying groups of highly similar consumers, a marketer is able to develop products and services specifically tailored to that group's needs that also closely match the capabilities of the organization, thus maximizing the chances of profit and success.

Marketers make two underlying assumptions related to market segmentation: first, consumer preferences vary, and second, by tailoring a product or service to a segment's needs, firms can make the offering so appealing that segment members are willing to pay a price that offsets the higher associated costs.

In addition to these assumptions, four factors influence a company's market segmentation strategy: consumer preference heterogeneity (the idea that consumer preferences vary), the majority fallacy (the risk of focusing on large average segments and neglecting smaller, less typical segments), the sales-cost trade-off (the fact that market segmentation increases sales and costs simultaneously), and potential for cannibalization (the case in which different products offered by the same company are so similar they compete with each other).

Bases of segmentation include demographic, geographic, psychographic, attributes/benefits, and behavioral. Demographic based segmentation divides customers along vital population statistics. In geographic based segmentation, the market is divided based on physical location of potential customers. An underlying assumption of this market segmentation base is that consumers located in geographic proximity share similar needs and preferences for some products. Geo-demographic segmentation combines geography and demographic segmentation bases. Psychographic based segmentation centers on customers' lifestyles, and one of the leading lifestyle segmentation systems is the VALS System. Behavioral based segmentation includes segmenting consumers based on consumer preference for a particular product attribute or benefit, usage occasion, user status, rate of product usage, and loyalty status.

Positioning is the process of communicating with our target market(s) through the use of marketing mix variables to help consumers differentiate a company's product from others and perceive how that product best satisfies their needs. Sometimes marketers use terms like *value proposition* or "*The Big Idea*" to describe a brand, product, or positioning strategy.

Like the bases of segmentation, there are several strategies companies use to position their products. The best positioning strategy depends on the characteristics of the product, market segmentation bases used, the competition, and the type of mental associations companies want their consumers to form. If a particular brand is the pioneer, the company should emphasize this in its promotion. If the brand is markedly different on a single easy-to-communicate and important dimension, a single core benefit proposition should be used. If the brand is highly similar to competitors' offerings or difficult to differentiate, the company may still be able to differentiate via price, usage situation, or user. If competing brands have an exploitable weakness, repositioning is a possible strategy. Finally, in order to measure how consumers envision a brand and develop competitive strategies, marketers can use perceptual mapping. Perceptual mapping measures the way products are positioned in the minds of consumers and show these perceptions on a graph whose axes are formed by product attributes.

Key Terms

behavior based segmentation
cannibalization
consumer preference heterogeneity
core benefit proposition
demographic characteristics

geo-demographic segmentation
geographic based segmentation
majority fallacy
market aggregation
market segmentation
perceptual mapping

positioning
premium pricing
psychographics
repositioning
sale-costs trade-off
target market

Review and Discussion

1. Clearly distinguish between the following terms: demographics, psychographic, lifestyle, and positioning.
2. What are the two underlying assumptions of market segmentation?
3. How do the majority fallacy and the potential for cannibalization influence market segmentation decisions?
4. According to the VALS technique, what type of consumer would probably buy a digital video camera? What type of consumer would take a fishing vacation trip? Justify your answer.
5. Describe how marketers of Tropicana orange juice could use usage situation to broaden the product's segment.
6. Why might the pioneering advantage be even stronger for services than it is for physical products? Give one example.
7. How might a leading brand of personal music players, such as Apple's iPod, best position itself? Give specific examples.
8. What steps might a follower brand of personal music players, such as Sony, do in terms of positioning to increase its chances of success? Give specific examples.
9. Describe when it is best to position using a core benefit proposition. Why?
10. Describe the three situations that gaps in perceptual maps represent.

Short Application Exercises

1. Find print advertisements that reflect segmentation based on the following:
   a. Demographic based using ethnicity/culture
   b. Attribute/benefit based
   c. Behavioral based on usage occasion
2. Visit the PRIZM website and enter your own zip code to see your neighborhood profile. Do you feel it accurately reflects your household and neighborhood? Why or why not?
3. Visit the VALS website and complete the online questionnaire to find out the segment to which you belong. Take some time to read the segment descriptions. Do you feel your segment accurately portrays your lifestyle? Next, take the survey again, but answer the questions from the perspective of someone else: your eccentric neighbor, you elderly uncle, or your conservative grandfather. (NOTE: Make sure to click the "yes" button that asks whether you have taken the survey before.) Again, are you satisfied with the profile? Why or why not?
4. Develop a questionnaire to measure some AIOs of your fellow college students. Administer the questionnaire to 20 students and generate lifestyle segments based on your results.
5. Identify one example in the marketplace of a brand that has repositioned either itself or a competitor. Was the campaign successful? Justify your opinion.
6. Watch the short video vignette for Chapter 2. Ethnicity is a demographic variable that marketers use to segment market segments. Identify an example of another brand that uses ethnicity to segment the market. Next, identify examples of brands that use other variables such as age, gender, and income.

Managerial Application

According to the U.S. Federal Research Division, the average U.S. credit card debt per household is $8,475, making credit card debt a large portion of all consumer debt. The use of credit cards varies extensively. For some, a credit card is a convenient substitute for cash, while others like to "buy now"—even if they can't afford it.

Imagine you have been hired as a consumer behavior consultant for JP Morgan Chase, one of the country's largest issuers of consumer credit card products. The company has decided one of the highest growth potential market segments for their credit card products is a "young influentials" segment. In light of this potential market segment, consider the following questions:

1. How would you define this market segment?

2. How would this segment use (and/or potentially abuse) credit cards?

3. What major benefits of owning a credit card should be stressed to this target segment?

4. What do you think is the best way to get information about your credit cards to these consumers?

5. What would be the primary message of your advertisements?

6. JP Morgan Chase is also concerned about the ethics of marketing credit card products to consumers who might abuse them. U.S. consumers' filings for personal bankruptcy are at an all-time high. In addition, in every major city, many people are flocking to classes and consultations designed to help them get out of consumer debt—a process that begins by cutting up credit cards. Besides the ethical issues, many consumers who abuse credit cards will never pay their credit card bills entirely. How can the company modify the advertising message to attract ONLY responsible credit card users?

End Notes

1 Sources for this article include: http://www.cafemom.com, and http://www.crunchbase.com/company/cafemom. Fung, A. (2008, May 4). Mothers' little helper. In Crain's New York Business. Retrieved from: http://www.crainsnewyork.com/article/20080504/FREE/876270075.

2 Information for this section taken from: Schumann, D. W. (1999, February 19). The transmission of prejudice: What do our marketing strategies really reinforce? *Presidential address presented to the membership of the Society for Consumer Psychology.*

3 Geary, S. P. (Producer) (1999). *Sell and Spin: A History of Advertising* [Film]. (Available from A&E Home Video, A&E Television Network, Cat. No AAE-17607).

4 Crow, J. J. (2005). Factors Influencing Product Customization. *International Journal of Internet Marketing and Advertising* (April). Crow, J. J., & Shenteau, J. (2005). Online product customization. In C. P. Haugtvedt, K. Machleit, R. Yalch (Eds.), *Online Consumer Psychology: Understanding and Influencing Behavior in the Virtual World.* Mahwah, NJ: Lawrence Erlbaum Associates, in press.

5 Starbucks. [Company Website]. (n. d.). Retrieved from: http://www.starbucks.co.jp/en/company.html.

6 Mahogany. On Hallmark Corporate Information. [Company Website]. (n. d.). Retrieved from: http://corporate.hallmark.com/Product/Mahogany.

7 7 Billion: Are there too many people on the planet? On National Geographic. [Magazine Website]. (n. d.). Retrieved from: http://ngm.nationalgeographic.com/7-billion.

8 Segment Lookup. On Nielsen. [Company Website]. (n. d.). Retrieved from: http://www.claritas.com/MyBestSegments/Default.jsp?ID=30&SubID=&pageName=Segment%2BLook-up.

9 US Frameworks and VALS Types. On Strategic Business Insights. [Company Website]. (n. d.). Retrieved from: http://www.strategicbusinessinsights.com/vals/ustypes.shtml.

10 Mordin, C., May 2005, Connecting with consumers, 4Cs Overview, www.4cs.yr.com. Reprinted by permission.

11 Reis, A., & Trout, J. (1981). *Positioning: The Battle for Your Mind.* New York: McGraw-Hill.

12 Kardes, F. R., & Gurumurthy, K. (1992). "Order of entry effects on consumer memory and judgment: An information integration perspective." *Journal of Marketing Research, 29,* 343–357. Kardes, F. R., Gurumurthy, K., Chandrashekaran, M., & Dornoff, R. J. (1993). "Brand retrieval, consideration set composition, consumer choice, and the pioneering advantage." *Journal of Consumer Research, 20,* 62–75.

13 Carpenter, G. S., & Nakamoto, K. (1989). "Consumer preference formation and pioneering advantage." *Journal of Marketing Research, 26,* 285–298.

14 Reis, A., & Trout, J. (1994). *The 22 Immutable Laws of Marketing.* New York: Harper Business.

15 Reis, A., & Trout, J. (1994). *The 22 Immutable Laws of Marketing.* New York: Harper Business.

16 Reis, A. (2005). The battle over positioning still rages to this day. *Advertising Age, April, 31,* 88. Did Mercedes-Benz Outsell BMW IN the U.S. Last Year? [Magazine Website]. (2013, February 19). Retrieved

from: http://www.motorauthority.com/news/1082427_did-mercedes-benz-outsell-bmw-in-the-u-s-last-year.

17 Reis, A. (2005). The battle over positioning still rages to this day. *Advertising Age, April, 31,* 88.

18 Cronley, M. L., Posavac, S. S., Meyer, T., Kardes, F. R., & Kellaris, J. J. (2005). A selective hypothesis testing perspective on price-quality inference and inference-based choice. *Journal of Consumer Psychology, 15 (2),* 159–169. Kardes, F. R., Cronley, M. L., Kellaris, J. J., & Posavac, S. S. (2004). The role of selective information processing in price-quality inference. *Journal of Consumer Research, 31 (2),* 368–374. See also, Kardes, F. R., Posavac, S. S., and Cronley, M. L. (2004). Consumer inference: A review of processes, bases, and judgment contexts. *Journal of Consumer Psychology, 14 (3),* 230–256.

19 Sunkist brand repositioning. On Brandsource. (2009, June 8). Retrieved from: http://www.labbrand.com /brand-source/sunkist-brand-repositioning.

MARKETING METRICS

Descriptive Statistics

Imagine that you are a consultant who has been asked to provide some insight into the market segment for your client CafeMom.com. You have collected the data related to CafeMom subscribers in the table shown below. The table provides data for 20 CafeMom users who have been active members of the social network for at least one year.

Column 1 shows the user number. Column 2 indicates the subscriber's age. Column 3 indicates the number of children that each subscriber has. Columns 4 and 5 indicate the number of posts the subscriber has posted in the last year, and the number of visits to the site, respectively.

Cafemom.Com Subscriber Data

User Number	Subscriber Age	# of Children	# of Posts	# of Site Visits
1	21	3	7	2
2	45	3	14	13
3	34	2	20	38
4	50	1	52	67
5	26	1	87	70
6	38	2	71	34
7	39	2	90	119
8	27	1	26	56
9	30	2	56	48
10	35	4	9	1
11	38	2	18	27
12	41	4	11	9
13	48	1	121	76
14	27	1	66	34
15	51	3	5	19
16	55	2	27	39
17	40	3	89	60
18	26	2	43	21
19	22	1	89	59
20	35	2	56	40

Your Task

Use the Excel file (DT2-1.xlsx) to execute the following analyses:

1. Calculate the age range and the mean age of CafeMom users based on this sample. Does it appear the actual customers match the target market described by the company?
2. Calculate the number of site visits made by the number of children each user has. (Recall that this is a cross-tabulation calculation.) Does there appear to be a pattern?
3. Calculate the correlation between the number of site posts and visits to the website. Is the correlation significant? Is the correlation negative or positive?
4. Calculate the correlations between the number of children a user has and the number of site posts and visits to the website made. Are the correlations significant? Are the correlations negative or positive? What conclusions can you draw from these analyses?

BRANDING STRATEGY AND CONSUMER BEHAVIOR

OBJECTIVES *After studying this chapter, you will be able to…*

1 Develop new products and entry strategies.

2 Develop appropriate brand strategies for each stage of the product life cycle and develop marketing strategies for extending the product life cycle.

3 Develop a strong brand name.

4 Develop appropriate marketing strategies for strong brands and weaker brands.

5 Develop consumer acquisition and retention strategies for a new brand.

Hyundai

When Hyundai automobiles were first introduced in the United States during the 1980s, they were unreliable and low in quality, and, not surprisingly, they developed a terrible brand image and brand reputation. Over the past few years, however, Hyundai has enjoyed one of the most successful turnarounds in automotive history. Today, Hyundai automobiles are reliable and high in quality, and Hyundai enjoys an excellent brand image and brand reputation. Managers at Hyundai use the term "modern premium" to reflect their new manufacturing philosophy and a marketing approach designed to build emotional ties that link consumers to the Hyundai brand name.[1] According to Innocean, Hyundai's ad agency located in Huntington Beach, California, the old view of luxury focused on exclusivity and

status. Hyundai wants to be inclusive, design oriented, and sensitive to economic conditions. Hyundai is attempting to enhance its overall brand name rather than specific models, and Hyundai is distancing itself from old ideas about luxury.

Over the past few years, Hyundai built its brand reputation for value by offering an "Assurance" powertrain warranty, a trade-in value guarantee, and a job-loss protection plan. Today, Hyundai is attempting to build a brand reputation for modern luxury, and in 2011, sales are up 20% from 2010. The Elantra and Sonata feature "fluidic sculpture" designs, the Veloster is a sporty, three-door model, the new Genesis is a performance model, and the top-of-the-line luxury model is the $60,000 Equus. The "New Thinking, New Possibilities" marketing campaign is designed to help the Equus compete with Lexus, Acura, and BMW. In 2012, Hyundai's aggressive marketing campaign included two Super Bowl spots and a 60-second ad before the Super Bowl kickoff.

What variables influence consumer perceptions of the value of a brand name like Hyundai? How can a company change consumer perceptions of its brand name? How do brand names reduce uncertainty and encourage consumers to make a purchase decision? What marketing activities are needed to acquire new consumers, and what marketing activities are required to retain current consumers? These are some of the key questions addressed in this chapter.

OBJECTIVE **(1)** # New Product Development

Although about 25% of most companies' sales come from new products, the new product failure rate is about 35%.[2] Hence, developing new products is risky, and the new product development process must be managed carefully. Companies need to decide whether they should pursue a **proactive strategy** or a **reactive strategy**. Proactive firms develop many new products and try to be first in the race to the market. Reactive firms wait to see what competitors offer and then develop me-too or copycat brands. The Ford Motor Company pursued a proactive strategy by inventing the automobile, and Ford dominated the automobile market for several decades. Eventually, General Motors' reactive strategy of developing their own automobiles—similar to Ford's but with greater variety in terms of sizes, shapes, and colors—turned out to be successful. In the 1930s, Ford's policy of letting consumers have any color they want as long as it was black turned out to be outdated, and GM was able to outsell Ford.

Proactive versus Reactive Strategies

Of course, proactive strategies are not always successful. The first light beer, Gablinger's, sold poorly and was pulled from the marketplace. Reactive strategies are not always successful either. P&G's Crest toothpaste copied Colgate by introducing gels, pumps, and tartar control varieties of Crest, but Crest's market share fell and Colgate's rose. When should firms pursue a proactive strategy, and when should firms pursue a reactive strategy? Five key factors should be considered: the potential for growth, protection for innovation, market size, competition, and the channel position. Growth opportunities are assessed using the opportunities matrix (see Figure 3.1).[3] The firm can either focus on

FIGURE 3.1 | **Opportunities Matrix**

Opportunities Matrix		
	New Products	Existing Products
New Markets	DIVERSIFICATION (e.g., product line extension, Arm & Hammer deodorant, detergent, carpet cleaner)	MARKET DEVELOPMENT (e.g., new uses, Arm & Hammer looking soda deodorizes refrigerators, freezers, sinks)
Existing Markets	PRODUCT DEVELOPMENT (e.g., variations on a theme, baking soda for cakes vs. cookies vs. breads)	MARKET PENETRATION (e.g., sales promotion)

Source: Ansoff, H. I. (1957). "Strategies for Diversification." *Harvard Business Review 35,* 113–124.

new products for the firm or on existing products; likewise, the firm can either focus on new markets or existing markets. The riskiest growth opportunity is diversification, in which the firm develops new products for new markets. For example, Arm & Hammer developed many new products with baking soda, including deodorant, detergent, and carpet cleaner. Arm & Hammer also pursued a market development strategy by developing new uses for its original baking soda. This product was not changed at all, but ads emphasized that baking soda is good for more than just baking. Baking soda can be used to deodorize refrigerators, freezers, and kitchen sinks. Another possibility for growth opportunity is to develop new products for existing markets by developing variations on a theme, such as several different types of baking soda for different uses (e.g., baking cakes versus baking cookies), but Arm & Hammer did not pursue this strategy. Yet another market development strategy is to sell existing products in a new markets overseas. Finally, aggressive promotion and advertising makes it possible to achieve growth or market penetration with existing products in existing markets.

In addition to analyzing growth opportunities, it is important to consider the amount of protection for innovation that is available. Innovations can be protected with patents or secrecy. For example, Polaroid's cameras were protected from imitation by patents, and Coca-Cola is famous for its secret formula. Market size is also important. The automobile market is huge, but niche markets are relatively small. Competition intensity should also be analyzed, as competition increases as the number of brands vying for the same market segment increases. Finally, power in the channel should be considered. Some firms enjoy a lot of power in their channels of distribution and are able to gain the cooperation of other channel members. Other firms are weaker and must attempt to accommodate other channel members. Walmart is a good example of a company with a lot of power in the channel. In general, proactive strategies are most successful when growth opportunities are high, protection for innovation is high, market size is large, competition is high, and when power in the channel is high. Reactive strategies are most successful when growth opportunities are low, protection for innovation is low, market size is small, competition is low, and when power in the channel is low.

The Pioneering Brand Advantage

Another important consideration, and one of the strongest arguments for pursuing a proactive strategy, is the **pioneering brand advantage**. Pioneering brands, or the first brands to enter a new market, often enjoy a long-term preference advantage over copycat brands. The pioneering brand advantage is remarkably robust, and this advantage has been observed in growing markets, mature markets, and even in markets with high switching costs.[4] Because pioneering brands are novel and interesting, consumers often are motivated to learn a lot about the features and benefits of pioneering brands.[5] On the other hand, copycat brands are more redundant and consequently receive less attention; therefore, consumers are likely to learn less about these brands. Because consumers form more favorable and more confidently-held judgments about brands they know a lot about, they are much more likely to form stronger preferences for pioneering brands than for copycat brands.

In addition to learning a lot about the attributes and benefits of pioneering brands, consumers also learn about ideal points for a product category.[6] Ideal points refer to the combination of attributes and benefits that are most preferred. When a product is totally new, consumers have no ideal points initially. However, if they try the new product and like it, the new product's combination of attributes and benefits become the most preferred combination. Other brands that have different shapes, sizes, colors, flavors, etc., seem inferior.

Consumer learning is not the only mechanism that contributes to the pioneering advantage. When consumers make a purchase decision, they often retrieve brand names from memory, form a consideration set consisting of a small set of brands that they would consider purchasing, and then choose one brand. Even when no information about attributes or benefits is available, the pioneering brand tends to be more memorable, more likely to be included in the consideration set, and more likely to be chosen.[7] Simply being first out of the gate creates a memory advantage, a consideration set advantage, and a choice advantage for the pioneering brand.

Some marketing researchers argue that market shares for pioneering brands have been overestimated because many pioneering brands fail; they contend that market shares of zero for brands that failed should be averaged with market shares of brands that survived.[8] When this is done, the average market share for pioneering brands is much lower. However, copycat brands also fail, and market shares of zero for brands that fail should be averaged with market shares of brands that survive. Because this analysis has not yet been performed, it is unclear whether pioneering brands and copycat brands fail at different rates. If copycat brands fail at a higher rate than pioneering brands, the pioneering advantage would be even larger than currently estimated.

OBJECTIVE (2)

Entry Strategy

Before managers can build a strong brand name for new products, they must develop appropriate **brand entry strategies** for bringing those products to market. The **diffusion of innovation**, or the rate at which a new product spreads or is adopted across the marketplace, differs among product categories. For example, diffusion was slow for black-and-white televisions when they were first introduced, but fast for color televisions when they hit the consumer marketplace. The reason for this is that diffusion is influenced by several factors, especially the relative advantage of the new product over the old product.[9] The advantages of black-and-white television over radio were not immediately obvious when black-and-white television was first introduced. However, after enjoying black-and-white television for decades, it was easy for consumers to imagine the relative advantages of color television over black-and-white.

Only about 2.5% of consumers are innovators, or the first to adopt new product innovations (see Figure 3.2). These consumers tend to be sensation seeking, open-minded, and heavy users of the product category that is being replaced by the innovation. For example, the first consumers to adopt DVD players watched a lot of TV, and used their VHS players frequently. Early adopters interact with innovators and with other early adopters, and these consumers are heavily influenced by word-of-mouth (WOM) communications

FIGURE 3.2 | Categories of Adopters of Innovations

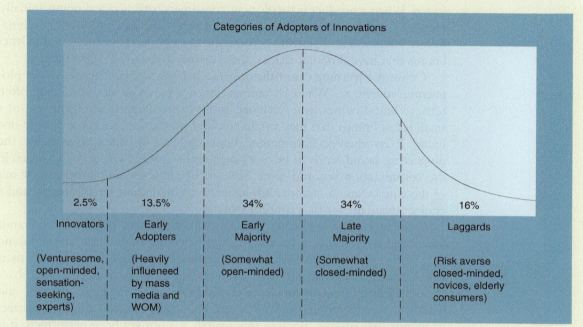

SOURCE: Iacobucci, D. (2013). *Marketing Models: Multivariate Statistics and Marketing Analytics* (p. 161). Mason, OH: South-Western.

with innovators and other early adopters. The early majority is influenced by the mass media. The late majority are late adopters, and laggards are very late adopters. In fact, by the time laggards adopt an innovation, the product has already been replaced by a newer innovation. In general, the later consumers are to adopt a new innovation, the more closed-minded and the more risk averse they tend to be.

Compatibility with consumers' beliefs, opinions, and lifestyles is another important factor that influences the diffusion rate. Wealthier consumers tend to travel and enjoy active lifestyles; in the past, sitting at home watching black-and-white television was incompatible with this way of life. This incompatibility slowed the diffusion of black-and-white TVs in the marketplace—because at the time, they were relatively expensive, i.e., only people with higher incomes were able to afford TVs. Complexity or user friendliness is another important factor. Black-and-white television was so novel when it was first introduced that consumers did not know how to use it. Incremental innovations, like color television, are often easier to use, so incremental innovations usually diffuse more quickly than totally new products.

Perceived risk also reduces the diffusion rate. This is true for financial risks (e.g., expensive products, such as black-and-white television when it was first introduced), social risks (e.g., embarrassment at being unable to use the product successfully), and physical risk (e.g., risk of harm). Trialability, or the ease with which consumers can try or use the new product, increases the diffusion rate. Trialability tends to be higher for inexpensive products than for expensive products, but it can vary across the board; not all products can be taken for a test drive. It is very common to test drive a new automobile, and now consumers can try out products like computers, mattresses, and even expensive rugs in their homes before finalizing purchases.

The typical diffusion curve is S-shaped; the proportion of potential adopters is low initially because it takes time for marketing programs to build awareness and stimulate trial (see Figure 3.3). The adoption rate typically increases dramatically during the growth phase as a result of the "snowball" effect from word-of-mouth communications. The more consumers talk favorably about a new product to other consumers, the more these other consumers want to try the product. Eventually, however, the market becomes saturated, and the product is replaced by a new innovation.

FIGURE **3.3** | Diffusion Curve

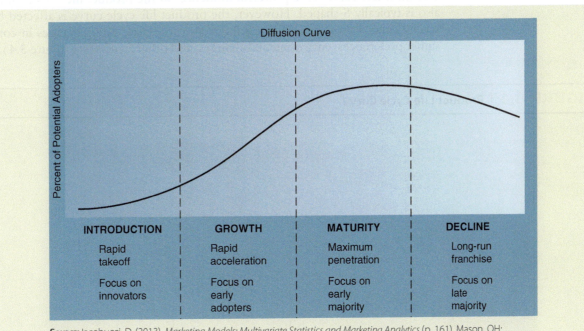

SOURCE: Iacobucci, D. (2013). *Marketing Models: Multivariate Statistics and Marketing Analytics* (p. 161). Mason, OH: South-Western.

Although the diffusion rate is affected by several factors outside of marketing managers' control, they can influence the diffusion rate by identifying innovator consumers and targeting marketing programs toward them. Innovator consumers are usually adventurous, open-minded, and sensation-seeking. They are willing to try new things. They also tend to be highly educated and upwardly mobile. Innovator consumers also tend to be heavy users of a product category and active seekers of information via specialty magazines and the Internet. In addition, focusing on innovator consumers helps firms increase initial sales and acceptance of a new product among other members of the channel of distribution. This is especially important when a firm is new and has relatively little power in the channel of distribution.

Heavy promotion and advertising can be used to influence early adopters and to stimulate word-of-mouth. This is particularly important when a product is expected to have a relatively short life cycle as a result of rapidly changing technology (e.g., computers and other high-tech products). If the product is expected to have a relatively long life cycle and if a firm has asymmetrical power in the distribution channel, then a long-term market leadership strategy should be pursued, including segmentation, targeting, positioning, and protection from imitation. Usually only the largest and most powerful firms can pursue this strategy (e.g., Disney, Sony, Coca-Cola).

OBJECTIVE ③ # Product Life Cycle Management

The diffusion curve has a powerful influence on the product life cycle, which also is typically S-shaped. However, the product life cycle curve is affected by several other factors as well, including repeat purchase rates, changes in consumer preferences, environmental changes, and other factors (see Figure 3.4).[10]

FIGURE 3.4 | **Product Life Cycle Curve**

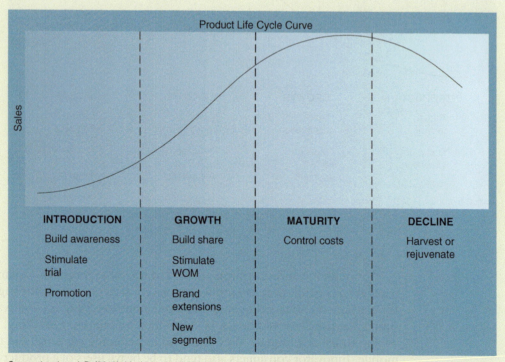

SOURCE: Iacobucci, D. (2013). *Marketing Models: Multivariate Statistics and Marketing Analytics* (p. 161). Mason, OH: South-Western.

As the product life cycle curve indicates, during the introduction stage, managers need to focus on creating awareness and stimulating trial. Promotion and advertising are important tools for achieving these goals. During the growth stage, managers need to build market share by stimulating word-of-mouth communication. New market segments and brand extensions (i.e., variations on a theme) tend to appear during this stage. During the maturity stage, managers need to focus on reducing production and marketing costs. Competition intensity also increases during this stage. Finally, during the decline stage, the product may be approaching obsolescence. If so, harvesting is appropriate; costs should be reduced to the bare minimum so future sales based on the reputation of the product yield high profits. Of course, harvesting shortens the product life cycle.

If the product is not yet obsolete, rejuvenation strategies can lengthen the product life cycle. One way to rejuvenate a product is to develop new uses for it. To return to the Arm & Hammer example, baking soda can be used to deodorize refrigerators, freezers, sinks, carpets, and clothing. It can also be used as an ingredient in toothpastes, deodorant, carpet fresheners, and even kitty litter. In other words, there are many uses for baking soda that do not involve baking. Similarly, DuPont continually develops new uses for its key product, nylon. Initially, nylon was used to make ropes and parachutes. Currently, it is also used in women's hosiery, clothing, tires, and carpets.

Commodities, or generic products, can sometimes be rejuvenated via branding. Sunkist oranges seem better than ordinary oranges. Purdue chickens seem better than ordinary chickens, and Idaho potatoes are positioned as high quality. Advertising can also rejuvenate a product, under the right circumstances. In the past, it was considered distasteful to run television ads for hygiene-related products, such as feminine goods and deodorants. Now such ads are common; axe and Old Spice grooming products for men and Always feminine hygiene products have benefited greatly from advertising exposure. Effective advertising can even turn disadvantages into advantages. For example, "Avis is number two so they try harder," and "With a name like Smucker's, it has to be good." Focusing on the correct advantages is also important. For example, Pampers disposable diapers originally sold poorly when advertising focused on benefits to the mother (i.e., convenience). Sales increased dramatically when advertising shifted its focus to benefits for the baby (i.e., helps keep baby drier and healthier).

Identifying new market segments or new potential users of a product can also rejuvenate a product. For example, Johnson & Johnson baby shampoo is not just for babies anymore. Its mild and gentle formula is also suitable for adults to use every day. Milk is not just for children anymore; it's healthy for adults, also. Lipton tea is not just for senior citizens; young people also enjoy drinking Lipton tea. Another way to rejuvenate a product is to reduce its price, as Datril did to compete more effectively against Tylenol. Social trends should also be analyzed. Increasing concerns among consumers about health, pollution, and the environment have increased sales of organic produce, health foods, vitamins, and environmentally friendly products.

Sometimes unused by-products from a manufacturing process can be marketed to increase the profitability of a product in the decline stage. For example, kitty litter is made from disposable sawdust from lumberyards. Mesquite wood was once destroyed by Texas farmers, but now they sell it for grilling. Cat food and dog food are made from the unused by-products of food for human consumption.

Finally, developing a new channel of distribution can be used to rejuvenate a product, as Hanes did for L'eggs panty hose. Originally, panty hose, and women's hosiery in general, were available primarily in department stores. But L'eggs became very successful when Hanes started selling them through grocery stores, drugstores, and mass merchandisers, using a clever egg-shaped plastic package—which also protected the relatively delicate product from damage and simplified display in store aisles. Direct marketing and Internet sales can also lengthen a product's life cycle.

OBJECTIVE # Brand Equity Management

The brand name of a product is often its most important asset.[11] A strong brand name triggers many important associations stored in consumers' memories, and a strong brand name also provides a promise of excellence. Strong brand names give consumers a good reason for buying. They also increase trust, repeat purchase rates, and the willingness of consumers to pay more for one brand than for another. Of course, these effects lead to greater sales, profits, and power in the distribution channel for companies.

How can managers build strong brand names for their products? The first step is to establish a strong *brand identity* (who are you?). For example, Disney has a strong brand identity; consumers know that Disney stands for excellence in children's entertainment. The second step is to establish a strong *brand meaning* (what are you?). Disney performs well on this dimension, too. Consumers know that Disney creates family-friendly cartoon characters, movies, and theme parks. The third step is to foster strong *brand responses*, or feelings, thoughts, and reactions from consumers. For example, Disney elicits warm family feelings, thoughts, and reactions. The fourth step is to build a strong *brand relationship* between the brand and the consumer. Many consumers have become so strongly attached and committed to Disney that they immediately buy whatever new product Disney develops, regardless of expense or whether they know much about the product.

Brand identity depends on the strength and the nature of the associations that come to mind whenever consumers encounter a brand. These associations can be linked to a product category, specific product attributes, specific product benefits, specific usage situations, or specific users of the product. When the associations are sufficiently strong, the relevant product category, attribute, benefit, usage situation, or user can prompt or automatically activate thoughts about the brand. This leads to a significant advantage for strong brands.

Brand meaning depends on the strength and the nature of the image of the brand in terms of objective quality and performance. Does the brand exceed consumers' performance expectations? Is the brand reliable, durable, and easy to service? Does the brand satisfy consumers' utilitarian, aesthetic, and economic needs and preferences? Building brand meaning takes a long time, and just a single bad experience with a product can erode many years' worth of goodwill. Therefore, managers need to ensure that the brand experience is consistently high in quality.

Brand responses are the feelings and judgments that come to mind when consumers think about a brand. Relevant feelings include warmth, fun, excitement, security, approval from others (won't the neighbors be impressed?), and self-esteem (I feel like an important person when I use this brand). Disney performs well on the warmth and fun dimensions, and BMW performs well on the approval from others and self-respect dimensions. Relevant judgments include subjective quality, credibility, consideration, and superiority. To perform well on these dimensions, the brand must deliver a unique and consistently high-quality experience. Uniqueness is especially important. Many companies have tried to copy Disney but have failed because Disney's uniqueness is preemptive; that is, it is difficult to copy.

Brand relationships take years to develop and can only occur after strong brand identities, brand meanings, and brand responses have been established. **Brand resonance** refers to a consumer's intense and actively loyal relationship with a brand. Brand resonance leads to high purchase frequencies and volumes, feelings of attachment, feelings of brand community or kinship with other users of the brand (e.g., anyone who uses my brand must be a good person), and active engagement, such as joining a fan club for the brand.

Brand equity is the value that a brand accrues based on the goodwill attached to associations with the brand name. One simple and direct approach to measuring brand equity is to compare consumers' evaluation of a product with no brand name to their evaluation of the same product with a brand name attached.[12] This approach is especially useful in the early stages of market research, when product concepts or ideas are tested for feasibility. For example, one group of consumers could be asked to evaluate a series of new product ideas (e.g., garden-vegetable flavored potato chips, Cajun-blackened steak frozen dinners, chunky peach cottage cheese, smoky bacon-flavored hotdogs, Italian spiced lunch meat, lemon mint soda). Another group could be asked to evaluate the same concepts with a brand name attached to each (e.g., Nabisco, Sealtest). If the same concepts are evaluated more favorably when a brand name is attached, the brand name adds value. Developing **brand extensions**, or different products with the same brand name (e.g., Coke Classic, Cherry Coke, Vanilla Coke, Coke Zero), is more problematic because the brand name becomes more variable and ambiguous. Consumers' perceptions as to why a company launches brand extensions are also important. Ideally, firms want consumers to assume that brand extensions were developed because they fit the unique skills of the manufacturer—and not because the manufacturer is simply copying competitors' products.

The Young & Rubicam Brand Asset Valuator is an instrument that uses a set of scales to measure differentiation (How unique is the brand?), relevance (How useful is the brand?), esteem (Is the brand the best?), and knowledge (Does the brand have a clear and consistent image?).[13] Multiplying differentiation scores by relevance scores provides a measure of brand *strength*. Usually, a high score on one dimension implies a low score on the other. Consequently, a compromise approach is often best; moderate levels of differentiation and relevance lead to high brand strength.

Multiplying esteem scores by knowledge scores provides a measure of brand *stature*. Again, a high score on one of these dimensions implies a low score on the other. As it was with brand strength, a compromise approach is therefore often best; moderate levels of esteem and knowledge result in high brand stature. Brands that are high in both brand strength and brand stature are the most successful brands. Of course, relatively few brands are able to achieve this high level of excellence. New brands are typically in the low brand strength/low brand stature quadrant because it takes time to build brand identity and brand reputation. Brands in the high brand strength/low brand stature quadrant are usually strong niche brands that have an opportunity to grow by improving their brand stature. Brands in the low brand strength/high brand stature quadrant are usually older brands that are resting on their laurels. These brands enjoyed high brand equity earlier in their product life cycles, but are now perceived as declining and unexciting (see Figure 3.5).

FIGURE 3.5 | **The Young & Rubicam Power Grid**

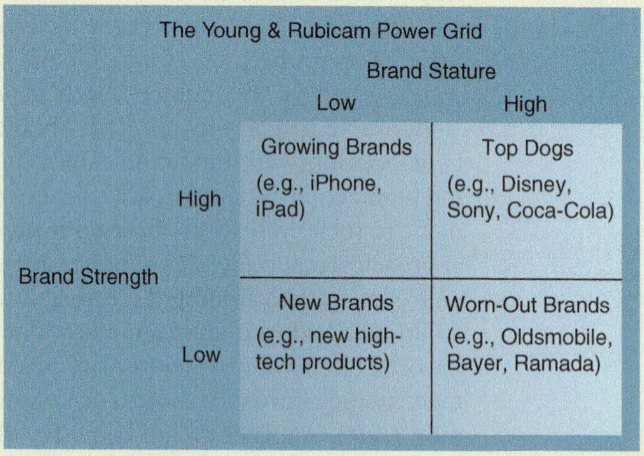

		Brand Stature	
		Low	High
Brand Strength	High	Growing Brands (e.g., iPhone, iPad)	Top Dogs (e.g., Disney, Sony, Coca-Cola)
	Low	New Brands (e.g., new high-tech products)	Worn-Out Brands (e.g., Oldsmobile, Bayer, Ramada)

Adapted from Kardes, F. R., Cronley, M. L., and Cline, T. W. (2011). *Consumer Behavior* (1st ed., p. 355). Boston: Cengage Learning.

Brand Extension Management

Brand name reputation is one of the most important cues consumers use to infer product quality, value, reliability, and risk. Consequently, a reputable brand name is an important asset that managers can use to increase demand for new products while controlling promotion, distribution, and other marketing costs. However, the effectiveness of a brand extension strategy depends critically on the degree of perceived similarity among the family of brands that share a brand name, and also on a host of important contextual variables. Perceived similarity depends on overlapping attributes, benefits, production processes, usage situations, and images.[14] The relative importance of different dimensions of similarity depends on contextual variables, such as involvement, mood, brand category breadth, thinking style, cultural background, and naïve theories or everyday assumptions about stability versus change.[15]

As the degree of similarity between the original parent brand (e.g., Coca-Cola) and a brand extension (e.g., Coke Zero) increases, the brand extension is evaluated more similarly to the parent brand. Consumers who like Coca-Cola a lot are likely to evaluate Coke Zero favorably (because both products are beverages, both are colas, and the two products even taste alike). However, similarity becomes less important as involvement, or the motivation to think about

great coke taste zero sugar

IT'S POSSIBLE

Coke Zero is one of Coca-Cola's recent brand extensions.

product information carefully, increases. Similarity also becomes less important when consumers are in a neutral mood. Consumers who are in a good mood are more creative and more likely to see non obvious parent-extension brand similarities that other consumers miss. In addition, similarity matters less when the category breadth of the parent brand is wide. For example, Mitsubishi has a wide category breadth. Mitsubishi makes automobiles and a wide variety of consumer electronic products. As parent brand category breadth increases, it becomes easier to extend into other new product categories. Similarity also depends on thinking style: whether a consumer usually thinks holistically and in terms of broad abstract generalizations, or analytically and in terms of specific concrete features. Holistic thinkers tend to see more similarities between objects, and this increases the degree to which evaluations of brand extensions match evaluations of parent brands. Cultural background also matters, because Easterners (consumers from China, Japan, Korea, India, and Eastern Europe) tend to be holistic thinkers, whereas Westerners (consumers from the United States, Canada, and Western Europe) tend to be analytic thinkers. Consequently, Easterners tend to have stronger preferences for brand extensions.

Naïve theories, or everyday assumptions about how the world works, are also important. Some consumers believe that the world is malleable or that change is possible (these consumers are known as **incremental theorists**). Other consumers believe that the world is rigid or fixed and that change is nearly impossible (these consumers are known as **entity theorists**). In general, incremental theorists are more optimistic, more able to change their bad habits, and more likely to prefer brand extensions. Hence, brand managers need to consider the influence of many different variables when evaluating the likelihood of success for a given brand extension strategy.

Global Perspectives

TBWA Hakuhodo

Japan was hit by a catastrophic earthquake and tsunami in March 2011. Despite this catastrophe, Advertising Age's International Agency of the Year, TBWA Hakuhodo, achieved 9% growth by helping to boost morale in Japan by developing upbeat ads for its clients (including Adidas, Apple, Ikea, Nissan, and P&G) based on its motto: "Think Happy."[16] For example, they developed P&G's Ariel detergent's "Cheers for You" program, which collected the laundry of people living in shelters and returned the laundry clean a few days later. For Adidas' ClimaCool apparel, TBWA Hakuhoda developed a campaign offering price discounts that matched the day's temperature. They also developed a shoe rental program for Adidas' AdiZero running shoes, which allowed consumers to rent the shoes for a few days and decide whether to buy them. They also helped Nissan shift to a more digital marketing strategy and helped launch Apple's iPad 2 and iPhone 4.

OBJECTIVE **5**

Product Line Management

Many firms are shifting from hiring brand managers to hiring product line managers who coordinate marketing and production activities across a product line or a family of products. As the number of products added to a product line increases, sales and costs increase. Managing the sales/costs trade-off can be difficult. Furthermore, if a product line is too large, product **cannibalization** may occur. This means that sales of one product on the line may "eat up" or reduce sales of another product on the same line. As a result, net sales do not necessarily increase with product line breadth.

However, research has shown that total market share increases with product line breadth.[18] For large Fortune 500 companies, however, product line breadth is not related to inventory costs and actually decreases manufacturing costs. As a result, many Fortune 500 companies have learned how to increase their product lines without increasing costs (although this study did not measure marketing costs) by incorporating cost-cutting procedures. For example, just-in-time, computer-aided supply and ordering procedures reduce inventory costs. Flexible manufacturing and manufacturing-cell-group-based technologies

Ethics

Brand names, trademarks, and product designs are valuable assets, and many firms attempt to protect these assets by filing lawsuits against competitors that use similar brand names, trademarks, and product designs. In fact, trademark infringement suits are fairly common. Recently, Gucci (an Italian company) filed a $124 million lawsuit against Guess? (an American company) for launching a fashion show featuring shoes that use colors and designs similar to those used by Gucci for their line of shoes.[17] However, the claim was dismissed on February 14, 2012 because Gucci was unable to prove that the Guess? show caused confusion in the marketplace that led consumers to buy Guess? shoes when they thought they were buying Gucci shoes. Gucci was also unable to provide sufficient evidence for a trademark dilution claim. How would you prove that confusion was created? How do you think international considerations complicate this case?

reduce manufacturing costs. Offering a wide range of products that share a large number of common parts also reduces manufacturing costs, especially if the common parts are used during the early stages of the manufacturing process.

Although many Fortune 500 companies have learned to control manufacturing costs, smaller companies may be less able to do so. Also, the problems of marketing costs and product cannibalization remain. Cannibalization is problematic when one product takes significant market share away from another product within the same product line. For example, Miller Lite takes share away from regular Miller. Coke Zero takes share away from Diet Coke. Cannibalization is likely to occur when **brand loyalty**, or the strong preference for a specific brand, is high. Consumers loyal to Miller Lite are likely to drink Miller when Miller Lite is unavailable. Consumers loyal to Coke Zero are likely to drink Diet Coke when Coke Zero is unavailable. On the other hand, consumers who are *attribute* loyal are less likely to create a cannibalization within a product line. Consumers loyal to light beer may switch to Bud Light when Miller Lite is unavailable. Similarly, consumers loyal to diet soft drinks may switch to Diet Pepsi when Diet Coke is unavailable. Thus, **attribute loyalty**, or the strong preference for a specific attribute, can create brand-switching, which is worse for a firm than cannibalization.

One way to determine if consumers are brand loyal or attribute loyal is to show them a set of brands and ask them to indicate their first and second choices.[19] Brand-loyal consumers indicate first and second choices that share the same brand name (e.g., Pepsi and Diet Pepsi). However, attribute-loyal consumers indicate first and second choices that share the same attribute rather than share the same brand name (e.g., Pepsi and Coke or Diet Pepsi and Diet Coke). If the vast majority of their consumers are brand loyal, marketers should maintain a relatively narrow product line to avoid cannibalization. On the other hand, if the vast majority of their consumers are attribute loyal, it makes sense to consider increasing a product line so that all relevant attributes are available under a particular brand name. The number of relevant attributes varies across product categories (e.g., diet versus nondiet, vanilla versus chocolate, decaf versus full strength, instant versus brewed, spicy versus nonspicy).

OBJECTIVE **6**

Managing Top Dogs and Underdogs

Market leaders, or the strongest brands with the largest market shares in their product categories, are the easiest brands to manage because success breeds success. Market leaders have large marketing, production, and R&D (research and development) budgets. Market leaders often have a large segment of loyal consumers and a great deal of power in the channel of distribution. Inertia benefits the market leader, and any change in the marketplace is potentially threatening. Therefore, market leaders often try to prevent change.[20]

One way to prevent change is to encourage consumers to "stick with what works"; remind them that "you get what you pay for," and emphasize that "we're always there when you need us." These types of claims discourage consumers from trying other brands because the status quo or current state of affairs seems safe and free of risk. Another way to prevent change is to increase ambiguity in the marketplace. Ambiguous information, or information that supports many different conclusions, is often interpreted as consistent with consumers' current conclusions. Of course, because most consumers buy the market leader, they have already concluded that the market leader is the best brand. Even when consumers try to be objective, they tend to interpret ambiguous evidence as consistent with their current beliefs. Known as the **confirmation bias**, this phenomenon occurs because people find it easier to identify and interpret information that supports their beliefs as opposed to information that fails to do so.

One way to increase ambiguity in the marketplace is to make it difficult to compare the prices of market leaders versus underdogs. This can be achieved through exclusive dealerships (many automobile dealers are allowed to sell only one brand), exclusive product displays (end-of-aisle displays in grocery stores), and confusing models (one dealer has model 505A and another has model 505B). Confusing model numbers, such as different numbers for products that are otherwise identical, increase ambiguity. Confusing brand names, such as the same appliances being sold under the Whirlpool name at H. H. Gregg stores and as Kenmore brand at Sears, also increase ambiguity.

Another way to increase ambiguity in the marketplace is to differentiate market leaders using irrelevant attributes. Budweiser beer is "beechwood aged," Bud Lite offers "drinkability," and Miller Genuine Draft is "cold filtered." These irrelevant attributes do not affect the taste of the beer, but they sound good to consumers who fall prey to confirmation bias. Similarly, Folger's coffee is "mountain grown," which is a meaningless attribute. Some powdered laundry detergents have blue specks in them that are supposed to give you whiter whites. The blue specks actually have no effect, but confirmation bias leads consumers to conclude that the blue specks increase the performance of the detergent.

Underdogs, or follower brands, need to do the opposite of market leaders. Market leaders promote the status quo, but underdogs need to disrupt it. Market leaders need to increase ambiguity in the marketplace, but underdogs need to decrease it. One way to disrupt the status quo is to encourage consumers to participate in blind taste tests and other evaluations that involve comparing underdogs to market leaders. Free samples, "try it, you'll like it" claims, websites that make it easy to compare prices, comparative ads, and side-by-side shelf placements with market leaders in grocery stores can potentially benefit underdogs.

Encouraging consumers to challenge their current beliefs can also be helpful to underdog brands. For example, a Stove Top Stuffing television commercial asked a stay-at-home mom if she could predict her family's preferences for potatoes or stuffing. The stay-at-home mom predicted confidently that her

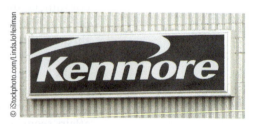

Which brand would you buy? Brand loyalty may lead you to choose one over the other, but in fact all Kenmore appliances are manufactured by Whirlpool.

husband, son, and daughters preferred potatoes. The narrator then asked the family which they preferred. Each family member responded, "Stuffing," much to the mom's surprise. Surprise is a useful weapon for inducing people to challenge their beliefs. Finally, unusual distribution channels such as home parties (e.g., Tupperware, Mary Kay) and unusual educational approaches (such as cooking classes, wine tasting classes, and cosmetic clinics) can also disrupt the status quo, increase consumer learning, and benefit underdog brands.

OBJECTIVE **(7)** # Acquisition versus Retention Strategies

Managers need to think carefully about their **source of volume**, or from where future purchases of their products will come. As Figure 3.6 indicates, increased volume can come from **acquisition strategies** or **retention strategies**.[21] Acquisition strategies focus on attracting new customers, while retention strategies focus on keeping current ones. This distinction is important because acquisition strategies and retention strategies involve the use of different marketing activities. It is also difficult to forecast sales accurately without considering all sources of volume.

One way to acquire new customers is to stimulate demand for an entire category of products (green tea, for example). Essentially, current nonusers need to be educated about the benefits of a product category over the products they are currently using (green tea is healthier than coffee). However, consumer educational programs are very expensive because they require large promotion and advertising budgets. It may also be necessary to give away free samples of a product to encourage nonusers to become users.

Another way to acquire new customers is to steal market share away from competitors. This approach is generally less expensive because competitors have already absorbed the costs of consumer education and of convincing nonusers to become users. Of course, one risk associated with this strategy is that competitors are likely to retaliate. Large competitors, such as P&G and Coca-Cola, have the resources to retaliate severely. For example, P&G's Ivory soap was the market leader for more than 100 years. When Lever 2000 launched a new soap that was very similar to Ivory, P&G retaliated by offering deeply discounted, 11-pack bundles of Ivory soap that took buyers out of the market for several purchase cycles.

Like acquisition strategies, retention strategies too can be used to build volume. One way to stimulate demand with current customers is to encourage them to use larger quantities or buy more frequently. Both goals can be achieved by selling the product in larger packages or by providing a price discount for larger packages. Typically, the more people buy, the more they consume. Anchoring can also be used to increase the number of packages that current customers purchase; claims emphasizing large numbers, such as "limit of 4 per household," "buy 12 for your freezer," or "101 uses," encourages consumers to buy larger quantities. Another way to stimulate demand is to encourage current customers to trade up. For example, satisfied customers who bought a relatively inexpensive cell phone in the past are likely to be interested in more feature-rich—and more expensive—cell phone models when it is time to purchase a new mobile phone.

Retention strategies can also be used to steal market share from competitors. For example, rather than eating the same brand of cereal every day, some consumers eat Kellogg's Corn Flakes on one day, Cheerios on another, and Kashi Good Friends on yet another. Kellogg's could attempt to steal market share by encouraging consumers to eat Kellogg's Corn Flakes more often and other brands less often. Of course, this strategy runs the risk of initiating competitive retaliation.

Acquisition and retention strategies influence all marketing activities by integrating each of the four Ps: product, promotion, price, and place. For the acquisition/increase demand strategy, the product should be designed so it has a relative advantage over other product categories. In addition, it is useful to focus on search attributes because quality can be evaluated more readily for these as opposed to other types of attributes. It is also useful to focus on alignable attributes, or attributes that are directly comparable. For example, a car that gets 30 miles per gallon is better than a similar model that gets only 25 miles per gallon. The quality of alignable attributes is easy to evaluate. A similar approach should be used for the acquisition/steal share strategy, except the focus here is on individual brand differences, rather than on product category differences.

For retention strategies, consumption among current users can be increased by developing new uses for the product, as Tums was able to do by promoting their antacid tablets as a calcium supplement. **Loyalty programs** that provide rewards for repeat purchases are also important. Examples include airline frequent flyer programs and hotel frequent user programs. Many grocery stores also provide points for purchases that accumulate and can be used for rewards. Satisfaction programs that provide excellent customer service for brands also facilitate retention. Retention strategies should also focus on experience attributes and nonalignable attributes. Current users are likely to overvalue their preferred brand's experience attributes because of confirmation bias. Also, nonalignable attributes seem unique, and current users are typically reluctant to give up a unique benefit of their preferred brand. For example, if one car brand offers rear motion detection systems and another offers heated steering wheels, it is more difficult for the consumer to compare these brands because these two attributes are not directly comparable.

Marketing managers can choose from many different promotion and advertising strategies. For the acquisition/increase demand strategy, category advertising that highlights the benefits of an entire product category is likely to attract new users. For the acquisition/steal share strategy, price advertising is likely to convince users of other brands to switch, especially if the brands are similar in quality. For retention/increase demand and retention/steal share strategies, **differentiating advertising** that emphasizes the differences in quality among brands may be effective.

Several different **pricing strategies** are possible. A large price discount on a single unit of a particular brand is referred to as **trial pricing**. The goal of trial pricing is to offer a price so low that it encourages potential new users to try the product. If they try the product and like it, they are more likely to continue purchasing it even at a higher price. Trial pricing is useful for acquiring new users for a category or brand. Offering a lower price for multiple units of a product or **continuity pricing** encourages current users to continue using a brand. If they buy a large number of units at a discounted price (11 bars of Ivory soap, say), these consumers will be committed to this particular brand for several purchase cycles. This is an excellent strategy for retaining current users.

Considering the vast volume of products in the marketplace, companies must continually evaluate their competitive strategies in order to retain and grow their customer base.

Fresh Picked/Alamy

Place strategies require careful planning of **channel length**, or the number of intermediaries (e.g., wholesalers, distributors, and retailers) needed to get the product from the manufacturer to the consumer. For example, Apple sells computers directly to consumers over the Internet, and no intermediaries are used. This is a good example of a *short* channel. Intel, on the other hand, uses many different intermediaries to get the product to the consumer, which is an example of a *long* channel. In general, a short channel is useful for acquiring both new category users and new brand users because it is easier to educate new users when the manufacturer and the users communicate directly. A long channel is riskier because consumers are more likely to encounter salespeople who may know little about the product. However, a long channel is useful for retaining existing customers. These customers are already familiar with the benefits of the product and therefore do not require education. In addition, long channels use many different outlets (e.g., grocery stores, drug stores, Walmart, Target, etc.) that facilitate product availability, which increases current users' convenience.

After identifying appropriate acquisition and retention strategies, marketing managers need next to develop an STP—Segmentation, Targeting, and Positioning—strategy. Segmentation involves dividing the market into smaller subgroups of consumers with different needs. The premise of segmentation is that "not all consumers are alike." If consumers within a specific segment respond similarly to a brand, then the marketer is able to better satisfy their needs, rather than attempt to satisfy a broader and more diverse market with the same brand. Targeting involves choosing the appropriate segments to pursue. Marketers are advised to target segments that are easy to measure, sufficiently profitable, and accessible. Positioning involves communicating the differences and the relative advantages of one's products over competitors' offerings. Positioning should focus on the firm's unique key competencies or strengths that are lacking in other firms. Importantly, acquisition and retention strategies should drive STP strategies, rather than the other way around.

FIGURE 3.6 | **Acqusition versus Retention Strategies**

	Acquisition		Retention	
	Increase demand	**Steal share**	**Increase demand**	**Steal share**
Goal	Attract new category users	Attract new brand users	Increase consumption among current brand users	Increase consumption among multibrand users
Product Strategy	Relative category advantage Satisfaction programs Search attributes Alignable differences	Relative brand advantage Satisfaction programs Search attributes Alignable differences	New uses Loyalty programs Experience attributes Nonalignable differences	New uses Loyalty programs Experience attributes Nonalignable differences
Promotion Strategy	Category advertising	Price advertising	Differentiation advertising	Differentiation advertising
Pricing Strategy	Trial pricing	Trial pricing	Continuity pricing	Continuity pricing
Place Strategy	Short channel	Short channel	Long channel	Long channel

Marketing in Action

Managing Consumers as Investments

Consumers are the most important assets of most firms. Without consumers, there would be no profits. Many companies spend $100 million or more on consumer satisfaction programs. Is this too much or too little? What is the best way to measure the value of consumers in the long run?[22] Recent research shows that it is possible to estimate customer lifetime value (CLV) using a simple equation:

$$CLV = m\,(r/1 + d - r)$$

where

m = margin or profit from a customer per quarter or year
r = retention rate
d = discount rate

The retention rate or repurchase rate is a function of product quality, price, service, etc. For most companies, retention rates are between 60 and 90 percent. The discount rate is a function of the company's cost of capital, which depends on its risk and debt-equity structure. For most companies, discount rates are between 8 and 16 percent. This equation can be used to determine if a firm is spending too much or too little on marketing programs. It can also be used to value firms to determine if stock prices are too high or too low.

One important implication of the CLV equation is that retention rates are often more important determinants of CLV than are acquisition rates. If this is true, firms should spend more on retention than on acquisition. Recently, however, it has been shown that the acquisition rate is more important than the retention rate when debt and nonoperating assets are considered.[23] CLV is an important concept, because in many industries, a 10% increase in CLV results in a 15% increase in shareholder value. This ratio is lower when a firm's debt level is high, and it is higher when a firm's nonoperating assets are high.

Chapter Summary

Product management involves monitoring and nurturing a product as it progresses through its life cycle. At first, managers must focus on building brand awareness. Later, promotion and advertising are used to stimulate growth. For mature products, it is important to reduce costs. Finally, during the decline phase, managers must decide whether to harvest the product or attempt to rejuvenate it.

Many managers view the reputation and image of a brand as its most important asset. Strong brand names help products through difficult times and provide unique opportunities during good times. Managers must also determine whether to reduce a product line to decrease brand cannibalization, or increase a product line through brand extensions to increase sales. In general, when consumers are brand loyal, the product line should be reduced to avoid cannibalization and diluting brand equity. When consumers are attribute loyal, firms should consider increasing their product lines to offer products that encompass all attributes under one brand name.

Acquisition strategies attempt to increase overall demand for a product category or to steal market share from competing brands. Retention strategies attempt to increase consumption among current brand users or among multi-brand users. Acquisition and retention strategies influence all aspects of brand management, including product strategy, promotion strategy, pricing strategy, and place strategy.

Key Terms

acquisition strategies
attribute loyalty
brand entry strategy
brand equity
brand extension
brand loyalty
brand resonance
cannibalization
channel length

confirmation bias
continuity pricing
differentiating advertising
diffusion of innovation
entity theorists
  incremental theorists
loyalty program
pioneering brand advantage
pricing stratgey

proactive strategy
reactive strategy
retention strategies
source of volume
The Young & Rubicam
  Brand Asset Valuator
trial pricing

Review and Discussion

1. Name and describe the four basic entry strategies that can influence the diffusion curve.

2. What type of entry strategy should be used to promote HDTV?

3. Think of a brand to which you are loyal. What experiences led to your brand loyalty in this case?

4. How can marketers extend the product life cycle of a worn-out product?

5. How does the Young & Rubicam Brand Asset Valuator help marketers?

6. What factors increase the likelihood of brand cannibalization?

7. How should marketers of a leading brand of coffee try to maintain their leadership position?

8. How should marketers of an underdog brand of furniture try to gain a stronger position in the marketplace?

9. What strategies should marketers use to acquire new customers?

10. What strategies should marketers use to retain old customers?

Short Application Exercises

1. Create a category advertisement, a price advertisement, and a differentiating advertisement.
2. Use the Young & Rubicam Brand Asset Valuator to evaluate the brand equity of Starbucks coffee.
3. Think of brand extensions that should be considered by KFC (fast-food restaurants), Panasonic (electronics), and Scion (automobiles).
4. Think of strategies to increase ambiguity in the marketplace to help Disney retain its leadership position.

Managerial Application

One of the authors (Frank R. Kardes) had the pleasure of meeting Les Behrens, the owner of Behrens and Hitchcock, in 2008. Previously, Les Behrens had owned a restaurant, and Bob Hitchcock was an accountant. Both gave up these relatively secure jobs to make wine on top of Spring Mountain in Napa Valley. Many of their wines received high ratings from Robert Parker, the most influential wine critic of all time (he has been nicknamed the Emperor of Wine), and the label very quickly became a success. Hitchcock retired and left the partnership in 2005, and Behrens changed the name of the label to Erna Schein, after his mother. According to Parker, Erna Schein wines are "fun-filled, fruit-driven, amazingly delicious wines."[24] Annual production is around 3,000 cases, which is quite small.

Your Challenge:

1. What are the dangers of changing the brand name of an already successful brand?
2. What strategies can be taken to try to minimize these dangers?
3. What marketing strategies would you recommend to Behrens for acquiring new customers?
4. What marketing strategies would you recommend to for retaining old customers?

End Notes

1 Williams, S. (2012). Hyundai – Yes, Hyundai – Aims to be New Badge of Luxury. *Advertising Age*, 83(2): 1–22.

2 Urban, G. L., and Hauser, J. (1993). *Design and Marketing of New Products*. Englewood Cliffs, NJ: Prentice Hall.

3 Ansoff, H. I. (1957). Strategies for Diversification. *Harvard Business Review*, 35: 113–124.

4 Gurumurthy, K., and Urban, G. (1992). Dynamic Effects of the Order of Entry on Market Share, Trial Penetration, and Repeat Purchases for Frequently Purchased Consumer Goods. *Marketing Science*, 11: 235–250; Urban, G. L., Carter, T., Gaskin, S., and Mucha, Z. (1986). Market Share Rewards to Pioneering Brands: An Empirical Analysis and Strategic Implications. *Management Science*, 32: 645–659.

5 Kardes, F. R., and Gurumurthy, K. (1992). Order-of-Entry Effects on Consumer Memory and Judgment: An Information Integration Perspective. *Journal of Marketing Research*, 29: 343–357.

6 Carpenter, G. S., and Nakamoto, K. (1989). Consumer Preference Formation and Pioneering Advantage. *Journal of Marketing Research*, 26: 285–298.

7 Kardes, F. R., Gurumurthy, K., Chandrashekaran, M., and Dornoff, R. J. (1993). Brand Retrieval, Consideration Set Composition, Consumer Choice, and the Pioneering Advantage. *Journal of Consumer Research*, 20: 62–75.

8 Golder, P. N., and Tellis, G. J. (1993). Pioneer Advantage: Marketing Logic or Marketing Legend? *Journal of Marketing Research*, 30: 158–170.

9 Rogers, E. M. (1983). *Diffusion of Innovations*. New York: Free Press.

10 Urban, G. L., and Star, S. H. (1991). *Advanced Marketing Strategy: Phenomena, Analysis, and Decisions*. Englewood Cliffs, NJ: Prentice Hall.

11 Aaker, D. A. (1991). *Managing Brand Equity*. New York: Free Press; Aaker, D. A. (1996). *Building Strong Brands*. New York: Free Press; Keller, K. L. (2007).

Strategic Brand Management: Building, Measuring, and Managing Brand Equity, 3rd ed. Upper Saddle River, NJ: Prentice Hall.

12 Kardes, F. R., and Allen, C. T. (1991). Perceived Variability and Inferences about Brand Extensions. *Advances in Consumer Research*, 18: 392–398.

13 Keller, K. L. (2007). *Strategic Brand Management: Building, Measuring, and Managing Brand Equity*, 3rd ed. Upper Saddle River, NJ: Prentice Hall.

14 Aaker, D. A., and Keller, K. L. (1990). Consumer Evaluations of Brand Extensions. *Journal of Marketing*, 54: 27–41; Boush, D., and Loken, B. (1991). A Process-Tracing Study of Brand Extension Evaluation. *Journal of Marketing Research*, 28: 16–28; Broniarczyk, S. M., and Alba, J. W. (1994). The Importance of the Brand in Brand Extension. *Journal of Marketing Research*, 31: 214–228; Herr, P. M., Farquhar, P. H., and Fazio, R. H. (1996). Impact of Dominance and Relatedness on Brand Extensions. *Journal of Consumer Psychology*, 5: 135–160; Keller, K. L., and Aaker, D. A. (1992). The Effects of Sequential Introduction of Brand Extensions. *Journal of Marketing Research*, 29: 30–50; Mao, H., and Krishnan, H. S. (2006). Effects of Prototype and Exemplar Fit on Brand Extension Evaluations: A Two-Process Contingency Model. *Journal of Consumer Research*, 33: 41–49; Park, C. W., Milberg, S. J., and Lawson, R. (1991). Evaluation of Brand Extensions: The Role of Product Level Similarity and Brand Concept Consistency. *Journal of Consumer Research*, 18: 185–193.

15 Barone, M. J., Miniard, P. W., and Romeo, J. B. (2000). The Influence of Positive Mood on Brand Extension Evaluations. *Journal of Consumer Research*, 26: 386–400; Gurhan-Canli, Z., and Maheswaran, D. (1998). The Effects of Extensions on Brand Name Dilution and Enhancement. *Journal of Marketing Research*, 35: 464–473; Meyvis, T., and Janiszewski, C. (2004). When Are Broader Brands Stronger Brands? An Accessibility Perspective on the Formation of Brand Equity. *Journal of Consumer Research*, 31: 346–357; Monga, A. B., and John, D. R. (2007). Cultural Differences in Brand Extension Evaluation: The Influence of Analytic Versus Holistic Thinking. *Journal of Consumer Research*, 33: 529–536; Monga, A. B., and John, D. R. (2010). What Makes Brands Elastic? The Influence of Brand Concept and Styles of Thinking on Brand Extension Evaluation. *Journal of Marketing*, 74: 80–92; Yorkston, E. A., Nunes, J. C., and Matta, S. (2010). The Malleable Brand: The Role of Implicit Theories in Evaluating Brand Extensions. *Journal of Marketing*, 74: 80–93.

16 Beattie, A. C. (2012). Agency A-List: International Agency of the Year. *Advertising Age*, 83(4): 26.

17 King, S. (2012). Sheppard Mullen Richter & Hampton LLP: Battle of the G's Rages On: Gucci's $124 Million Trademark and Trade Dress Infringement Lawsuit Against Guess? Withstands Summary Judgment, www.lexisnexis.com.

18 Kekre, S., and Srinivasan, K. (1990). Broader Product Line: A Necessity to Achieve Success? *Management Science*, 36: 1216–1231.

19 Urban, G. L., Johnson, P. L., and Hauser, J. R. (1984). Testing Competitive Market Structures. *Marketing Science*, 3: 83–112.

20 Hoch, S. J., and Deighton, J. (1989). Managing What Consumers Learn From Experience. *Journal of Marketing*, 53: 1–20.

21 Nordhielm, C. L. (2006). *Marketing Management: The Big Picture*. New York: John Wiley & Sons.

22 Gupta, S., and Lehmann, D. R. (2005). *Managing Customers as Investments: The Strategic Value of Customers in the Long Run*. Upper Saddle River, NJ: Wharton School Publishing (division of Pearson Education).

23 Schulze, C., Skiera, B., and Wiesel, T. (2012). Linking Customer and Financial Metrics to Shareholder Value: The Leverage Effect in Customer-Based Valuation. *Journal of Marketing*, 76: 17–32.

24 Parker, R. M. (2008). *Parker's Wine Buyer's Guide*, 7th ed. New York: Simon & Schuster, 1121.

PART 2

CONSUMER INFORMATION PROCESSING

POSITIONING

EMOTION

© iStockphoto.com/rsm_web

CHAPTERS

AN INTERVIEW WITH ROBERT S. WYER, JR.

Professor of Marketing
University of Illinois

Robert S. Wyer, Jr., is a Professor Emeritus of Psychology at the University of Illinois and Visiting Professor at Chinese University of Hong Kong. He studies information processing; the representation of narrative information in memory and its use in judgment; priming effects on comprehension, judgment, and decisions; memory processes; and affect and cognition.

Q. Please describe the information processing paradigm and what this paradigm offers to the field of consumer behavior.

Consumers' behavior is influenced to a large extent by the information they receive about the products they consider purchasing. It is therefore important to know how this information is used. An information processing approach to understanding consumer behavior breaks down the effects of information on judgments and decisions into a number of steps:

1. Attention to the information
2. Interpretation of its features in terms of preexisting concepts
3. Organization of these features into a representation of the referent as a whole
4. Storage of this representation in memory
5. Later retrieval of the representation, along with other knowledge acquired about the referent
6. Assessment of the implications of this knowledge for a subjective evaluation or behavioral decision
7. Translation of these implications into an overt response.

The effects of information about a product or responses to it and the way situational factors influence these effects can be mediated by its effects at any one or more of these stages.

Information processing researchers try to understand the cognitive processes that operate at each stage and the factors that affect them. In addition, they attempt to develop theoretical models that specify how the various stages of processing interface.

Most conceptualizations of information processing are metaphorical and do not pretend to describe the physiology of the brain. Thus, they should be evaluated on the basis of their utility and not their validity. The theories that have been proposed in cognitive and social psychology, many of which have been applied in the consumer area, have generally been very successful in explaining known phenomena and generating predictions of new ones.

Q. Please explain the priming effect and the different types of priming effects that you have studied.

People normally do not use all the knowledge they have acquired about an object to evaluate it or decide how to respond to it. Rather, they only use a small subset of this knowledge that happens to be easily accessible in memory at the time. "Priming" refers to a procedure used in the laboratory to increase the accessibility of different subsets of knowledge and to investigate the effects of their use. Any number of procedures can be used, depending on the particular type of knowledge of concern. Single concepts can often be primed by having individuals construct sentences in which exemplars of the concepts are used. However, activating more general types of knowledge (stereotypes, affective reactions, procedures, and implicit theories) requires different techniques.

In many cases, concepts and knowledge can be primed subliminally. It is critical, however, to ensure that individuals are unaware of the relationship between the priming task and the task that they are asked to perform subsequently. Individuals should not realize that the primed knowledge comes to mind for reasons that have anything to do with the judgments or decisions they are called upon to make. If individuals *are* aware, they often intentionally avoid using the concepts or knowledge to prevent bias, and this can lead the priming to have a contrast effect.

My own and others' work was initially designed to test various theoretical assumptions concerning the effects of priming *per se*. For example, we showed that the likelihood of using a trait concept to interpret a person's behavior increased with how recently and how frequently the concept had been primed in a prior, unrelated task. Once the person's behavior was interpreted in terms of this concept however, its effect on evaluations of the person described by the behavior increased over time.

The effects of priming are now well established. In our more recent work, we have used priming as a methodological tool to examine phenomena of interest for other reasons. Research with Catherine Yeung, for example, used priming techniques to examine the role of affect in product impression formation. We showed that priming positive or negative affect influenced consumers' initial impressions of a product formed on the basis of a picture. This impression, once formed, was used as a basis for later judgments of the product independent of the attribute information presented subsequently. A series of studies with Hao Shen has used priming techniques to demonstrate that cognitive procedures, if activated in one situation, can persist to influence the processing of information in a later, totally unrelated, situation. Thus, for example, individuals who have been induced to give the same answer to each of a series of questions about animals are less likely than other participants to choose a variety of different products in a later, multiple-choice decision task. Furthermore, the rate at which individuals are required to speak while shadowing a speech affects the speed with which they complete a marketing survey in an unrelated situation they encounter subsequently.

Of particular interest is a series of studies with Jing Xu. She finds that individuals who are induced to make comparative judgments in an initial situation develop a "which-to-choose" mindset that increases their likelihood of deciding which of two products to purchase in a later situation without considering the option of not buying anything at all. This is apparently true even when the comparative judgments are totally unrelated to purchase behavior. Thus, for example, comparing the physical attributes of wild animals or judging the similarity of foreign countries can increase the likelihood of making a purchase in a product choice situation.

Q. How does priming occur outside the laboratory? What is the role of television, advertising, and other types of marketing communication?

Although the concepts and knowledge that are primed in the laboratory are intentionally manipulated, the effects of knowledge accessibility generally occur without awareness. Consequently, numerous experiences that fortuitously occur in daily life can influence the concepts and procedures consumers apply in evaluating products and making purchase decisions a short time later. Perhaps more important, concepts and knowledge that have been applied very frequently in the course of individuals' daily lives can become *chronically* accessible in memory, and therefore can have effects that generalize over a number of situations.

L. J. Shrum and his colleagues provide a particularly interesting demonstration of these effects in their research on the impact of television on perceptions of social reality. They found that individuals tend to overestimate the incidence of persons, objects, and events in the real world that are overrepresented on television. Shrum also found that the degree of their overestimation increases with the amount of television individuals watch. Although other explanations of this effect have been suggested, Shrum provides convincing evidence that it results from the fact that objects and events seen on television are more accessible in memory and are used as a basis for frequency estimates without considering the context in which they were encountered. So, heavy television viewers, relative to light viewers, overestimate the number of policemen and doctors in the general population, the incidence of violent crime, and the number of households with swimming pools in the backyard.

The chronic accessibility of concepts and knowledge can also vary with individuals' cultural backgrounds. A series of studies by Donnel Briley, Michael Morris, and Itamar Simonson show that Asians, who are more inclined than Westerners to think of themselves in relation to one another, exhibit a tendency to choose the "compromise" option in a multiple-alternative product decision task. Put another way, they are more inclined to choose options that minimize the negative consequences of their decision, independently of the positive outcomes that might accompany them. Interestingly, these differences are not evident unless cultural norms are made more accessible in memory, either by asking participants to give reasons for their choices or, in the case of bilingual consumers, by varying the language in which the product decision task is administered.

Q. How do consumers get into a buying mindset? Can marketers trick consumers into buying more than they should?

Jing Xu's research provides one possible answer. It suggests that consumers who are asked by a salesperson to make comparative judgments before considering a purchase are more likely to make a purchase than they otherwise would. I'm reminded of my personal experiences with Oriental rug salesmen. After displaying a number of rugs, they frequently ask you to indicate which one you prefer, thus attempting to induce a "which to buy" mindset that will stimulate a purchase without considering the option of buying nothing.

A more common situation may be exemplified by the shopping momentum effect identified by Dhar, Huber, and Kahn. Inducing individuals to make a small purchase early in the experiment increases their willingness to make a second purchase later on. They argue that the process of making the first purchase activates an "implemental" mindset that persists over time.

However, one could speculate about numerous other real-world priming phenomena that have implications for marketing strategy. Nunes and Boatright found that customers in a beachfront shopping area were more willing to pay a higher price for CDs being sold if the sweaters at an adjacent booth were priced relatively high than if they were priced relatively low. Although the specific process underlying this effect is unclear, it provides yet another example of the effects of concept activation on purchase behavior outside the laboratory.

Having said this however, I personally believe that our objective as consumer behavior researchers is not to provide marketers with tools for tricking the public into buying more than they should, but to provide consumers with tools they can use to avoid being tricked. Because the effects of knowledge accessibility are largely unconscious, this is a challenging problem.

CHAPTER

4

CONSUMER PERCEPTION

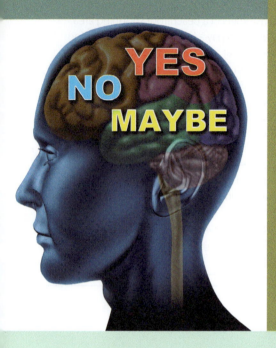

OBJECTIVES   *After studying this chapter, you will be able to...*

1 Define perception, attention, cognitive capacity, and comprehension and describe how the perceptual process works.

2 Explain how sensory thresholds influence perception.

3 Describe the physical influences on attention and perception.

4 Discuss how selective attention is both voluntary and involuntary, and provide examples of how marketers appeal to the senses to obtain and maintain consumers' attention.

Digital Display Energizes Consumer Perceptions

Display signage is as old as civilization itself. Early Egyptians used stone obelisks to display notifications to its citizens. With the invention of movable type press by Gutenberg in the 1400s, advertising in the modern sense was born. And, by the late 1800s the modern, large outdoor advertising billboard was part of the American roadside, its goal being to grab the consumer's attention and interest.

Today, the signage industry has come a long way, and digital display is taking over the industry as the market approaches 20 million digital signs in the marketplace. What's more, the goal has changed as technology changes. In the age of marketing clutter, it's not enough to catch the consumer's attention; marketers must engage and interact with the consumer in meaningful and entertaining way.

For example, consider the marketing campaign run by Plan UK in London bus shelters that could sense a viewer's gender using facial recognition technology and then adapted displayed advertising content accordingly. Alternatively, retailer Forever 21 created a digital billboard in Times Square that interacts with the crowd. The company that created the digital sign used computer technology and live cameras to simulate larger-than-life on-screen fashion models interacting with people in the crowd. And, cable provider Clear Channel Communications created an interactive hub where pedestrians on the Las Vegas Strip could post Twitter updates and Foursquare check-ins to digital billboards.

Eye Ubiquitous/Alamy

To achieve this level of entertainment and interactivity, the digital display field will continue to evolve. LCD (liquid crystal display in a flat screen) technology is the new standard display of today and E Ink, the technology behind eReaders, will continue to drive the world of digital display forward. These technologies and marketing ingenuity will continue to energize consumers' senses.[1]

OBJECTIVE 1 ## Defining the Perceptual Process

Why do some product packages stick out on grocery store shelves, while others barely get noticed? Why do some television commercials generate attention, while others are ignored? This chapter describes how consumers physically acquire and interpret information about products, services, and the world around them through the perceptual process.

Perception is a process of receiving, selecting, and interpreting environmental stimuli involving the five senses. Through perception, we define the world around us and create meaning from our environment. For example, consumers eat ice cream, and it feels cold and tastes sweet. People look upward, see blue, and know that they are viewing the sky. But how cold or sweet or blue is different for every individual because each person's perceptual process is unique. This chapter demonstrates that myriad factors influence consumers' perceptions. That no two people perceive the world in the same way is a challenging concept because it is difficult for people to step outside their own physical senses, i.e., to try to see things as others see them. The erroneous assumption that everyone else perceives the world as we do is called **phenomenal absolutism**.

The steps in the perceptual process are shown in Figure 4.1. Although the process appears sequential from sensory exposure through comprehension, the entire process occurs almost instantaneously, and the steps of the process interact and overlap seamlessly.

FIGURE 4.1 | **The Perceptual Process**

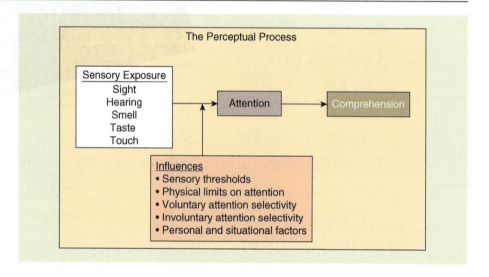

Perception of the environment requires consumers to use their physical senses. *Sensory exposure* occurs when a stimulus, like the smell of pretzels in the shopping mall or seeing a print ad in the newspaper, is detected by the physical senses. Although the senses include dozens of secondary sensory systems, consumers' primary senses are sight, hearing, smell, taste, and touch. The body's first and immediate response to a stimulus is called **sensation**. Sensation involves gathering data from the sensory organs and nervous system and sending them to the brain for processing and interpretation. But not all stimuli receive attention. People perceive only a fraction of the stimuli to which they are exposed. In other words, consumers are not passive recipients of the world around them. To avoid being overwhelmed by the sheer volume of stimuli available in the marketplace, consumers are selective about stimuli. Thus, an important part of the perceptual process is discriminating among stimuli and selecting those to receive further processing. This step represents the act of attention.

Attention means focusing on one or more environmental stimuli while potentially ignoring others. Attention is highly selective in nature. If consumers didn't have *selective attention* (also called *perceptual selection*), they would be so overloaded with information in the marketplace that they wouldn't be able to function effectively. For example, in the United States there are more than 1,800 television stations, more than 16,000 radio stations, and over 8,000 newspapers and magazines.[2] The average U.S. consumer is exposed to up to 5,000 ad messages per day.[3] In addition, the typical American watches about 4.5 hours of television per day, spends about 2.0 hours per day online, and according to phone maker Nokia, the average person looks at their cell phone about 150 times per day.[4]

Adding to this state of media overload, American firms spend over $150 billion a year on advertising, with over $500 billion spent worldwide.[5] Obviously, consumers cannot attend to all product information to which they are exposed. **Cognitive capacity**, or the ability to pay attention to and think about information, is limited. Consequently, marketers need to understand what guides consumers' allocation of cognitive capacity and their selective attention.

Consumers today are in a state of media overload and have limited cognitive capacity, which is why selective attention is so important.

Yellow Dog Productions/Photodisc/Getty Images

The last step in the perceptual process involves providing meaning to the sensory data that gets processed. **Comprehension** is the ability to interpret and assign meaning to the new information by relating it to knowledge already stored in memory. The ways new environmental stimuli are categorized, interpreted, and experienced are influenced by existing knowledge. Ask two people with radically different political opinions to interpret a political speech, and the answers will differ dramatically. To revisit the ice cream example from earlier in this discussion, when consumers taste chocolate ice cream, their senses take in sweetness, cold, chocolate flavor, the smell of chocolate, and wet stickiness. Consumers' ability to organize, categorize, and interpret these sensations help them recognize that, indeed, they are eating chocolate ice cream. After comprehension, preferences and choice follow.

Marketing in Action

Marketing to the Senses: The Ingenious Ways Marketers Use Color

Marketers have long realized the importance of perception and appealing to our physical senses; and perhaps our most important physical sense is sight. Through sight we perceive colors, sizes, and the position of objects in the environment. In fact, the majority of our sensual perception occurs through sight. Visual tools related to perception are used by marketers to increase attention to marketing messages.

An important tool for marketers related to sight is the use of color. According to color experts, color sells. Color catches attention, conveys meaning, and elicits emotions from consumers. Let's look at some common colors and how they are perceived:

- Red is typically associated with appetite and sexual arousal; it is attention-getting and exciting. Red can also convey a warning or signify rescue from danger—think of the American Red Cross or a bright red fire engine.
- Orange is also a high-energy color associated with appetite and power. Tide laundry detergent uses an orange package to signify its strength.
- Blue is considered relaxing; it is associated with sky, water, trust, and the future. Blue is America's favorite color, according to the makers of Crayola crayons.

- Green is representative of health, refreshment, and the environment. The Healthy Choice packaged food brand uses green as its signature color to symbolize its low-fat content and healthfulness. On the downside, green is also associated with money, greed, and envy, so it isn't a good color to wear if you want someone to trust you.
- Yellow sends a message of optimism, happiness, and nature. Yellow is symbolic of light, the sun, and cleanliness. Cleaning products are often packaged in yellow.

Marketers know that colors speak to people and give them messages about the product, making color an important part of the overall marketing message.

AP Images/PR NEWSWIRE

Perception is important to marketers because it is the communication gateway to the consumer. Understanding perception and how it influences consumers' attention to the environment, their interpretation and comprehension of stimuli, and ultimately their behavior, are essential to developing successful products and marketing messages. The rest of the chapter explores the influences and limits of the perceptual process of importance to marketers, including sensory thresholds, physical limits on attention, and voluntary and involuntary attention selectivity.

OBJECTIVE ② ## Sensory Thresholds

The Absolute Threshold

Have you ever watched a dog sniff the ground as he tracks some secret scent? Or listened to your cat move around the dark house at night, able to see every obstacle? There are some stimuli that people simply cannot perceive. Overall, however, the sensory limits or *thresholds* for animals—including humans—are relatively high. The minimum level of stimuli needed for an individual to experience a sensation is called the **absolute threshold**. It is the lowest point at which a person can detect "something" on a given sensory receptor. The smells that dogs can use for tracking are too slight to be detected by humans, so this stimulus is beyond our olfactory absolute threshold. Likewise, the farthest point at which a person can read a billboard advertisement from a moving car represents an absolute threshold.

In addition to the overall physical strengths and weaknesses of human senses, individual differences in sensory ability also exist. For example, children tend to experience lower absolute thresholds, which might explain why infants often react to startling noises and bright lights by crying or showing distress. Research demonstrates that women also tend to have lower absolute thresholds than men. Some people may have their senses impaired or altered because of disability or aging; some people often have one sense that they feel is particularly strong, such as a keen sense of smell or sharp vision. For example, two consumers riding together in a car may see a billboard advertisement at different times from different distances. Consequently, advertisers need to make sure that the type on the billboard is large enough and brief enough to maximize the number of people capable of reading it. (As a general industry rule of thumb, because a billboard is read by the average person in six seconds or less, it should contain no more than six words in the primary message.) Pharmaceutical companies and other industries that must include details and fine print in their advertisements must design the type large enough for the average person to read—particularly if the target market is seniors, who typically prefer 16 point font. These examples all demonstrate that the absolute threshold is an important consideration for marketers when designing marketing stimuli for targeted audiences.

Marketers need to consider consumers' absolute thresholds when designing marketing materials.

The Just Noticeable Difference

Another important sensory threshold is the ability to detect changes in relative levels of stimuli. The **just noticeable difference (j. n. d.)**, also called the *differential threshold,* is the amount of incremental change required for a person to detect a difference between two similar stimuli. For example, the number of pounds you have to put on before your friends notice you've gained weight is the j. n. d., as is the amount you have to raise your voice in a crowded restaurant until you can be heard by your companions.

In the middle of the nineteenth century, German scientist Ernst Weber found that the magnitude of the j. n. d. between two stimuli was systematically related to the intensity of the first stimulus, rather than some absolute amount. In other words, Weber discovered that the ability to sense a change in stimulus level depends on the original magnitude of that stimulus. The greater or stronger the initial stimulus was, the greater was the amount of change required for it to be noticed. This is known as **Weber's Law**. For instance, consider a product just put on sale. A rule of thumb in retailing maintains that a price should be marked down at least 20% for consumers to notice the price change. So, if a grocer marks down a can of pineapple that normally costs $1.00, the sales price should be $0.80 cents (0.80 × $1.00, or a $0.20 discount). However, that same $0.20 discount won't benefit a package of steaks that cost $10.00; the steaks would have to be marked down to $8.00 (a $2.00 discount) to be noticed by consumers.

Consumers' abilities to detect change in stimuli and j. n. d. are critical to marketers, particularly when the goal is to ensure that negative product changes (e.g., increases in price or reductions in product quality) go unnoticed, falling below the j. n. d. Conversely, when positive product changes occur (e.g., sales discounts or updated product features), a marketer wants to ensure that the change is readily apparent, exceeding the j. n. d., without being excessive or wasteful.

Marketers also use j. n. d. in an attempt to increase the profit margin on a product by decreasing the amount of product offered in the package, rather than by increasing the price. Reducing the volume in a product's package reduces the firm's cost per unit. Here, understanding the amount of change that can be made to the product's volume, while remaining below consumers' j. n. d., can generate incremental profits. This practice is called *package-pricing*. It's a way for a company to enact an "invisible" price increase. In recent years, packages of Doritos and Fritos and Tostitos are about 20% lighter than they were a few years ago; Tropicana shifted from a 64-ounce to 59-ounce container as the price of oranges rose; and Edy's Grand Ice Cream cut package sizes from 2 liters (a half-gallon) to 1.5 liters.[6]

But this tactic is not without risk. When Kimberly-Clark implemented a 5% package reduction while holding prices steady on its Huggies Diapers, rival Procter & Gamble flooded the market with coupons and price promotions on its Pampers and Luvs diaper brands. Consumers often feel cheated if they figure out that a brand has applied package-pricing. Nevertheless, research shows that while consumers prefer a straightforward price increase over reductions in package quantity, if a company can employ package-pricing and effectively fall below the j. n. d., most customers may never notice the change in price.[7]

Marketers also often use j. n. d. estimations to help update existing package designs or brand symbols without losing any brand recognition that has been cultivated through expensive marketing communication. When this is the case, small successive changes are made, each carefully designed to fall below the j. n. d. For example, Tony the Tiger, Betty Crocker, Aunt Jemima, and Wendy from Wendy's Old Fashioned Hamburger Restaurants, have all been subtly refreshed and modernized over the years. While the new version of the Wendy's mascot, for example, still has the trademark pigtails and freckles, with the same color scheme in terms of clothing and her trademark red hair, the surrounding design of the logo and prior saturation of cluttered taglines has been updated to a fresh, simplistic design aligned to today's market standards.

The recent evolution of the Wendy's image is a result of evolving market trends.

Of course, sometimes the marketer's goal is to exceed the j. n. d. with package and message changes in order to generate attention and create "buzz." For example, Pepsi has periodically introduced obvious and significant changes to its packaging as part of its marketing campaigns.

Adaptation

Another concept related to sensory thresholds is **adaptation**, the process of becoming desensitized to sensual stimuli. Over time, if a stimulus doesn't change, we adapt or orient to it and notice it less. This is important to marketers because as advertisements and other marketing stimuli become familiar, they are less likely to attract attention. The following conditions can increase adaptation:

- **High Repetition:** High repetition of a perceptual stimulus increases adaptation. When an advertisement is overexposed, it loses the ability to attract attention and interest; this is also known as **advertising wear-out**.
- **Simplicity:** Simple stimuli tend to encourage adaptation because they don't require much cognitive capacity to process. A billboard with no words is easy to comprehend, but may quickly become part of the scenery.
- **Low Intensity:** Soft sounds, faint smells, and dull colors all produce quick adaptation because they require little input from human sensory systems.

Marketers work hard to discourage adaptation. For example, how frequently an ad appears is typically monitored closely to avoid wear-out. In contrast, a marketer may try to increase the intensity of sensory input. For example, Cadillac recently purchased all the ad time for a season premiere episode of A&E Channel's *Mad Men* to ensure that their message wouldn't get lost in advertising clutter. Additional information about how marketers design messages to rise above the clutter is provided later in the chapter.

Subliminal Perception and Advertising

In a typical college marketing class today, if a professor were to ask how many students believed that subliminal messages are effective in influencing people, the majority would answer in the affirmative. That's because the public has been fascinated with the topic of subliminal perception for years. The popular press has taken advantage of this interest, perpetuating speculations and inaccuracies about the use of subliminal messaging in marketing. Thus, many people believe in subliminal advertising, even though no substantial body of research shows that subliminal messaging has any practical behavioral influence on consumers. The practice is banned in Great Britain and Australia and can result in licensure penalties in the United States.

Subliminal perception is the unconscious awareness of a stimulus. Technically, "subliminal" means beneath the absolute threshold (*limen* is another word for threshold). Nevertheless, many subliminal messages are actually *supraliminal*, meaning they fall above the absolute threshold, but are consciously repressed by the recipient. In other words, consumers don't consciously engage these messages; they process them at a subconscious level.

Subliminal advertising has a notorious history. Although the basic terminology and concept of subliminal messaging has been around for more than a century, its close association to advertising emerged in the 1950s, due to James Vicary.[8] In 1957, Vicary conducted a six-week subliminal message experiment in movie theatres in New Jersey during a showing of the movie *Picnic*. He flashed subliminal messages, "Drink Cola-Cola" and "Hungry? Eat Popcorn" during a movie, at 1/3000 of a second—far too quickly to be recognized via conscious awareness. Vicary claimed that popcorn sales increased by 57.7%, and Coke sales increased by 18.1% as a result of the subliminal embedded message. He coined the term "subliminal advertising" to describe this form of messaging. His findings launched a flurry of research into subliminal marketing messages, a national debate on the ethics of subliminal messaging, and the perception among many consumers that subliminal messages are commonly (and successfully) employed by marketers. Regrettably, Vicary's results were fabricated to promote his business. After years of other researchers failing to replicate his experiments, Vicary finally admitted that he had done little research and did not have enough data to draw meaningful conclusions.

In the 1970s, Wilson Bryan Key reignited interest in the topic of subliminal advertising.[9] His books focused on identifying supposed sexual symbols, images, and words embedded in advertising, so-called *subliminal embeds*. He claimed that marketers included the sexually themed subliminal embeds to physically arouse viewers to increase attention and persuasion.

In 1989, a lawsuit was filed against the musical group Judas Priest for supposedly planting the hidden phrase "Do It" in their song "Better You Than Me." The subliminal phrase could be heard when the record album was played backward. The parents of two teenage boys brought the lawsuit and alleged that the phrase pushed their sons to commit suicide. The group argued they didn't intentionally place the message on the album and if they had, it should be protected by the First Amendment to the U.S. Constitution, which protects freedom of speech. However, the judge ruled that subliminal messages are not protected by the First Amendment because people can't avoid them, so the messages constituted an invasion of privacy. But the judge also ruled that actual persuasion via subliminal messaging had never been proven, and the case was ruled in favor of the band.

Over the years, companies have tried to profit from the *open* use of subliminal messaging. In the 1950s, Chevrolet used a jingle about subliminal advertising to promote a new car. Similarly, Absolut Vodka has a famous print advertisement entitled "Absolut Subliminal," which features a glass of vodka with ice. Embedded in the ice, the words "Absolut Vodka" are written. In the 1980s, a rash of companies selling self-help subliminal message audio tapes sprang up, promising everything from weight loss to a job promotion. And a few years ago, KFC planted a hidden coupon in frames of television commercials. These were specifically designed for users of DVRs; when the commercials were played frame-by-frame, the coupon was revealed.

Recently, researchers have returned to the subject of the potential influence of subliminal stimuli. Some research has shown that under controlled circumstances, subliminal stimuli can influence attitudes and behaviors. Still, applications for subliminal messaging in a mass-marketing environment have not been demonstrated because the conditions needed to generate subliminal perception are very difficult to produce outside the laboratory. Unfortunately however, misconceptions about the use of subliminal messaging still persist today. In reality, the majority of marketers do not intentionally use subliminal messaging because it would be a waste of time and money.

Now that we have examined the physical thresholds of the senses, let's look at two other physical influences on the perceptual process: cognitive limitations related to short-term memory and physical arousal.

The Truth about Perfume Marketing

Ethics

The marketing of perfume is the marketing of scent, perception, memory, emotion, mystery, and magic. However, despite being a billion-dollar industry and a product that millions of people put on their bodies on a regular basis, many consumers are unaware of how fragrances are often developed and marketed.

One big misconception is that if a perfume lists a "note" of an exotic ingredient, such as lilac, cedar, jasmine, or vanilla, then the perfume actually contains some of that ingredient. The reality is that those scents are usually artificial and synthetic, manufactured by a chemist in a lab. The ad copy may not be clear on this point, as its job is to pull the consumer in, ignite the imagination, and entice the consumer to purchase.

Another misconception around the manufacture and marketing of perfume is that famous celebrities, athletes, and designers actually create their own perfumes. Perfumes are created by experts called "noses" who work for large fragrance companies. The famous names are usually just licensing their name to the product. This is a win-win situation for both the company and the celebrity because the perfume company can leverage the celebrity brand and marketing network, and the celebrity can create another point of connection with his or her fan base. For example, when the singer Rihanna launched the perfume Re'l Fluer, she reached out to over 4.5 million Twitter followers and 30 million Facebook fans. While there are exceptions to the rule and some celebrities provide extensive input into the development of the fragrance, more typically the celebrity may just provide a brief description of what they might like (e.g., make it smell spicy; or give it a nautical note).[10]

OBJECTIVE ③ # Physical Influences on Attention

Beyond the physical limitations of our senses, consumers possess limited cognitive capacity and mental resources for information processing, particularly with respect to attention. People are able to attend to and think about only a small amount of information at a time, and attention varies from person to person and from situation to situation. The next section examines two pervasive physical influences on attention: short-term memory limits and physical arousal.

Short-Term Memory

From a cognitive psychology perspective, memory is divided into three main types: sensory memory, short-term memory, and long-term memory. **Sensory memory** is the preliminary, very brief recording of information that happens during sensation in the perceptual process. Sensory memory has a large capacity for processing stimuli but lasts only a few seconds unless the information is transferred into short-term memory. **Short-term memory** is the part of memory where small bits of information are paid attention to and processed for short periods of time. All information that is actively and consciously considered is processed in short-term memory. This is why short-term memory is often called *"working memory," "active memory,"* or *"conscious awareness."* Recently received sensory input utilizes short-term memory in the perceptual process.

According to well-known Harvard psychologist George Miller, people are able to consider approximately five to nine (seven plus/minus two) units of information at one time in working memory. This is often referred to as **Miller's Rule**.[11] A unit of information can be very small, such as a single number, letter, or word, or very large, such as a string of numbers, letters, words, or ideas. It is easy to test Miller's Rule. Quickly, off the top of your head, recall as many brands of breakfast cereal as you can. How many brands do you recall? For most, the number will fall between five and nine.

Because people can attend to only about seven units of information at a time, it is easy to overwhelm or overload consumers with too much information. For example, a grocery store may carry a dozen or more different brands of laundry detergent. In addition, detergents are often available in large (e.g., 150 ounces), medium (e.g., 100 ounces), and small (e.g., 50 ounces) containers. If 12 brands are available in each of these three sizes, consumers are faced with 36 different alternatives from which to choose. To compare all possible pairs of these 36 alternatives, consumers would have to make over 1,200 comparisons ($36!/(36 - 2)! = 1,260$). Few consumers are willing to commit the time and effort necessary to choose among a set of just 12 alternatives (resulting in $12!/(12 - 2)! = 132$ pairwise comparisons).

Interestingly, one factor that influences the amount of information people can attend to at one particular moment is prior knowledge or expertise.[12] People who are knowledgeable about a topic are able to attend to more pieces of information, and as knowledge increases, unit size increases. Consequently, compared with novices, experts attend to and think about larger units of information. Ultimately, this processing advantage enables experts to solve problems more effectively and efficiently compared to novices.

Arousal

Arousal, a state of physical wakefulness or alertness, also influences consumers' attention.[13] When arousal is extremely low, people are asleep. The level of wakefulness or alertness people experience during the normal course of a day is moderate. Viewing exciting events such as action movies, rock concerts, basketball games, and football games (and, yes, even stimulating lectures) produce high levels of arousal. Consumption of caffeine products (e.g., coffee, tea, cola, energy drinks), as well as exposure to loud noises, flashing lights, and unexpected events, also produces high levels of arousal. Similarly, physical exertion from roller coaster rides, sports activities, and aerobic exercise produces high arousal.

An inverted U-shaped relationship exists between arousal and consumers' ability to attend to information. Consumers' ability to pay attention to information is low when arousal is extreme (low or high). When arousal is too low, the amount of cognitive capacity and mental resources available for information processing is also low. It is difficult to attend to much information when people are tired, drowsy, or completely disinterested. Surprisingly, when arousal is high, cognitive capacity is also low. Under conditions of high arousal, consumers are overstimulated, and this arousal competes with their ability to attend to large amounts of information. On the other hand, when consumers are moderately aroused, they are alert but not overstimulated, freeing up cognitive capacity, which can be used to attend to information (see Figure 4.2).

Consider the results of an interesting field experiment on attention and memory for television commercials aired during the Super Bowl.[14] Fans from the two cities represented in the Super Bowl were highly aroused and overstimulated, and as a consequence, attention and memory for the television commercials aired during the game were poor. In contrast, viewers from other cities across the country were only moderately aroused, and these viewers exhibited much better attention and memory for the same television commercials. Under moderate levels of arousal, attention and memory are at their best.

FIGURE 4.2 | **The Relationship between Attention and Physical Arousal**

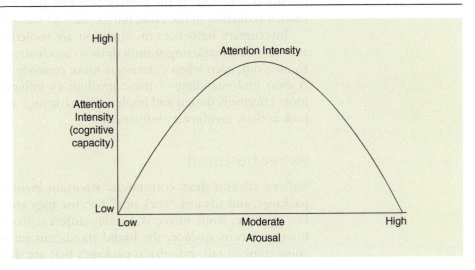

OBJECTIVE 4

Voluntary and Involuntary Selective Attention

Consumers are exposed to so much marketplace information that they cannot possibly process and think about each and every product-related piece of data they encounter. If consumers had to think carefully about every ad, each package label, and every marketing communication they saw or heard, little time would be left for anything else. According to famous researcher Daniel Kahneman, the allocation of attention is influenced by both voluntary and involuntary factors.[15] People voluntarily attend to information consistent with their current knowledge and expertise and to information relevant to their motivations, plans, intentions, and goals. Specifically, we manage our perceptual exposure by focusing our attention to things in the environment that are meaningful and appealing. For example, people who dislike country music avoid tuning in to country-music radio stations. Likewise, consumers shopping for new laptops purposefully seek out marketing information about computers. Furthermore, our perceptual comprehension and retention is shaped by our existing knowledge and memories. Thus, we tend to interpret and retain perceptual information through the lens of what we already know and believe.

One real concern for marketers today is how to win the battle for broadcast advertising exposure in this age of the remote control and the ability to watch content online and with mobile devices. With the growing popularity of DVRs, consumers can mute, fast-forward, and skip over commercials entirely. Some advertisers are trying to adapt to these technologies, as seen in the KFC coupon example described earlier. Other practitioners are trying to make their advertisements more interesting and entertaining to discourage viewers from zapping past ads; still others are simply opting out of television advertising altogether. For content shown online and over mobile devices, advertisers often force consumers to watch an advertising message before or during the show, but that doesn't stop viewers from muting the message. Some industry experts speculate that cable providers and advertisers will eventually be forced to provide incentives to encourage consumers to watch their messages. These incentives may come in the form of coupons, patronage rewards, or in extreme cases, a reduction in the cable bill for each ad watched.

Involuntary influences on attention are rooted in the very nature of the stimuli. Some marketing stimuli draw so much attention that they are difficult to tune out, even when consumers make concerted attempts to ignore them. A clear understanding of these involuntary influences enables marketers to more effectively design and implement marketing strategies. Let's take a closer look at these involuntary influences.

Salient Stimuli

Salient stimuli draw consumers' attention involuntarily.[16] Some products, packages, and ads just "stick out" because they are different and interesting. For example, Rolls Royce is notably different from other types of automobiles; as a consequence, the brand stands out on the road. Pringles potato chips come in tall, cylindrical packages that are distinguishable from typical potato chip bags. Consequently, Pringles snack packages are conspicuous on grocery store shelves.

However, salience depends on context. In other words, stimuli that stand out in one context or situation may not stand out in another. For example, while a Rolls Royce automobile might be quite noticeable driving through most typical American college campuses, it would not be very salient in the parking lot of an exclusive country club in Beverly Hills, where the members all drive luxury automobiles. Stimuli are salient only when they are very different from other stimuli in a specific context. From a perception perspective, when a stimulus is salient, it is figural or focal, and everything else fades into the background. This is known as the **figure-ground principle** of perception. Marketers create salience through novelty, intensity, and complexity.

Through its use of cutting-edge design and fluid consumer experiences, Apple makes use of salient stimuli that are novel, intense, and complex.

Novelty A novel stimulus is one that is new, original, different, or unexpected. Sometimes the product itself is novel. Rust-Oleum offers a paint-on counter-top transformation system. Sumseeds are roasted sunflower seeds that are ener-gized with caffeine. Replenish cleaners use twist-on concentrated pods that attach to spray bottles you fill with water.

Placing marketing messages in unexpected places also increases novelty. Suprette, a New Zealand clothing store, put metal plates in benches so that when people sat on them, an ad message would be pressed onto their bare legs. In another example, Billboard Magazine enhanced the bathroom experi-ence by installing strings and an amp to urinals so people could make music while in the bathroom.[17] Charmin Toilet Tissue opened a Charmin-themed public restroom in Times Square in New York. Other unexpected advertising venues can be found on eggs, airsickness bags, airplane tray tables, the sides of straws, and even tattooed onto other willing consumers.[18] Advertisers con-stantly experiment with novel advertising and promotional executions. New characters, themes, and scenarios are constantly under development.

AP Images/Mary Altaffer

Intensity The intensity of a stimulus affects salience, and in turn, induces attention. Intensity can be influenced through several stimulus characteristics, including overall size, height, length, weight, volume, color/brightness, odor, temperature, and position. Scents that catch your attention may increase intensity. Larger print ads, longer radio and television ads, and bigger retail displays tend to be more intense. Ever notice that sometimes a television ad is louder than the show you're watching? Bright colors are exciting, and warm colors (e.g., red, yellow, and brown) are more arousing than cool colors (e.g., blue, green, and grey). Position is the place an object occupies in space or time. A stimulus that is easy to see is more likely to be noticed, which is why marketers jockey for the eye-level shelf or the displays at the end of aisles in stores. In magazines, ads placed either on the front or back covers or near the front of the magazine on the right-hand page are more likely to be noticed than their counterparts.

While more intense stimuli generally draw more attention, the goal is to generate a level of intensity that results in that product or message standing out from surrounding stimuli. Thus, having a silent television ad among a series of loud ones or using a black-and-white print ad in a colorful magazine can also create intensity based on simple contrast.

Complexity Stimuli that require substantial cognitive processing or that challenge consumers to make sense of them can be intriguing and draw attention. Dynamic stimuli—with constant change and movement—can be perceived as different and salient. Spokespersons in television commercials typically move or walk while they talk because presentations delivered by stationary speakers are much less engaging. Moving signs, like the famous Las Vegas cowboy sign with the arm that moves up and down, also draw more attention than stationary signs. Neon signs often display letters that light up one at a time and appear to move. Digital billboards that shift and change make the eye linger longer. Such stimuli are difficult to ignore.

Two perceptual concepts also related to complexity are closure and grouping. **Closure** is the tendency for a person to perceive an incomplete picture as complete, either consciously or subconsciously. People like to fill in missing pieces when a puzzle is incomplete (see Figure 4.3). Incomplete messages from marketers beg for completion, thus drawing the perceiver in, and messages where closure is required tend to elicit strong recall.

Grouping is the tendency to arrange stimuli together to form well-organized units. Thus, objects viewed in close proximity tend to be grouped together, as do stimuli that move in the same direction together. Marketers can use grouping to create positive associations for their brands. For instance, placing an attractive, well-liked celebrity endorser in an advertisement with the brand can create a positive association to that brand. If marketers want an audience to associate the product with the presenter, they should place them close together; likewise, if marketers want consumers to perceive two ideas as associated, they should present them in close proximity.

Both closure and grouping help provide salient attention-drawing stimuli. Next, we examine another attribute of stimuli that draws attention involuntarily—vividness.

Vividness

Vivid stimuli, like salient stimuli, draw attention automatically and involuntarily.[19] However, unlike salient stimuli, vivid stimuli are attention-drawing across *all* contexts. Because vividness is context independent, but dependent upon a person's interests, perspective, and situation, it does not matter what other stimuli are present in a given situation. Vivid stimuli are:

- emotionally interesting
- concrete and imagery provoking
- proximate in a sensory, temporal, or spatial way[20]

Let's examine more closely these characteristics of vivid stimuli.

FIGURE **4.3** | Closure: There are no complete shapes, but we fill in the missing pieces.

Emotional Interest Consumers' goals, hobbies, and interests determine what information is emotionally interesting and vivid. Stimuli that are interesting to one person may not be interesting to another, but a stimulus that is emotionally interesting tends to get noticed. Stamp collectors find stamps incredibly fascinating. They spend hours studying their collections, examining watermarks, postmarks, and even perforations. Stamp collectors have been known to dream about stamps and see stamps when looking at plaid shirts (the plaid squares turn into stamps). To these individuals, stamps are very vivid and emotionally interesting. By contrast, people who are not stamp collectors might find stamps hopelessly boring.

Although both salient and vivid stimuli draw attention involuntarily, what is salient in one situation may not be salient in another, and what is vivid to one person may not be vivid to another. Salient stimuli capture the attention of all of the people some of time, while vivid stimuli grab the attention of some of the people all of the time. Unfortunately, marketers can't make their products

Marketers try to make their advertisements as concrete, and thus vivid, as possible.

RICHARD B. LEVINE/Newscom

interesting to everyone, just like stamp collectors can't make stamps interesting to everyone. Emotional interest is but one factor that influences the vividness of a product, ad, promotion, or package. Vividness is also affected by concreteness and proximity.

Concreteness Concrete information is specific and easy to picture, imagine, and visualize, versus abstract information, which is conceptual or theoretical. For instance, seeing and smelling a hot, juicy hamburger is more concrete than a picture of a hamburger, whereas the taste of a hot, juicy hamburger is more concrete than just seeing and smelling it. All of these instances are more concrete than just a written description. Research demonstrates that making product attributes more concrete in a marketing message increases the amount of attention paid to the attributes and subsequently increases the perceived importance of the attributes.[21]

The use of scent can also increase concreteness, in part because scents can trigger memories, moods, and emotion, thus increasing interest. *Scent marketing*—associating your brand with a specific smell—helps brands connect with consumers on an emotional level. The logic behind this assumption is that our olfactory system is tied into the limbic system. When we smell something, it directly enervates the limbic system, which is the part of the brain that controls emotion, moods, and memory. This is sometimes referred to as the "Proustian Effect," after Marcel Proust, a French author who wrote about how smell is emotionally powerful. Thus, whether scent is used to create a pleasant ambient aroma, create a *signature* for a brand, or convey a specific scent naturally associated with a product, scent can increase vividness of a stimulus through concreteness.[22]

Global Perspectives

Harrods Sniffs out Ways to Appeal to Customers

Scent marketing is one way in which marketers try to appeal to consumers' senses in order to attract attention, engage consumers, and create memorable brands. Harrods, a premier European retailer, has been a leader in scent marketing strategies. One strategy used by the retailer involves injecting tailored aromas into its stores to try to extend the multisensory buying experience for its customers. The scent marketing tactics are designed to encourage customers to look, touch, smell, taste, and listen more while they shop.

The luxury retailer, working with The Aroma Company and the Brand Sense Agency, injected scents into several store areas. Vanilla and chocolate have been featured in ladies shoes. The ladies swimwear department has sported the scent of coconut oil. Basil and lime scents have perfumed store

entrances as well as the paper receipts that customers receive after making a purchase (so they took the scents home). The garden living department has featured the fragrance of freshly mown grass. In one area, customers were able to sample all 12 different aromas from around the store.

Harrods' effort follows those of several U.S. retailers, including Macy's, Bloomingdales, and Saks Fifth Avenue, which all have adopted scent-marketing strategies to some extent. *Scent marketing* has a variety of applications and can help brands connect with consumers on an emotional level. This type of marketing isn't new—real-estate agents have long known about the value of popping fresh chocolate chip cookies into the oven before showing a house—but marketers are particularly interested in leveraging this perceptual sense in more and more sophisticated ways.[23]

Face-to-face communications are also typically more concrete and vivid than written communications, an important advantage of a field-based sales force. One research study investigated the effects of face-to-face versus written messages on judgment by presenting subjects with a description of a new personal computer.[24] The exact wording of the description was held constant. However, the description was presented either in a face-to-face format or in a written format. Even though the words presented in each situation were exactly the same, the face-to-face message had a much stronger impact on subjects' evaluations of the described product. However, results also showed that the vividness effect was weaker when subjects had a strong prior opinion about the described product and when a lot of negative information was available. When a product is described with many negative descriptions, strongly negative opinions are formed regardless of whether information is presented in a vivid or pallid manner.

Proximity Information that is proximal, or close to a consumer, is more vivid and has more impact than information that is distant or not immediately relevant. Three different kinds of proximities are important: sensory, temporal, and spatial. *Sensory proximity* refers to firsthand (proximal) versus second-hand (distant) information. Information that is perceived by consumers' own eyes and ears is more vivid than information perceived and relayed by another person. When consumers see for themselves that a product works, they are more convinced than if they receive secondhand, hearsay evidence. This is one reason marketers encourage consumers to sample products. *Temporal proximity* refers to how recently an event occurred. Events that occurred recently are much more vivid and draw more attention compared with events that occurred a long time ago. People are much more aware of and concerned about the awful flight they had the last time they flew on a particular airline than about the great flight they had five years ago. Finally, *spatial proximity* refers to the location of events. Events that occur near consumers' homes, work, or personal spaces are much more vivid than events that occur far away.

To summarize, information can be made more vivid and draw more attention in many different ways. Vividness is increased by making information more emotionally interesting, more concrete, or more proximal to the consumer. Obviously, information that grabs our attention has a stronger influence on judgment and choice relative to information that is virtually ignored.

Chapter Summary

This chapter looks at perception—the process through which we define the world and create meaning from our environment. Broken down, the perceptual process includes sensory exposure, attention, and comprehension. The process first relies on physical senses, such as sight, sound, smell, touch, and taste, to take in stimuli. Through attention and comprehension, those sensations are processed into meaningful and useful information and knowledge.

Not all stimuli to which consumers are exposed receive attention. People pay attention to a fraction of the stimuli to which they are exposed. In other words, attention is highly selective, and there are important limits and influences on attention and the perceptual process. The first of these influences deals with the thresholds of our sensory systems, including the absolute threshold, the just-noticeable-difference (j.n.d), and adaptation. Subliminal perception, the unconscious perception of stimuli, is an interesting topic related to these sensory thresholds.

Beyond the physical limitations of the senses, people also have limited cognitive capacity to devote to attention. Because of sensory memory and short-term memory limitations, people are able to attend to and think about a relatively small amount of information at a time, usually between five and nine pieces of information. This ability varies from person to person and from situation to situation.

Finally, the allocation of attention is also voluntarily and involuntarily influenced by factors unique to each individual. Consumers voluntarily pay attention to stimuli consistent with their existing knowledge and expertise and their plans, intentions, and goals. People involuntarily pay attention to stimuli that are salient and/or vivid. Stimuli that are salient draw attention involuntarily but are context dependent. Novel, intense, and complex stimuli tend to be salient. Vivid stimuli are emotionally interesting, concrete, and proximal, and these stimuli are vivid, regardless of the contextual background. Combined, the influences on attention and perception are pervasive, but these influences help us to function in an environment of information overload.

Key Terms

absolute threshold	comprehension	salient stimuli
adaptation	figure-and-ground principle	sensation
advertising wear-out	grouping	sensory memory
arousal	just noticeable difference (j. n. d.)	short-term memory
attention	Miller's Rule	subliminal perception
closure	perception	vivid stimuli
cognitive capacity	phenomenal absolutism	Weber's Law

Review and Discussion

1. Clearly distinguish among the following terms: perception, attention, cognitive capacity, and comprehension.
2. Why is sensation important in the perceptual process?
3. In what ways does selective attention differ for each person?
4. How does the absolute threshold influence the potential effectiveness of subliminal advertising?
5. What implications does the perceptual phenomenon of adaptation have for advertisers?
6. Do you think superstores that specialize in one type of product, such as office supplies, shoes, or electronics, run the risk of overloading consumers with too much information? Why or why not?
7. What is Miller's Rule?
8. What is the primary difference between salient and vivid stimuli?
9. How does closure in an advertisement increase salience?
10. How can marketers increase vividness for their advertisements?

Short Application Exercises

1. Ask five different friends to freely recall as many brands of hotel chains, pizza restaurants, and NFL teams as they can, and see if Miller's Rule regarding short-term memory applies. Do the results vary by level of knowledge or interest?

2. Find print advertisements that include salient stimuli and justify your choices.

3. Find a print advertisement that includes stimuli that are vivid (for you) and justify your choice.

4. Describe how marketers of Levi's Jeans could use sensory-based marketing messages to increase sales. Identify one technique for each of the five senses.

5. Read the Marketing In Action feature on the ways marketers use color and identify four brands that you feel effectively incorporate color into their marketing strategies. Explain why.

6. Watch the short video vignette for Chapter 4. Recalling the discussion of sensory stimuli and perceptual attention discussed in the chapter, what type of stimuli is the grocery store creating by using the scenting machines? Why are these machines effective?

Managerial Application

Imagine you work in the marketing department for a mid-sized regional bakery that sells doughnuts, cookies, and snack cakes in retail grocery stores. Your company would like to increase sales of its doughnuts and is considering an in-store sampling campaign to generate more interest in the product. This campaign would involve offering retail customers free samples of doughnuts in stores, along with a coupon for a discount on a box of doughnuts. You know that taste is a powerful sense and would like to engage the consumer in as many ways as possible to entice them to buy the product.

For this campaign to be implemented, you need to convince your superiors in the company that giving away free doughnut samples, a sizable investment in product and labor, may actually increase sales. In addition, you suspect that retail grocery store managers are likely to be interested in how this in-store sampling campaign may influence overall store sales. You realize that some marketing research is needed.

You decide to run an experiment in one local grocery store.

Your challenge:

1. Design an experiment to test whether in-store doughnut sampling influences sales of the doughnuts and/or the overall store sales. What should the independent and dependent variables be?

2. Given what we have studied in this chapter about sensory marketing, what experimental outcomes do you predict will occur?

3. How might a participant in your experiment who is very hungry affect the results?

4. Based on your answers above, is in-store food sampling a smart marketing technique for your company's product? Why or why not?

End Notes

1 Sources for the article: Fischer, M. (2012, March 30). The next generation of digital signs will interact with you. On Ad Age Digital. Retrieved from: http://adage.com/article /digitalnext/generation-digital-signs-interact/233778/. History of outdoor. On Outdoor Advertising Association of America. (n. d.). Retrieved from: http://www.oaaa.org /about/historyofoutdoor.aspx. Choices for girls – interactive bus shelter ad. On Youtube.com. [Video Content]. (n. d.). Retrieved from: http://www.youtube .com/watch?v=BHnpSGdIGAI. Forever 21 Times Square billboard. [Video Content]. (n.d.). Retrieved from: http://vimeo.com/32114343. Book of Tens: Coolest out-of-home ideas. On AdvertisingAge. (2010, December 13). Retrieved from: http://adage.com/article/special -report-the-book-of-tens-2010/advertising-coolest-home -ideas-2010/147611/.

2 Waits, J. (2013, January 11). Latest FCC statistics show increase in number of licensed ratio stations in 2012 [website]. (n. d.). Retrieved from: http://radiosurvivor.com/2013/01/11 /latest-fcc-statistics-show-increase-in-number-of-licensed

-radio-stations-in-2012/. Newspapers in the United States. On Wikipedia. [Open-source Website]. (n. d.) Retrieved from: http://en.wikipedia.org/wiki/Newspapers_in_the_United _States#cite_ref-2. [Industry research website]. (n. d.) Retrieved from: http://www.firstresearch.com/Industry-Research /Magazine-Publishers.html.

3 Story, L. (2007, January 15). Anywhere the eye can see, it's likely to see an ad. On *The New York Times* website. Retrieved from: http://www.nytimes.com/2007/01/15 /business/media/15everywhere.html?pagewanted=all.

4 Average person looks at their phone 150 times per day. On Techcraver.com (n. d.). Retrieved from: http://techcraver .com/2012/02/16/average-person-glances-at-their-phone -150-times-per-day/. Fredricksen, C. (2010, December 15). Time spent watch TV sill tops internet. On Emarketer Digital Intelligence. Retrieved from: http://www.emarketer .com/blog/index.php/time-spent-watching-tv-tops -internet/.

5 GroupM revises global 2013 ad spending forecast to 4.5% growth. [company website]. Retrieved from: http://www .groupm.com/pressandnews/details/864.

6 Clifford, S., and Rampell, C. (2011, March 28). Food inflation kept hidden in tinier bags. On *The New York Times*. Retrieved from: http://www.nytimes.com/2011/03/29 /business/29shrink.html?pagewanted=all.

7 Howard, T. (2003). Pay the same, get less as package volume falls. *USA Today, March 17*, 3b.

8 Pratkanis, A. R., Eskenazi, J., and Greenwald, A. G. (1994). What you expect is what you believe (but not necessarily what you get): A test of the effectiveness of subliminal self-help audiotapes. *Journal of Applied Social Psychology, 15 (3)*, 251–276. Haberstroh, J. (1994). *Ice cube sex*. Notre Dame: Cross Roads Books. Rogers, S. (1993). How a publicity blitz created the myth of subliminal advertising. *Public Relations Quarterly*, 12–17.

9 Key, W. B. (1973). *Subliminal seduction*. Englewood Cliffs, NJ: Signet. Key, W. B. (1976). *Media sexploitation*. Englewood Cliffs, NJ: Signet. Key, W. B. (1980). *The clam-plate orgy*. Englewood Cliffs, NJ: Signet.

10 Sources for the article: Hamilton, D. (2012, January). Whiff of truth: Exploding the 10 biggest myths in the perfume world. On Lost Angeles Times Magazine. Retrieved from: http://www.latimesmagazine.com/2012/01/image -uncommon-scents-whiff-of-truth.html. Pomerantz, D. (2011, April 13). Top-selling celebrity perfumes. On Forbes. com. Retrieved from: http://www.forbes.com/2011/04/13 /top-selling-celebrity-perfumes-business-entertainment.html.

11 Miller, G. A. (1956). The magical number seven, plus or minus two: Some limits on our capacity for processing information. *Psychological Review, 63*, 81–97.

12 Alba, J. W., and Hutchinson, J. W. (1987). Dimensions of consumer expertise. *Journal of Consumer Research, 13*, 411–454.

13 Kahneman, D. (1973). *Attention and Effort*. Englewood Cliffs, NJ: Prentice-Hall.

14 Pavelchak, M. A., Antil, J. H., and Munch, J. M. (1988). The Super Bowl: An investigation into the relationship among program context, emotional experience, and ad recall. *Journal of Consumer Research, 15*, 360–367.

15 Kahneman, D. (1973). *Attention and Effort*. Englewood Cliffs, NJ: Prentice-Hall.

16 Greenwald, A. G., and Leavitt, C. (1984). Audience involvement in advertising: Four levels. *Journal of Consumer Research, 11*, 581–592. Nisbett, R. E. and Ross, L. (1980). *Human inference: Strategies and shortcomings of social judgment*. Englewood Cliffs, NJ: Prentice-Hall.

17 Pathak, S., and Bruell, A. (2012, April 30). The 10 most unexpected media placements we've seen. On Ad Age. Retrieved from: http://adage.com/article/agency-news /10-unexpected-media-placements/234338/.

18 Pisani, J. (2006, August 1). Ad placement gets extreme. *BusinessWeek* [Online]. Available: BusinessWeek.com.

19 Kisielius, J., and Sternthal, B. (1984). Detecting and explaining vividness effects in attitudinal judgments. *Journal of Marketing Research, 21*, 54–64.

20 Nisbett, R. E., and Ross, L. (1980). *Human inference: Strategies and shortcomings of social judgment*. Englewood Cliffs, NJ: Prentice-Hall, 45.

21 MacKenzie, S. B. (1986). The role of attention in mediating the effect of advertising on attribute importance. *Journal of Consumer Research, 13*, 174–195.

22 Dowdey, S. (n. d.). Does what you smell determine what you buy? On Howstuffworks.com. Retrieved from: http:// money.howstuffworks.com/scent-marketing.htm.

23 Sources for the article: Dowdey, S. (n. d.). Does what you smell determine what you buy? On Howstuffworks.com. Retrieved from: http://money.howstuffworks.com /scent-marketing.htm. Harrods introduces scent marketing. On UTalkMarketing.com. (2008, February 29). Retrieved from: http://utalkmarketing.com/Pages /Article.aspx?ArticleID=4492&Title=Harrods_introduces _scent_marketing.

24 Herr, P. M., Kardes, F. R., and Kim, J. (1991). Effects of word-of-mouth and product-attribute information on persuasion: An accessibility-diagnosticity perspective. *Journal of Consumer Research, 17*, 454–462.

MARKETING METRICS

Interpreting Experimental Results

Continuing from the scenario from the Marketing Application feature above, let's say you conducted an experiment to examine how an in-store sampling campaign may influence overall store sales.

Column 1 shows the subject number. Column 2 indicates the sample condition for the independent variable of whether the subject received a doughnut sample or not. (1 = no sample; 2 = sample). Column 3 indicates the amount of overall sales the subject purchased in the store (in $). Column 4 indicates the subject's rating of hunger upon entering the store (ranging from 1 = not at all hungry to 7 = extremely hungry).

In-Store Doughnut Sampling Data

Subject Number	Sample Condition	Overall Sales	Subject's Rating of Hunger
1	1	65	3
2	1	100	3
3	1	99	5
4	2	80	3
5	1	23	5
6	2	140	6
7	2	110	4
8	2	45	2
9	2	35	4
10	1	150	3
11	1	60	4
12	1	178	4
13	2	200	7
14	1	12	2
15	2	178	7
16	2	19	5
17	2	90	4
18	2	210	7
19	1	25	6
20	1	43	5

(continued)

Subject Number	Sample Condition	Overall Sales	Subject's Rating of Hunger
21	1	9	2
22	1	15	3
23	2	89	6
24	2	260	7
25	2	190	5

Your Task

Use the Excel file (DT4-1.xlsx) to execute the following analyses:

1. Calculate the amount of sales by the experimental condition. (Recall that this is a cross-tabulation calculation.) Does there appear to be a pattern?
2. Determine whether the presence or absence of the sample impacted overall sales. (To do this, you will need to perform an F-test.) Is the result significant? What conclusion do you draw from this finding?
3. Calculate the correlations between hunger ratings and overall sales. Is the correlation significant? Is the correlation negative or positive? With this conclusion in hand, speculate on what potential role a person's hunger may play on the results of the experiment. (*Hint*: this is called moderation.) Draw a graph to show the possible relationship.

LEARNING AND MEMORY

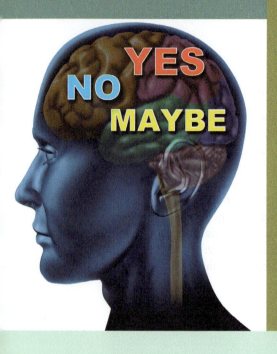

OBJECTIVES   *After studying this chapter, you will be able to...*

1 Explain how classical conditioning works in advertising.

2 Explain how operant conditioning works in sales promotion.

3 Identify misleading ads that encourage consumers to form incorrect inferences.

4 Define the seven sins of memory.

Dos Equis

We all know that The Most Interesting Man in the World prefers Dos Equis. How did we learn this? Why is this knowledge so memorable? These are the types of questions we are going to address in this chapter. But first, let's talk about Dos Equis. In 2005, Dos Equis did not sell very well in the United States.[1] Back then, Dos Equis was an obscure beer that sold primarily in Texas and California, but was virtually unknown throughout the rest of the United States. And Dos Equis had no idea that the Most Interesting Man in the World advertising campaign would be so successful. In 2012, this campaign was in its sixth year, and the Most Interesting Man in the World is so famous that Michael Jordan asked to have his picture taken with him. In 2011, Dos Equis' sales increased by 15.4%, compared to a meager 2.7% for the other top ten beer imports. Why is The Most Interesting Man in the World campaign so wildly successful?

The Most Interesting Man in the World is portrayed by actor Jonathan Goldsmith, now 73 years of age. He started out as a starving actor who drove a garbage truck. His first big break was on *Gunsmoke*, and the Bronx-born actor had to ride a horse for the role even though he didn't know how. He appeared on *Gunsmoke* 16 times, and also appeared on *Bonanza*, *Hawaii Five-O*, *Knight Rider*, and *Dallas*. He usually played bad guy-types who ended up getting shot. He even got shot by the legendary John Wayne in *The Shootist* in 1976.

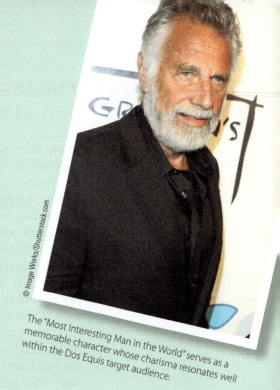

The "Most Interesting Man in the World" serves as a memorable character whose charisma resonates well within the Dos Equis target audience.

The original idea behind the "Most Interesting Man in the World" campaign was to help Dos Equis go beyond its image as a niche Mexican beer. Dos Equis was looking for actors who could improvise and who could offer a James Bond/Ernest Hemmingway-type image. Jonathan Goldsmith was perfect for the part. In real life, he had saved a girl from drowning and rescued a man during a snowstorm on a mountain. He prefers martinis and Scotch to beer, but when he drinks beer, he prefers Dos Equis ("I don't always drink beer, but when I do, I prefer Dos Equis"). The advertising campaign features The Most Interesting Man in the World in many different situations, ranging from parachuting out of an airplane on a kayak to winning trophies for his "game face" alone. His mother has a tattoo that reads "Son," and he has a lot of excellent advice for speed-dating ("I assure you, most women would not consider speed a virtue") and for partying ("the after party is the one you want to attend"). Jonathan Goldsmith describes his character as, "every guy's fantasy." He's a teacher. He's a sage. He's a shaman. He's a fantasy. He's an illusion of things past. He reminds one of the authors (Kardes) of the charismatic Baron Phillipe Rothschild, who made one of the world's finest wines (Mouton Rothschild), and drove race cars in Monte Carlo. He is an adventurer, who all men respect and all women admire. As you will see in this chapter, conveying an idea using an unexpected character, and using many different scenarios, plots, and stories, is an outstanding way to facilitate learning and enhance memory performance.

OBJECTIVE (1)

The Importance of Learning and Memory

In our continuing discussion of consumer information processing, this chapter discusses the role of learning and memory in consumer behavior. *Learning*, as it pertains to consumer behavior, is the process of acquiring new information and knowledge about products and services for application to future behavior. As learning increases, the amount of knowledge about products and services stored in a consumer's memory also increases. *Memory* enables past experiences and learning to influence current behavior. Without memory, we cannot physically function in society. People often underestimate how important memory is for everyday behavior; most people don't fully appreciate how essential memory is until this function is seriously impaired as a result of health conditions such as Alzheimer's, Korsakov's syndrome, or serious head trauma.

Consumer behavior research shows that learning plays an important role in preference formation.[2] Learning changes the way consumers think about and use products. The more consumers learn about a product category, the more likely they are to use new words and phrases to describe their consumption experiences, and the more likely they are to focus on product attributes that didn't seem as important when they first tried the product. In other words, learning enriches consumers' experiences with products and services, and of course, influences their potential future behavior related to the product.

Types of Learning

People learn in many ways. How people learn has been studied extensively in medicine, psychology, sociology, and education, and a number of learning theories have been developed. Two of these theories, classical conditioning and operant conditioning, are discussed next.

Classical Conditioning

Learning leads to knowledge. *Knowledge* is created when a person makes associations between concepts. For example, associating touching a hot stove burner with pain creates knowledge about how to behave around stoves. One way associations between concepts are formed is by simply thinking about the concepts. Thinking about two objects or ideas (like the hot stove burner and pain) at the same time is enough to form an association in memory; repeatedly thinking about two things at the same time increases the strength of the association. The nature of the objects or ideas and the timing are also crucial for learning, as we will discuss shortly.

Classical conditioning (or Pavlovian conditioning) is a learning theory centered on creating associations between meaningful objects or ideas (or what researchers call *stimuli*) to elicit desired responses. In a classic example, a researcher named Ivan Pavlov in the 1920s illustrated classical conditioning with a dog, some food, and a bell. Pavlov would place food in front of a dog, which naturally made the dog salivate. Every time Pavlov fed the dog, he would also ring a bell. Eventually, the dog would begin to salivate simply at the sound of the bell even when the food was not presented.

According to the theory, learning results when a meaningful or important object, called an **unconditioned stimulus** (US, or the dog's food in this example), is paired with a neutral object, called a **conditioned stimulus** (CS, or the bell in this example). The unconditioned stimulus has a known response called an **unconditioned response** (UR, or salivation in this example). Over time, the pairing leads to the response, without the original unconditioned stimulus, and this response is called the **conditioned response** (CR, or salivation at the sound of the bell even when no food is presented).[3]

In a consumer behavior setting, advertisers use a wide variety of meaningful unconditioned stimuli, including catchy music, attractive models, likable celebrities, cute animals, pretty scenery, exciting sporting events, and so on.[4] These positive unconditioned stimuli produce positive unconditioned responses, such as amusement, joy, happiness, attraction, etc. Negative unconditioned stimuli produce negative unconditioned responses or feelings. The brand serves as the conditioned stimuli (just like the bell in Pavlov's experiment). By pairing meaningful unconditioned stimuli with the brand, the advertiser hopes to *condition* consumers to feel positively about the brand. Hence, it is crucial for advertisers to select unconditioned stimuli that appeal to the target market. For example, many consumers think that the Geico Gecko and Progressive's Flo are cute and attention drawing.

© iStockphoto.com/Lanier

Pairing a conditioned stimulus with an unconditioned stimulus repeatedly leads to *stimulus generalization*, or similar responses to both stimuli. This means that people learn to associate the unconditioned stimuli or the background elements of the ad with the conditioned stimulus, the brand itself. Once an association is learned, people respond similarly to the conditioned stimulus and to the unconditioned stimulus. Importantly, this occurs even when the conditioned stimulus is presented alone. After learning an association between an advertised brand and the positive background elements of an ad, consumers often encounter the advertised brand alone in a store. To the extent that learning or conditioning was effective, the same feelings generated by the advertisement should occur when the brand is encountered in the store without any advertising.

The Role of Timing Timing is crucial. Greater learning or conditioning occurs when the conditioned stimulus is presented before the unconditioned stimulus. This is known as **forward conditioning** because the presence of the conditioned stimulus can be used to predict the subsequent occurrence of the unconditioned stimulus. Many advertisements, however, use **backward conditioning**. That is, the conditioned stimulus (the advertised brand) is presented after the unconditioned stimulus (e.g., likable music, people, places, or things). Learning still takes place, but the associations are weaker; higher levels of repetitive advertising are needed for learning to occur. Furthermore, many ads use unconditioned stimuli that are ineffective because they were previously encountered alone without pairing (the unconditioned stimulus **pre-exposure effect**). For example, a popular song that has been repeatedly encountered alone is not a good candidate for classical conditioning because consumers have been pre-exposed to the music. The familiar song is not likely to become associated with a brand. Classical conditioning is also less effective for old, familiar brands than for new, less familiar brands.[5]

FIGURE 5.1 | Classical Conditioning

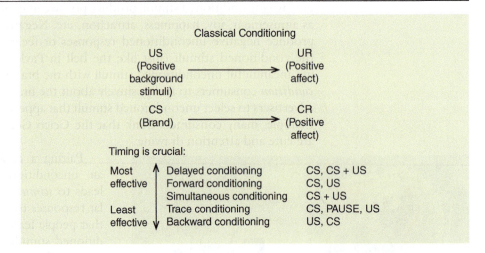

Classical conditioning is also less effective when multiple conditioned stimuli predict the subsequent occurrence of an unconditioned stimulus.[6] Conditioned stimuli compete with one another for predictive strength. Consequently, as the predictive strength of one stimulus increases, the predictive strength of other stimuli decreases. Again, timing is paramount. The order in which stimuli are presented has an important influence on subsequent learning. For example, after consumers learn that a target attribute (e.g., brand name) is useful for predicting quality, other cues (i.e., other attributes) seem unpredictive. This is known as **blocking** because the first predictive stimulus blocks or prevents learning for other predictive stimuli encountered later. During the learning phase of a recent study on blocking, participants received attribute (AireCell or closed-cell compartments) and brand name (Hypalon or Riken) information for several products in an unfamiliar category (rafts).[7] Either the type of compartment or the brand name predicted quality ratings. During a second learning phase, a redundant cue (tubular or I-beam floor) also predicted quality ratings. During the test phase, participants judged the quality of several new raft products. Learning about the importance of a redundant cue was blocked by prior learning about the first predictive cue, regardless of whether the first predictive cue was a brand name or an attribute.

In a follow-up study, researchers investigated the competition between attribute versus brand name information as signals for quality by manipulating the predictive strength of attribute and brand cues (experimental conditions) or brand cues only (control conditions).[8] During the learning phase, participants received attribute (Alpine class down filling or regular down filling) and brand name (Hypalon or Riken) information for several products in an unfamiliar category (down jackets). During the test phase, participants judged the quality of several new products. The results showed that the brand name had a weaker effect on quality judgments when the target attribute was predictive (versus unpredictive) of product quality. This pattern was observed for new products in the original product category (down jackets), as well as in a different product category (wool sweaters). This effect is reduced when brand–quality associations are learned prior to attribute–quality associations or when no information about quality is provided during the learning phase. Although conventional wisdom suggests that building strong brands requires marketers to design products with high-quality attributes, the results of these studies show that attribute equity undermines brand equity when unambiguous information about quality is available.

Learning via classical conditioning is important in advertising and in many other situations as well. Think about the importance of timing for learning about the benefits and costs of using credit cards to buy products. The benefits of credit card use are immediate: the product or service is yours to enjoy as soon as you use your card. Consequently, strong credit card–benefit associations are learned by consumers. However, the costs of credit card use are delayed: the credit card bill arrives days or weeks after the credit card purchase is made. Consequently, weak credit card–cost associations are learned by consumers. In other words, the benefits of using credit cards are more strongly associated with credit cards than are the costs of using credit cards. This conditions or brainwashes consumers into spending more when they use their credit cards.

To test this idea, a study of credit cards and classical conditioning examined the average size of tips left by restaurant patrons who paid using a credit card versus those using cash.[9] Customers who paid by credit card left larger tips. In a follow-up study, consumers were asked to play a "Price Is Right" game by guessing the prices of several products shown on a computer monitor. In the experimental condition, a small plastic MasterCard sign was placed next to the computer monitor. In the control condition, the sign was removed. Higher price estimates were formed when the MasterCard sign was present than when the MasterCard sign was absent. In another follow-up study, several products and their prices were displayed on a computer monitor, and consumers were asked to press one key if they were willing to buy each product and a different key if they were unwilling to buy the product. Decision times to buy the product were faster when the MasterCard sign was present than when the MasterCard sign was absent. A final study found that college students donated more to charity (The United Way) when the request to donate was made in a room containing credit-card logos, despite the fact that the donations had to be cash! Together, these results show that consumers spend more and reach the decision to spend faster when credit card symbols are present rather than

Consumers' willingness to spend generally increases when credit card logos are included near the point of sale.

absent. As a result, retailers, catalog marketers, and Internet marketers should prominently display credit card symbols in menus, point-of-purchase displays, catalogs, web pages, and other marketing communications, because it is very likely that their customers will make larger purchases if they know they can use their credit cards.

The Role of Surprise In Pavlov's original theory of classical conditioning, the animal responds to the conditioned stimulus as if it were the unconditioned stimulus due to stimulus generalization: the bell acquires the properties of the food (the bell seems tasty). The modern view downplays stimulus generalization and up-plays prediction: the bell predicts that food is coming. According to the Rescorla-Wagner model, little learning occurs when animals (and people) predict events perfectly.[10] However, when animals (and people) predict one event and a different event occurs, animals (and people) are motivated to learn how to better predict the unexpected event. The following equation puts it more formally:

$$\Delta S = B(o-p)c,$$

where ΔS refers to the change in strength of the association between the conditioned stimulus and the unconditioned stimulus, B refers to the learning rate, o refers to the actual outcome, p refers to the prediction, and c refers to the presence or absence of the predictive cue.[11] Importantly, when perfect prediction occurs, $o - p = 0$ and no learning takes place. As the discrepancy between p and o increases, learning increases. Hence, learning requires prediction and discrepancy or surprise. Research shows that the Rescorla-Wagner model describes consumer learning quite well.[12] Consumers frequently make predictions about product quality using a wide variety of predictive cues—including brand name, price, warranty, store reputation, and other variables. If a prediction is accurate, little learning takes place and ΔS, or the change in strength of the association between the conditioned stimulus and the unconditioned stimulus, is close to zero. For example, if you predict that a new Sony product will be high in quality and you buy it and see that it is, little learning will take place and you will continue to believe that Sony makes high-quality products. If a prediction is inaccurate, however, the consumer is surprised and ΔS increases as the difference between o and p increases. For example, if you predict that a new Sony product will be high in quality and it breaks the first day you use it, your opinion about Sony will change. The magnitude of the change depends on how surprised you were, or on how much o differed from p. In addition to explaining associative strength, the Rescorla-Wagner model can explain blocking and other learning phenomena.

Exemplar-Based Learning The learning process described by the Rescorla-Wagner model is forward looking: cues are used to predict outcomes, and feedback is used to update associative strength on a trial-by-trial basis. However, sometimes learning is more passive and backward looking: no predictions are formed and all experienced stimuli are stored together in memory and are more likely to be retrieved together if they co-occurred.[13] If a new product reminds you of a product you have tried before, you are more likely to assume that the new product will be similar in quality to the product you already tried. Similarity is more important than surprise when exemplar-based learning occurs. Forward looking learning is more likely to occur when consumers are motivated and able to learn, and backward looking learning is more likely to occur when consumers are unmotivated or unable to learn. Hence, exemplar-based learning is more likely in uninteresting product categories or when distractions and interruptions prevent consumers from thinking carefully about the relationships between predictive cues and outcomes.

Evaluative Conditioning In traditional classical conditioning, the conditioned response is a behavioral response, such as salivation (as in Pavlov's original experiments). However, pairing conditioned stimuli (e.g., brands) with positive unconditioned stimuli (e.g., celebrity advertising, humor in advertising, event sponsorship, product placement) can also influence consumers' attitudes or evaluative judgments.[14] Although classical conditioning can contribute to evaluative conditioning, evaluative conditioning is more sensitive to the absolute number of CS–US pairings and less sensitive to the proportion of nonpairings (presentations of the CS alone and presentations of the US alone). Evaluative conditioning is also longer lasting than classical conditioning, which is good news for marketers. This is because presentations of the CS alone produce **extinction**, or a reduced CR, in classical conditioning. If the CS is presented alone frequently enough, the CR is eventually eliminated. Because evaluative conditioning is less sensitive to the proportion of nonpairings, evaluative conditioning is more resistant to extinction. Evaluative conditioning is even more resistant to extinction if several different USs are paired with the CS.

Evaluative conditioning differs from classical conditioning because the CR is different (i.e., an attitude rather than a behavior), and because other psychological mechanisms also contribute to evaluative conditioning. Specifically, inferences or beliefs that go beyond the information given influence evaluative conditioning.[15] For example, pairing Domino's pizza with a race car in television ads encourages consumers to infer that Domino's pizza delivery is speedy. Pairing Charmin bathroom tissue with a soft bear cub in ads and on product packages encourages consumers to infer that Charmin is soft. Recent research has discovered a third mechanism: misattribution, or confusion of the CS with the US, contributes to evaluative conditioning.[16] Eye tracking experiments show that when consumers switch their eye gaze between the CS and the US more frequently, greater levels of evaluative conditioning occur. Hence, three different psychological processes influence evaluative conditioning: (1) classical conditioning, (2) inferential reasoning, and (3) misattribution.

OBJECTIVE ② **Operant Conditioning**

In classical conditioning, the stimulus precedes the response, but in **operant conditioning** (or instrumental conditioning), the stimulus follows the response.[17] **Positive reinforcement**, or the presence of a reward, increases the probability of a response, while **negative reinforcement**, or the absence of **punishment**, also increases the probability of a response. **Extinction**, or the absence of a reward, decreases the probability of a response. The presence of punishment also decreases the probability of a response. Learning via operant conditioning is faster under conditions of **continuous reinforcement**, or when reinforcement occurs every time the desired response occurs. However, learning via operant conditioning is more persistent under conditions of **partial reinforcement**, or when reinforcement occurs only some of the times the desired response occurs.

Rewards used in marketing include coupons, bonus points, rebates, and prizes given to consumers who buy your product. Rewards increase the probability of repeat purchase. Operant conditioning can also be used to influence consumers who do not currently use your product. Negative reinforcements in marketing include eliminating expensive shipping terms, reducing paperwork associated with rebates and warranties, or eliminating long waiting lines or delivery times. **Shaping**, or reinforcing successive approximations of the desired response, also can be used to encourage current nonusers to buy your product. For example, a retailer may first reward nonusers to visit the mall where the store is located by offering a free fashion show. Then, the retailer may encourage nonusers to visit the store by offering a door prize. Next, the retailer may encourage nonusers to buy products by offering a discount on products purchased in the store using a store credit card. Finally, when consumers buy products, the retailer can reward them by offering frequent-user bonus points for each purchase.

Global Perspectives

Private Label Brands

Private label brands, or store brands, are exclusive to specific retail outlets and are designed to compete with national brands, or manufacturer's brands. Consumers often learn that private label brands are similar to but less expensive than national brands, and many retail outlets carry both types of brands. In the United States, private label brands account for 15% of sales of consumer packaged goods, but in some European countries, private label brands are much more important.[18] For example, private label brands account for 43% of sales in the United Kingdom, and 46% of sales in Switzerland. Some retailers believe that private label brands help consumers learn about the different offerings available at different stores, and that private label brands help to differentiate stores and enhance store loyalty. Recent research conducted in the Netherlands, however, suggests that this is not always true. For dish soaps and breakfast cereals, high levels of cross-brand learning were observed for private label brands, but not for national brands. In other words, all private label brands were perceived as similar, and what consumers learned about one private label brand spilled over to other private label brands. By contrast, all national brands were perceived as different, and consumer learning about one national brand did not apply to other national brands. Hence, private label brands do not always help to differentiate stores, and they do not always help to build store loyalty.

OBJECTIVE **3**

Comprehension and Miscomprehension

Comprehending or understanding information requires relating new information presented in the environment to old information stored in memory.[19] Because new information is typically incomplete, consumers must form inferences to fill in missing details to make sense out of the new information. For example, when reading a story stating that Bob pounded a nail into the wall, people automatically infer that Bob used a hammer even though the story never stated this.[20] Similarly, when reading an ad for a new automobile, consumers automatically infer that the automobile has standard features, such as automatic transmission, anti-lock brakes, etc., even if the ad never mentions these features. Background knowledge helps people fill in missing details to make sense of new information. However, sometimes new information is so extreme, it invites consumers to form specific inferences. For example, the features of a Lexus are so luxurious that it is difficult not to infer that the Lexus is a luxury automobile while examining it. Consumers' goals also influence what inferences they are likely to form. For example, consumers with the goal of purchasing a luxury automobile are likely to evaluate all automobiles in terms of the attributes that mean luxury to them.

As comprehension increases, memory performance also increases. It is difficult to remember meaningless information. This is why professors use memory tests (e.g., multiple choice exams, fill-in-the-blank questions, short essay questions) to assess comprehension. If a student does not understand the course material, the student is not likely to remember much and will probably perform poorly on the exam. Controlled laboratory studies show that students have great difficulty memorizing meaningless statements, such as "the notes went sour because the bag was ripped."[21] However, these statements were easy to remember when the students were given a theme word (e.g., "bagpipe") that made the statements more meaningful. Ideally, students should always try to make new course material more meaningful by relating it to prior knowledge.

Because consumers use background knowledge to fill in missing details, ads can mislead consumers by presenting claims that are literally true but figuratively false. Claims stating that a product *may* be effective, or is *more* effective, or is *recommended* by experts often lead consumers to assume that the product is better than it actually is.[22] When consumers see an ad stating, "Be popular! Brush with UltraBrite!" they often assume that brushing with UltraBrite will make them more popular, even though the ad never directly stated this. When consumers see an ad stating, "Women who look younger use Oil of Olay," they often assume that using Oil of Olay will make them look younger, even though the ad never stated this. Advertisements often imply much more than what is actually stated, and such implications can be misleading.

Some ads take advantage of consumers' assumptions about advertising claims that are literally true but figuratively false. Because the claims are literally true, advertisers can argue that they are not lying. However, consumers' assumptions about the meaning of the advertised claims can make the claims misleading. For example, the word "may" implies maybe yes and maybe no. However, consumers often assume that "may" probably means yes. So, when an ad states that Brand X may relieve pain, consumers often assume that yes, Brand X does relieve pain.

Comparison omission can also mislead consumers. When an ad states that Brand Y gasoline gives you greater mileage, consumers typically assume that this means that Brand Y gives you greater mileage than other brands of gasoline. The ad never stated this directly, and after all, Brand Y does give you greater mileage than water. Piecemeal information can also make a product seem better than it actually is. For example, an ad stating that a Brand Z car has more head room than a Mercedes Benz, more leg room than a BMW, and more trunk space than a Lexus implies that Brand Z is better than each of these luxury automobiles. In reality, the differences were trivial: Brand Z has 1/10th of an inch more head room than a Mercedes Benz, 1/5th of an inch more leg room than a BMW, and 1/15th of an inch more trunk space than a Lexus. Thus, each of the piecemeal claims are literally true, but the actual differences are trivial.

Visual images can also contain false implications.[23] For example, a Milky Way ad transforms a glass of milk into a candy bar, implying that the candy bar is as nutritious as a glass of milk. A Mattel advertisement uses extreme close-ups and camera angles that make Hot Wheels toy cars appear much faster than they actually are. A Campbell's soup ad shows a bowl of soup with meat, potatoes, and vegetables bursting above the broth level. What consumers do not know is that marbles are in the bottom of the bowl, pushing the solid ingredients above the broth level.

Why would all those ingredients overflow from the can on the product packaging but in reality be resting in a seemingly smaller quantity all the way at the bottom of the can when the consumer opens it for dinner?

A Black Flag ad shows two glass tanks filled with cockroaches. One tank is sprayed with Black Flag, and most of the cockroaches die. The other tank is sprayed with another leading brand, but few cockroaches die. What consumers are not told is that the cockroaches in the second tank are bred to be resistant to the other leading brand of insecticide.

Ethics

Most consumers think that breakfast cereals are healthy. However, some children's cereals contain up to 50% sugar.[24] Honey Smacks contain 15 grams of sugar per serving, which is more than the amount contained in a glazed donut. Many outraged parents have filed suits against cereal companies. Some cereal companies, like Kellogg's, have proactively changed the ingredients of their cereals and have stopped advertising cereals that fail to meet the World Health Organization's recommended guidelines for cereal.

Cereal companies have also been sued for deceptive advertising. General Foods lost a lawsuit for airing television ads that made it seem like children who eat its cereals could become stronger, happier, and could even acquire magical powers. Before Kellogg's changed its advertising policies, it formed an alliance with Nickelodeon and used cartoon characters from movies and television shows aired on Nickelodeon on Kellogg's cereal boxes.

Unhealthy products and misleading advertising targeted for children raise serious ethical concerns. Do children require greater protection than adults from unethical business practices? What should the ethical guidelines be for marketing products to children? Do children have a powerful influence on what products their parents buy for them? How would you encourage companies to do the right thing and make healthier products for children and to promote these products using nondeceptive advertising?

Misleading advertising practices are unfair because consumers must form inferences and make assumptions to comprehend advertising claims. Sometimes the Federal Trade Commission (FTC) orders advertisers to air **corrective advertising** that states that a previous ad was misleading, as in the famous Listerine case. A Listerine ad stated that Listerine kills germs that cause colds, which simply was not true. Listerine's corrective ad stated that Listerine does not help prevent colds. Nevertheless, extensive research has shown that corrective advertising is typically ineffective[25] because consumers have difficulty changing their beliefs dramatically, even when they realize that those beliefs are wrong.[26]

Memory

Memory researchers often use a computer metaphor to explain how memory works.[27] A computer has a hard drive that can store a large number of inactive files. A computer also allows users to retrieve a file from the hard drive and bring it into active memory so the file can be processed (e.g., edited or used). Similarly, people have a long-term memory system that stores a large amount of inactive data or knowledge. To use such knowledge, however, people must retrieve a "file" from long-term memory and bring it into short-term memory to process it further. All thinking and reasoning occurs in short-term memory, but only a small amount of information can be held in short-term memory at any given time (7 plus-or-minus 2 chunks or units). If this information is not used, it is lost less than 18 seconds later (hence, the name "short-term memory"). By contrast, long-term memory appears to store an unlimited amount of information for a long period of time. Nevertheless, three different types of forgetting can occur in long-term memory:

1. Original information is not maintained.
2. New information is not successfully stored in memory.
3. New knowledge overrides existing information, or vice-versa.

Information held in long-term memory can also be distorted or changed over time. Furthermore, sometimes consumers can't forget things that they would prefer to forget. We discuss how consumers forget information in the next section.

The Seven Sins of Memory

Although memory influences nearly every thought and action we take, memory can also be fallible. There are seven basic mistakes or "sins" of memory: transience, absent-mindedness, blocking, misattribution, suggestibility, bias, and persistence.[28] The first three sins refer to three different types of *forgetting*. The second three refer to three different types of *distortion*. Persistence refers to the inability to forget things one wants to forget.

Transience People tend to forget details over time, and this type of forgetting is known as **transience**. If you don't use it, you lose it: if knowledge is not used for a long period of time, information loss can occur. Recently processed information is more **accessible** or easy to retrieve than is information that was processed long ago, relatively speaking. Information accessibility decreases with the passage of time. Hence, it is easier to remember commercials we viewed recently than to remember commercials we viewed long ago. However, the passage of time is not the only variable that influences forgetting. Forgetting can also occur as a result of shallow processing (absent-mindedness) or interference from other information stored in memory (blocking).

Absent-mindedness Shallow or superficial processing of information during encoding or retrieval leads to poor memory performance. This type of forgetting is known as **absent-mindedness**. People are often distracted by multiple tasks they wish to perform, and it is relatively easy to walk into a room to look for something and forget what you were looking for when you are distracted. **Encoding** refers to attention, comprehension, and the transference of information from short-term memory to long-term memory. **Retrieval** refers to the transference of information from long-term memory to short-term memory. Lapses of attention or effort during encoding or retrieval can lead to forgetting. If consumers are unmotivated to process information carefully because of a lack of interest in a product, or if they are unable to process information carefully because of distractions or attempts to perform several cognitive tasks simultaneously (divided attention), absent-mindedness and the forgetting associated with it are likely to occur.

Depth-of-processing research shows that memory performance improves with effort.[29] A given word is easier to remember if it is processed at a deep level rather than at a shallow level. Level of processing can be manipulated experimentally by varying the difficulty of the questions we are asked about a word. For example, shallow encoding occurs when people are asked a simple question: Is TIDE printed in uppercase letters? Deeper encoding occurs when people are asked a more difficult question: Is TIDE a type of detergent? The word TIDE is more likely to be remembered when it is processed intensely rather than superficially. Consequently, ads that encourage consumers to think deeply about a product are more memorable than ads that encourage cursory processing.

A name and a logo are intensely important aspects of a brand's identity, but consumers will easily forget those superficial qualities if the company doesn't attach a deeper purpose for the consumer to associate with it in long-term memory.

In a similar vein, simply reading a bunch of words is a bad way to prepare for an exam. Thinking deeply about the concepts, generating examples of the concepts, and relating the concepts to prior knowledge and experience is a much better way to study. Research on the **generation effect** shows that memory performance is enhanced when people generate their own answers to questions rather than simply reading them.[30] This occurs because generating answers requires more effort than simply reading answers, and memory improves as effort increases.

Absent-mindedness can also occur at the time of retrieval. When distracted, consumers often forget to perform actions they intended to perform. Consumers forget to take their medicine, pick up certain items at the grocery store, or keep appointments; that is, consumers forget to perform a future action even though they intended to do so. Memory aids such as post-it notes, pocket calendars, cell phone reminders, and even tying string around a finger are often used to prevent this type of forgetting.

Blocking Forgetting frequently occurs because the information one is trying to retrieve is temporarily inaccessible as a result of blocking or interference from related information. The information one is trying to retrieve is stored in memory; it has not been lost over time—it is encoded deeply, but the search for it in one's memory is not always successful. Sometimes people know they know the answer to a question, but they cannot quite put their finger on it. This is known as the **tip-of-the-tongue effect**: the answer seems to be on the tip of your tongue, but you can't quite retrieve it.[31] Students often complain that they knew the answer to an exam question, but couldn't retrieve it until after the exam was over. The answer was temporarily inaccessible because "ugly sisters" blocked or prevented retrieval of the correct answer. The name "ugly sisters" comes from the story of Cinderella, in which the nice Cinderella was dominated by her mean older sisters. In memory research, ugly sisters are incorrect answers related to the correct answer, and they are retrieved repeatedly instead of the correct answer.

The tip-of-the-tongue effect shows that forgetting can occur even when the answer to a question is stored somewhere in long-term memory. The answer did not fade or decay over time. Instead, the answer is temporarily inaccessible because of interference from related information. Studies of very long-term memory show that people can remember information learned in high school (e.g., foreign languages, mathematics) for more than 50 years![32] Again, this shows that long-term memories do not necessarily fade or decay over time.

Studies of relearning provide the best evidence for forgetting without information loss. Relearning something you thought you forgot (e.g., foreign languages, mathematics) is easier than learning something for the first time.[33] In classic relearning studies, participants learned 20 pairs of numbers and words (e.g., 43/dog). Two weeks later, participants forgot about 25% of this material. In the relearning condition, participants relearned the same 20 pairs of numbers and words. In the control condition, participants learned new words paired with old numbers for all forgotten pairs (e.g., the original 43/dog was changed to 43/house). Memory performance was far better in the relearning condition than in the control condition. This result could not occur if the forgotten information were lost forever.

According to the association principle of long-term memory, each **node**, idea, or piece of information stored in memory is connected to other nodes that are conceptually related by links known as **associations**.[34] Associations are learned via classical conditioning and operant conditioning. Related nodes are connected in a complex **associative network**, in which closely related nodes are connected directly by a single association, and distantly related nodes are connected by a chain or series of associations. **Activation**, or retrieval, refers to the transfer of information from inactive long-term memory to active short-term memory. **Spreading activation** refers to the idea that when people retrieve a particular node, they automatically think about other closely related nodes. An associative network is like a complex system of irrigation ditches; each node is like a pool of water connected to other pools via a system of ditches. When one pool is filled with water, the water spills out to other nearby pools. The more water poured into a pool, the farther the spillage spreads. Eventually, the water runs out and the spreading stops.

FIGURE 5.2 | **Associative Network**

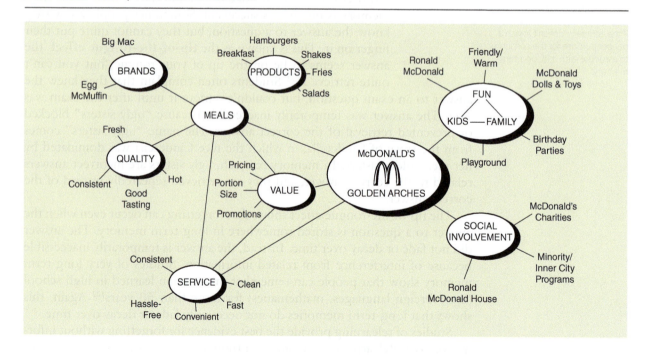

For example, whenever consumers think about a brand name, like McDonald's, they start thinking about associations with the brand (e.g., Big Macs, fries, shakes, Ronald McDonald). A strong association leads to a **priming effect**: simply thinking about the brand leads consumers to think about closely related concepts. The priming effect can be reduced or eliminated by adding new associations to consumers' associative networks. As the number of new associations increases, the likelihood that consumers will think about a particular old association decreases. New associations increase the complexity of consumers' associative networks and produce **associative interference**, in which the new associations compete with and block old associations.

Associative interference is commonly observed in advertising.[35] Old ads compete with new ads, and vice versa. **Proactive interference** occurs when information learned earlier blocks memory for information learned later. **Retroactive interference** occurs when information learned later blocks memory for information learned earlier. Both types of interference are common in advertising. Furthermore, greater proactive and retroactive interference occurs with advertisements for brands in the same product category (e.g., ads for different brands of cereal) than for brands in different product categories (e.g., ads for cereal and for cars).

Blocking is often frustrating because people realize that they know the answer they're looking for, but they can't find it. How can blocking be reduced? According to the **encoding-specificity principle**, memory is context dependent.[36] Contextual or background cues have a surprisingly powerful influence on memory performance. During encoding, contextual cues are encoded along with the target information one is trying to remember. Later, during retrieval, the contextual cues may be the same or different. Memory performance is enhanced when the contextual cues at the time of encoding and at the time of retrieval match or are highly similar. As the degree of similarity decreases, memory performance decreases.

For example, students typically attend lectures and take exams in the same classroom. In this case, the contextual cues (e.g., lighting, seating, background noise level) are the same during encoding (learning) and retrieval (taking an exam), and this improves memory. If a professor wants to be mean, he or she could lecture in one room and give exams in a different room. In this case, the contextual cues present during encoding and during retrieval are different, and this reduces memory performance. Even small, seemingly irrelevant background differences can have dramatic effects on memory performance. Larger background differences have even more dramatic effects. For example, students often do themselves a disservice by studying for an exam late at night while drinking lots of coffee. They then take the exam in the morning without coffee. Nighttime contexts differ from daytime contexts in many respects (e.g., lighting, seating, fatigue levels, hunger levels) and high caffeine contexts also differ from low caffeine contexts in many respects (e.g., alertness levels, thirst levels). The greater the differences between encoding contexts and retrieval contexts, the more memory performance decreases.

Marketers can use the encoding-specificity principle to their advantage by trying to increase the similarity of contextual cues present during encoding and during retrieval. Consumers often encode information about products while watching TV at home. Later, while shopping at a grocery store, they are likely to retrieve information about products to make informed purchase decisions. Obviously, large contextual differences exist between the home environment and the grocery store environment. These differences can be reduced by placing characters from advertisements viewed at home in the grocery store

environment. For example, a long-running TV commercial for Life cereal features Little Mikey, and Little Mikey's picture appears on boxes of Life cereal
in grocery stores. Other advertising characters (e.g., the Pillsbury doughboy,
Tony the tiger, the Keebler elves, Juan Valdez) are also featured on product
packages or point-of-purchase displays to help consumers remember information from advertisements they viewed in different contexts.

The encoding-specificity principle also suggests that it is better to learn
information in many different contexts and many different brief sessions over
time, rather than in one long cramming session. This effect is known as the
spacing effect. Spacing is beneficial because the context for learning is likely
to vary over time, and because people are likely to use different encoding strategies and different cues for encoding over time. Furthermore, advertising is
more effective when it is spaced out over time rather than massed in one television program or one print medium.[37]

Recent research suggests that forgetting due to blocking is the most common type of forgetting.[38] People often assume that transience or decay over
time is the most common type of forgetting, but this is not true. People's
assumptions about how memory works, and more generally, how the mind
works, are often wrong. Laboratory research is needed to uncover the truth.
To test the frequency with which forgetting occurs due to transience and the
frequency with which it occurs due to blocking, memory researchers developed
a "recent probes task." This task has the advantage of testing people's memory
without their knowledge. This is an important advantage because people often
rehearse information when they know their memory is being tested. For example, suppose you knew you were participating in a memory test and were asked
not to think about white bears. This is surprisingly difficult to do, and chances
are, you the reader will continue to think about white bears for several minutes.
However, with the recent probes task, subjects are shown four target words.
Next, they are shown one probe word. After that, they are asked to indicate if
the probe word matches one of the earlier four target words. Response times
to the matching task are faster if the probe word is completely new and unrelated to the target words than if the probe word is related but not identical to
the target words. This effect occurs even if there is a relatively lengthy delay
between the presentation of the target words and the presentation of the probe
word. The absence of delay effects is consistent with blocking, but inconsistent
with transience.

Misattribution Forgetting isn't the only memory problem consumers encounter. Memory can also be distorted from **misattribution**. Three different types
of memory misattributions or confusions are possible:

1. Source confusion
2. Feelings of familiarity
3. False memories

Source confusion occurs when consumers remember reading a fact about
a product but misremember where they read it.[39] Sometimes consumers
believe that they read the information from a credible source (e.g., *Consumer
Reports*), but they actually read it from a noncredible source (e.g., *National
Enquirer*). Sometimes consumers believe that the conclusions they drew after

reading a message about a product were actually stated in the message. In short, source confusion can lead consumers to trust product information more than they should.

The second type of memory misattribution is the tendency to confuse feelings of familiarity with a wide variety of possible judgments, including fame, confidence, liking, and truth.[40] The more familiar a brand name seems, the more famous and popular the brand seems to be. Answers to questions that come to mind readily are held with greater confidence. The more familiar an initially neutral product becomes, the more consumers like the product. This is known as the **mere exposure effect** because repeated exposure to a product increases familiarity and liking. This is one reason why consumers learn to like novel foods (e.g., sushi), beverages (e.g., martinis), words (e.g., afworbu), and songs (e.g., new tunes heard on the radio) more over time. As the familiarity of a product claim increases, the more consumers believe the claim. This is known as the **truth effect**.[41] Simple repetition (e.g., repetitive advertising) is one way to increase the familiarity of a product, a claim, or an idea, and simple repetition can increase judgments of fame, confidence, liking, or truth. Increasing the ease with which consumers can perceive, read, or comprehend product information also increases familiarity. Consumers are most likely to confuse familiarity with fame, confidence, liking, or truth when their attention is divided during encoding, retrieval, or both.

The third type of memory misattribution is a false memory, or the tendency to remember items or events that never happened.[42] In a typical false memory experiment, people study a list of words that are closely related to a nonpresented word. For example, the words "sugar," "sweet," "chocolate," and "tasty" are closely related to the nonpresented word "candy." When people are later asked to recall as many words from the list as possible, they frequently recall the word "candy," even though it was not presented. This occurs because it is easier to remember the gist or the general meaning of the presented words than to remember the specific presented words themselves.

Suggestibility Misleading questions and suggestions can also lead to a form of memory distortion known as **suggestibility**.[43] For example, people who witness an automobile accident remember different events when they are asked, "How fast was the car going when it ran past the stop sign?" versus "How fast was the car going when it ran past the yield sign?" They also remember different events when they are asked, "How fast was the car going when it smashed into the other car?" versus "How fast was the car going when it bumped into the other car?" Similarly, adults asked to remember their childhood experiences are more likely to remember instances of child abuse if they receive suggestions of child abuse from a psychotherapist. Advertising can also produce memory distortion for past experiences with a product. For example, after tasting a bland orange juice, consumers are more likely to misremember the orange juice as flavorful after seeing an ad suggesting that the product is flavorful than after seeing no ad.

Bias Previously viewed advertising can also influence what is learned from current product experiences.[44] Advertising influences consumers' expectations, and expectations subsequently color what consumers see. To the extent that product experiences are ambiguous or open to multiple interpretations, expectations guide the interpretation of product experiences. Products seem larger, smaller, heavier, lighter, tastier, or more comfortable if consumers expect them to be larger, smaller, heavier, lighter, tastier, or more comfortable, respectively. Prior beliefs can **bias** current beliefs and experiences.[45] Consequently, learning from experience becomes difficult because prior beliefs and current experiences are perceived as more consistent than they actually are.

The opposite is also possible. Current beliefs can bias memory for prior beliefs and experiences. In a recent study, marketers were led to prefer supplier A over supplier B. Three weeks later, the same marketers were led to prefer supplier B over supplier A. When they were asked about their earlier preference, the marketers indicated that they always preferred supplier A.[46] Even when preferences change dramatically over time, people often assume that their earlier preferences were the same as their current preferences. Consequently, people often believe that their preferences are more consistent than they actually are.

Persistence Sometimes people can't forget things they want to forget. Traumatic events are often difficult to forget. Some songs and advertising jingles get stuck in our heads. This is known as "earworm."[47] Try not to think about a catchy song (such as "Who Let the Dogs Out") or advertising jingle (such as the Subway jingle) that you've heard recently. Simple, catchy, repetitive tunes are especially likely to produce earworm. Trying not to think about a specific song, object, or issue is surprisingly difficult. After trying not to think about a specific topic, people are more likely to think about it later when they are no longer trying not to think about it! Momentary distractions can also lead people to think more about a topic they are trying not to think about. The **persistence** of unwanted thoughts can be frustrating, distracting, and sometimes depressing.

Marketing in Action

Really New Products

Because of the mere exposure effect, consumers often prefer familiar products to unfamiliar products. They also tend to prefer incrementally new products to really new products. Incrementally new products are similar to products consumers already use, so they do not need to learn a lot about these new products. Really new products, however, are often so completely new and different that consumers have a hard time appreciating the benefits of such products, and frequently do not even know how to use such products. In other words, relatively little learning is needed for incrementally new products, but much learning is needed for really new products. Really new products tend to have much higher failure rates. Crystal Pepsi, Colgate Kitchen Entrees, and Premier smokeless cigarettes were all really new products that failed. Recent research, however, suggests that it might be possible to induce consumers to learn more about really new products and thus decrease the failure rate for this type of product.[48] The key is to increase cognitive flexibility, or to motivate consumers to think about really new products in more creative ways. Increasing cognitive flexibility helps consumers to see nonobvious similarities between really new products and other more familiar products. For the research, three different techniques for increasing cognitive flexibility were used, and all three lead to more favorable evaluations of really new products: Positive affect, or a good mood, increases cognitive flexibility. Imagining using a really new product in the distant future rather than in the near future also increases cognitive flexibility. Finally, encouraging consumers to think about a product using multiple perspectives also increases cognitive flexibility. In all three cases, increasing cognitive flexibility increased learning and preference for really new products.

Chapter Summary

Learning produces knowledge about products, and memory determines how knowledge about products is accessed and used. Associations between unconditioned and conditioned stimuli are learned via classical conditioning. Associations between responses and consequences are learned via operant conditioning. Associations are the building blocks of knowledge stored in memory. Although memory influences nearly all aspects of consumer behavior, most consumers underestimate the importance of memory. The seven sins of memory are side effects of an otherwise adaptive memory system. The sins of *forgetting* are transience (forgetting over time), absent-mindedness (forgetting because of a lack of effort during encoding or during retrieval), and blocking (forgetting as a result of interference caused by cue competition). The sins of *distortion* are misattribution (distortion as a result of confusion), suggestibility (distortion as a result of the questions and suggestions of others), and bias (distortion because of overestimating the consistency of the past and the present, and vice versa). The sin of persistence refers to the inability to forget what one wants to forget. Despite these sins, memory enables consumers to perform remarkably complex thinking, reasoning, and decision-making activities.

Key Terms

absent-mindedness
accessibility
activation
associations
associative interference
associative network
backward conditioning
bias
blocking
classical conditioning
conditioned response
conditioned stimulus
continuous reinforcement
corrective advertising

encoding
encoding-specificity principle
extinction
forward conditioning
generation effect
mere exposure effect
misattribution
negative reinforcement
node
operant conditioning
partial reinforcement
persistence
positive reinforcement
pre-exposure effect

priming effect
proactive interference
punishment
retrieval
retroactive interference
shaping
spacing effect
spreading activation
suggestibility
tip-of-the-tongue effect
transience
truth effect
unconditioned response
unconditioned stimulus

Review and Discussion

1. What are the differences between classical conditioning and operant conditioning?

2. How does learning influence memory?

3. How does memory influence learning?

4. Discuss three different ways forgetting occurs.

5. Discuss three different ways memory distortion occurs.

6. Discuss some ways that forgetting influences consumer behavior.

7. Discuss some ways that memory distortion influences consumer behavior.

8. What are the three types of memory misattribution?

9. When and how does previously viewed advertising influence current beliefs?

10. When and how does advertising viewed today influence memory for past product experiences?

Short Application Exercises

1. Think of some ways you could use classical conditioning in advertising.

2. Think of some ways you could design an advertisement that would improve memory for the advertised brand and for claims about the advertised brand.

3. Think of some ways you could design an advertisement that would block memory for competing brands and for claims about competing brands.

4. Organize several small groups and create a memory test for them. Each group should pick a product category, write down a list of ten brands, and purposely omit one leading brand. Read the list quickly to the memory test takers and ask them to count backwards from 100 by threes for about 20 seconds. Then ask the test takers to recall as many brand names as possible. How many test takers mention the omitted leading brand? Is it possible to create false memories in only 20 seconds?

Managerial Application

Imagine that you work for the Consumers Union, the consumer protection organization that publishes *Consumer Reports*. Your supervisor has asked you to test the effectiveness of several subliminal self-help CDs that are currently on the market. Before designing your experiment, you perform a literature review and find a classic experiment on the effectiveness of subliminal self-help audiotapes. In this experiment, students were randomly assigned to conditions in a 2 × 2 factorial design in which expectations and audiotape contents were manipulated experimentally.[49] Half the students were told that the audiotape improved memory performance. The other half were told that the audiotape improved self-esteem.

Half of the students received the memory audio-tape, and half received the self-esteem audiotape, regardless of what they were told earlier. Hence, in half of the conditions, expectations and content matched (e.g., students expected the audiotape to improve memory and the audiotape was supposed to actually improve memory). For the remaining half, expectations and content were mismatched (e.g., students expected the audiotape to improve memory, but the audiotape was

supposed to actually improve self-esteem). The results showed that expectations influenced memory performance and self-esteem ratings and that the content of the audiotapes had no effect. Now imagine that you conduct a replication experiment using currently available subliminal self-help CDs, and that you obtain the same pattern of results.

Your Challenge:

1. Explain your results. Which of the seven sins of memory is at work here and how is it operating?

2. Placebo effects are common in medical research. Which of the seven sins of memory is responsible for placebo effects? How do medical researchers design experiments to test for placebo effects?

3. How are marketing expectation effects and medical placebo effects similar?

4. How would you protect consumers from subliminal self-help CDs that don't work?

End Notes

1 Schultz, E. J. (2012). How This Man Made Dos Equis a Most Interesting Marketing Story. *Advertising Age*, 83(10): 1–11.

2 West, P. M., Brown, C. L., and Hoch, S. J. (1996). Consumption Vocabulary and Preference Formation. *Journal of Consumer Research*, 23: 120–135.

3 Mackintosh, N. J. (1974). *The Psychology of Animal Learning*. London: Academic Press.

4 Gorn, G. J. (1982). The Effects of Music in Advertising on Choice Behavior: A Classical Conditioning Approach. *Journal of Marketing*, 46: 94–101; Kim, J., Allen, C. T., and Kardes, F. R. (1996). An Investigation of the Mediational Mechanisms Underlying Attitudinal Conditioning. *Journal of Marketing Research*, 33: 318–328; McSweeney, F. K., and Bierley, C. (1984). Recent Developments in Classical Conditioning. *Journal of Consumer Research*, 11: 619–631; Shimp, T. A., Stuart, E. W., and Engle, R. W. (1991). A Program of Classical Conditioning Experiments Testing Variations in the Conditioned Stimulus and Contents. *Journal of Consumer Research*, 18: 1–12.

5 Cacioppo, J. T., Marshall-Goodell, B. S., Tassinary, L. G., and Petty, R. E. (1992). Rudimentary Determinants of Attitudes: Classical Conditioning Is More Effective When Prior Knowledge about the Attitude Stimulus Is Low Than High. *Journal of Experimental Social Psychology*, 28: 207–233.

6 van Osselaer, S. M. J., and Janiszewski, C. (2001). Two Ways of Learning Brand Associations. *Journal of Consumer Research*, 28: 202–223.

7 van Osselaer, S. M. J., and Alba, J. W. (2000). Consumer Learning and Brand Equity. *Journal of Consumer Research*, 27: 1–16.

8 van Osselaer, S. M. J., and Alba, J. W. (2003). Locus of Equity and Brand Extension. *Journal of Consumer Research*, 29: 539–550.

9 Feinburg, R. A. (1986). Credit Cards as Spending Facilitating Stimuli. *Journal of Consumer Research*, 13: 348–356.

10 Rescorla, R. A., and Wagner, A. R. (1972). A Theory of Pavlovian Conditioning: Variations in the Effectiveness of Reinforcement and Nonreinforcement. In A. H. Black and W. F. Prokasy (eds.), *Classical Conditioning II: Current Research and Theory*, 64–99. New York: Appleton-Century-Crofts.

11 Gluck, M. A., and Bower, G. H. (1988). From Conditioning to Category Learning: An Adaptive Network Model. *Journal of Experimental Psychology: General*, 117: 227–247.

12 van Osselaer, S. M. J. (2008). Associative Learning and Consumer Decisions. In C. P. Haugtvedt, P. M. Herr, and F. R. Kardes (eds.), *Handbook of Consumer Psychology*, 699–729. New York: Psychology Press.

13 van Osselaer, S. M. J., and Janiszewski, C. (2001). Two Ways of Learning Brand Associations. *Journal of Consumer Research*, 28: 202–223; van Osselaer, S. M. J., Janiszewski, C., and Cunha, M. (2004). Stimulus Generalization in Two Associative Learning Processes. *Journal of Experimental Psychology: Learning, Memory, and Cognition*, 30: 626–638.

14 Allen, C. T., and Janiszewski, C. (1989). Assessing the Role of Contingency Awareness in Attitudinal Conditioning with Implications for Advertising Research. *Journal of Marketing Research*, 26: 30–43; De Houwer, J., Thomas, S., and Baeyens, F. (2001). Associative Learning of Likes and Dislikes: A Review of 25 Years of Research on Human Evaluative Conditioning. *Psychological Bulletin*, 127: 853–869; Gibson, B. (2008). Can Evaluative Conditioning Change Attitudes toward Mature Brands? New Evidence from the Implicit Association Test. *Journal of Consumer Research*, 35: 178–188; Sweldens, S., van Osselaer, S. M. J., and Janiszewski, C. (2010). Evaluative Conditioning Procedures and the Resilience of Conditioned Brand Attitudes. *Journal of Consumer Research*, 37: 473–489.

15 Kim, J., Allen, C. T., and Kardes, F. R. (1996). An Investigation of the Mediational Mechanisms Underlying Attitudinal Conditioning. *Journal of Marketing Research*, 33: 318–328.

16 Jones, C. R., Fazio, R. H., and Olson, M. A. (2009). Implicit Misattribution as a Mechanism Underlying Evaluative Conditioning. *Journal of Personality and Social Psychology*, 96: 933–948.

17 Nord, W. R., and Peter, J. P. (1980). A Behavior Modification Perspective on Marketing. *Journal of Marketing*, 41: 36–47; Skinner, B. F. (1969). *Contingencies of Reinforcement: A Theoretical Analysis*. New York: Appleton-Century-Crofts.

18 Szymanowski, M., and Gijsbrechts, E. (2012). Consumption-Based Cross-Brand Learning: Are Private Labels Really Private? *Journal of Marketing Research*, 49: 231–246.

19 Alba, J. W., and Hutchinson, J. W. (1987). Dimensions of Consumer Expertise. *Journal of Consumer Research*, 13: 411–454; Wyer, R. S. (2008). The Role of Knowledge Accessibility in Cognition and Behavior: Implications for Consumer Information Processing. In C. P. Haugtvedt, P. M. Herr, and F. R. Kardes (eds.), *Handbook of Consumer Psychology*, 31–76. New York: Psychology Press.

20 Bransford, J. D., and Johnson, M. K. (1972). Contextual Prerequisites for Understanding: Some Investigations of Comprehension and Recall. *Journal of Verbal Learning and Verbal Behavior*, 11: 717–726.

21 Ibid.

22 Harris, R. J. (1977). Comprehension of Pragmatic Implications in Advertising. *Journal of Applied Psychology*, 62: 603–609; Harris, R. J., and Monaco, G. E. (1978). Psychology of Pragmatic Implications in Advertising: Information Processing between the Lines. *Journal of Experimental Psychology: General*, 107: 1–22.

23 Preston, I. L. (1977). The FTC's Handling of Puffery and Other Selling Claims Made "By Implication." *Journal of Business Research*, 5: 155–181.

24 Ferrell, O. C., and Hartline, M. D. (2012). Marketing Strategy (5th edition). Cincinnati, OH: South-Western Cengage Learning.

25 Mazis, M. B., and Adkinson, J. E. (1976). An Experimental Evaluation of a Proposed Corrective Advertising Remedy. *Journal of Marketing Research*, 13: 178–183; Mazursky, D., and Schul, Y. (1988). The Effects of Advertisement Encoding on the Failure to Discount Information: Implications for the Sleeper Effect. *Journal of Consumer Research*, 15: 24–36; Schul, Y., and Mazursky, D. (1990). Conditions Facilitating Successful Discounting in Consumer Decision Making. *Journal of Consumer Research*, 16: 442–451; Wilkie, W., McNeill, D., and Mazis, M. (1984). Marketing's "Scarlet Letter": The Theory and Practice of Corrective Advertising. *Journal of Marketing*, 48: 11–31.

26 Gilbert, D. (1991). How Mental Systems Believe. *American Psychologist*, 46: 107–119.

27 Anderson, J. R. (1983). *The Architecture of Cognition*. Cambridge, MA: Harvard University Press; Atkinson, R. C., and Shiffrin, R. M. (1968). Human Memory: A Proposed System and Its Control Processes. In K. W. Spence and J. T. Spence (eds.), *Advances in the Psychology of Learning and Motivation Research and Theory* (Vol. 2). New York: Academic Press.

28 Schacter, D. L. (1999). The Seven Sins of Memory: Insights from Psychology and Cognitive Neuroscience. *American Psychologist*, 54: 182–203.

29 Craik, F. I. M., and Lockhart, R. S. (1972). Levels of Processing: A Framework for Memory Research. *Journal of Verbal Learning and Verbal Behavior*, 11: 671–684; Craik, F. I. M., and Tulving, E. (1975). Depth of Processing and the Retention of Words in Episodic Memory. *Journal of Experimental Psychology: General*, 104: 268–294.

30 Slamecka, N. J., and Graf, P. (1978). The Generation Effect: Delineation of a Phenomenon. *Journal of Experimental Psychology: Learning, Memory, and Cognition*, 4: 592–604.

31 Brown, A. S. (1991). A Review of the Tip-of-the-Tongue Experience. *Psychological Bulletin*, 109: 204–223; Schacter, D. L. (1999). The Seven Sins of Memory: Insights from Psychology and Cognitive Neuroscience. *American Psychologist*, 54: 182–203.

32 Bahrick, H. P., Bahrick, L. E., Bahrick, A. S., and Bahrick, P. E. (1993). Maintenance of Foreign Language and the Spacing Effect. *Psychological Science*, 4: 316–321; Bahrick, H. P. and Hall, L. K. (1991). Lifetime Maintenance of High School Mathematics Content. *Journal of Experimental Psychology: General*, 104: 54–75.

33 Nelson, T. O. (1971). Savings and Forgetting from Long-Term Memory. *Journal of Verbal Learning and Verbal Behavior*, 10: 568–576; Nelson, T. O. (1978). Detecting Small Amounts of Information in Memory: Savings for Nonrecognized Items. *Journal of Experimental Psychology: Human Learning and Memory*, 4: 453–468.

34 Anderson, J. R. (1983). *The Architecture of Cognition*. Cambridge. MA: Harvard University Press; Tybout, A. M., Calder, B. J., and Sternthal, B. (1981). Using Information Processing Theory to Design Marketing Strategies. *Journal of Marketing Research*, 18: 73–79.

35 Aaker D. A. (1996). *Building Strong Brands*. New York: Free Press; Burke, R. R., and Srull, T. K. (1988). Competitive Interference and Consumer Memory for Advertising. *Journal of Consumer Research*, 15: 55–68.

36 Tulving, E. (1983). *Elements of Episodic Memory*. Oxford, England: Oxford University Press; Keller, K. L. (1987). Memory in Advertising: The Effect of Advertising Memory Cues on Brand Evaluations. *Journal of Consumer Research*, 14: 316–333.

37 Appleton-Knapp, S. L., Bjork, R. A., and Wickens, T. D. (2005). Examining the Spacing Effect in Advertising: Encoding Variability, Retrieval Processes, and Their Interaction. *Journal of Consumer Research*, 32: 266–276; Janiszewski, C., Noel, H., and Sawyer, A. G. (2003). A Meta-Analysis of the Spacing Effect in Verbal Learning: Implications for Research on Advertising Repetition and Consumer Memory. *Journal of Consumer Research*, 30: 138–149.

38 Berman, M. G., Jonides, J., and Lewis, R. L. (2009). In Search of Decay in Verbal Short-Term Memory. *Journal of Experimental Psychology: Learning, Memory, and Cognition*, 35: 317–333.

39 Johnson, M. K., and Rahe, C. L. (1981). Reality Monitoring. *Psychological Review*, 88: 67–85; Johnson, M. K., Hastroudi, S., and Lindsay, D. S. (1993). Source Monitoring. *Psychological Bulletin*, 114: 3–28; Pham, M. T., and Johar, G. V. (1997). Contingent Processes of Source Identification. *Journal of Consumer Research*, 24: 249–265.

40 Jacoby, L. L., Kelley, C. M., and Dywan, J. (1989). Memory Attributions. In H. L. Roediger and F. I. M. Craik (eds.), *Varieties of Memory and Consciousness: Essays in Honor of Endel Tulving*, 391–422. Hillsdale, NJ: Lawrence Erlbaum Associates; Schwarz, N. (2004). Metacognitive Experiences in Consumer Judgment and Decision Making. *Journal of Consumer Psychology*, 14: 332–348.

41 Hawkins, S. A., and Hoch, S. J. (1992). Low-Involvement Learning: Memory Without Evaluation. *Journal of Consumer Research*, 19: 212–225; Hawkins, S. A., Hoch, S. J., and Meyers-Levy, J. (2001). Low-Involvement Learning: Repetition and Coherence in Familiarity and Belief. *Journal of Consumer Psychology*, 11: 1–12; Law, S., Hawkins, S. A., and Craik, F. I. M. (1998). Repetition-Induced Belief in the Elderly: Rehabilitating Age-Related Memory Deficits. *Journal of Consumer Research*, 25: 91–107; Skurnik, I., Yoon, C., Park, D. C., and Schwarz, N. (2005). How Warnings about False Claims Become Recommendations. *Journal of Consumer Research*, 31: 713–724.

42 Roediger, H. L. III. (1996). Memory Illusions. *Journal of Memory and Language*, 35: 76–100; Roediger, H. L. III. (1995). Creating False Memories: Remembering Words Not Presented in Lists. *Journal of Experimental Psychology: Learning, Memory, and Cognition*, 21: 803–818.

43 Braun, K. (1999). Postexperience Advertising Effects on Consumer Memory. *Journal of Consumer Research*, 25: 319–334; Loftus, E. F. (1993). The Reality of Repressed Memories. *American Psychologist*, 48: 518–537.

44 Ha, Y., and Hoch, S. J. (1989). Ambiguity, Processing Strategy, and Advertising-Evidence Interactions. *Journal of Consumer Research*, 16: 354–360; Hoch, S. J., and Ha, Y. (1986). Consumer Learning: Advertising and the Ambiguity of Product Experience. *Journal of Consumer Research*, 13: 221–233.

45 Alba, J. W., and Hasher, L. (1983). Is Memory Schematic? *Psychological Bulletin*, 93: 203–231; Alba, J. W., and Hutchinson, J. W. (1987). Dimensions of Consumer Expertise. *Journal of Consumer Research*, 13: 411–454; Hoch, S. J., and Deighton, J. (1989). Managing What Consumers Learn from Experience. *Journal of Marketing*, 53: 1–20; Sanbonmatsu, D. M., Posavac, S. S.,

Kardes, F. R., and Mantel, S. P. (1998). Selective Hypothesis Testing. *Psychonomic Bulletin & Review*, 5: 197–220.

46 Kardes, F. R., Chandrashekaran, M., and Kellaris, J. J. (2002). Preference Construction and Reconstruction. In R. Zwick, and A. Rapoport (eds.), *Experimental Business Research,* 301–327. Boston, MA: Kluwer.

47 Kellaris, J. J. (2008). Music and Consumers. In C. P. Haugtvedt, P. M. Herr, and F. R. Kardes (eds.), *Handbook of Consumer Psychology*, 837–856. New York: Psychology Press.

48 Jhang, J. H., Grant, S. J., and Campbell, M. C. (2012). Get It? Got It. Good! Enhancing New Product Acceptance by Facilitating Resolution of Extreme Incongruity. *Journal of Marketing Research*, 49: 247–259.

49 Greenwald, A. G., Spangenberg, E. R., Pratkanis, A. R., and Eskanazi, J. (1991). Double-Blind Tests of Subliminal Self-Help Audiotapes. *Psychological Science*, 2: 119–122.

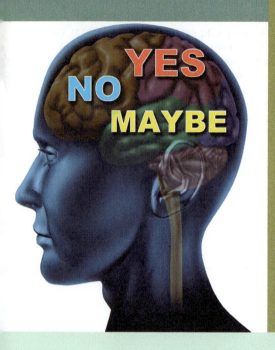

CHAPTER 6

AUTOMATIC INFORMATION PROCESSING

OBJECTIVES   *After studying this chapter, you will be able to…*

1 Define automatic information processing.

2 Explain the benefits of unconscious thought.

3 Explain thin slice theory.

4 Identify many different types of priming effects.

5 Identify key regions of the brain that influence different types of information processing.

Mars Bars

Mars, Inc. makes several different types of candy products and also other food and pet food products. Mars is best known, however, for its candy bars: Snickers, Twix, Milky Way, 3 Musketeers, and, of course, Mars Bars. The company was founded in 1911 by Frank C. Mars, and the company is still owned by the Mars family. In 2010, the company enjoyed $30 billion in sales. Although the company has nothing to do with the planet Mars, consumers buy more Mars Bars when the planet Mars is featured in the news. This is exactly what happened when NASA landed the Pathfinder spacecraft on the surface of Mars. Presumably, if the planet Mars is again featured in the news, Mars Bars will enjoy another temporary spike in sales. Why might this be?

Recent research suggests that when environmental cues that remind us of specific products are encountered frequently or recently, evaluations of those products become more favorable.[1]

Lightspring/Shutterstock

The planet Mars has absolutely nothing in common with the Mars candy company, but because of the priming effect, whenever the planet makes news headlines, the candy company enjoys a spike in its sales.

NASA Images

This occurs because of the **priming effect**, or a temporary increase in the ease with which ideas can be retrieved from memory. Information that is easy to retrieve often seems more relevant, familiar, and accurate or valid. As we will see in this chapter, many different types of ideas can be primed and many different types of priming effects are possible. Interestingly, priming effects occur automatically, or without awareness or intention. That is, consumers do not realize that watching a news story about the planet Mars will influence their thoughts about Mars Bars. Furthermore, consumers do not intentionally allow news stories about the planet Mars to influence their judgments about Mars Bars.

Priming effects are surprisingly common. Think about what happens every Halloween: orange pumpkins are everywhere and they prime the color "orange." To test the effects of priming "orange" on consumers, shoppers at a supermarket were asked to list as many candy/ chocolate products they could think of quickly and to list as many soft drinks as they could off the top of their heads. Shoppers were more likely to list orange candies, like Reese's (which have orange packaging), and orange sodas, like Orange Crush and Sunkist, the day before Halloween (when the color orange was highly accessible from memory) than one week after Halloween (when the color orange was less accessible). In a follow-up study, consumers were randomly given an orange pen or a green pen, and they were asked to choose between two products in 20 different product categories (e.g., candies, beverages, detergents). Consumers using an orange pen chose more orange products, and consumers using a green pen chose more green products.

In another follow-up study, students randomly received a luggage slogan ("Luggage carries your gear, ePlay carries what you want to hear") or a dinner tray slogan ("Dinner is carried by a tray, music is carried by ePlay") via email. One week later, the students received another email in which they were asked to evaluate the ePlay digital music player. Students who were preparing to travel back to campus were more likely to purchase the ePlay and were willing to pay a greater amount, compared to students who were already on campus and not thinking about luggage. In another follow-up study using the same slogans, the ePlay was rated more highly by students living in a dorm that used trays than by students living in a dorm that did not use trays.

Yet another follow-up study that used slogans showed that linking fruits and vegetables to a tray ("Each and every dining hall tray needs five fruits and vegetables a day") led students to eat more fruits and vegetables when students encountered trays frequently, but not when students encountered trays infrequently. In a final study, the researchers took advantage of a natural association stored in memory: the association between cats and dogs. Students rated 20 photos, and the number of dog photos presented was manipulated experimentally. Later, students familiar with Puma sneakers recognized the sneakers more quickly and rated them more favorably as the number of dog photos presented increased. Together, these studies show that linking a product to a frequently or recently encountered environmental stimulus leads to faster and more favorable evaluations of the product, and consumers do not even realize that this is occurring.

OBJECTIVE **1** ## Two Styles of Thinking

In his recent book, *Thinking, Fast and Slow*, Nobel laureate Daniel Kahneman describes two styles of thinking that he refers to as System 1 thinking and System 2 thinking.[2] System 1 is fast and automatic, which means that it occurs without awareness or intention. System 1 is also intuitive, which means that it reaches judgments and decisions quickly, and that people are unable to explain precisely how they arrived at these judgments and decisions. System 1 is good at categorizing objects quickly—identifying prototypes or typical categories— and averaging large amounts of information. By contrast, System 2 is slow and deliberative, which means that it occurs with awareness and intention. System 2 also uses up cognitive resources, which means that we experience mental fatigue when we engage in high levels of System 2 thinking. System 2 is good at logical reasoning and performing mathematical operations.

The idea that there are two styles of thinking has had a profound effect on research on judgment, decision making, attention, reasoning, and persuasion. Theoretical frameworks that describe the two styles of thinking are referred to as **dual-process models**.[3] Such models maintain that information processing sometimes occurs quickly and effortlessly, and sometimes occurs slowly and with great effort. Different names for the two styles of information processing are used by researchers investigating different topics, but all of these models are similar to Kahneman's System 1 versus System 2 model. Table 6-1 summarizes the names used by different dual-process models. The important thing to remember is that thinking is sometimes fast and automatic, and sometimes slow and deliberative.

TABLE 6.1 | Dual-Process Models

System 1	System 2
Automatic	Deliberative (or controlled)
Fast	Slow
Intuitive	Computational (or rule based)
Effortless	Effortful
Low involvement	High involvement
Peripheral	Central
Heuristic	Systematic
Category based	Attribute based
Experiential	Rational
Holistic	Analytic
Reflexive	Reflective

This chapter focuses on System 1 thinking, or automatic information processing. This topic is difficult to study because people often do not realize that they rely heavily on automatic processing, and people are unable to describe or explain their automatic thought processes. How do you study thought processes that occur without awareness or intention? How can we scientifically investigate subconscious thought processes that people do not even realize are occurring? These are the key questions addressed in this chapter.

What Is Automatic Information Processing?

Automatic information processing refers to mental processes that occur without awareness or intention, but nevertheless influence judgments, feelings, goals, and behaviors.[4] Consumers do many things without their conscious awareness. For example, in a classic study, consumers were shown four pairs of nylon stockings and were asked to choose the best pair.[5] The stockings were arranged from left to right on a table, and the results showed that most consumers preferred the right-most pair. However, when they were asked why they liked this pair best, they were unable to explain it. Some said that they thought that this pair of stockings was higher in quality than the other pairs. This was not correct, however; the study participants were tricked: all four pairs of stockings were identical. So, when consumers are not sure why they like one product better than another, they often make up an answer that seems reasonable, but may be—and often is—wrong.

When shopping for groceries, consumers often buy impulsively. These impulse purchases are usually made with little or no conscious thought; later, when it's time to pay for the groceries, consumers are often surprised by how high their bills are. Impulse buys are sometimes made without awareness. That is, consumers sometimes do not realize that they are putting certain items into their shopping carts. Impulse buys are usually made without intention. That is, consumers usually do not intend to make impulse purchases. Research shows that grocery shoppers are more likely to make impulse purchases when they are hungry and even more when they don't have a shopping list.[6]

Impulse purchases are more likely when consumers don't use a shopping list.

How do consumers make decisions with minimal thought? Some decisions are based on attitudes that come to mind automatically whenever consumers see or think about a particular product.[7] Rather than thinking about all the pros and cons associated with a product, consumers simply think about whether they like the product. This does not occur for all products, but it does occur for highly familiar products. For example, consumers do not need to think about the pros and cons of Snickers candy bars if they already know that Snickers bars are among their favorites. Consumers do not need to think about the pros and cons of canned spinach if they already know that they detest canned spinach. For products associated with strong attitudes that are highly accessible from memory, responses come to mind quickly and unintentionally whenever these products are encountered.

OBJECTIVE **2** ## The Adaptive Unconscious

How does a mental process become automatic? The answer is practice. Learning how to drive a car for the first time is painstakingly difficult. It is important to pay close attention to the road, to other cars, to the pedals, and to the controls on the dashboard. However, with lots of practice, driving becomes easy because it becomes automatic. Instead of paying close attention to everything, practice makes it possible to receive all the information you need with just a glance. Practice can also make it easy to play a new sport, solve math problems, or make purchase decisions.

What are the benefits of automatic information processing? When a mental process becomes automatic and subject to unconscious control, it becomes easier to pay attention to novel objects and ideas that require careful attention and thought. Here, the subconscious mind frees up mental resources for the conscious mind. It would be difficult, if not impossible, for the conscious mind to navigate our complex environment without assistance from the unconscious mind.

Note that this view of the unconscious is quite different from the Freudian view. Sigmund Freud thought that the unconscious hid important thoughts and ideas from us, and that this causes mental illness. The purpose of psychotherapy, according to Freud, was to uncover these hidden thoughts and ideas. In sharp contrast, the modern view of the **adaptive unconscious** suggests that the unconscious mind can be trained to perform routine mental activities. This is beneficial, rather than harmful, because it enables people to devote more attention and thought to non-routine mental activities. For example, shopping for routine products, such as milk, butter, and eggs, requires little time or energy. So, time and energy are thus freed up for thinking more carefully about non-routine purchases, such as the special ingredients for a new dish you want to try.

It becomes easier to appreciate the importance of the unconscious mind when one compares normal people to people whose brain injuries prevent them from experiencing emotions and learning unconsciously.[8] In an important experiment, groups of participants were asked to play a gambling game in which they drew cards from four decks. Two of the decks were high-risk decks with high payoffs or high losses, with losses more likely to occur than payoffs. Two decks were low-risk decks with low payoffs or low losses, but in this case, payoffs were more likely. Normal people quickly and unconsciously learned to draw mainly from the low-risk decks. Interestingly, they learned to do this long before they could explain why they did this. People with brain injuries that blocked emotions, but who were otherwise highly intelligent, drew mainly from the high-risk decks and lost more money. The absence of emotional responses and gut feelings prevented them from learning to avoid high-risk situations.

OBJECTIVE **3** # Thin Slice Inferences

People can learn a surprisingly large amount of information from very quick first impressions. "Thin slices," or brief observations of another person's behavior, provide surprisingly accurate information about this person's personality traits and current feelings and goals.[9] Research shows that what people learn from thin slices of behavior typically occurs in less than five minute intervals. Ironically, first impressions are often more accurate when they are based on very brief observations than when they are based on longer observations.

Also, first impressions are often more accurate when people focus on non-verbal information, such as facial expressions, gestures, voice tone, and body movements, than when they focus on verbal information. This occurs because people have less control over nonverbal cues than they do over their verbal communication.

In a recent study of thin slicing, consumers were asked to make inferences about sales management job applicants based on 20-second audiotapes of random portions of job interviews. These inferences were compared to those of the expert sales managers who conducted the interviews. The results showed that consumers formed remarkably accurate inferences about the social skills and the anxiety levels of the job applicants based on thin slices of behavior. Accuracy was even higher when the audiotapes were content-filtered, so that consumers could listen to voice tone but the verbal message was garbled. Sometimes less is more.

Sometimes snap judgments are more accurate than judgments resulting from a great deal of thought. In a strawberry jam taste test, some consumers were asked simply to indicate which jams they liked best.[10] Other consumers were asked to explain why they liked one particular jam better than the others. The researchers then compared the ratings of these consumers to the ratings of experts. The results showed that the consumers who simply indicated their preferences without explaining them were more accurate than the consumers who were asked to explain their preferences. In a follow-up study, consumers were asked to choose one of several decorative posters to keep for free.[11] Again, half simply indicated their preferences, and half explained their preferences. Three weeks later, the consumers who simply indicated their preferences were more satisfied with their decisions than the consumers who explained their preferences. Sometimes too much thinking can lead to bad decisions.

When should consumers trust their **intuition** and when should they think carefully about a decision problem? Some types of decisions, like picking strawberry jams or decorative posters, should be made intuitively. Other types of decisions, like buying a car or a kitchen appliance, should be made deliberatively. In a study of intuitive versus deliberative judgment, participants were asked either to provide simple answers to various questions or to explain their answers.[12] Some of the questions were subjective, such as "Which advertisement would consumers like best?" Other questions were more objective, such as "What is the length of the Amazon River?" The results showed that intuition worked best for questions with subjective answers, and deliberation worked best for questions with objective answers.

Thin-slice inferences are more accurate for questions with subjective answers. Thin-slice inferences are also more accurate when consumers have a lot of practice forming these inferences and when they receive a good deal of accurate feedback about the quality of their inferences.[13] The best type of feedback occurs frequently and quickly. A great deal of learning takes place under these conditions. On the other hand, learning is difficult when feedback is infrequent or delayed. Learning also depends on the consequences of one's mistakes. It is easier to learn from one's mistakes when mistakes are obvious. However, it is difficult to learn from one's mistakes if it is unclear whether a mistake actually was made. For some types of decisions, nearly any reasonable judgment turns out well. For example, most brands of portable music players are very good. Consequently, consumers are likely to be satisfied with nearly any brand of portable music player they choose, even if they make a mistake and fail to choose the best brand.

OBJECTIVE **4**

Implicit Memory

Sometimes consumers purposefully try to retrieve information from memory. When consumers are aware that they are searching for information stored in memory and/or when they intend to do so, they are performing an **explicit memory** task. However, sometimes consumers are not aware that they are using memory as a tool to perform some task. When memory is used as a tool without awareness or intention, consumers are performing an **implicit memory** task. The priming effect is the most common type of implicit memory phenomenon.

Priming Effects Priming occurs in situations in which consumers are subtly led to think about a concept, such as a brand name, a product category, an attribute, a benefit, or any idea.[14] For example, watching TV primes concepts related to products (e.g., information conveyed in ads), politics (e.g., information conveyed in news shows), and entertainment (e.g., television shows featuring sex, violence, comedy, action, etc.). Crossword puzzles and other types of intellectual puzzles (e.g., word searches, scrambles) also prime ideas. Fiction and non-fiction books and magazines also prime ideas. Once an idea has been primed, it influences how people think about related ideas. People are usually unaware of this influence.

Simply thinking about a concept activates that concept from memory. Once a concept has been activated, it influences how consumers think about subsequent topics. For example, in a study on pricing, consumers were asked to complete a word search.[15] In expensive prime conditions, the puzzle contained brand names of expensive automobiles (e.g., Mercedes-Benz, Rolls Royce, Ferrari, Porsche). In inexpensive prime conditions, the puzzle contained brand names of inexpensive automobiles (e.g., Chevette, VW Beetle, Ford Pinto, Ford Fiesta). Participants were asked to find the hidden names and circle them. This simple task resulted in the activation of either expensive or inexpensive automobiles in the minds of the participants. Later, consumers were asked to judge the expensiveness of a moderately priced automobile, called the target. In the ambiguous condition, participants were asked to rate a moderately priced car with a concealed brand name. In the unambiguous condition, different participants rated the same car, except the brand name was clearly exposed. Results of the study revealed that the previous puzzle task had a surprising influence on subsequent consumer judgments.

Participants who completed the puzzle containing inexpensive brands rated the ambiguous automobile (no brand name) as inexpensive, while participants who completed the puzzle with expensive brand names rated the ambiguous automobile as expensive. This is known as an **assimilation effect** because the target was perceived as similar in price to the automobiles primed in the puzzle. In other words, consumers assimilated the target with the prime. The results were very different when the ad contained an unambiguous automobile. In this case, participants who were primed with inexpensive brands rated the moderately priced target (with a clearly visible brand name) as expensive, while participants who were primed with expensive brands rated the target as inexpensive. This is known as a **contrast effect** because consumers contrasted the target with the prime. In summary, priming produced assimilation effects when the target was ambiguous and contrast effects when the target was unambiguous. The results also showed that consumers did not think that the puzzles influenced their judgments.

Previously viewed ads can also prime ideas that influence the interpretation of currently viewed ads. In an important study, participants received one of two ads for a personal computer: the Versa-Com computer, a versatile machine that can perform many functions, or the EZ-Com computer, a very easy-to-use machine.[16] Hence, either "versatile" or "easy to use" was primed. Next, participants received an ad for another computer, the PC-3000, which stated that this computer had numerous features. "Numerous features" can be good or bad depending on what specific benefits consumers are seeking. The results of the study showed that the PC-3000 was evaluated more favorably when "versatile" was primed than when "easy to use" was primed. This occurred because "numerous features" seemed good when consumers focused on versatility, but "numerous features" seemed bad when consumers focused on ease of use.

The average American watches more than four hours of television per day, and television can distort consumers' opinions in very subtle ways via the priming effect.[17] Watching television leads people to overestimate crime, violence, affluence, and marital discord rates, as well as the number of doctors, lawyers, and police officers working in the real world. Furthermore, the more TV people watch, the more distorted their judgments become. Fortunately, these distortions are reduced when people estimate how much television they watch before they provide crime and occupation estimates. Distortions are also reduced when people are warned that watching television can distort their judgments.

Priming can influence behavior as well as judgment. Many studies have shown that people mimic or imitate other people during social interaction.[18] People tend to like other people who are similar to them in terms of mannerisms, speech patterns, gestures, and facial expressions. Mimicry often happens unintentionally and without awareness, and it often helps social interactions go more smoothly. Mimicry even happens when people are eating together. In an ice cream taste test, people ate more ice cream when their partner consumed a a lot of it than when their partner consumed only a little, provided their partner was not obese.[19] The partners were actually study confederates who were instructed by the experimenter about how much ice cream they should eat.

Scrambled sentence puzzles can also prime a surprisingly wide variety of behaviors.[20] In studies of this phenomenon, participants received a set of words and were asked to construct sentences out of them. In "rude" prime conditions, the words related to rudeness (i.e., rude, bold, aggressive). In "polite" prime conditions, the words related to politeness (i.e., polite, respect, patient).

After performing either the rude or polite scrambled sentence priming task, participants were asked to meet with another experimenter who was talking with someone else. The results showed that participants were more likely to interrupt when they were in rude prime versus polite prime conditions. In a follow-up study, participants were either primed with words related to older people (i.e., gray, bingo, Florida) or participated in a no-prime control condition. The results showed that when the study was over, participants walked more slowly to the nearest elevator when they were in the old prime condition than in the no-prime condition.

In another similar study, participants were asked to write down everything that came to mind when they thought about college professors in the professor prime condition.[21] No-prime control participants did not perform this task. Next, all participants played the game "Trivial Pursuit." The person who answered the greatest number of trivia questions correctly won (e.g., Question: "Who painted La Guernica?" Answer choices: a. Dali, b. Velasquez, c. Picasso, d. Miro). Participants answered more questions correctly in the professor prime condition than in the no-prime condition. Hence, merely thinking about stereotypes can influence behavior.

Other types of priming effects have been observed. For example, **procedural priming effects** occur when situations are linked to cognitive or motor processes via "if X, then Y" linkages, where X refers to a specific situation and Y refers to a cognitive or behavioral activity. If the linkage or association is sufficiently strong, Y is performed whenever X occurs. For example, in one study consumers were asked to rank product attributes from either the most favorable to the least favorable, or vice versa.[22] Ranking from most to least favorable led consumers to focus on the best attributes first. Ranking from least to most favorable led consumers to focus on the worst attributes first. Later, consumers were asked to indicate whether they would buy a computer described by a large amount of information (i.e., 10 attributes), and they had to do so either under time pressure (i.e., making a decision in 15 seconds) or no time pressure. The results showed that the ranking task performed in the first session influenced purchase decisions in the second. When the ranking task led consumers to focus on the most favorable attributes first, consumers were more likely to buy the computer when the decision had to be made under time pressure. This effect was reversed when the decision was made without time pressure because consumers were more likely to focus on the attributes considered last.

Simply indicating a preference can increase the probability of purchasing a brand.

Digital Vision/Getty Images

In the **mindset priming effect**, the cognitive activity performed during the first session tends to be performed again in the second, even if the products considered during the two sessions are completely different. For example, when consumers were given the opportunity to buy a pen for a low price or for a high price, they typically chose to buy the pen for a low price, but not a high price. Later, when given the opportunity to buy a moderately expensive key chain, consumers were more likely to buy in the second session if they chose to buy in the first.[23] Putting consumers in a buying mindset leads them to continue buying.

Clever salespeople can get consumers into a buying mindset simply by asking them to indicate their preferences for different brands, models, or colors. After indicating a preference, consumers are more likely to buy. In a recent study, some consumers were asked to indicate their preferences between two computers; another group of consumers was simply asked whether they wanted to buy a computer.[24] Later, these consumers received descriptions of two vacation packages and were asked to choose one or neither. Consumers who indicated their preferences between the two computers in the first session were more likely to buy a vacation package in the second session. A preference mindset leads consumers to buy and to overlook the option of buying nothing. A follow-up study showed that this mindset effect occurs even when the first session preference task does not involve products or services.[25] Merely indicating preferences for pairs of animals or performing comparisons of pairs of animals (e.g., Which animal is heavier, faster, or more ferocious?) in the first session increases purchase decisions in the second session.

In addition to buying, preference, and comparison mindsets, it is also possible to induce a generating alternatives mindset.[26] People frequently focus on one alternative at a time, and this can lead to poor predictions. For example, when asked to predict whether a leading basketball team is likely to win the championship, people typically overestimate the likelihood of this team winning. More accurate predictions are formed when people are asked to consider the likelihood of many different teams winning, rather than focusing on only one team. Considering the likelihood of many different football teams winning the Super Bowl, or the likelihood of many different sitcoms winning an award, leads to more accurate predictions of a basketball team winning the championship.

Even something as complex as **naïve theories**, or theories or assumptions about how the world works, can be primed.[27] For example, consumers have naïve theories about the relationship between the amount of effort required to produce a piece of artwork and the quality of the artwork.[28] Most consumers assume that it takes a great deal of time and effort to produce a masterpiece. However, most consumers also assume that a master artist, like Picasso, can produce a masterpiece very quickly. Hence, if you ask consumers which painting is better, a painting that was produced in one day or a painting that was produced in one week, most consumers conclude that the latter painting is better. However, if you ask consumers which artist is more talented, an artist that produced a painting in one day or an artist that produced a painting in one week, most consumers conclude that the artist that produced a painting in one day is better. These conclusions are logically inconsistent because the painting produced in one day cannot be the best and the worst painting at the same time.

Recent research shows that consumers also have multiple, contradictory naïve theories about how marketing works.[29] For example, consumers believe that expensive products tend to be high in quality. However, at the same time, consumers also believe that expensive products are often overpriced and are therefore poor value for money. When the importance of quality was primed in a magazine article about an unrelated product, consumers inferred that the more expensive target product was the better product. However, when the importance of value was primed in a magazine article about an unrelated product, consumers inferred that the less expensive target product was the better product. Hence, a high price can be good or bad depending on which naïve theory consumers use to think about price.

In a follow-up study, some consumers read an article about an unrelated product arguing that *popular* products are good products. After all, one million satisfied customers cannot be wrong. However, consumers also believe that *scarce* products are good products, i.e., rare, valuable products like diamonds, Ferraris, and so on. The other consumers in the study read an article about an unrelated product arguing that scarce products are good products. When the importance of product popularity was primed, consumers preferred the popular target product. However, when the importance of product scarcity was primed, consumers preferred the scarce target product. Again, different naïve theories lead to different conclusions based on the same evidence.

Technical jargon in an ad can be interpreted either as a good thing or a bad thing. Technical information, like "This multivitamin contains the recommended daily doses of beta-carotene, ascorbic acid, anuerine, riboflavin, pyridoxal, dibencozide, calcium, potassium, zinc, and magnesium," seems useful when consumers rated how detailed and informative the ad was before they evaluated the multivitamin. However, when consumers rated how easy it was to understand the ad, the technical information seemed less informative and consumers gave the multivitamin less favorable overall evaluations. Hence, technical jargon can be interpreted either positively or negatively, depending on which naïve theory consumers bring to bear at the time of judgment.

Subliminal priming, or presenting priming stimuli below the level of conscious awareness, can also influence consumer judgment and choice.[30] In a classic study of subliminal priming, participants were asked not to eat or drink for three hours prior to the experiment. At the beginning of the experiment, participants were randomly assigned to a thirsty condition (i.e., they were not allowed to drink any water) or a non-thirsty condition (i.e., they were allowed to drink as much water as they wanted). Next, words were flashed for 16 milliseconds on a computer screen followed by a mask, or a string of letters that makes it even more difficult to see a briefly flashed word. Participants were randomly assigned to a thirst-related words condition (i.e., thirst, dry) or a control condition in which neutral words were flashed (i.e., pirate, won). Finally, participants were asked to perform a taste test for two different kinds of Kool-Aid and they were allowed to drink as much as they wanted. The results showed that thirsty participants exposed to thirst-related subliminal primes drank more Kool-Aid than did participants in the other conditions.

When combined with accessible needs, subliminal priming can increase persuasion.

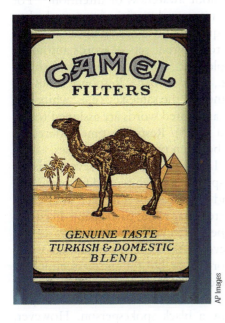

AP Images

Global Perspectives

Effects of French versus German Music on Purchase Behavior

Can the background music played in a store prime different thoughts and influence consumer behavior? To answer this question, an experiment was conducted in which either French music or German music was played in a store.[31] The results showed that consumers bought more French wine when French music was played. The results also showed that consumers bought more German wine when German music was played. These results were surprising because the consumers did not think that the music had any influence on them. Furthermore, France is famous for dry red wines, such as cabernet sauvignon-merlot blends from Bordeaux and pinot noir from Burgundy. However, Germany is famous for sweet white wines, like Riesling, Gewurtztraminer, and Kabinett. Even though the styles of wine are very different, background music influenced choices and did so without consumers' awareness or intention.

In a follow-up experiment, thirst-related primes increased preferences for a drink that was advertised as thirst-quenching ("SuperQuencher") over a drink that was advertised as energizing ("PowerPro"). Again, however, this effect was observed only for participants who were already thirsty. Hence, subliminal priming by itself does not increase persuasion. However, subliminal priming combined with an already accessible need or goal can increase persuasion.

The Implicit Association Test (IAT) People are often unwilling to admit that they have stereotypes or prejudices. How can researchers measure beliefs about stereotypes if people are unwilling to answer questions about stereotypes truthfully? The **Implicit Association Test (IAT)** is a new procedure for measuring sensitive beliefs, including those held without awareness or intention.[32] For example, words appear on a computer monitor, and participants are asked to press one of two keys (left or right key) as quickly and as accurately as possible. The computer records response latencies to different sets of words automatically. Sometimes the words relate to people (e.g., white or black) and sometimes the words relate to evaluations (e.g., good or bad). Response times are faster when two associated words are assigned to the same key (e.g., white and good, black and bad) than when two non-associated words are assigned to the same key (e.g., white and bad, black and good). Response time differences increase as the strength of the association between two words increases.

In a recent advertising study using the IAT, participants saw several ads for sneakers.[33] For some of the ads, the spokesperson was white, and for some, the spokesperson was black. A different brand logo was used in each ad. Scores on standard, explicit attitude scales suggested that white participants liked the sneakers associated with the white spokesperson as well as the sneakers associated with the black spokesperson. However, IAT scores showed that white participants' **implicit attitudes** were more favorable for sneakers endorsed by the white spokesperson than for sneakers endorsed by the black spokesperson. In contrast, scores on explicit attitude scales indicated that black participants preferred the brand endorsed by a black spokesperson. However, black participants' implicit attitudes were equally favorable for white and black endorsers. Hence, **explicit attitudes** and implicit attitudes can and do sometimes differ. Marketers could benefit greatly by understanding consumers' underlying (or implicit) attitudes and designing communication to match these attitudes.

Familiarity Effects Repetitive advertising can have surprising effects on consumer judgment. The more consumers see a product or hear a claim about a product, the more familiar that product or claim becomes. Familiarity can be furthered by increasing the clarity or the size of a picture of a product, presenting the picture or message for a longer time, or by presenting the product in sharper focus than the background. As familiarity increases, a brand name seems more famous, liking for the brand increases, judgments about the brand are held with greater confidence, and product claims seem more likely to be true (the **truth effect**).[34] Distraction can also make claims seem more believable because it prevents consumers from thinking carefully about the source of a feeling of familiarity.

Familiar products and ideas are easy to think about, and products and ideas that are easy to think about seem more famous, likable, and true. In other words, consumers can confuse familiarity with fame, liking, confidence, and truth. Consequently, even seemingly trivial manipulations of familiarity (e.g., priming, repetition, clarity, rhyming) can increase judgments of fame, liking, confidence, and truth. The truth effect is a particularly interesting case in point: The more consumers see or hear a product claim, the more they believe it.[35] Repetition increases familiarity, which then increases believability. In short, familiar statements that "ring a bell" with consumers often appear to be true. All of these familiarity effects are likely to occur when consumers use familiarity as a basis for judgment without awareness or intention. This is especially likely when involvement is low or when distractions are present. However, when consumers think more carefully about why a product or a claim seems familiar, familiarity effects disappear. Furthermore, when consumers are highly knowledgeable about a product, the truth effect disappears.[36]

Distraction Effects According to social psychologist Dan Gilbert, comprehension and beliefs are inseparable.[37] Consumers *initially* believe everything they see and hear. Unbelieving, or rejecting a false claim, is a separate process. It comes later, perhaps only seconds later, but later nevertheless. In other words, believing is as easy and automatic as seeing and understanding. Unbelieving, however, requires more time and effort. To demonstrate this, Gilbert and his colleagues asked participants to learn a new language by studying statements presented on a computer monitor. After reading a statement, such as "a monishna is a star," participants were told the statement was either true or false. In addition, sometimes the true or false feedback was interrupted by a distracting tone-detection task (i.e., participants were asked to multi-task during the experiment). Later, all the statements were presented again, and participants were asked to indicate whether each statement was true or false. It is no surprise that because a great many statements were presented, participants made lots of errors. However, some errors were more common than others. In fact, participants were more likely to believe false statements to be true than true statements to be false. This is because believing is easier than unbelieving.

Naturally, consumers do not ultimately believe everything they see and hear, but the important point is that unbelieving or rejecting false claims requires an additional step beyond simply understanding the claim. When consumers are overloaded with too much information, when they need to make a judgment or decision quickly, or when they try to do too many things at once, they are less able to engage in the extra effort required for unbelieving. So, under these circumstances, they are more likely to believe false claims to be true. Information overload, time pressure, and multi-tasking are facts of contemporary everyday life, so consumers may have difficulties rejecting false claims even more today than in previous decades.

Can distraction affect important decisions? Evidence indicates that it can. In a fascinating study, participants read statements about two crime reports that crawled across the bottom of a television screen, just like a weather, business, or sports bulletin. True statements were printed in black and false statements were printed in red. The false statements suggested that the first defendant was innocent and the second was guilty, or vice versa. Participants were sometimes distracted by multi-tasking while they read the crime report. The distraction greatly influenced their judgments. On average, distracted participants recommended 11 years in prison for the accused party when the false statements were exacerbating (made to appear worse) and only six years in prison when the false statements were extenuating (accompanied by an explanation). In contrast, participants who were not distracted recommended approximately the same prison sentence (about six years) in both cases. Thus, distracted participants had difficulty unbelieving false statements, despite the fact that true statements were printed in black, and false statements were printed in red. Of course, unbelieving false statements is even more difficult when the real-world mass-media fails to tell us which information is true and which is false.

Habit Theory

Habits are repetitive behaviors that are relatively uninfluenced by current intentions, goals, and attitudes.[38] Habits are cued instead by the environment. When behaviors are performed repeatedly in the same context over time, a behavior-context association is formed in memory, and this association is surprisingly resistant to change. Furthermore, whenever this context is encountered in the future, the habit is cued automatically and alternative actions are inhibited. Habits are important because about 45% of consumer behavior is repeated almost daily. Consumers tend to buy the same brands, shop in the same stores, and eat similar meals routinely every week.

Habit formation requires the performance of repetitive behaviors in stable contexts. Daily behaviors—like making coffee, having breakfast, watching TV, driving to work, and so on—are frequently performed in the same contexts (e.g., performed in the same room around the same time) and, over time, they are performed automatically, with little conscious intention or awareness. By contrast, infrequently performed behaviors—like donating blood, going to the doctor's office, voting, and so on—tend to be performed in unstable contexts. A meta-analysis of studies examining the correlations between past behavior, intentions, and future behavior showed that in stable contexts, past behavior was strongly correlated with future behavior and intentions were weakly correlated with future behavior.[39] However, this pattern was reversed for behaviors performed irregularly in unstable contexts: past behavior was weakly correlated with future behavior and intentions were strongly correlated with future behavior.

Additional evidence for the importance of stable contexts was provided by a study examining response latencies, or the speed with which people can answer questions presented on a computer monitor. Participants were asked to press one key on their keypad if string of letters presented on the monitor was a word (e.g., running, jogging), and to press another key if the string of letters was a non-word (e.g., afworbu, lemphor). Before the letter string was presented, different contexts for running and jogging were presented subliminally (e.g., gym, forest). For participants who jogged frequently in the same location, response times were faster when the prime matched this location. No priming effect was found for non-runners or for people who ran in several different locations.

A recent field experiment also tested the role of stable contexts in the cuing of habitual behaviors.[40] Many consumers frequently eat popcorn while watching movies in a movie theater. For these people, a strong popcorn–theater association should be stored in memory. No such association should be available for people who rarely eat popcorn in theaters. In the experiment, habitual or non-habitual popcorn eaters watched a movie in a theater or watched music videos in a campus meeting room. In addition, participants were either given fresh, tasty popcorn or one-week-old stale popcorn. While watching a movie in a theater, habitual popcorn eaters ate a lot of popcorn regardless of whether the popcorn was fresh or stale. However, when watching music videos in a meeting room, habitual popcorn eaters and non-habitual popcorn eaters ate more popcorn when it was fresh than when it was stale. Hence, habits lead people to repeat behaviors performed in stable contexts even when the behaviors are unrewarding. Changing the context breaks the habit and allows attitudes and intentions to guide behavior instead.

One important implication of **habit theory** is that the best time to break a bad habit is when the context changes, like when a person moves to a new apartment or a new house, or when a person starts a new job. Another important implication of habit theory is that the best way to develop new good habits

Habits are powerful behavioral drivers that people oftentimes continue to act upon, even when the results may be unfulfilling.

© Foodio/Shutterstock.com

is to form **implementation intentions**, or behavioral intentions to perform specific actions at specific times and places.[41] The more specific the preplanned actions and contexts are, the better the new habits are likely to be. Forming implementation intentions creates behavior-context associations in memory, and the stronger these associations are, the more likely a person is to perform the behavior automatically when the appropriate context is encountered. For example, in one study consumers were asked to form implementation intentions regarding when and how they will use a healthy cleansing product during the upcoming two weeks.[42] Compared to consumers in the control condition, consumers in the implementation intentions condition were more likely to use the product, and they actually consumed three times more of the product. Forming implementation intentions and forging strong and specific behavior-context associations in memory is a good way to develop good habits.

FIGURE 6.1 | Correlations among Past Behavior, Intentions, and Future Behavior for Frequently versus Infrequently Performed Behaviors

---

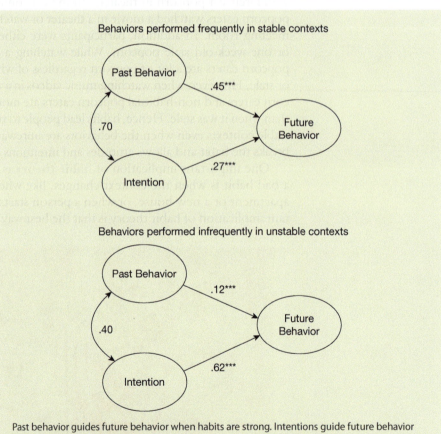

Past behavior guides future behavior when habits are strong. Intentions guide future behavior when habits are weak.

***Larger numbers indicate stronger correlations. For behaviors performed frequently in stable contexts, future behavior is more strongly correlated with past behavior than with intentions. However, for behaviors performed infrequently in unstable contexts, future behavior is more strongly correlated with intentions than with past behavior.

OBJECTIVE ⑤ ## Cognitive Neuroscience

Scientists are beginning to understand how the brain influences thinking and behavior. The scientific study of this topic is known as cognitive neuroscience. As Figure 6.2 indicates, the brain consists of three main structures: the forebrain, the midbrain, and the hindbrain.[43] The forebrain includes the cerebral cortex, the basal ganglia, the limbic system, the thalamus, and the hypothalamus. The cerebral cortex controls thinking, reasoning, judgment, and decision making. The basal ganglia are groups of neurons that control motor movements. The limbic system influences motivation, emotion, learning, and memory. This system helps people adapt to changes in the environment, and it has three main parts: the septum, the amygdala, and the hippocampus. The septum and the amygdala influence anger and fear. The hippocampus influences learning and memory, and when damaged, people are often unable to form new memories. The word hippocampus is Greek for seahorse, which describes the

FIGURE 6.2 | Structures of the Brain

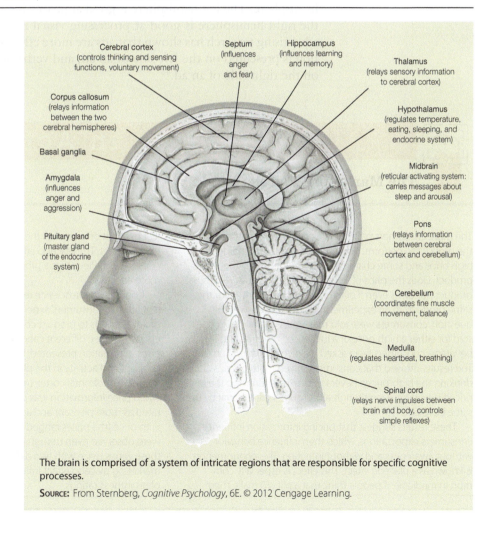

The brain is comprised of a system of intricate regions that are responsible for specific cognitive processes.

SOURCE: From Sternberg, *Cognitive Psychology*, 6E. © 2012 Cengage Learning.

general shape of this brain structure. The thalamus is the main relay station for sensory information transmitting to the brain. The hypothalamus controls the endocrine system, which influences feeding, fighting, fleeing, and mating.

The midbrain consists of the reticular activating system, which influences consciousness, alertness, sleep patterns, and partially influences respiration and heart rate. Finally, the hindbrain consists of the cerebellum, the pons, and the medulla oblongata. The cerebellum influences motor movements, balance, and coordination. Pons is Latin for bridge, and the pons serves as a type of bridge or relay station. The medulla oblongata controls respiration and heart rate, as well as swallowing and digesting food.

Neuroscientists have also shown that the cerebral cortex is divided into two halves: the left hemisphere and the right hemisphere. The left hemisphere influences language and movement, whereas the right hemisphere influences spatial visualization and comprehension. The two hemispheres are connected by the corpus collosum, a collection of neurons that allows the two hemispheres to communicate with each other. This is important because information processed in the right visual field is transmitted to the left hemisphere, and information processed in the left visual field is transmitted to the right hemisphere. The left hemisphere is good at processing verbal information, and the right hemisphere is good at processing visual information. Consequently, advertising research has shown that ads are more effective when visual information is presented on the left side of an ad, and verbal information is presented on the right side of an ad.[44]

Marketing in Action

The Marketing Placebo Effect

The more consumers pay for a product, the better they expect the product to perform. However, some retailers charge a high price and some charge a low price for exactly the same product. Does the price of a product influence how well the product performs even if different prices are charged for the same product? In an experiment designed to answer this question, consumers were told that SoBe Adrenaline Rush sold for either a high price or a low price.[45] After tasting this beverage, consumers were asked to solve intellectual puzzles. The results showed that consumers solved more puzzles after drinking the high-priced beverage than after drinking the low-priced beverage, even though all consumers drank exactly the same beverage.

These results suggest that pricing information influences consumers' expectations, which then influence behavior without awareness and without intention. This phenomenon is known as a placebo effect. This effect is especially common in medicine: if people think that a pill will make them

feel better, it often makes them feel better, even if the pill has no real effect. The placebo effect also occurs in marketing: if consumers believe that a product will be effective, it seems more effective.

Cognitive neuroscience research using fMRI brain scanning reveals that consumers' expectations also influence how the brain responds to product consumption.[46] When consumers tasted three different cabernet sauvignon wines with no price information presented, the wines were rated as equally pleasant and activity in the pleasure center of the brain, the medial orbitofrontal cortex (mOFC), did not differ. However, when price information was presented, the wines were rated as more pleasant and activity in the mOFC increased with price (the prices ranged from $5 to $90). These results were observed even though participants tasted two of the three wines twice with two different price levels! Hence, the marketing placebo effect influences brain activity as well as pleasantness ratings.

Ethics

There are many different types of marketing placebo effects. If a consumer believes that a product will be highly effective, the product is often more effective. Marketing placebo effects have been observed for self-help tapes, energy drinks, coffee, and other products. Even when two products are identical, the higher-priced product or the product with the more prestigious brand name often seems better. Is it ethical to market subliminal self-help tapes that don't work? Is it ethical to market products that produce placebo effects, like homeopathic medicines, herbal remedies, and New Age cures? Where should the FDA draw the line?

Each cerebral hemisphere is divided into four lobes: the frontal lobe, the parietal lobe, the temporal lobe, and the occipital lobe.[47] The frontal lobe influences higher-order thought processes, such as abstract reasoning, problem solving, planning, and decision making. Broca's area, which is crucial for speech, is located in a small section of the left frontal lobe. The parietal lobe, in the upper back portion of each hemisphere, influences attention, touch, pain, temperature, and limb position. The temporal lobe, on the side of each hemisphere, influences language on the left side and visual memories on the right side. Wernicke's area, which is crucial for language comprehension, is located in a small section of the left temporal lobe. Finally, the occipital lobe is located at the back of the head and is important for visual information processing. Brain scanning procedures, such as functional magnetic resonance imaging (fMRI), are enabling cognitive neuroscientists to develop increasingly more precise maps of brain structures and functions.

Chapter Summary

Automatic information processing refers to mental processes that influence judgments, feelings, and behaviors, but occur without awareness or intention. Automatic information processing is useful and adaptive because it enables people to perform some simple tasks without thinking. This allows people to think more carefully about other tasks they need to perform. A response becomes automatic through practice and repetition. One particularly useful skill that people have learned automatically is thin-slice inferencing. Thin slices or brief observations of another person's behavior often tell us a surprisingly large amount of information about the person.

The priming effect is another important example of automatic information processing. Recent or frequent exposure to an idea presented on television, on the radio, in a magazine, in a book, or in a conversation can change the way people think about subsequently encountered ambiguous information. An unfamiliar product can seem expensive or inexpensive, versatile or easy to use, or good or bad depending on what information was primed before examining the product. Priming can also influence behavior as well as judgment. People often behave in a manner consistent with the implications of a prime and do so without awareness or intention.

Key Terms

adaptive unconscious
assimilation effect
automatic information
    processing
contrast effect
distraction effect
explicit attitudes

explicit memory
habit theory
implementation intentions
Implicit Association Test (IAT)
implicit attitudes
implicit memory
intuition

mindset priming effect
naïve theory priming effect
placebo effect
procedural priming effect
subliminal priming
thin-slice inferences
truth effect

Review and Discussion

1. What is automatic information processing?
2. Give some examples of automatic information processing.
3. When are attitudes likely to come to mind automatically?
4. How does a mental process become automatic?
5. What are the benefits of automatic information processing?

6. Why do people trust their intuition more than they should?
7. Give some examples of thin-slice inferences.
8. Give some examples of the priming effect.
9. What is the IAT?
10. When is the IAT most useful?

Short Application Exercises

1. Subliminal sexual images are sometimes used in ads for alcohol. Do people have a strong association in memory between sex and alcohol? Why are people afraid of subliminal advertising? Should they be afraid?
2. Discuss ads for Cialis, Viagra, and other drugs for erectile dysfunction. What automatic information processing principles would be most useful for selling these types of products?
3. Describe the ways the priming effect could influence you after watching TV, reading the newspaper, or reading a novel.
4. Visit the website for the IAT (www.implicit. harvard.edu) and take the test. What have you learned from this test?

Managerial Application

"What's in a name? A rose by any other name would smell as sweet." Although this may be true in Shakespeare, it's not true in marketing. Because of thin-slice inferences, a brand name often tells consumers quite a bit about the brand, including information about its identity and personality.

A good brand name is easy to pronounce, because brand names that are easy to pronounce are easier to think about and are more memorable. A good brand name also primes product applications, the appearance of the product, the key features of the product, and an appropriate mindset. A good brand name could also prime a specific consumer lifestyle, so as to appeal to members of a target consumer segment.

Your Challenge:

Keeping all of these thin-slice inferences and priming effects in mind, generate three good brand names for each of the following products, and explain why each brand name could be effective.

1. Personal computer
2. Smartphone
3. 3-D TV
4. Hawaiian vacation package

End Notes

1 Berger, J., and Fitzsimons, G. (2008). Dogs on the Street, Pumas on Your Feet: How Cues in the Environment Influence Product Evaluation and Choice. *Journal of Marketing Research*, 45: 1–14.

2 Kahneman, D. (2010). *Thinking, Fast and Slow*. New York: Farrar, Straus and Giroux.

3 Chaiken, S., and Trope, Y. (1999). *Dual-Process Theories in Social Psychology*. New York: Guilford; Shiffrin, R.M., and Schneider, W. (1977). Controlled and Automatic Human Information Processing: II. Perceptual Learning, Automatic Attending, and a General Theory. *Psychological Review*, 84: 127–190.

4 Bargh, J. (2002). Losing Consciousness: Automatic Influences on Consumer Judgment, Behavior, and Motivation. *Journal of Consumer Research*, 29: 280–285.

5 Nisbett, R. E., and Wilson, T. D. (1977). Telling More Than We Can Know: Verbal Reports on Mental Processes. *Psychological Review*, 84: 231–259.

6 Gilbert, D., Gill, M. J., and Wilson, T. D. (2002). The Future Is Now: Temporal Correction in Affective Forecasting. *Organizational Behavior and Human Decision Processes*, 88: 430–444.

7 Fazio, R. H., Sanbonmatsu, D. M., Powell, M. C., and Kardes, F. R. (1986). On the Automatic Activation of Attitudes. *Journal of Personality and Social Psychology*, 50: 229–238.

8 Damasio, A. (1994). *Descartes' Error: Emotion, Reason, and the Human Brain*. New York: Grosset/Putnam.

9 Ambady, N., Krabbenhoft, M. A., and Hogan, D. (2006). The 30-Sec Sale: Using Thin-Slice Judgments to Evaluate Sales Effectiveness. *Journal of Consumer Psychology*, 16: 4–13.

10 Wilson, T. D., and Schooler, J. W. (1991). Thinking Too Much: Introspection Can Reduce the Quality of Preferences and Decisions. *Journal of Personality and Social Psychology*, 60: 181–192.

11 Wilson, T. D., Lisle, D. J., Schooler, J. W., Hodges, S. D., Klaaren, K. J., and LaFleur, S. J. (1993). Introspecting About Reasons Can Reduce Post-Choice Satisfaction. *Personality and Social Psychology Bulletin*, 19: 331–339.

12 McMackin, J., and Slovic, P. (2000). When Does Explicit Justification Impair Decision Making? *Journal of Applied Cognitive Psychology*, 14: 527–541.

13 Kardes, F. R. (2006). When Should Consumers and Managers Trust Their Intuition? *Journal of Consumer Psychology*, 16: 20–24.

14 Wyer, R. S. (2008). The Role of Knowledge Accessibility in Cognition and Behavior: Implications for Consumer Information Processing, 31–76. In C. P. Haugtvedt, P. M. Herr, and F. R. Kardes (eds.), *Handbook of Consumer Psychology*. Mahwah, NJ: Lawrence Erlbaum Associates.

15 Herr, P. M. (1989). Priming Price: Prior Knowledge and Context Effects. *Journal of Consumer Research*, 16: 67–75.

16 Yi, Y. (1990). The Effects of Contextual Priming in Print Advertisements. *Journal of Consumer Research*, 17: 215–222.

17 Shrum, L. J., Wyer, R. S., and O'Guinn, T. C. (1998). The Effects of Television Consumption on Social Perceptions: The Use of Priming Procedures to Investigate Psychological Processes. *Journal of Consumer Research*, 24: 447–458.

18 Dijksterhuis, A., Smith, P. K., van Baaren, R. B., and Wigboldus, D. H. J. (2005). The Unconscious Consumer: Effects of Environment on Consumer Behavior. *Journal of Consumer Psychology*, 15: 193–202.

19 Johnston, L. (2002). Behavioral Mimicry and Stigmatization. *Social Cognition*, 20: 18–35.

20 Bargh, J. A., Chen, M., and Burrows, L. (1996). The Automaticity of Social Behavior: Direct Effects of Trait Concept and Stereotype Activation on Action. *Journal of Personality and Social Psychology*, 71: 230–244.

21 Dijksterhuis, A., and van Knippenberg, A. (1998). The Relation Between Perception and Behavior or How to Win a Game of Trivial Pursuit. *Journal of Personality and Social Psychology*, 74: 865–877.

22 Shen, H. (2008). Procedural Priming and Consumer Judgments: Effects on the Impact of Positively and Negatively Valenced Information. *Journal of Consumer Research*, 34: 727–737.

23 Dhar, R., Huber, J., and Khan, U. (2007). The Shopping Momentum Effect. *Journal of Marketing Research*, 44: 370–378.

24 Xu, A. J., and Wyer, R. S. (2007). The Effect of Mindsets on Consumer Decision Strategies. *Journal of Consumer Research*, 34: 556–566.

25 Xu, A. J., and Wyer, R. S. (2008). The Comparative Mindset: From Animal Comparisons to Increased Purchase Intentions. *Psychological Science*, 19: 859–864.

26 Hirt, E. R., Kardes, F. R., and Markman, K. D. (2004). Activating a Mental Simulation Mindset through Generation of Alternatives: Implications for Debiasing in Related and Unrelated Domains. *Journal of Experimental Social Psychology*, 40: 374–383.

27 Schwarz, N. (2004). Metacognitive Experiences in Consumer Judgment and Decision Making. *Journal of Consumer Psychology*, 14: 332–348.

28 Cho, H.J., and Schwarz, N. (2008). Of Great Art and Untalented Artists: Effort Information and the Flexible Construction of Judgmental Heuristics. *Journal of Consumer Psychology*, 18: 205–211.

29 Deval, H., Mantel, S.P., Kardes, F.R. and Posavac, S.S. (2012). Flexible Inferences: How Naïve Theory Activation Leads Consumers to Draw Different Conclusions from the Same Information. Unpublished manuscript, Dalhousie University.

30 Strahan, E. J., Spencer, S. J., and Zanna, M. P. (2002). Subliminal Priming and Persuasion: Striking While the Iron Is Hot. *Journal of Experimental Social Psychology*, 38: 556–568.

31 North, A. C., Hargreaves, D. J., and McKendrick, J. (1997). In-Store Music Affects Product Choice. *Nature*, 390: 132.

32 Greenwald, A. G., McGhee, D. C., and Schwarz, J. (1998). Measuring Individual Differences in Implicit Social Cognition: The Implicit Association Test. *Journal of Personality and Social Psychology*, 74: 1464–1480; Maison, D., Greenwald, A. G., and Bruin, R. H. (2004). Predictive Validity of the Implicit Association Test in Studies of Brands, Consumer Attitudes, and Behavior. *Journal of Consumer Psychology*, 14: 405–415.

33 Brunel, F. F., Tietje, B. C., and Greenwald, A. G. (2004). Is the Implicit Association Test a Valid and Valuable Measure of Implicit Consumer Cognition? *Journal of Consumer Psychology*, 14: 385–404.

34 Schwarz, N. (2004). Metacognitive Experiences in Consumer Judgment and Decision Making. *Journal of Consumer Psychology*, 14: 332–348.

35 Hawkins, S. A., and Hoch, S. J. (1992). Low-Involvement Learning: Memory Without Evaluation. *Journal of Consumer Research*, 19: 212–225; Hawkins, S. A., Hoch, S. J., and Meyers-Levy, J. (2001). Low-Involvement Learning: Repetition and Coherence in Familiarity and Belief. *Journal of Consumer Psychology*, 11: 1–12; Law, S., Hawkins, S. A., and Craik, F. I. M. (1998). Repetition-Induced Belief in the Elderly: Rehabilitating Age-Related Memory Deficits. *Journal of Consumer Research*, 25: 91–107; Skurnik, I., Yoon, C., Park, D. C., and Schwarz, N. (2005). How Warnings about False Claims Become Recommendations. *Journal of Consumer Research*, 31: 713–724.

36 Richter, T., Schroeder, S., and Wohrmann, B. (2009). You Don't Have to Believe Everything You Read: Background Knowledge Permits Fast and Efficient Validation of Information. *Journal of Personality and Social Psychology*, 96: 538–558.

37 Gilbert, D. T., Tafarodi, R. W., and Malone, P. S. (1993). You Can't Not Believe Everything You Read. *Journal of Personality and Social Psychology,* 65: 221–233.

38 Wood, W., and Neal, D.T. (2007). A New Look at Habits and the Habit-Goal Interface. *Psychological Review*, 114: 842–862;Wood, W., and Neal, D.T. (2008). The Habitual Consumer. *Journal of Consumer Psychology*, 19: 579–592.

39 Ouellette, J. A., and Wood, W. (1998). Habit and Intention in Everyday Life: The Multiple Processes by Which Past Behavior Predicts Future Behavior. *Psychological Bulletin*, 124: 54–74.

40 Neal, D. T., Wood, W., Wu, M., and Kurlander, D. (2011). The Pull of the Past: When Do Habits Persist Despite Conflict with Motives? *Personality and Social Psychology Bulletin*, 37: 1428–1437.

41 Gollwitzer, P. M., and Sheeran, P. (2009). Self-Regulation of Consumer Decision Making and Behavior: The Role of Implementation Intentions. *Journal of Consumer Psychology*, 19: 593–607.

42 Kardes, F. R., Cronley, M.L., and Posavac, S.S. (2005). Using Implementation Intentions to Increase New Product Consumption: A Field Experiment. In F. R. Kardes, P. M. Herr, and J. Nantel (eds.), *Applying Social Cognition to Consumer-Focused Strategy.* Mahwah, NJ: Erlbaum, 219–233.

43 Sternberg, R. J., and Sternberg, K. (2009). *Cognitive Psychology,* 6th ed. Belmont, CA: Wadsworth, Cengage Learning.

44 Janiszewski, C. (1990). The Influence of Print Advertisement Organization on Affect Toward a Brand Name. *Journal of Consumer Research*, 17: 53–65.

45 Shiv, B., Carmon, Z., and Ariely, D. (2005). Placebo Effects of Marketing Actions: Consumers May Get What They Pay For. *Journal of Marketing Research*, 37: 383–393.

46 Plassmann, H., O'Doherty, J., Shiv, B., and Rangel, A. (2008). Marketing Actions Can Modulate Neural Representations of Experienced Pleasantness. *Proceedings of the National Academy of Sciences*, 105: 1050–1054.

47 Sternberg, R. J., and Sternberg, K. (2009). *Cognitive Psychology,* 6th ed. Belmont, CA: Wadsworth, Cengage Learning.

MOTIVATION AND EMOTION

OBJECTIVES   *After studying this chapter, you should be able to …*

1 Define motivation and emotion.

2 Explain approach and avoidance.

3 Match advertising approaches to attitude functions.

4 Explain the role of consistency in motivation and persuasion.

5 Explain how emotions evoked by one stimulus influence emotional responses to other stimuli.

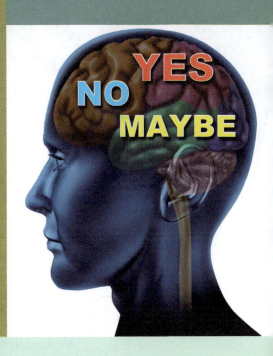

DIRECTV

DIRECTV recently ran a series of television commercials using an unusual mix of logic and humor. Case in point: In the 2012 Charlie Sheen commercial, the narrator says, "When you have cable and can't record all your shows you feel unhappy. When you feel unhappy you go to happy hour. When you go to happy hour you're up for anything. When you're up for anything you head to a Turkish Bath House. When you head to a Turkish Bath House you meet Charlie Sheen and when you meet Charlie Sheen you re-enact scenes from *Platoon* with Charlie Sheen. Don't re-enact scenes from *Platoon* with Charlie Sheen. Get rid of cable and upgrade to DIRECTV."[1]

When logical arguments build on one another, as they do in this commercial, you have a syllogism. If the premises of a syllogism are true, the conclusion that follows must be true.

This commercial is funny because the likelihood of the premises being true is very low, but the chain of events is described as if it was inevitable. Charlie Sheen is also known for being a wild and crazy guy, and this adds to the humor. But does humor work? Does it make sense to mix logic and emotion in a television commercial? When does humor increase persuasion by making us feel good, and when does humor decrease persuasion by distracting us? What other types of emotions are important in advertising? These are the types of questions addressed in this chapter.

By connecting the viewer to a product's message through humor or other emotional means, advertisers gain a unique opportunity for connection with their target market.

OBJECTIVE **1**

An Overview of Motivation and Emotion

Motivation (needs or drives) and emotions (feelings or affective responses) encourage consumers to act. **Motivation** is a driving force that moves or incites us to act and is the underlying basis of all behavior. Individuals are driven to satisfy their needs, wants, and desires. **Emotion** (or *emotional* and *affective responses*) is a person's affect—feelings and moods—plus arousal.

Motivation and emotion are linked in a number of ways, which is why they are covered together in this chapter. Motivations and emotions are linked because consumers feel positive emotions when motivations are satisfied and negative emotions when motivations are not satisfied. Consumers also often describe motivations and emotions similarly, saying, "I feel like eating some Pizza Hut pizza," or "I feel like drinking Coca-Cola," or "I feel like reading my Consumer Behavior textbook," and so on. Furthermore, motivations and emotions focus attention and energize behavior. Motivations focus attention on goal-relevant objects, and emotions focus attention on emotional objects. This chapter examines how motivation and emotion influence consumer behavior by examining the process of motivation and several motivation and emotion theories.

The Process of Motivation

What creates the driving force of motivation in a person? Motivation begins when a person feels a need that requires satisfaction. In general, **needs** are desires that arise when a consumer's current state does not match the consumer's preferred state. Physiological needs, such as the need for air, water, food, sex, and protection from the environment (clothing and shelter), are *innate needs* or *primary needs*. Psychological needs are learned as we grow and are socialized, such as needs for affection, companionship, power, self-esteem, and intellectual stimulation. These are *secondary needs*. Needs should also be distinguished from *wants*. Although some people tend to use these two terms synonymously, there are differences. Needs are automatic and required; if you wake up at 2 A.M. "dying" of thirst, for instance, you need something to quench it. Wants are learned manifestations of our needs, e.g., only a glass of chocolate milk will take care of your 2 A.M. problem. Some marketers also distinguish between needs and wants by classifying wants as product-specific needs.

Craving chocolate milk is a product-specific need.

Needs are aroused via three routes: physiological, emotional, and cognitive. We have already touched on physiologically based needs. Physical changes in the body trigger need **arousal**. For example, your stomach growls when you haven't eaten in several hours; you shiver when your body temperature drops; and your eyes blur and feel scratchy when you are deprived of sleep. Emotions also lead to need arousal. For example, feeling bored or frustrated at work may lead to the need for a vacation; feeling lonely may lead to a need to go to a social event. Finally, arousal can come from our thoughts. Recalling the date of your mother's birthday may prompt a need to purchase and send her a gift. Cognitive arousal is tied closely to the environment because environmental situations and stimuli often trigger cognitive arousal. For example, seeing your roommate's new pair of running shoes may remind you of how old your own shoes are and trigger the need to shop.

Once a need is aroused, a state of tension is created that energizes a person to reduce or eliminate the need, returning to a preferred state, called the **goal** (or *goal-object, goal-state*). This tension is called a **drive**, and the degree or amount of tension influences the urgency with which actions are taken to return to the desired goal-state. Thus, motivation focuses attention on goals and drives us to act.

Motivations focus attention by producing a **valuation effect** and a **devaluation effect**.[2] When consumers are extremely hungry, they rate food products as more desirable (the valuation effect), and they rate nonfood products as less desirable (the devaluation effect). Similarly, when consumers are extremely thirsty, they rate beverages as more desirable (the valuation effect), and they rate non-beverages as less desirable (the devaluation effect). Surprisingly, hungry or thirsty consumers devalue money, even though money can be used to buy food or beverages. Furthermore, the devaluation effect is usually larger than the valuation effect, and these effects occur only when powerful motivations are present. For example, a famished consumer is motivated to attain one goal—to satisfy his hunger immediately. Thus, he will devalue any objects (including money) in an attempt to reduce hunger. This is one reason some consumers stand in line and pay exorbitant prices for food and beverages at amusement parks and sporting events. In this situation, they value food and beverages and devalue both time and money.

When faced with a desperate situation such as extreme thirst or hunger, consumers will sacrifice time and be willing to pay higher prices to satisfy that urgent need.

Neil Tingle/Alamy

Motivations also influence the direction of behavior. Two directions are possible: **approach**, or movement toward a desired object or outcome, and **avoidance**, or movement away from an undesired object or outcome. For example, most consumers seek good entertainment; lack of such entertainment causes dissatisfaction. On the other hand, many consumers don't enjoy shopping in crowded retail environments and are likely to avoid shopping at peak times unless forced to do so. Motivations also influence what goals consumers pursue and how intensely and persistently consumers pursue these goals. In other words, our hobbies, interests, and needs influence what goals we pursue and how intensely and persistently we pursue these goals. Consumers who love collectible objects (e.g., wine, comic books, stamps, coins, works of art) pursue these objects frequently (e.g., they search for these objects often), intensely (they search everywhere, including stores, flea markets, and the Internet), and persistently (they search for years).

OBJECTIVE ## Motivation and Human Needs

Whatever the direction of motivation, needs are the root of the motivational process. Several psychologists and researchers have developed theories and models related to human needs. Some of the most popular are reviewed in the following subsections.

Drive Theory and Maslow's Hierarchy of Needs **Drive theory** is one of the earliest theories of motivation.[3] Drive theory maintains that people have several basic physiological needs, such as needs for food, water, air, etc. When people do not get enough food, water, air, or other basic requirements for survival, a source of energy known as drive compels people to behave in ways that reduce these drives. For example, eating reduces the drive for food. Drinking reduces the drive for water, and breathing reduces the drive for air.

Physiological needs are the most basic needs experienced by people. Building on drive theory, Abraham Maslow suggested that people also have higher-order needs and desires.[4] After all physiological needs are met, people become preoccupied with safety and security needs, including needs for shelter and protection. Once safety and security needs are met, people move on to the next level of social needs, i.e., the need for belongingness and love. At this level, social relationships, affection, belonging, and choosing the right spouse become important. After these needs are met, people advance to the ego or esteem level. At this level, people need to feel competent and important. Finally, the highest level is self-actualization, which is the state of mind of people who feel that they have reached their full potential. Theoretically, relatively few people have reached this ultimate level. It should be noted that while each need is defined separately, overlap occurs among the categories. No need is ever completely satisfied, but a person cannot progress upward along Maslow's hierarchy until lower level needs are primarily satisfied. The full hierarchy is shown in Figure 7.1.

Marketers design clever promotions to appeal to all levels of needs in Maslow's hierarchy. For instance, watch any late night television show, and you will see big, juicy hamburgers and hot, crispy fries floating across the screen to tempt late night cravings. Companies that market home security systems, insurance policies, and even clothing, promote safety and security needs. The Land's End clothing catalog has featured a story about how one of the brand's winter coats kept a person stranded in the wilderness alive. Products consumed in social groups in social gathering places, such as food and beverages, stress good friends, good times, and a feeling of belonging. eHarmony, an online dating service, emphasizes the importance of finding "that true soul mate," while in the 1980s AT&T encouraged you to "reach out and touch someone." Examples of esteem needs are everywhere from health and beauty ads to automobile ads. L'Oreal says that you're "worth it"; Lexus is for when "you've arrived"; Maybelline asks, "Maybe she's born with it?" Finally, self-actualization needs, while realized by relatively few, are certainly pursued, and marketers use

FIGURE 7.1 | Maslow's Hierarchy of Needs

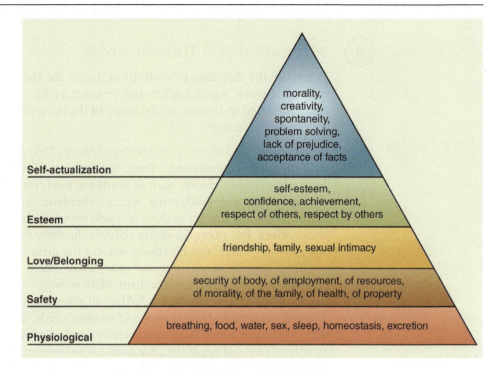

these needs to help people reach for more. The U.S. Army and Air Force tap into this need with their slogans, "Be all that you can be," and "The sky's the limit." Gatorade asks, "Is it in you?" and Nike says, "Just Do It!"

Self-Determination Theory This theory builds on **Maslow's hierarchy of needs** by distinguishing between intrinsic motivation and extrinsic motivation.[5] Intrinsic motivation refers to the desire to pursue an activity or goal for its own sake, rather than for an extrinsic reward, such as money. Extrinsic motivation refers to the desire to pursue an activity or goal in order to receive a reward, such as money or praise. This distinction is important because people are usually more creative, hard-working, and more fulfilled and happy when they pursue intrinsic goals rather than extrinsic goals. According to self-determination theory, intrinsic motivation is highest when autonomy, belongingness, and competence (the ABCs of self-determination) are high. This means that intrinsic motivation is greater when people feel that they have free choice (i.e., they are not forced to do something), are part of an important group or organization, and feel that they are very good at what they do. For example, consumers who view themselves as knowledgeable about wines and have income adequate to purchase high quality wines are more likely to enjoy shopping for and consuming these products.

The Trio of Needs Some consumer researchers believe that Maslow's list of needs can be simplified to three key elements particularly important for consumer behavior. The need for *power* refers to the consumer's desire to control other people, objects (e.g., money), and the environment (e.g., one's home or work)

Some product advertisements appeal to the need for achievement.

Image Courtesy of The Advertising Archives

because power increases the likelihood that the consumer can acquire the things he or she wants. The need for *affiliation* refers to the need for belongingness and friendship or the desire to be a member of a personally important social group. People with high affiliation needs are socially dependent and choose products they feel others will approve of. The need for *achievement* refers to the need to accomplish difficult tasks (e.g., completing a college degree, getting a high-paying job) and to be successful. After all, no one wants to be a "loser." High achievement is a valuable promotional tool when targeting well-educated and affluent consumers.

So far, we have seen that consumers have many different motivations and needs. Some are physical (e.g., food, water, air) and some are emotional (e.g., belongingness). Next, let's switch gears and discuss cognitive needs. Cognition refers to purposeful thinking or information processing. Some types of thoughts and ideas "feel right" and make consumers feel at ease and comfortable. Others feel bad and make consumers feel awkward or uncomfortable. People have a need for cognitive consistency.[6] Typically, consistent thoughts feel right, and inconsistent thoughts feel wrong. Three consistency theories provide explanations for consumers' need for consistency in their thinking: attitude function theory, balance theory, and cognitive dissonance theory.

OBJECTIVE (3)

Attitude Function Theory This theory describes four major types of attitudes.[7] Attitudes that serve the *knowledge function* summarize large amounts of information to simplify the world and help consumers make decisions. Attitudes that serve the *value-expressive function* communicate important beliefs to others and help consumers interact with each other more efficiently. Attitudes that serve the *ego-defensive function* help consumers feel safe and secure and good about themselves. Finally, attitudes that serve the *adjustment function* help consumers approach pleasure and avoid pain more quickly and efficiently. Persuasive messages that are positive and consistent with the underlying function of a consumer's attitude are more likely to feel right and be effective. On the other hand, persuasive messages that are inconsistent with an attitude function are more likely to be ignored. Thus, it is critical for marketers to understand which functions consumers draw on when evaluating their products.

Different persuasion techniques are needed for different attitude functions. Information and facts are useful for changing attitudes that serve the **knowledge function**, but not for changing attitudes that serve other functions. Image appeals are useful for changing attitudes that serve the **value-expressive function**. Authority and fear appeals are useful for changing attitudes that serve the **ego-defensive function**. Finally, hedonic (or pleasure/pain) appeals are useful for changing attitudes that serve the **adjustment function**. Should anyone doubt the power of attitude functions, observe someone trying to change another person's religious attitudes (which serve the ego-defensive function) with facts (which serve the knowledge function). Similarly, try changing someone's attitudes about a favorite guilty pleasure such as smoking (which serves the adjustment function) with imagery such as yellow teeth (which serves the value-expressive function).

Understanding a consumer's regulatory focus is also important. **Regulatory focus theory** suggests that consumers regulate or control their behavior by using either a **promotion focus** or a **prevention focus**.[8] A promotion focus is concerned with the presence or absence of positive outcomes and with aspirations and accomplishment. A prevention focus is concerned with the presence or absence of negative outcomes and with protection and responsibilities. Some consumers are usually more promotion-focused, while others tend to be more prevention-focused. Messages that encourage consumers to think about their aspirations and accomplishments foster a promotion focus. Messages that encourage consumers to think about protection and responsibilities foster a prevention focus.

Combining attitude function theory and regulatory focus theory results in a 4 × 2 matrix of persuasion techniques.[9] For maximum effectiveness, persuasive messages must match consumers' attitude functions and regulatory focus. Figure 7.2 lists major persuasive message types and the conditions under which each is most effective.

FIGURE 7.2 | Types of Advertisements and the Conditions Under Which Each Will Be Most Effective

Attitude Function	Promotion-Focused Ads	Prevention-Focused Ads
Knowledge	Factual appeals Logical arguments Comparative advertising	Mystery ads Surprise Confusion
Value expression	Image appeals Celebrity advertising	Nerd alert ads
Ego defense	Authority figures Experts	Fear appeals
Adjustment	Pleasure	Pain

Source: Adapted from Kardes & Cronley (2000).

For example, many ads for personal computers and other high-tech products provide information about brand attributes and benefits to inform consumers about these complex products. Usually, consumers need to be at least somewhat knowledgeable about these products to makes sense of the information. Rather than try to inform consumers, prevention-focused knowledge appeals attempt to confuse consumers by using unfamiliar technical information or surprising and unexpected information that leads consumers to rethink their attitudes. Mystery ads, or ads that do not reveal what is being advertised until the end of the message, can also encourage consumers to think more diligently about their attitudes.[10] Many dot.com companies use this approach, as did early ads for the Infiniti automobile.

Clynt Garnham Lifestyle/Alamy

Promotion-focused value-expressive appeals.

© iStockphoto.com/Squaredpixels

Promotion-focused ego-defensive appeal.

Promotion-focused, ego-defensive appeals use authority figures (e.g., political leaders, religious leaders, police officers) or experts (e.g., doctors, lawyers, executives) to convince consumers to change their attitudes about products and services that offer protection against accidents (e.g., insurance), theft (e.g., home and car security systems), and other uncertain, negative events. Such appeals are particularly useful for influencing political attitudes. Stereotypes, or negative attitudes toward specific groups, also serve an ego-defensive function by helping people feel better when they compare themselves to a group they perceive as inferior.

Adjustment appeals focus on simple hedonism, or the pleasure/pain principle. Consumers buy some types of products simply because they taste good (e.g., ice cream, candy, and other unhealthy but tasty foods and beverages) or feel good (e.g., alcohol, caffeine, cigarettes). In the same vein,

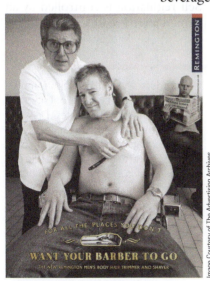

Image Courtesy of The Advertising Archives

Prevention-focused ego-defensive appeal.

consumers avoid some types of products because they taste bad (e.g., mouthwash, fiber cereals), or feel bad (e.g., pharmaceuticals that improve one's health despite aversive side effects, such as blood pressure medicines). Promotion-focused adjustment appeals focus on the benefits of guilty pleasures, such as high-calorie foods and beverages and entertainment products that no one wants to admit they like (e.g., movies such as *Dumb and Dumber* and gossip magazines). Facts and figures do not promote such products effectively (e.g., statistics do not convince consumers to quit smoking). Neither does image, because many guilty pleasures are consumed privately rather than publicly. Ego-defensive appeals are similarly ineffective because people like what they like, no matter what authorities or experts think.

Prevention-focused adjustment appeals are particularly useful for products that help consumers avoid pain, such as pain relievers (e.g., aspirin, acetaminophen, antacids, seltzers, laxatives, ointments). A recent ad for Excedrin, for example, shows an actor saying he does not know why or care how the product works,

Global Perspectives

Culture and Regulatory Focus

Most of the research published in leading scientific consumer behavior journals reports the results of experiments conducted in the United States. Of course, the United States is a western culture dominated by people with an independent self-view (Canada and Western Europe are similar in this outlook). This means that western consumers are primarily interested in maximizing their own outcomes and are not always concerned about what happens to other people. By contrast, in eastern cultures, such as those of Japan, China, and Eastern Europe, people have a more interdependent self-view. This means that these consumers are primarily interested in maximizing the outcomes of important groups in their lives, such as their families, friends, and co-workers.

Recent research on culture and regulatory focus shows that consumers with independent self-views often adopt a promotion focus.[11] These consumers are therefore more sensitive and responsive to promotion-focused ads because these ads match their promotion-focused regulatory orientation. By contrast, consumers with interdependent self-views often adopt a prevention focus. These consumers are more sensitive and responsive to prevention-focused ads because these ads match their prevention-focused regulatory orientation. Hence, cultural backgrounds have a powerful influence on regulatory focus, and regulatory focus in turn has a powerful influence on the relative effectiveness of promotion- versus prevention-focused advertisements.

it just works. In other words, no complex arguments, celebrities or experts are needed. Consumers want a product that eliminates headaches, and they don't care how or why the product works.

Self-Regulation Consumers often have admirable goals (such as avoiding unhealthy foods, exercising more, watching less mindless television, drinking less alcohol, quitting smoking, and quitting other bad habits) that they fail to reach due to problems with **self-regulation**, or self-control or willpower.[12] Self-regulation is necessary for making good decisions and avoiding bad ones—such as overeating, overspending, impulsive buying, compulsive spending, and making decisions that one will later regret. Self-regulation is controlled by an inner psychological resource called the *ego* (named after Freud's ego), and the

Ethics

Approximately 25% of the population of the United States is clinically obese. Obesity is a huge (pardon the pun) social problem because of the health risks associated with it, including increased risk for heart attacks, diabetes, and other health problems.

Of course, fast food restaurants, such as McDonald's, Burger King, and Wendy's, are very popular in the United States, and this popularity very likely contributes to the obesity problem. Recently, some morbidly obese U.S. consumers have brought lawsuits against McDonald's based on the fact that much of McDonald's food is very fattening and unhealthy and is therefore a major cause of the plaintiffs' obesity problems. The plaintiffs claim that McDonald's is slowly killing them. Does McDonald's have a moral responsibility to produce and market healthier food to help reduce the serious obesity problem in the United States? Or is it up to the individual consumer to decide what foods and how much of it is reasonable to consume? What do you think? What is the role of motivational psychological processes in wanting to eat unhealthy food in large quantities? Can individual consumers be expected to control the physiological and motivational processes that regulate their urge to eat?

availability of this resource at any particular time depends on several important psychological variables.

For example, imagine that you had to choose between a delicious looking slice of chocolate cake versus a healthy but less appetizing fruit salad. What would you do in this situation? If you choose with your heart and focus on your feelings, you will be more likely to choose the chocolate cake. However, if you choose with your head and focus on making a healthy choice, you will be more likely to choose the fruit salad. This experiment was actually conducted and the results showed that when consumers had unlimited time and energy for thinking about this problem, they were more likely to choose the healthy fruit salad.[13] However, if they were distracted and asked to memorize a string of numbers while performing this choice task, they were more likely to focus on feelings and choose the unhealthy chocolate cake.

Depleting or using up cognitive resources during a choice task often results in poorer choice decisions. However, depleting resources for one task can also leave fewer resources for subsequent tasks. In a classic demonstration of **ego depletion**, participants entered a lab filled with the wonderful aroma of fresh-baked chocolate chip cookies.[14] In the control condition, participants got to taste these cookies and rate them. However, in the experimental condition, participants were asked to taste and rate radishes. Next, all participants were asked to solve unsolvable anagrams, and the amount of time participants spent on this task served as the major dependent variable. The results showed that participants gave up sooner in the radish condition than in the cookie condition. Eating radishes while smelling chocolate chip cookies uses up **self-regulatory** resources, leaving fewer resources for follow-up tasks. It should be noted that this carry-over effect was not influenced by mood or by mental or physical fatigue. Instead, when one task depletes self-regulatory resources, people perform more poorly on subsequent tasks that require self-regulation or restraint.

Any task that uses up self-regulatory resources leaves fewer resources for tasks that come later. Ego depleting tasks come in many forms, and the radish task is just one example. Similar results were observed when self-regulatory resources were depleted by a complicated proofreading task. In the control condition, participants were asked to cross out every "e" in one page of text. In the experimental condition, participants were asked to cross out every "e" in one page of text except for those that preceded or followed a vowel. This type of task takes restraint because the first impulse is to cross out every "e," and not crossing out some of them uses up willpower. Similar results were also observed when participants performed a **Stroop task**, or a color naming task in which color words were printed in different colors. For example, the word "green" could be printed in the color red. In the control condition, participants were asked to name the color word and to try to ignore the color that the word is printed in. In the experimental condition, participants were asked to name the color that the word is printed in and to try to ignore the color word. The latter task is much more difficult and requires greater willpower, because the first impulse is to name the color word. Whenever ego depletion occurs, however, people perform more poorly on subsequent tasks. Ego depletion has been shown to lead to poorer consumer choice decisions in many different settings. In other words, ego depletion leads consumers to make a wide variety of gut decisions that rely on intuitions and feelings, rather

A Stroop task can lead to ego depletion which in turn can lead to poor consumer decisions.

than deliberative decisions that require making difficult trade-offs among attributes.[15] This occurs because gut decisions are quick and easy, and they do not require self-regulatory resources. Trade-off decisions, however, are slow and difficult, and they cannot be made without self-regulatory resources.

OBJECTIVE **4**

Balance Theory This theory focuses on the degree of consistency among three elements:

- p, the person or consumer who receives a persuasive message
- o, the other person (e.g., a friend, salesperson, or spokesperson) who recommends a particular product or service
- x, a stimulus such as a particular product or service[16]

Balance exists when the relationships among all three elements are positive (e.g., p likes o; o likes x; therefore, p should like x) or if two relations are negative and one is positive (e.g., my enemy's enemy is my friend). Balanced relationships are learned more quickly, are more memorable, and are rated as more pleasant. Consumers like balanced triads. However, the converse is also true. Consumers do not like imbalanced triads, where all three relations among the elements are negative (e.g., p dislikes o, o dislikes x, and p dislikes x) or two relations are positive and one is negative (e.g., p likes o, o likes x, and p dislikes x). Imbalanced triads produce unpleasant tension, and consumers are motivated to reduce this tension by changing one (or more) of the perceived relations within the p-o-x triad.

Let's look at an example. A recent Capital One Venture Card commercial shows actor Alec Baldwin endorsing the card while making fun of airlines by saying you should always turn off your electronic devices during takeoff and landing, even though he recently refused to do this in real life. If p is you, o is Alec Baldwin, and x is Capital One, imbalance exists if you like Baldwin (p likes o), Baldwin uses Capital One (o likes x), and you dislike Capital One (p dislikes x). There are three ways that you can bring about balance to this triad:

1. Change your attitude.
2. Deny the relationship.
3. Differentiate the relationships.

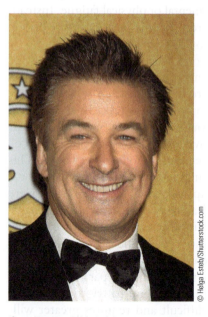

If you like Alec Baldwin but not necessarily the company Capital One, an advertisement with Baldwin endorsing Capital One's credit card may lead you to shift your attitudes toward the company and perhaps become a new customer for them.

© Helga Esteb/Shutterstock.com

First, you could change your attitude toward Capital One (p likes x) or change your attitude toward Baldwin (p dislikes o). Second, you could deny Baldwin's relationship with Capital One by suggesting that he doesn't really prefer Capital One; he just uses the card to gain huge endorsements. Third, you could resolve the imbalance through differentiation by indicating that you like Alec Baldwin the actor, but not Alec Baldwin the celebrity.

This type of analysis can be applied to almost any set of three elements. For example, consumer, p, likes cigarettes, o, which are linked to heart disease, x. It seems reasonable to assume that the consumer dislikes heart disease (p dislikes x). Therefore, the consumer must resolve the imbalance through attitude change (e.g., disliking cigarettes and thus quit smoking), denial (e.g., cigarettes do not cause heart disease), or differentiation (e.g., the consumer likes the way cigarettes make him feel but dislikes the long-term side effects). Many ads feature a likable celebrity, *o*, endorsing a new product, *x*. If the consumer, *p*, likes *o*, and if *o* likes *x*, subtle pressure toward consistency induces the consumer to form a favorable attitude toward *x* so that the triad is in balance. It's easy to see how balance theory explains why celebrity advertising can be highly effective (see Figure 7.3).

FIGURE **7.3** | **Balance Theory**

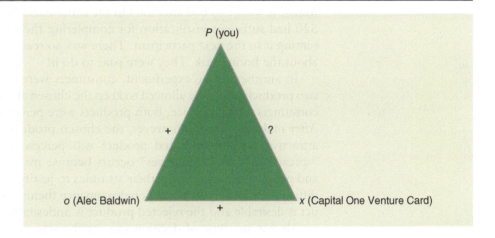

Cognitive Dissonance Theory Most people assume that attitudes influence behavior, but **cognitive dissonance theory** suggests the reverse: behavior can also influence attitudes. According to cognitive dissonance theory, consumers strive for consonance, or consistency between a specific behavior and an attitude related to that behavior. Dissonance, or behavior-attitude inconsistency, produces an unpleasant tension, referred to as dissonance arousal. When it occurs, people are motivated to reduce the dissonance by changing their attitude to match the behavior that was performed. The shift in attitude that increases behavior-attitude consistency is known as the dissonance effect. It often involves effort justification, or attempts to rationalize the initially undesirable behavior. Sometimes people are persuaded to do things that they really don't want to do. For example, parents talk children into cleaning their rooms, professors talk students into doing their homework, and bosses talk employees into doing their jobs. As the amount of effort involved in performing a disliked activity increases, the more people change their attitudes to convince themselves that the effort was worthwhile. This attitude change then leads to future behavior change.

In a classic experiment, college students were asked to perform a senseless and boring task: to turn a series of pegs on a pegboard one quarter of a turn.[17] After turning each peg, they were asked to return the peg to its beginning point and repeat the task. This continued for about a half hour. In the high-dissonance condition, each subject was asked to tell the next participant that the task was "exciting and fun." These students received $1 for performing the task and describing it as "fun" to the next participant. In the low-dissonance condition, a separate group of students received $20 for performing the task and telling the next participant that it was "fun." Which group do you think rated the task more favorably, the group who received $1 or the group who received $20? At first glance, one might think the low-dissonance group (those who received $20) rated the task more favorably because they were happy to receive $20. But the opposite was true. Students in the high-dissonance condition (those who received only $1) rated the task more favorably.

Why? Describing the task as "fun" when they knew it was boring is inconsistent, and $1 is insufficient justification for lying. Thus, they had to reduce their dissonance arousal by changing their attitudes toward the boring task. Maybe it wasn't so bad after all. On the other hand, the students who received $20 had sufficient justification for completing the boring task and misrepresenting it to the next participant. There was no reason to change their attitude about the boring task. They were paid to do it!

In another classic experiment, consumers were asked to choose between two products and were allowed to keep the chosen alternative as a gift.[18] Before consumers made a choice, both products were perceived as equally attractive. After making a choice, however, the chosen product was perceived as highly attractive, and the rejected product was perceived as less attractive. This "spreading of the alternatives" occurs because making a decision is difficult, and people need to readjust their attitudes to justify their decisions. The more difficult a decision, the more people convince themselves that the chosen product is desirable and the rejected product is undesirable.

Almost any type of decision can set the stage for dissonance effects. For example, suppose a consumer makes a bad decision and buys a product that performs poorly. This behavior is likely to produce dissonance arousal because the behavior is inconsistent with the belief or desire to make good purchase decisions. Post-purchase dissonance is especially likely when the decision

- is important.
- involves giving up positive features of a rejected alternative or accepting negative features of a chosen alternative.
- involves alternatives that are similar in terms of overall desirability.

Making purchase decisions is not the only difficult activity that people perform. Joining a fraternity or sorority, getting into college, getting a job, landing a sale, and losing weight are also difficult activities. Research has shown that the more difficult the activity is (e.g., hazing, interviewing, negotiating), the more people value their fraternities, sororities, universities, jobs, clients, and health clubs. Consequently, people are more likely to remain loyal members of these establishments for longer periods of time.

Emotion

The previous sections in this chapter have described how motivations focus attention and influence a wide variety of consumer behaviors. We will now show how feelings and emotions also focus attention and influence consumer behavior. Even very simple feelings, such as **positive affect** or positive mood, can have surprisingly powerful and complex effects on behavior. Little things—like nice weather, finding a dollar on the sidewalk, receiving a small gift or a compliment, remembering a positive event, and so on—can induce positive affect. When people are in a good mood, they are more helpful, more creative, and more willing to try new products.[19] Positive affect also helps consumers make better and more satisfying purchase decisions.

Feelings-as-Information Theory

This theory suggests that mood and other types of feelings are often treated like any other piece of information, and this information is integrated along with other information when consumers form an overall evaluation of a product.[20] Consequently, a good mood often results in a more favorable evaluation, while a bad mood is likely to result in a less favorable evaluation, even when mood has nothing to do with the product. For example, nice weather, finding a dollar, receiving a compliment, remembering a positive event, and other extraneous sources of mood can enhance product evaluations. This effect can backfire, however, when consumers recognize that their mood may have influenced their evaluation. In this case, consumers attempt to subtract the mood effects. The mood-as-information effect is also qualified by the type of product consumers evaluate. The effect is more pronounced for **hedonic products**, or products consumers use to enjoy positive experiences, than for **instrumental products**, or products consumers use to solve a problem.[21]

Consumers often pay attention to their feelings and regard them as relevant to the task at hand, even when these feelings stem from irrelevant sources, like the weather or other incidental mood-altering sources.[22] When consumers realize that their feelings were influenced by irrelevant sources, however, they discount the informational value of their feelings and try to ignore them. Usually, however, feelings are perceived as relevant and the influence of feelings on judgment and choice increases with perceived relevance. Inferences about feelings depend on consumers' naïve theories about the meaning of these feelings. For example, consumers often assume that thinking about favorable products puts them in a good mood, so if they are in a good mood, the product they are thinking about is likely to be a good product. Other types of feelings are also important. For example, consumers often assume that feelings of fluency or ease imply that the information they are reading is valid and informative, and that judgments that spring to mind quickly and easily are also likely to be valid and informative. Consequently, consumers tend to be overconfident when information seems familiar or easy to read or when judgments are formed quickly and easily.

When it is easy to think of reasons for liking a product, consumers often infer that there must be many reasons for liking the product. Conversely, when it is difficult to think of reasons for liking a product, consumers often infer that there must be few reasons for liking the product. For example, consumers often form more favorable overall evaluations of a BMW after generating one reason for liking the BMW than after generating ten reasons for liking the BMW![23] Generating one reason seems easy and this suggests that there are many reasons for liking the BMW. Generating ten reasons seems like a lot of work, and this suggests that there are few reasons for liking the BMW even though ten reasons were just generated.

Other types of feelings are also important. Feelings such as bodily sensations have also been shown to influence consumer judgment and choice. Reading information or forming judgments while smiling or nodding often leads to greater perceptions of validity and more favorable judgments. The opposite has also been observed: reading information or forming judgments while frowning or shaking one's head "no" often leads to lower perceptions of validity and less favorable judgments. Using cleansing products can also change people's feelings. For example, after telling a lie, people often feel guilty. However, using an appropriate cleansing product can make people feel less guilty. When people lie with their hands by sending a lie via e-mail, they feel less guilty after washing their hands with hand sanitizer. When people lie with their mouths by delivering a lie via voicemail, they feel less guilty after washing their mouths with mouthwash.[24]

Feelings can also influence how other types of information are processed.[25] When people feel nervous, irritable, or sad, they sometimes infer that their judgments are incorrect, and this leads them to search for more information and think about this information more carefully to avoid forming incorrect judgments. When people feel content, happy, or confident, they sometimes infer that their judgments are correct, and this can lead to reduced information search and a greater reliance on categorical knowledge.

Affect Confirmation Theory

This theory suggests that affect or mood can also influence how consumers use product attribute information.[26] Instead of a direct input for judgment, as the mood-as-information model suggests, mood can alter the weighting of product attribute information. When consumers are in a good mood, positive attributes tend to be weighted more heavily. When consumers are in a bad mood, negative attributes tend to be weighted more heavily. For example, a consumer who is in a good mood may consider a positive feature of Polo Ralph Lauren clothing (e.g., prestige) more important than when he is in a bad mood. Alternatively, a consumer who is in a bad mood may think more about a negative feature of Polo (e.g., expensive). Hence, mood can have many different effects on consumer judgment.

Affective experiences or feelings are intensified when they are accompanied by physiological arousal or excitation of the sympathetic nervous system. As stated previously, emotion is defined as intense affect or affect plus physiological arousal. Emotion is more specific than affect because it reflects an appraisal process (e.g., happiness, sadness, anger, fear).[27] Exciting events like action movies, major sporting events, and intense interpersonal interactions produce emotion. Exercise also increases physiological arousal levels and can produce emotion. Chemicals, such as caffeine, adrenalin, norepinephrine (synthetic adrenalin), and other stimulants also produce emotion. Figure 7.4 illustrates the vast array of emotions.

Although people are good at detecting changes in their arousal levels, they are often surprisingly bad at interpreting their own emotions. For example, in a classic study, people were injected with norepinephrine (which produces arousal) and were asked to stay in a waiting room for the next phase of the experiment.[28] Another person was also waiting there. Although this person seemed like another participant in the experiment, he was actually an accomplice of the experimenter. In "happy" conditions, the accomplice seemed to be

FIGURE 7.4 | Types of Affect and Emotion

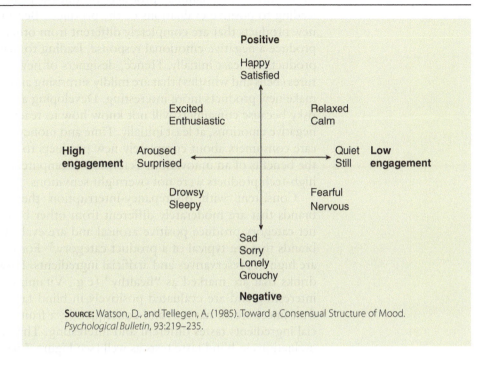

SOURCE: Watson, D., and Tellegen, A. (1985). Toward a Consensual Structure of Mood. *Psychological Bulletin*, 93:219–235.

overjoyed: he smiled a lot and threw paper airplanes. In "angry" conditions, the accomplice seemed to be annoyed and mad: he frowned a lot and complained about having to wait for so long. During the next phase of the experiment, participants were asked to fill out a questionnaire asking them about their current emotional states. Participants who received norepinephrine and saw the happy accomplice perceived themselves to be happy. Participants who received norepinephrine and saw the angry accomplice perceived themselves to be angry, just like him. In other words, people used the accomplice's behavior as a contextual cue to help them interpret their own emotions. In general, studies like this have found that people are bad at interpreting their own emotions without the help of such contextual cues.

Discrepancy-Interruption Theory

Discrepancies or surprises and interruptions or unexpected events that prevent us from pursuing a goal that we are currently trying to achieve also increase arousal and emotion.[29] Discrepancies increase arousal or alertness and wake us up because they often require our immediate attention. Interruptions also increase arousal and require immediate attention. Small discrepancies or small surprises produce positive emotions because they are usually mildly interesting and thought-provoking. On the other hand, large discrepancies or big surprises usually produce negative emotions because they suggest that our current expectations are completely wrong. No one likes to be completely wrong. Similarly, no one likes to be interrupted while working on something. So, the more important the task is, the more intense our negative emotional reaction is when we are interrupted.

Because small surprises are good, new products that are slightly different from other, more familiar products produce a positive emotional response, leading to positive evaluations of the products. Because big surprises are bad, new products that are completely different from other, more familiar products produce a negative emotional response, leading to negative evaluations of the products, at least initially. Hence, designers of new products should add features (bells and whistles) that are mildly surprising and interesting because these make new products more interesting. Developing a completely new product is risky because consumers will not know how to react to it or use it, leading to negative emotions, at least initially. Time and money are often required to educate consumers about completely new products to help them fully appreciate the benefits of an innovation. Televisions, computers, smartphones, and other high-tech products were not overnight sensations.

Consistent with discrepancy-interruption theory, research shows that brands that are moderately different from other brands in a particular product category produce positive arousal and are evaluated more favorably than brands that are typical of a product category.[30] For example, most soft drinks are high in preservatives and artificial ingredients. However, new fortified soft drinks that are marked as "healthy" (e.g., Vitaminwater) taste different and interesting and are evaluated positively in blind taste tests. Conversely, most fruit juices are all natural, and consequently, a fruit juice that is high in artificial ingredients tastes different and interesting. This results in more favorable evaluations in blind taste tests as well (see Figure 7.5).

FIGURE 7.5 | **Discrepancy-Interruption Theory**

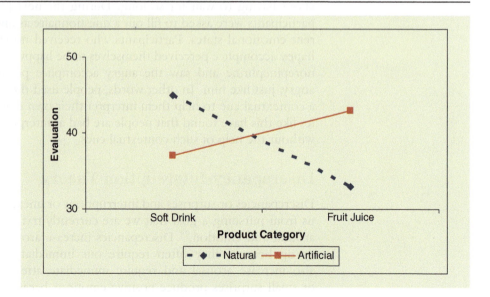

Recent research shows that, relative to male consumers, female consumers have better visuospatial skills and are better at detecting and categorizing incongruent products.[31] As a result, female consumers evaluate incongruent products more favorably than male consumers. Furthermore, when consumers focus on utilitarian attributes, moderately incongruent products are preferred over congruent products.[32] However, when consumers focus on experiential or hedonic attributes, congruent products are preferred over moderately incongruent products. This pattern of results suggests that utilitarian functions are primary to hedonic functions: consumers must first figure out how to use a product before they can fully appreciate its hedonic benefits.

Excitation Transfer Theory

OBJECTIVE **5**

Because consumers are bad at interpreting their emotional states, the excitation or arousal produced by one stimulus (e.g., exciting media events, exercise, stimulants, discrepancies, interruptions) can transfer or spillover to other stimuli.[33] **Excitation transfer theory** rests on four key principles of emotion:

1. Arousal is nonspecific with respect to emotion (i.e., arousal intensifies both positive and negative emotions).
2. People are insensitive to small changes in arousal.
3. People often look for a single cause for their arousal, even when there are multiple causes.
4. Physiological arousal dissipates at a slower rate than perceived arousal.

These principles suggest that a narrow window exists in which arousal can transfer from one stimulus to the next, thereby intensifying the emotional experience attributed to the second stimulus. Initially, little transfer occurs because a single, salient stimulus is perceived to be the cause of the arousal (e.g., an exciting movie). After a long period of time, arousal goes away, and nothing is left to be transferred. After a moderate period of time, however, excitation transfer is possible.

At this intermediate point in time, an individual is still aroused from the original stimulus, but because the stimulus event has passed (e.g., the movie is over), the person doesn't perceive that he is still aroused. For example, an exciting sporting event or action movie is likely to produce arousal that could—potentially—transfer to an advertisement embedded in the program. Ads aired during the Super Bowl and other exciting events may benefit from this excitation transfer process: the advertised product may seem more exciting if its ad is aired during an exciting program. But timing is crucial. If consumers attempt to interpret their emotions while watching an exciting movie or TV program, they would recognize that the source of their arousal is the program, not the products advertised during commercial breaks. However, if people attempt to interpret their emotions shortly after an exciting event, they are more likely to confuse their arousal from the event with interest in the advertised brand.

Tetra Images/Jupiter Images

Advertising time during sporting events is oftentimes costly, though the potential benefit to marketers gained from consumers confusing their sporting excitement with excitement for advertised products can potentially offset those higher costs when those heightened emotions translate into more product revenue.

It's no surprise that watching a scary movie at a theater can produce arousal, and this arousal can later be transferred to your date! In fact, transference produces a more intense emotional response than the original arousal. Furthermore, because people are bad at interpreting their emotional states, the fear produced by a horror movie can be misinterpreted as romantic attraction to the date. Again, timing is crucial. If people attempt to interpret their emotions *while* watching a horror movie, they should recognize that they are feeling fear. If people attempt to interpret their emotions shortly *after* a horror movie, however, they are more likely to confuse romantic attraction for fear. Of course, the mass media can produce all kinds of emotions (e.g., love, hate, fear, anger, sadness), and if the timing is right, arousal will transfer to other stimuli (e.g., other people, advertised products, products consumed while watching an exciting event)—see Figure 7.6.

FIGURE 7.6 | **Misattribution of Arousal**

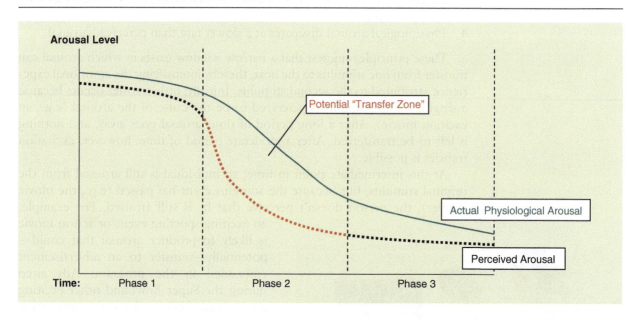

Emotional Appeals in Advertising

Advertisements often use feelings such as fear, guilt, nostalgia, humor, and sexual excitement to sell products. It is often tempting to try to create ads that appeal to everyone by using emotional appeals and rational appeals, or logical arguments. However, research shows that mixing emotional appeals with rational appeals often fails because the two types of appeals tend to compete and interfere with each other.[34] Think about how disruptive it is when you watch a scary or suspenseful movie on TV, and the movie is interrupted by a funny beer commercial. Research shows that mixed appeal ads are more difficult to comprehend and to remember.[35] Furthermore, fear appeals in ads can be so aversive that consumers try not to think about the ads or about the problems mentioned in the ads. As discussed earlier in this chapter, fear appeals are effective only when consumers' attitudes serve an ego-defensive function. Furthermore, consumers need to believe that they can cope with the fearful event and that the advertised product is effective for eliminating the problem completely.[36]

Advertisements sometimes use feelings of guilt and sorrow to encourage consumers to donate to nonprofit organizations that help feed hungry children or prevent animal abuse. For example, in "Save the Children" ads, starving African children are shown living in squalid conditions while a narrative voiceover says that you can help. When these ads included statistics about how the donations would help, however, consumers inferred that they were just one person and one person cannot do anything to alleviate such a huge problem.[37] Again, mixing emotional appeals with rational information like statistics appears to backfire.

Humor in advertising can be persuasive, provided that consumers are already familiar with and like the brand and need little additional information. In addition, the humor should be related to the product and also be simple, appropriate, and not offensive.[38] Extreme humor can be offensive, as the writers of *South Park* know full well. Furthermore, experiments using several different versions of mock ads for fictitious brands showed that humor works better for simple messages than for complex messages, and that subtle but product-relevant humor improves memory for product information.[39]

Marketing in Action

Sex in Advertising

Like other types of emotional appeals, sexual appeals can attract attention to an ad but distract consumers from thinking about the advertised brand.[40] Hence, sex works best when it is relevant to the advertised brand, and when the advertising message is simple. When sex is not product relevant, television commercials have lower scores on comprehension, memory, and persuasion.[41] A meta-analysis, or a study that statistically combined the results of 53 academic journal articles and 23 dissertations, revealed that physically attractive models increased persuasion for messages related to social competence and impression management, slightly increased persuasion for messages related to intellectual competence, and had no effect on messages pertaining to integrity or compassion for others.[42]

Research has also investigated the effects of the types of television programs in which commercials were embedded. In one study, consumers saw nine commercials for common grocery store products embedded in a television show that had sex, violence, or neutral content. Memory performance—immediately after watching the program and 24 hours later—was higher in the neutral program condition than in the sex or violence conditions.[43] In a follow-up study, consumers saw 12 ads for inexpensive, unfamiliar products embedded in television programs with sex, violence, or neither. Again, memory performance was better in the neutral program condition than in the sex or violence conditions.[44] Hence, advertisers need to focus on the content of the television programs that they sponsor as well as on the content of their own ads.

Chapter Summary

Motivation and emotion focus attention and energize behavior. When consumers desperately need something, goal-relevant products are overvalued (the valuation effect) and goal-irrelevant products are undervalued (the devaluation effect). Basic physiological needs must be satisfied before consumers pursue higher-order goals, such as safety, belongingness, and, finally, self-actualization. In addition to these needs and goals, consumers need cognitive consistency. Several types of cognitive consistency are important, including attitude function consistency, balance (consistent relationships among *p-o-x* elements), and behavior-attitude consistency. According to cognitive dissonance theory, when behaviors and attitudes are inconsistent, consumers are motivated to change their attitudes to make them consistent with their behaviors.

Positive affect increases helpfulness, creativity, and the quality of decision making. Emotion is intense affect or affect plus arousal. Exciting or unexpected events, interruptions, exercise, and stimulants all increase arousal and intensify emotional experiences. Because consumers are bad at interpreting their emotions without the help of contextual cues, one emotion can be confused for another, and arousal produced by one stimulus can be transferred to another. In addition, emotional appeals can draw attention to an ad, but distract the viewer from thinking about the content of the ad.

Key Terms

adjustment function
affect confirmation theory
approach
arousal
attitude function theory
avoidance
balance theory
cognitive dissonance theory
devaluation effect
discrepancy-interruption theory

drive theory
drives
ego depletion
ego-defensive function
emotion
excitation transfer theory
feelings-as-information theory
goals
hedonic product
instrumental product

knowledge function
Maslow's hierarchy of needs
motivation
needs
positive affect
regulatory focus theory
self-determination theory
self-regulatory
valuation effect
value-expressive function

Review and Discussion

1. How does motivation focus attention?
2. How does motivation energize behavior?
3. List the hierarchy of needs from the most basic level to the most advanced level.
4. What factors increase self-determination and intrinsic motivation?
5. Use balance theory to analyze how a specific consumer segment should be linked with a specific celebrity and a specific brand.
6. Provide some examples of how people can be tricked into behaving in ways that are not consistent with their attitudes.
7. Think of an ad that, in your opinion, is particularly good at making you feel a strong emotion. How did the advertiser accomplish this?
8. Think of a product so new and different that it made you feel negative emotions at first. How do you feel about this product now?
9. In what ways are motivations and emotions similar?
10. In what ways are motivations and emotions different?

Short Application Exercises

1. Managers are constantly trying to develop ways to motivate their employees to work harder without paying them more. Think of some ways you might be able to accomplish this.

2. Think of some ways you could use advertising to motivate consumers to find out more about your product.

3. Think of some ways excitation transfer theory can be used to make your product more exciting.

4. Form a small group and take turns pretending one person is an actor and the others are the audience. The actor should think of a past emotional event and make a face consistent with the emotion. The actor should use only facial expressions and no verbal communications. The actor should pretend to have several different emotions (e.g., happiness, sadness, anger, fear, anxiety). How good is the actor at expressing emotions nonverbally, and how good is the audience at interpreting the actor's emotional expressions?

Managerial Application

Imagine that you work for a large advertising agency. Your supervisor has asked you to analyze the attitude functions of large consumer segments for several different clients. For each client, you need to analyze the need or the desire served by the client's product or service. This provides clues about the attitude function that is most likely to be associated with each product or service. Based on this functional analysis, design an ad that tailors different persuasion techniques to different attitude functions.

Your Challenge:

Perform a functional analysis and design appropriate ads for each of the following clients:

1. General Motors
2. Carnival Cruises
3. A local hospital
4. A candidate for U.S. Senator from your state
5. Your university

End Notes

1 Lybio.net/directv-charlie-sheen-commercial-2012.

2 Brendl, C. M., Markman, A. B., and Messner, C. (2003). Devaluation of goal-unrelated choice options. *Journal of Consumer Research, 29*, 463–473; Markman, A. B., and Brendl, C. M. (2005). Goals, policies, preferences, and actions. In F. R. Kardes, P. M. Herr, and J. Nantel (Eds.), *Applying Social Cognition to Consumer-Focused Strategy* (pp. 183–199). Mahwah, NJ: Lawrence Erlbaum Associates.

3 Hull, C. L. (1943). *Principles of Behavior.* New York: Appleton-Century-Crofts.

4 Maslow, A. H. (1970). Motivation and Personality. New York: Harper.

5 Ryan, R. M., and Deci, E. L. (2000). Self-Determination Theory and the Facilitation of Intrinsic Motivation, Social Development, and Well-Being. *American Psychologist, 55*, 68–78.

6 Cialdini, R. B., Trost, M. R., and Newsom, J. T. (1995). Preference for Consistency: The Development of a Valid Measure and the Discovery of Surprising Behavioral Implications. *Journal of Personality and Social Psychology, 69*, 318–328.

7 Katz, D. (1960). The Functional Approach to the Study of Attitudes. *Public Opinion Quarterly, 24*, 163–204; Petty, R. E., and Wegener, D. T. (1998). Matching versus Mismatching Attitude Functions: Implications for Scrutiny of Persuasive Messages. *Personality and Social Psychology Bulletin, 24*, 227–240; Smith, M. B., Bruner, J. S., and White, R. W. (1956). Opinions and Personality. New York: Wiley.

8 Higgins, E. T. (1998). Promotion and Prevention: Regulatory Focus as a Motivational Principle. In M. P. Zanna (Ed.), Advances in Experimental Social Psychology. San Diego, CA: Academic Press; Higgins, E. T.

(2002). How Self-Regulation Creates Distinct Values: The Case of Promotion and Prevention Decision Making. *Journal of Consumer Psychology, 12,* 177–192.

9 Kardes, F. R. (2005). The Psychology of Advertising. In T. C. Brock, and M. C. Green (Eds.), Persuasion: Psychological Insights and Perspectives. Thousand Oaks, CA: Sage Publications; Kardes, F. R., and Cronley, M. L. (2000). The Role of Approach/Avoidance Asymmetries in Motivated Belief Formation and Change. In S. Ratneshwar, D. G. Mick, and C. Huffman (Eds.), The Why of Consumption: Contemporary Perspectives on Consumer Motives, Goals, and Desires. London: Routledge.

10 Fazio, R. H., Herr, P. M., and Powell, M. C. (1992). On the Development and Strength of Category-Brand Associations in Memory: The Case of Mystery Ads. *Journal of Consumer Psychology, 1,* 1–13.

11 Aaker, J. L., and Lee, A. Y. (2001). "I" Seek Pleasures and "We" Avoid Pains: The Role of Self-Regulatory Goals in Information Processing and Persuasion. *Journal of Consumer Research, 28,* 33–49.

12 Vohs, K. D., Baumeister, R. F. and Tice, D. M. (2008). Self-Regulation: Goals, Consumption, and Choices. In C. P. Haugtvedt, P. M. Herr, and F. R. Kardes (Eds.), *Handbook of Consumer Psychology* (pp. 349–366). New York: Psychology Press.

13 Shiv, B., and Fedorikhin, A. (1999). Heart and Mind in Conflict: The Interplay of Affect and Cognition in Consumer Decision Making. *Journal of Consumer Research, 26,* 278–292.

14 Baumeister, R. F. (2002). Yielding to Temptation: Self-Control Failure, Impulsive Purchasing, and Consumer Behavior. *Journal of Consumer Research, 28,* 670–676; Baumeister, R. F., Bratslavsky, E., Muraven, M., and Tice, D. M. (1998). Ego Depletion: Is the Active Self a Limited Resource? *Journal of Personality and Social Psychology, 74,* 1252–1265.

15 Pocheptsova, A., Amir, O., Dhar, R., and Baumeister, R.F. (2009). Deciding Without Resources: Resource Depletion and Choice in Context. *Journal of Marketing Research, 46,* 344–355; Wang, J., Novemsky, N., Dhar, R., and Baumeister, R. F. (2010). Trade-Offs and Depletion in Choice. *Journal of Marketing Research, 47,* 910–919.

16 Heider, F. (1958). *The Psychology of Interpersonal Relations.* New York: Wiley.

17 Festinger, C. (1957). A *Theory of Cognitive Dissonance.* Evanston, IL: Row and Peterson.

18 Brehm, J. W. (1956). Post-Decision Changes in Desirability of Alternatives. *Journal of Abnormal and Social Psychology, 52,* 384–389.

19 Isen, A. M. (2001). An Influence of Positive Affect on Decision Making in Complex Situations: Theoretical Issues with Practical Implications. *Journal of Consumer Psychology, 11,* 75–86; Isen, A. M. (2008). Positive Affect and Decision Processes: Some Recent Theoretical Developments with Practical Implications. In C. P. Haugtvedt, P. M. Herr, and F. R. Kardes (Eds.), *Handbook of Consumer Psychology* (pp. 273–296). New York: Psychology Press.

20 Cohen, J. B., Pham, M. T., and Andrade, E. B. (2008). The Nature and Role of Affect in Consumer Behavior. In C. P. Haugtedt, P. M. Herr, and F. R. Kardes (Eds.), *Handbook of Consumer Psychology* (pp. 297–348). New York: Psychology Press; Pham, M. (1998). Representativeness, Relevance and the Use of Feelings in Decision Making. *Journal of Consumer Research, 25,* 144–159; Schwarz, N. (2012). Feelings-as-Information Theory. In P. A. M. Van Lange, A. W. Kruglanski, and E. T. Higgins (Eds.), *Handbook of Theories of Social Psychology* (Vol. 1, pp. 289–308). Thousand Oaks, CA: Sage; Schwarz, N., and Clore, G. L. (2007). Feelings and Phenomenal Experiences. In A. W. Kruglanski, and E. T. Higgins (Eds.), *Social Psychology: Handbook of Basic Principles* (pp. 385–407). New York: Guilford.

21 Yeung, C. W. M., and Wyer, R. S. (2004). Affect, Appraisal, and Consumer Judgment. *Journal of Consumer Research, 31,* 412–424.

22 Schwarz, N. (2012). Feelings-as-Information Theory. In P. A. M. Van Lange, A. W. Kruglanski, and E. T. Higgins (Eds.), *Handbook of Theories of Social Psychology* (Vol. 1, pp. 289–308). Thousand Oaks, CA: Sage.

23 Wanke, M., Bohner, G., and Jurkowitsch, A. (1997). There Are Many Reasons to Drive a BMW: Does Imagined Ease of Argument Generation Influence Attitudes? *Journal of Consumer Research, 24,* 170–177.

24 Lee, S. W. S., and Schwarz, N. (2011). Wiping the Slate Clean: Psychological Consequences of Physical Cleansing. *Current Directions in Psychological Science, 20,* 307–311.

25 Schwarz, N. (2012). Feelings-as-Information Theory. In P. A. M. Van Lange, A. W. Kruglanski, and E. T. Higgins (Eds.), *Handbook of Theories of Social Psychology* (pp. 289–308). Thousand Oaks, CA: Sage

26 Adaval, R. (2001). Sometimes It Just Feels Right: The Differential Weighting of Affect-Consistent and Affect-Inconsistent Product Information. *Journal of Consumer Research, 28,* 1–17.

27 Watson, D., and Tellegen, A. (1985). Toward a Consensual Structure of Mood. *Psychological Bulletin, 98,* 219–235.

28 Schwarz, N., and Clore, G. L. (2007). Feelings and Phenomenal Experiences. In A. W. Kruglanski, and E. T. Higgins (Eds.), *Social Psychology: Handbook of Basic Principles* (pp. 385–407). New York: Guilford.

29 Schacter, S., and Singer, J. E. (1962). Cognitive, Social, and Physiological Determinants of Emotional State. *Psychological Review, 69,* 379–399.

30 Mandler, G. (1982). The Structure of Value: Accounting for Taste. In M. S. Clark, and S. T. Fiske (Eds.), *Affect and Cognition: The 17th Annual Carnegie Symposium on Cognition.* Hillsdale, NJ: Erlbaum; Meyers-Levy, J., and Tybout, A. M. (1989). Schema Congruity as a Basis for Product Evaluation. *Journal of Consumer Research, 16,* 39–54. Stayman, D. M., Alden, D. L., and Smith, K. H. (1992). Some Effects of Schematic Processing on Consumer Expectations and Disconfirmation Judgments. *Journal of Consumer Research, 19,* 240–255.

31 Noseworthy, T. S., Cotte, J., and Lee, S. W. (2011). The Effects of Ad Context and Gender on the Identification of Visually Incongruent Products. *Journal of Consumer Research, 38,* 358–375.

32 Noseworthy, T. S., and Trudel, R. (2011). Looks Interesting, But What Does It Do? Evaluation of Incongruent Product Form Depends on Positioning. *Journal of Marketing Research, 48,* 1008–1019.

33 Zillmann, D. (1978). Attribution and Misattribution of Excitatory Reactions. In J. H. Harvey, W. Ickes, and R. F. Kidd (Eds.), *New Directions in Attribution Research* (Vol. 2). Hillsdale, NJ: Erlbaum.

34 Armstrong, J. S. (2010). *Persuasive Advertising: Evidence-Based Principles.* New York: Palgrave MacMillan.

35 Mehta, A., and Purvis, S. C. (2006). Reconsidering Recall and Emotion in Advertising. *Journal of Advertising Research, 46,* 49–56; Stewart, D. W., and Furse, D. H. (1986). *Effective Television Advertising: A Study of 1000 Commercials.* Lexington, MA: Lexington.

36 Witte, K., and Allen, M. (2000). A Meta-Analysis of Fear Appeals: Implications for Effective Public Health Campaigns. *Health Education and Behavior, 27,* 591–615.

37 Small, D. A., Loewenstein, G., and Slovic, P. (2006). Sympathy and Callousness: The Impact of Deliberative Thought on Donations to Indentifiable and Statistical Victims. *Organizational Behavior and Human Decision Processes, 102,* 143–153.

38 Armstrong, J. S. (2010). *Persuasive Advertising: Evidence-Based Principles.* New York: Palgrave MacMillan; Madden, T. J., and Weinberger, M. G. (1984). Humor in Advertising: A Practitioner View. *Journal of Advertising Research, 24,* 23–29.

39 Cline, T. W., and Kellaris, J. J. (1999). The Joint Impact of Humor and Argument Strength in a Print Advertising Context: A Case for Weaker Arguments. *Psychology & Marketing, 16,* 69–86; Cline T. W., and Kellaris, J. J. (2007). The Influence of Humor Strength and Humor-Message Relatedness on Ad Memorability: A Dual Process Model. *Journal of Advertising, 36,* 55–67.

40 Armstrong, J. S. (2010). *Persuasive Advertising: Evidence-Based Principles.* New York: Palgrave MacMillan.

41 Stewart, D. W., and Furse, D. H. (1986). *Effective Television Advertising: A Study of 1000 Commercials.* Lexington, MA: Lexington.

42 Eagly, A. H., Ashmore, R. D., Makhijaniand, M. G., and Longo, L. C. (1991). What is Beautiful is Good, but … A Meta-Analytic Review of Research on the Physical Attractiveness Stereotype. *Psychological Bulletin, 110,* 109–128.

43 Bushman, B. J., and Bonacci, A. M. (2002). Violence and Sex Impair Memory for Television Ads. *Journal of Applied Psychology, 87,* 557–563.

44 Bushman, B. J. (2005). Violence and Sex in Television Programs Do Not Sell Products in Advertisements. *Psychological Science, 16,* 702–708.

ATTITUDE AND JUDGMENT FORMATION AND CHANGE

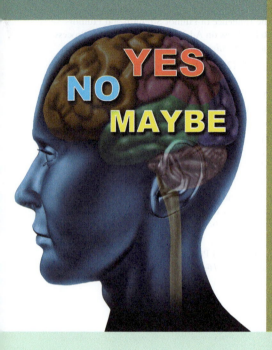

OBJECTIVES   *After studying this chapter, you will be able to…*

1   Define search, experience, and credence attributes.

2   Define descriptive, informational, and inferential beliefs.

3   Calculate numerical values for attitudes using expectancy-value models.

4   Use dual-process models of persuasion to design more effective marketing communications.

5   Use multiple strategies to develop more effective marketing communications.

The Truth

One of the most important jobs of marketers is to develop effective techniques for changing the beliefs and attitudes of consumers. Everyone knows that persuasion is an important topic, and this chapter focuses on the science of persuasion. Effective ads can dramatically increase market shares and revenues for companies. Effective ads influence election outcomes and attitudes toward one's country and its leaders. They can also encourage people to adopt healthier lifestyles. In 2012, the Centers for Disease Control (CDC) and the Food and Drug Administration (FDA) received $100 million in federal funding to develop more effective anti-smoking public service announcements.[1] This is money well spent because these public service announcements work: the teen smoking rate dropped 40% between 1997 and 2003, and the teen smoking rate continued to drop by 21% between 2005 and 2009. The overall smoking rate also dropped by 20% between 2005 and 2009.

One of the most important national anti-smoking campaigns is The Truth campaign. The Truth ran several different versions of a public service announcement attempting to show, in a concrete fashion, how many people have died from smoking. The Truth print ads and online ads also reveal tobacco company memos ordering factories to add more chemicals that increase the addictive properties of cigarettes, and referring to the target 18- to 25-year-old market segment as the "Scum" segment. This segment consists of sensation seekers with nose rings, tattoos, shabby clothes, and anti-establishment attitudes, and it was reasoned that this segment would be the easiest segment to persuade to achieve cigarette market growth. The Truth campaign was introduced in 2000, and its cost between 2000 and 2002 was $324 million. This cost was trivial considering that the campaign reduced medical costs for tobacco-related illnesses by $1.9 billion. The campaign was developed by the Arnold Agency in Boston, which won several awards for it.

© Barnaby Chambers/Shutterstock.com

The once-vibrant, glamorous allure of smoking has rather quickly evolved into a national health improvement campaign whereby cigarettes are now regarded as public enemies.

The national smoking rate is currently around 20%, and over the next five years, the CDC and FDA will be spending $390 million to reduce this rate further. The CDC and FDA will also be sponsoring ads from other agencies, including new television commercials showing sick and dying smokers providing advice on how to deal with tracheotomies.

OBJECTIVE ① # Nonevaluative Judgment

Beliefs are nonevaluative **judgments**, or ratings about product attributes and benefits. Marketers define attributes as specific features or characteristics of a brand (e.g., size, price, style), and benefits as the outcomes or consequences that follow from each attribute (e.g., safety, exclusivity, trendiness). Beliefs capture consumers' assessments about a specific relationship between a brand and an attribute or benefit. "Starbucks coffee is strong" describes a belief about the relationship between a brand and an attribute, without making judgments about whether strong coffee is good or bad. Similarly, "McDonald's hamburgers do not contain soy" describes a belief about how much of an attribute is present in a brand,

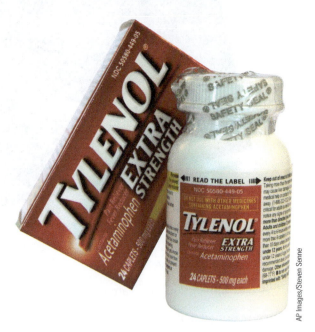

Following the 1982 poisonings, Johnson & Johnson introduced tamper-proof packaging to reduce perceptions of the likelihood of tampering.

also without placing a positive or negative value on soy in hamburgers. Some people like soy for health reasons; others find the taste objectionable.

More generally, beliefs entail assessments about probability or the likelihood of something occurring.[2] Because consumers often have imperfect information regarding products and brands, they sometimes think about the *likelihood* that a product contains a particular attribute or provides a specific benefit. For example, how likely is it that Bufferin has caffeine or that Tums relieves heartburn quickly? Likelihood judgments can also pertain to past events in the marketplace (e.g., how likely is it that competitors tampered with Tylenol capsules in the 1982 Tylenol crisis?), future events (e.g., what is the probability that a price reduction will occur?), or current events (e.g., how likely is it that aspirin therapy prevents heart attacks?). Likelihood judgments can also pertain to the probability of a cause-effect relationship (e.g., how likely is it that smoking cigarettes causes lung cancer?). In summary, beliefs represent judgments about the likelihood that a particular product claim, event, state of events, or relationship is true.

In addition to having beliefs about how likely it is that a product possesses a given attribute or benefit, consumers also maintain beliefs about the *importance* of a particular attribute or benefit. For example, snacks brands differ from each other in terms of saltiness, automobile brands differ in terms of fuel efficiency, and clothing brands differ in terms of softness and fashion. For some consumers, healthiness is more important than saltiness, style is more valued than fuel efficiency, and comfort is more important than fashion.

Many different product attributes are potentially important to consumers. Most of these attributes belong to one of three possible attribute categories. **Search attributes** are attributes that can be judged or rated simply by examining a product without necessarily buying it.[3] Brand name, price, and appearance-related attributes (e.g., design and color) are good examples of search attributes. **Experience attributes** are attributes that can be judged or rated only by using a product. Sensory attributes that pertain to the taste, smell, and feel of products are good examples of experience attributes. **Credence attributes**, a special type of experience attributes, are attributes that can be judged or rated only after *extended* use. Reliability, durability, and safety are good examples of credence attributes.

OBJECTIVE (2) ## Types of Beliefs

Consumers establish beliefs on the basis of several different types of information. **Descriptive beliefs** are based on direct experience with a product or what we see with our own eyes or hear with our own ears.[4] Search attributes and experience attributes are used to form descriptive beliefs. Simply by

Consumers shopping for clothes evaluate search attributes such as design, color, and fabric.

examining the physical dimensions of a laptop, consumers can form descriptive beliefs about the laptop's size and weight. In the same vein, consumers who have experience with a plasma television develop descriptive beliefs about the TV's refresh rate or side-angle viewing.

In contrast, **informational beliefs** are based on indirect experience or on what other people tell us. Friends, relatives, acquaintances, spokespersons, and salespeople have beliefs about products, and they usually are eager to share their viewpoints. In addition, consumers often rely on word-of-mouth to form beliefs about the attributes and benefits of new or unfamiliar products and brands. For example, if a trusted friend describes a brand as durable, a consumer may adapt this belief. **Inferential beliefs** are beliefs that go beyond the information given.[5] Consumers often draw their own conclusions, or infer beliefs about attributes and benefits based on both direct and indirect experiences. For example, if a particular automobile is judged to be sturdy or durable, consumers might infer or assume that it is also safe, even though they were never told this specifically. If a product is expensive, consumers often infer that it is high in quality. Conversely, if a product is inexpensive, consumers often infer that it is low in quality. To the extent that two attributes, such as price and quality, are perceived or expected to be related (or correlated), information about one attribute permits consumers to draw inferences about the other.[6]

Correlation is not the only basis for inferential beliefs. Inferences can also be formed on the basis of overall evaluations about a product.[7] For example, if a consumer's overall evaluation of an Olympus digital camera is very favorable, the consumer may infer that the camera has a high quality zoom lens even if he or she never received any information about this camera's zoom lens specifically. Similarly, if a consumer's overall evaluation of the camera is unfavorable, the consumer may infer that this camera has a low quality zoom lens. The former is referred to as a "halo effect" (if a brand is judged favorably on one key attribute, it must be good on other attributes), while the latter is called the "negative halo effect" (if a brand is judged unfavorably on an important attribute, its other attributes must also be poor). Finally, inferences can be based on prior knowledge.[8] For example,

Global Perspectives

Superstitious Beliefs

Chinese consumers tend to be very superstitious.[9] Many Chinese consumers believe that the number 8 and the color red are lucky. Many also believe that the number 4 and the color black are unlucky. As a result, many products in China have prices with the number 8 featured, and few products in China have prices with the number 4 featured. In the United States, a Continental Airlines ad targeted for Chinese American consumers stated, "$888 to Beijing. Lucky You." In China, a person paid 54,000 yuan for an APY888 license plate, and a Chinese airline paid 2.4 million yuan for an 8888 8888 telephone number. Also, some buildings in China have no fourth floor, just as some buildings in the United States have no thirteenth floor. Furthermore, the Beijing Summer Olympics opened on August 8, 2008, at 8 P.M.

In a recent experiment performed with Chinese consumers, superstitious beliefs were either primed or not primed, and participants were asked to rate tennis balls, a rice cooker, and a digital camera with lucky price numbers (8) or unlucky price numbers (4). The products were evaluated more favorably when superstitious beliefs were primed and when lucky price numbers were presented. Follow-up studies showed that consumers were more likely to choose safe options over risky options when negative superstitious beliefs were primed.

consumers typically know a good deal about familiar product categories, such as cars. The typical car has four wheels, an engine, an exhaust system, and so on. Consequently, consumers do not need to be told that a brand new car model has four new wheels, a reliable engine, or a quiet exhaust system. Consumers infer or assume that the car has these features by default, even if they receive no information about them.

Overall, inferential beliefs basically involve some type of *evaluative judgment*, whereas descriptive and informational beliefs simply describe likelihoods or relationships between objects. Think of inferential beliefs as a bridge between beliefs and attitudes. In the next section, we discuss attitudes in greater depth.

Evaluative Judgment

Attitudes are evaluative judgments, or ratings of how good or bad, favorable or unfavorable, or pleasant or unpleasant consumers find a particular person (e.g., salesperson, spokesperson), place (e.g., retail outlet, website, vacation site), thing (e.g., product, package, advertisement), or issue (e.g., political platform, economic theory).[10] Evaluative judgments have two main components: *direction* (positive, negative, or neutral) and *extremity* (weak, moderate, or strong). Attitudes often follow from beliefs. When consumers believe that a new product has many features that match their needs, they are likely to form positive attitudes about the new product. For example, suppose consumers believe that Verizon offers a relatively simple service, and these consumers value simplicity. It follows that they will form favorable attitudes toward Verizon.

Marketers need to understand that all consumer attitudes are not created equally. Typically, consumers develop some attitudes that are strongly held or held with conviction and other attitudes that are weakly held or held with low confidence.[11] Strong attitudes tend to be highly accessible from memory, maintained with high confidence, held with little uncertainty, and highly correlated with beliefs. The last property is referred to as high **evaluative-cognitive consistency**. On the other hand, weak attitudes are relatively inaccessible from memory (or difficult to retrieve from memory), kept with low confidence, held with high uncertainty, and exhibit low evaluative-cognitive consistency. Attitude strength is important because strong attitudes are difficult to change and have a great deal of impact on other judgments and on behavior. In other words, strong attitudes guide consumers' thoughts and actions, while weak attitudes do not. So, it's no surprise that marketers strive to elicit strong, favorable attitudes from their target markets toward their brands and limit or reduce strong, negative attitudes.

In addition, marketing practitioners cannot simply assume that all favorable attitudes are the same. For example, two different consumers may express positive evaluations of the Verizon brand, and yet only the first consumer purchases a long-term service contract. This situation may occur because, even though both consumers indicated a liking for Verizon, the first consumer's attitudes were strongly held, whereas the second consumer felt only mildly positive about the brand.

Zanna and Rempel's Model

Research on evaluative-cognitive consistency shows that attitudes are often based on beliefs. However, attitudes can be based on other types of information as well. **Zanna and Rempel** developed a theory suggesting that attitudes can be based on cognition (beliefs), affect (feelings, moods, and emotions), or behavior.[12] Let's look at an example. A consumer's attitude toward a Dairy Queen hot fudge sundae is likely to be influenced by her cognitions, such as beliefs about the sundae's properties (e.g., features, taste, size), affect, or how she feels when she eats a Dairy Queen hot fudge sundae (e.g., good mood, refreshed, rewarded). In addition, her attitudes may be influenced by the very act of buying hot fudge sundaes. If a consumer buys a Dairy Queen hot fudge sundae as a reward for completing a difficult task, this *behavior* may encourage strong, favorable attitudes toward the brand. This is not unusual. After buying a product or service (behavior), consumers' attitudes toward brands are often more favorable than their attitudes prior to making the purchase.

In addition to being formed on the basis of cognition, affect, or behavior, attitudes can also *influence* or change cognition, affect, and behavior. In other words, there is a reciprocal relationship between attitudes and the bases of attitudes. Favorable attitudes lead consumers to focus on favorable beliefs (e.g., sundaes are made from milk and milk is healthy), rather than unfavorable beliefs (e.g., sundaes have a high fat content and are therefore unhealthy). Favorable attitudes also lead consumers to focus on positive feelings rather than on negative feelings. Finally, favorable attitudes toward sundaes increase the likelihood that consumers will buy and consume sundaes.

Attitudes can be based on one's own beliefs, especially if consumers consider themselves to be knowledgeable about a product category.[13] However, attitudes can also be based on the beliefs of other people, especially when consumers consider themselves to be less knowledgeable about a product category than other people. Television advertising often uses experts as spokespersons because experts are more knowledgeable about a topic than the typical person. The beliefs of experts can have a powerful influence on the attitudes of consumers, provided that consumers trust that experts are providing truthful and accurate information. On the other hand, consumers attempt to avoid expert influence when they suspect that an expert is lying in order to take advantage of them.

Mood can also influence attitudes, even if mood has nothing to do with the products or services that consumers evaluate.[14] For example, a sunny day might put people in a good mood, and this can lead people to evaluate products and services more favorably. However, when consumers suspect that their moods might be biasing their judgments, they attempt to avoid letting their moods influence them. So overall, attitudes can be influenced by many different variables—including cognition, affect, behavior, the opinions of others, and unrelated moods. Now that we've discussed attitudes, let's examine the importance of consumer involvement.

FIGURE **8.1** | **The Reciprocal Relationship between Attitudes and Their Bases**

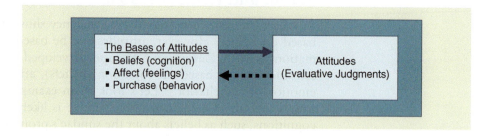

The Inclusion/Exclusion Model Attitudes are also heavily influenced by the context in which they are formed. Any attitude object—including a person, place, or thing—can seem good or bad, hot or cold, big or small, expensive or inexpensive, and so on—depending on what it is compared to. The same average car seems good when compared to a Yugo and seems bad when compared to a Mercedes Benz. The same average temperature seems hot when the previous day was cold and seems cold when the previous day was hot. The same house seems big when the neighboring house is small and seems small when the neighboring house is big. The mass media also influence the context in which objects are judged. In the famous "Charlie's Angels" study, male undergraduates rated the physical attractiveness of a female undergraduate in a photo.[15] The woman was rated as less attractive after the guys watched an episode of Charlie's Angels than after the guys watched a nature documentary. All of these effects are examples of **context effects**, because the background or context in which an object is judged influences judgments. Two types of context effects are possible: an **assimilation effect**—a shift in judgment of the target toward the reference point (or standard or point of comparison)—or a **contrast effect**—a shift in judgment of the target away from the reference point.

The Inclusion/Exclusion Model is the most complete theory of assimilation effects and contrast effects.[16] This model suggests that judgment requires two mental representations: one of a target and one of a reference point. The information that is most accessible from memory is used as a basis for judgment. Information used to form a representation of the target results in assimilation effects: as the amount of favorable information used increases, more favorable judgments of the target are formed, and vice versa. Assimilation effects differ in magnitude depending on the amount of favorable information included in the representation of the target and on the extremity of the favorable information included in the representation of the target (e.g., highly favorable information is more extreme than slightly favorable information).

Information that is excluded from the representation of the target results in contrast effects. Two types of contrast effects are possible: a **subtraction-based contrast effect**, in which information is excluded from the representation of the target, or a **comparison-based contrast effect**, in which information is included in the representation of the reference point or standard of comparison. In the former case, as the amount and extremity of the favorable information excluded from the representation of the target increases, less favorable judgments of the target are formed. In the latter case, as the amount or extremity of the favorable information included in the representation of the standard increases, less favorable judgments of the target are formed. For example, the Republican Party is rated more positively when popular Republicans are included in the representation of the target (an assimilation effect) than when popular Republicans are excluded from the representation of the target (a subtraction-based contrast effect). To elaborate, less positive ratings of the Republican Party were formed when people were reminded that Colin Powell declined to run for President in 1996. When people are asked to rate the trustworthiness of politicians in general, politicians are rated as more trustworthy when no political scandals come to mind than when they are reminded of Nixon and the Watergate scandal.[17] These effects are assimilation effects. However, when people are asked to rate the trustworthiness of a specific politician, Newt Gingrich for example, Gingrich is rated as more trustworthy when Nixon comes to mind than when Nixon does not come to mind. In this case, Nixon influences the representation of the standard, which results in a comparison-based contrast effect.

Inclusion and exclusion effects also influence judgments of products manufactured in different countries.[18] The country of origin is more likely to be included in representations of a target product when the country of origin is presented first, before other product attribute information is presented. Hence, assimilation effects should be observed when the country of origin is presented first. However, the country of origin is more likely to be included in representations of the standard when country-of-origin information is presented last, after other product attribute information is presented. Hence, comparison-based contrast effects should be observed when country-of-origin information is presented last. To test these predictions, participants rated a watch manufactured in a country known for making high-quality watches (e.g., Switzerland) or not (e.g., Mexico), and rated a computer made in a country known for making high-quality computers (i.e., Japan) or not (e.g., Brazil). Even though the other product attribute information was held constant, country of origin had a strong impact on product evaluations: assimilation effects were found when country-of-origin information was presented first, and comparison-based contrast effects were found when country-of-origin information was presented last.

The inclusion/exclusion model is elegant because it integrates the effects of a large set of variables—including ambiguity, typicality, and similarity—and explains their influence on assimilation and contrast effects.[19] When ambiguity (i.e., general categories are more ambiguous than specific examples), typicality (i.e., moderate examples are more typical than extreme examples), or similarity (i.e., similarity increases as the amount of feature overlap between the target and the standard increases) are high, assimilation effects are likely. When ambiguity, typicality, or similarity are low, contrast effects are likely. Subtraction-based contrast effects occur when examples are excluded from the representation of the target, and comparison-based contrast effects occur when examples are included in the representation of the standard.

Overview of Involvement

Sometimes consumers think carefully about their beliefs and attitudes, and sometimes they reflect very little. One of the most important determinants of the amount or extent of thinking is the level of **involvement**, or the personal relevance and importance of an issue or situation.[20] When an issue or situation is relevant and important, higher levels of consumer involvement follow, and consumers think very carefully about the implications of the available information. When an issue or situation is not relevant or important, involvement is low, and consumers reflect very little. Involvement with a particular issue or topic is called *enduring involvement*. Here, consumers' levels of interest in the topic are fundamental—either high or low, and hence, their interest (or lack of interest) endures. For example, consumers who ski regularly become fundamentally involved with many aspects of skiing, including products, services, events, and weather conditions. As a result, their high levels of involvement with skiing endure through many winter seasons and over a variety of product life cycles. On the other hand, consumers who never ski demonstrate very low levels of involvement, which also endure, as even the newest, most interesting ski products and skiing events are likely to elicit only a passing glance.

A second type of involvement, based solely on special circumstances or specific conditions, is known as *situational involvement*. Here, any personal relevance that a consumer develops for a situation is ephemeral or short lived. When the situation goes away, the consumer's interest decreases correspondingly. For example, a consumer who travels infrequently is not likely to be concerned about luggage products in a serious or enduring manner. However, if an important travel opportunity suddenly arises, this same consumer may increase his situational involvement with luggage products. But, when this consumer returns from the trip, his interest in luggage will decrease to its prior, low level. His involvement with luggage is not enduring; it is strictly situational.

When a purchase decision is important or consequential, situational involvement is typically high and consumers are likely to think very carefully about the decision. For example, buying a car is consequential for most people, and they think carefully about what characteristics of a car are right for them. However, when a purchase decision is unimportant or inconsequential, situational involvement is low and consumers aren't likely to think carefully about the decision. For example, buying a candy bar is a fairly trivial exercise, and most consumers buy the brand they usually buy without thinking a lot about the purchase decision. Furthermore, when information is complex, inconsistent, or difficult to evaluate, a high degree of situational involvement is needed to appreciate the implications of the information for attitudes. However, when information is simple and easy to evaluate, a high level of situational involvement is not needed to determine its relevance or its implications.

Attitude Models Based on High or Low Consumer Involvement

Several key models of attitude formation deal primarily with high involvement conditions. These models propose that consumers think a good deal about their evaluations of products and services, integrating a relatively large amount of information in a manner consistent with mathematical models. Examples include **expectancy-value models**, the **theory of reasoned action**, and **information integration theory**. Expectancy-value models suggest that attitudes toward a product depend on consumers' subjective evaluation of the product's attributes multiplied by the expectancy that the product possesses each attribute. The theory of reasoned action is one specific type of expectancy-value model that explains how beliefs are combined to influence attitudes and how social norms or rules and attitudes influence behavior. The information integration theory is another type of expectancy-value model that explains how beliefs are combined to influence attitudes. The two theories differ in at least one important way: the theory of reasoned action suggests that beliefs are *added* together, but information integration theory suggests that beliefs are *averaged* together.

Dual-process models of attitude formation assume that consumers think a great deal when involvement is high but they don't think much when involvement is low.[21] The **elaboration likelihood model** and the **heuristic/systematic model** are the most famous examples of dual-process models. Both models suggest that there are two different routes to persuasion: a high involvement route in which consumers think a lot (i.e., the central route of the elaboration likelihood model and the systematic route of the heuristic/systematic model), and a low involvement route in which consumers think very little (i.e., the peripheral route of the elaboration likelihood model and the heuristic route of the heuristic/systematic model). The next section of this chapter looks at the use of expectancy-value models to compute actual values for attitudes.

OBJECTIVE **3**

Expectancy-Value Models

Early expectancy-value models were used to determine the value of gambles. For example, would you rather play a gamble that offers a 30% chance to win $100 or a gamble that offers a 25% chance to win $125? The answer is simple if you compute the expected values of each gamble. The expected value is the probability of success multiplied by the monetary outcome. So, the value of the first gamble is $0.30 \times \$100 = \$30$. The expected value of the second gamble is $0.25 \times \$125 = \$31.25$. Now it's obvious that the second gamble is the better deal.

Expectancy-value models can also be used to compute attitudes toward products. For example, would you rather buy car A, which offers low maintenance, good gas mileage, and reliability, or car B, which offers quick acceleration, excellent handling, and a quadraphonic sound system? First, you need to rate each attribute on a scale ranging from very bad (1) to very good (7). Next, you need to rate the likelihood that car A actually has the attributes of low maintenance, good gas mileage, and reliability, and the likelihood that car B actually offers quick acceleration, excellent handling, and a superior sound system. Finally, you multiply the attribute ratings by the likelihood ratings and add these ratings up separately for each car. The final calculations represent a specific consumer's attitudes toward each car.

The Theory of Reasoned Action

This type of expectancy-value model suggests that beliefs are added together to form attitudes and, as the number of favorable beliefs increases, the amount of favorable attitude also increases.[22] Specifically, $A = \Sigma be$, where A is the attitude toward a product or an attitude toward buying the product, b is the belief that the product has a given attribute considered important to consumers, and e is the evaluation or the extent to which consumers like each specific attribute. Beliefs (b) and evaluations (e) are measured for each important attribute. To compute an attitude, consumers multiply their b (beliefs) by their e (evaluations) for each attribute, and add these ratings.

For example, suppose a market researcher wanted to compute a group of consumers' attitudes toward Clarks shoes. Consumers would rate the shoes on all important attributes, such as comfort, support, and style. Suppose the belief ratings for these attributes were 4, 3, and 5, respectively, on a scale from 1 (very low likelihood) to 7 (very high likelihood). Furthermore, suppose the evaluation ratings for these attributes were 5, 4, and 5, respectively, on a scale from 1 (very bad) to 7 (very good). $b \times e$ for each attribute is $4 \times 5 = 20$, $3 \times 4 = 12$, and $5 \times 5 = 25$, respectively. The overall attitude rating is $20 + 12 + 25 = 57$. If Clarks shoes return a higher overall rating than other brands of shoes, a consumer develops more favorable attitudes toward Clarks shoes than for other brands (see Figure 8.2). This model also suggests

FIGURE 8.2 | **Theory of Reasoned Action Attitude Formation for Clarks Shoes**

Attribute	Belief (b)		Evaluation (e)		Attitude (A)
Comfort	4	×	5	=	20
Support	3	×	4	=	12
Style	5	×	5	=	25
Overall Attitude					57

that marketers can change consumers' attitudes by changing beliefs (*b*) about the level of the attribute present in a brand, changing evaluations (*e*) about whether the attribute is important, or both. This particular model also informs marketing researchers about the specific attributes that perform well and perform poorly for their brands.

The theory of reasoned action is a simple *additive* model—as the number of favorable beliefs increases, overall attitudes increase. This theory also suggests that attitudes influence intentions, which subsequently influence behavior. This should be straightforward: as attitude favorableness toward a product increases, intentions to buy the product increase, and as a result, consumers are more likely to actually purchase the product.

However, variables other than attitudes also influence intentions. Specifically, subjective norms or social rules for behavior also influence consumer intentions. Specifically, $SN = \Sigma(NB \times MC)$, where SN refers to subjective norms, NB refers to normative beliefs or beliefs about what other people think of you if you use a product, and MC refers to the motivation to comply or how concerned you are about what other groups of people think of you if you use a product. For example, to measure normative beliefs about what other people think of you if you wear Clarks shoes, you could rate how much you think your (1) friends, (2) parents, and (3) co-workers would like your Clarks shoes on a scale from 1 (strongly dislike) to 7 (strongly favorable). You could also rate your own motivation to comply with the wishes of your friends, parents, and co-workers on a scale from 1 (very low motivation) to 7 (very high motivation).

Subjective norms influence consumers' intentions to purchase products and brands.

Suppose your ratings were 5, 7, and 6, respectively, for normative beliefs, and 7, 1, and 6, respectively, for the motivation to comply. Note that the motivation to comply is low (rating of 1) for your parents because you don't really care what they think of your shoes. However, your motivation to comply is high (a 7 rating) for your friends because you really care about what they think of your shoes. $NB \times SN = (5 \times 7) + (7 \times 1) + (6 \times 6) = 78$. The higher this number is, the more likely are normative beliefs to influence intentions. Attitudes plus normative beliefs influence intentions, and as intentions increase, consumers are more likely to buy a product (see Figure 8.3). Taken together, consumers use attitude formation and subjective norms to form their intentions to purchase, and purchase intentions often predict actual purchase. A flowchart for the theory of reasoned action is provided in Figure 8.4.

FIGURE 8.3 | Theory of Reasoned Action Subjective Norms for Clarks Shoes

Source of Compliance	Normative Beliefs (*NB*)		Motivation to Comply (*MC*)		Subjective Norm (*SN*)
Friends	5	×	7	=	35
Parents	7	×	1	=	7
Co-workers	6	×	6	=	36
Overall Subjective Norms					78

FIGURE 8.4 | The Theory of Reasoned Action

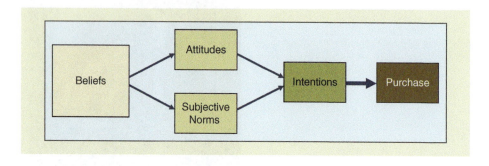

Information Integration Theory

The theory of reasoned action suggests that beliefs are *added* together to form attitudes. However, information integration theory suggests that beliefs are *averaged* together to form attitudes.[23] This distinction is important because an addition-based model implies that more is better: as the number of favorable attributes increases, attitude favorableness increases. However, an averaging model implies that *less is more*. Here, advertisers should encourage consumers to focus only on the very best attributes of their products and services, because attributes with lower than average ratings pull the overall rating down. The theory of reasoned action and information integration theory differ in another important respect. The theory of reasoned action computes attitudes as a function of beliefs and evaluations. However, information integration theory estimates, or weights, how important an attribute is on the basis of overall attitude ratings and individual attribute ratings. Specifically,

$$A = \Sigma ws, \text{ with } \Sigma w = 1$$

where A is the attitude toward the product, w is the importance weight of each attribute, and s is the evaluation of each attribute. The weights (w) must sum to one (1.00), and this makes the model an averaging model. The weights (w) are estimated using a statistical analysis—usually analysis of variance (ANOVA) or multiple regression. This procedure is useful because consumers can't always tell researchers how important a particular attribute really is to them. Consumers sometimes overestimate the importance of some attributes and underestimate the importance of others. Information integration theory suggests that marketers can change consumers' attitudes by changing w, s, or both. The model also informs marketers about which attributes perform well, which attributes perform poorly, and which attributes are most important.

Suppose you are forming attitudes toward Clarks shoes by using information integration rather than the theory of reasoned action. You consider style to be most important, followed by comfort and support. Accordingly, you allocate style 50% of the total importance weights ($w = 0.50$), comfort 30% ($w = 0.30$), and support 20% ($w = 0.20$). Note that the weights total 1.00, or 100%. Next, you evaluate style, comfort, and support on a scale of −3 (very bad) to +3 (very good), 2, −1, and 3, respectively. By multiplying each importance weight (w) by each evaluation (s), you arrive at an overall attitude via information integration of +1.3 (see Figure 8.5).

FIGURE 8.5 | **Information Integration Theory Attitude Formation for Clarks Shoes**

Attribute	Weights (w)		Evaluation (s)		Attitude (A)
Comfort	0.50	×	2	=	1.0
Support	0.30	×	−1	=	−0.3
Style	0.20	×	3	=	0.6
Overall Attitude					1.3

Note that information integration theory suggests that overall values below zero indicate unfavorable attitudes, while overall values greater than zero indicate favorable attitudes. Unlike the theory of reasoned action (an additive model), in information integration (an averaging model), adding attributes doesn't guarantee higher overall attitudes. Consumers must rate any new attributes both important *and* positive for their overall attitudes to increase. Now, let's turn our attention to dual-process models, where high involvement is not always assumed.

OBJECTIVE

The Elaboration Likelihood Model

The name, elaboration likelihood, implies that consumers are sometimes likely to think about and elaborate on ads and other persuasive messages and are sometimes unlikely to do so. When consumers think a great deal, they are likely to consider supportive arguments if they agree with a message or counterarguments if they disagree with it. The elaboration likelihood model also suggests that there are two different routes to persuasion, the **central route** and the **peripheral route** (see Figure 8.6).[24] When involvement is high, and when the ability to think about a marketing claim is high, consumers are likely to follow the central route to persuasion by focusing on information most central to or important for forming an accurate attitude. Strong arguments and reasons for forming a particular attitude are most persuasive when consumers follow the central route to persuasion.

On the other hand, when involvement is low or when the ability to think about a marketing claim is low because of distraction, a lack of relevant knowledge, time pressure, and so on, consumers are likely to follow the peripheral route to persuasion. They focus on peripheral cues or superficial information that makes it easy to form an opinion without much thought. Good examples of peripheral cues include attractive, likeable, and expert sources and positive moods and feelings. Attractive, likable, and expert sources seem trustworthy, so if these sources say that an advertised product is good, consumers often believe these sources rather than spend time thinking about the attributes and benefits of the product themselves. Furthermore, positive moods and feelings often transfer to the advertised brand when consumers follow the peripheral route to persuasion.

FIGURE 8.6 | The Elaboration Likelihood Model of Persuasion

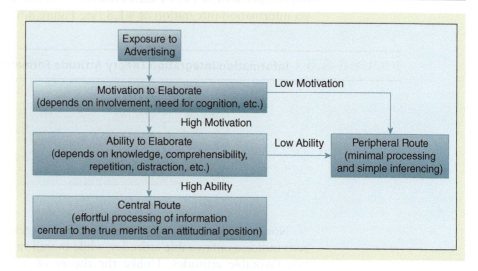

The elaboration likelihood model indicates that facts and reason are important when consumers follow the central route to persuasion, but not when consumers follow the peripheral route to persuasion. The model also indicates that celebrities, authority figures, humor, and pleasant background music and scenery are important when consumers follow the peripheral route to persuasion, but not when consumers follow the central route to persuasion. In other words, consumers use different types of information depending on which route to persuasion they are following. Furthermore, the central route to persuasion leads consumers to form strong attitudes that are accessible from memory, persistent, resistant to change, and that have a strong influence on other judgments and behavior. Conversely, the peripheral route to persuasion leads consumers to form weak attitudes that are not accessible from memory, not long-lasting, not resistant to change, and that have a weak influence on other judgments and behavior.

The elaboration likelihood model suggests that a persuasion variable can influence attitudes in one of five ways: (1) by serving as a peripheral cue, (2) by serving as a substantive argument, (3) by influencing the amount of information processing that is performed, (4) by influencing the direction of information processing (e.g., positive information leads consumers to focus on other positive information, whereas negative information leads consumers to focus on other negative information), and (5) by influencing the confidence with which attitude-relevant thoughts are held. The confidence idea is now referred to as the self-validation hypothesis, and recent research has shown that a large number of source related, message related, recipient related, and context related variables influence thought confidence.[25] Confidence is important because thoughts have a greater impact on attitudes and lead to stronger attitudes as thought confidence increases. Credible sources, sources similar to the recipient, and majority opinions tend to increase thought confidence. Feelings, including feeling of ease of processing, affective responses, and bodily feedback can also increase thought confidence. Matching effects (e.g., matching messages to consumers' preferred information processing styles) can also increase thought confidence. Finally, contextual variables such as repetition, distraction, and resource depletion can also influence thought confidence.

The Heuristic/Systematic Model

Another dual-process model of persuasion, the heuristic/systematic model, also suggests two routes to persuasion.[26] When involvement is high and when consumers are able to think carefully about a persuasive message, consumers follow the systematic route to persuasion. In so doing, they analyze all information for its relevance to an attitude and integrate all relevant information into an attitude.

When involvement is low or when consumers are unable to think carefully about a message, consumers follow the heuristic route to persuasion and use persuasion heuristics or shortcuts to form an attitude. A heuristic or mental shortcut is quick and simple; it allows consumers to form an attitude rapidly, but it also encourages them to overlook a good deal of information that they might have needed to form an accurate attitude. Good examples of persuasion heuristics are "experts are usually correct," the "majority is usually correct," and "length implies strength," i.e., long messages imply there are a lot of valid reasons for liking an advertised product. Strong brand names on a product, such as Sony, Disney, and so on, imply that these products are good. Weak or unfamiliar brand names imply that an advertised product is a bad product.

Marketing in Action

When Is Celebrity Advertising Effective?

According to the elaboration likelihood model and the heuristic/systematic model, celebrity advertising is effective only when involvement is low. When involvement is high, money spent on celebrities is often wasted. It is also important to choose the right celebrity for your brand. For example, L'Oreal Garnier decided they needed a glamorous, intelligent, and approachable spokesperson for their products. Sarah Jessica Parker used to be their spokesperson, but their new spokesperson is Tina Fey, the former star of Saturday Night Live and the star of *30 Rock*, *Baby Mama*, *Mean Girls*, and *Date Night*. Several marketing consultants say that this was a good decision. Tom Julian says that she is today's wholesome, scandal-free Mary Tyler Moore, and Randall Stone says, "She's every man's smart person. She has a directness, a dry unpretentiousness, and comes across as very approachable."[27]

John Allen says that she's, "funny in a very classy, sophisticated Rodney Dangerfield way."

Liz Lemon, Tina Fey's character on *30 Rock*, also makes fun of product placements on *30 Rock*, thereby drawing even more attention to products placed on the show. In one episode, Liz Lemon and Jack Donaghy (played by Alec Baldwin) extolled the virtues of Verizon Wireless, and Lemon asked, "Can we have our money now?" In another episode promoting Snapple, Donaghy said, "Everyone loves Snapple. Lord knows I do," as a person wearing a walking Snapple bottle costume exited an elevator. Tina Fey has also promoted the American Express Platinum card, and her popularity appears to be growing. Prior to its recent cancellation, about 4.8 million viewers watched *30 Rock* every week.

All persuasion heuristics enable consumers to form attitudes quickly without much thinking. If consumers are sufficiently confident that their attitudes are correct, they stop thinking about a persuasive message. If they're not as confident, however, they think more carefully and follow the systematic route to persuasion. When both routes to persuasion point to the same conclusion (i.e., both routes imply that the advertised product is a good product), both routes influence attitudes. However, when the two routes to persuasion point to opposite conclusions (i.e., one route implies that the product is good, and the other implies that the product is bad), the systematic route overrules the heuristic route to persuasion. Now that we've evaluated various models of attitude formation, let's consider the range of information used in judgment and some general approaches for changing consumer attitudes.

OBJECTIVE ⑤ # Parameters of Judgment

Nearly all types of information can be used in consumer judgment. Information from marketing communications, consumer magazines, other consumers, and prior knowledge and experiences retrieved from memory influence judgment. The information used and how it is used, however, depend on five important parameters:

- perceived relevance of the information
- task demands
- cognitive resources
- nondirectional motivation
- directional motivation[28]

The greater the perceived relevance of a piece of information, the more heavily that information is weighted or used in judgment. For example, word-of-mouth communications are often weighted more heavily than marketing communications because consumers trust their friends and other consumers more than they trust marketers. As the difficulty or complexity of a judgment task increases, consumers are more likely to rely on information that is easy to use (e.g., simple information with straightforward implications). As cognitive resources, or the ability to think carefully about a judgment task or choice task decrease, consumers are more likely to rely on information that is easy to use.

Motivation also influences how extensively consumers use information. Nondirectional motivation refers to a preference to acquire and to think carefully about all judgment-relevant information, regardless of its direction or its implications. As nondirectional motivation increases, consumers typically use more information and think more carefully about the implications of this information. Nondirectional motivation also encourages balanced information processing, or an attempt to use all relevant information, regardless of its ease of use. Directional motivation, on the other hand, refers to a preference for information that supports a consumer's preferred conclusion. This is also known as wishful thinking. For example, after buying an expensive automobile, a consumer usually focuses only on information that suggests that he or she made a wise purchase. The consumer typically prefers to avoid information that discusses potential problems with the car or that better alternatives are available. Wishful thinking often leads a consumer to use less information and to use one-sided information that supports a preferred conclusion, rather than taking a more balanced approach. Together, the five parameters of judgment determine how much information is used, what information is used, and how heavily or lightly this information is weighted in consumer judgment.

The Message-Learning Approach to Persuasion

All complete theories of persuasion or attitude change suggest that it is important to choose an appropriate source or spokesperson, to use a suitable message or type of message, and to tailor the message to appeal to the intended audience or market segment. Source factors, message factors, and recipient factors are all important, and the study of persuasion concerns the study of who says what to whom. *Who* refers to the source, *what* refers to the message, and *whom* refers to the recipient.[29]

Effective sources tend to be attractive, likable, knowledgeable, trustworthy, and credible. The effectiveness of a particular type of source depends on the situation. For example, expert sources are most effective when the message is complex, and attractive sources are most effective when the message is simple. Factual messages are most effective when consumers are likely to think carefully about the message, but emotional messages are most effective when consumers are unlikely to think carefully.

Factual messages are most effective when consumers think carefully about an advertisement.

Two-sided messages that discuss the pros and cons of an advertised product are most effective for knowledgeable consumers. On the other hand, one-sided messages that discuss the pros only are most effective for consumers who know little about the product. Comparative advertising argues that the advertised brand is superior to competitors' brands in important ways, whereas noncomparative advertising presents information about the advertised brand only. Research shows that comparative advertising should not be used by leading brands because comparative advertising increases the perceived similarity of the brands that are compared.[30] On the other hand, new brands and unfamiliar brands benefit from comparison to leading brands.[31] Comparative ads are also more effective when they focus on positive differences (rather than negative differences) and when these differences pertain to the same attribute dimension (e.g., 30 miles per gallon versus 25 miles per gallon).[32] Hence, a wide variety of source related, message related, and recipient related variables should be considered when designing a persuasive message.

To a large extent, persuasion depends on the likelihood that consumers will receive and comprehend a message and on the probability and strength of counterarguments.[33] More formally, $A = R (1 - CA)$, where A refers to attitude, R refers to the likelihood of receiving and comprehending a message, and CA refers to the likelihood of counterarguing. This equation implies that persuasion is greater when R and CA are moderate than when both are high or both are low. Consequently, distraction can increase persuasion when it decreases the ability to counterargue more than it decreases the ability to receive and comprehend a message. Counterarguing is most likely when a message is inconsistent with consumers' prior beliefs. However, when a message is consistent with what consumers already believe, consumers are likely to think of support arguments rather than counterarguments. When this is the case, distraction decreases persuasion.

Consumers differ on many persuasion-relevant individual difference dimensions—including intelligence, knowledge, and self-esteem. For most individual difference variables, comprehension and counterarguing counteract.[34] For example, as the intelligence of the message recipient increases, comprehension increases and this facilitates persuasion, but counterarguments also increase and this inhibits persuasion. As a result, these processes tend to cancel each other out, especially when intelligence is very high (because counterarguing will be very high) or very low (because comprehension will be very low). At moderate levels of intelligence, however, comprehension is moderate and counterarguing is moderate. Furthermore, similar relationships between comprehension and counterarguing should occur for all individual difference variables. Hence, the type of consumer that is most susceptible to persuasion is the consumer who is moderate or average on many different individual difference variables. This is good news for advertisers because the average segment is also the largest segment.

The media used to convey persuasive messages are also important. Because audiovisual messages (e.g., television ads, Internet ads) and audio messages (e.g., radio ads) are brief and must be processed quickly, simple messages are more persuasive than complex messages for these media.[35] However, because print messages (e.g., magazine and newspaper ads) can be processed at the consumer's own pace and because the opportunity to deliberate is greater, complex messages are more persuasive than simple messages for print media. Furthermore, the likability of the message source is more important for audiovisual messages and audio messages because the source is more salient for these media.

Resistance to Persuasion

Most persuasion models—including the message-learning approach, the elaboration likelihood model, and the heuristic/systematic model—focus mainly on approach forces, such as developing more or stronger reasons for buying, using a more credible source, providing incentives for buying, etc. In many situations, however, these approach forces are canceled out by avoidance forces that lead consumers to avoid, resist, or reject persuasion attempts.[36] Several types of avoidance forces have been identified: (1) exposure control, (2) counterarguing, (3) reactance, and (4) correction. Exposure control involves avoiding the unwanted message by not reading it, changing the channel, leaving the room, or otherwise disengaging. Many consumers pay for premium television channels with no commercial interruptions, and many consumers do not want to be exposed to marketing communications in print media, television, radio, or on the Internet.[37] Consumers also resist persuasive messages by counterarguing, or by generating reasons why the messages cannot be true. Reactance involves doing the opposite. If a parent tells a child that a place is off limits, the child often sneaks into the place. If someone tells you not to step across a line in the sand, you often step across the line. If someone is too forceful in telling you that you must buy Brand X, you often buy Brand Y instead. Reactance occurs when an important freedom is threatened. People often try to reinstate their freedom by doing the opposite. Finally, when consumers believe that their judgments have already been contaminated by an unwanted message, they often correct or adjust their judgments in the opposite direction in an attempt to remove the bias.

The **persuasion knowledge model** suggests that when consumers suspect ulterior motives on the part of marketers, they attempt to resist the marketers' persuasion attempts.[38] Consumers use persuasion knowledge (or knowledge about the tactics of marketers and their appropriateness), topic knowledge (or knowledge about the product), and agent knowledge (or knowledge about the traits, characteristics, and goals of a specific marketer, such as a particular salesperson) to develop coping responses to persuasive messages. When the intent to persuade on the part of marketers is too obvious, consumers often suspect ulterior motives and unfair marketing practices. Suspicion is aroused by many different "hard sell" approaches—including flattery from salespersons, rhetorical questions in ads, incongruent product placements in movies and television programs, cause-related marketing, negative comparative advertising (e.g., mudslinging), partially comparative pricing, expensive default options, and obviously biased sources (e.g., a Hair Club for men ad for hair replacement asking, "why should I lie to you? I'm the President of the company."). When suspicion is aroused, consumers form negative evaluations of marketers and their tactics. Consumers' coping responses include resistance to persuasion (e.g., leaving the store, counterarguing, becoming more closed-minded), and attempting to negotiate with the marketer to get a better deal.

How can marketers reduce consumer resistance to persuasion? One approach is to use a "soft sell" approach instead of a "hard sell approach." A "soft sell" approach involves providing consumers with information and letting them draw their own conclusions, rather than using a "hard sell" approach in which marketers tell consumers what conclusions they must believe.[39] The "soft sell" approach reduces reactance and counterarguing, but if consumers are insufficiently motivated or able to draw their own conclusions they often miss the main point of the marketing message. Hence, the "soft sell" approach is effective only when consumers are motivated and able to draw their own conclusions, and when they are likely to draw the conclusions marketers wish them to draw.

Using a soft-sell approach, marketers present consumers with the tools to make their own decisions.

Dave and Les Jacobs/Blend Images/Getty Images

Fortunately, extensive research on consumer inference processes has made it possible to predict what conclusions consumers are likely to infer in many different situations.[40] An inference is a conclusion derived from available information based on a rule that associates the information to the conclusion in a subjectively logical fashion. If a marketer understands consumers' subjective rules for linking information and conclusions, the marketer can guide consumers' inference processes by leading them down the garden path.

For example, one inference rule used by consumers is the syllogistic inference rule. Syllogistic arguments have the following form: if A implies B, and B implies C, then A implies C. For instance, a Burger King ad stated that, "People prefer their hamburgers at home flame-broiled" (if A, then B). "Now if McDonald's and Wendy's fry their hamburgers and Burger King flame-broils theirs" (if B, then C), "where do you think people should go for a hamburger?" No answer was provided to this question; instead, consumers were invited to draw their own conclusions. Consumers who believe that these arguments are true will also believe that people should go to Burger King (A implies C).

In a study on syllogistic reasoning in advertising, consumers received print ads about a compact disc player called the CT-2000.[41] The ads contained three sets of arguments implying three conclusions about the benefits of the CT-2000. For example, the first set stated that the CT-2000 has a motorized drawer and inserting a disc is easy when the CD player has a motorized drawer. These arguments imply the conclusion that inserting a disc is easy with the CT-2000. A second set of arguments implied the conclusion that the CT-2000 filters out sampling frequency distortions at less cost, and the third set implied the conclusion that the CT-2000 reduces distortion from surface irregularities. All three conclusions were either presented explicitly or implied by omission, allowing consumers to draw their own conclusions. Involvement was also manipulated within the ad. In high involvement conditions, the header stated: "You will own a Compact Disc Player Sooner than you Think, Some CD Players are Very Bad and Some are Very Good." This header implied that product relevance is high and product variability is high, which suggests that consumers should think carefully about their purchase decision. In low involvement conditions, the header merely stated, "Compact Disc Players." The results showed that when involvement was high, consumers inferred the appropriate conclusions spontaneously (or on their own without any prompting or encouragement) and consumers formed stronger, more accessible brand attitudes. When involvement was low, however, consumers missed the main point of the message and explicit conclusions were more persuasive than implicit conclusions.

Other techniques can also be used to reduce resistance to persuasion. For example, consumers are more likely to watch and be influenced by pleasant ads (i.e., amusing, humorous, entertaining ads) than by neutral or unpleasant ads.[42] Furthermore, marketing communications are more persuasive when consumers believe that other people are more influenced by these messages than they themselves are.[43] Ironically, when consumers believe that marketing communications do not influence them personally, they are more likely to be influenced because they lower their guards and stop trying to resist persuasion when they think resistance is unnecessary. Marketers can also address resistance directly by addressing consumers' concerns, lowering costs, or by offering guarantees.[44] Another approach is to address resistance indirectly by building consumer self-confidence, self-esteem, or self-efficacy. Another approach is to sidestep resistance by creating the illusion that the situation is not a social influence situation. This can be achieved by using product placement, stealth marketing, or by calling the salesperson a consultant or an advisor. Distraction can also be used to reduce counterarguing and other forms of resistance. For example, the disrupt-then-reframe technique involves providing a confusing message and then restating the message in a manner that makes sense.[45] Asking consumers to donate 100 pennies to a worthy cause confuses them, and restating the message to donate one dollar, which seems like a bargain, un-confuses them and reduces resistance. Asking consumers to make many decisions or to perform many activities that use up self-regulatory resources also decreases resistance to persuasion.[46] Finally, acknowledging resistance can be effective paradoxically. Statements such as, "Most people don't think so, but …" "It's really weird and sounds bizarre, but …" "You're not going to believe this, but …" and "I know you won't want to agree with this, but …" have been shown to reduce resistance to persuasion. This technique is interesting because it involves attitude change without persuasion: there is no attack or counterargument. Merely acknowledging resistance can reduce resistance.

Skechers Toning Shoes

Ethics

Misleading ads for Skechers toning shoes claimed that simply wearing these shoes will tone your legs, butt, and abs.[47] In 2012, the FTC forced Skechers to pay $40 million for refunds to resolve consumer complaints about the deceptive ads. The ads featured celebrity spokespersons Kim Kardashian and Brooke Burke, who claimed that Skechers Shape-Ups, Resistance Runners, Toners, and Tone-Ups could give you toned legs, better buttocks, and a slimmer body without setting foot in a gym. Skechers' executives continue to deny making false claims and argue that they paid the $40 million settlement to avoid even more costly court fees. In 2010, toning shoes enjoyed $1.1 billion in sales, and Skechers had 49% of the market share. Skechers is the second toning shoe manufacturer that was forced by the FTC to pay a settlement. In September 2011, Reebok had to pay $25 million for refunds for deceptive ads for their Easy Tones sneakers.

Chapter Summary

Beliefs are nonevaluative judgments, and attitudes are evaluative judgments. Marketers frequently try to change consumers' beliefs and attitudes through using advertising and other persuasion techniques. Attitudes influence and are influenced by cognition, affect, and behavior. The theory of reasoned action suggests that attitudes and subjective norms influence intentions, and intentions influence behavior. This theory also suggests that beliefs are added together to form attitudes. Information integration theory suggests that beliefs are averaged together to form attitudes, and consequently, it is better to tell consumers about a few very positive features of a product than to tell consumers about many fairly positive features of a product.

Dual-process models of persuasion suggest that consumers think carefully about a persuasive message when involvement is high and when they are able to think carefully. The most famous dual-process models are the elaboration likelihood model and the heuristic/systematic model. The elaboration likelihood model predicts that consumers will follow the central route to persuasion when they think carefully about a message and the peripheral route to persuasion when they don't think carefully about a message. The heuristic/systematic model predicts that consumers follow the systematic route to persuasion when they think carefully, but the heuristic route when they don't think carefully. Both theories suggest that it is important to predict how carefully consumers will think about a message before designing a persuasive message. An effective persuasive message uses an appropriate source and an appropriate argument and targets appropriate recipients.

Key Terms

assimilation effect
attitudes
belief
central route
credence attribute
comparison-based contrast effect
context effects
contrast effect
descriptive beliefs

dual-process models
elaboration likelihood model
evaluative-cognitive consistency
experience attribute
expectancy-value models
heuristic/systematic model
Inclusion/Exclusion Model
inferential beliefs
informational beliefs

information integration theory
involvement
judgment
search attribute
subtraction-based contrast effect
theory of reasoned action
peripheral route
persuasion knowledge model
Zanna and Rempel's model

Review and Discussion

1. How do beliefs influence attitudes?

2. How do attitudes influence beliefs?

3. When are search attributes likely to be more important than experience attributes?

4. When are experience attributes likely to be more important than search attributes?

5. What is involvement? What variables influence involvement? How can you create an ad that increases involvement?

6. Think of questions you would ask to measure brand awareness using several semantic differential scales.

7. Think of questions you would ask to measure beliefs about advertising using several Likert scales.

8. When are factual arguments likely to be important? When are emotional appeals likely to be important?

9. In what ways are the elaboration likelihood model and the heuristic/systematic model similar?

10. In what ways are the elaboration likelihood model and the heuristic/systematic model different?

Short Application Exercises

1. Design an ad for a car using the theory of reasoned action. What attributes should you use and how many should you describe? Remember, an adding model implies that more is better.

2. Design an ad for a digital camera using information integration theory. What attributes should you use and how many should you describe? Remember, an averaging model implies that less is more.

3. Design an ad for a new product using the elaboration likelihood model and the heuristic/systematic model.

4. Form groups of two and ask each other which food is disliked the most. Then, take turns trying to convince the other person that the food he or she dislikes is excellent. What persuasion principles did each of you use?

Managerial Application

Imagine you work for a well-known market research firm. Your supervisor has asked you to calculate numerical values for consumer attitudes using the Fishbein expectancy-value model, $A = \Sigma be$. In your preliminary research for a client that manufacturers LCD HDTVs, you learned that the key attributes are picture resolution, screen size, viewing angles, reliability, and easy-to-use inputs.

Attribute	Consumer A		Consumer B	
	b	e	b	e
1080i	7	7	3	4
47-inch screen	6	6	7	7
Viewing angles	6	5	4	3
Reliability	5	6	3	3
Inputs	7	7	2	3

Using the data below, compute attitude scores for consumer A, a highly knowledgeable consumer, and for consumer B, a consumer who knows relatively little about HDTVs.

Your Challenge:

1. Compute attitudes for both consumers. Which consumer likes the product more and why?

2. For the knowledgeable consumer, which attribute(s) need improvement?

3. For the consumer who knows little about the product, which attribute(s) need improvement?

4. Explain how to influence b and how to influence e for consumer A and for consumer B.

End Notes

1 Creamer, M. (2012). These Ads Work, So Don't Quit Now. *Advertising Age, 83,* 1–19.

2 Wyer, R. S. (2004). *Social Comprehension and Judgment: The Role of Situation Models, Narratives, and Implicit Theories.* Mahwah, NJ: Erlbaum; Wyer, R. S. and Srull, T. K. (1989). *Memory and Cognition in Its Social Context.* Hillsdale, NJ: Erlbaum.

3 Darby, M. R. and Karni, E. (1973). Free Competition and the Optimal Amount of Fraud. *Journal of Law and Economics, 16,* 66–86; Wright, A. and Lynch, J. G. (1995). Communication Effects of Advertising versus Direct Experience When Both Search and Experience Attributes are Present. *Journal of Consumer Research, 21,* 708–718.

4 Fishbein, M. and Ajzen, I. (1975). *Belief, Attitude, Intention, and Behavior: An Introduction to Theory and Research*. Reading, MA: Addison-Wesley.

5 Kardes, F. R., Posavac, S. S., and Cronley, M. L. (2004). Consumer Inference: A Review of Processes, Bases, and Judgment Contexts. *Journal of Consumer Psychology, 14*, 230–256.

6 Kardes, F. R., Cronley, M. L., Kellaris, J. J., and Posavac, S. S. (2004). The Role of Selective Information Processing in Price-Quality Inference. *Journal of Consumer Research, 31*, 368–374; Cronley, M. L., Posavac, S. S., Meyer, T., Kardes, F. R. and Kellaris, J. J. (2005). A Selective Hypothesis Testing Perspective on Price-Quality Inference and Inference-Based Choice. *Journal of Consumer Psychology, 15*, 159–169.

7 Sanbonmatsu, D. M., Kardes, F. R., and Sansone, C. (1991). Remembering Less and Inferring More: The Effects of the Timing of Judgment on Inferences about Unknown Attributes. *Journal of Personality and Social Psychology, 61*, 546–554.

8 Sujan, M. (1985). Consumer Knowledge: Effects on Evaluation Processes Mediating Consumer Judgments. *Journal of Consumer Research, 12*, 31–46; Sujan, M. and Dekleva, C. (1987). Product Categorization and Inference Making: Some Implications for Comparative Advertising. *Journal of Consumer Research, 14*, 372–378.

9 Kramer, T., and Block, L. (2008). Conscious and Nonconscious Components of Superstitious Beliefs in Judgment and Decision Making. *Journal of Consumer Research, 34*, 783–793.

10 Albarracin, D., Johnson, B. T. and Zanna, M. P. (Eds.) (2005). *The Handbook of Attitudes*. Mahwah, NJ: Erlbaum.

11 Fazio, R. H. (1989). On the Power and Functionality of Attitudes: The Role of Attitude Accessibility. In A. R. Pratkanis, S. J. Breckler, and A. G. Greenwald (Eds.), *Attitude Structure and Function* (pp. 153–179). Hillsdale, NJ: Erlbaum; Kruglanski, A. W. and Stroebe, W. (2005). The Influence of Beliefs and Goals on Attitudes: Issues of Structure, Function, and Dynamics. In D. Albarracin, B. T. Johnson, and M. P. Zanna (Eds.), *The Handbook of Attitudes* (pp. 323–368). Mahwah, NJ: Erlbaum.

12 Zanna, M. P. and Rempel, J. K. (1988). Attitudes: A New Look at an Old Concept. In D. Bar-Tal and A. W. Kruglanski (Eds.), *The Social Psychology of Knowledge* (pp. 315–334). Cambridge, UK: Cambridge University Press.

13 Kardes, F. R., Kim, J. and Lim, J. S. (1994). Moderating effects of prior knowledge on the perceived diagnosticity of beliefs derived from implicit versus explicit product claims. *Journal of Business Research, 29*, 219–224.

14 Clore, G. L. and Schnall, S. (2005). The Influence of Affect on Attitude. In D. Albarracin, B. T. Johnson, and M. P. Zanna (Eds.), *The Handbook of Attitudes* (pp. 437–489). Mahwah, NJ: Erlbaum; Kruglanski, A. W. and Stroebe, W. (2005). The Influence of Beliefs and Goals on Attitudes: Issues of Structure, Function, and Dynamics. In D. Albarracin, B. T. Johnson, and M. P. Zanna (Eds.), *The Handbook of Attitudes* (pp. 323–368). Mahwah, NJ: Erlbaum.

15 Kenrick, D.T., & Gutierres, S.E. (1980). Contrast Effects and Judgments of Physical Attractiveness: When Beauty Becomes a Social Problem. *Journal of Personality and Social Psychology, 38*, 131–140.

16 Bless, H., & Schwarz, N. (2010). Mental Construal and the Emergence of Assimilation and Contrast Effects: The Inclusion/Exclusion Model. In M.P. Zanna (Ed.), *Advances in Experimental Social Psychology* (vol. 42, pp. 319–373). San Diego: Academic Press.

17 Schwarz, N., & Bless, H. (1992). Scandals and the Public's Trust in Politicians: Assimilation and Contrast Effects. *Personality and Social Psychology Bulletin, 18*, 574–579.

18 Li, W., & Wyer, R. S. (1994). The Role of Country of Origin in Product Evaluations: Informational and Standard-of-Comparison Effects. *Journal of Consumer Psychology, 3*, 187–212.

19 Bless, H., & Schwarz, N. (2010). Mental Construal and the Emergence of Assimilation and Contrast Effects: The Inclusion/Exclusion Model. In M. P. Zanna (Ed.), *Advances in Experimental Social Psychology* (vol. 42, pp. 319–373). San Diego: Academic Press.

20 Chaiken, S. and Trope, Y. (Eds.) (1999). *Dual-Process Theories in Social Psychology*. New York: Guilford; Albarracin, D., Johnson, B. T., and Zanna, M. P. (Eds.), *The Handbook of Attitudes*. Mahwah, NJ: Erlbaum; Zaichowsky, J. (1985). Measuring the Involvement Construct, *Journal of Consumer Research, 12*, 341–352.

21 Chaiken, S. and Trope, Y. (Eds.) (1999). *Dual-process Theories in Social Psychology*. New York: Guilford.

22 Fishbein, M. and Ajzen, I. (1975). *Belief, Attitude, Intention, and Behavior: An Introduction to Theory and Research*. Reading, MA: Addison-Wesley.

23 Anderson, N. H. (1981). *Foundations of Information Integration Theory*. New York: Academic Press; Anderson, N. H. (1982). *Methods of Information Integration Theory*. New York: Academic Press; Lynch, J. G. (1985). Uniqueness Issues in the Decompositional Modeling of Multiattribute Overall Evaluations: An Information Integration Perspective. *Journal of Marketing Research, 22*, 1–19.

24 Petty, R. E., and Brinol, P. (2012). The Elaboration Likelihood Model. In P. A. M. Van Lange, A.W. Kruglanski, and E. T. Higgins (Eds.), *Handbook of Theories of Social Psychology* (Vol. 1, pp. 224–245). Thousand Oaks, CA: Sage; Petty, R. E., Caciopppo, J. T., and Schumann, D. (1983). Central and Peripheral Routes to Advertising Effectiveness: The Moderating Role of Involvement. *Journal of Consumer Research, 10*, 135–146; Petty, R. E. and Wegener, D. T. (1999). The Elaboration Likelihood Model: Current Status and Controversies. In Chaiken, S. and Trope, Y. (Eds.). *Dual-Process Theories in Social Psychology* (pp. 41–72). New York: Guilford.

25 Brinol, P., and Petty, R. E. (2009). Persuasion: Insights from the Self-Validation Hypothesis. *Advances in Experimental Social Psychology, 41*, 69–118; Brinol, P., Petty, R. E., and Tormala, Z. L. (2004). The Self-Validation of Cognitive Responses to Advertisements. *Journal of Consumer Research, 30*, 559–573; Clarkson, J. J., Tormala,

Z. L., and Leone, C. (2011). A Self-Validation Perspective on the Mere Thought Effect. *Journal of Experimental Social Psychology*, 47, 449–454; Clarkson, J. J., Tormala, Z. L., and Rucker, D. D. (2011). Cognitive and Affective Matching Effects in Persuasion: An Amplification Perspective. *Personality and Social Psychology Bulletin*, 37, 1415–1427; Wan, E. W., Rucker, D. D., Tormala, Z. L., and Clarkson, J. J. (2010). The Effect of Regulatory Depletion on Attitude Certainty. *Journal of Marketing Research*, 47, 531–541.

26 Chaiken, S., and Ledgerwood, A. (2012). A Theory of Heuristic and Systematic Information Processing. In P. A. M. Van Lange, A. W. Kruglanski, and E. T. Higgins (Eds.), *Handbook of Theories of Social Psychology* (Vol. 1, pp. 224–245). Thousand Oaks, CA: Sage; Chen, S. and Chaiken, S. (1999). The Heuristic/Systematic Model in Its Broader Context. In Chaiken, S. and Trope, Y. (eds.). *Dual-process Theories in Social Psychology* (pp. 73–96). New York: Guilford; Maheswaran, D., Mackie, D. M., and Chaiken, S. (1992). Brand Name as a Heuristic Cue: The Effects of Task Importance and Expectancy Confirmation on Consumer Judgments. *Journal of Consumer Psychology*, 1, 317–336.

27 Steinberg, B. (2012). As Pitchwomen, Tina Fey Trades Geeky for Glam. *Advertising Age*, 83, 6.

28 Kruglanski, A. W. and Orehek, E. (2007). Partitioning the Domain of Social Inference: Dual Mode and Systems Models and Their Alternatives. *Annual Review of Psychology*, 58, 291–316.

29 Hovland, C. I., Janis, I. L., and Kelley, H. H. (1953). *Communication and Persuasion*. New Haven, CT: Yale University Press; Hovland, C. I., Lumsdaine, A. A., and Sheffield, F. D. (1949). *Experiments on Mass Communication*. Princeton, NJ: Princeton University Press.

30 Johnson, M.D., and Horne, D.A. (1988). The Contrast Model of Similarity and Comparative Advertising. *Psychology & Marketing*, 5, 211–232.

31 Grewal, D., Kavanoor, S., Fern, E. F., Costley, C., and Barnes, J. (1997). Comparative versus Noncomparative Advertising: A Meta-Analysis. *Journal of Marketing*, 61, 1–15.

32 Jain, S. P., and Posavac, S. S. (2004). Valenced Comparisons. *Journal of Marketing Research*, 41, 46–58; Zhang, S., Kardes, F. R., and Cronley, M. L. (2002). Comparative Advertising: Effects of Structural Alignability on Target Brand Evaluations. *Journal of Consumer Psychology*, 12, 303–312.

33 Wyer, R. S. and Albarracin, D. (2005). Belief Formation, Organization, and Change: Cognitive and Motivational Influences. In Albarracin, D., Johnson, B. T., and Zanna, M. P. (Eds.), *The Handbook of Attitudes* (pp. 273–322). Mahwah, NJ: Erlbaum.

34 McGuire, W. J. (1972). Attitude Change: The Information-Processing Paradigm. In C. G. McClintock (Ed.). *Experimental Social Psychology* (pp. 108–141). New York: Holt, Rinehart & Winston; Rhodes, N., & Wood, W. (1992). Self-Esteem and Intelligence Affect Influenceability: The Mediating Role of Message Reception. *Psychological Bulletin*, 111, 156–171.

35 Chaiken, S., and Eagly, A. H. (1976). Communication Modality as a Determinant of Message Persuasiveness and Message Comprehensibility. *Journal of Personality and Social Psychology*, 34, 605–614; Chaiken, S., and Eagly, A. H. (1983). Communication Modality as a Determinant of Persuasion: The Role of Communicator Salience. *Journal of Personality and Social Psychology*, 45, 241–256.

36 Knowles, E.S., and Linn, J.A. (Eds.) (2004). *Resistance and Persuasion*. Mahwah, NJ: Erlbaum.

37 Wilson, T. D., and Brekke, N. C. (1994). Mental Contamination and Mental Correction: Unwanted Influences on Judgments and Evaluations. *Psychological Bulletin*, 116, 117–142; Wilson, T. D., Gilbert, D. T., and Wheatley, T. P. (1998). Protecting Our Minds: The Role of Lay Beliefs. In V. Y. Yzerbyt, G. Lories, and B. Dardenne (Eds.), *Metacognition: Cognitive and Social Dimensions* (pp. 171–201). Thousand Oaks, CA: Sage.

38 Campbell, M. C., and Kirmani, A. (2008). I Know What You're Doing and Why You're Doing It: The Use of Persuasion Knowledge Model in Consumer Research. In C. P. Haugtedt, P. M. Herr, and F. R. Kardes (Eds.), Handbook of Consumer Psychology (pp. 549–573). New York: Psychology Press.

39 Kardes, F. R. (1988). A Nonreactive Measure of Inferential Beliefs. *Psychology & Marketing*, 5, 273–286; Kardes, F. R. (1988). Spontaneous Inference Processes in Advertising: The Effects of Conclusion Omission and Involvement on Persuasion. *Journal of Consumer Research*, 15, 225–233; Kardes, F. R., Cronley, M. L., Pontes, M. C., and Houghton, D. C. (2001). Down the Garden Path: The Role of Conditional Inference Processes in Self-Persuasion. *Journal of Consumer Psychology*, 11, 159–168; Kardes, F. R., Kim, J., and Lim, J. (1994). Moderating Effects of Prior Knowledge on the Perceived Diagnosticity of Beliefs Derived from Implicit versus Explicit Product Claims. *Journal of Business Research*, 29, 219–224; Stayman, D., and Kardes, F. R. (1992). Spontaneous Inference Processes in Advertising: Effects of Need for Cognition and Self-Monitoring on Inference Generation and Utilization. *Journal of Consumer Psychology*, 1, 125–142.

40 Kardes, F. R., Posavac, S. S., and Cronley, M. L. (2004). Consumer Inference: A Review of Processes, Bases, and Judgment Contexts. *Journal of Consumer Psychology*, 14, 230–256; Kardes, F. R., Posavac, S. S., Cronley, M. L., and Herr, P. M. (2008). Consumer Inference. In C. P. Haugtvedt, P. M. Herr, and F. R. Kardes (Eds.), *Handbook of Consumer Psychology* (pp. 165–191). New York: Psychology Press.

41 Kardes, F. R. (1988). Spontaneous Inference Processes in Advertising: The Effects of Conclusion Omission and Involvement on Persuasion. *Journal of Consumer Research*, 15, 225–233

42 Batra, R., and Stayman, D. M. (1990). The Role of Mood in Advertising Effectiveness. *Journal of Consumer Research*, 17, 203–214; Brown, S. P., Homer, P. M., and Inman, J. J. (1998). A Meta-Analysis of Relationships between Ad-Evoked Feelings and Advertising Response. *Journal of Marketing Research*, 35, 114–126; MacKenzie, S. B., Lutz, R. J., and Belch, G. E. (1986). The Role of Attitude toward

the Ad as a Mediator of Advertising Effectiveness: A Test of Competing Explanations. *Journal of Marketing Research, 23,* 130–143; Mitchell, A. A., and Olson, J. C. (1981). Are Product Attribute Beliefs the only Mediator of Advertising Effects on Brand Attitudes? *Journal of Marketing Research, 18,* 318–322.

43 Sagarin, B. J., Cialdini, R. B., Rice, W. E., and Serna, S. B. (2002). Dispelling the Illusion of Invulnerability: The Motivations and Mechanisms of Resistance to Persuasion. *Journal of Personality and Social Psychology, 83,* 526–541.

44 Knowles, E. S., and Linn, J. A. (2004). Approach-Avoidance Model of Persuasion: Alpha and Omega Strategies for Change. In Knowles, E. S., and Linn, J. A. (Eds.) (2004). *Resistance and Persuasion* (pp. 117–148). Mahwah, NJ: Erlbaum.

45 Kardes, F. R., Fennis, B. M., Hirt, E. R., Tormala, Z. L., and Bullington, B. (2007). The Role of the Need for Cognitive Closure in the Effectiveness of the Disrupt-then-Reframe Influence Technique. *Journal of Consumer Research, 34,* 377–385.

46 Knowles, E. S., and Linn, J. A. (2004). Approach-Avoidance Model of Persuasion: Alpha and Omega Strategies for Change. In Knowles, E. S., and Linn, J. A. (Eds.) (2004). *Resistance and Persuasion* (pp. 117–148). Mahwah, NJ: Erlbaum.

47 O'Connor, A. (2012). Skechers Toning Shoe Customers to Get Refund. *New York Times,* May 16, 2012.

PART 3

CONSUMER DECISION MAKING

CONSIDERATION

PREFERENCE

CHOICE

SATISFACTION

© iStockphoto.com/csm_web

CHAPTERS

AN INTERVIEW WITH BABA SHIV

Professor of Marketing
Stanford University

Baba Shiv is Professor of Marketing at Stanford University. He studies consumer decision making and decision neuroscience, with specific emphasis on the role of emotion in decision making, the neurological basis of emotion, and nonconscious mental processes in decision making.

Q. Please describe the role of affect in consumer decision making.

All emerging evidence seems to suggest that by and large, affect is fundamental to and essential for making decisions that one can live with and be committed to. In several of my recent studies, I show that individuals with a more muted emotional circuitry have trouble making committed decisions, which manifests in a greater propensity to change one's mind following a decision. Affect seems to play its role in making committed decisions by promoting what is called pre-decisional distortion—distorting information in favor of the affect-laden option. The result is a clear dominance structure, where the affect-laden option clearly dominates the other options in the choice set.

Q. Recently, you conducted some fascinating work on neuroimaging and the marketing placebo effect. Please describe this work and its implications for understanding the consumer.

For a number of years, I had been puzzled by the widespread use of the price-leadership strategy, wherein the marketer focuses on lowering prices to create a super customer value proposition. Given that price affects quality perceptions, I was puzzled with the ubiquity of the use of this strategy across different categories. When I would meet with marketers who use this strategy, I would ask them if this price-quality relationship is something that concerns them. The common response was that, indeed, lower prices can affect *perceptions* of quality, but then these

perceptions would be corrected by the marketplace; once consumers use the product, they would realize that the product is of good quality, and the word will then spread around. In other words, what these marketers were assuming was that predicted utility (predictions of the utility one would derive from a product) has no impact on experience utility (the actual utility one derives from a product). I embarked on this research topic essentially to question the validity of this assumption—that price affects not merely perceptions and thus predicted utility, but can shape experience utility as well.

One of the studies I conducted on this topic was with Hilke Plassmann, John O'Doherty, and Antonio Rangel. Test subjects were told that they would be consuming five different wines ranging in price from $5 to $90. The wines were delivered in random order through a mouthpiece while the test subjects were in an fMRI scanner. A trial would begin with the price of the wine being flashed on a monitor. The wine was then delivered and the test subject was told to swirl the wine in the mouth for five seconds and then swallow the wine when prompted. Water was then delivered through the mouthpiece to rinse the mouth, following which the next trial began. The activity in the entire brain was recorded across trials and across various phases within each trial. We then compared the brain activation across trials (different price levels), and what we found was that the activation of an area of the brain called the medial orbitofrontal cortex (mOFC) was greater when the wine was at a higher price than a lower price (the mOFC is the area of the brain that measures experienced pleasure). Now, here is the twist in the story: unbeknownst to the test subjects, the same wine was delivered across trials!

The accumulated evidence across different studies suggests that the core assumption behind the price-leadership strategy—that predicted utility does not influence experience utility—is invalid. In reality, from the consumer's point of view, *Pro tali numismate tales merces* [One gets what one pays for].

Q. What type of advances do you predict with respect to neuroscience and consumer behavior? What should we expect to learn in the near future? What should we expect to learn in the distant future?

An obvious advantage of integrating research in neuroscience with that in consumer behavior is that neuroscientific methods such as fMRI offer the promise of localizing neural activity associated with various phenomena. These methods offer the advantage of providing direct tests for existing as well as new theories. This is particularly important for furnishing process-level evidence, especially when the underlying processes are nonconscious and thus difficult to tap using conventional psychological techniques. Apart from providing new methodologies for testing theories, neuroscience offers considerable promise in terms of

- Providing confirmatory evidence about the existence of a phenomenon
- Generating a more fundamental (i.e., neural-level) conceptualization and understanding of underlying processes
- Refining existing conceptualizations of various phenomena

AN INTERVIEW WITH GEORGE LOEWENSTEIN

Professor of Economics and Psychology
Carnegie Mellon University

George Loewenstein is the Herbert A. Simon Professor of Economics and Psychology at Carnegie Mellon University. He studies intertemporal choice decisions involving trade-offs between costs and benefits occurring at different points in time, negotiation, and people's predictions of their own future feelings and behavior.

Q. How does the field of behavioral economics enhance our understanding of consumer decision making?

Traditional economics assumes that people make rational, self-interested decisions. It doesn't shed much light on commonly observed self-destructive patterns of behavior, such as smoking and other forms of drug abuse, overeating, and overspending except to say that if people are doing them, they must be rational.

Behavioral economics attempts to provide a more realistic account of consumer behavior by recognizing that people make certain types of systematic mistakes. For example, people overweight immediate, relative to delayed, costs and benefits (a phenomenon known as "present-biased preferences"); they overweight small probabilities (which helps to explain the appeal of lottery tickets); and they tend to take the path of least resistance, going with the status quo or default options even when superior alternatives are available. By providing a more realistic account of human decision making, behavioral economics can account for a much wider range of consumer behavior, including self-destructive patterns of behavior that traditional economics assumes don't exist.

Q. What role does behavioral economics play in the administration of U.S. President Barack Obama?

By assuming that behavior is rational and self-interested, traditional economics doesn't provide many useful ideas for policies aimed at helping people overcome self-destructive patterns of behavior and is, in fact, generally hostile to such interventions. Recognizing these limitations of traditional economics, the Obama administration, which includes many behavioral economists, has incorporated insights from behavioral economics into the policies it has been promoting. For example, their proposal to require employees to make enrollment in tax-protected IRAs (individual retirement accounts) automatic, i.e., the default upon employment, plays on the default bias. Likewise, legislation to encourage employers to offer immediate incentives for employees to engage in healthy behaviors plays on present-biased preferences, because it introduces an immediate reward for self-beneficial behavior where the delayed rewards of better health seem insufficient to motivate behavior change. Yet a third example is the proposal to require credit card companies which specify a minimum

payment in the monthly bill to also report how long it would take to pay off the credit card balance making payments of this magnitude.

Q. How does the field of neuroeconomics enhance our understanding of consumer behavior?

Ultimately, knowing how the brain solves the problem of consumer decision making cannot fail to enhance our understanding not only of the triggers that lead to purchasing but also the ways that consumer behavior can go wrong. However, the field of neuroeconomics is still in its infancy. Despite the rise of firms offering to provide retailers and manufacturers with data from brain scans and other neuroscience measures, I believe that at present this type of information provides, at best, limited value to businesses.

Q. What advances do you expect to see in the future of neuroeconomics and consumer behavior?

As neuroeconomics matures as a field, we are likely to see the emergence of theoretical models of behavior that are much more closely tied to what we know about how the brain processes information. Currently, behavioral economists tend to begin with the rational choice model, modifying it to incorporate the types of insights I mentioned above, e.g., present-biased preferences, overweighting of small probabilities, etc. As neuroeconomics advances, it is likely that we will see the emergence of new models of economic behavior that bear little resemblance to rational choice models and that are able to accommodate the full range of economic behavior in more comprehensive fashion, rather than as deviations from the rational choice model.

THE CONSUMER DECISION MAKING PROCESS

OBJECTIVES   *After studying this chapter, you will be able to...*

1 Define the four primary types of consumer decisions

2 Describe the traditional model of consumer decision making

3 Understand the nature of problem recognition

4 Understand the nature of information search

5 Discuss the Uncertainty-Reduction Model

6 Provide examples of how marketers manage post-purchase evaluation

Kellogg's Company: Cereal with Disclosure

The marketplace is filled with information about brands—some useful, some superfluous. In fact, so much brand information exists today that consumers often feel overwhelmed and confused. Kellogg's Company, the Battle Creek, Michigan, breakfast cereal giant known for Special K, Froot Loops, and Rice Krispies, is trying to change all of that—for the better. Recently, Kellogg's unveiled new cereal boxes designed to make it easier for consumers to find nutritional information about the brands. All Kellogg's ready-to-eat cereals sold in the United States feature "Nutrition at a Glance" banners on the front of its boxes. The nutritional banners display information about fat, sugar, sodium, and calorie content. In addition, the banners indicate whether the cereals contain 10% of an adult's recommended daily allowance of magnesium, calcium, potassium, fiber, and vitamins A, C or E.

Kellogg's now provides easy-to-read graphics of how their cereals satisfy requirements of consumers' daily diets. The "Nutrition at a Glance" banners provide a quick overview of the nutritional data, tailored to the product's front-facing placement on grocery shelves. More details about those figures are located on the traditional "Nutrition Facts" labels. The new packaging follows Kellogg's effort to raise the nutritional value of the cereals and snacks it markets to children. In addition, the Kellogg's Company reformulated its products that contained high levels of sugar, such as Apple Jacks, Corn Pops, and Pop-Tarts toaster pastries and introduced a new brand, Kellogg's Frosted Flakes Reduced Sugar. Kellogg's is striving to produce products that meet the U.S. Department of Agriculture's 2,000-calories-a-day guidelines. And if reduced-sugar versions of the products don't pass the taste test, Kellogg's will not market them to children.[1]

People make hundreds of decisions each day, from very mundane (e.g., choosing what socks to wear) to extremely important (e.g., selecting a graduate school). As consumers, we constantly make decisions regarding the purchase of products and services. Some of these decisions are trivial, such as clicking a website for the daily news, and others are complex, like deciding on an anniversary gift. Thus, consumer decision making is a multifaceted process that ranges from nearly automatic to highly structured problem solving. In this chapter, we discuss how consumers recognize problems, define markets of interest, gather information for consideration and purchase decisions, and evaluate satisfaction.

OBJECTIVE ① # Types of Consumer Decisions

One way to characterize consumer decision making is on an *effort continuum,* ranging from very low to very high. **Routine choice** is carried out automatically, with little conscious effort. As such, it involves no information search or deliberation. Frequently purchased, low-cost products, such as chewing gum and milk, generally involve habitual responses. These purchase decisions are highly familiar and relatively trivial because they involve little risk. **Intermediate problem solving** usually involves limited information search and deliberation. Consumers are not motivated to rigorously evaluate each alternative, so they use simple decision rules or heuristics to aid their decision making. Products such as snack foods and soft drinks, for which consumers typically have established preferences, generally entail intermediate effort. Finally, **extensive problem solving** requires a deliberate and systematic effort. Here, consumers generally do not have well-established criteria to evaluate brands or may be unfamiliar with the product category. Consumers generally engage in extensive problem solving for infrequently purchased, expensive products such as automobiles, investment services, and home security systems. Because these decisions involve high levels of risk, consumers normally dedicate a great deal of time and effort in gathering information and evaluating alternatives prior to actually making a purchase.

A more complete way to think about consumer decision making entails two separate factors: processing effort and involvement.[2] The first factor, *processing effort,* represents a continuum from automatic to systematic processing. At one extreme, consumers may process no information and simply respond intuitively. At the other extreme, consumers gather and evaluate a large amount of product information prior to choice. Processing effort closely parallels the routine–intermediate–extensive continuum discussed above.

The second dimension, *involvement,* represents a continuum ranging from decisions that entail low levels of consumer involvement or personal relevance to decisions that elicit much higher levels of interest and concern. It may be helpful to think of processing effort as primarily cognitive or thinking-oriented and involvement as more affective or feeling-oriented. Figure 9.1 depicts this two-dimensional model of consumer decision making, with its quadrants of brand laziness, brand loyalty, variety seeking, and problem solving. Figure 9.2 provides product examples.

Involvement is the personal relevance or importance of an issue or situation. Accordingly, high involvement decisions are characterized as important to consumers. High involvement is often associated with emotional outcomes. Consumers seek not only functional benefits, such as the warmth of a new jacket, but also the social rewards of compliments on their good taste or fitting in with group norms.[3] Finally, if a decision involves a high level of **perceived risk**, i.e., the possibility of negative outcomes, then consumers are more likely to demonstrate higher levels of involvement.[4] Perceived risk comes in a variety of forms: financial, physical, performance, psychological, and social. Figure 9.3 provides definitions and examples of these five forms of risk. In the following sections, the four quadrants shown in Figures 9.1 and 9.2 are examined in detail.

FIGURE 9.1 | Types of Consumer Decision Making

		Involvement	
		Low	High
Information Processing	Low	**1. Brand Laziness** *Commodity Products*	**2. Brand Loyalty** *Self-Concept Enhancing Products*
	High	**3. Variety Seeking** *Parity Products*	**4. Problem Solving** *Complicated big-Ticket Items*

SOURCE: Adapted from Assael, H. (1998). *Consumer Behavior and Marketing Action.* Cincinnati, OH: South-Western Publishing.

FIGURE 9.2 | Product Examples by Decision Type

		Involvement	
		Low	High
Information Processing	Low	**1. Brand Laziness** *butter, ammonia, salt, flour, cheese, toothpaste**	**2. Brand Loyalty** *jeans, athletic shoes, TV programs, cigarettes, magazines, toothpaste**
	High	**3. Variety Seeking** *beer, candy, sports drinks, chewing gum, breakfast cereal, toothpaste**	**4. Problem Solving** *automobiles, appliances, furniture, airlines, consumer electronics, toothpaste**

*some products, such as toothpaste, can appear in multiple quadrants.

SOURCE: Adapted from Assael, H. (1998). *Consumer Behavior and Marketing Action.* Cincinnati, OH: South-Western Publishing.

Brand Laziness

When both involvement and information processing are low (Figure 9.1, quadrant 1), consumers typically make choices as a matter of habit, requiring little effort. This is referred to as **brand laziness**, a consumer's natural inertia toward a product or service based on familiarity and convenience, rather than a fundamental commitment to the brand. Consumers sometimes stick with old, familiar brands for no apparent reason other than the fact that they purchased it before, and it seems fine. Most consumers' daily market decisions lack interest, risk, and emotion. So, brand laziness is quite pervasive.

FIGURE **9.3** | Categories of Perceived Risk

Risk Type	Risk Capital	Perceived Consequences	Risk Target	Examples
Financial	Time and money	The costs of the product or service will exceed the benefits	Consumers whose investment in time or money is large relative to their resources	1. Real estate 2. Automobile 3. Graduate school
Functional	Task performance	The product fails to provide the desired functional benefits	Consumers who are dependent on the product to do a job, especially technologically driven consumers	1. Laptop computer 2. Home security system 3. Automobile
Physical	Personal health and safety	Product failure causes physical harm	Unhealthy consumers or sensation-seeking	1. Pharmaceuticals 2. Food and beverages 3. Motorcycles
Psychological	Self-concept	Product will be inconsistent with a consumer's self-concept	Compulsive shoppers and consumers with low self-esteem	Privately consumer luxury items (e.g., HDTV)
Social	Self-esteem	Product will not meet the standards of the consumer's reference group	High self-monitors	Publicly consumed luxury items (e.g., fashion clothing)

Source: Adapted from a variety of sources, including Assael, H. (1998). *Consumer Behavior and Marketing Action*. Cincinnati, OH: South-Western Publishing.

Consumers have been described as *cognitive misers*; we rarely think about all of the criteria surrounding a brand choice.[5] Furthermore, people are often pressed for time, distracted, or confused about brand information. Accordingly, consumers often reduce their information processing to the bare minimum. Similarly, when a purchase decision is not particularly important or relevant, consumers' emotional involvement is low. Most of the time, we just don't care which brand of ammonia we buy. In short, consumers rarely have the motivation, ability, or opportunity to respond to marketing communication in a thoughtful manner.[6]

In fact, brand laziness is not necessarily irrational because carefully evaluating low-risk decisions could steal valuable time from the consideration of important issues and concerns. However, brand laziness is dangerous for marketers because consumers quickly shift their preferences when a better deal comes along. With no underlying commitment to a brand, competitors can disrupt consumers' inertia with promotional activities such as samples, rebates, buy-one-get-one-free offers, price discounts, and end-of-aisle displays. The result is brand switching and potentially a new cycle of brand laziness.

Although brand laziness varies from consumer to consumer (along with motivation, ability, and opportunity), commodity-type products such as flour, butter, and cheese are often associated with low involvement and minimal processing. It's important to point out, however, that while one consumer may be highly involved with the purchase of cheese if he or she is a cheese aficionado, another consumer may engage in detailed information processing of butters because of nutritional concerns. Notice that *toothpaste* is present in all four quadrants of Figure 9.2 because different consumers may exhibit each of the four decision types for this product category. For example, a college student may buy the brand offering the best deal (brand laziness), but a parent may be loyal to Crest on the basis of its historical association with cavity prevention (brand loyalty). A single professional may seek a variety of brands depending on her changing desires (variety seeking), and a senior citizen may carefully evaluate toothpaste brands if he needs something for sensitive teeth (problem solving).

Brand Loyalty

Brand laziness is often confused with brand loyalty. The former describes a habitual response that lacks underlying reasons or motivation for buying a particular brand. In contrast, **brand loyalty** involves intrinsic commitment to a brand based on the distinctive benefits or values it provides consumers. Both brand laziness and brand loyalty consist of minimal information processing. The difference between the two types of decisions can be explained by involvement.[7] Consumers who exhibit brand loyalty are more highly involved in a decision than those who display laziness. Faced with repetitive but relatively important decisions, loyal consumers may perceive that they already possess sufficient information to make quick decisions. Thus, limited information processing is likely to occur, and consumers rely on earlier experience to make decisions. But brand loyal consumers choose their brands because of previous experience with them, not because of deals or convenience.

For example, even the purchase of relatively low cost items such as dishwashing detergent and coffee may be highly involving as a result of perceived performance risk. If the dishwashing detergent doesn't function properly, embarrassment could ensue (Have you ever served dishes with dried food stuck to the plate?). Likewise, coffee that disappoints can ruin a consumer's entire morning. Nevertheless, consumers make these purchases (dishwashing detergent and coffee) at least several times a year, and they don't need to think deeply about the decisions. Instead, they rely on prior brand evaluations. If those evaluations are positive, brand loyalty is likely to follow. Quadrant 2 of Figure 9.1 depicts brand loyalty as a combination of low information processing and high involvement. Brand loyalty is manifest in both attitudes and behaviors. Attitudes reflect consumers' overall feelings toward a brand, and behaviors deal with consumers' tendency to repeat a purchase. Consumers often exhibit brand loyalty with products that enhance their self-concepts.

Variety Seeking

Thus far, we've discussed decisions that involve only low levels of information processing—brand laziness and brand loyalty. On the other hand, consumers sometimes make low involvement decisions that require higher levels of information processing. With this type of decision making, consumers may understand the criteria for evaluating a product category, but they haven't yet established clear brand preferences. Thus, even with low levels of interest, consumers' limited past experience with brands may require higher levels of information processing. We refer to this type of decision as **variety seeking**, typically defined as the desire to choose new alternatives over more familiar ones. It is represented as quadrant 3 in Figure 9.1. Variety seeking is the opposite of brand loyalty. Unlike brand loyalists—who have clearly developed preferences—variety seekers must gather additional information to discriminate among their choice alternatives. Also in contrast to brand loyalty, involvement is low with variety seeking, and consumers often switch brands to reduce boredom.[8]

Variety seeking has generated considerable attention from researchers. Let's examine two important types of variety seeking, derived varied behavior and intrinsic variety seeking.[9] **Derived varied behavior** describes situations where consumers' brand switching is either *externally imposed* or *extrinsically motivated*. In both cases, variety is not its own virtue. Instead, variety behavior is a by-product of other constraints or goals.[10] For example, a consumer may switch brands of candy because her most recently purchased brand is not available in the vending machine (out-of-stock condition). Similarly, while enjoying a ball game at Bush Stadium, a consumer may switch from Samuel Adams beer to Budweiser because Anheuser-Bush maintains an exclusive contract with the St. Louis Cardinals. Both examples depict externally imposed switching behavior, i.e., the consumers had little choice in the matter. Consumers also switch brands as a result of situation-specific preferences. Perhaps a consumer generally buys white bread, but she purchases whole wheat to improve her health. Similarly, consumers may switch brands to obtain specific benefits or values not offered by their previous selection. For example, a new brand of toothpaste may offer long-term whitening benefits. The last two cases depict extrinsically motivated switching behavior because the incentive to switch derives not from an inherent need for variety, but to attain a specific consumption goal (better health and whiter teeth).[11]

In contrast, **intrinsic variety seeking** begins with a consumer who seeks variety for the inherent pleasure of change and the positive stimulation it

Most products are available from multiple brands, providing an abundance of choices for variety seekers.

brings.[12] *Intrinsically motivated* variety seeking can occur out of curiosity,[13] because of a need for change, to reduce boredom, or because consumers have become satiated with a particular attribute offered by a brand.[14] For example, a consumer may wonder what a new chewing gum tastes like or switch to a brand of cereal that contains nuts or raisins. Variety seeking can be a powerful internal force for consumers. Fascinating research shows that individuals sometimes switch from their preferred brands to new ones, even though they predict that the new brands are likely to bring less enjoyment than their preferred brand.[15] These findings highlight the inherent value in variety; consumers actually forego the satisfaction of a highly predictable, favorable experience just for the sake of variety. Change is good, if you will.

Research also reveals that consumers' positive feelings can lead to increased variety seeking within safe, enjoyable product categories such as crackers, soup, and snack foods.[16] What is also interesting is that when people make multiple choices for future consumption, they seek more variety than if they make each choice in sequence—one at a time.[17] For example, consumers who buy a year's worth of canned soups are more likely to buy a variety of brands than if they buy the same quantity of soup, but shop weekly for it. A recent study provides evidence that consumers expect boredom associated with making the same choice to occur more quickly with others than with themselves. Therefore, consumers demonstrate more variety seeking when they buy products for others, especially when they are held accountable for their choices.[18]

Is there an upper boundary to variety seeking? Research demonstrates that when the degree of novelty and complexity in a purchase situation is extreme, consumers diminish these complexities by simplifying their buying decisions.[19] Ironically, by decreasing information processing, consumers reduce variety seeking and usher in brand laziness, i.e., choosing the same brand over and over, with little rationale except to reduce unwanted stimulation. Another stream of research argues that most consumers desire an intermediate level of stimulation.[20] Thus, clever marketers who provide variety on the premises, say in a retail environment, can encourage brand laziness within a product class. For example, a retailer such as Macy's may constantly change the store décor and limit the number of non-store brands offered. In this way, the shopping environment may satisfy consumers' need for stimulation, and subsequently, routine buying behavior is encouraged, i.e., the Macy's brand becomes the choice. Similarly, a restaurant might provide a wide variety of appetizers, but limit the entrée choices to high-margin items, such as steak and lobster. Variety seeking can also depend on individual differences. Those individuals who crave variety are more likely to engage in variety seeking behavior than in repeat purchasing.[21]

The introduction of low-involvement product categories and brands can elicit variety seeking behavior. For example, Gatorade's powder packets, a single-serving water beverage mix, may require more than minimal information processing because consumers have no prior exposure to the product. However, the category is low risk, so consumers are likely to exhibit low levels of emotional involvement. Here, consumers might examine the package and purchase the

Some traditional products are inherently limited in the amount of variety that they can offer to consumers.

Steve Cukrov/Alamy

product on a trial basis as a substitute for a more familiar product (e.g., lemonade or other sports drinks), or as a complement to an existing product, like bottled water.

Variety seeking is also prevalent among products offering hedonic rewards, such as beer and candy,[21] particularly if the category is comprised of **parity products**, i.e., brands that possess functionally equivalent attributes, making one brand a satisfactory substitute for most others. Some researchers maintain that advertising and promotion messages are especially effective for this type of decision making (quadrant 3 in Figure 9.2). They reason that in low-involvement product categories, such as sports drinks and chewing gum, consumers either don't care which brand they buy, or their propensity to seek variety leaves them open to minimal involvement. Put simply, consumers just look for interesting new items. Thus, repetitive advertising and promotional incentives can tip the balance in favor of a heavily exposed brand.[22]

Problem Solving

The fourth type of decision combines high involvement with high levels of information processing. Represented in quadrant 4 of Figures 9.1 and 9.2, this is referred to as **problem solving**. Decision making of this type often involves unfamiliar, expensive products that are purchased infrequently. Consumers who shop for their first automobile, home, or insurance policy often exhibit problem solving. Because their involvement is high and the search task is new, consumers try to collect as much information as possible and carefully evaluate each brand. At this level of decision making, consumers need extensive information to understand the various brand attributes as well as the relative performance of these attributes for each brand. For example, a consumer who shops for dining room furniture first needs to determine which attributes to include in the decision process. Does furniture construction make a difference—veneer or solid? Does the type of wood matter (cherry versus oak)? Is the warranty important? Is the source of the wood significant (domestic versus imported)? How critical is price? What about architecture, delivery, size, weight, and brand name? Considering all criteria can be difficult, particularly if competing brands closely resemble one another. Consequently, consumers typically identify one or more **determinant attributes**, characteristics of a product that are most likely to affect the buyer's final choice.[23] Attributes can be described according to their *importance* and *uniqueness*. Important attributes matter deeply to consumers, often producing emotional responses. For instance, a consumer may insist, "I've always wanted oak," or "I'm not putting veneer in my new dining room." On the other hand, some attributes can be trivial. For example, a consumer may proclaim, "Money is no object," or "Color doesn't matter much to me." Uniqueness, on the other hand, embodies the perceived variation among alternatives on a particular attribute. If all brands offer a solid oak finish, then wood type is not a unique attribute. In contrast, if only one brand features Alaskan spruce and another firm exclusively offers wormy chestnut, then wood type is a unique attribute. Figure 9.4 provides an overview for assessing determinant attributes.[24]

Consumers could, potentially, place any attribute in one of the four quadrants of this figure. For example, a consumer shopping for a set of golf clubs might consider spin-milled technology important to iron play; Titleist, TaylorMade,

FIGURE 9.4 | **Assessing Determinant Attributes**

		Perceived Attribute Variation (Uniqueness)	
		Low	High
Perceived Attribute Importance	Low	**1. Irrelevant Attribute** *Who cares?*	**2. Optional Feature** *That's nice.*
	High	**3. Defensive Attribute** *Keep up with the competition*	**4. Determinant Attribute** *A positioning opportunity*

Source: Based on Guiltinan, J. P., Paul, G.W., and Madden, T. J. (1997). *Marketing Management: Strategies and Programs*, 6th ed. New York: The McGraw-Hill Companies, Inc.

and other brands offer this important feature. Thus, a spin-milled iron surface is categorized as a defensive attribute, and brands not offering it would be at a disadvantage. Alternatively, a consumer may consider forged (versus cast iron) construction inconsequential with respect to the performance of an iron. All brands offer this feature. Thus, forged technology is labeled an irrelevant attribute. In other words, who cares? In contrast, when brands provide unique attributes that matter very little to consumers, they are known as optional features. For example, if a consumer doesn't care whether golf clubs feature a "blade" style (versus cavity back), then a firm that differentiates itself by offering this option may elicit a humdrum "that's nice" response. Finally, when a firm is fortunate enough to develop a unique attribute important to consumers, it has a potentially powerful positioning opportunity. Let's say that a firm develops a golf club with an innovative, dual-angle hosel for independent loft and lie adjustments. Most consumers care deeply about the accuracy of their ball flight. Thus, if only one firm offers this technology, then it becomes a distinctive competency around which the firm is likely to position a brand.

Consumer problem solving corresponds closely to the traditional perspective in consumer behavior, where consumers are thought to proceed through a series of deliberated steps prior to and after making a purchase.[25] This approach views consumers as highly involved information processors, i.e., *problem solvers*. Next, we'll examine the traditional model of consumer decision making.

OBJECTIVE **The Traditional Model of Consumer Decision Making**

All consumer purchase decisions are not alike. Routine decisions involve little risk and low involvement. At the other extreme, emotionally involving decisions entail substantial risk and extensive problem solving. Figure 9.5 shows the five sequential stages of consumer problem solving:

1. Problem recognition
2. Information search

FIGURE 9.5 | The Traditional Model of Consumer Decision Making

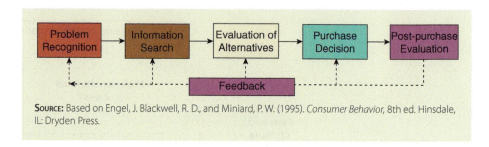

SOURCE: Based on Engel, J. Blackwell, R. D., and Miniard, P. W. (1995). *Consumer Behavior*, 8th ed. Hinsdale, IL: Dryden Press.

3. Evaluation of alternatives
4. Purchase decision
5. Post-purchase evaluation.[26]

Problem recognition takes place when consumers experience a disparity between what they have and what they want. This inconsistency creates arousal and motivation to act, leading to information search, which involves both the active and passive processing of data aimed at solving the problem. Information search is closely linked to evaluation of alternatives, where consumers must determine which characteristics or attributes of a product are important and which brands to evaluate on the basis of these criteria. Eventually, consumers cease gathering information and comparing alternatives, and they make a purchase decision. Purchase decisions do not always result in actual purchases. Instead, they represent consumers' predispositions or intentions to buy a brand. Finally, post-purchase evaluation provides an opportunity for consumers to assess their decisions. This traditional model of consumer decision making flows in a linear fashion, one stage following the next. Let's examine these stages in detail.

OBJECTIVE ③ # The Nature of Problem Recognition

The first step in the traditional model of consumer decision making is problem recognition. It occurs when a consumer acknowledges a significant difference between what is perceived as the desired state and what is perceived as the actual state. In short, a *discrepancy* exists between what the consumer wants the situation to be and what the situation really is. We call this discrepancy a **want-got gap** (see Figure 9.6).[27]

FIGURE 9.6 | The Want-Got Gap

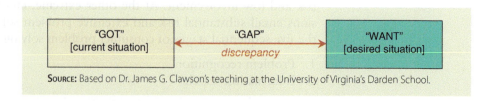

SOURCE: Based on Dr. James G. Clawson's teaching at the University of Virginia's Darden School.

These gaps between consumers' acceptable and actual states do not always trigger problem recognition. First, the gap must be substantial. After all, consumers rarely attend to trivial differences between their desired and actual states. For example, a consumer may momentarily perceive a gap between her actual and desired states of hunger. But, it's just a small grumble in her stomach, and she doesn't give it a second thought. On the other hand, sometimes the psychological or physical discomfort derived from a discrepancy is of sufficient magnitude to compel us to action. For example, if the same consumer experiences the effects of low blood sugar (e.g., mild shaking, grouchiness), she may be motivated to reduce her hunger immediately. Not coincidentally, Snickers implemented a successful campaign targeting consumers' mild afternoon hunger. The strategy was simple but effective: they encouraged consumers to pay attention to their want-got gap. Snickers' prominent tagline, coupled with familiar packaging, ensured that consumers would connect the "want" of midday hunger with the "got" of a tasty candy bar.

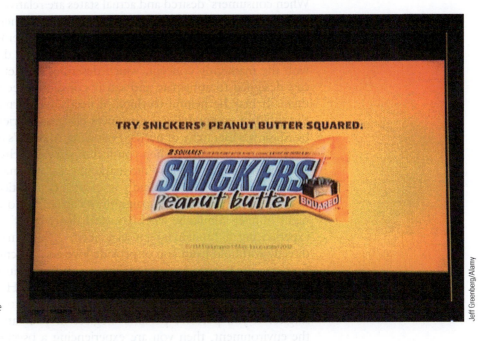

Snickers captured an *opportunity* by acknowledging consumers' late afternoon hunger.

Jeff Greenberg/Alamy

Second, the discrepancy must relate to a problem that is readily solvable. In other words, dreams and fantasies rarely constitute want-got gaps. As far as the psychological process of problem recognition is concerned, consumers must reasonably understand the desired state as one that he or she can attain. Let's say you perceive a want-got gap regarding your automobile. You've "got" a 2000 Ford Focus, and you "want" a new Bentley. Assuming you're a typical college student, this discrepancy is not likely to be recognized as a problem, because college students rarely possess the means to obtain a Bentley. Alternatively, if you envision a more realistic trade-up to a 2010 Toyota Camry, true problem recognition is more likely to follow.

Given that the want-got gap is substantial and attainable, problem recognition is triggered in three ways: the actual state changes, the desired state changes, or the actual and desired states change simultaneously.[28] All three situations are depicted in Figure 9.7.[29]

FIGURE 9.7 | **Problem Recognition: Needs, Wants, and Opportunities**

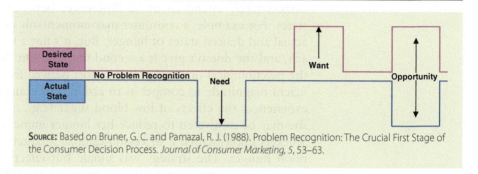

SOURCE: Based on Bruner, G. C. and Pamazal, R. J. (1988). Problem Recognition: The Crucial First Stage of the Consumer Decision Process. *Journal of Consumer Marketing, 5,* 53–63.

Needs

When consumers' desired and actual states are relatively close together, *problem recognition* does not occur. However, when consumers' actual states fall below their desired states, *needs* emerge. A **need** is a fundamental state of felt deprivation. Thus, needs are not created by marketing efforts directly. This is consistent with the marketing concept, which describes marketing as an outside-in process designed to anticipate and satisfy consumer needs and wants—not create them. It may be helpful to think of needs as internal states that fall below a threshold of acceptability. Consumers possess a variety of needs, as described by Maslow's hierarchy of needs. Following Maslow's approach for understanding human motivation, when you feel hungry or dehydrated, you experience a basic physiological need. While marketing cannot make you hungry or thirsty, marketing activities can remind you of your deprivation. For example, Wendy's "Eat great—open late" campaign draws attention to consumers' potential late night hunger. Similarly, when you feel deprived of love or affection, you are experiencing a fundamental social need. Again, marketing activities cannot directly withhold from you or provide love and affection. Those satisfiers come from people. But marketing activities can indirectly influence perceptions about your current state of belonging. Not surprisingly, eHarmony.com advertises its patented compatibility matching system designed to reduce loneliness among singles. If you perceive personal neglect in your attitude toward conserving the environment, then you are experiencing a psychological need, i.e., a gap between a current and desired way of thinking. Marketing is not capable of dictating your thoughts, but marketing activities often trigger latent psychological problem recognition. For example, Shell Oil boasts of its partnership with the National Fish and Wildlife Foundation. Given that most consumers consider gasoline brands at parity, Shell may appear to be a good choice for environmentally conscious consumers. In the same way, Honda advertises, "Accord drivability with a hybrid heart" for those concerned about global warming.

A "need" depicted in Figure 9.7 shows an actual state that has dropped below the threshold of acceptability, a baseline ideal state. Given that the need is substantial, problem recognition occurs, and consumers are motivated to reduce this gap. Some researchers describe needs as *informational* or *negative-oriented motives* because when a consumer's actual state drops below the ideal, it creates a negative condition and a desire for information.[30] **Motives** are internal drives that push people to resolve a problem or reduce a need. The greater the disparity between a consumer's actual and ideal state, the stronger the motive is to satisfy the need. Informational motives come in a variety of forms, including problem removal, problem avoidance, incomplete satisfaction, and normal depletion.

Although marketing activities cannot create needs directly, marketers are eager to identify and satisfy needs. For example, if your car's transmission breaks down, your actual state of affairs will fall dramatically below the acceptable level, and you will follow a problem removal motive. Fortunately, the market stands ready to offer services (automobile repair), products (automobiles), and substitutes (public transportation) to help bring into equilibrium your ideal and actual states. Similarly, problem avoidance motives occur when consumers proactively avoid negative outcomes such as burglary (e.g., installing ADT Systems), heartburn (e.g., taking Prilosec), or drowsiness (e.g., drinking Red Bull). Here, consumers take action to prevent their actual states from declining. In contrast, incomplete satisfaction motives arise when products fail to live up to our expectations. Perhaps a consumer's laundromat has become too busy, or her hairdresser now keeps odd hours. Maybe a consumer's favorite restaurant recently increased prices, or a new brand of shampoo makes her hair too dry. Each of these examples creates a need on the basis of dissatisfaction. Consequently, a consumer's motive is to reverse this condition, i.e., to bring her actual state back to an acceptable level. Consumers also experience normal depletion when they exhaust supplies of products such as aspirin, orange juice, and frozen vegetables. Marketers are eager to replenish those supplies through well-established distribution systems.

In some cases marketers come very close to creating consumer needs. For example, producers of personal hygiene products, such as mouthwash, antiperspirants, and beauty aids, sometimes enlist marketing programs to create insecurities that consumers can resolve by purchasing these products.[26] Sports franchises regularly alter their logos to encourage the sales of new licensed products. Fashion clothiers also change styles in order to draw attention to consumers' outdated wardrobes. Nevertheless, assuming that marketers obey the regulatory system and follow ethical guidelines set forth by their appropriate trade associations, consumers ultimately determine whether their actual state has dropped below the threshold of adequacy.

Wants

When consumers' ideal states rise above their actual states, *wants* occur. **Wants** are *need satisfiers* that are shaped by a consumer's personality, experiences, and culture—including marketing. In fact, marketing activities deliberately create wants. The distinction between needs and wants is important. Needs occur when consumers' real conditions decline while their desired conditions remain stable. On the other hand, wants occur when consumers perceive an increase in their desired states while their actual states remain constant. As depicted in Figure 9.7, wants represent a consumer's perceptions that they can improve their current situations by obtaining better goods and services. Earlier, needs were depicted as *informational* motives, because they are negatively reinforcing, i.e., the motive is to remove something negative. In contrast, wants can be thought of as *transformational motives* and positively reinforcing. Here, consumers are driven to purchase products and services that will produce benefits beyond their normal states.[31]

Marketing activities famously influence consumers' perceptions as to what their ideal states should be via advertising, promotion, endorsements, product placements, buzz marketing, and the like. For example, Dell tells us how much more productive we can be with Bluetooth and mobile broadband options; Verizon elevates our ideal states regarding mobile communication with VZ Navigator and Family Locator apps; and Subaru raises our perceptions of automobile reliability via exceptional service history.

By exposing consumers to new and better products, marketers induce problem recognition and provide a means for consumers to attain their ideal states or wants. But want creation also has a dark side. Targeting vulnerable audiences such as children, the elderly, and disadvantaged consumers can produce a wide range of deleterious effects on society. Likewise, a plethora of ethical concerns such as puffery and stereotyping surround the advertising business. Unscrupulous practices such as spamming, spyware, pyramid schemes, planned obsolescence, telemarketing fraud, and infomercial schemes also dot the marketing landscape with unsightly blemishes. Each of these unethical practices, though beyond the scope of this text, has generated considerable research in marketing.[32]

Some researchers have linked marketing to various problems in society, including pollution, materialism, alcohol and nicotine addictions, obesity and poor nutrition, and the denigration of cultural values.[33] Others argue that marketing has positively contributed to consumers' quality of life by reducing search costs, fostering innovation and broad product choices, facilitating product acquisition (e.g., e-commerce), and reducing prices via increased price competition. The overarching philosophy of this text maintains that individuals, businesses, and public policy can benefit from the study of consumer behavior. Following this perspective, the reader is encouraged to evaluate both sides of this complicated, global debate.[34]

Marketers are not alone in creating wants. Life changes also influence consumers' perceptions of their actual and ideal states. By virtue of time and circumstance, consumers' lives do not stand still. Human bodies and minds mature with age, people's relationships change, and consumer preferences shift accordingly. When you were in high school, you probably desired less autonomy and independence than you do today. If so, your ideal state has increased over time, creating a "want" for independence. Also, when you graduate from college, your lifestyle, financial situation, and employment status will change, altering perceptions of both your ideal and actual states. A steady job may trigger a desire for more expensive clothing, a sporty automobile, and a wider range of food choices (wants). In short, your standards of comparison will change, and firms such as Brooks Brothers, BMW, and Foods of All Nations will be eager to provide products and services to help you attain your wants. Marketers are also keenly aware of major life changes in the family life cycle, such as marriage, having children, and divorce. For example, Procter & Gamble dedicates an entire website to *Pampers,* which includes advice on pregnancy and preparing for the arrival of new babies. Life insurance firms encourage customers to consider increasing their levels of coverage as family size increases. Taken together, both marketing activities and various aspects of consumers' lives trigger problem recognition in the form of wants.

Opportunities

When a consumer's ideal and actual states simultaneously move in opposite directions, this combination creates a sizable want-got gap, or an **opportunity**. See Figure 9.7. Perhaps disenchantment with a current job is accompanied by a desire to experience a more promising future. Many non-traditional students describe their motivation to attend college in these terms. Alternatively, if a personal relationship begins to feel stifling at a time when a person's need for autonomy increases, she is likely to perceive a significant want-got gap and the motivation to close it. In a market context, if a consumer's favorite running shoes split and separate (a reduced actual state), and at the same time Nike introduces shoes with more advanced features and improved durability (an elevated ideal state), the consumer may feel motivated to pursue the new product offer. In this sense, an opportunity can be viewed as a chance to dramatically shift a consumer's reduced state to an elevated, ideal state.

Firms spend considerable time and effort identifying tactical opportunities in the marketplace. For example, Americans have repeatedly indicated their interest in fitness and health and at the same time, have reported feeling time-impoverished. As a consequence, clever marketers now offer time-saving, low-calorie foods (e.g., Lean Cuisine and Weight Watchers) and home fitness equipment (e.g., Nordictrack and Bowflex). Opportunities to close want-got gaps are emerging also in markets like China, whose 800 million rural citizens both need and want access to personal computing. In sum, opportunities depict the joint interplay of needs and wants because consumers' actual and ideal states diverge concurrently.

Researching consumers' discomforts and desires enables marketers to design and implement strategies that satisfy needs, wants, and opportunities, which is the essence of target marketing. Whether our want-got gaps are physiological, safety-oriented, social, or psychological in nature, marketers attempt to communicate benefits that shrink the gap between our ideal and actual states. But marketers are not always successful at closing these gaps completely. Consumers must perceive the benefits to be real (not just fluff), better than what they currently possess, and affordable. Furthermore, marketers must be able to articulate the benefits of their products. For example, despite millions of dollars aimed at educating consumers about its benefits, TiVo's digital video recorders (DVRs) initially generated disappointing market share because consumers did not understand what problems it would solve. Is the benefit of digital recording really worth the extra cost? How does "time shifting" work? Can consumers watch other programs while recording their favorite shows? Furthermore, many consumers would rather walk on hot coals than program a VCR, and TiVo was perceived to be *more* complicated than traditional recording devices. By the time consumers understood the benefits of DVRs, cable companies began offering similar features to their current customers—a captive audience.

AP Images/Paul Sakuma, file

TiVo failed to capitalize on an *opportunity* by inadequately communicating its benefits to consumers.

Global Perspectives

Lenovo Builds Computers for Chinese Farmers

Incorporated in Hong Kong, and headquartered in Raleigh, North Carolina, Lenovo Group Ltd. has a personal computer for China's 800 million rural inhabitants. Lenovo Group is the world's third-largest computer company by shipments and wants to increase global market share. Enter the bare-bones, low-cost PC aimed at China's farmers. The PC will sell for between $199 and $399, and include only a keyboard and processor. Televisions will have to substitute as monitors. Software designed to help farmers gather information about agricultural products is included.

As PC sales reach the maturity phase of the product life cycle in the United States, computer manufacturers are beginning to develop simple, lower-cost products aimed at first-time buyers in emerging markets, such as rural areas of China and India. China is now the largest PC market in the world (The United States is second). PC sales in China exceeded $11 billion during the second quarter of 2011. However, less than 10% of Chinese people own a computer. In contrast, more than 86% of Americans own a PC.

Lenovo's marketing plan is not without challenges. Although a $199 PC may appear to be a bargain to Westerners, it may be a difficult sell in rural China, where the average annual income is less than $600. However, Lenovo hopes to establish a dominant presence in China, despite new competition from Hewlett-Packard. and Dell. Currently, about one-third of all computers sold in China are made by Lenovo. Some experts claim that the PC may not be the triumphant technology in the developing world. For instance, in India, the rapid adoption of cell phones in rural areas suggests that high-tech handheld mobile devices could surpass the personal computer as the primary method for gaining access to the Internet.[35]

OBJECTIVE # The Nature of Information Search

Once a problem is recognized, consumers often gather information to inform their purchase decisions. Researchers refer to this activity as **prepurchase search** because the information gathered relates directly to a consumption problem at hand.[36] Prepurchase search follows the linear pattern of decision making outlined by the traditional model, where consumers first recognize a want-got gap and subsequently perform search activities to help close it. During prepurchase search efforts, consumers may access information from their long-term memories to recall past experiences with brands, potential options, and relevant evaluative criteria.[37] This deliberate retrieval of information, known as **internal search**, is common with low involvement decisions that comprise much of consumers' day-to-day activities. When internal search fails to provide adequate problem-solving information, consumers actively seek external sources of information. **External search** can engage personal sources (e.g., colleagues, friends and relatives), market sources such as advertisements and brochures, public sources (e.g., *Consumer Reports, Epinions,* and *ConsumerSearch.com*), and product trials, i.e., examining or testing products on a limited basis.

Consumers also obtain product information *without* recognizing a consumption problem. In these situations, consumers are not yet in the market for the products they examine and consider. Instead, they simply browse through catalogs, window shop, surf the Internet, or read specialty magazines without the intent of making a purchase. This type of information gathering, known as **ongoing search**, involves external search activities independent of solving an immediate purchase problem.[38]

Influences on Search

The extent of information processing is determined by consumer involvement, the marketing environment, situational influences, and individual differences. Researchers have identified two distinct types of consumer involvement: enduring and situational.[39] **Enduring involvement** describes a consumer's long-term and continuous interest in a brand or product category. Here, personal relevancy resides in the product itself and the inherent satisfaction that consumption or use brings to a consumer.[40] Most of us maintain enduring involvement with certain products. Fashion-conscious consumers enjoy clothes and jewelry, so they sustain long-term relationships with these products. Golf enthusiasts are drawn to new golf clubs, training aids, and apparel, and they relish the opportunity to play new golf courses. Wine connoisseurs seek out new varieties, build wine cellars, collect rare vintages, and visit vineyards. They are deeply and permanently involved with their avocation.

In contrast, **situational involvement** reflects a consumer's relatively temporary and context-dependent interest in a product or category. For example, an infrequent flyer who decides to visit a foreign country may suddenly find airline services and luggage products personally relevant. However, the level of involvement is related only to this specific situation. After returning from her trip, her involvement with travel-related products and services all but disappears—until the next journey. In a prepurchase situation, search generally derives from situational involvement with the consumption problem. To a large extent, consumers enlist prepurchase search strategies to reduce perceptions of risk.[41] Quite the reverse, ongoing search necessitates enduring involvement. This reflects more permanent interest and enthusiasm for a product or category on the part of the consumer, and not just a temporary concern triggered by immediate needs.

The marketing environment influences both prepurchase and ongoing search. Product information from advertising, salespeople, promotions, and the Internet can increase consumers' search efforts, along with highly accessible distribution channels (e.g., well-placed stores, retail catalogues, and e-commerce). Research shows that the location, availability, and distance between retail stores in a given geographic area can affect the number of visits consumers make prior to purchase. Thus, close proximity among stores can increase consumers' external search efforts.[42] Consumers' perceptions of wide price ranges can also increase external search. A recent study shows that consumers reduce information search when retailers offer *price-matching refunds*, because such policies are seen as a signal of low store prices.

External information search is not free—it takes time and effort. Traveling, parking, and dealing with crowds extract both monetary and psychological costs. Thus, consumers weigh the benefits of additional search against the costs of conducting it. Not surprisingly, the Internet can be an effective tool at reducing search costs, especially for those who are relatively young and well educated.[43] As a general rule, the greater the number of products in a category, the greater the external search is. More brands require more information processing. Too many choices, however, can cause psychological distress for consumers, causing them to end their search and select the most recognizable brand, a special case of brand laziness. Have you ever felt overwhelmed by the sheer number of available brands and as a result quickly grabbed the one most familiar to you? We call that type of information overload **brand overload**, a condition brought on by the proliferation of brands that offer few distinctive attributes or benefits.

Situational variables (separate from the market environment) can affect consumers' information search. For example, *time constraints* can pressure consumers into reducing their information processing. A recent study demonstrates that, under time constraints, consumers evaluate fewer alternatives and tend to ignore moderately important attributes.[44] Perceptions of crowding also cause people to reduce external search. As more people enter a store or restaurant, or as the store becomes packed with displays and merchandise, consumers are likely to experience discomfort. As a result, they process less information, make quicker decisions, and spend less time in the store. In addition, satisfaction with their shopping experience declines.[45] Other research reveals that consumers increase external search efforts when the purchase is important, information is highly accessible, and perceived risk is high.[46]

Individual differences influence both prepurchase and ongoing search activities. In general, younger, better-educated consumers expend more effort searching than those who are older and less educated. Also, middle-income consumers engage in more external search than both lower- and upper-income groups. For some individuals, gathering information about products and services is a full-time hobby. If you need to replace your cell phone or want a laptop, to whom would you turn for product information? You might seek out **market mavens**, people who search, accumulate, and share product knowledge with others. In some circles, market mavens are known as "price vigilantes" because they keep the marketplace honest through their vigilant watch over marketers' pricing tactics and trends. They are also regarded as product data banks. Market mavens are not just passive collectors of information; they also initiate discussions with other consumers and eagerly respond to requests

A single shopping center can offer dozens of stores stocked with a seemingly infinite number of brands, which sometimes results in brand overload for the consumer.

Oleksiy Maksymenko/Alamy

for information. They read more magazines and newspapers than the average consumer; they examine junk mail; and they regularly scrutinize *Consumer Reports*.[46] Because market mavens collect information for future use, they are experts at conducting ongoing search.

In contrast, some consumers enjoy shopping just for the sake of shopping. For them, it's the journey that counts. Research reveals that women are more likely to indicate that shopping is relaxing and enjoyable than are men. Specifically, only 29% of men say they enjoy shopping for clothes, compared with 48% of women. Stores with a wide selection appeal less to men. Apparently for men, it's convenience that counts. Also, stores that are easy to browse, are close to one's home or office, or have knowledgeable salespeople, appeal more to men than to women.[47] It therefore follows that women typically conduct more external search than men.

Prior knowledge and experience also affect the extent to which consumers conduct external search. Intuitively, one might expect those with low levels of expertise to spend the most time gathering product information. After all, they have the most to learn. On the other hand, you might say that consumers who possess product expertise might find external search easy to process and also search the most. Research supports neither of these views. In fact, moderately knowledgeable consumers process more product information than either the low or high knowledge groups.[48] These counterintuitive results can be explained as a function of two determinants of information processing: motivation and ability. Those low in product knowledge and experience are likely to be motivated to gather information, but without requisite knowledge, they couldn't make sense of the data even if they gathered them. Thus, because they view the task as too difficult, they give up searching and seek a simple solution. In contrast, those high in experience and knowledge—although perfectly capable of understanding the information—are not motivated to search. Instead, they rely on their past experiences and memory to guide their decisions. The moderately experienced consumer, on the other hand, may possess just enough motivation and ability to devote substantial search effort to the decision task. Figure 9.8 depicts search effort as a joint function of motivation and ability. The inverse U function illustrates that consumers who are both low and high with respect to product knowledge are less likely to conduct extensive search than those with moderate levels of product knowledge. This is consistent with classic personality research, which demonstrates that the greatest attitude change occurs at an intermediate level of a personality trait (e.g., knowledge).[49]

Motivation to Search

Regarding prepurchase search, consumers' motives are straightforward—to make a better purchase decision. For ongoing search, however, two separate motives emerge: to acquire a data bank of product information for future use[50] and pleasure or recreation. The first motive centers on consumers' desire for product knowledge, while the second motive derives from consumers' consumption experience.[51] Building a warehouse of product knowledge involves increasing product expertise for reasons other than optimizing an immediate decision. It can make consumers feel well informed, improve future choices, and enhance self-actualization.[52] Ongoing search activities can also be fun.

FIGURE 9.8 | Search Effort and Product Knowledge

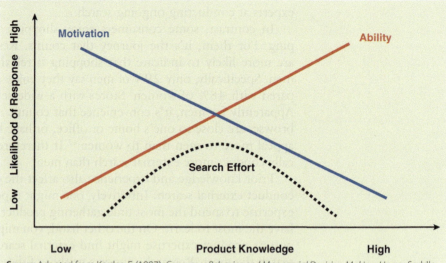

SOURCE: Adapted from Kardes, F. (1997). *Consumer Behavior and Managerial Decision Making.* Upper Saddle River, NJ: Prentice Hall.

Many consumers simply enjoy seeking information about products, whether by surfing the Internet or browsing through a traditional bricks-and-mortar store. For these consumers, shopping doesn't need to be purposeful. Shopping represents a leisure pursuit in and of itself, similar to attending a concert or movie or participating in a softball game. As the weekend approaches, listen to your friends discuss their alternatives plans. They are likely to include shopping—in terms of ongoing search—in the same consideration set as watching a movie, taking a road trip, or going to a sporting arena. Shopping is similar to other activities that compete for consumers' time; it's considered an *event*.

Results of Search

The outcomes or results of information search differ for prepurchase versus ongoing search. When consumers search for product information explicitly to solve a problem, prepurchase search can increase knowledge, optimize brand choice, and heighten satisfaction. For example, a consumer dedicates considerable prepurchase search effort to finding a brand of moisture-rich cosmetics to keep her delicate skin comfortable during a grueling business conference. If successful, she will have attained important information to reduce her search the next time she's in the market for cosmetics (e.g., Elizabeth Arden's Flawless Finish Radiant Moisture Makeup SPF 8 works well for her skin type). Perhaps most important, this consumer will have made a good choice, giving rise to satisfaction, i.e., comfortable skin.

Ongoing search can increase consumers' efficiency by allowing them to rely on less costly internal sources of information (e.g., memory). For example, most consumers realize that they will eventually need to replace their automobile tires. Ongoing searchers keep their "antennae" active long before the decision is necessary. They may read blogs on the Internet, pay attention to magazine and newspaper ads, and query friends who enthusiastically relay their experiences with various brands. Thus, when the decision is imminent (the tires won't pass the penny test!), ongoing searchers may be prepared to make a wise choice, without costly external search. Ongoing searchers also like to disseminate their stored knowledge to friends and family. Perhaps this is how market mavens are born. Being regarded as a product expert or opinion leader can enhance self-esteem. Finally, ongoing search engenders **impulse buying**, i.e., purchases made without prior planning. The more frequently consumers surf the Web and browse through traditional stores, the higher the probability is that they will eventually purchase on impulse.[53]

Economics of Search

Economic psychologists often describe two extreme cases of industry structure. In *perfect competition*, there are many firms, but competition among them is so intense that anytime one of them achieves a market advantage, the others quickly duplicate it. As a result, the firms end up producing identical products. In perfect competition, brands do not have identities because the "sameness" of the products makes the concept meaningless. For example, while you are likely to recall the brand of cereal you ate for breakfast this morning, you probably do not know the brand of the milk you poured on the cereal. Milk comes close to satisfying the requirements of a perfectly competitive product; a gallon of milk from one producer is virtually identical to a gallon of milk from any other producer. At the other extreme of industry structure is *monopoly*, in which case, there is only one producer. For example, almost everyone who owns a PC needs a copy of the *Windows* operating system, and that is offered by only one producer, Microsoft Corp.

What do these two extremes of industry structure have in common? In both cases, the consumer decision making process is simple, and information search is virtually eliminated. In the case of perfect competition, while there are many competing brands (e.g., gasoline), the fact that the products are virtually identical means that consumers need not compare brands. Instead, consumers only need to answer the question, "Do I want this product at the going price?" In the case of monopoly (e.g., a local electric company), there is only one brand and so again, the only relevant question is, "Do I want this product?"

Most consumer choices take place in the intermediate case of industry structure known as *monopolistic competition*. In a monopolistically competitive industry, consumers are faced with many competing brands, each of which is different from the other in one or several attributes. Monopolistic competition creates a unique problem for consumers: it is nearly impossible to obtain full information about all competing brands prior to making a purchase decision. In fact, fully aware that they may choose the wrong brand, consumers try to make the *best* choice, given limited information search. In general, researchers refer to this concept as **bounded rationality**, the idea that consumers can only make rational decisions within the limits of time and cognitive capability.[54] Economic psychologist Antony Davies has developed a way to explain how consumers interpret the marketplace, given their limited rationality. The model provides a foundation for examining product consideration, evaluation, and choice.

Milk comes very close to being a perfectly competitive product, as a gallon of milk from one supplier will likely taste nearly identical to a gallon of milk from another supplier.

OBJECTIVE **5**

Evaluation of Alternatives: An Uncertainty-Reduction Model

We have discussed why consumers conduct information search. But exactly what information do consumers need? There are three pieces of information necessary to conduct prepurchase and ongoing search: the number of available brands, the determinant attributes for the product category, and how an individual thinks he will reacts to a brand after it is purchased. In practice, consumers almost never know even one of these three pieces of information. For example, how many brands of beer can the average consumer recall? Beer connoisseurs (product experts) might recall as many as 20 or more brands. Nevertheless, approximately 500 brands of beer exist in U.S. markets alone. Even the most avid beer expert would not be aware of all these! Next, suppose that a consumer considers six important attributes for the product category, beer: color, aroma, taste, alcohol content, carbonation, and price. Can this consumer rate each brand on these six attributes? Probably not (unless the consumer's list is very short). Lastly, this consumer probably does not know exactly how well he would like these brands, even if he could rate them all. For example, he may claim not to like dark beer, but it's possible that he might like a dark beer brewed with a lot of hops, or a dark beer with heavy carbonation. Thus, consumers' inability to perfectly predict how much they will like a brand is another source of uncertainty.

Given enough search effort, consumers could, potentially, acquire all the information necessary to make a rational purchase decision. The term *rational* means that, with complete information, consumers would make decisions that maximize their satisfaction. However, the cost of acquiring information often exceeds the benefits of making the best decision.[55] For example, no one is willing to spend five years of research just to find the single best cereal. Instead, we settle for the good-though-perhaps-not-best cereal. Gathering and using product information under uncertainty is the focus of the **uncertainty-reduction model**.

Consumer Uncertainty

The uncertainty-reduction model describes how consumers attempt to reduce their uncertainty when they search and evaluate product information. Like the traditional model of consumer decision making, the uncertainty-reduction model views consumers as relatively involved problem solvers. Accordingly, consumers must come to terms with the actual brands available in the market. The set of **actual brands** represents all brands that exist along with measures of each of their attributes. The set of actual brands is an objective reality. Because it is prohibitively costly to gather complete and fully accurate information about all existing brands and their attributes, what is in a consumer's head is not the set of actual brands but a set of **perceived brands**. The set of perceived brands includes only those brands that a consumer acknowledges—whether real or not. Three sources of **external uncertainty** create noise during information search and cause a consumer's perceived brands to differ from actual brands. The sources of external uncertainty are incomplete information, measurement error, and obsolete information. *Incomplete information* suggests that consumers may be unaware of all the existing or actual brands. For example, if you have never heard of Castle Rock beer, then your perceived brand set suffers from incomplete information. Quite the reverse, if you mistakenly perceive a brand that doesn't exist, your perceived brand set also contains incomplete information. *Measurement error* describes a condition in which consumers may measure brands' attributes inaccurately or may be unaware of a particular attribute. For example, you may believe that all dark beers are sour tasting. However, because some are actually sweet, your perceived brand set suffers from measurement error. Finally, *obsolete information* describes a situation such that consumers fail to update their perception of the actual brand set as quickly as the actual brand set evolves. Perhaps the last time you purchased an Apple laptop computer, the price was double that of other brands. Since then, Apple has lowered its prices to be more competitive with Dell and other brands. If you do not revise your perception of Apple's price to match the changed reality, your perceived brand set suffers from obsolete information.

Consumers must also come to understand the *true pleasure* they are likely to derive by using various combinations of brands or brand attributes. For example, some consumers obtain more pleasure from coffee than tea. In the same way, a consumer may gain more pleasure from a dark roast Columbian variety versus a decaffeinated coffee. A consumer's **true preference** is the actual pleasure she will obtain from consuming various brands, i.e., another objective reality. However, consumers don't know as much about their own preferences as they think they do. It is time-consuming and expensive to sample every existing brand. So, even when consumers fully understand a brand's attributes, their reactions to those attributes may be different from what they anticipated. Thus, a consumer's **perceived preference**, what she believes her reaction will be to various brands and their attributes, differs from her true preference.

Two sources of **internal uncertainty**—uncertainty about the consumer himself—cause a consumer's perceived preference to differ from his true preference: absolute error and relative error. *Absolute error* describes a consumer's uncertainty regarding satisfaction that a particular attribute will deliver. Through experience, consumers learn how much pleasure they will gain by using or consuming various products. For example, a consumer may have full information about a car's auto parking system, but he may incorrectly believe that auto parking is less important than it truly is. It may not be until he has driven the car for a while that he realizes auto parking is very rewarding. In contrast, *relative error* describes situations where consumers are uncertain about the relative influence or weight of *each* attribute on his true preference. For example, a consumer may be fully aware of a car's gas mileage and engine power. However, he may incorrectly gauge his willingness to reduce mileage to increase performance. It may not be until he has purchased the car and filled it up a few times that he realizes he would have preferred to give up some engine power in exchange for more miles per gallon.[56] In sum, because consumers cannot know every brand in the market or how much they will like those brands, they cannot know either the set of actual brands or their true preferences. Accordingly, consumers construct a mental picture of their reactions (perceived preference) and the world around them (perceived brands). Bounded by our rationality, consumers then organize that mental picture to form their notion of the overall market, or the perceived product market.

The Perceived Product-Market

Regardless of whether consumers conduct prepurchase or ongoing search, their perceptions of existing brands, along with their perceived preferences, influence how they construe the marketplace (see Figure 9.9). Here, the old adage, "perceptions are greater than reality" holds true. A consumer's **perceived**

FIGURE 9.9 | An Uncertainty-Reduction Model

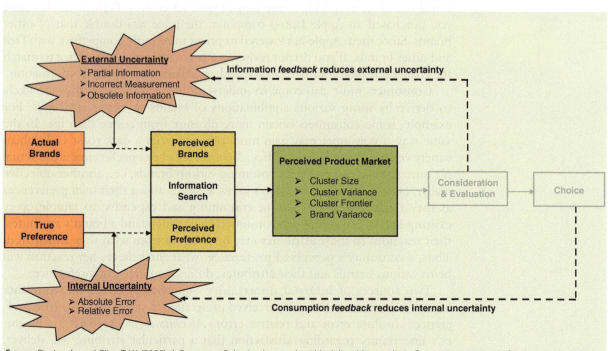

Source: Davies, A., and Cline T. W. (2005). A Consumer Behavior Approach to Modeling Monopolistic Competition. *Journal of Economic Psychology, 26*, 797–826.

product-market represents a patterned organization of brands in her mind. Consider the market for ice cream. Suppose a consumer views the product-market as possessing two determinant attributes: taste and calories. Furthermore, let's assume she is aware of six brands: Weight Watchers, Carvel, Edy's, Häagen-Dazs, Ben & Jerry's, and Breyers. These brands and the consumer's belief about their attributes constitute the consumer's perceived brands. Although limited by internal uncertainty, this consumer is also aware how she "feels" about ice-cream taste and ice-cream calories. These feelings constitute the consumer's perceived preference. When this consumer combines her perceived brands with her perceived preference, she forms an intuitive image of the product-market. Her perceived product-market for ice cream is represented in Figure 9.10. Each dot represents the consumer's perception as to the pleasure she will obtain from the attributes she perceives each brand to have. The further up and to the right a dot is located, the more (perceived) pleasure the consumer obtains from the brand's attributes.

Notice that in the consumer's mind, the brands naturally fall into two *clusters*. The three brands at the top left (Weight Watchers, Carvel, and Edy's) score high on pleasure from fewer calories but low on pleasure from taste. Together, these brands comprise the *low-calorie cluster*. The other three brands (Häagen-Dazs, Ben & Jerry's, and Breyers) score high on pleasure from taste but low on pleasure obtained from fewer calories. Together, these brands comprise the *high taste cluster*. This clustering of brands is the first step the consumer takes in looking, either consciously or subconsciously, for patterns among brands. By **clustering**, the consumer simplifies the task of choosing a brand by thinking not of many individual brands, but of a few clusters of brands, each with a key attribute. Consumers naturally think of brands this way. People talk about domestic versus imported beer, vans versus SUVs, houses versus apartments, city versus suburb, and so on.

Four important characteristics of the consumer's perceived product-market describe something about the product-market that is relevant to the consumer's subsequent choice:

1. **Cluster size**, the number of brands the consumer places in the cluster
2. **Cluster variance**, the degree to which brands within a single cluster are dissimilar from each other
3. **Cluster frontier**, the best possible combination of attributes observed within a cluster
4. **Brand variance**, a consumer's awareness of uncertainty as to an individual brand's attributes

Consideration and Choice

After constructing perceptions of the product-market, consumers follow a two-stage choice process of *consideration* and *choice*. In the consideration stage, consumers often select a single cluster of brands via a non-compensatory process.[57] A **non-compensatory process** is a simple, although error-prone, way to make a decision in which the person does not consider trade-offs. For example, it is easier to decide whether to drink a caffeinated drink or a caffeine-free drink (a non-compensatory decision) than it is to decide *which* caffeinated drink or *which* caffeine-free drink to drink (a compensatory decision). The non-compensatory decision is easy because it is binary—"I want caffeine" versus "I don't want caffeine."

FIGURE **9.10** | **Two-Dimensonal Preceived Product-Market for Ice Cream**

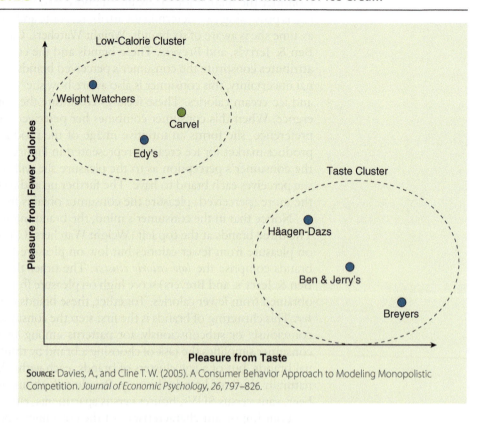

Source: Davies, A., and Cline T. W. (2005). A Consumer Behavior Approach to Modeling Monopolistic Competition. *Journal of Economic Psychology, 26,* 797–826.

In the choice stage, consumers evaluate the brands in the considered cluster via a **compensatory process**. The compensatory process is difficult because it requires weighing trade-offs—"Red Bull tastes better than Hype, but Hype is less expensive," and "Is Red Bull's additional taste worth the additional price?" While a non-compensatory process requires less thought and fewer facts, a compensatory process requires the person to consider and weigh much more information. Why do consumers use this two-stage process? When faced with many competing brands, the consumer is confronted with the conflicting goals of making a decision with little effort and making an optimal decision. The consumer balances these two conflicting goals by employing a non-compensatory process so as to "whittle down" the field of competing brands to a manageable subset. The consumer then applies a compensatory process to evaluate the smaller set of brands and select a single brand for purchase.[57] For example, when looking for student housing, one person may begin by considering only apartments with two or more bathrooms, while another student may begin by considering only locations convenient to the university.

In terms of the perceived product-market, consumers apply non-compensatory decision making in selecting a single cluster ("consideration") followed by compensatory decision making to select a single brand from within the considered cluster (choice). The product-market characteristics suggest heuristics—or "rules of thumb"—that the consumer will use in consideration and choice. Let's focus on a set of heuristics that derives from consumers' perceptions of a product-market.

Cluster Size Consumers may interpret larger cluster size as an indication of lesser *external uncertainty* because:

1. Observing more brands can imply that a greater proportion of the actual brands has been observed (reducing partial information).
2. Observing more brands with similar attributes (i.e., brands in the same cluster) can provide confirmation that the consumer has correctly observed attribute levels (reducing measurement error).
3. Observing more brands in a specific cluster can imply a lesser probability of a brand having altered its attributes; the cluster may be stable over time (reducing obsolete information).

For example, suppose a consumer observes ten cars, all with reported gas mileage in the 25 to 30 miles per gallon (mpg) range and one car with a reported gas mileage of 60 mpg. All else being equal, this consumer is more likely to question the 60 mpg because all the other cars she has seen are in the 25 to 30 mpg range. Observing more brands with similar attributes provides confirmation that the consumer has correctly observed the attributes. Interestingly, during the 1970s, consumers may have believed that the VHS format would supplant the Betamax format because there were a greater number of brands using the VHS format (which indeed proved to be the case). Similarly, despite being more user-friendly and employing a more powerful microprocessor, the Apple Macintosh brand lost substantial market share to IBM clones during the 1980s. One possible explanation is that there were a large number of brands in the IBM clone cluster, and consumers interpreted this as a signal of greater survival probability for the PC cluster. See Figure 9.11—Cluster 1 is the largest because it contains the most brands.

Consumers may also interpret the number of brands in a cluster as a proxy for the demand for brands in that cluster.[58] Thus, a larger cluster size can signal less *internal uncertainty* because observing more brands implies that consumers' preferences are being satisfied. This is consistent with evidence that consumers make use of other people's experience when making purchase decisions.[59] For example, suppose a consumer investigates ten cell phone plans, nine of which come with free texting, with one plan charging for texting. All else being equal, the consumer is likely to judge that other consumers like free texting and that, consequently, he will also like free texting. In addition, people have inherent motives to justify their decisions to others and to themselves,[60] i.e., to bolster self-esteem,[61] to alleviate cognitive dissonance,[62] and to reduce anticipation of regret.[63] A larger set of brands in a cluster can help consumers justify their behavior to others and confirm their behavior to themselves. In sum, because a large cluster size decreases both perceived internal and external uncertainties, as the size of a cluster increases, the likelihood that a consumer will consider that cluster increases.

Cluster Variance Consumers may interpret larger cluster variation as an indication of greater *external uncertainty* because observing large differences among brands within a cluster could indicate:

1. Consumers have incorrectly grouped dissimilar brands into the same cluster.
2. Consumers have erroneously measured some of the attributes of the brands in the cluster.

FIGURE 9.11 | **Characteristics of the Perceived Product Market**

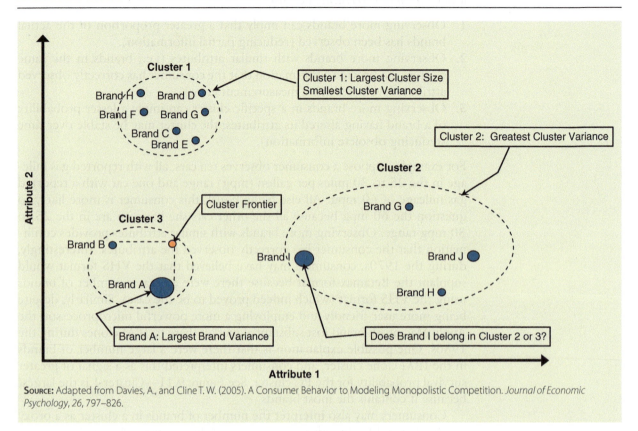

SOURCE: Adapted from Davies, A., and Cline T. W. (2005). A Consumer Behavior to Modeling Monopolistic Competition. *Journal of Economic Psychology, 26,* 797–826.

Consumers may also interpret larger cluster variance as an indication of greater *internal uncertainty* because

1. Observing a large difference among brand attributes within a cluster implies greater uncertainty regarding the consequences of a purchase from this cluster.
2. High cluster variance may send confusing signals about the *importance* of the various attributes.

For example, suppose a consumer observes four brands of hair coloring. The brands require that the coloring treatment be left in for 1 minute, 5 minutes, 10 minutes, and 20 minutes, respectively. The large variation among the treatment times can make the consumer less certain as to the benefit of treatment time, increasing internal uncertainty. In sum, cluster variance increases the likelihood of a consumer making a bad purchase decision. Therefore, as cluster variance increases, the likelihood of the consumer considering that cluster decreases (see Figure 9.11). Because the brands in Cluster 1 are relatively similar, i.e., close together, Cluster 1 has the smallest cluster variance. In contrast, Cluster 2 shows the greatest variation. In fact, one might argue that Brand I belongs in Cluster 3, not Cluster 2.

Cluster Frontier (The Ideal Brand) Once the consumer has selected a single cluster for consideration, the consumer then employs compensatory decision making to select a single brand from within the considered cluster. The cluster frontier represents a hypothetical brand that contains the best attributes of all brands within the cluster. It may be helpful to think of the cluster frontier as the perceived *ideal brand* in a given cluster. For example, suppose a consumer sees two water heaters within a single cluster. Brand A has an annual electricity usage of $400 (efficiency) and a 40-gallon capacity. Brand B has an annual electricity usage of $500 and a 60-gallon capacity. If there were no uncertainty in the consumer's mind as to these attributes, then the consumer would assume that the ideal water heater would have a 60-gallon capacity and cost $400 annually to operate. This combination of efficiency and capacity would represent the *cluster frontier,* or the best possible case for a water heater (see Figure 9.11). Cluster 2 shows a frontier that combines the best of Brands A and B.

Brand Variance Consumers are rarely certain about a brand's true attributes. For example, a consumer can see that a water heater is rated to use $400 in electricity annually. But the consumer knows that this figure is only an estimate; differences in electric rates, in hot water usage, and a unit's efficiency cause the actual electricity usage to vary. The greater the brand variance, the less able the consumer is to infer the cluster frontier, or ideal brand. Suppose that the consumer is unsure about the attributes of Brand A in Figure 9.11. What if the consumer perceives that the operating cost for Brand A could be off by as much as $200 per year, and that the capacity could be off by as much as five gallons? This means that the perceived ideal water heater in the best-case scenario could have a 65-gallon capacity and cost $200 per year, or, in the worst-case scenario, could have a 35-gallon capacity and a cost of $600 per year. Because the consumer is less certain as to the cluster frontier, the consumer is less certain as to how far from the cluster frontier these two brands are. Thus, the greater the brand variance, the less useful the cluster frontier is as a benchmark for making a choice. The larger size for Brand A in Figure 9.11 indicates a greater brand variance.

In summary, consumers, when faced with incomplete information, construct perceptions of a product-market. After consuming a chosen product, consumers revise information about both the product's attributes and the pleasure gleaned from the attributes in an attempt to reduce uncertainty. Consumers then adapt their perception of the product-market by mentally repositioning the consumed brand and, possibly, reforming clusters. The consumer bases a subsequent purchase decision on this revised mental mapping of the product-market.

OBJECTIVE **6** # Post-Purchase Evaluation

The uncertainty-reduction model emphasizes that consumers continuously process information about brands and their attributes *after* purchase and consumption. This feedback is depicted with dashed lines returning from "choice" to external and internal uncertainty in Figure 9.9. By potentially reducing uncertainties, consumers allow for updated product-market perceptions and, potentially, better future decisions. The traditional model also acknowledges consumers' feedback loop. Figure 9.5 shows that, after consumers conduct "post-purchase evaluation," they integrate this information into their future decisions by informing any of the previous processes. In some cases, post-purchase evaluation may send consumers back to the drawing board with problem recognition. Perhaps the purchase created a new problem or failed to solve the old one. In either case, the extensive information processing and high levels of involvement necessitate an entirely new problem-solving process. On the other hand, a successful choice may require only that consumers loop back to the "choice" phase. Perhaps a successful low involvement purchase decision leads to brand laziness, or a higher involvement purchase encourages brand loyalty. In any event, consumers are not likely to conduct new search or re-evaluate alternatives. The intermediate case of variety seeking suggests that, even with a moderately successful post-purchase evaluation, consumers may return to the "evaluation of alternatives" or "information search" phases of decision making, seeking and processing new information that will lead to a different choice. How do consumers decide if the purchase was successful? In a word—*satisfaction*.

Consumer Satisfaction

Consumer satisfaction is determined by consumers' post-purchase evaluations of their decisions. Consumers constantly evaluate their choices as they integrate products into their daily lives.[64] Satisfaction is important to marketers because it influences future purchases. The marketing concept suggests that consumer satisfaction should be the focal point of marketing activities. Research shows that satisfaction positively influences consumers' repeat purchase intentions and leads to higher spending. Another study demonstrates that satisfied customers are willing to spend more on a brand that they like.[65] But these effects can be offset by competitive intensity, i.e., the number of available alternatives.[66] In the same vein, research demonstrates that customer retention is driven by a brand's advantage over other choices, not just consumers' overall evaluations of the chosen brand.[67] Finally, a recent study reveals that extremely high levels of satisfaction can translate into brand loyalty, the most important strategic objective of marketing managers worldwide. However, consumers who have a longstanding relationship with a brand demonstrate a high risk of switching when their loyalty is weakly held.[68]

Dissonance-Reduction Consumers ask themselves a number of questions after purchasing a brand. Was this brand the right choice? Is it better than alternative choices? One of the strategies consumers use to assess their satisfaction is to compare the chosen brand with a rejected alternative. The chosen brand is the product the consumer actually purchased, while the rejected alternative is a brand considered, but not chosen. If the chosen brand seems superior to the rejected alternative during post-purchase evaluation, then consumers experience satisfaction and minimal cognitive dissonance. The converse is also true: if the chosen product appears inferior to a rejected alternative, then cognitive dissonance sets in, leading to dissatisfaction. Evidence of post-purchase dissonance may include comments such as, "Gee, I wish I had purchased the other brand," and, "I paid too much. I should have searched more stores." Cognitive dissonance involves behavior-attitude inconsistency

Marketing in Action

Ben and Jerry's and Miller Brewing: Changing Consumer Perceptions

At the height of the weight-conscious 1990s, Ben and Jerry's launched an ad campaign highlighting the fact that their brand was *not* low in calories. The ad went on to claim that Ben and Jerry's great taste was worth the higher calories. Perhaps unwittingly, the campaign altered consumers' perceptions of the cluster frontier among premium ice creams. Let's take a look at Figure 9.12, which shows a hypothetical consumer's perceived product-market for ice cream.

Among the high taste cluster, the consumer is aware of Häagen-Dazs, Ben and Jerry's, and Breyers. The consumer also perceives that the "ideal" premium ice cream is one that has the flavor of Breyers, but the calories of Häagen-Dazs. This point is labeled *original cluster frontier*. The point of the Ben and Jerry's ad campaign was to convince consumers that there is a trade-off between taste and calories, such that it is impossible for a brand to posses the taste of Breyers and the calories of Häagen-Dazs. As a result, Ben and Jerry's hoped that consumers

would shift their perceptions of the cluster frontier to the point labeled *new cluster frontier*. Why? Given that Ben and Jerry's is positioned between Häagen-Dazs and Breyers, moving the cluster frontier in this way puts Ben and Jerry's closer to this ideal point, resulting in an increase in market share for Ben and Jerry's at the expense of Häagen-Dazs and Breyers.

Similarly, in the early 1990s, the Miller Brewing Company introduced a new brand, Red Dog. With respect to taste and price, two of the most salient attributes for beer, Miller positioned Red Dog to be similar, although inferior, to its flagship brand, Miller Genuine Draft (MGD). Market analysts warned that, by introducing a new brand so similar to its flagship brand, Miller risked siphoning off market share from the flagship brand, a phenomenon known as *cannibalization*. What happened, however, was the reverse—Red Dog attained market presence while increasing MGD's market share. The uncertainty-reduction model offers an explanation for these unexpected

FIGURE 9.12 | Cluster Frontiers for Ice Cream

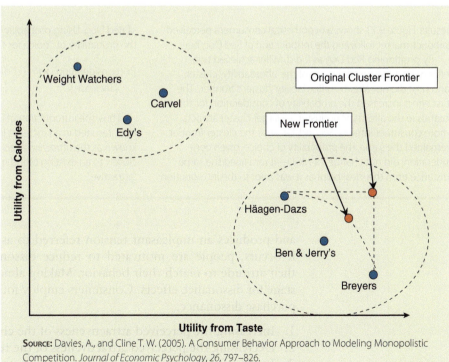

SOURCE: Davies, A., and Cline T. W. (2005). A Consumer Behavior Approach to Modeling Monopolistic Competition. *Journal of Economic Psychology, 26,* 797–826.

FIGURE **9.13** | **Cluster Frontiers For Beer**

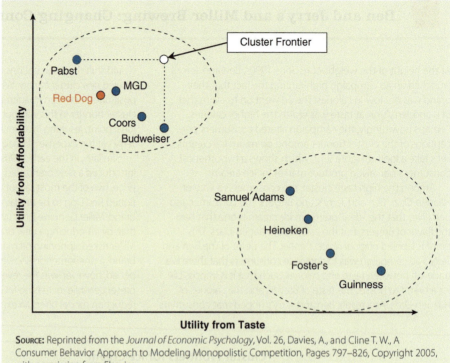

Source: Reprinted from the *Journal of Economic Psychology*, Vol. 26, Davies, A., and Cline T. W., A Consumer Behavior Approach to Modeling Monopolistic Competition, Pages 797–826, Copyright 2005, with permission from Elsevier.

results. Figure 9.13 shows a hypothetical consumer's perceived product-market following the introduction of Red Dog beer.

By positioning Red Dog as it did, Miller achieved two effects: (1) it increased the size of the "affordability" cluster, and (2) it did not alter the affordability cluster's frontier. The first effect increased the probability of consideration for the brands in the affordability cluster—a larger cluster attracts more consumer interest. Second, because the cluster frontier remained the same, the probability of choice, given consideration, did not change for MGD—it remained the same distance from the ideal point as it was prior to the introduction

of Red Dog. Using probability notation, the overall impact on the probability of choice for MGD is:

$$\text{Pr (consideration)} \times \text{Pr (choice | consideration)} = \text{Pr (choice)}$$
$$\text{[Increase]} \qquad\qquad \text{[No Change]} \qquad\qquad \text{[Increase]}$$

Thus, the introduction of Red Dog, an objectively inferior beer, resulted in an increase in market share for MGD. This is known as the *attraction effect*: an inferior brand positioned closely to an existing brand makes the existing brand more "attractive."

and produces an unpleasant tension referred to as dissonance arousal. When it occurs, people are motivated to reduce dissonance arousal by changing their attitude to match their behavior. Making almost any decision can set the stage for dissonance effects. Consumers employ four strategies to reduce post-purchase dissonance:

1. Increasing the perceived attractiveness of the chosen alternative
2. Decreasing the perceived attractiveness of the rejected alternative
3. Increasing the perceived similarity among alternatives
4. Revoking the decision

The first strategy, known as *sweet lemons,* involves attempts to raise the positive qualities of the chosen alternative. The second strategy, called *sour grapes,* entails disparaging the qualities of rejected alternatives. The third strategy attempts to level the playing field by interpreting all alternatives as similar. The final strategy involves reversing the choice. For example, you might attempt to return the chosen brand in exchange for one of the alternatives.

In a classic study of post-purchase dissonance, consumers were asked to rate the attractiveness of several products, including a stopwatch, silk screen print, portable radio, and fluorescent lamp.[69] They were also told that, at the end of the study, they would receive one of these products as a gift. In the high-dissonance condition, consumers were asked to choose between two products they rated nearly equal in desirability. In the low-dissonance condition, consumers were asked to choose between a product they rated highly and a product they rated much lower in desirability. After receiving their gifts, consumers were asked again to rate all the products. Large shifts in attitude occurred in the high-dissonance condition. The chosen product was rated slightly higher and the rejected product was rated much lower after the decision was made. In contrast, smaller shifts in attitude occurred for the low-dissonance condition. Only the chosen product was rated slightly higher after the choice occurred.

Expectancy Disconfirmation Model In assessing their satisfaction, consumers may also want to know the extent to which their chosen product lived up to its expectations. The **expectancy disconfirmation model** suggests that consumers form expectations about product performance prior to purchasing a brand.[70] After buying a product, people compare their perceptions of its performance on various key attributes against the level of performance that was expected on those same attributes. If consumers' perceptions of the brand's performance are in line with their expectations, they are more likely to be satisfied. If the brand performs more poorly than expected, dissatisfaction sets in. But if performance exceeds expectations, consumers may experience supra-satisfaction, or *customer delight.* Note that consumers' prior expectancies are confirmed if the product performs as anticipated, while expectancies are disconfirmed if the brand performs more poorly or better than expected. This model can be expressed statistically as:

$S = \Sigma w(p - e)$, where satisfaction (S) is a function of the importance weights that consumers assign to each attribute (w) and the difference between perceptions and expectations on those attributes ($p - e$).

When the sum of all the perceptions minus expectations equals zero, consumers are perfectly satisfied. When this sum dips below zero, consumers become dissatisfied, and when the function returns a value greater than zero, consumers are supra-satisfied. The expectancy disconfirmation model suggests that consumers will be dissatisfied with excellent products if their expectations are too high. Conversely, consumers may be pleased with mediocre products that exceed expectations. So, whatever expectations that exist in the minds of consumers prior to purchase are as important as consumers' perceptions of a brand's performance. This line of thinking creates a potential *satisfaction paradox,* a conundrum in which marketers must create sufficiently high expectations to induce brand trial, but not so high as to engender disappointment. In other words, brands that generate extremely low expectations will experience difficulty in getting consumers to try them. Conversely, when marketers build unrealistic expectations for brands, they are destined to disappoint.

Performance-Based Satisfaction The expectancy disconfirmation model assumes that product performance is always compared to consumers' *initial* expectations or goals. When those goals are met, satisfaction results; if they are not met, dissatisfaction follows. This model also implies that consumers who attain low expectations will be just as satisfied as consumers who achieve higher expectations. Recent research on **performance-based satisfaction** shows the opposite can be true: consumers who set and meet lower expectations are typically less satisfied than consumers who set and meet higher expectations. This occurs because consumers' initial expectations do not always serve as the standard of comparison for evaluating performance.[71] Instead, consumers often compare the performance of a product with the product's best possible outcome, or its *potential*. For example, let's say John invests in a low-risk mutual fund and expects an 8% annual return. Jane, on the other hand, picks a riskier portfolio and a target return of 14%. Both investors believe that the best possible annual return of mutual fund is about 20%. At the end of the year, John's fund earned 8% and Jane's earned 14%, exactly meeting their expectations. Whereas the expectancy disconfirmation model predicts that John and Jane will be equally satisfied, performance-based satisfaction research demonstrates that this will only be the case if John is reminded of his initial, *lower* goal. Without a deliberate reminder from his fund adviser, John is likely to use the fund's potential (20%) as a standard of comparison, and he will see a relatively higher gap between performance and potential than will Jane. Why do consumers use a brand's potential rather than their initial expectations or goals? Some psychologists believe that people are wistful of "what could be," particularly if they believe they cannot attain the best possible outcome. If consumers are naturally forward-looking, it is easier for them to think about a brand's potential, which relates to the future rather than their expectations, which relate to the past.[72]

Complaining Behavior Because consumers are not always satisfied with their product experiences, effective resolution of consumer complaints can have a dramatic effect on customer retention, reduce the spread of damaging word-of-mouth, and improve profitability.[73] Complaint handling strategies are particularly critical in the service industry, where customer satisfaction leads to long-term trust with and commitment to an organization. One framework for managing complaining behavior views customer complaints as a sequence of three events: (1) a *procedure* beginning with communicating the complaint, (2) an *interaction* between the customer and representatives of the organization, and (3) a *distribution* of benefits to the dissatisfied customer.[74] From a consumer's perspective, each of these events translates into a specific *justice. Procedural justice* indicates that the company has assumed responsibility for the problem and is providing a timely resolution. *Interactional justice* involves a polite, honest, and empathetic response from the service provider. *Distributive justice* focuses on compensation issues such as refunds, replacements, and repairs, along with an apology. In order to achieve even a modest level of satisfaction with complaint handling, an organization must perform relatively high on all three justice components. Failure on just one of the three leads to consumer dissatisfaction.

Research dealing with online complaining behavior demonstrates the potential for customers to punish and avoid firms that fail to resolve their complaints.[75] While customers' feelings for revenge eventually dissipate over time, their avoidance behavior increases with time. In other words, online complainers maintain grudges through their increasing desire to completely disengage with firms. Most alarming, a firm's best customers—those who believe they have a strong relationship with the firm—feel more betrayed and show stronger revenge and avoidance desires than do customers who have a weaker relationship with the firm. Postcomplaint resolution can reduce consumers' desire for revenge, but only if the resolution immediately follows the complaint. Moreover, best customers do not need expensive compensation (e.g., refund) to assuage their feelings of revenge. On the other hand, resolving online complainers' problems does not seem to bring back their business. The implications are clear: the best marketers can do with online complainers is eliminate their desire to punish with additional public complaints. Accordingly, marketers should encourage consumers to resolve complaints directly with the firm, demonstrating a positive resolution process that engenders trust and commitment. By the time complaints reach the Internet, it may be too late.

Ethics

Would you like a better deal when negotiating the price of a car, a house, or a service contract? Would it be ethical for a consumer to fake anger if it got him a better deal? According to professors Eduardo B. Andrade and Teck-Hua Ho from the University of California, Berkeley, showing anger can

work to a haggler's benefit.[76] These researchers set up a series of "emotion gaming" experiments and discovered that not only does displaying emotions work to a haggler's benefit, but those who show emotions often pretend they're upset for the purposes of financial gain.[77] One particular experiment simulated a retail environment. Sellers offered to divide a pot of money and receivers now had the option of accepting or rejecting the offer. A rejected offer, just like in the consumer world, meant that both the seller and buyer received no gains.

Researchers told half of the angry buyers that their irateness would be shown to the sellers. The results show that those who knew that their anger would be revealed added a little drama. Equally interesting, buyers received a better offer from sellers as long as sellers thought that the buyer's feelings were genuine. When sellers learned that buyers might be inflating their anger, the effect attenuated. Have you ever faked anger to get a better deal? Did it work? Is it ethical?

Chapter Summary

This chapter focused on how consumers recognize problems, define their markets, gather information related to their consideration and purchase decisions, and determine their satisfaction. Consumer decision making can be defined by the amount of effort people exert to solve a problem. Routine response behavior involves minimal effort, intermediate problem solving entails mid-level effort, and extensive

problem solving requires a great deal of effort. Consumer decision making can also be characterized as a joint function of processing effort and involvement, which creates four distinct types of decisions. When both involvement and information processing are low, consumers typically make choices as a matter of habit, or exhibit brand laziness, as opposed to a fundamental commitment to the brand. When consumer involvement is high and information processing is low, consumers exhibit brand loyalty, an intrinsic commitment to a brand based on the benefits or values it provides consumers. When consumers experience low involvement and high information processing, they exhibit variety seeking behavior, the desire to choose new alternatives over more familiar ones—just for the sake of change. Finally, when both involvement and information processing are high, consumers engage in genuine problem-solving strategies. Because consumers cannot consider all the features of a brand, they must identify one or more determinant attributes, characteristics of a product that are both important and unique, and thus, most likely to affect the buyer's choice. Problem solving is the focus of the traditional model of consumer decision making because the decision involves relatively high levels of risk.

The traditional model of consumer decision making involves five stages of consumer problem solving. Problem recognition takes place when consumers experience a disparity between what they have and what they want. This is known as a want-got gap. Needs, wants, and opportunities trigger problem solving. Information search involves both the active and passive processing of data aimed at solving the problem. The level of search is determined by consumer involvement, the marketing environment, situational influences, and individual differences. Evaluation of alternatives requires consumers to determine which product attributes are important and which brands to evaluate on the basis of these attributes. Purchase decisions represent consumers' predispositions or intentions to buy a brand. Finally,

during post-purchase evaluation, consumers compare their perceptions of a brand with their expectations and determine their satisfaction.

The uncertainty-reduction model recognizes that consumers can only make rational decisions within the limits of time and cognitive capability. This approach to decision making involves four stages that specifically deal with consumers' bounded rationality. First, consumers develop perceptions of what the product-market looks like. Next, they whittle down the vast number of brands into a single subset of brands for consideration. Then, consumers choose one brand from the consideration set. Finally, based on their consumption experiences, consumers adjust their perceptions of product-markets in an attempt to make better future decisions. This model emphasizes that consumers continuously sort out and manage information about their chosen brands in an attempt to reduce uncertainty. One of the ways that consumers evaluate their purchases is by assessing their satisfaction. A popular strategy that consumers use to assess their satisfaction is to compare the chosen brand with a rejected alternative. This strategy is known as dissonance-reduction. Another way consumers determine satisfaction is by comparing a brand's performance against expectations of that performance. If the performance equals expectations, then consumers are satisfied. If it exceeds expectations, consumers are delighted. And if the brand fails to live up to expectations, people become dissatisfied. Some consumers imagine a product's best possible outcome to determine their satisfaction. Here, expectations are less important than whether the product achieved its potential.

Key Terms

actual brands
bounded rationality
brand laziness
brand loyalty
brand overload
brand variance
cluster frontier
cluster size

cluster variance
clustering
compensatory process
derived varied behavior
determinant attributes
enduring involvement
expectancy disconfirmation
    model

extensive problem solving
external search
external uncertainty
impulse buying
intermediate problem solving
internal search
internal uncertainty
intrinsic variety seeking

market mavens
motives
need
non-compensatory process
ongoing search
opportunities
parity products

perceived brands
perceived preference
perceived product-market
perceived risk
performance-based satisfaction
prepurchase search
problem solving

routine choice
true preference
situational involvement
uncertainty-reduction model
variety seeking
want-got gap
wants

Review and Discussion

1. What distinguishes *brand loyalty* from *brand laziness*? Which of the two is more likely to result in long-term repeat purchase behavior?

2. How are consumers' perceptions of *risk* related to their level of product *involvement*?

3. Which categories of risk do you think have the greatest influence on the purchase of: (a) fashion clothing, (b) a laptop, (c) real estate, (d) sushi, and (e) a smartphone?

4. Why is variety seeking prevalent among parity product categories?

5. What's the difference between a *defensive* and *determinant* attribute? Both types of attributes are important to consumers.

6. Under what conditions are consumers likely to follow the five stages of the traditional model of Consumer Decision Making?

7. What are the two conditions necessary for problem recognition to occur?

8. Discuss the differences among *needs, wants,* and *opportunities.*

9. Predict the level of search for

   a. A beginning skier interested in new skis

   b. A frequent flyer looking for a flight to New York

   c. A stay-at-home-dad who has moderate knowledge regarding baby foods

10. How do *external* and *internal* uncertainties cloud consumers' perceptions of the true brand universe and their true utility functions, respectively?

11. Review the two types of satisfaction models: dissonance-reduction versus expectancy disconfirmation. Which model would a consumer most likely use if she recently switched to a new brand after years of loyalty to one brand? Which model would a consumer use if he were processing information from advertisements and opinion leaders' word-of-mouth?

Short Application Exercises

1. Use Figure 9.4 (Assessing Determinant Attributes) to identify attributes in each of the four quadrants for *blue jeans.* On the basis of your analysis, what are the determinant attributes?

2. Identify a product category for which you feel *enduring involvement* and a product category for which you show only *situational* *involvement.* Explain why these product categories affect you differently.

3. Interview a friend regarding her search activities in a recently purchased, high-involvement product (e.g., automobile, computer, graduate school). Identify whether she relied primarily on *prepurchase* or *ongoing* search to make her choice.

Managerial Application

Imagine that you work for a well-known marketing research firm. Your supervisor has asked you to use the expectancy disconfirmation model to evaluate a consumer's post-hoc satisfaction level for a recent purchase of running shoes.

Your Challenge:

1. Identify three determinant attributes for this consumer (e.g., comfort, style, durability).

2. Determine the consumer's importance weights for each attribute, such that they total 100%. For example, comfort = 30%, style = 10%, and durability = 60%.

3. On a 1 to 7 scale, ask the consumer to rate how he expected the

brand to perform on each of these attributes, *prior* to purchase (for example, comfort = 6, style = 4, and durability = 6).

4. Also on a 1 to 7 scale, ask the consumer to rate his actual perceptions of how the shoe has performed on each of these attributes.

5. Plug in the weights, expectations, and perceptions into the formula: $S = \Sigma w(p - e)$. Does the outcome of the function suggest that this consumer is satisfied, delighted, or dissatisfied? To see if the model is consistent with the consumer's response, ask the consumer if he is satisfied.

End Notes

1 Associated Press (2007, August 17). Reported in *The Wall Street Journal* [Online]. Available: http://online.wsj.com/article/SB118737017784201124.html.

2 Assael, H. (1998). *Consumer Behavior and Marketing Action.* Cincinnati, OH: South-Western Publishing.

3 Laurent, G., and Kapferer, J-N. (1985). Measuring Consumer Involvement Profiles, *Journal of Marketing Research, 22,* 41–53.

4 Dowling, G. R., and Staelin, R. (1994). A Model of Perceived Risk and Risk-Handling Activity. *Journal of Consumer Research, 21,* 119–134.

5 Cacioppo, J. T., Petty, R. E., and Kao, C. F. (1986). Central and Peripheral Routes to Persuasion: An Individual Difference Perspective. *Journal of Personality and Social Psychology, 51,* 1032–1043.

6 Batra, R., and Ray, M. L. (1986). Situational Effects of Advertising Repetition: The Moderating Influence of Motivation, Ability, and Opportunity to Respond. *Journal of Consumer Research, 12,* 432–445.

7 Robertson, T. S. (1976). Low-commitment Consumer Behavior. *Journal of Advertising Research, 16,* 19–27.

8 Venkatesan, M. (1973). Cognitive Consistency and Novelty Seeking. In S. Ward and T. S. Robertson (eds.), *Consumer Behavior: Theoretical Sources,* (pp. 354–384). Englewood Cliffs, NJ: Prentice Hall.

9 Van Trijp, H. C. M., Hoyer, W. D., and Inman, J. J. (1996). Why Switch? Product Category-Level of Explanations

for True Variety-Seeking Behavior. *Journal of Marketing Research, 33,* 281–292.

10 Holbrook, M. B. (1984). Situation-Specific Ideal Points and Usage of Multiple Dissimilar Brands. In J. N. Sheth (Ed.), *Research in Marketing,* vol. 7, 93–131. Greenwich, CT: JAI Press.

11 McReynolds, P. (1971). The Nature and Assessment of Intrinsic Motivation. In P. McReynolds (ed.), *Advances in Psychological Assessment,* vol. 2, (157–177). Palo Alto, CA: Science and Behavior Books.

12 McAlister, L., and Pessemier, E. A. (1982). Variety Seeking Behavior: An Interdisciplinary Review. *Journal of Consumer Research, 9,* 311–322.

13 Sheth, J. N., and Raju, P. S. (1974). Sequential and Cyclical Nature of Information Processing Models in Repetitive Choice Behavior. In S. Ward and P. Wright (Eds.), *Advances in Consumer Research,* vol. 1, 348–358.

14 Zuckerman, M. (1979). *Sensation Seeking: Beyond the Optimal Level of Arousal.* Hillsdale, NJ: Lawrence Erlbaum Associates.

15 Ratner, R. K., Kahn, B. E., and Kahneman, D. (1999). Choosing Less-Preferred Experiences for the Sake of Variety. *Journal of Consumer Research, 26,* 1–15.

16 Kahn, B. E., and Isen, A. M. (1993). The Influence of Positive Affect on Variety Seeking among Safe, Enjoyable Products. *Journal of Consumer Research, 20,* 257–270.

17 Simonson, I. (1990). The Effect of Purchase Quantity and Timing on Variety Seeking Behavior. *Journal of Marketing Research, 27,* 150–162.

18 Choi, J., Kim, B. K., Choi, I., and Yi, Y. (2006). Variety-Seeking Tendency in Choice for Others: Interpersonal and Intrapersonal Causes. *Journal of Consumer Research, 32,* 590–595.

19 Howard, J. A., and Sheth, J. N. (1969). *The Theory of Buyer Behavior.* New York: Wiley.

20 Leuba, C. (1955). Toward Some Integration of Learning Theories: The Concept of Optimal Stimulation. *Psychological Reports, 1,* 27–33.

21 Menon, S., and Kahn, B. (1995). The Impact of Context on Variety Seeking in Product Choices. *Journal of Consumer Research, 22,* 285–295.

22 Sutherland, M., and Sylvester, A. K. (2000). *Advertising and the Mind of the Consumer,* 2nd ed. St. Leonards NSW, Australia: Allen & Unwin.

23 Myers, J. H., and Alpert, M. (1968). Determinant Buying Attitudes: Meaning and Measurement. *Journal of Marketing, 32,* 13–20.

24 Guiltinan, J. P., Paul, G. W., and Madden, T. J. (1997). *Marketing Management: Strategies and Programs,* 6th ed. New York: The McGraw-Hill Companies, Inc.

25 Dewy, J. (1910). *How We Think.* Boston, MA: D. C. Health; Brim, O. G. Jr., Glass, D. C., Lavin, D. E., and Goodman, N. (1963). Personality and Decision Processes. *The American Journal of Sociology, 69,* 96.

26 Engel, J. Blackwell, R. D., and Miniard, P. W. (1995). *Consumer Behavior,* 8th ed. Hinsdale, IL: Dryden Press.

27 We credit James G. Clawson with popularizing the "want-got gap" model while teaching organizational behavior at the University of Virginia's Darden School of Business.

28 Bruner, G. C. II (1986). Problem Recognition Styles and Search Patterns: An Empirical Investigation. *Journal of Retailing, 62,* 281–297.

29 Bruner, G. C., and Pamazal, R. J. (1988). Problem Recognition: The Crucial First Stage of the Consumer Decision Process. *Journal of Consumer Marketing, 5,* 53–63.

30 Rossiter, J. R., Percy, L., and Donovan, R. J. (1991). A Better Advertising Planning Grid. *Journal of Advertising Research, 31,* 11–21.

31 Rossiter, J. R., and Percy, L. (1997). *Advertising Communications and Promotion Management.* New York: The McGraw-Hill Companies, Inc.

32 Gundlach, G. T., Block, L. G., and Wilkie, W. L. (2007). *Explorations of Marketing in Society.* Mason, OH: Thomson Higher Education.

33 Pollay, R. W., and Banwari, M. (1993). Here's the Beef: Factors, Determinants, and Segments in Consumer Criticism of Advertising. *Journal of Marketing, 57,* 99–114.

34 Wilkie, W. L., and Moore, E. S. (2007). Marketing's Contributions to Society. In G. T. Gundlach, L. G. Block, and W. L. Wilkie (Eds.) *Explorations of Marketing in Society* (pp. 2–39). Mason, OH: Thomson Higher Education.

35 Spencer, J. (2007, August 6). In China, Lenovo Sets Sights on Rural Market. *The Wall Street Journal* [Online] Available: http://online.wsj.com/article/SB118634998647088589.html.

36 Punj, G. N., and Staelin, R. (1983). A Model of Consumer Information Search for New Automobiles. *Journal of Consumer Research, 9,* 366–380.

37 Bettman, J. R. (1979). Memory Factors in Consumer Choice: A Review. *Journal of Marketing, 43,* 37–53.

38 Bloch, P. H., Sherrell, D. L., and Ridgeway, N. M. (1986). Consumer Search: An Extended Framework. *Journal of Consumer Research, 13,* 119–126.

39 Houston, M. J., and Rothschild, M. L. (1978). Conceptual and Methodological Perspectives on Involvement. In S. C. Jain (Ed.), *Educator's proceedings* (pp. 184–187). Chicago, IL: American Marketing Association.

40 Celsi, R. L., and Olson, J. C. (1988). The Role of Involvement in Attention and Comprehension Processes. *Journal of Consumer Research, 15,* 210–224.

41 Clarke, K., and Belk, R. (1979). The Effects of Product Involvement and Task Definition on Anticipated Consumer Effort. In W. L. Wilkie (Ed.). *Advances in Consumer Research,* vol. 6, 313–318. Ann Arbor, MI: Association for Consumer Research.

42 Dellaert, B. G. C. (1998). Investigating Consumers' Tendency to Combine Multiple Shopping Purposes and Destinations. *Journal of Marketing Research, 35,* 177–189.

43 Ratchford, B. T., Lee, M-S, and Talukdar, D. (2003). The Impact of the Internet on Information Search for Automobiles. *Journal of Marketing Research, 40,* 193–209.

44 Weenig, M. W. H., and Maarleveld, M. (2002). The Impact of Time Constraint of Information Search Strategies in Complex Choice Tasks. *Journal of Economic Psychology, 23,* 689–702.

45 Machleit, K. A., Eroglu, S. A., and Mantel, S. P. (2000). Perceived Retail Crowding and Shopping Satisfaction. *Journal of Consumer Psychology, 9,* 29–42.

46 Gladwell, M. (2002). *The Tipping Point: How Little Things Can Make a Big Difference.* New York: Back Bay Books.

47 Klein, M. (1998). He Shops, She Shops. *American Demographics, 20,* 83–95.

48 Bettman, J. R., and Park, C. W. (1986). Effects of Prior Knowledge and Experience and Phase of the Choice Process on Consumer Decision Processes: A Protocol Analysis. *Journal of Consumer Research, 7,* 234–248.

49 McGuire, W. J. (1968). Personality and Susceptibility to Social Influences. In E. F. Borgatta and W. W. Lambert (Eds.), *Handbook of Personality Theory and Research* (pp. 1130–1187). Chicago, IL: Rand McNally; McGuire, W. J. (1972). Attitude Change: The Information-processing Paradigm. In C. G. McClintock (Ed.), *Experimental Social Psychology* (pp. 108–141). New York: Holt, Rinehart & Winston; McGuire, W. J. (1976). Some Internal Psychological Factors Influencing Consumer Choice. *Journal of Consumer Research, 2,* 302–319.

50 Hirschman, E. C., and Wallendorf, M. R. (1982). Motive Underlying Marketing Formation Acquisition and Transfer. *Journal of Advertising, 11*, 25–31.

51 Hirschman, E. C. (1980). Innovativeness, Novelty Seeking, and Consumer Creativity. *Journal of Consumer Research, 7*, 283–295.

52 Fleischmann, G. (1981). Sources for Product Ideas: A Proactive View on the Consumer. In K. B. Monroe (Ed.), *Advances in Consumer Research*, vol. 8, (pp. 386–390). Ann Arbor, MI: Association for Consumer Research.

53 Bellenger, D. N., and Korgoankar, P. (1980). Profiling the Recreational Shopper. *Journal of Retailing, 58*, 58–81.

54 Simon, H. A. (1982). *Models of Bounded Rationality*. Cambridge, MA: MIT Press.

55 Kahneman, D. (1973). *Attention and Effort*. Englewood Cliffs, NJ: Prentice Hall; Beatty, S. E. and Smith, S. M. (1987). External Search Effort: An Investigation across Several Product Categories, *Journal of Consumer Research, 14*, 83–95; Brucks, M. (1985). The Effect of Product Class Knowledge on Information Search Behavior. *Journal of Consumer Research, 12*, 1–6.

56 Simonson, I. (1989). Choice Based on Reason. The Case of Attraction and Compromise Effects. *Journal of Consumer Research, 16*, 158–174.

57 Bettman, J. R. (1979). *An Information Processing Theory of Consumer Choice*. Reading, MA: Addison-Wesley; Kardes, F. R., Kalyanaram, G. Chandrashekaran, M., and Dornoff, R. J. (1993). Brand Retrieval, Consideration Set Composition, Consumer Choice, and the Pioneering Advantage. *Journal of Consumer Research, 20*, 62–75.

58 Dhar, R., and Glazer, R. (1996). Similarity in Context: Cognitive Representation and Violation Preference and Perceptual Invariance in Consumer Choice. *Organization Behavior and Human Decision Processes, 67*, 280–293; Nosofsky, R. M. (1987). Attention and Learning Processes in Identification and Categorization of Integral Stimuli. *Journal of Experimental Psychology: Learning, Memory, and Cognition, 13*, 87–108.

59 Pinsky, J., and Slade, M. E. (1998). Contracting in Space: An Application of Spatial Statistics to Discrete Choice Models. *Journal of Econometrics, 85*, 125–154.

60 Baumeister, R. E. (1982). Self-Esteem, Self-Preservation, and Future Interaction: A Dilemma of Reputation. *Journal of Personality, 50*, 29–45.

61 Hall, C. S., and Lindzey, G. (1978). *Theories of Personality*. New York: Wiley.

62 Festinger, L. (1957). *A Theory of Cognitive Dissonance*. Evanston, IL: Row, Peterson & Company.

63 Bell, D. E. (1982). Regret in Decision Making under Uncertainty. *Operations Research, 30*, 961–981.

64 Tse, D. K., Nicosia, F. M, and Wilton, P. C. (1990). Consumer Satisfaction as a Process. *Psychology & Marketing, 7*, 177–193.

65 Homburg, C. Koschate, N., and Hoyer, W. D. (2005). Do Satisfied Customers Really Pay More? A Study of the Relationship between Customer Satisfaction and Willingness to Pay. *Journal of Marketing, 69*, 84–96.

66 Seiders, K., Voss, G., Grewal, D., and Godfrey, A. L. (2005). Do Satisfied Customers Buy More? Examining Moderating Influences in a Retail Context. *Journal of Marketing, 69*, 26–43.

67 Gustafson, A., Johnson, M. D., and Roos, I. (2005). The Effects of Customer Satisfaction, Relationship Commitment Dimensions, and Triggers on Customer Retention, *Journal of Marketing, 69*, 210–218.

68 Chandrashekaran, M., Rotte, K., Tax, S. S., and Grewal, R. (2007). Satisfaction Strength and Customer Loyalty. *Journal of Marketing Research, 44*, 153–163.

69 Brehm, J. W. (1956). Postdecision Changes in the Desirability of Alternatives. *Journal of Abnormal and Social Psychology 52*, 384–389.

70 Oliver, R. L. (1980). A Cognitive Model of the Antecedents and Consequences of Satisfaction Decisions. *Journal of Marketing Research, 17*, 460–469; Oliver, R. L. (1981). Measurement and Evaluation of Satisfaction Process in Retail Settings. *Journal of Retailing, 57*, 25–48; Oliver, R. L., and DeSarbo, W. S. (1988). Response Determinants in Satisfaction Judgments. *Journal of Consumer Research, 14*, 495–507.

71 Cho, C. K, and Johar, G. V. (2011). Attaining Satisfaction, *Journal of Consumer Research, 38*, 622–631.

72 Van Boven, L., and Ashworth, L (2007). Looking Forward, Looking Back: Anticipation is More Evocative than Retrospection, *Journal of Experimental Psychology: General, 136 (2)*, 289–300.

73 Reichheld, F. F. (1993). Loyalty-Based Management, *Harvard Business Review, 71* (March/April), 64–74.

74 Tax, S. S., Brown, S. W., and Chandreshekaran, M. (1998). Customer Evaluations of Service Complaint Experiences: Implications for Relationship Marketing, *Journal of Marketing, 62*, 60–76.

75 Gregoire, Y., Tripp, T. M., and Legoux, R. (2009). When Customers Love Turns into Lasting Hate: The Effects of Relationship Strength and Time on Customer Revenge and Avoidance, *Journal of Marketing, 73*, 18–32.

76 Andrade, E., and Ho, Tack-Hua. (2009). Gaming Emotions in Social Interactions, *Journal of Consumer Research, 36 (4)*, 539–552.

77 Pilon, M. (2009, May, 15). Does It Pay to Be an Angry Customer? *The Wall Street Journal* [Online]. Available: http://blogs.wsj.com/wallet/2009/05/15/does-it-pay-to-be-an-angry-customer/

78 Johnson, M. D., and Fornell, C. (1991). A Framework for Comparing Customer Satisfaction Across Individuals and Product Categories, *Journal of Economic Psychology, 12 (2)*, 267–86.

79 Dwyer, F. R., Schurr, P. H., and Oh, S. (1987). Developing Buyer-Seller Relationships, *Journal of Marketing, 51* (April), 11–27.

MARKETING METRICS

Measuring Consumer Satisfaction

Imagine that you are a consultant who is building a statistical model to predict how long a customer will remain with a firm (i.e., customer retention). Research demonstrates that both consumer satisfaction and calculated brand commitment should help predict customer retention. Consumer satisfaction is defined as a customer's overall evaluation of the performance of a product or service to date.[78] Calculated brand commitment is a consumer's dependence on a brand's benefits due to a lack of choices or switching costs.[79] The following table provides data for twenty wireless phone customers. All twenty have used wireless services for 10 years. Column 1 shows the customer number. Column 2 provides consumers' ratings for overall satisfaction to date on a seven-point scale, where 7 represents the highest rating for satisfaction, and 1 represents the lowest. Column 3 shows consumers' estimated switching costs, i.e., the cost of switching from their current wireless service provider to a competitor. Finally, column 4 shows how long consumers have been with their current wireless service provider, a surrogate for customer retention.

Wireless Phone Customer Data [DT9-1.Xls}

(1) Customer Number	(2) Overall Satisfaction (1–7 Scale)	(3) Switching Costs ($)	(4) Months with Firm (Customer Retention)
1	6	120	28
2	4	25	6
3	7	200	48
4	2	20	12
5	5	75	18
6	3	0	2
7	6	50	24
8	4	50	16
9	5	70	20
10	1	0	2
11	6	180	48
12	5	85	20
13	4	80	18
14	2	40	2

(continued)

(1) Customer Number	(2) Overall Satisfaction (1–7 Scale)	(3) Switching Costs ($)	(4) Months with Firm (Customer Retention)
15	7	90	48
16	7	110	30
17	1	0	8
18	5	75	12
19	3	60	6
20	6	90	24

Your Task

Use the Excel file (DT9-1.xls) to execute the following analyses:

1. Conduct a Pearson correlation for (1) *switching costs* and (2) *retention*. Recall that a correlation (r_{xy}) measures the extent to which two variables are associated with each other. The value of r_{xy} always falls between -1 and 1. A positive correlation would indicate that higher switching costs are associated with longer customer retention, whereas a negative correlation would indicate the opposite. A correlation of $r_{xy} > 0.75$ would be considered large. What is r_{xy}? Does it indicate that higher switching costs are associated with customers' duration with the firm?

2. Conduct a univariate, multiple linear regression analysis using *retention* as the dependent (y) variable and (1) *satisfaction* and (2) *switching costs* as the independent, or predictor (x) variables. Find the data analysis tab and click "regression." Use the third column (retention) for the y-range and the first two columns for the x-range. Click "labels" so that Excel knows the column titles aren't data. Click "new worksheet ply" and provide a name. Then click "OK." Examine the output.

   - *Adjusted R-square* indicates the proportion of variation in retention explained by satisfaction and switching costs. An adjusted R-square greater than 0.50 means that satisfaction and switching costs account for more than 50% of the number of months consumers remain with the firm. What is the adjusted R-square in your model? Does it indicate that satisfaction and switching costs explain customer retention?

   - The *Satisfaction Coefficient* indicates the number of *additional* months a consumer would remain with his wireless provider if he were to rate the firm one point higher on the 7-point satisfaction scale. According to your model, how many additional months of retention will one satisfaction point bring a wireless provider?

   - Now it's time to predict how long a customer will remain with a wireless provider based on a specific satisfaction score and switching cost. Use 5 as the customer satisfaction score and $100 as the switching cost, and plug these two numbers into your model: *Intercept Coefficient* + (5) × *Satisfaction Coefficient* + (100) × *Switching Costs Coefficient* = *Retention* (in months). What is your prediction for how long this particular customer will be retained?

PRODUCT CONSIDERATION, EVALUATION, AND CHOICE

CHAPTER 10

OBJECTIVES *After studying this chapter, you will be able to…*

1 Explain the stages of consumer choice.

2 Describe several marketing techniques for influencing consumers' consideration sets.

3 Define stimulus-based, memory-based, and mixed choice.

4 Explain the MODE model.

5 Explain how many different heuristics or shortcuts are used to simplify prediction and choice.

Walmart

Walmart is the largest retailer in the world, with over $400 billion in sales per year.[1] Walmart's famous "everyday low prices" appeal to consumers, and has enabled Walmart to become the largest buyer of products from Disney, Gillette, Kellogg's, Mattel, Procter & Gamble, and others. Some argue that Walmart is too powerful, and that it destroys communities, small businesses, and even previously successful manufacturers such as Rubbermaid and Vlassic. Walmart's rise to power reflects recent trends of significant increases in power in the channel of distribution for retailers and decreases in power for manufacturers.

A 2012 study of the influence of Walmart on manufacturers' profits conducted over a five-year period shows that Walmart increases manufacturers' profits by an average of 18%. Although low prices reduce manufacturers' profits, this reduction is offset by the increase in sales due to market expansion. Hence, Walmart's policies are not as harmful to

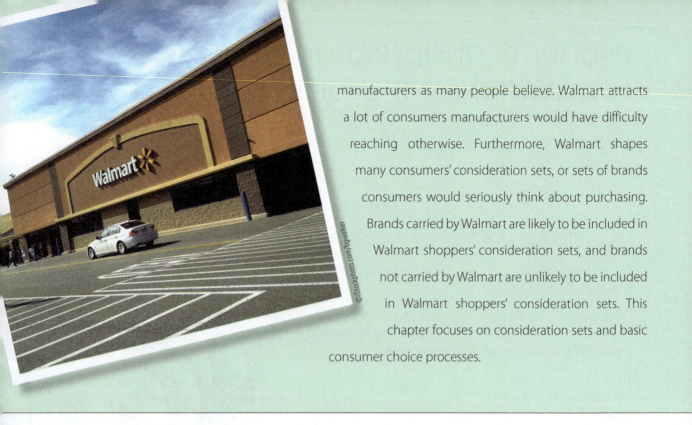

manufacturers as many people believe. Walmart attracts a lot of consumers manufacturers would have difficulty reaching otherwise. Furthermore, Walmart shapes many consumers' consideration sets, or sets of brands consumers would seriously think about purchasing. Brands carried by Walmart are likely to be included in Walmart shoppers' consideration sets, and brands not carried by Walmart are unlikely to be included in Walmart shoppers' consideration sets. This chapter focuses on consideration sets and basic consumer choice processes.

OBJECTIVE ①

The Consideration Set: Determining Choice Alternatives

Before a person can make a purchase, or even make evaluations of various alternative brands, they generate a set of brands to consider and evaluate—even if it's just one. A **consideration set** is the group of brands that consumers think about buying when they need to make a purchase.[2] The brands included in the consideration set can come from the *evoked set* of brands, from brands discovered during external information search, and from point-of-purchase. This is discussed further when we examine consumer choice later in the chapter.

Because consumers can't select a brand unless it is included in their consideration sets, the first job of a marketer is to encourage the consumer to consider buying his or her brand. This is often difficult because the consideration set for many products is quite small. Although consideration set size can range from one (a very brand-loyal customer may consider only one brand) to as many brands as are available in the market—dozens or even hundreds for some products—consumers rarely consider more than seven brands (see Figure 10.1). Aside from the fact that consumers just don't have the time or the desire in many cases (given the limited utility of evaluating 15 different brands of toilet paper, for instance) to carefully consider dozens of brands, limited information processing capacity also prevents people from considering more than Miller's magic number of seven plus or minus two.[3] Although there are always exceptions to every rule, this tendency to have small consideration sets exists across product categories, from toothpaste and breakfast cereal to cars and computers.

Because people consider so few brands, marketers have to be creative in order to encourage consumers to consider their brands over competitors' offerings. One way marketers get consumers to consider brands is by drawing attention to the brand and making it memorable. When a marketer uses the principles of attention, learning, and memory to increase the likelihood that a brand is included in a consumer's consideration set, the marketer is one step closer to a potential sale.

FIGURE 10.1 | **Consideration Sets**

| Brands Available in the Marketplace (> 20 brands) | Consideration Set (7+2 brands) | Choice (1 brand) |

Source: Kardes, F. (1997). *Consumer Behavior and Managerial Decision Making.* Upper Saddle River, NJ: Prentice Hall.

Ensuring that a brand is simply included in consumers' consideration sets is an important first step to influencing brand evaluation and ultimate choice, but how many and what other brands are also included in the consideration set are also important factors. As the number of brands in the consumer's consideration set increases, the likelihood of a brand being chosen decreases. Thus, the next step should be to control the number of competitors' brands in the consideration set. Three techniques for influencing consumers' consideration sets are part-list cuing, the attraction effect, and the compromise effect.

OBJECTIVE ## Influencing the Consideration Set

Part-List Cuing One way marketers influence the consideration set is to decrease its overall size while at the same time maintaining their brand presence in the set. Marketers can reduce the number of brands considered for a purchase through **part-list cuing**, which involves presenting the names of just some brands when consumers are trying to recall as many brands as possible.[4] This technique is designed to make some brands more prominent than others by using a competitive advertisement or by listing the names of only a few competing brands in a promotional campaign or selling situation. As the partial list of brands becomes more conspicuous and more strongly connected with the product category, it becomes more difficult for the consumer to think of other brands. For example, let's imagine that a consumer want to purchase a new car. The consumer knows she wants a small, sporty car, but she doesn't know what brand of car she wants, and she knows that at least a dozen brands in the market fit her general purchase criteria. The consumer heads to a nearby new car dealer to "browse around." Of course, a salesperson quickly approaches her. After a few minutes of discussing the features available in a new car, the sales associate directs the consumer to a brand model that best fits her needs. The salesperson may then proceed to compare his brand to one or two other brands in the market. Of course, the salesperson will likely focus on competing brands that are inferior in some way to his brand. As the consumer focuses on these three brands—the one on the lot and the other two mentioned by the salesperson—it becomes more difficult for her to recall other brands that might also fit her needs. Suddenly, her consideration set has been reduced to three brands. The comparative advertisement for ID Patrol on page 271 works in a similar fashion. The ad tries to create a consideration set of just four, one in which ID Patrol is the only brand to offer all five, key attributes.

The part-list cuing effect is important because it can help consumers quickly and efficiently come to a decision, plus it can also lead them to focus on some brands while ignoring others that are potentially better. As a result, consumers may make choices they later regret.[5]

The Attraction Effect Marketers also attempt to influence which specific brands consumers are likely to compare and evaluate. A target brand seems more attractive when it is compared to inferior brands and less attractive when compared to superior brands. This is called the **attraction effect**.[6] Marketers want consumers to compare their brands to inferior brands—remember the car salesperson? Again, this can be done in a selling situation or by using comparative advertising and promotion that show the target brand as superior to other brands on some dimension. Alternatively, the attraction effect can unintentionally occur when a firm has multiple brands in its product line (see Figure 10.2).

For example, Williams-Sonoma sold a home bread-baking machine for $275 and at first, sales were poor. Later, Williams-Sonoma added a much more expensive home bread-baking machine to its product line. When consumers compared the $275 machine to the much more expensive machine, the $275 machine seemed very attractive because of the price, and sales of this machine almost doubled! This occurred because $275 seemed like a more reasonable price when it was compared to an even higher price, and consumers like to save money.

The Compromise Effect Another way to improve the evaluation of a particular brand is to make the brand appear as an average (or a good compromise) brand against other brands in the consideration set. A compromise brand seems average on all important attributes or features. While other brands often have some really good and some really bad features, a compromise brand appears to not have any very bad features and is at least acceptable on all features. Thus, a compromise brand seems like a safe choice. This **compromise effect**, or the increased probability of buying a compromise brand, is especially likely to occur when consumers are concerned about making a bad decision (see Figure 10.2).[7] For example, consider a consumer who wants to purchase a camera and is deciding between an inexpensive model and a moderately priced model. If a third camera, a high-priced model, is added to the consideration set,

FIGURE 10.2 | The Attraction Effect and the Compromise Effect

Two Equally Preferred Brands	Attraction Effect	Compromise Effect
Dimension A	**Dimension A**	**Dimension A**
• Brand A	• Brand A	• Brand A
		• Brand B
• Brand B	• Brand B	• Brand C
	• Decoy	
Dimension B	**Dimension B**	**Dimension B**
Brand A is better on dimension A (one attribute or one cluster of attributes). Brand B is better on dimension B. The dimensions are equally important.	Adding a decoy similar but inferior to Brand B increases preference for Brand B.	Adding a Brand C, which is excellent on dimension B but poor on dimension A, increases preference for Brand B.

SOURCE: Kardes, F. (1997). *Consumer Behavior and Managerial Decision Making.* Upper Saddle River, NJ: Prentice Hall.

ID Patrol™ — new from Equifax.

Our whole team behind you and your identity. Count on ID Patrol. Only from Equifax.

EQUIFAX

COMPARE FEATURES	*EQUIFAX	*TrueCredit™ by TransUnion®	*Experian®	*LifeLock®
Credit File Monitoring	✓	✓	✓	✗
Credit File Lock	✓	✓	✗	✗
Internet Scanning	✓	✗	✗	✓
ID Theft Resolution Specialist	✓	✗	✗	✓
Fraud Alert	*FREE*†	*FREE*†	*FREE*†	✓

*Comparisons are based on the following products: Equifax ID Patrol™; Experian's Triple Advantage℠ credit monitoring, TrueCredit by TransUnion 3-Bureau Credit Monitoring, and Lifelock.

†The ability to place an initial 90-day fraud alert on your credit file is not a part of the above product, but is available for free from the national credit reporting agency affiliate of each company if you believe that you are a victim of identity theft. Once you place an alert on your credit file with one of the national credit reporting agencies, your alert request will automatically be forwarded to the other two so you don't need to contact each of them separately.

All marks, service marks, and trademarks are the property of their respective owners.

When comparing their products to their competitors' products, marketers often use the attraction effect to make their product seem more desirable than the others.

AP Images/PRNewsFoto/Equifax Inc.

Marketing in Action

Mid-Calorie Soft Drinks

Due to health concerns about obesity and diabetes, soft drink sales have been dropping in the United States. How can soft drink companies get soft drinks back into consumers' consideration sets? One possibility is to introduce new ten-calorie soft drinks to the market.[8] Consumers already understand that regular soft drinks have a lot of calories and diet soft drinks typically have one calorie, but they need to be educated about mid-calorie soft drinks—such as Dr. Pepper Ten, 7Up Ten, A&W Ten, Canada Dry Ten, RC Ten, and Sunkist Ten. All of these products are owned by the Dr. Pepper Snapple Group. Dr. Pepper Ten is positioned for men only, and commercials for this product show a rugged man in an action movie drinking Dr. Pepper Ten. The slogan is: "It's Not for Women." The product is targeted at 25- to 34 year-old men who prefer regular Dr. Pepper but want to cut down on calories. 7Up Ten is targeted at men and women, and a recent ad shows a young couple getting into a pink monster truck and watching a cooking show in which the host is tackled by a football player. The slogan is: "Great Taste, 10 Calories, Get Both."

then the moderately priced model seems like a reasonable compromise. Brands that are intermediate or "average" in terms of price, quality, and number of features are frequently chosen from the consideration set. They are chosen even more frequently when consumers need to justify their choice to others, such as a spouse, boss, or friends. It is often easier to justify the purchase of intermediate rather than extreme brands.

Of course, nearly any brand can appear to be a compromise brand depending on the brands to which it is compared. Advertising and promotion campaigns that encourage consumers to compare a seemingly average brand to more extreme brands increase the influence of the compromise effect.

The choices that consumers make follow their evaluations and judgments of the brands in their considerations sets (see Figure 10.1). Now that we have examined how consumers establish consideration sets and how marketers attempt to influence brand evaluations within these considerations sets, we turn our attention to the desired outcome of the consumer decision-making process: *consumer choice*.

Constructing Evaluations to Make Choices

Consumer choice involves selecting one product or brand from a set of possibilities. Marketers who want to influence consumers must understand three critical issues:

1. The brands in the consideration set
2. The types of information used to detect and evaluate the differences among the considered alternatives
3. How this information is ultimately used in the choice process[9]

The first point has already been discussed. The other two issues are discussed throughout the rest of the chapter. First, three types of consumer choice based on the physical presence or absence of the brand during choice are reviewed: stimulus-based, memory-based, and mixed choice.

OBJECTIVE **3**

Stimulus-Based, Memory-Based, and Mixed Choice

After the consideration set has been determined, consumers need to evaluate the differences in the attributes among the considered brands to make a choice. When consumers can directly and physically observe all relevant brands in the consideration set and their brand attributes, they make a **stimulus-based choice**.[10] For example, in a grocery store, it is easy to compare brands and attributes simply by examining the different packages on a shelf.

When none of the relevant brands and attributes is directly and physically observable, however, consumers make a **memory-based choice.** Here, consumers must retrieve brand and attribute information from memory. An example is a consumer at home trying to decide what restaurant to go to for dinner. Finally, in **mixed choice**, consumers can see some brands but must remember others. This is the most common type of choice scenario. When this occurs, *stimulus brands*—the brands that are physically observed—usually have an advantage over *memory brands*—the brands not observed but drawn from memory—because consumers tend to forget specific details about memory brands.[11] For example, when shopping for a new car, a consumer is likely to visit an automobile dealership. While on the premises, the consumer may attempt to compare model brands on the dealership lot (stimulus brands) to model brands that she examined earlier at a different dealership (memory brands). If all the brands are similar in quality, the consumer is more likely to choose the stimulus brand because she might not be able to remember the exact price or the exact level of performance on an important attribute of the memory brands.

Car shopping typically involves a mixed choice situation.

Although consumers usually choose stimulus brands over memory brands, marketers can reverse this effect when memory brands have a very large number of favorable attributes. Consumers are likely to remember that these brands are very good even if they can't remember specific details about the brands.[12] "Puffery" or exaggerated advertising claims about a memory brand such as, "This brand is rated number 1 in its class," can also increase the likelihood that consumers will choose it. Thus, stimulus brands are preferred over memory brands except in special cases where memory brands seem too good to be ignored.

Now that we have looked at the differences in stimulus versus memory brands, let's examine some common ways consumers evaluate brand information and how the amount of effort expended on the decision-making process influences choice.

Attitude versus Attribute-Based Choice

Sometimes, consumers make choices based on general impressions about a brand and sometimes on specific brand attribute information. In **attitude-based choice**, they form overall evaluations and general impressions of brands in the consideration set based on a combination of everything they know about all the brands, and then select the one with the highest evaluation. Formally, an *attitude* is an evaluative judgment that a person forms of people, objects, and issues. In contrast to attitude-based choice, when consumers make **attribute-based choices**, they compare the specific attributes or features of each brand and select the one that performs best on key attributes.

When do consumers use attitude-based versus attribute-based choice strategies? One determinant is *accessibility*, or ease of retrieving either attitude or attribute information from memory. Research shows that, when drawing information from memory, a person usually finds it easier to use attitude-based choice because attitudes are easier to retrieve from memory than are specific brand attributes.[13] For example, it is easier for consumers to recall that they generally like the Skippy brand of peanut butter more than Jif than it is to recall attributes of both brands (e.g., price, nutty taste, smoothness) and individual preferences for each attribute. Of course, attitude-based choice can occur only if the attitudes exist; a person must have a previously formed attitude toward a brand to pull it from memory.

On the other hand, usefulness of information is important too. When brands are very similar overall, small differences among them are easier to detect when comparing them along specific attributes. In this case, attribute-based choice may be preferable because the attribute information is more *diagnostic*, which means it is more relevant for distinguishing among brands. Therefore, while attitudes are often more *accessible*, attributes are often more *diagnostic*. In general, the information that is most accessible *and* diagnostic is the information that is used in a consumer's choice decision.

The accessibility and diagnosticity of information are not the only factors that influence the type of information that consumers use in their choices. The more important the product choice, the more consumers want to think about it, and this too influences the type of information they use. For example, purchasing an engagement ring, selecting a university, or even choosing a new cologne are probably more important than purchasing a bottle of ketchup or selecting a movie rental. According to a theory called the **MODE model**, **M**otivation and **O**pportunity to deliberate are key **DE**terminants of the processes that influence consumer choice.[14] Motivation is high when the decision is more personally relevant (motivation is synonymous with high involvement).

Opportunity is high when people can take time and have the ability to think carefully and to deliberate about the decision. When both motivation and opportunity are high, consumers are likely to deliberate about the decision. This careful deliberation is more consistent with attribute-based choice because brands are carefully evaluated along every relevant product attribute. Recall that small differences among brands are easier to detect when comparing them along specific attributes, and even small differences between brands may be crucial when the purchase choice is very important. If either motivation or opportunity is low, attitude-based choice is more likely. See Figure 10.3.

FIGURE 10.3 | The MODE Model

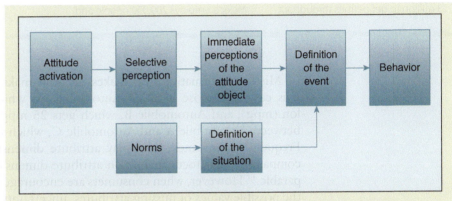

SOURCE: Reprinted from *Advances in Experimental Social Psychology*, M. P. Zanna (Ed.), Vol. 23, Fazio, R. H., Multiple Processes by which Attitudes Guide Behavior: The MODE Model as an Integrative Framework, pages 75–109, Copyright 1990, with permission from Elsevier.

Choice Deferral Choice deferral refers to the decision to choose nothing. When the choice decision becomes too difficult because there are too many options or because the choice decision requires too many trade-offs among options, consumers often decide to choose nothing.[15] Decision difficulty increases uncertainty, and uncertainty encourages consumers to decide not to decide. This is bad news for marketers, because marketers do not want consumers to go home empty-handed. Hence, it is important for marketers to understand the factors that influence choice deferral.

Uncertainty appears to be one of the most important factors because uncertainty encourages consumers to postpone decision making, search for additional information before making a decision, or ask someone else to make the decision—someone like a spouse or an advisor. For example, many people hire financial advisors so they do not need to think about difficult financial decisions. Similarly, many consumers buy *Consumer Reports'* "Best Buys" so they do not need to make difficult trade-offs among attributes, such as the trade-off between price and quality. Most consumers want to purchase a high-quality brand, but they do not want to pay too much. How much would you be willing to pay for a 10% increase in quality? This is a common but difficult trade-off that consumers must deal with frequently. *Consumer Reports* helps consumers avoid making this trade-off by labeling some brands as "Best Buys."

Walmart de Mexico

Walmart de Mexico is Walmart's largest foreign subsidiary.[16] A former Walmart de Mexico executive recently revealed that his company paid bribes in excess of $23 million to get permits throughout Mexico. Specifically, the bribes paid for zoning approvals, reduced environmental protection fees, and support from neighborhood leaders. He gave precise details regarding names, dates, and bribe amounts. Furthermore, Walmart de Mexico's top executives knew about the bribes and attempted to conceal this information from Walmart headquarters in Bentonville, Arkansas. Walmart de Mexico employs 209,000 people and is Mexico's largest private employer. Walmart headquarters in Bentonville is currently attempting to strengthen compliance with the Foreign Corrupt Practices Act in Mexico. Some argue that Walmart should adopt the highest possible ethical standards. Others argue that Mexico, not the United States, should investigate Walmart's practices in Mexico. What do you think?

Missing information also makes decision making difficult. For example, it is easy to choose between Automobile A, which gets 35 miles per gallon (mpg), and Automobile B, which gets 25 mpg. But how do you choose between Automobile A and Automobile C, which has unknown gas mileage? Frequently, consumers downplay attribute dimensions that are not directly comparable, and focus mainly on attribute dimensions that are directly comparable.[17] However, when consumers are encouraged to form inferences about the possible values of missing attributes, uncertainty decreases, and consumers are more likely to make a decision.[18]

Research also shows that consumers tend to overestimate the quality of the brands included in their consideration sets, and this decreases choice deferral.[19] When one group of consumers receives three brands to consider, and another group of consumers receives three completely different brands to consider, both groups believe that the best brand is likely to be included in their consideration sets. This effect is even greater when consumers have a high need for cognitive closure, or the preference to reach a firm decision as quickly as possible. When the need for cognitive closure is high, consumers underestimate the quality of brands not included in their consideration sets even when they are reminded about several high-quality brands that were not included in their consideration sets.

OBJECTIVE **4**

Heuristic Processing

The MODE model is an example of a *dual process model*. This model suggests that sometimes consumers think carefully about decisions and sometimes they don't. As we saw in the discussion of the MODE model, motivation and opportunity are important determinants as to how much careful thinking people do when making a product choice. Also important are processing factors related to involvement, ability, and situational factors. In general, when consumers think carefully about decisions, using all relevant information and considering all implications, they are engaging in **systematic processing**. In contrast, sometimes people are unwilling or unable to use careful and effortful decision-making strategies, such as when motivation or opportunity—according to the MODE model—is low. Instead, consumers use simple **heuristics** that enable them to make decisions quickly and easily. This is known as **heuristic processing**.[20] Heuristics are mental shortcuts that help consumers simplify their decision-making tasks. There are three types of heuristics—persuasion, prediction, and influence. All heuristics aid in simplifying cognitive tasks, but the type of heuristic consumers use depends on the specific task at hand.

Persuasion heuristics influence consumers' beliefs and attitudes. They come in three forms.[21] The *length-implies-strength heuristic* suggests "size matters." For example, advertisements and sales pitches filled with facts and figures appear more compelling than just a few claims. So consumers tend to evaluate the quality of the brand according to the number of favorable attributes it possesses. The *liking-agreement heuristic* is based on the assumption that consumers usually agree with people they like. This heuristic is embodied in balance theory. Finally, the *consensus-implies-correctness heuristic* is synonymous with "the bandwagon effect." It implies that if everyone is doing it, then it must be good, i.e., it offers social validation.

Prediction heuristics are used to form likelihood judgments (e.g., representativeness, availability, simulation, and anchoring-and-adjustment). The third heuristic type, **influence or choice heuristics**, affects consumers' decisions directly (e.g., lexicographic, additive-difference, conjunctive, disjunctive, frequency of good/bad features). Prediction and choice heuristics are discussed in detail later in this chapter.

Heuristic processing occurs most often when a decision is perceived as unimportant—which ketchup brand to buy, for instance—or when decision making is stressful or difficult as a result of time pressure or information overload. Consumers' use of heuristics becomes even more prevalent as the amount of information available to them increases, as potential choice alternatives increase, and as the pace of life increases.

There are many ways consumers use heuristics when evaluating brands. Consumers often use heuristics to predict what will happen if they buy or don't buy a particular product or brand. For example, "If I buy the most expensive laundry detergent, my clothes will be extra clean." Heuristics also influence what and how much choice-related information consumers use to make a decision and how they use that information. For example, many consumers assume that price and quality are strongly related; that is where the idea that "you get what you pay for" comes from. This assumption leads consumers to predict that expensive products are high in quality, and inexpensive products are low in quality. When consumers use price as a heuristic cue for predicting quality, they base their judgment of quality on price alone. However, many other variables also influence quality, such as product reliability, durability, appearance, ease of use, cost of use, and the number of different uses of a product. Price is just one variable. Here lies a potential pitfall of using heuristic processing. Although it simplifies decision making and enables consumers to make choices quickly and easily, heuristic thinking often oversimplifies choice and leads consumers to overlook important information. Consequently, when consumers focus only on price, they over-simplify prediction and make poor decisions. For example, for many different products, price is only weakly related to quality.[22] This means that some brands are high in price but low in quality, and some brands are low in price but high in quality. Relying too heavily on the price-quality heuristic can lead consumers to buy a high-priced brand that is low in quality. Of course, price is not the only cue that consumers use to predict the quality of a product. People also rely on brand name, store reputation, warranty, the Good Housekeeping seal of approval, and company membership in the Better Business Bureau, among other heuristic cues.

In addition to using the specific heuristic cues noted above, people also use *general* heuristic cues. In their path-breaking research on the use of general heuristics, Tversky and Kahneman researched four important general cues that people use for simplifying predictions related to decision making: the representativeness heuristic, the availability heuristic, the simulation heuristic, and the anchoring-and-adjustment heuristic (see Figure 10.4).[23] Each of these heuristics can lead all people, including consumers and marketers, to make bad predictions and, thus, bad decisions.

FIGURE 10.4 | **Prediction Heuristics**

Representativeness Heuristic	
Concept	Example
Assessing the likelihood that a particular target belongs to a category based on the degree to which the target and category appear similar.	If a consumer believes that Honda automobiles are high quality, he may conclude that Honda motorbikes are similarly high in quality.

Availability Heuristic	
Concept	Example
Searching memory for relevant examples of a particular event and basing one's prediction of that event on how easily these examples come to mind.	If a consumer recalls many floods, then he or she will predict that future floods are likely. As a result, this consumer may be inclined to buy flood insurance.

Simulation Heuristic	
Concept	Example
An event or sequence of events that is easy to imagine also seems very likely to occur.	Consumers who imagine a brand performing well are more likely to believe that this brand will actually satisfy their needs.

Anchor-and-Adjustment Heuristic	
Concept	Example
Random anchors or "starting points" influence probability estimates.	Real estate agents' estimates of the value of a property are very close to the prior observed list price (anchor).

OBJECTIVE ⑤

Prediction Heuristics

Good consumer decision making often requires accurate probability or likelihood judgments about events, such as accurate predictions about future product performance (will the product do what I need it to do?), about when a product needs replacement (Should I buy a new car now or risk future repair bills?), about the behavior of others (Will my sister like this gift? Will this salesperson try to trick me?), and about one's own future behavior (Will I still like this color of paint two years from now?). However, although the ability to make predictions is very important, research suggests that people are not very good at making them, largely because they often unknowingly use heuristics to generate those predictions.

Representativeness Heuristic Predictions are sometimes based on similarity or representativeness. People using the **representativeness heuristic** make predictions based on perceived similarities between a specific target and a general category. For example, if a new product has a similar name, package, or appearance to another product we like a lot, we usually predict that we will like the new product, too. If a person we just met reminds us of another person that we do not like—perhaps because the two people have similar glasses, clothing, gestures, or mannerisms—we often predict that we will dislike the new person, as well. Because whales have many traits and characteristics similar to those possessed by fish—such as fins, tails, and the ability to swim and live in water—children often believe that whales are fish. Consumers make similar mistakes when they focus on superficial similarities between an object and a category. In the same way, marketers can use the representativeness heuristic to their advantage. For example, a private store brand often packages products in boxes with sizes, colors, and graphics similar to that of leading national brands, hoping that the superficial package similarities will lead consumers to predict that the store brands are similar to leading national brands on more important dimensions.

Private labels such as Kroger can appear to be similar to or representative of national brands.

AP Images/Al Behrman, file

Unfortunately, consumers often focus on these irrelevant similarities—package color and graphics—so their predictions may suffer.

Important information often overlooked because of the representativeness heuristic is the *base rate*, which is the incidence rate of an event. If consumers know that 10% of the products in a particular industry fail or need repair, then they can predict a 10% chance of a randomly selected product from this industry failing. In the absence of other information, that prediction should be based entirely on the base rate. However, Tversky and Kahneman have shown that even a small amount of marginally useful information can lead people to rely too heavily on the representativeness heuristic and subsequently neglect, overlook, or ignore the base rate.[24] For example, in a classic study, Tversky and Kahneman told research participants that a panel of psychologists administered personality tests to 30 engineers and 70 lawyers. Participants were asked to predict the likelihood that a randomly selected person from this sample was an engineer. When no other information was provided, most participants predicted correctly that there was a 30% chance that the randomly selected person was an engineer. However, in another experimental condition, participants received a brief, marginally informative description of the randomly selected person:

Jack shows no interest in political and social issues and spends most of his free time on hobbies, which include home carpentry, sailing, and mathematical puzzles.

Sweepstakes can appeal to the *gambler's fallacy*.

When participants received this brief description, they categorized Jack as an engineer, and they predicted that it was highly likely that Jack was an engineer. Even marginally relevant descriptive information can lead people to ignore highly relevant base rate information.

Another bias related to the representativeness heuristic deals with the *law of large numbers*, which states that the larger the sample size, the more likely it is that statistics estimated from a sub-sample apply to the larger population from which the sub-sample was drawn. Unfortunately, people expect even very small samples to be representative of larger populations, but this may not be the case. For example, a small group of friends may tell you that a new movie is really good or a particular new restaurant is bad. It is very likely that you will rely on this information received from a small group and ignore that fact that the opinion of such a small group may not be representative of what the majority of people think.

The representativeness heuristic also encourages people to commit the *gambler's fallacy*. Gamblers often foolishly believe that events alternate frequently in random sequences and that long streaks of the same event must be nonrandom. Consequently, if a basketball player makes several baskets in a row, gamblers believe the player is more likely to make the next basket.[25] The streak seems nonrandom because it does not correlate with people's conceptions of chance. Similarly, when betting on whether a coin will turn up heads or tails, gamblers often believe that tails is more likely after a string of heads (e.g., four heads in a row). However, the actual likelihood of tails after four heads in a row is still the base rate: 50%. In the long run, the number of times tails turns up is 50%, but in small samples, random streaks are highly likely to be observed. Marketers use the gambler's fallacy to convince people to buy lottery tickets, enter sweepstakes, and look for winning game tokens, based on the idea that if consumers purchase enough tickets, etc., they will eventually win.

In business, a string of successes seems nonrandom, and lucky marketing managers often conclude that they have beaten the odds. Consequently, they predict that they will continue to beat the odds. This is another example of the gambler's fallacy. After a string of failures, unlucky marketing managers often predict that the odds will even out and, therefore, they are due for a success. Again however, marketing managers can get lucky or unlucky as a result of chance, and the laws of chance never change. Fortunately, many business outcomes are influenced by both skill and chance. What marketers should hope is that the skill component is great enough to increase the probability of success, regardless of chance. But whenever chance exists, no matter how small, the probability of success cannot be 100%.

Finally, the representativeness heuristic influences how consumers might use information prematurely to make decisions. The likelihood of one specific extreme or unusual event is very low, by definition. Usually, extreme or unusual events are followed by less extreme or less unusual events. This is known as *regression to the mean*. In the long run, the average or typical level of a variable is observed. For example, many top athletes have remarkable rookie years and much less remarkable second years (the so-called sophomore slump). Many restaurants seem to serve outstanding meals once, but less exciting meals over subsequent visits. Regression to the mean occurs for extreme negative events, also. A store where you received terrible customer service when you visited it the first time may offer better service over the long term. In each of these examples, an initial extreme or unusual performance is followed by a more moderate, typical, or average performance. This is because the initial extreme performance was influenced by random factors (e.g., the rookie's style of play just happened to click well with the other players; the chef had especially fresh and delicious ingredients). However, in the long run, individuals, groups of people, and organizations perform at an average or typical level.

The representativeness heuristic makes it difficult to fully appreciate the statistical concept of regression to the mean. Good performances seem to come from skill, and skill seems to ensure continued success. Poor performances seem to stem from mediocrity, and mediocrity seems to ensure continued failure. However, chance factors can lead consumers to jump to conclusions. Prematurely categorizing customer service, products, or organizations on the basis of their initial performance can lead to poor predictions. Thus, it is important for marketers to limit the number of unusual events that can happen when dealing with customers, and to strive for consistently good performance from their products and services.

To summarize, the representativeness heuristic encourages people to focus on simple similarities and to ignore complex but highly relevant statistical concepts, such as base rates, gambler's fallacy, and regression to the mean.

In order to minimize the loss of customers due to poor customer service experiences, retailers must strive to maintain consistently good performance in the minds of their customers.

Availability Heuristic People use the **availability heuristic** to make predictions based on how easily they can retrieve information from memory.[26] Events that are highly memorable because of media exposure, frequent exposure, or recent exposure are easily recalled. Easily recalled events tend to be overestimated. For example, let's suppose a consumer is booking a flight reservation and is trying to determine the likelihood that his flight will be delayed. If his flight was delayed the last time the consumer flew with a particular airline, then that event will be easily recalled. As a result, this consumer will be more likely to predict that his upcoming flight will be delayed, also. Likewise, events that are unmemorable tend to be underestimated. For example, is it more likely to be killed by a shark or by falling airplane parts? Most people believe that shark attacks are more likely because of movies featuring giant sharks and media reports of shark attacks. Deaths resulting from falling airplane parts, however, receive much less media attention. In reality, a person is 30 times more likely to die from falling airplane parts than from a shark attack.[27]

It is also important to distinguish between the *ease* with which examples of a to-be-predicted event can be retrieved from memory and the *number* of examples of a to-be-predicted event that can be retrieved from memory.[28] If it is easy to retrieve examples, the event seems likely. If it is possible to retrieve many examples, the event also seems likely. In many situations, ease of retrieval and the number of examples that can be retrieved are confounded. That is, ease and number are either both high or both low. When this is the case, it is impossible to determine whether ease of retrieval or the number of examples that can be retrieved has a stronger influence on predictive judgment.

In some circumstances, however, ease and number are *inversely related* (i.e., as one variable increases, the other variable decreases). In an important experiment that separates the effects on prediction of ease of retrieval versus number of examples retrieved, participants were asked to generate either ten (difficult task) or one (easy task) reason that a BMW is better than a Mercedes-Benz.[29] The results revealed that the BMW was more strongly preferred over the Mercedes-Benz when one reason was generated than when participants offered ten reasons. These results are surprising because ten reasons are better than one. However, one reason is easier to retrieve, and ease of retrieval is more important than the number of items retrieved when the availability heuristic is used as a basis for prediction.[30]

Simulation Heuristic People use the **simulation heuristic** to make predictions based on how easily an event or a sequence of events can be imagined or visualized.[31] If an event or sequence of events is easy to imagine, it tends to be overestimated. If an event or sequence of events is difficult to imagine, it tends to be underestimated. In one study of this phenomenon, participants were asked to imagine how likely they were to contract a disease called Hyposcenia-B.[32] In the easy-to-imagine condition, participants were told that the symptoms of the disease were headaches, muscle aches, and low energy. Most of us have experienced these symptoms at some point in our lives, and consequently, it is easy to imagine suffering from them. By contrast, in the difficult-to-imagine condition, participants were told that the symptoms of the disease were disorientation, a malfunctioning nervous system, and an inflamed liver. Most of us have not experienced these symptoms, so they are difficult to imagine. The results indicated that people believed they were personally more likely to contract Hyposcenia-B when the symptoms of the disease were easy to imagine as opposed to difficult to imagine. These effects disappeared, however, when participants did not attempt to imagine experiencing any of the symptoms.

These findings have important implications to marketers. For example, the simulation heuristic affects healthcare marketing. Consumers with high blood pressure often forget to take their medicine because the symptoms usually aren't that bad, so it is difficult to imagine that their condition is serious. Consequently, their health deteriorates, and marketers at pharmaceutical firms sell fewer pills. Similarly, consumers suffering from infections often take antibiotics for a few days and then stop before finishing the course because they feel better and it is difficult for them to imagine that they are still sick. Consequently, antibiotic-resistant infections develop, and pharmaceutical firms have to spend millions on the development of new antibiotics.

Anchoring-and-Adjustment Heuristic People using the **anchoring-and-adjustment heuristic** make predictions based on a first impression or an initial judgment (or anchor) and then shift (adjust or fine-tune) this judgment upward or downward depending on the implications of the imagined possibilities.[33] Unfortunately, people often do not adjust enough, and as a result, final judgments tend to be too close to initial judgments. For example, thinking about big numbers leads to big judgments, and thinking about small numbers leads to small judgments. Consequently, if you are asked to think of a big number first, such as 975, you would be more likely to overestimate the price of an inexpensive product that you don't buy frequently. If you are asked to think of a small number, such as 1, you would be more likely to underestimate the price of the same product. Similarly, expert real estate agents who receive a high list price (or high anchor value) for a house overestimate the value of a house, while agents who receive a low list price (or low anchor value) underestimate the value of the same house.[34]

The anchoring-and-adjustment heuristic can be used to trick consumers into buying more at a grocery store. In many cases, consumers intend to buy only one unit of a product when they enter the store (e.g., one container of milk); obviously the number one is a relatively low anchor. However, merely mentioning larger numbers can encourage consumers to consider higher anchors.[35] For example, multiple-unit pricing such as 3 for $1.99, or 12 for the price of 10, encourages consumers to buy more than one unit for two reasons: first, to obtain the volume discount, and second, multiple units suggest an anchor value that is higher than one. Ironically, purchase quantity limits (e.g., a limit of 10 per customer) can also encourage consumers to think about higher anchors and buy more than one unit, even if they do not come close to purchasing the amount implied by the limit. Suggestive selling (grab six for studying, buy eight and save a trip, buy 12 for your freezer, etc.) and expansion anchors (e.g., 101 uses around the house) also encourage consumers to consider larger anchors and to purchase multiple units.

Grocery store marketers oftentimes use the anchoring-and-adjustment heuristic to convince consumers to buy more than one unit of a particular product.

Consumers and marketers could make better predictions and better decisions if they relied more heavily on statistics and less on perceptions of similarity, ease of retrieval, ease of imagination, and first impressions. However, statistical knowledge requires training and effort, while heuristic thinking does not. Consequently, heuristic thinking is common despite the fact that it usually leads to poor predictions and poor decisions. The next section examines heuristics further in how consumers use them when selecting products.

Choice Heuristics

The Lexicographic Heuristic Consumers using the **lexicographic heuristic** (or single-attribute heuristic) compare all brands on one *key* attribute, such as price, size, weight, reliability, durability, calories, sugar, etc., and choose the brand that performs the best on that single attribute, while generally ignoring the other attributes.[36] If there is a tie, consumers examine the next most important attribute to break the tie. Assume that a particular consumer views style as the most important attribute for a new pair of blue jeans and comfort as the second most important attribute. This consumer will select the brand that appears to be most stylish, ignoring price, durability, colorfastness, and other attributes.

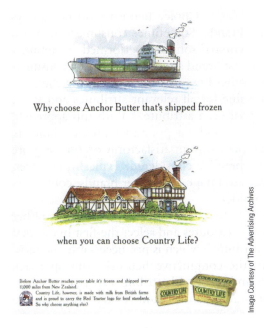

Why choose Anchor Butter that's shipped frozen

when you can choose Country Life?

Before Anchor Butter reaches your table it's frozen and shipped over 11,000 miles from New Zealand. Country Life, however, is made with milk from British farms and is proud to carry the Red Tractor logo for food standards. So why choose anything else?

Consumers often compare brands on one key attribute.

Image Courtesy of The Advertising Archives

Style is the key attribute; it is all that matters. If two brands appear equally desirable with respect to style, then this consumer chooses the brand from these two that performs best on comfort.

The lexicographic heuristic is a *non-compensatory choice strategy* because a high score on one attribute cannot compensate for a low score on another attribute. In this particular case, no other attribute can compensate for inadequacy on the key attribute. In fact, most choice heuristics are non-compensatory because attributes are evaluated one at a time. Unfortunately, this leads consumers to sometimes choose brands that are not the best choice because trade-offs are ignored. Consumers typically don't like making trade-offs because it is difficult to determine how much they should give up on one attribute to gain on another. For example, it is difficult for a consumer to express how much he would pay for a 10% improvement in the speed of his computer. But ignoring trade-offs can lead to bad decisions. Nevertheless, consumers assume this risk when they use quick-and-dirty heuristics that oversimplify the choice process.

The Elimination-By-Aspects Heuristic Another non-compensatory choice heuristic is the elimination-by-aspects heuristic. Consumers using the **elimination-by-aspects heuristic** reject all brands that do not have a key feature they want.[37] For example, if a consumer wants to buy a hybrid automobile, she might reject all non-hybrid cars. Next, she would focus on a different attribute and reject all brands that did not meet her requirements on that particular feature. For example, if the consumer prefers front-wheel drive, she might reject all hybrid automobiles that are rear-wheel drive. The process continues until only one brand remains. Rejecting brands is often easier than accepting multiple brands and then choosing among them. Consumers rarely need to examine a large set of attributes when using this choice heuristic. Furthermore, thinking about the attributes you do not want (a rejection frame of mind) often leads to different choices than thinking about the attributes you want (an acceptance frame of mind). The former focuses on avoiding negative outcomes from the purchase, while the latter emphasizes attaining positive outcomes.

The Additive-Difference Heuristic Consumers using the **additive-difference heuristic** compare two brands at a time, one attribute at a time, and subtract the evaluative differences.[38] Subtraction is performed on all relevant attributes, and each attribute is weighted for importance, i.e., each difference is multiplied by the importance of the attribute. Each weighted score is then summed to arrive at an overall score for each brand. The brand that performs the best on the most important attributes is selected. For example, if a consumer is evaluating automobiles and Brand *A* gets 35 mpg, but Brand *B* gets 30 mpg, the difference is 5 mpg. If fuel economy is judged to be very important for this consumer (e.g., 5 on a scale of 1 to 5), then the weighted difference between Brand *A* and *B* = 25 (5 × 5). This method of multiplying the weights times the differences continues for all relevant attributes, and the differences are summed for a total score. This heuristic requires more effort because math (subtraction, multiplication, and addition) is used. However, more effort can lead to better decisions.

The Conjunctive and Disjunctive Heuristics Choice heuristics do not always involve making comparisons among brands. Sometimes consumers focus on one brand at a time, and no brand comparisons are performed. Examining one brand at a time is easy, and if the first brand seems satisfactory, a consumer might buy it without examining any other brands. Consumers using the **conjunctive heuristic** set a minimum value for all relevant attributes and select the first brand that meets this value for each attribute.[39] With this approach, all the attributes are considered together, and one poor attribute can eliminate the brand. In other words, if a brand performs unsatisfactorily on one or more attributes, it is rejected, and another brand is considered. Typically, however, the first brand considered has a large advantage over other brands; consumers often choose the first brand they consider.

Consumers using the **disjunctive heuristic** set an acceptable value, rather than a minimum value, for all relevant attributes and select the first brand that meets this value on one particular attribute—which is not necessarily the most important attribute. In contrast to the conjunctive heuristic, this approach focuses on each attribute separately, and one good attribute can save the alternative. Again, the first brand has a large advantage and is likely to be chosen unless it is clearly unsatisfactory.

The Frequency Of Good and Bad Features Heuristic While all the heuristic choice strategies we've considered thus far have been non-compensatory choice strategies, consumers also use *compensatory choice strategies*. With a compensatory choice strategy, good attributes can compensate for bad attributes. When using the **frequency of good and bad features heuristic**, consumers form a simple attitude toward each brand alternative by counting the number of good and bad product features and choosing the brand with the greatest difference between good product features and bad product features. For example, if Brand A appears to have six good attributes and three bad attributes ($6 - 3 = 3$), and Product B has nine good features and seven bad features ($9 - 7 = 2$), then

While various tools can help consumers make purchase decisions, relying solely on those resources oversimplifies the choice task.

Product *A* is chosen. This heuristic is easy to apply because counting is easy and relatively little information is needed. Consumers are concerned only with the number of attributes, not the importance of each attribute. In other words, all attributes are treated equally.

As we've seen, choice heuristics help consumers make purchase decisions quickly and easily. Unfortunately, these approaches also often reduce the likelihood of making the best possible decision because they oversimplify and minimize the amount of information involved in the choice task. See Figure 10.5 for a summary of choice heuristics.

FIGURE 10.5 | **Choice Heuristics**

Lexicographic Heuristic
A consumer chooses the brand that appears best on the most important feature, ignoring all other attributes. If two or more brands are viewed as equal on this important feature, then the consumer chooses the brand that appears best on the second most important feature, and so on.
Elimination by Aspects Heuristic
A consumer rejects all brands that lack a key feature or possess an undesirable feature. Then, the remaining brands are evaluated on another important dimension in a similar manner. Eventually, only one brand remains.
Additive-Difference Heuristic
A consumer assigns important weights to all relevant attributes for a product and then compares brands, two at a time. Values for each attribute are then assigned to each brand. Next, the importance weights are multiplied by the differences in the values of the two brands' attributes and summed. More formally, $P = \Sigma w_i (A_i - B_i)$, where P = preference w_i = importance weight for attribute i, A_i = value of attribute i for brand A B_i = value of attribute i for brand B A positive score for P indicates a preference for Brand A, a negative score for P indicates a preference for Brand B, and a score of zero for P indicates no preference.
Conjunctive Heuristic
A consumer sets a minimum value for all relevant attributes and selects the first brand that meets these values for each attribute.
Disjunctive Heuristic
A consumer sets an acceptable value (usually higher than minimum) for all relevant attributes and selects the first brand that meets this value on one particular attribute (not necessarily the most important attribute).
Frequency of Good-Bad Features Heuristic
A consumer counts both the number of good product features and bad product features for each brand. The brand with the largest difference between its number of good and bad product features is chosen.

Global Perspectives

Decision-Making Styles Vary across Cultures

When making decisions, many North Americans are said to be analytical, relying on factual information, and individualistic, making one choice independently of others. Similarly, the French tend to consider many alternatives, and are highly rational and thorough in their decision making, while Russians are said to place more emphasis on values and appearance than facts. Germans are said to be deductive, and the Danes tend to be pragmatic when making decisions. In contrast, in Japan and other Asian cultures, logic and rationality seem less important; instead, one's "gut feeling" needs to be right, and the collective consensus is more important than the individual's opinion. Similarly, many Saudi Arabians are more intuitive in their decision making and avoid persuasion in favor of empirical evidence.[40]

In recent years, researchers have extensively examined cultural differences in decision making. While cross-cultural research related to decision making covers a broad range of topics, the overall results show that cultural differences are pervasive, not just along Eastern and Western philosophies, but also between countries and cultures within those countries. Additionally, within individuals, cultural influences are thought to influence consumers at all stages of the decision process.[41]

Developing a fuller understanding of how people from different cultures make decisions is essential for marketers as they expand globally. As our world becomes smaller as a result of information technology and the political opening of borders and economies, understanding cross-cultural differences in consumer behavior, decision making, and choice will become essential. Only by understanding cross-cultural differences can marketers effectively craft products and messages to satisfy global consumers.

Chapter Summary

Consumer choice involves choosing one brand from a set of products. The set of products that consumers think about and evaluate—the consideration set—usually consists of fewer than seven brands, and the best brand is not always included in the consideration set. The more consumers think about some brands, the more difficult it is to think about other brands (the part-list cuing effect). Moreover, a given brand can seem attractive (the attraction effect) or unattractive depending on what other brands are included in the consideration set. Compromise brands, or brands that are average on multiple dimensions, often have an advantage over brands that are good on some dimensions and bad on others (the compromise effect). Attraction and compromise effects are often more pronounced when consumers feel the need to justify or explain their decisions to themselves or others.

After the consideration set has been determined, consumers need to evaluate the differences in features and attributes between the considered brands in order to make a choice. When consumers can directly and physically observe all relevant brands in the consideration set and the brand attributes, they make a stimulus-based choice, but when brand alternatives are drawn from memory, choice is memory-based. Mixed choice combines both stimulus-based and memory-based choices. In addition, choice often involves focusing on differences among brands and using these differences as reasons or justifications for making decisions. These differences may be general (attitude-based choice) or specific (attribute-based choice), depending on the accessibility (salience in memory) and the diagnosticity (relevance) of the information used as a basis for choice.

Choice heuristics are mental shortcuts that simplify difficult decisions. Consumers use many different choice heuristics. Sometimes consumers focus on only one attribute (the lexicographic heuristic), and sometimes consumers eliminate brands that do not have a desired feature (the elimination-by-aspects heuristic). On other occasions, consumers compare two brands at a time and subtract the difference in the values of the attributes (the additive-difference heuristic). In other circumstances, consumers can focus on only one brand and choose the brand if it is satisfactory on all attributes (the conjunctive heuristic) or satisfactory on one attribute (the disjunctive heuristic). Finally, consumers may simply add up a product's good and bad

features and choose the best overall brand (the frequency of good and bad features heuristic). Choice heuristics can lead to bad decisions when consumers overlook important information. Nevertheless, consumers are often forced to use choice heuristics when information overload, time pressure, or other stresses make decision making difficult.

Key Terms

additive-difference heuristic
anchoring-and-adjustment
   heuristic
attraction effect
attribute-based choices
attitude-based choice
availability heuristic
choice deferral
compromise effect
conjunctive heuristic

consideration set
disjunctive heuristic
elimination-by-aspects heuristic
frequency of good and bad
   features heuristic
heuristics
heuristic processing
influence or choice heuristics
lexicographic heuristic
memory-based choice

mixed choice
MODE model
part-list cuing
persuasion heuristics
prediction heuristics
representativeness heuristic
simulation heuristic
stimulus-based choice
systematic processing

Review and Discussion

1. How can marketers increase the likelihood that their brands are included in consumers' consideration sets?

2. How can marketers use the part-list cuing effect to decrease the likelihood that competitors' brands are included in consumers' consideration sets?

3. Why does the trade-off contrast occur?

4. Describe a situation in which you purchased a compromise brand. Why does compromise seem like such a compelling reason on which to base a choice?

5. How does the availability heuristic influence how consumers make predictions about products?

6. How might the law of large numbers be related to word-of-mouth marketing? (*Word-of-mouth* marketing occurs when

marketing messages, product information, and/or people's opinions of the product are passed from person to person through informal conversation).

7. When are consumers likely to use a choice heuristic? When are they unlikely to do so?

8. Choice heuristics are often non-compensatory. Explain what this means and how it can lead to bad choices.

9. Some choice heuristics involve comparing several brands on the same attribute or set of attributes. Describe a situation in which you used one of these choice heuristics.

10. Some choice heuristics involve focusing on one brand at a time rather than making comparisons across brands. Describe a situation in which you used one of these choice heuristics.

Short Application Exercises

1. Find three advertisements that use puffery. Do you think that puffery or exaggeration is an effective advertising tactic? Do you think the use of puffery is ethical? Why or why not?

2. Choose three products you purchased recently. Identify whether your choice of the product was stimulus-based, memory-based, or the result of mixed choice. How could a marketer use package information to better appeal to you for any of the products under conditions of stimulus-based choice?

3. Find two advertisements, one that appeals to consumers using attitude-based choice and one that focuses on attribute-based choice.

4. Identify a product for which you think people generally use price as a prediction of quality. Design an experiment to test this idea. Can you find evidence from the Internet that supports or refutes the price-quality relationship for this product?

Managerial Application

In the early 1980s, a format war took place between VHS and Betamax videotapes for video storage. VHS ultimately won. History always repeats itself. Between 2000 and 2008, another format war took place between Sony's Blu-Ray and Toshiba's HD DVD (high density optical disc for video storage). Blu-Ray ultimately won. But why? HD DVD had several advantages over Blu-Ray. HD DVD was the pioneering brand, or the first brand to enter the market, plus it was less expensive than Blu-Ray. Initially, almost as many movie titles appeared in HD DVD as did in Blu-Ray. Using the concepts in Chapter 10, how would you compare and evaluate these differences?

In January 2008, an important event tipped the scale in favor of Blu-Ray when Warner Brothers Studios decided to support Blu-Ray exclusively. Because Sony Blu-Ray already had the exclusive support of Sony Pictures (including MGM/Columbia Tristar), Disney (including Touchstone and Miramax), Fox, and Lions Gate, the Warner decision gave Blu-Ray the support of 70% of the movie studios. Toshiba was unable to overcome this advantage. In addition, Blu-Ray discs hold more data than HD DVD discs (50 GB versus 30 GB). The Sony PlayStation 3 can also play PS3 games, Blu-Ray discs, and standard DVDs. Using the concepts in Chapter 10, how would you compare and evaluate these differences?

Your Challenge:

1. What strategies could HD DVD have used to beat Blu-Ray?

2. What strategies could Blu-Ray have used to beat HD DVD more quickly?

3. After Warner Brothers decided to support only Blu-Ray in January 2008, Toshiba reduced the price of HD DVD players to $150. Explain why this was too little, too late. In February 2008, Net Flix, BestBuy, and Walmart announced that they would phase out HD DVD. After these announcements, Toshiba announced that they would stop producing HD DVD players. Explain why Toshiba needed the support of Warner Brothers, Net Flix, BestBuy, and Walmart.

4. In what other product categories do you currently see a format war? What steps can competing companies take to try to avoid format wars?

End Notes

1 Huang, Q., Nijs, V. R., Hansen, K., and Anderson, E. T. (2012). WalMart's Impact on Supplier Profits. *Journal of Marketing Research, 49,* 131–143.

2 Nedungadi, P. (1990). Recall and Consumer Consideration Sets: Influencing Choice without Altering Evaluations. *Journal of Consumer Research, 17,* 263–276.

3 Miller, G. A. (1956). The Magical Number Seven, Plus or Minus Two: Some Limits on Our Capacity for Processing Information. *Psychological Review, 63,* 8–97; Russo, J. E. (1977). The Value of Unit Price Information. *Journal of Marketing Research, 141,* 193–201.

4 Alba, J. W., and Chattopadhyay, A. (1985). Effects of Context and Part-Category Cues on Recall of Competing Brands. *Journal of Marketing Research, 22,* 340–349; Alba, J. W., and Chattopadhyay, A. (1986). Salience Effects on Brand Recall. *Journal of Marketing Research, 23,* 363–369.

5 Nedungadi, P. (1990). Recall and Consumer Consideration Sets: Influencing Choice without Altering Evaluations. *Journal of Consumer Research, 17,* 263–276.

6 Huber, J., Payne, J. W., and Puto, C. (1982). Adding Asymmetrically Dominated Alternatives: Violations of Regularity and the Similarity Hypothesis. *Journal of Consumer Research, 9,* 90–98; Huber, J., and Puto, C. (1983). Market Boundaries and Product Choice: Illustrating Attraction and Substitution Effects. *Journal of Consumer Research, 10,* 31–44; Simonson, I., and Tversky, A. (1992). Choice in Context: Trade-off Contrast and Extremeness Aversion. *Journal of Marketing Research, 29,* 281–295.

7 Simonson, I. (1989). Choice Based on Reasons: The Case of Attraction and Compromise Effects. *Journal of Consumer Research, 16,* 158–174; Simonson, I., and Tversky, A. (1992). Choice in Context: Trade-off Contrast and Extremeness Aversion. *Journal of Marketing Research, 29,* 281–295.

8 Zmuda, N. (2012). Five More Join Midcal 'Ten' Lineup in Bid to Lure Back Soda Drinkers. *Advertising Age, 83,* 2–19.

9 Kardes, F. R. (2002). *Consumer Behavior and Managerial Decision Making,* 2nd ed. Upper Saddle River, NJ: Pearson Education/Prentice Hall.

10 Lynch, J. G., Marmorstein, H., and Weigold, M. F. (1988). Choices from Sets Including Remembered Brands: Use of Recalled Attributes and Prior Overall Evaluations. *Journal of Consumer Research, 15,* 169–184; Lynch, J. G., and Srull, T. K. (1982). Memory and Attentional Factors in Consumer Choice: Concepts and Research Methods. *Journal of Consumer Research, 9,* 18–37.

11 Biehal, G. J., and Chakravarti, D. (1983). Information Accessibility as a Moderator of Consumer Choice. *Journal of Consumer Research, 10,* 1–14.

12 Alba, J. W., Marmorstein, H., and Chattopadhyay, A. (1992). Transitions in Preference over Time: The Effects of Memory on Message Persuasiveness. *Journal of Marketing Research, 29,* 406–416.

13 Kardes, F. R. (1986). Effects of Initial Product Judgments on Subsequent Memory-Based Judgments. *Journal of Consumer Research, 13,* 1–11.

14 Fazio, R. H. (1990). Multiple Processes by Which Attitudes Guide Behavior: The MODE Model as an Integrative Framework. In M. P. Zanna (Ed.), *Advances in Experimental Social Psychology* (pp. 75–109). New York: Academic Press; Sanbonmatsu, D. M., and Fazio, R. H. (1990). The Role of Attitudes in Memory-Based Decision Making. *Journal of Personality and Social Psychology, 59,* 614–622.

15 Dhar, R. (1997). Consumer Preference for a No-Choice Option. *Journal of Consumer Research, 24,* 215–231; Dhar, R., and Nowlis, S. M. (1999). The Effect of Time Pressure on Consumer Choice Deferral. *Journal of Consumer Research, 25,* 369–384; Greenleaf, E. A., and Lehmann, D. R. (1995). Reasons for Substantial Delay in Consumer Decision Making. *Journal of Consumer Research, 22,* 186–1999.

16 Barstow, D. (2012, April 21). Vast Mexico Bribery Case Hushed Up by WalMart after Top-Level Struggle. *New York Times.*

17 Kivetz, R., and Simonson, I. (2000). The Effects of Incomplete Information on Consumer Choice. *Journal of Marketing Research, 37,* 428–448; Sanbonmatsu, D. M., Kardes, F. R., Posavac, S. S., and Houghton, D. C. (1997). Contextual Influences on Judgment Based on Limited Information. *Organizational Behavior and Human Decision Processes, 69,* 251–264.

18 Gunasti, K., and Ross, W. T. (2009). How Inferences about Missing Attributes Decrease the Tendency to Defer Choice and Increase Purchase Probability. *Journal of Consumer Research, 35,* 823–837.

19 Kardes, F. R., Sanbonmatsu, D. M., Cronley, M. L., and Houghton, D. C. (2002). Consideration Set Overvaluation: When Impossibly Favorable Ratings of a Set of Brands are Observed. *Journal of Consumer Psychology, 12,* 353–361.

20 Chaiken, S., and Trope, Y. (Eds.) (1999). *Dual-Process Theories in Social Psychology.* New York: Guilford.

21 Stec, A. M., and Bernstein, D. A. (1999). The Scope of Psychology: More Than Meets The Eye. In Stec, A. M. and Bernstein, D. A. (Eds.), *Psychology: Fields of Application* (pp. 1–16). Boston, MA: Houghton Mifflin Company.

22 Kardes, F. R., Posavac, S. S., and Cronley, M. L. (2004). Consumer Inference: A Review of Processes, Bases, and Judgment Contexts, *Journal of Consumer Psychology, 14,* 3, 230–256; Kardes, F. R., Cronley, M. L., Kellaris, J. J., and Posavac, S. S. (2004). The Role of Selective Information Processing in Price-Quality Inference, *Journal of Consumer Research, 31,* 368–374; Lichtenstein, D. R., and Burton, S. (1989). The Relationship between Perceived and Objective Price-Quality. *Journal of Marketing Research, 26,* 429–443.

23 Tversky, A., and Kahneman, D. (1974). Judgment under Uncertainty: Heuristics and Biases. *Science, 185,* 1124–1131; Gilovich, T., Griffin, D., and Kahneman, D. (2002).

Heuristics and Biases: The Psychology of Intuitive Judgment. Cambridge, UK: Cambridge University Press.

24 Tversky, A., and Kahneman, D. (1974). Judgment under Uncertainty: Heuristics and Biases. *Science, 185*, 1124–1131; Gilovich, T., Griffin, D., and Kahneman, D. (2002). *Heuristics and Biases: The Psychology of Intuitive Judgment.* Cambridge, UK: Cambridge University Press.

25 Gilovich, T., Vallone, R., and Tversky, A. (1985). The Hot Hand in Basketball: On the Misperception of Random Sequences. *Cognitive Psychology, 17*, 295–314.

26 Tversky, A., and Kahneman, D. (1974). Judgment under Uncertainty: *Heuristics and Biases.Science, 185*, 1124–1131; Gilovich, T., Griffin, D., and Kahneman, D. (2002). *Heuristics and Biases: The Psychology of Intuitive Judgment.* Cambridge, UK: Cambridge University Press.

27 Plous, S. (1993). *The Psychology of Judgment and Decision Making.* New York: McGraw-Hill.

28 Schwarz, N. (1998). Accessible Content and Accessibility Experiences: The Interplay of Declarative and Experiential Information in Judgment. *Personality and Social Psychology Review, 2*, 87–99.

29 Schwarz, N. (1998). Accessible Content and Accessibility Experiences: The Interplay of Declarative and Experiential Information in Judgment. *Personality and Social Psychology Review, 2*, 87–99.

30 Schwarz, N. (1998). Accessible Content and Accessibility Experiences: The Interplay of Declarative and Experiential Information in Judgment. *Personality and Social Psychology Review, 2*, 87–99.

31 Kahneman, D., and Tversky, A. (1984). Choice, Values, and Frames. *American Psychologist, 39*, 341–350.

32 Sherman, S. J., Cialdini, R. B., Schwartzman, D. F., and Reynolds, K. D. (1985). Imagining Can Heighten or Lower the Perceived Likelihood of Contracting a Disease: The Mediating Effect of Ease of Imagery. *Personality and Social Psychology Bulletin, 11*, 118–127.

33 Tversky, A., and Kahneman, D. (1974). Judgment under Uncertainty: Heuristics and Biases. *Science, 185*, 1124–1131; Gilovich, T., Griffin, D., and Kahneman, D. (2002). *Heuristics and Biases: The Psychology of Intuitive Judgment.* Cambridge, UK: Cambridge University Press.

34 Northcraft, G. B., and Neale, M. A. (1987). Experts, Amateurs, and Real Estate: An Anchoring and Adjustment Perspective on Property Pricing Decisions. *Organizational Behavior and Human Decision Processes, 39*, 84–97.

35 Wansink, B., Kent, R. J., and Hoch, S. J. (1998). An Anchoring and Adjustment Model of Purchase Quantity Decisions. *Journal of Marketing Research, 35*, 71–81.

36 Payne, J. W., Bettman, J. R., and Johnson, E. J. (1993). *The Adaptive Decision Maker.* Cambridge, UK: Cambridge University Press.

37 Payne, J. W., Bettman, J. R., and Johnson, E. J. (1993). *The Adaptive Decision Maker.* Cambridge, UK: Cambridge University Press; Tversky, A. (1972). Elimination by Aspects: A Theory of Choice. *Psychological Review, 79*, 281–299.

38 Payne, J. W., Bettman, J. R., and Johnson, E. J. (1993). *The Adaptive Decision Maker.* Cambridge, UK: Cambridge University Press; Tversky, A. (1969). Intransitivity of Preferences. *Psychological Review, 76*, 31–48.

39 Payne, J. W., Bettman, J. R., and Johnson, E. J. (1993). *The Adaptive Decision Maker.* Cambridge, UK: Cambridge University Press.

40 Ardichvili, A., and Kuchinke, K. P. (2002). Leadership Style and Cultural Values among Managers and Subordinates: A Comparative Study of Four Countries of the Former Soviet Union, Germany, and the US. *Human Resources Development International, 5*, 1, 99–117; DuPraw, M. E., and Axner, M. (2005, January 11). Working on Common Cross-cultural Communication Challenges. *A More Perfect Union* [Online]. Available: www.wwcd.org; Guss, C. D. (2002). Decision Making in Individualistic and Collectivistic Cultures. In W. J. Lonner, D. L. Dinnel, S. A. Hayes, and D. N. Sattler (Eds.), *Online Readings in Psychology and Culture.* Center for Cross-Cultural Research, Western Washington University, Bellingham, Washington, [Online]. Available: www.wwu.edu; Schramm-Nielsen, J. (2001). Cultural Dimensions of Decision Making: Denmark and France Compared. *Journal of Managerial Psychology, 16*, 6, 404–423.

41 Ardichvili, A., and Kuchinke, K. P. (2002). Leadership Style and Cultural Values among Managers and Subordinates: A Comparative Study of Four Countries of the Former Soviet Union, Germany, and the US. *Human Resources Development International, 5*, 1, 99–117.

BEHAVIORAL DECISION THEORY

CHAPTER 1

OBJECTIVES *After studying this chapter, you will be able to…*

1 Explain expected value theory and how the framing effect violates this theory.

2 Develop marketing strategies for segregating gains and aggregating losses.

3 Explain several different ways preference reversals can occur.

4 Define singular evaluation and comparative evaluation.

5 Analyze the pros and cons of selective thinking.

McCormick

Executives at McCormick & Company, Inc. say that, "our mission is to save the world from boring food."[1] The company is 123 years old and it currently has a 49% share of the $169 million pepper market. Of course, McCormick also sells a wide variety of other spices and herbs. In their recent television and print ads, McCormick has claimed that cinnamon, pepper, turmeric, oregano, and other herbs and spices are high in antioxidants that are essential for good health. The McCormick website, "Spices for Health," also argues that spices can reduce inflammation, reduce hunger, increase metabolism, and even reduce the risk of cancer. Stephen Gardner, the litigation director for the Center for Science in the Public Interest, says that it is illegal for companies to claim that their "food products can be used to prevent, cure, treat, or mitigate disease. That is precisely what [McCormick] are saying on the website." What is the likelihood or probability that McCormick products promote good

health? What is the probability that McCormick will be sued over their health claims? How should people think about probabilities?

Behavioral decision research focuses mainly on **risky decision making**, or decision making under uncertainty. Uncertainty means that the probabilities of various possible outcomes are unknown. How should people think about unknown probabilities? How should people think about risk? What level of risk is acceptable? What is the best way to manage risk? These are the types of questions addressed by behavioral decision research, and they are important questions to ask because decision making often requires an attempt to predict the likelihood of various future outcomes. Decision makers prefer to choose courses of action that are highly likely to lead to desirable outcomes.

OBJECTIVE # Expected Utility Theory

How should people think about risk? According to expected utility theory, people should think about uncertain events in terms of "gambles." All gambles have two components: a probability component called p, and a value component called v.[2] The predicted or expected value of a gamble is simply p times v. For example, the expected value of a gamble that offers a 25% chance of winning $100 is $0.25 \times 100 = \$25$. This means that people should be willing to pay up to $25 to play this gamble, but no more than $25. Expected utility theory also shows how people should rank different gambles. For example, should a person play a gamble that offers a 25% chance of winning $100 or a gamble that offers a 20% chance of winning $130? As $0.25 \times \$100 = \$25$, and $0.20 \times \$130 = \$26$, the second gamble is the better deal.

People face similar decisions in the marketplace daily. Considering only the durability of a product, would a consumer rather purchase a $100 brand with a 50% probability of failure after two years or a $300 brand with a 20% probability of failure after two years? Perhaps surprisingly, the cheaper product is the better choice. The expected replacement cost of the first product is $\$100 \times 0.50 = \$50$, but the expected replacement cost of the second product is $\$300 \times 0.20 = \$60$.

Expected utility theory suggests that all alternatives can be ranked from worst to best. It also suggests that alternatives with higher expected values **dominate** or are better choices than alternatives with lower expected values. In gambles with different stages, such as a game show in which you need to win in stage one in order to advance to stage two, stage one should cancel out, or be ignored, if it is identical for two different gambling games. This is called

Marketing in Action

Accenture

Accenture is marketing research firm that tracks consumer satisfaction, brand loyalty, and brand switching rates.[3] In a global study involving 10,000 consumers and 10 industries conducted in September and October 2011, it was found that satisfaction scores were rising, but so were brand switching rates. The switching rate was 66% for the entire sample, and 51% for the U.S. sample. Why would consumers switch when satisfaction scores were so high? The research showed not only that just one bad customer service experience was enough to lead to a switch, but also that consumers' expectations about product performance and customer service continue to rise. Furthermore, only 24% of the consumers surveyed indicated that they were brand loyal, and 23% said that they had no brand loyalty.

---

cancellation. In addition, preferences should be **transitive**; in other words, if you prefer A to B, and B to C, then you must prefer A to C. Finally, according to the **invariance principle**, preferences should remain the same no matter how preferences are measured or how decision alternatives are described.

Framing Effects

In direct violation of the invariance principle, extensive research shows that preferences change when decision alternatives are described in terms of different **frames**, or perspectives.[4] For example, imagine you are a manager for a hospital preparing for a flu epidemic that is expected to kill 600 people. Your staff has developed two programs to combat the flu, but because of cost constraints you can implement only one of these two programs. If program A is selected, 200 people will be *saved*. If program B is selected, there is a 33% chance that all 600 people will be saved and a 67% chance that no one will be saved. Which program would you choose?

Now consider the very same problem with a slight change of wording. A flu epidemic is expected to kill 600 people. If program A is selected, 400 people will *die*. If program B is selected, there is a 33% chance that no one will die and a 67% chance that all 600 will die. Now which program would you choose? To be consistent, if you chose program A for the first version of the problem you must choose program A for the second version because the outcomes are identical. And if you chose program B for the first version of the problem, you must choose program B for the second version. However, most people are inconsistent. Most people choose program A when the problem is worded in terms of lives *saved*, and most people choose program B when the problem is worded in terms of *deaths*. Program A is the sure-thing alternative: 200 will be saved for sure and 400 will die for sure. Program B is the risky alternative: there is a 33% chance all 600 will be saved (i.e. no one will die), and a 67% chance that no one will be saved (i.e., all 600 will die).

When people think about a choice problem in terms of positive outcomes, such as lives saved or money gained, people typically prefer the sure thing. This is known as **risk aversion**; people typically prefer to avoid risky alternatives when outcomes are framed positively. However, when people think about a choice in terms of negative outcomes, such as deaths or money lost, people typically prefer the risky alternative. This is known as **risk seeking**; people are more likely to accept risk when outcomes are framed negatively. When people are inconsistent, i.e., sometimes risk averse and sometimes risk seeking, **preference reversals** occur. A preference reversal means that people prefer option A over option B at one point in time but can prefer option B over option A at another point in time.

Importantly, even experts are susceptible to the framing effect. Expert physicians were asked to recommend either radiation therapy or surgery for lung cancer based on information presented using a loss frame (probability of dying) or a gain frame (probability of surviving).[5] The loss frame stated that out of 100 people having surgery, 10 will die during treatment, 32 will die within one year, and 66 will die within five years. Out of 100 people having radiation therapy, none will die during treatment, 23 will die within one year, and 78 will die within five years. The gain frame stated the opposite: out of 100 people having surgery, 90 will survive the treatment, 68 will survive one year, and 34 will survive five years. Out of 100 people having radiation therapy, 100 will survive the treatment, 77 will survive one year, and 32 will survive five years. The physicians were more likely to recommend surgery in the gain frame condition than in the loss frame condition. Even experts making life and death decisions fail to use information about probabilities consistently.

Reference Dependence Consider a marketing manager who has experienced a run of product failures in a difficult economy. For strategic reasons, the firm continues to maintain one of two poorly performing brands in the market. When considering which of these poorly performing brands to support, the manager may be evaluating the decision with a negative frame (i.e., the firm has already lost money on several products, and the economy is in recession). Given a negative frame, would this manager choose to support Brand A, a brand that is certain to lose $1 million, or Brand B, a brand that has a 40% probability of losing $2.5 million and a 60% probability of breaking even or losing nothing? Framing theory suggests that the marketing manager would choose to support Brand B. The manager will choose the riskier option because the decision has been framed negatively.

What if the frame were reversed? Consider a marketing manager who has had a string of successes with product introductions, and the economy has become robust. Given a choice between two brands, would this manager provide additional marketing support for Brand A, which is guaranteed to produce $1 million in profits, or Brand B, which offers a 40% probability of generating $2.5 million in profits and a 60% probability of breaking even or generating no profits? Given the positive frame, this manager is likely to support Brand A and avoid unnecessary risks.

Loss Aversion Expected utility theory cannot explain the framing effect or preference reversals. According to expected utility theory, people should be consistent and choose the same alternative regardless of how the outcomes are framed or described. Expected

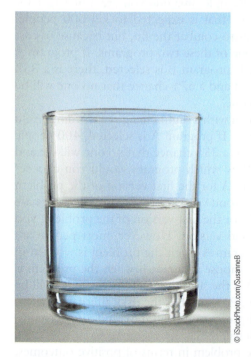

A positive stance may instigate a completely different decision than a negative stance.

utility theory also suggests that the pleasure experienced from winning $100 should be just as intense as the pain experienced from losing $100. However, prospect theory suggests that all outcomes are evaluated with respect to a neutral reference point, and that preferences change as reference points change. This is known as **reference dependence**. For example, $100 seems like a lot of money to poor people who use low reference points (e.g., $5). However, $100 seems like not a lot of money to rich people who use high reference points (e.g., $1 million).

In Figure 11.1, the reference point is in the middle. Outcomes above the reference point are perceived as gains or positive outcomes. Outcomes below the reference point are perceived as losses or negative outcomes. As Figure 11.1 shows, the value function is much steeper for losses than for gains. This means that losses have a bigger impact on people, relative to equivalent gains. This is called **loss aversion** (e.g., losing $100 has a bigger impact on people's feelings, relative to winning $100). Finally, Figure 11.1 shows that outcomes have weaker effects on people as distance from the reference point increases. This is called **diminishing sensitivity** (e.g., the difference between $100 and $0 seems larger than the difference between $1,100 and $1,000).

Loss aversion is so powerful that it can lead people to violate the dominance principle.[6] For example, when asked to choose between A and B below, most people recognize that B dominates A:

A. 25% chance to win $240 and 75% chance to lose $760

B. 25% chance to win $250 and 75% chance to lose $750

FIGURE 11.1 | **Reference Dependence and Loss Aversion**

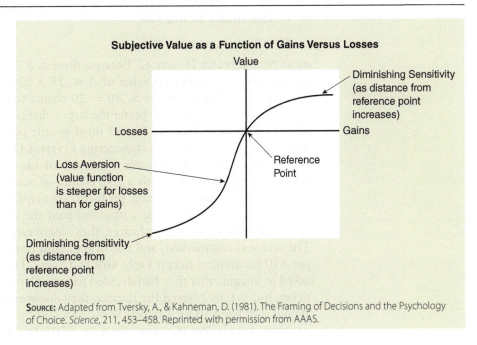

SOURCE: Adapted from Tversky, A., & Kahneman, D. (1981). The Framing of Decisions and the Psychology of Choice. *Science*, 211, 453–458. Reprinted with permission from AAAS.

B is better than A because you could win more or lose less with B than with A, so B dominates A. However, imagine you were asked to choose among the following back-to-back options:

C. a sure gain of $240

D. 25% chance to gain $1,000; 75% chance to gain nothing versus the following back-to-back options:

E. a sure loss of $750

F. 75% chance to lose $1,000; 25% chance to lose nothing

Now, most people prefer C over D because focusing on the sure gain makes people risk averse. Furthermore, most people prefer F over E because focusing on the sure loss makes people risk seeking. This violates the dominance principle because combining C and F gives you A in the previous choice problem, as does combining D and E to give you B. But in the previous choice problem, it was obvious that B was better than A.

Research on framing also shows that people overestimate the likelihood of very small probabilities, which is what makes lotteries seem more attractive than they really are. People also underestimate the likelihood of moderate and large probabilities. This also leads to violations of the invariance principle, as shown in the following choice problem.

Consider the following two-stage game. In the first stage, there is a 75% chance to end the game without winning anything and a 25% chance to move into the second stage. If you reach the second stage you have a choice between:

A. a sure win of $30

B. 80% chance to win $45

Most people prefer A over B. However, when the gamble is changed to a one-stage choice between:

C. 25% chance to win $30

D. 20% chance to win $45

most people prefer D over C. Because there is a 25% chance to move to the second stage, the expected value of A is .25 × $30, which is the same as C. The expected value of B is .25 × .80 = .20 chance to win $45, which is the same as D. However, most people prefer the larger chance to win the smaller amount when considering A versus B, and most people prefer the smaller chance to win the larger amount when considering C versus D. This occurs because most people ignore stage one and this makes A look like a sure gain, even though it is not a sure gain; there is only a 25% chance of reaching stage two.

In another famous framing problem, participants were asked to imagine that they had decided to see a play and paid the admission price of $10 per ticket. As they entered the theater, they discovered they had lost the ticket. The seat was not marked, and the ticket could not be recovered. Would they pay $10 for another ticket? Only 46% said "yes." However, when people were asked to imagine that they had decided to see a play where admission is $10 per ticket, but as they entered the theater, they discovered they had lost a $10 bill. Would they pay $10 for a ticket? Some 88% said "yes." In both versions of this problem, people lost the same amount ($10), but this loss seems like part of the price of the ticket in the first case but not in the second. The difference between the response to losing the ticket and losing $10 can be explained by *mental accounting*. The purchase of another $10 ticket is entered into the "ticket account," and thus, the cost of seeing the play is interpreted as $20. In contrast, the loss of $10 was not specifically linked to the "ticket account," so the cost of seeing the show is interpreted as only $10.

OBJECTIVE (2)

The Endowment Effect Even slight variations in the framing or wording of choice problems can change people's preferences dramatically, resulting in surprisingly inconsistent choices. Loss aversion and the framing effect also contribute to the **endowment effect**, or the tendency to view a product as more valuable if one owns it than if one does not own it.[7] Obviously, the value of an object should stay the same, but after buying a product or receiving it as a gift, consumers are surprisingly reluctant to sell the object. Selling the object is equivalent to losing it, and people are reluctant to give up what they have now. Consider the following examples:

- Example 1. Mr. Jones bought a case of good wine in the late 1950s for about $5 a bottle. A few years later his wine merchant offered to buy the wine back for $100 a bottle. Mr. Jones refused, although he has never paid more than $35 for a bottle of wine.

- Example 2. A neighbor's son offers to mow Mr. Smith's lawn for $8. Mr. Smith refuses and mows his own lawn, despite the fact that he wouldn't mow his neighbor's same-sized lawn for less than $20.

In these examples, consumers are reluctant to sell what they currently own or to pay much less for a service than their perceived value of the service. In both cases, consumers underestimate the importance of **opportunity costs**. Selling the wine would provide Mr. Jones with the opportunity of buying many bottles of wine in his usual price range, and paying the neighbor's son would provide Mr. Smith with the opportunity of doing something more enjoyable or productive than mowing his lawn.

The Sunk Cost Effect The sunk cost effect also results from insensitivity to opportunity costs because as the amount of time or money invested in a product or a service increases, people are more reluctant to give up the product or service. Consider the following examples:

- Example 1. A family pays $40 for tickets to a basketball game to be played 60 miles from their home. On the day of the game, there is a snowstorm. They decide to go anyway, but note in passing that had the tickets been given to them, they would have stayed home.

- Example 2. A consumer joins a tennis club and pays a $300 yearly membership fee. After two weeks of playing, he develops tennis elbow. He continues to play (in pain) saying, "I don't want to waste the $300!"

Once people own something, the endowment effect makes them reluctant to sell it, even if it isn't providing them with a measurable, direct benefit.

In poker, there's a famous saying: "don't throw good money after bad" At some point, people should cut their losses and avoid doing what they don't want to do even though they already paid for the activity. By performing a less preferred activity, people give up the opportunity to do something they enjoy more. Once again, opportunity costs are undervalued or neglected.

Loss aversion also implies that marketers should segregate gains and aggregate losses.[8] Many small gains are more pleasant than one large gain, even when the small gains add up to the same value as the large gain. The opposite is true for losses; many small losses are more unpleasant than one large loss, even when the small losses add up to the same value as the large loss. For example, most people are happier if they win $10 five times than if they win $50 once; conversely, most people would be more upset by losing $10 five times than losing $50 once. So, based on these factors, marketers should aggregate losses because asking consumers to pay one large payment is less painful to consumers than asking them to pay several small payments. For example, based on this information, hotels would likely have better guest relations if they charged one fee covering several services, such as HBO, breakfast, and the use of the hotel's exercise equipment. Asking consumers to pay for each service individually is irritating. Most consumers would rather pay one lump sum. This one-fee-for-all approach is used by cruise lines, Club Med, and Tire Discounters. On the other hand, airlines have become infamous for tacking on separate, annoying surcharges for checking luggage, food, and beverages.

Price bundling is used by some firms to aggregate losses.[9] For example, instead of charging $40 per day for four days on ski-lift tickets, a resort could charge one lump sum of $160 for a four-day ski pass. If the weather is poor on the fourth day, consumers are likely to exhibit the sunk cost effect and go skiing anyway. However, the sunk cost effect is perceived as smaller to the consumer who paid one lump sum than to the consumer who bought four separate tickets. Price bundling is also used for complementary products, such as razors and razor blades and electronic products and batteries.

Although it is usually beneficial to aggregate losses, this is not true when the individual losses are extremely small.[10] For example, in a public service announcement for a children's charity, Alyssa Milano tells us that we can feed

Price bundling is a strategy used by marketers to sell complementary products.

a starving child for "only 50 cents a day," and a mattress retailer tells us that we can sleep comfortably for "only 10 cents a night." This is known as the pennies-a-day approach. Segregating losses makes sense when the individual losses are so small that they can be considered trivial. Of course, even trivial expenses can add up.

The Status Quo Effect Another type of framing effect is the status quo effect, or the preference to keep one's current options.[11] Consumers tend to keep their current jobs, insurance policies, investment plans, cars, and other products, even when they could do better. It seems safer to accept the status quo because change usually involves risk. Loss aversion often makes consumers reluctant to accept risk. However, framing manipulations can change the way consumers define the status quo, and this can produce dramatic changes in preferences. For example, in one study, consumers learned about an unfamiliar anti-clotting drug called Carozile. Like most drugs, Carozile had dangerous side effects. Half of the participants were told that Carozile is currently on the market. The remaining half were told that Carozile is currently not on the market but is being considered by the FDA for approval. Participants' preferences tended to match the status quo: they preferred to keep the drug on the market if it was currently on the market, and they preferred to keep the drug off the market if it was currently off the market. This effect was more pronounced as risk increased or as accountability increased. Accountability was manipulated by requiring or not requiring participants to justify their judgments and decisions to the experimenter at the conclusion of the study.

The Default Option Effect Another type of framing effect is the default option effect, or the preference for the fallback choice option or the choice option one accepts if one does nothing.[12] Doing nothing is attractive because it requires little thought or effort, and because change often involves risk. For example, U.S. drivers have to opt-in and sign forms to become organ donors, so the default option is to not be an organ donor. In some European countries, however, the opposite is true: drivers are automatically organ donors unless they opt-out and sign forms to not be an organ donor. The default option matters: only 12% of Germans agree to become organ donors because not donating is the default option, whereas 99% of Austrians agree to become organ donors because donating is the default option. Changing the default option changes people's preferences.

In some U.S. companies, contributing to one's retirement plan is the default option and employees need to opt-out and sign forms to not contribute to their retirement plans. In other U.S. companies, not contributing to one's retirement plan is the default option and employees need to opt-in and sign forms to contribute to their retirement plans. Because of the default option effect, the former group saves more for retirement than the latter group. In both cases, people choose the easy path or the path of least resistance. However, this path is arguably more beneficial for the first group than for the second group.

Libertarian paternalism refers to the idea that people should have free choice; however, choice options should be arranged in a manner to help people make the best choices. Default choice options should be the options that are the best for most people, but all people should have the choice to choose as they wish. Empirical research should determine what options are the best options for the most people. Policymakers should then structure the choice options in a manner that helps people to make informed decisions. This type of structuring is known as **choice architecture**. Choice architects should use consumer psychology, social psychology, and behavioral decision research to structure people's choice options.

OBJECTIVE **3**   ## Preference Reversal

The framing effect is a type of preference reversal. Consumers prefer the safe alternative when options are framed in terms of gains. However, consumers prefer the risky alternative when options are framed in terms of losses. Thus, preferences reverse or switch when consumers think about a choice problem differently. One option looks better at one point in time, and the other option looks better at another point in time. Framing is not the only way to produce preference reversals, however. Preference reversals can occur anytime consumers weigh information inconsistently.

For example, when evaluating gambles, people sometimes weigh the probability of winning higher than the value of the amount of money they can win.[13] This is called a p-bet, or a probability-based bet. At other times, however, consumers weigh value more heavily than probability. This is called a v-bet, or a value-based bet. Of course, there is typically a negative correlation between p and v: As p increases, v decreases. Consumers prefer a p-bet, or a bet that offers a high probability of winning a small amount of money, when they are asked to choose among gambles. However, consumers prefer a v-bet, or a bet that offers a low probability of winning a large amount of money, when they are asked to indicate a minimum selling price for each bet. Interestingly, this preference reversal has been documented for gamblers using their own money in Las Vegas. Different procedures for measuring preferences can change consumers' preferences, which violates the invariance principle discussed earlier. This pattern of results suggests that marketing managers prefer a p-bet when deciding whether to launch a new product or service and a v-bet when assessing the value or cost of a new product concept.

How serious is preference reversal? Consider the decision faced regularly by oil company executives. Any given drilling site has some probability of success (p) and some level of profit potential (v). Research shows that oil companies paid over $1 billion for the privilege of drilling in the Baltimore Canyon (in the Atlantic Ocean), even though leading oil geochemists determined that the probability of finding oil there was extremely low. This suggests that oil company executives often focus on the extremely large size of potential profits (v) and neglect the probabilities provided by the geochemists.[14] Ideally, of course, billion-dollar decisions should be based on both probabilities and potential earnings.

Why do different measurement techniques lead to different preferences? One reason is the **compatibility principle**.[15] According to this principle, different measurement techniques highlight different aspects of the choice options. For example, any measure that emphasizes money or value increases the importance of v and the likelihood that consumers will make a v-bet. Research also shows that the most important attribute seems even more important when a choice measure is used (e.g., choose or select the best bet) than when a judgment measure is used (e.g., rate the attractiveness of each bet). A choice task encourages consumers to focus on the most important attribute, but a judgment task requires them to think about all the attributes.

For many consumers, price is the most important attribute, and consequently, consumers are more likely to choose lower-price/lower-quality products (e.g., a $139 Goldstar microwave oven) when choosing one brand from a set of brands than when rating purchase intentions for each brand.[16] Purchase intention ratings or judgments encourage consumers to consider all the attributes of all the brands—which leads them to prefer a higher-price/higher-quality product (e.g., a $179 Panasonic microwave oven). This preference reversal occurs even when price range information (e.g., microwave ovens range from $99 to $299) is provided to consumers.

OBJECTIVE **Singular versus Comparative Evaluation** Consumers often evaluate products one at a time, a process known as **singular evaluation**, or singular judgment. Sometimes, however, consumers compare two or more products concurrently, which is known as **comparative evaluation**, or comparative judgment. Surprisingly, consumers' preferences frequently change depending on whether they are forming a singular judgment or a comparative judgment. In singular judgment, familiar attributes that are easy to evaluate have a greater impact on preference.[17] Conversely, in comparative judgment, unfamiliar attributes that are difficult to evaluate carry more weight. This leads to a preference reversal when easy-to-evaluate attributes favor one brand and difficult-to-evaluate attributes favor a different brand.

For example, in one study, consumers were asked to evaluate two compact disc (CD) players:

	CD capacity	THD
CD player C:	Holds 5 CDs	0.003 percent
CD player S:	Holds 20 CDs	0.01 percent

The consumers were told that THD refers to total harmonic distortion, a measure of sound quality (smaller numbers are better). However, THD is difficult to evaluate because most consumers are unfamiliar with this attribute and do not know if a THD of 0.01 percent is good or bad. Consequently, in singular evaluation, most consumers ignored THD. Thus, when consumers evaluated each CD player separately, most consumers preferred CD player S. Conversely, in comparative evaluation consumers were less likely to ignore THD because they could see that 0.003 percent was better than 0.01 percent. Consequently, when consumers compared the two CD players, most consumers preferred CD player C.

In another study of singular evaluation versus comparative evaluation, consumers rated two dictionaries:

	Number of entries	Any defects?
Dictionary C:	20,000	Yes, the cover is torn
Dictionary S:	10,000	No, it's like new

In singular evaluation, consumers preferred Dictionary S because the presence or absence of defects is easy to evaluate. In comparative evaluation, however, consumers preferred Dictionary C because the number of entries is difficult to evaluate. However, when comparisons are performed, it is easy to see that 20,000 entries are better than 10,000 entries.

In another study, consumers saw a picture of an overfilled cup of ice cream (i.e., 7 ounces of ice cream in a 5-oz. cup) or a picture of an under-filled cup of ice cream (i.e., 8 ounces of ice cream in a 10-oz. cup):

	Amount	Filling
Serving C:	8 oz.	Under-filled
Serving S:	7 oz.	Overfilled

In singular evaluation, consumers preferred Serving S because an overfilled cup looks really good, but an under-filled cup seems stingy. In comparative evaluation, however, consumers preferred Serving C because directly comparing the brands made it clear that 8 ounces was better than 7 ounces.

To summarize, consumers are remarkably inconsistent in the way they use different pieces of information. Inconsistency leads to preference reversals when consumers weigh one piece of information heavily at one point in time and weigh another piece of information heavily at another point in time. Different frames, different measures, and different judgment tasks (singular versus comparative judgment tasks) also lead to different preferences. Consumers are likely to make choices that they regret later when they prefer one brand initially and later prefer a different brand.

Global Perspectives

Culture and Overconfidence

A great deal of research on behavioral decision making shows that decision makers are often overconfident. Imagine you were asked trivia questions such as, "Which contains more calories per unit of weight: (a) bread or (b) rice?" After selecting an answer, imagine you were asked to indicate how confident you were that your answer was correct on a scale from 50% confident to 100% confident.

When the average percentage of correct answers is compared to the average percent confidence ratings, the confidence ratings are typically higher than the percentage of correct answers. Thus, people are typically overconfident about the accuracy of their answers to trivia questions. Although overconfidence is very common, even among experts, research shows that Asian consumers are typically even more overconfident than American consumers.[18] This pattern was found even when participants were given the opportunity to win a gift certificate for $2.20 at their university's bookstore if they could provide confidence ratings that matched their percentage of correctly answered questions.

Construal Level Theory

According to construal level theory, people think about near-future decisions differently than they think about distant-future decisions. Similarly, people think about near-past decisions differently than they think about distant-past decisions.[19] Why do people think differently about decisions about outcomes occurring at different points in time? Standard economic theory suggests that time discounting follows a hyperbolic function: as the temporal distance of an outcome increases, devaluation of the outcome is steep initially and then becomes moderate for more distant outcomes. For example, most people would rather win $100 today than $120 six months from now. It is easy to imagine how one would use $100 today, and hard to imagine how one would use $120 six months from now. Longer delays (e.g., one year, two years, etc.) also produce devaluation, but they produce less devaluation than short delays.

Construal level theory is the most complete theory of how consumers evaluate the same outcome at different points in time. Furthermore, construal level theory explains how consumers evaluate outcomes at many different levels of psychological distance. Psychological distance is shortest for outcomes that affect "me, here and now." Psychological distance increases for events that affect other people (rather than oneself), that affect people in other locations (rather than here), and that affect people at other times (in the distant future or distant past rather than now). That is, psychological distance increases with social distance (oneself versus similar others versus dissimilar others), spatial distance (here versus somewhere else), and temporal distance (now versus the distant future or the distant past). In addition, psychological distance increases with hypothetical possibility: likely events seem closer than unlikely events. As psychological distance increases on any dimension, people think about events in higher-level, more abstract terms. Construal level, or the abstractness of a mental representation, increases with social, spatial, temporal, or hypothetical distance. Interestingly, construal level increases with psychological distance, and psychological distance increases with construal level.

The implications of construal level theory are far reaching. Higher-level construals lead to abstract and general mental representations that lack contextual detail, whereas lower-level construals lead to concrete and specific mental representations rich in contextual detail. Higher-level construals focus on abstract, superordinate goals and categories, and also focus on the primary reasons for pursuing a particular course of action. By contrast, lower-level construals focus on concrete, subordinate goals and categories, and on the secondary reasons for pursuing a particular course of action. In other words, different types of information are weighed heavily when people think abstractly versus concretely. All risky decisions have two components: a value component (how much you win or lose, or the primary reason for playing a gamble), and a probability component (the likelihood of winning or losing, or the secondary reason for playing a gamble). Although both components are equally important, the value seems more important in the distant future and distant past, whereas the probability seems more important in the near future and near past. This leads to a preference reversal where people prefer risky gambles (i.e., gambles with a high value and a low probability of winning) in the distant future and distant past, but prefer safe gambles (i.e., gambles with a low value and a high probability of winning) in the near future and near past.

Similarly, students prefer interesting lectures and challenging assignments in the distant future, but prefer boring lectures and easy assignments in the near future. Students also prefer interesting lectures at inconvenient times (e.g., 7 A.M. Saturday morning) in the distant future, but prefer boring lectures at convenient times (e.g., noon on Monday) in the near future. Consumers also prefer high-quality products in the distant future, but low-price products in the near future. In a classic study, students were asked to evaluate a radio that had high sound quality (i.e, the main reason for buying a radio) and a low-quality clock (i.e., a secondary reason for buying a radio), or vice versa.[20] In the distant future, sound quality had a stronger influence than clock quality on consumer preferences. However, in the near future, sound quality had a weaker influence and clock quality had a stronger influence on consumer preferences. Hence, secondary features and contextual details matter more in near-future decisions than in distant-future decisions. Similarly, strong arguments matter more in distant-future decisions, and peripheral features matter more in near-distant decisions.[21]

Recent research also suggests that consumers think differently about products that are physically present versus absent but represented by an abstract brand name.[22] The physical presence of a product changed the way consumers thought about the product. Consumers formed lower-level and more concrete representations of unfamiliar Canadian candy bars (e.g., Zero Cool) that were physically present versus absent. Consequently, preference stability was higher, preference-behavior consistency was greater, and product category-identification latencies for competing brands were slower when the products were physically present.

Concrete versus abstract thinking also influences the way consumers think about product claims.[23] There are many different ways to manipulate concrete versus abstract mind-sets. For example, asking consumers a series of "how" questions (e.g., "How do you open a new bank account?") encourages consumers to think in concrete, lower-level terms, and this thinking style influences performance of subsequent tasks. By contrast, asking consumers a series of "why" questions (e.g., "Why would you open a new bank account?") encourages consumers to think in abstract, higher-level terms, and this thinking style influences performance of subsequent tasks. Perceptual tasks can also influence mind-sets. For example, showing consumers a series of large letters composed of different smaller letters (e.g., a large A composed of many Hs) and asking them to identify the small letters encourages concrete thinking, whereas asking them to identify the large letters encourages abstract thinking. Both styles of thinking carry over to subsequent tasks. When the subsequent task involves judging the validity of marketing claims, the claims seem more valid in concrete mind-set than in abstract mind-set conditions. Table 11.1 summarizes the key ideas of construal level theory.

TABLE 11.1 | **Construal Level Theory**

Properties of Lower-Level and Higher-Level Mental Representations

Lower-Level Mental Representations	Higher-Level Mental Representations
Low psychological distance	High psychological distance
Concrete	Abstract
Vivid	Pallid
Easy to imagine	Difficult to imagine
How	Why
Subordinate categories	Superordinate categories
Secondary features	Primary features
Contextual details	No contextual details
Immediate implications for behavior	Distant implications for behavior

Adapted from Trope, Y., and Liberman, N. (2003). Temporal Construal. *Psychological Review*, *110*, 403–421.

OBJECTIVE (5)

Selective Thinking

Singular versus comparative judgment tasks change the way consumers evaluate products, and these different judgment tasks can lead to different preferences. Singular evaluation is easier, so it is therefore more common than comparative evaluation.[24] It is easier to focus selectively on one brand at a time than to compare two or more brands on many attribute dimensions concurrently. When consumers attempt to test the idea that a particular brand is a good brand, they focus selectively on information that confirms or supports this idea, and neglect information that disconfirms or fails to support it. Consumers also tend to interpret ambiguous information as supportive and to integrate information so a preferred brand is cast in a favorable light. This is known as **selective thinking**, or one-sided thinking, because singular evaluation often leads consumers to focus selectively on favorable information while neglecting unfavorable information.

In a classic study of selective thinking, people were asked to imagine they were serving on the jury of a child custody case following a divorce.[25] Using the information below, which parent would you *choose*?

Parent A: average income
average health
average working hours
reasonable rapport with the child
relatively stable social life

Parent B: above-average income
very close relationship with the child
extremely active social life
lots of work-related travel
minor health problems

Most people chose parent B because the best way to choose an alternative is to focus on the most favorable information. When people focus selectively on favorable information, parent B has the advantage because of some very favorable attributes, while parent A has only moderately favorable attributes.

Another group of people were asked a slightly different question. Instead of asking which parent they would choose, they were asked which parent they would *reject*. The best way to reject an alternative is to focus selectively on unfavorable information. When people focus on unfavorable information, they are likely to notice that parent B has some very unfavorable attributes, but parent A has only moderately unfavorable attributes. Consequently, most people recommend rejecting parent B.

But wait a minute. Why did most people choose parent B when they performed a choice task, but reject parent B when they performed a rejection task? How can people both choose and reject the same alternative? The answer is selective thinking. Selective thinking makes parent B look very good when people focus on the positives, but makes parent B look very bad when people focus on the negatives. Thus, parent B is the best alternative *and* the worst alternative.

The same process occurs for products and services. Imagine that you had to choose between one of two different ice cream flavors. Flavor A is good, and flavor B is excellent, but high in cholesterol. When asked to choose a flavor, most consumers prefer B because it is excellent. When asked to reject a flavor, most consumers reject B because it is high in cholesterol. Consumers choose and reject the same alternative because it is the best and the worst alternative.

Imagine that you are planning a vacation and have to choose between two vacation spots:

Spot A: average weather
           average beaches
           medium-quality hotel
           medium-temperature water
           average nightlife

Spot B: lots of sunshine
           gorgeous beaches and coral reefs
           ultra-modern hotel
           very cold water
           very strong winds
           no nightlife

Which spot would you *choose*? If you are like most people, you would choose B because it has some extremely favorable attributes. Which spot would you *reject*? If you are like most people, you would reject B because it has some extremely unfavorable attributes. Focusing selectively on mainly favorable information or on mainly unfavorable information leads to biased or lopsided decisions.

Asking consumers to reject alternatives is not the only way to encourage them to focus selectively on negative attributes. Whenever consumers attempt to reduce the size of their consideration sets, they are likely to focus on negatives. For example, the elimination-by-aspects heuristic reduces consideration sets by rejecting brands that do not have a particular feature of interest. Furthermore, recent research shows that when consumers expect to fill out a customer satisfaction survey, they focus on negatives to help firms improve their products and services.[26] Focusing on negatives leads consumers to form less favorable evaluations than they would have formed if they did not expect to fill out a customer satisfaction survey after using a product or service. This result was found for a wide range of products and services, including computers, electric utilities, supermarkets, drugstores, and magazines.

Selective thinking influences many other types of judgments as well. For example, selective thinking is much more likely in singular evaluation than in comparative evaluation. Furthermore, singular evaluation is very common. Noncomparative advertising encourages singular evaluation, as do end-of-aisle displays in grocery stores. Exclusive dealerships, such as automobile dealerships that offer only one brand, also encourage singular evaluation. Even when it is painfully obvious that many different brands are available, consumers often focus singularly on one brand at a time when forming product evaluations.

Consumers often fall prey to the price-quality heuristic, assuming that higher priced brands offer superior quality and that lower priced brands offer inferior quality.

Recent research on the **brand positivity effect** shows that consumers form unrealistically favorable evaluations of moderately favorable brands when they form singular evaluations, but not when they form comparative evaluations.[27] In one experiment, consumers were shown the brand names for four first-class hotels. They were told that they would be asked to evaluate one hotel, which would be selected randomly. Consumers formed unrealistically positive evaluations of the focal hotel no matter which hotel was selected. Furthermore, consumers acknowledged that the focal hotel was selected randomly. Similar results were found for laundry detergents. Follow-up studies showed that the brand positivity effect is reduced when consumers are encouraged to form comparative evaluations or when consumers happen to be very knowledgeable about a product category.

Selective thinking also influences the degree to which consumers rely on the **price-quality heuristic**.[28] Most consumers believe that as price increases, quality also increases. This belief becomes stronger when consumers are encouraged to test this belief, because the testing process encourages consumers to focus on information consistent with this line of thinking. For example, consumers often pay more attention to and have better memory for high-price/high-quality brands and low-price/low-quality brands than for exceptions (i.e., high-price/low-quality brands and low-price/high-quality brands). Thinking selectively about brands that support the price-quality heuristic is easier than thinking about exceptions that fail to support it. As a consequence, consumers often overestimate the magnitude of the correlation between price and quality by a factor of three! This result is reduced, however, when the amount of information presented is small, when time pressure is low, or when consumers are motivated or encouraged to consider exceptions.

General Evaluability Theory

Some attribute values are relatively easy to evaluate, and some are relatively difficult to evaluate. According to general evaluability theory, consumers are more sensitive to attribute values that are easy to evaluate.[29] Furthermore, several different variables influence ease of evaluation: (1) mode of evaluation (i.e., singular evaluation versus comparative evaluation), (2) knowledge (i.e., distributional knowledge about the values of an attribute), and (3) the nature of the attribute (i.e., some attributes have a natural, innate psychophysical scale and some do not). Attribute values are easier to evaluate in comparative evaluation, when distributional knowledge is high, and when the attribute has a natural, innate psychophysical scale. In comparative evaluation, it is easy to determine that a high attribute value is greater than a low attribute value, even when the attribute values are unfamiliar. College students are familiar with grade point averages, and know the typical mean and range of scores on this measure. However, most college students are unfamiliar with body-mass index scores, and learning is needed to acquire distributional knowledge of this measure. Finally, some attributes have a natural, innate psychophysical scale—such as temperature, sleep, and social connectedness. We know what levels of these attributes are pleasant or unpleasant. However, other attributes lack a natural, innate psychophysical scale and can only be evaluated with training—such as the size of a diamond or the power of a car.

According to general evaluability theory, sensitivity to attribute values will be low only when ease of evaluation is low for all three factors (mode, knowledge, and nature). The theory also hypothesizes that people will mispredict their own value sensitivity or the value sensitivity of others when evaluability differs over time or across individuals. For example, consumers should not buy groceries when they are hungry because they are likely to buy more than they need due to misprediction. The opposite might also be true: consumers should not buy groceries when they are full because they are likely to buy less than they need due to misprediction. Both types of errors are interesting because people should realize that they will not always feel hungry or full, but current feelings influence predictions about the future.

General evaluability theory is useful because it can explain a surprisingly wide range of behavioral decision phenomena—including preference reversals due to singular versus comparative evaluation, scope insensitivity, duration neglect, and affective forecasting. Unfamiliar attributes are easier to evaluate and are weighed more heavily in comparative evaluation than in singular evaluation, and this leads to systematic preference reversals when familiar attributes and unfamiliar attributes have opposite evaluative implications. **Scope insensitivity** occurs when people lack distributional knowledge about attributes that are inherently difficult to evaluate. For example, people are often willing to pay the same amount of money to save 2,000 endangered birds versus 200,000 endangered birds. However, this bias is observed only in singular evaluation, not in comparative evaluation. **Duration neglect** occurs when people are asked to indicate their preferences for two events that are similar, but differ in terms of temporal duration. For example, in some studies, participants were asked to place their hands in water that was so cold it was painful. In one trial, participants placed their hands in the water for 60 seconds. In another trial, participants placed their hands in the water for 60 seconds and kept their hands in the water for an additional 30 seconds in which the water temperature was less cold but still painful. Later, participants remembered the longer trial as being less painful even though it was more painful (i.e., 90 seconds of pain is worse than 60 seconds of pain). Similar results were observed in other studies of memory for colonoscopies, a painful medical procedure. Participants prefer more pain to less pain when the ending is less painful. Duration neglect occurs due to the **peak-end effect**, or due to better memory for the worst part of the procedure (the peak) and the end, relative to the rest of the procedure. It also occurs because duration is inherently difficult to evaluate.

Affective forecasting studies compare the predictions of forecasters with the evaluations of experiencers.[30] Forecasters attempt to predict future reactions to positive or negative events, whereas experiencers rate current reactions to positive or negative events. Typically, a **durability bias** is found where people believe they will be happy or sad for a long time following a positive or negative event. The bias tends to be stronger for negative events. In reality, affective reactions tend to be relatively short-lived. For example, professors predicted they would be happy for years after achieving tenure or sad for one year if they did not. Both predictions were wrong: professors were equally happy a year after the tenure decision regardless of the decision. Voters predicted they would be much happier one month later if their preferred candidate won rather than lost. Again, one month later, happiness was not influenced by the election outcome. Students predicted they would be much happier one day later if their football team won rather than lost. Again, one day later, happiness was not influenced by the outcome of the game. Consumers predicted that they would be more satisfied with a poster of a famous painting if they could exchange the poster for another one. However, consumers were actually more satisfied if they were not allowed to exchange the product. These mispredictions occur due to *focalism* and due to immune neglect. Focalism refers to the idea that people tend to ruminate on a single, focal event, and to underestimate the influence of other events. Immune neglect refers to the idea that cognitive dissonance and other psychological processes tend to temper our responses to negative events over time, but people fail to recognize this. In addition, duration is inherently difficult to evaluate. Attributes that are easy (versus difficult) to evaluate are weighed more heavily in judgment and decision

Marketers attempt to predict consumer behavior, but the art becomes challenging when consumers do not even understand their own preferences.

making, even though the attributes that are the easiest to evaluate are not necessarily the most important attributes.

Misprediction also occurs when consumers make simultaneous choices at one point in time, versus sequential choices over time.[31] When consumers are asked to choose three candy bars now, one each for consumption today, one week from today, and two weeks from today, they often choose several different brands. However, when consumers are asked to choose one candy bar today, they tend to choose their most preferred brand. When asked again one week later, they again tend to choose their most preferred brand. Another week later, they again tend to choose their most preferred brand. Hence, variety seeking is greater in simultaneous choice than in sequential choice because consumers predict that they will prefer more variety than they actually will prefer. Prediction is difficult when consumers do not understand their own preferences very well.

Ethics

For six years in a row, Enron was *Fortune* magazine's "America's Most Innovative Company." But after its fraudulent accounting activities came to light, Enron went bankrupt, thus wiping out its shareholders' life-time savings. Today, the Sarbanes-Oxley Act is supposed to prevent the same thing from happening again. But does greed usually win when pitted against honesty? To address this question, a study of honesty was conducted at the prestigious Harvard Business School.[32] About 20% of the top three positions in Fortune 500 companies are held by its graduates. Harvard undergraduates and MBAs were asked to take a 50-item multiple choice quiz on a variety of topics (e.g., What is the longest river in the world? Who wrote *Moby Dick*?), and were paid ten cents for each correct answer. They were randomly assigned to one of four conditions. In the control condition, there was no opportunity to cheat, and the students correctly answered 32.6 questions. In the self-check condition, the students received the correct answers and were asked to re-enter their original answers on a scoring sheet. They claimed they correctly answered 36.2 questions. In the self-check plus shredding condition, the students received the correct answers, re-entered their original answers, and shredded their original answers. They claimed they correctly answered 35.9 questions. The final condition was the self-check plus shredding plus money jar condition. The students received the correct answers, re-entered their answers, shredded the original answers, and paid themselves from a jar that contained $100 while exiting the experiment. They claimed they correctly answered 36.1 questions. Hence, cheating levels increased when the opportunity presented itself, but the probability of getting caught had little influence on the results. Small amounts of cheating seemed okay, but no one claimed to get 100% of the answers correct and no one took too much money from the jar.

Chapter Summary

Behavioral decision research focuses mainly on risky decision making, or decision making under uncertainty. To reduce uncertainty, consumers often attempt to predict the future. What will happen if I buy one brand instead of another? What will happen if I choose one course of action instead of another? Will I be satisfied with my decision one month from now, one year from now, or several years from now? Unfortunately, consumers' predictions are biased by framing effects and by selective thinking. Gain frames lead to risk aversion, but loss frames lead to risk seeking. The inconsistent weighting of information resulting from framing, measurement, or selective thinking leads to systematic preference reversals where consumers prefer one option initially and another option later. Consumers are remarkably inconsistent in their use of information, leading to inconsistent preferences and choices they later regret.

Key Terms

affective forecasting
brand positivity effect
cancellation
choice architecture
comparative evaluation
compatibility principle
diminishing sensitivity
dominate
durability bias
duration neglect

endowment effect
expected utility theory
frames
invariance principle
lebertarian paternalism
loss aversion
opportunity costs
peak-end effect
preference reversals
price bundling

price-quality heuristic
reference dependence
risk aversion
risky decision making
risk seeking
scope insensitivity
selective thinking
singular evaluation
transitive

Review and Discussion

1. What is risky decision making?
2. Why are consumers often unable to explain how they arrived at a prediction?
3. Why do consumers often fail to maximize expected value?
4. Give an example of a situation in which you chose a safe option.
5. Give an example of a situation in which you chose a risky option.
6. Why are consumers sometimes risk averse and sometimes risk seeking?
7. Why do different types of preference measures change preferences?
8. Describe the compatibility principle. How does this principle change people's preferences? Can you think of a situation in which this principle changed your preferences?
9. What is a preference reversal?
10. How do preference reversals lead to decisions that consumers later regret?

Short Application Exercises

1. Most consumers do not realize that information that initially seems very important may seem less important later. Think of some ways that marketers can influence the perceived importance of different types of information.
2. Think of some ways marketers can use preference reversals to their advantage.
3. Selective thinking occurs frequently. Think of some ways marketers can use selective thinking to their advantage.
4. Design an ad that gets consumers to think of the positive features of products while ignoring the negative features.

Managerial Application

The most recent recession is encouraging consumers to focus more on price in their decision making. One major consequence of this price focus is an increase in the market share of private labels at the expense of name brands.[33] The same thing happened in the U.K. and Canada in the 1970s. Tom Falk, CEO of Kimberly-Clark, says, "One thing you don't want to do is create a consumer who shifted to private label and then have to spend a lot to get them back." A. G. Lafley, CEO of Procter & Gamble (P&G), says, "Of course there's a shift to private label at this point, but it's not nicking us." In the past, P&G has fought against private labels by increasing promotions advertising, but in the current recession, consumers are buying private labels in categories that have been resistant to them in the past, such as feminine protection and skin care products. Furthermore, even relatively wealthier households with annual incomes greater than $100,000 have spent more on private labels. Across package-goods categories and retailers, private-label market share increased by 0.8% to 21.9% in 2008. This trend is likely to continue until the economy improves significantly.

Your Challenge:

1. If you were a brand manager at P&G, what strategies would you pursue to encourage consumers to focus less heavily on price?

2. If you were a brand manager at P&G, what strategies would you use to protect product categories that are usually resistant to private labels?

3. If you were a manager at The Kroger Co., what strategies would you pursue to encourage consumers to focus more heavily on price?

4. If you were a manager at The Kroger Company, what strategies would you use to encourage consumers to buy private labels in more product categories? In what product categories do you see opportunities for private labels?

End Notes

1 Schultz, E. J. (2012). In Search of New Consumers, McCormick Sprinkles Health Message into Marketing. *Advertising Age*, 83, 3–36.

2 von Neumann, J., and Morgenstern, O. (1947). *Theory of Games and Economic Behavior*. Princeton, NJ: Princeton University Press.

3 Bulik, B. S. (2012). Why Brand Love, Satisfaction Aren't Keeping Shoppers Faithful. *Advertising Age*, 83, 8.

4 Kahneman, D., and Tversky, A. (1979). Prospect Theory: An Analysis of Decision under Risk. *Econometrica*, 47, 263–291; Tversky, A., and Kahneman, D. (1981). The Framing of Decisions and the Psychology of Choice. *Science*, 211, 453–458.

5 McNeil, B. J., Pauker, S. G., Sox, H.C., and Tversky, A. (1982). On the Elicitation of Preferences for Alternative Therapies. *New England Journal of Medicine*, 306, 1259–1262.

6 Kahneman, D., and Tversky, A. (1984). Choices, Values, and Frames. *American Psychologist*, 39, 341–350.

7 Thaler, R. H. (1985). Mental Accounting and Consumer Choice. *Marketing Science*, 4, 199–214.

8 Thaler, R. H. (1985). Mental Accounting and Consumer Choice. *Marketing Science*, 4, 199–214.

9 Soman, D., and Gourville, J. (2001). Transaction Decoupling: How Price Bundling Affects the Decision to Consume. *Journal of Marketing Research*, 38, 30–44.

10 Gourville, J. (1998). Pennies-a-Day: The Effect of Temporal Reframing on Transaction Evaluation. *Journal of Consumer Research*, 24, 395–408.

11 Tetlock, P.E., and Boettger, R. (1994). Accountability Amplifies the Status Quo Effect When Change Creates Victims. *Journal of Behavioral Decision Making*, 7, 1–23.

12 Thaler, R.H., and Sunstein, C.R. (2008). *Nudge: Improving Decisions about Health, Wealth, and Happiness*. New Haven, CT: Yale University Press.

13 Grether, D. M., and Plott, C. R. (1979). Economic Theory and the Preference Reversal Phenomenon. *American*

Economic Review, 69, 623–638; Lichtenstein, S., and Slovic, P. (1971). Reversal of Preferences between Bids and Choices in Gambling Decisions. *Journal of Experimental Psychology, 89*, 46–55.

14 Kerr, R. A. (1979). Petroleum Explorations: Discouragement about the Atlantic Outer Continental Shelf Deepens. *Science, 204*, 1069–1072.

15 Tversky, A., Sattah, S., and Slovic, P. (1988). Contingent Weighting in Judgment and Choice. *Psychological Review, 95*, 371–384.

16 Nowlis, S. M., and Simonson, I. (1997). Attribute-Task Compatibility as a Determinant of Consumer Preference Reversals. *Journal of Marketing Research, 34*, 205–218.

17 Hsee, C. K. (1996). The Evaluability Hypothesis: An Explanation of Preference Reversals Between Joint and Separate Evaluations of Alternatives. *Organizational Behavior and Human Decision Processes, 46*, 247–257; Hsee, C. K., and LeClerc, F. (1998). Will Products Look More Attractive When Evaluated Jointly or When Evaluated Separately? *Journal of Consumer Research, 25*, 175–186; Hsee, C. K, Loewenstein, G. R., Blount, S., and Bazerman, M. H. (1999). Preference Reversals between Joint and Separate Evaluation of Options: A Review and Theoretical Analysis. *Psychological Bulletin, 125*, 576–590.

18 Yates, J. F., Lee, J. W., and Bush, J. G. (1997). General Knowledge Overconfidence: Cross-National Variations, Response Style, and "Reality." *Organizational Behavior and Human Decision Processes, 70*, 87–94.

19 Trope, Y., and Liberman, N. (2003). Temporal Construal. *Psychological Review, 110*, 403–421; Trope, Y., and Liberman, N. (2010). Construal-Level Theory of Psychological Distance. *Psychological Review, 117*, 440–463; Trope, Y., and Liberman, N. (2012). Construal Level Theory. In P.A.M. Van Lange, A.W. Kruglanski, and E.T. Higgins (Eds.), *Handbook of Theories of Social Psychology* (pp. 118–134). Thousand Oaks, CA: Sage.

20 Trope, Y., and Liberman, N. (2000). Temporal Construal and Time-Dependent Changes in Preference. *Journal of Personality and Social Psychology, 79*, 876–889.

21 Fujita, K., Eyal, T., Chaiken, S., Trope, Y., and Liberman, N. (2008). Influencing Attitudes toward Near and Distant Objects. *Journal of Experimental Social Psychology, 44*, 562–572.

22 Kardes, F. R., Cronley, M. L., and Kim, J. (2006). Construal-Level Effects on Preference Stability, Preference-Behavior Correspondence, and the Suppression of Competing Brands. *Journal of Consumer Psychology, 16*, 135–144.

23 Wright, S., Manolis, C., Brown, D., Guo, X., Dinsmore, J., Chiu, C. Y. P., and Kardes, F. R. (2012). Construal-Level Mind-Sets and the Perceived Validity of Marketing Claims. *Marketing Letters, 23*, 253–262.

24 Sanbonmatsu, D. M., Posavac, S. S., Kardes, F. R., and Mantel, S. P. (1998). Selective Hypothesis Testing. *Psychonomic Bulletin & Review, 5*, 197–220.

25 Shafir, E. (1993). Choosing versus Rejecting: Why Some Options Are Both Better and Worse Than Others. *Memory & Cognition, 21*, 546–556.

26 Ofir, C., & Simonson, I. (2001). In Search of Negative Customer Feedback: The Effect of Expecting to Evaluate on Satisfaction Evaluations. *Journal of Marketing Research, 38*, 170–182.

27 Posavac, S. S., Kardes, F. R., Sanbonmatsu, D. M., and Fitzsimons, G. J. (2005). Blissful Insularity: When Brands Are Judged in Isolation from Competitors. *Marketing Letters, 16*, 87–97; Posavac, S. S., Sanbonmatsu, D. M., Kardes, F. R., and Fitzsimons, G. J. (2004). The Brand Positivity Effect: When Evaluation Confers Preference. *Journal of Consumer Research, 31*, 643–651.

28 Cronley, M. L., Posavac, S. S., Meyer, T., Kardes, F. R., and Kellaris, J. J. (2005). A Selective Hypothesis Testing Perspective on Price-Quality Inference and Inference-Based Choice. *Journal of Consumer Psychology, 15*, 159–169; Kardes, F. R., Cronley, M. L., Kellaris, J. J., and Posavac, S. S. (2004). The Role of Selective Information Processing in Price-Quality Inference. *Journal of Consumer Research, 31*, 368–374.

29 Hsee, C.K., and Zhang, J. (2010). General Evaluability Theory. *Perspectives on Psychological Science, 5*, 343–355.

30 Wilson, T.D., and Gilbert, D.T. (2003). Affective Forecasting. *Advances in Experimental Social Psychology, 35*, 345–411.

31 Simonson, I. (1990). The Effect of Purchase Quantity and Timing on Variety Seeking Behavior. *Journal of Marketing Research, 32*, 150–162.

32 Amir, O., Ariely, D., and Mazur, N. (2008). The Dishonesty of Honest People: A Theory of Self-Concept Maintenance. *Journal of Marketing Research, 45*, 633–634.

4

CONSUMER SOCIAL INFLUENCES AND CONTEMPORARY STRATEGIES FOR MARKETERS

PERSONALITY

SOCIAL MEDIA

© iStockphoto.com/csm_web

C H A P T E R S

AN INTERVIEW WITH THOMAS O'GUINN

Professor of Marketing
University of Wisconsin
Executive Director, Brand and Product Management Center

Thomas O'Guinn is Professor of Marketing at the University of Wisconsin. He is also executive director of the Brand and Product Management Center at UW. He studies brands and their communication as well as aspects of the sociology of consumption, i.e., how membership in various groups and social strata affect consumer behavior. He is the author of several award-winning articles and a leading book on advertising and integrated brand communication.

Q. Could you comment on the role of the many different paradigms or "camps" in the field of consumer behavior and your position with respect to these camps?

I don't fit particularly well in any of these camps. I had the opportunity to study several different paradigms when I was in graduate school and did some qualitative work on how people watch television and use advertising. A lot of that work was federally funded to understand how children watch television. Those methods, in that context, became very accepted, even with NSF [National Science Foundation] money, to really understand how kids watch TV and how advertising works in real homes with real kids. At the same time, I was working in social and developmental psychology labs doing experiments—again, federally funded. So, I got a wonderful opportunity to cross paradigms in the same substantive domain. That was an education. I loved the clean nature of experiments AND the messy nature of *in situ* observation. Television viewing is one of those social behaviors that is so hard to replicate in the lab. It's very hard to bring people into a lab and say "watch this—pretend you are at home." And there are long-term processes; the significant effects of television do not occur in an hour, or a day, or even a year. I was always one of those people who was inclined, just by virtue of chance and by training, to be very multidisciplinary and to use multiple methods. I'm very driven by the phenomena, so sometimes it's entirely appropriate to be in the lab; it's

the only way you can get it done. Other times, there are phenomena that I don't know how you could possibly do in a lab. So, to me, it's always the question that tells you which are the tools out of the toolbox you need to apply. And I think, in my work I've always been less concerned about, "I am an experimentalist; I should do it this way," than I was about, "this is the phenomena; how am I going to understand it?" I also like to work with other people because they bring something to the project, and they make me stay on deadline. I get bored pretty easily.

Q. How did you get interested in the topic of consumer compulsiveness, and what insights does your research provide on this important topic?

That came about literally when Ron Faber and I were at ACR [Association for Consumer Research] in Las Vegas. And we're watching people gamble. I said to Ron, "I know people who shop like these people gamble." And we started this conversation. And on the way home I'm reading an in-flight magazine, and [in the magazine] there is this woman talking about people who shop too much and this and that. So I get back home and I think, you know this is a pretty interesting thing. And that was one of those things we knew nothing about. And we spent a good two-and-a-half years learning it before we ever put anything on paper because we didn't want to look like idiots. We found this group out in the Bay Area that was the largest self-help group for shopaholics. But at first it had this kind of carnival-esque feel about it—I didn't like this. When you really saw the suffering, it was no longer funny. And we went out there, and we spent a lot of our own money, a lot of time. I remember sleeping on the floor at San Francisco International Airport one night because we were both young and didn't have money. We went out there and got with these self-help groups and spent I don't know—a good two and a half years doing qualitative work, trying to understand what it was and what it wasn't. And then we went into a more quantitative phase where we used our qualitative data to develop instruments. And then we were able to piece together enough money through different funding to do a big sample—the State of Illinois matched to a national list of self-reported compulsive buyers. We went to a Survey Research Lab in Illinois and did the adjustment to make these comparable. Seymour Sudman [Walter H. Stellner, Distinguished Professor of Marketing, Deputy Director and Research Professor, Survey Research Laboratory] helped us. When we finally came out with a series of papers, we felt really good about them because we had done the work. We had used the qualitative data largely in a developmental phase. Although I don't want to say that was all it was used for, because that would diminish the nature of those data. We did use verbatims from it occasionally as exemplars of what we were talking about. But, we also used those data as you would any data—to drive understanding. I came out of a survey research background, and Ron came out of an experimental background. I think that we both, at least on that project, saw that the qualitative results could have stood alone. But I don't think so now. I think it needed the numbers side as well; their convergence helped. So when we wrote two or three, four or five papers from it, we really felt good about it. We thought they were solid. We felt like we could actually go talk at a conference and not look foolish because you know the topic was so easy to lampoon or dismiss. And we didn't want that because we had actually seen these people. You know these people literally had impulse control disorders; they couldn't not do this. And the co-morbidity between them and compulsive gamblers, most of these people, they just floated from one impulsive control to another. These were a lot of people who were in a lot of serious trouble. And the other thing that we didn't want made light of was that they were 90 percent women. There are two reasons for that. One is the self-report bias for women: they are much more likely to seek therapy (and report it) than

men. If you go back to the 1940s, a woman is upset with a man, [the man says] "Here, honey, here's some money, go buy a hat." We didn't want to contribute to that. Stratification differences in income and work status, as well as gender stereotyping, kind of made it "a woman's problem." So when the *New York Times* and National Public Radio and *The Wall Street Journal* start calling you for interviews, you are very aware of the potential for harm. The first thing out of our mouths was, "We're not clinicians, we are not . . ." But I think we were able to talk about it in a sensitive enough way that we didn't just run out, do some kind of goofy study, make fun of these people and leave, which does happen in the field. I think there are people in our field that I think regrettably do that. They see something in the news, they run out, they do a study. And it's topical, but I think sometimes if you don't do the work, if you don't do the two or three years of homework on it, you can either make a fool of yourself or you can make light of something that's actually serious.

Q. Does your work have implications for helping consumers to adopt healthier lifestyles?

Yes, but my co-author Ron Faber is much better at talking about that. Ron and I are still working on some things together, but he's more interested in psychological issues. He's hooked up with some people at the medical school at [the University of] Minnesota and has done some brilliant work on this. I was more interested in the "why consumption" question, the social question. Why does this manifest as buying? And that turned out to be a substantive but easy answer: because we live in a consumer culture. And I think Ron's work, the work that came out of our work that I have some part of, I think it does help. He's gotten involved in—well, our screener that we developed for the second paper, third paper. One of the cool things about that is that's becoming the preferred clinical and diagnostic screener. The psychometrics of it are just very strong, and it's a lot of luck. Then a guy at the Stanford Medical School got very fascinated in this topic. They adopted it as their screener. And then once they adopted it, so did a lot of folks. And so, that helps people screen for compulsive buying. And then I think just what Ron has been able to do with understanding the co-morbidity of this with other impulse control disorders and their response to certain anti-depressants—I mean Ron and his MD colleagues actually do help people; a lot of these people do respond really well to certain antidepressants. And I think our work also informs how therapists talk to people about compulsive buying. I think the most interesting thing we found out is that these people, at least on materialism scales, are no more materialistic than anybody else. What's interesting is they don't use the products. It's all about the acquisition. They store them under their beds, they hide them. They will go out and buy ten of the same thing. And it is about their relationship with the store. It's about the thrill of shopping; it's not the thrill of owning or using. It's the buying. To me, that really challenged what were then the dominant models of consumer behavior. I'm proud of that. The things purchased often remain unopened. And their social networks often are, not surprisingly, comprised of shopping clerks and delivery people. Compulsive buyers often consider the shopping clerks their friends. So there's more to the phenomenon than simple acquisition. It's the buying. That, I think, has helped clinicians. I think we have helped some consumers and I'm proud of that.

Q. Let's switch gears and talk about your work on advertising.

You know, it's funny—I hardly ever wrote about advertising until this book and then lately, for whatever reason, I've started doing more advertising-related research. I've always been interested in mass media, but mostly program content, consumption in program content. But now that those lines between ads and content have started to disappear, I've become interested in branded entertainment. Also, I've always been fascinated how different social strata—stratification issues, social class issues—play out in ads and through ads. Target is one of the brands I use as an example because of how they have leveraged those sociological phenomena and how they do it with their ads and other ways. Here's a retailer that has done what was thought to be impossible. Sears tried to be everything to everybody for a hundred and something years. And I knew a lot of people who worked on Sears' business, and the problem was always that not many people wanted to buy a little black dress where they bought their socket sets. It just didn't work.

Target, however, has been able to do that, at least much more effectively. Part of the reason they have is what has happened demographically and how those demographics relate to what we call taste. So, it used to be we identified the wealthy through their display of certain types of consumption. For a long time, "handmade" had a certain social marker status. Well, now robots make much better things than handmade. Handmade is actually inferior. Several people write about this in sociology—the democratization or collapse of traditional status hierarchies in consumption.

John Seabrook [NOBROW] writes about the case where high-end brands are now replicating low-end stuff like the sort of torn, beaded jeans for $3,500 from Gucci to look like something you would see, you know, in a very different social milieu from 5th Avenue. And this collapse of traditional status hierarchy is flattening taste cultures. Target management picked up on this beautifully, this whole design for the masses that Target has done so well.

Some of this matches up with my interest in design thought. I got lucky because when I came to the University of Wisconsin–Madison to run this brand center, one of my donors earmarked some money to look into design issues. I took a group out to the design school at Stanford, and now UW–Madison is partnering with a wonderful design company in Madison, Design Concepts, Inc. And one of the things we're all interested in, companies as well, is how do these things convey social meaning, map onto strata; how do they convey taste and culture? So, here again, a lot of interests: visual thought, design thought, social strata, and markers of taste all converge. I'm lucky: lots of nice toys.

Q. This leads into the next question. What are some of the key implications of the sociological and anthropological perspectives for marketing managers?

You don't have to convince managers of the value of qualitative research. It's one of the funniest things. In the academic field, it's been harder to convince people; they want so desperately to be real scientists. Well, maybe it's not that hard now, but there was a time when it was difficult to convince academic marketing colleagues that there was any value at all in doing fieldwork. I understand that because I came out of that tradition, too, and people want to see hard numbers and heavily controlled experiments, and I'm a believer in that too. But you know, I was listening to Scott Cook from Intuit talk. He is such a believer in going out and watching people use the product. You have to go see people actually use products and figure out what it is that they need. Eric von Hippel's [MIT] early work on using lead users and not being trapped by the present was so right. I've yet to run into a company that thinks that doing fieldwork is weird, in fact quite the opposite. It's more an academic concern. Now, the implications I think come in a lot of forms. Usually it's called, you know, consumer insights. They almost always think of fieldwork and in-home visits and all that as consumer insight. And that's just a big basket term for what they are learning in the field. But I think it's more the exception to hear them say that they didn't do that. They all sort of believe that. Now, some of them still do a lot of attitude work . . . particularly tracking studies. But I think they drive the front end with qualitative work. They all want metrics; some remain attitudinal, but I don't think they get used much beyond that sort of behavioral bean-counting. I do think, in my experience over the last 20 years, that there has been increasing skepticism about some of the metrics. Not about *doing* metrics, but about some of the metrics.

And how sometimes their internal metrics on a brand mix will get in the way. We need to think about brands in terms of meaning rather than mere attitudes. Now, do I think attitudes and any of those other things are valuable? Sometimes.

Academic research often has different goals than managerial research. I try not to confuse them, but I also try to let one at least partially inform the other when that makes sense.

AN INTERVIEW WITH ROBERT CIALDINI

Regents' Professor of Psychology and Marketing,
Distinguished Graduate Research Professor
Arizona State University

Robert Cialdini is the Regents' Professor of Psychology and Marketing at Arizona State University, where he is also a Distinguished Graduate Research Professor. He is a recipient of the Distinguished Scientific Achievement Award of the Society for Consumer Psychology, the Donald T. Campbell Award for Distinguished Contributions to Social Psychology, and the Peitho Award for Distinguished Contributions to the Science of Social Influence. He studies persuasion and influence, altruism, and the tactics of favorable self-presentation.

Q. How did you get interested in social influence?

As I say at the outset of a book I wrote on the topic, I think my initial interest in social influence was grounded in a personal weakness: I was always finding myself contributing to charities I knew nothing about or buying things I didn't really want from salespeople at my door. So, out of self-defense, I figured I'd better learn how this worked.

Q. What role does social influence have in consumer behavior and marketing?

I believe there is a central role for social influence in these areas. After all, social influence involves the ability of one person to change the attitudes, beliefs, or behaviors of another, and this is frequently the primary goal of consumer-related messaging and marketing.

Q. You once told me that the timing of the various elements of a request is crucial. Can you elaborate on this point?

I believe that there are particular moments in the course of an interaction when a request, recommendation,

or proposal is likely to be most successful. In fact, I am planning to write a book on the subject titled *Moments of Power*. It will not be so much about what to say for optimal influence as when to say it.

Q. There are some publications in marketing literature suggesting that high self-monitors are more effective salespersons relative to low self-monitors. Does this finding apply to the application of the weapons of influence, or can anyone learn to apply these tools? Do some types of individuals have an advantage in terms of their ability to influence consumers?

For a long time, persuasion was thought to be an art, something people were just naturally good (or not so good) at. I do believe that's true. At the same time, we now know that persuasion is also a science; consequently, it can be taught and learned. Therefore, even those of us who were not born with the artist's touch of a persuasion master can be trained to use scientifically proven principles of persuasion to become significantly more influential at work, at home, and beyond.

CHAPTER

12

SELF-CONCEPT AND PERSONALITY

OBJECTIVES *After studying this chapter, you should be able to …*

1 Define self-concept, extended self, and love objects.

2 Explain how self-monitoring is related to consumer behavior.

3 Describe the three components of impression management.

4 Describe multiple trait theory and how it is linked to brand personality.

5 Discuss cognitive factors relating to single-trait theory of personality.

Kia Soul Has Personality

A favorable brand personality can be critical to the success of any product. Many of the world's top brands seem to possess human-like traits, providing a vehicle for consumers to express their own personalities. For example, Disney is cheerful; Coca-Cola is reliable; IBM is intelligent; McDonald's is friendly; Apple is creative and edgy; Volkswagen is down-to-earth; and Harley-Davidson exudes rugged individuality. Firms have even branded commodities, such as chicken (Purdue), potatoes (Idaho), and fruits (Sunkist). Automobile manufacturers rely heavily on brand personality to communicate a sustainable point of differentiation. Apparently, nobody does it better than Kia Soul—a youthful, irreverent, unpretentious, and reliable brand targeted at likeminded drivers.

The Kia Soul has become somewhat of a rock star on YouTube. In a recent television advertisement, the small, quirky Soul is driven by hip-hop hamsters through a sea of

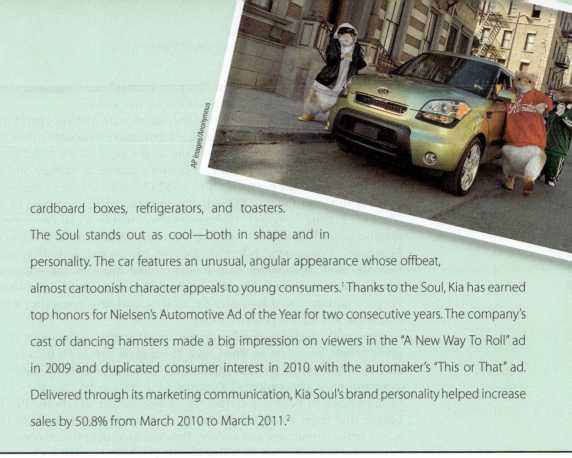

cardboard boxes, refrigerators, and toasters. The Soul stands out as cool—both in shape and in personality. The car features an unusual, angular appearance whose offbeat, almost cartoonish character appeals to young consumers.[1] Thanks to the Soul, Kia has earned top honors for Nielsen's Automotive Ad of the Year for two consecutive years. The company's cast of dancing hamsters made a big impression on viewers in the "A New Way To Roll" ad in 2009 and duplicated consumer interest in 2010 with the automaker's "This or That" ad. Delivered through its marketing communication, Kia Soul's brand personality helped increase sales by 50.8% from March 2010 to March 2011.[2]

OBJECTIVE # Self-Concept Defined

Most people are preoccupied with discovering who they are. Indeed, "Who am I?" is a question that most of us consider throughout our lives. Our unique answers to this question provide insight into our **self-concept**, the beliefs and attitudes we hold about ourselves. Although no precise definition of self-concept exists in the consumer behavior literature, self-concept is often described as the totality of an individual's thoughts and feelings regarding him or herself as an object.[3] Self-concept is complicated and multidimensional. Consumers have been character-ized as describing themselves on three dimensions: role identities, personal qualities, and self-evaluations.[4]

Role identities represent the numerous *positions* that people occupy in society such as student, friend, son or daughter, and consumer. People construct these identities by observing how they behave and the reactions that others form about them in each of their roles.[5] Although society imparts role expectations on its members (e.g., friends should be loyal), individuals usually have plenty of room to improvise. It may be helpful to think of consumers as *shaping* their role identities within the broad boundaries set by society. For example, all people playing the role of customer do not respond the same way to sales promotions. Some people are passionate "bargain-hunters," while others play a more indifferent role toward sales. Because people create roles in unique ways, each person derives a different role identity even when they occupy the same position. Moreover, these differences vary widely across product category.

For example, a person who is a "bargain hunter" for shoes may demand an expensive brand when it comes to coffee, or vice versa.

When people identify their roles, they often start with occupational or educational groups (e.g., college student). Consumers have convenient acronyms that provide ready shortcuts, especially in the professions. "She's an MBA" labels someone as having obtained a master's degree in business and someone who is probably quite practical. "I'm an M.D." self-identifies a medical doctor, which is different than a D.O. (doctor of osteopathic medicine) or a D.D.S. (doctor of dental surgery). Consumers also identify social categories such as religion (e.g., Protestant), race (e.g., African American), and ethnicity (e.g., Lebanese). Consumers' role identities are played out in public, and hence, they are more transparent than their personal qualities and self-evaluations, which describe idiosyncratic parts of the self-concept and are not so clear-cut. People's notions about how friendly, athletic, and easy-going they are may not match the way others perceive them.

Personal qualities involve modes of interpersonal behavior that distinguish people from one another, such as sense of humor or friendliness. They also include internal psychological styles that influence role identities, such as optimism or cheerfulness.[4] Personal qualities can be thought of as **traits**, or tendencies to behave a certain way across similar situations. Psychologists believe that traits are developed at an early age, remain relatively consistent across similar situations, and endure. Personal qualities provide consumers with opportunities to play out their role identities. For example, people respond differently to product failures and malfunctions. Some people exhibit anger and aggression, while others are more "laid back" in response to these disappointments. Similarly, consumers who are technologically savvy may play the role of the expert whom friends and family members contact when it is time to shop for a personal computer or digital video recorder. Consumer psychologists also know that traits play out differently in different contexts. For example, a person who is classified as anxious is unlikely to express anxiety in the same way in all contexts, e.g., with a friend versus a policeman or professor. Thus, using personality traits to predict consumer behavior can be a tricky business.

People also perform **self-evaluations** by considering the adequacy of their performances in various role identities. Am I a good student or a thoughtful boyfriend/girlfriend? Am I a smart shopper? Usually, these evaluations focus on competence, perseverance, morality, and social unity. Self-evaluations also influence role identities. For example, people who perceive themselves as "athletic" are more likely to engage in organized sports than those with poorer self-evaluations. In a similar vein, consumers who see themselves as competent Internet shoppers often share their knowledge with less experienced friends. One consumer might say to another, "Just type in www.fedex.com, click 'track by number,' and type in your tracking number. You can follow your package all the way to its destination." If this advice is well received, then the e-shopper's self-evaluation is enhanced and he or she is more likely to perform this role identity in the future.

The sum of all self-evaluations determines **self-esteem**, the overall evaluative component of a person's self-concept. Self-esteem can be considered a person's general attitude toward him or herself. Research shows that high self-esteem is associated with active and comfortable social interactions, and that low self-esteem can be depressing and debilitating. People with low self-esteem tend to view social situations as threatening, feel more negative toward others, and hence, are easily wounded by criticism. In addition, they yield more to other's requests.[3] It is probably best to think of self-esteem and behavior as a two-way street. People with high self-esteem tend to be more confident and consequently more influential. And yet, the behavior of influencing others may lead to increased self-esteem, a virtuous cycle.

The opposite may be true for those with low self-esteem. With little faith in their ability to succeed, people with low self-esteem may fulfill their low expectations, which leads to even lower self-esteem—a vicious cycle. Research provides evidence that marketing activities can affect a consumer's self-esteem. Exposure to idealistic standards can produce unpleasant consequences regarding how we view ourselves.[6] On the other hand, marketing stimuli can also cause our self-evaluations to converge toward these higher standards, subsequently increasing self-esteem.[7] Some marketers have attempted to enhance image-related self-esteem through the inclusion of more realistic and attainable role models. See this chapter's Ethics box feature regarding Unilever's "Real Beauty" and "Body Language" campaigns for Dove.

A consumer's self-concept is comprised of two key dimensions: (1) *focus* (actual versus the ideal) and (2) *domain* (private versus public). Each dimension has two parts. Regarding private domain, the **actual self-concept** represents how consumers in fact perceive themselves, while the **ideal self-concept** describes how consumers would like to be. The gap between the two is referred to as self-discrepancy. In the public domain, the **actual public-concept** embodies others' perceptions of a consumer, while the **ideal public-concept** represents how consumers would like others to see them. The gap between actual public- and ideal public-concepts is known as a public-discrepancy. This four-part self-concept is shown in Figure 12.1.

FIGURE 12.1 | A Two-Dimensional Self-Concept

Domain	Focus	
	Actual	**Ideal**
Private	Actual self-concept "Who I think I am"	Ideal self-concept "Who I want to be"
Public	Actual public-concept "Who they think I am"	Ideal public-concept "Who I want them to think I am"

SOURCE: Cline, T. W. (2012). Working paper, Saint Vincent College, Latrobe, PA.

Brands offer a variety of opportunities for consumers to express who they are and who they would like to be.[8] Depending on the purchase situation, consumers are likely to emphasize a different self-concept. For privately consumed products, consumers may simply rely on their private-concepts. In contrast, when purchasing products that will be consumed in public, consumers may draw on their actual public-self concept to appear consistent with others' expectations, or they may employ their ideal public-concept to change how others view them. Let's take a closer look at the joint interplay of marketing activities and self-concept, with particular emphasis on the actual versus ideal self-concepts.

The Role of Self-Concept

Self-concept is important to marketers because consumers' self-perceptions influence their attitudes toward product categories and specific brands and subsequent purchase behavior.[8] Consequently, brands deliberately convey images that extend beyond their purely functional characteristics. For example, Harley-Davidson evokes mental imagery quite distinct from that of Honda or Suzuki, and Nordstrom conveys a different image than Kmart or Sears. Research suggests that some consumers like to express themselves in their brand choices. Thus, promotional efforts to image-conscious consumers are more effective if they portray product images that are consistent with consumers' self-concepts.[9] But which self-concept should marketers embrace—the actual or ideal? The answer is, "it depends."

Because self-concept is relatively important to everyone, consumers tend to maintain or protect their self-concepts on the one hand and enhance them on the other. The former is referred to as the self-consistency motive; the latter is called the self-esteem motive. Consumers motivated by self-consistency act in accordance with their self-concepts—even in the face of challenging evidence. In contrast, consumers motivated by self-esteem engage in activities that lead to more positive self-evaluations.[10] Both motives coexist within an individual, but they can tug us in different directions, depending on the task at hand.

Advertisers want us to remember their brands and evaluate them favorably, but recall and evaluation are two different tasks. If a consumer's task is to recall the brand name or its attributes, then she is more likely to remember information consistent with her *actual* self-concept, rather than information consistent with her *ideal* self-concept. Why? Consumers generally possess well-developed, actual self-schema with rich associative networks in their memories. **Self-schemas** are cognitive structures that help us make sense of who we are. Schemas can be thought of as basic sketches of what people know about something. People are generally knowledgeable (if not altogether happy) about who they are. Consequently, people are likely to attend to and retrieve information congruent with their actual self-schema.[11] Recalling congruent information also enables consumers to maintain a state of cognitive consonance. In general, consumers are motivated to maintain harmony in their belief systems and between their attitudes and behavior. Thus, if marketing communication fits with consumers' understanding of who they are, the communication facilitates this desired balance.

The situation is quite different if a consumer is focused on evaluating or judging a product. Because consumers are aware of not only who they are, but also who they would like to be, a gap between the actual and ideal self-concepts represents a state of inconsistency. As such, the ideal self-concept can serve as an important moving target, a goal that consumers seek to attain. Thus, when consumers evaluate a brand, they are more likely to be influenced by whether the brand fills the gap, i.e., advances them toward their ideal self-concepts. It follows that brands congruent with a consumer's ideal self-concept are evaluated more favorably than those congruent with a consumer's actual self-concept. For example, a consumer who wants to feel "intelligent" and "in-the-know" may meet that goal by purchasing a smartphone. On the other hand, if a consumer's ideal self-concept is more "artsy," he may buy an iPad. In sum, if marketers want consumers to remember their brand names, attributes, and benefits, they should create communications that are consistent with consumers' actual self-concepts. In contrast, if changing attitudes is important, marketers should communicate information that is congruent with consumers' ideal self-concepts.

In a public context, a consumer who wants to be seen as "preppy" may meet that goal by endorsing J. Crew or Polo Ralph Lauren. If a consumer's ideal public-concept is more "edgy," he may wear clothing from Karl Kani or Timberline. Connecting with consumers' ideal public-concepts is *particularly* important for individuals who have a relatively negative view of self. Recent research shows that consumers who are anxious about relationships are likely to use brands as a means for signaling their ideal public-concepts to potential relationship partners. In addition, high anxiety consumers tend to avoid brands that don't match their ideal public-concepts to avoid the risk of being viewed as unattractive by others.[12]

The notion of positioning brand images to be congruent with consumers' self-concepts reflects the general practice of market segmentation (see Chapter 2). Marketers identify patterns of self-concepts residing in specific demographic groups and find media that communicate directly to these

groups. This practice is not new. For decades, Virginia Slims cigarettes attempted to match their slogan, "You've come a long way, baby," with women's ideal self-concepts regarding social independence. Similarly, Harley-Davidson motorcycles convey raw excitement to consumers seeking to improve their ideal self-concepts regarding freedom and adventure. Non-profits and government organizations have also used this approach. The U.S. Army's recent ad campaign, "Symbol of Strength," targets prospects with messages of self-empowerment and self-determination. Other military services also rely on slogans to appeal to consumers' ideal self-concepts. The U.S. Air Force recently abandoned its "Cross Into the Blue" for

Harley-Davidson ads target consumers who seek excitement in their lives.

Marketing in Action

The U.S. Army's "Symbol of Strength" Targets Recruits' Self-Esteem

Early in 2001, the U.S. Army abandoned its 20-year ad campaign, "Be All You Can Be." Instead, the Army committed its $150 million advertising budget and its recruiting goals to "An Army of One." The campaign emphasized that young people could maintain their sense of identity and attain self-fulfillment while serving in the Army. One promotion featured a solitary soldier running outdoors while a voiceover says, "I am an army of one, even though there are 1,045,690 soldiers like me."

The change in campaign was not without controversy. Advertising expert Jerry Della Famina thought it was a mistake. He argued that the Army benefited from one of the greatest campaigns in history. *Advertising Age*, an industry publication and information leader, ranked the "Be All You Can Be" campaign as the second best of the 20th century.

Although "Be All You Can Be" was embedded in the culture of the nation, apparently it had lost its connection with the Army's target audience of over 20 million young adults between the ages of 18 and 24. During the fall of 2006, however, "Army of One" was retired. Army officials said the "Army of One" campaign had not been highly effective. The Army missed its recruiting target in 2005 by the widest margin in more than 20 years.

In 2006, the Army, hoping to better connect with potential recruits, introduced a new pitch, "Army Strong," accompanied by a $200 million annual advertising contract with McCann Worldgroup. This campaign, developed after numerous focus groups and interviews with soldiers, was designed to communicate the idea that if you join the Army, you will gain physical and emotional strength as well as strength of character and purpose.[13]

In May 2011, the U.S. Army extended "Army Strong" through its newest advertising campaign, "Symbol of Strength." This campaign highlights the ultimate benefit of becoming a soldier—participating in new opportunities and serving missions available only to members of the Army.[14] The U.S. Army is connecting with potential recruits through Facebook, Twitter, MySpace, YouTube, and armystrongstories.com, where soldiers blog about their day-to-day life in the Army. These marketing communications are aimed directly at recruits' ideal self-concepts.

Dates	Campaign Slogan[15]
1971–1973	*Today's Army Wants to Join You*
1973–1979	*Join the People Who've Joined the Army*
1979–1981	*This is the Army*
1981–2001	*Be All You Can Be*
2001–2006	*Army of One*
2006–2011	*Army Strong*
2011–present	*Symbol of Strength*

Slogans of historical U.S. Army advertising campaigns

"Do Something Amazing." Since 2001, the U.S. Navy has promoted itself with "Accelerate Your Life," and the Marines have relied on "The Few...The Proud," targeting prospects who are motivated to enhance their self-esteem. Similarly, luxury brands such as BMW and Rolex play on consumers' desires to bridge the gap between actual public- and ideal public-self concepts.

The Extended Self

Some products are so important to consumers that they are used to confirm their self-concepts. The direct link between a consumer's self-concepts and her possessions is called the **extended self**.[16] The idea that our belongings represent an extension of ourselves dates back to 1890, when psychologist and philosopher William James claimed that we are the sum of our possessions.[17] In a more recent and highly regarded essay, the academic Russell Belk maintains that the extended self is not limited to personal possessions, but also includes people, places, and group possessions. This view is consistent with the notion that external objects become a part of us when we are able to exercise significant control over them. In this sense, even body parts are viewed as part of the extended self.[18] Research confirms that people consider the following categories as possessions:

- Their bodies
- Personal space
- Consumable goods
- Durable goods
- Home and property
- Significant others
- Children
- Friends
- Mementos
- Pets[19]

Thus, marketers need to understand the variety of ways consumers express themselves through their possessions. And they do. For example, Unilever appeals to consumers' view of their bodies with Lever 2000, "for your 2000 body parts." An enormously successful campaign, Unilever extended the Lever 2000 brand to include body washes with ginseng and vitamins (Energize), cucumber extracts (Fresh Aloe), and a rain scent (Refresh). The computer security company Malwarebytes understands consumers' need for privacy. They developed a series of products designed to protect computers by completely removing all forms of malware, including viruses, Trojans, spyware, adware, and rootkits. For consumers who view their pets as an extension of themselves, PetSmart, Inc., the world's largest specialty pet retailer of products and services, offers in-store PetsHotels, Doggie Day Camps, pet training, pet grooming, and adoption programs.

While acquiring and investing in possessions can extend who consumers think they are, the loss of important belongings can reduce their extended selves. Burglary victims report a diminished sense of self when their possessions are lost to theft. Research suggests that grief and mourning follow theft, just as it does when someone loses a loved one.[20] Similarly, natural disaster victims report going through a grieving process, including denial, anger, depression, and finally acceptance.[21] The security system company ADT knows that homeowners fear the loss of possessions resulting from burglary. In fact, ADT advertises that its customer monitoring centers "help protect the people and things you value most," i.e., the extended self. Insurance companies like Allstate understand that natural disasters can damage more than homeowners' property. They can also destroy a consumer's extended self. Accordingly, these firms offer catastrophe and disaster insurance for those willing to pay the premiums.

Research also suggests that for many Americans, the automobile is an important part of their extended selves and ideal self-concepts.[22] The process of creating one's extended self through an automobile occurs when people customize their cars or painstakingly wash and maintain them. Some consumers build special sound systems for their cars; others spend hours washing and waxing their vehicles. To these consumers, their automobiles represent a significant part of their extended selves. Marketers of Turtle Wax and 3M Car Care run advertisements that encourage people-car relationships. They feature beautifully conditioned automobiles, lavishly maintained by their owners, who caress and talk to their cars as though they are lovers. When car aficionados damage their vehicles, they often behave as though their own bodies have been wrecked, and they work anxiously to restore the automobiles to their original condition. Not surprisingly, for car aficionados, collision centers act as surrogate "emergency rooms."

Ethics

Launched nearly a decade ago, Dove's "Real Beauty" campaign purported to celebrate women of all shapes, sizes, and colors. It was conceived based on the results of a multinational study of 3,500 women. The study revealed that two-thirds of women believed that the media endorsed an image of beauty unattainable by most women. Moreover, just 2% of respondents reported that they considered themselves beautiful. Consequently, Unilever overhauled Dove's global advertising message to challenge the imagery traditionally associated with beauty and personal care products. "Real Beauty" arrived in the United States in 2005 with ads for hair, skin, and body products featuring images of mature skin for skin care; curvier bodies for moisturizers; and short, curly coifs for hair care products. TV ads in the series featured women old and young and of different complexions promoting Dove's Body Nourishers lotion line, as well as curvy women dressed in underwear endorsing a new Dove Intensive Firming Lotion.[23] In 2006, Dove ran its first Super Bowl ad with an inspirational message designed to raise girls' self esteem. Helping girls accept themselves is a mission of Dove's five-year marketing strategy.[24]

But is the "Real Beauty" campaign for real? Some consumers see it as just another marketing stunt aimed at selling soap. In June 2010, *Jezebel* uncovered a Craigslist ad for a New York casting call for Dove's Real Beauty campaign. Ironically, Dove's definition of "real women" narrowly adheres to typical beauty standards. It called for women who are "naturally fit," with "flawless skin," free of tattoos or scars, and who have "nice bodies," and "beautiful hair."[25]

Perhaps the heart of the issue is whether the campaign makes women feel good about themselves.[26] On one hand, there are certain classic looks that women would all secretly love to possess. When they see a beautiful model promoting a brand, women respond imaginatively and, for a moment or two, feel beautiful, too. Although they know the product will not change them, the power of association is so great that, deep down, women feel as though a little of the model's magic has rubbed off—this is the ideal self-concept speaking. On the other hand, contemporary, self-confident women want to see figures and faces like their own featured and celebrated in advertising—this is the actual self-concept speaking. Which self-concept wins? Research suggests that when evaluating brands, it's usually the ideal—not the real—that matters, which was an ominous sign for *Dove's* "Real Beauty" campaign. Early 2011, Dove decided to dump the "Real Beauty" campaign in favor of a less preachy "Body Language" campaign aimed at convincing women that Dove products will make them feel attractive and confident.[27]

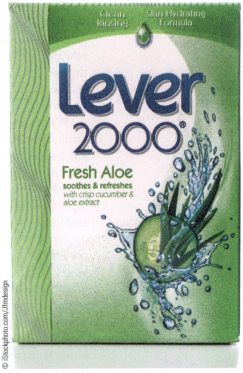

© iStockphoto.com/Jfmdesign

How do possessions become extensions of consumers? First, they facilitate *action* by allowing consumers to do things they otherwise couldn't do. For example, without an iPod, consumers would not be able to share their favorite songs with their friends, songs that also represent part of the extended self. Second, consumers' belongings *symbolically* extend who they are. For instance, trophies and awards highlight individual accomplishments; diplomas exhibit academic credentials; and photographs and artwork present vivid illustrations of what people deem important. Third, possessions bring consumers *power* and *prestige*. Accumulating antiques and other scarce items, for example, conveys a certain status, because rare items can be expensive. Fourth, possessions allow consumers to associate themselves with desirable *people, places,* or *times.* Autographs of a favorite celebrity, memorabilia acquired on a trip to Paris, and family heirlooms—these types of things extend who consumers are by linking them to these desirable entities.[13] Some possessions are so important that consumers develop a deep affection for them. These items are known as "loved objects."

Loved Objects

The people and things that consumers love impart a strong influence on their self-concepts. The word "love" is commonly used to describe activities, places, and possessions: "I love to golf," "I love Paris," "I love your hair style," "I love that movie." Research shows that consumers not only "love to shop," but they also "fall in love" with the products they buy.[28] In fact, love is the second most common word consumers use to describe their feelings about possessions (happiness ranks first). Of all the possessions that consumers acquire and divest throughout their lives, only a few attain loved status. Loved objects, a special subset of all possessions that comprise the extended self, play a central role in our knowledge of who we are as people. Recent research provides evidence that loved objects can be part of a synthesizing solution to a specific identity conflict. In fact, **loved objects** are shown to derive much of their emotional status by helping to resolve these internal conflicts.[29] For children, a favorite stuffed animal provides comfort during times of psychological conflict. For adults, beloved sports cars can compensate for lack of physical stature, and chocolates can be used as rewards. Loved objects can also resolve role conflicts. For example, if a man experiences a psychological conflict between his role as a businessperson and his role as an art connoisseur, he might come to love his paintings and sculptures as a way of preserving his artistic persona and compartmentalize his business as simply a pragmatic choice. "It's just a job," he says. He might also identify his unloved objects, such as furniture, as practical and mundane—like his job. Similarly, if a woman has a conflict between her feminist and traditional ideals, she may identify loved objects to help resolve this conflict. Perhaps her collection of antique and delicate porcelain figurines raises good feelings about a time (the 1950s) in which women were relatively repressed.[29]

Even a favorite pair of blue jeans can resolve internal role conflict. Perhaps a young manager has misgivings about working on Saturday. By dressing in her favorite, well-worn blue jeans, she can exercise some autonomy. "If I have to work on the weekends, at least I'll be comfortable," she says. In a positive sense then, loved objects can provide a mechanism for psychological conflict resolution. Now that we've discussed the importance of the extended self and loved objects, let's examine how individuals manage their social behavior.

In times of emotional conflicts, people oftentimes focus on loved objects to ease their struggles.

OBJECTIVE ## Self-Monitoring

The extent to which consumers use situational cues to guide their social behavior is known as **self-monitoring**. People who routinely modify their behavior to meet the expectations of others are known as *high self-monitors*. Conversely, people who act primarily on the basis of their internal beliefs and attitudes are known as *low self-monitors*.[30] Put simply, high self-monitors tend to behave like social chameleons, constantly changing and adapting their behaviors to different situations and different people. Low self-monitors march to the beat of their own drums. Research shows that *low* self-monitors exhibit greater attitude-behavior consistency than high self-monitors.[31] Research also demonstrates that *high* self-monitors show more concern for the self-image they project in social situations.[32] As a result, high self-monitors are more likely to respond to image-based appeals that promise to make them look good, while low self-monitors are more likely to evaluate the functional benefits of a product.[33] Self-monitoring typically involves three somewhat distinct individual differences:

- Willingness to be the center of attention
- Concern about the opinions of others
- Ability and desire to adjust one's behavior to induce positive reactions in others

Like many individual difference variables, self-monitoring can be measured by a survey instrument. Low self-monitors tend to endorse statements like, "My behavior is usually an expression of my true inner feelings, attitudes, and beliefs." High self-monitors agree with statements such as, "When I am uncertain how to act in a social situation, I look to the behavior of others for cues."

Self-monitoring can be helpful in resolving the personality-versus-situation debate in consumer behavior, which focuses on the relative influence of personality traits versus situational factors on consumers' attitudes and behaviors. Advocates of the personality approach argue that an individual's personality traits determine his or her behavior. Conversely, advocates of the situation approach believe that the nature of circumstances drives behavior.[34] Research suggests that both approaches can be correct, depending on an individual's self-monitoring. The importance of personality traits is discussed later in this chapter.

The term **malleable self** refers to a multifaceted self-concept that includes a *good self, bad self, not-me self, desired self, ideal self,* and *ought-to-be self.* Any of these **self-conceptions** are accessible at any given moment.[35] In this sense, self-concept is regarded as both stable and malleable. On one hand, the self-concept contains an enduring set of self-conceptions. On the other hand, consumers access and use different self-conceptions, depending on the task at hand—like tools in a toolbox. Classic research indicates that people prefer brands that match their self-conceptions. But which self-conceptions do consumers use to compare themselves to brands? Recent research shows that high self-monitors use social cues to select self-conceptions, and low self-monitors draw on their internal traits.[36]

Let's take a real-world example. Suppose a first-year college student goes dancing three nights during the first week of school. Does this mean that she is extroverted (a stable personality trait) or did she go dancing to reduce the stress associated with her new school environment (a temporary situation)? Self-monitoring provides a possible explanation. Perhaps this individual is neither unusually extroverted nor extraordinarily stressed. She is, however, interested in joining a social sorority (a brand), whose members have been frequenting the night clubs this week. As a high self-monitor, she evaluated the situation and drew on her "desired self," i.e., her desire to be a member of this sorority. Next, she adapted her behavior to appear extroverted and outgoing because she believes this would increase her chances of being invited to join the sorority. Alternatively, if she were a low self-monitor, she would probably stay at home. Her choice of a sorority would be guided predominately by her internal beliefs and attitudes, and she would not attempt to construct a desired image. Perhaps charity is an important part of her self-schema, or actual self. If this is the case, she might evaluate sororities on the basis of their community service record and search for a sorority accordingly.

Consider also a high self-monitoring consumer who wants to project an image of intellect and culture to his dinner party guests. In addition to choosing appropriate words and mannerisms, he selects and displays the brands of food, wine, and music that support an intellectual and cultured image. Conversely, the low self-monitor would not be influenced by these social cues. Instead, he would select a decorum that fits his actual self-concept, i.e., who he really is.[37] Some level of self-monitoring is inherent in all social situations. People must adapt to their environments in order to interact. Nevertheless, some individuals present themselves in such a way as to create exaggerated or misleading images. Motivation for this behavior is explored next in a discussion of impression management theory.

OBJECTIVE ③ **Impression Management Theory**

The process of creating desirable images of ourselves for others is known as **impression management**. In general, people practice impression management to increase control over valued outcomes, such as praise, approval, sympathy, and special treatment. Individuals engage in impression management to make people like them (ingratiation); to generate fear (intimidation); respect (self-promotion); to lift up their morals (exemplification); and to engender pity (supplication).[38] Consumers employ at least three tactics to manage the images that others form about them:

1. Appearance management
2. Ingratiation
3. Aligning activities

Appearance Management By controlling the selection of clothes, grooming, habits (e.g., smoking), verbal communication (e.g., jargon, accents), and the display of possessions, consumers convey desired images to others.[39] The decisions regarding how consumers control their physical appearances and surroundings comprise their **appearance management**. Research supports the notion that consumers pay close attention to their physical appearance in order to claim certain identities. Job applicants have been shown to manage their physical appearance to match the interviewer's stereotyped expectations. If the interviewer is thought to be conservative, the applicants dress more traditionally than if the interviewer is thought to be progressive.[40] Likewise, salespeople spend considerable time and money on clothing and grooming. People also pay close attention to their props (items in their physical environments). Do you arrange your dormitory or apartment differently depending on whether your parents or friends will be visiting? You are not alone; most consumers use props. Executives arrange their offices to convey prestige; children prop their bedrooms with colorful posters; and professors always seem to have piles of books on their desks and tables (they must be busy). Have you noticed that U.S. politicians always have the American flag propped in the background and an American flag pin in their lapels for photo ops and speeches? The retail website *Fathead* targets consumers who want to prop their surroundings with sports and entertainment figures.

Ingratiation It is inherently pleasing to be liked by others. One of the tactics people use to get others to like them is **ingratiation**, a set of strategic behaviors designed to increase the probability of gaining benefits or favors from another person. One can ingratiate with self-presentation, opinion conformity, and flattery.

Self-presentation involves either *self-enhancement* or *self-deprecation*. The former occurs when people promote their good qualities, such as during interviews or on first dates. Self-enhancement can backfire, however, if the claims are viewed as conceited[41] or exaggerated and are later discredited.[42] When employing

Fathead appeals to consumers who like to prop their surroundings with sports and entertainment figures.

Courtesy of Fathead

self-deprecation, people make humble or modest claims about themselves, often downplaying their positive attributes or their role in a successful outcome. This tactic can also backfire if the self-deprecation is excessively negative and perceived as an attempt to elicit reassurance from others.[43] Taken together, self-presentation is a trade-off between favorability and plausibility—modest claims may signal incompetence, and yet, highly favorable claims may not be credible.

Think about your strategy on a first date. On one hand, if you describe all of your accomplishments and talents, you may be perceived as boastful and turn off your date. On the other hand, if you fail to mention your positive capabilities, your date may regard you as mediocre. Either way, you probably don't get a second date. Thus, self-presentation involves striking a balance between the opposing forces of self-enhancement and self-deprecation.[44] Research demonstrates that the optimal balance shifts, depending on whether people are interacting with friends or strangers.[45] Self-presentations are more likely to be self-enhancing to strangers and modest to friends. Why? Strangers usually have little information, so an individual's performance record may be difficult to verify. Consequently, by presenting highly favorable information to strangers, people willingly sacrifice likeability in exchange for perceptions of competence. The strategy is different with friends. Because they have more background information about you, friends can easily disconfirm an exaggerated claim. Moreover, people share common interests with friends and expect many future interactions. Thus, people maintain friendships by increasing likeability through a more modest self-presentation. Let's return to the strategy for a first date. Research suggests that if a new acquaintance is aware of something you've done well, he or she will like you more if you are modest about it. On the contrary, if the other person is completely unaware of a particular talent, modesty is simply interpreted as mediocrity.[46] In sum, if you've got it, flaunt it—but only if your date doesn't already know about it.

Opinion conformity entails expressing insincere agreement on important issues. Subordinates often use this tactic with supervisors, because people generally like those who share their opinions.[47] But it can backfire if the target of opinion conformity perceives the ingratiator as pandering. Thus, a clever mix of disagreement on unimportant issues and agreement on critical issues reduces suspicion.

Flattery involves excessive compliments or praise designed to make someone feel good about him or herself. Flattery does not have to be insincere. In fact, effective flattery should be targeted at important attributes where people feel uncertain about their abilities or performance. For example, if a friend expresses anxiety about his performance on an important and recently delivered speech, an earnest comment such as, "I appreciate that you spoke slowly and clearly," is likely to gain favor for the ingratiator. Similarly, when a salesperson flatters a potential customer regarding an important but uncertain attribute, the customer is likely to respond favorably. For example, a consumer may have reservations about his weight and expresses those concerns while trying on business suits. A clever salesperson may flatter the customer by remarking that he is "in better shape than most men his age." Recent research demonstrates that if customers perceive flattery to be sincere, it doesn't matter whether the remark is perceived to be accurate, as both genuine compliments (sincere and accurate) and opaque flattery (sincere and inaccurate) appear to generate positive intentions to continue working with a salesperson.[48] Figure 12.2 provides a multi-dimensional model of Consumer Ingratiation.

FIGURE 12.2 | A Multi-Dimensional Model of Consumer Ingratiation

POSITIVE INGRATIATION		**Sincerity** [Perception of the Ingratiator's Motive]	
		Insincere [self-enhancement] *manipulative*	**Sincere** [other-enhancement] *genuine*
Accuracy [Perception of the accuracy of the remark]	**Accurate** [true positive]	**Phony Compliment** *[smooth talk]*	**Genuine Compliment** *[positive feedback]*
	Inaccurate [false positive]	**Transparent Flattery** *[brown-nosing]*	**Opaque Flattery** *[friendly behavior]*

NEGATIVE (anti) INGRATIATION		**Sincerity** [Perception of the Ingratiator's Motive]	
		Insincere [self-enhancement] *manipulative*	**Sincere** [other-enhancement] *genuine*
Accuracy [Perception of the accuracy of the remark]	**Accurate** [true negative]	**Disparagement** *[malicious Criticism]*	**Negative Feedback** *[useful Criticism]*
	Inaccurate [false negative]	**Sarcasm** *[harmful Criticism]*	**Hyper Critique** *[ineffectual Criticism]*

Source: Thomas W. Cline, D.P. Mertens, N.S. Vowels, and A. Davies, "All Ingratiation Is Not Equal: A Two Dimensional Model of Consumer Ingratiation," Society for Consumer Psychology 2009 Winter Conference. Reprinted by permission of Thomas W. Cline.

Aligning Activities Sometimes consumers behave in ways that violate existing cultural norms. **Aligning activities** consist of comments that attempt to realign our behavior with norms.[49] **Disclaimers** are verbal assertions, made in advance, to offset the potential negative effects of a behavior.[50] A celebrity endorser may use a disclaimer such as, "I'm no expert, but …" to avoid responsibility for a product's performance. A salesperson may remark, "Please hear me out before you refuse this offer" to keep potential customers from prematurely rejecting an offer. **Accounts** entail *excuses* and *justifications*. The former reduce or deny one's responsibility for inappropriate actions; the latter acknowledge responsibility but rationalize the behavior as appropriate, given the circumstances.[51] Both excuses and justifications are designed to reduce perceptions of wrongdoing. For example, a customer service representative from Dell, who claims that your computer crashed because you installed incompatible software, is excusing Dell from any responsibility for the problem. In contrast, the service rep may justify the computer crash on grounds that the computer is seven years old and well beyond its useful life. In a similar vein, one salesperson may explain a late delivery as a shipping or supplier problem—an excuse; another may explain the late delivery as a function of building a custom order—a justification. Accounts work best when the individual delivering them is of superior status and when the violating behavior is not serious.[52] What about students, who are not in a superior position to account for serious violations such as late assignments and missed exams? Research suggests that students' excuses and justification are better received if they are truthful and apologetic. It also helps if the account is reasonable.

It should be clear that people employ various tactics to manipulate the impressions others form of them. Consumers and salespeople manage their appearances; they ingratiate themselves through selective presentation, opinion conformity, and flattery; and they try to repair their identities when their conduct is questionable. Next, let's take a look at what makes an individual unique and how that influences his or her behavior as a consumer.

Personality

Personality is a set of unique psychological characteristics that influences how a person responds to his or her environment, including cognitive, affective, and behavioral tendencies. Understanding a consumer's personality can help predict his or her responses to marketing activities—but it is a tricky business. People don't necessarily behave the same way in all situations, and an individual's personality can change over time. Consumers' personalities mature along with their physical growth. For example, advanced education may affect consumers' personalities by teaching them to be more open-minded and inquisitive. Similarly, the process of aging often ushers in self-reflection, increasing consumers' desire for reading and experiential travel. Some people become more cynical over time, while others become more trustful. Few consumers respond to products and services today as they did as children or teenagers.

Major life events can also produce "shocks" in a consumer's personality. A full-time job can increase a person's need to be conscientious, and marriage frequently brings a spirit of cooperation (at least initially!). Having children, changing occupations, chronic illness, and the death of loved ones can also engender significant shifts in one's personality. Nevertheless, it's difficult to ignore the enduring qualities of personality; in fact, personality has uniformly been considered to be constitutional, i.e., an essential and stable characteristic of individuals. Some people just seem consistently grouchy, while others routinely act pleasingly. In the same vein, some of your friends probably assert themselves without fail, while others predictably withdraw from confrontations. Earlier in this chapter, we described these individual nuances as traits. Indeed, scholars have approached the study of personality from a variety of angles, producing many interesting theories, including Freudian Systems,[53] Neo-Freudian Theories,[54] and trait theories.[55] The most useful approach for consumer behavior is multiple trait theory.

OBJECTIVE ## Multiple Trait Theory

Multiple trait theory maintains that **personality traits** represent consumers' tendencies to respond in a certain way across similar situations. Traits vary from one person to another, and although an individual's traits can shift, they are generally stable over a reasonable time frame. Think of traits as those specific qualities and mannerisms that distinguish one person from another. Consider, for a moment, your best friend. How would you describe his or her personality? Is this person generally outgoing, smart, shy, or moody? How does he or she respond to new situations? Is he or she optimistic, dramatic, or indifferent? How does this individual react to marketing stimuli? Is he or she a bargain hunter or an impulsive shopper? Longstanding research interest in personality and consumer psychology has produced a host of measurable personality traits. Among the most popular multiple trait theory taxonomies is the **Five-Factor Model**.[56] This multi-factor structure identifies five basic traits that derive primarily from an individual's genetics and early childhood learning.[57] The five basic traits have traditionally been numbered and labeled as:

1. Surgency (outgoingness)
2. Agreeableness
3. Conscientiousness
4. Emotional stability
5. Intellect

Figure 12.3 provides specific characteristics of the five core traits.[56]

The Five-Factor Model enables marketers to categorize consumers into different groups based on several traits. Thus, trait theory is a special case of market segmentation. Research shows that important personality traits can be linked to specific consumption behavior, such as **compulsive buying**, i.e., the drive to consume uncontrollably and to buy in order to avoid problems. Specifically, consumers who score low on conscientiousness or high on agreeability demonstrate a propensity to shop compulsively.[58] This negative link between conscientiousness and compulsive buying suggests that individuals who have difficulty controlling their buying may also lack organization, precision, and efficiency. The positive relationship between agreeability and compulsive buying implies that uncontrolled shopping is associated with tendencies to be kindhearted, sympathetic, and not rude to others.[59] The Five-Factor Model has also been used to explain consumers' bargaining and complaining behavior,[60] voting behavior,[61] and alcohol abuse.[62] Research also shows that the Five-Factor Model can provide a framework to tap the dimensions of a brand's personality.

FIGURE 12.3 | The Five-Factor Model of Personality

Those scoring low are...	DIMENSION	Those scoring high are...
	Surgency	
Introverted		Extraverted
Shy		Talkative
Quiet		Assertive
Reserved		Verbal
Untalkative		Energetic
Inhibited		Bold
Withdrawn		Active
Timid		Daring
Bashful		Vigorous
Those scoring low are...	**Agreeableness**	*Those scoring high are...*
Cold		Kind
Unkind		Cooperative
Unsympathetic		Sympathetic
Distrustful		Warm
Harsh		Trustful
Demanding		Considerate
Rude		Pleasant
Selfish		Agreeable
Uncooperative		Helpful
Those scoring low are...	**Conscientiousness**	*Those scoring high are...*
Disorganized		Organized
Careless		Systematic
Unsystematic		Thorough
Inefficient		Practical
Undependable		Neat
Impractical		Efficient
Negligent		Careful
Inconsistent		Steady
Those scoring low are ...	**Emotional Stability**	*Those scoring high are ...*
Anxious		Unenvious
Moody		Unemotional
Temperamental		Relaxed
Envious		Imperturbable
Emotional		Unexcitable
Irritable		Undemanding
Those scoring low are...	**Intellect**	*Those scoring high are...*
Unintellectual		Intellectual
Unintelligent		Creative
Unimaginative		Complex
Uncreative		Imaginative
Simple		Bright
Unsophisticated		Philosophical
Unreflective		Artistic

SOURCE: Adapted from Goldberg, L. R. (1992). The Development of Markers for the Big Five-Factor Structure. *Psychological Assessment, 4*, 26–42.

Brand Personality

Earlier in this chapter, we learned that consumers prefer brands that enhance their self-concepts. In some cases, consumers prefer products that reflect who they are, i.e., their actual self-concepts. For example, "These blue jeans aren't for me. They're too risqué." In other cases, consumers buy products that help them express who they'd like to be, i.e., their ideal self-concepts. For example, "I'll take these preppy jeans; I need to upscale my image." Brands such as Nike and Nokia often conjure up specific **brand images**, which comprise all the thoughts and feelings consumers have about a particular brand. Consumers' thoughts and feelings are evoked through the stimuli they associate with a brand, such as logos, slogans, endorsers, price, distribution channel, typical users, and use situations. Though somewhat elusive, brand image can be estimated by asking consumers the first words that come to mind when the think about a brand. What comes to mind when consumers think of Mountain Dew, Google, Apple, Ford, McDonald's, and Louis Vuitton?

A considerable amount of research demonstrates that, like people, brands exhibit personality traits. **Brand personality** refers to the set of human characteristics associated with a brand. Brand personality comprises the human side of a brand's image. For example, Absolut vodka is typically described as a cool, contemporary, 25-year old, while Stolichnaya vodka is an intellectual, conservative, older man. Would consumers describe the personality of SKYYvodka any differently? Drawing on the Five-Factor Model of personality, Jennifer Aaker, General Atlantic Professor of Marketing at Stanford Graduate School of Business, developed a framework to measure a brand's personality. She identified five distinct personality traits:

1. Sincerity
2. Excitement
3. Competence
4. Sophistication
5. Ruggedness[63]

Each of these factors includes various descriptors, as shown in Figure 12.4.

Three of the five dimensions of brand personality relate to the "Big Five" human personality dimensions. *Agreeableness* matches up with *sincerity* to capture warmth and acceptance; *conscientiousness* parallels *competence,* as both embody responsibility, security, and dependability; and *extroversion* and *excitement* mutually describe energy, activity, and sociability. However, two dimensions of brand personality (*sophistication* and *ruggedness*) stand apart from the Five-Factor Model. This suggests that consumers may not recognize these particular traits in themselves, but rather aspire to attain them. This notion is consistent with existing marketing activities surrounding archetypal sophisticated brands such as Gucci, Lexus, Hennessy, and Rolex that feature glamorous, high-class images. Similarly, rugged brands such as Marlboro, Timberline, Jeep, and L.L. Bean symbolize tough, outdoorsy ideals that appeal to consumers' ideal self-concepts.[63]

Brand personality traits maintain an important relationship with human personality traits. First, human traits are characterized based on a consumer's observable behavior, manifest beliefs and attitudes, and physical and

FIGURE 12.4 | The Dimensions of Brand Personality

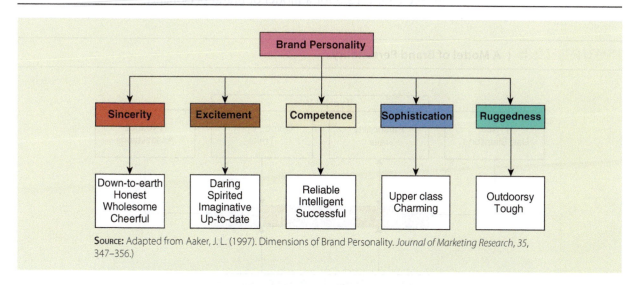

SOURCE: Adapted from Aaker, J. L. (1997). Dimensions of Brand Personality. *Journal of Marketing Research*, *35*, 347–356.)

demographic characteristics.[64] For example, "He's a sophisticated manager, always up-to-date with technology." In contrast, brand traits are characterized based on a brand's *typical user*, i.e., the set of human characteristics associated with those who routinely endorse the brand. Thus, if technologically inclined, sophisticated managers are typical users of Bluetooth technology, then these particular personality traits are likely to be transferred to the Bluetooth brand.[65]

Consumers also extract cultural meaning from the brands they purchase. Thus, the process is a paradoxical two-way street. A brand's image is shaped by those who use it, and yet the users construct their identities through a brand's personality. Research also suggests that brand personality includes the demographic characteristics of the typical users, such as gender, class, and age. For example, Revlon is predominately female; Budweiser is male; and Starbucks is gender-neutral. Chevy is middle-class; but Cadillac is upper-class. Apple's Mac is young; and HP is older.

Brand traits can also be inferred through *typical use situations*, which represent the various ways a brand is consumed or used. For example, McDonald's is a popular destination for single parents to treat their children to a pre-made meal in a colorful, quick-serve environment. Big Boy also appeals to this demographic, offering a similar menu and remarkably comparable brand symbols (Ronald McDonald versus Big Boy). However, the use situation at Big Boy is sit-down and typically includes the entire family. For another example, consider the desktop computer. Apple computers are typically used for creative applications and hobbies. Quite the opposite, PCs tend to be all about business applications. The popular "I'm a Mac/I'm a PC" ads by Apple attest to this dichotomy.

Like human traits, brand traits can also be inferred indirectly through *product associations*, such as attributes (e.g., the iPhone's apps are imaginative), product-category (e.g., motorcycles are daring), names (e.g., Smucker's is down-to-earth), and logos (e.g., Nike's swoosh is spirited).[66] Finally, a brand's personality can be formed by using characters and celebrities to endorse the brand. See Figure 12.5 for a model of brand personality.

FIGURE 12.5 | A Model of Brand Personality

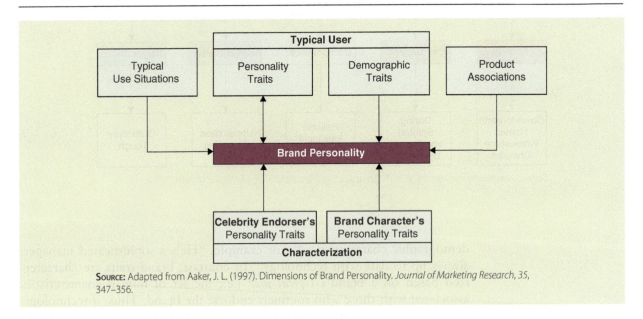

Source: Adapted from Aaker, J. L. (1997). Dimensions of Brand Personality. *Journal of Marketing Research, 35,* 347–356.

In contrast to a brand's tangible attributes (e.g., dress or pants size), brand personality tends to serve a symbolic or self-expressive function for consumers.[67] The symbolic use of brands occurs because consumers instill brands with human personality traits. Marketers understand the importance of symbolic meaning and often use characterization to communicate brand personality.

Characterization

Two strategies provide brands with characterization. **Brand personification** involves giving non-humans human-like traits, while **brand anthropomorphism** assigns both human traits and *form* to non-humans. Marketers use both strategies to build brand personality. For example, Geico's talking gecko represents brand personification. The gecko's English accent and delightful mannerism are unmistakably human, but he retains the form of a lizard. In fact, this laid-back ambassador of great customer service and quick insurance rate quotes was voted America's favorite advertising icon in 2005.[68] The idea for the gecko emerged from a creative session at the Martin Agency in Richmond, Virginia. For years, the company's name, "Geico," an acronym for Government Employees Insurance Company, had been incorrectly pronounced as "Gecko." Thus, the gecko was created to turn consumers' mispronunciations into an amusing memory aid. The famous gecko first aired on national television in

The M&M characters represent brand personification.

1999. But the gecko had, and still has, competition—in the form of the Aflac Insurance duck. Also debuting in 1999, Aflac's duck—voiced by Gilbert Gottfried—"quacks" out the company's name in frustration to prospective policyholders who can't seem to remember it. This is a deliberate attempt to facilitate brand name recall and link the zany character traits of the duck to an otherwise boring product, supplemental insurance.

Brand personification need not involve animals. The M&M characters appear in lighthearted commercials for Mars, Inc., one of the largest privately owned businesses in the world. The M&M characters have been assigned human traits but their forms are primarily non-human, i.e., they have faces on a body reminiscent of actual M&Ms. To emphasize the M&M's brand personality, Mars has even named their "spokescandies." The cynical and sardonic *red* duo serve as mascots for milk chocolate M&Ms, and the happy and gullible *yellow* duo represent peanut M&Ms.

In a recent online poll sponsored by *USA Today* and *Yahoo!*, the M&M candy characters were voted America's favorite advertising icons.[69] Their popularity even gave rise to Planet M&Ms, a website where customers could create their own look-alike M&M characters. There are many more brand personifications out there, including classics such as the Budweiser Clydesdales, the Energizer Bunny, Star-Kist's Charlie the Tuna, and the Michelin Man, along with the more contemporary Taco Bell Chihuahua, Cheetos Chester Cheetah, and Chic-fil-A cows.

In contrast to brand personification, brand anthropomorphization enlists fictitious characters with both human traits and human form. In one of the most fascinating cases of brand anthropomorphization, the California Raisin Advisory Board, working with its advertising agency, Foote Cone and Belding, employed claymation (stop-motion animation) to bring its dried and shriveled commodity to life. In 1987, the agency created The California Raisins, a fictitious rhythm and blues musical group, that debuted singing Marvin Gaye's 1968 classic, "Heard It through the Grapevine." The annual advertising budget was estimated at $40 million. The dancing raisins created such a popular brand image that the licensed dolls, toys, and mugs bearing their likenesses generated nearly $200 million in revenue. Although estimates vary, raisin sales increased dramatically during the first two years of the campaign, largely as a result of cereal marketers Post Cereal Co. and Kellogg Company bolstering the raisin content of their brands. Fewer than five years later, however, the characters lost their charm, and sales of raisins had decreased to below pre-campaign levels.[70] Perhaps the California Raisins overpowered the image of Sun-Maid, the very brand they were enlisted to help. Unlike the M&M characters, the California Raisins' faces were sculpted with distinctly human features.

Longstanding brand anthropomorphizations dot the marketing landscape, including the Jolly Green Giant, The Pillsbury Dough Boy, Mr. Clean, McGruff the Crime Dog (National Crime Prevention Council), Planter's Mr. Peanut, Froot Loops' Toucan Sam, Mrs. Butterworth, the Quaker Oats man, and the Kool-Aid man. Each is designed to "humanize" and distinguish the brand from its competitors. In a more recent example of brand anthropomorphization, the ABC network developed a comedy called "Cavemen," adapted from

Geico Insurance commercials as an offbeat commentary on ethnic prejudice from the perspective of three prehistoric guys trying to make their way in the modern world. The television show debuted in fall 2007, but didn't survive the entire season.

In sum, brand personality has long held the attention of marketing professionals, who are interested in "striking the right chord" with their target markets.[71] Humanizing a brand empowers it to play a more central role in the consumer's life, potentially allowing consumers to project a desirable aspect of him or herself.[12] Research has demonstrated that consumers purchase brands not only for their functional benefits, but also for their symbolic roles. Brand personality dimensions can affect consumer behavior as a result of self-expressive needs expressed when consumers choose brands representing an extension of their actual or ideal-self concepts. Furthermore, brands are also capable of affecting consumers' self-concepts. Recent research provides evidence that a brand's personality can be transferred to consumers. Specifically, when consumers think about "sincere" brands, they view themselves as more agreeable. When consumers consider "competent" brands, they see themselves as more sophisticated.[72] This is particularly true for consumers who believe that their personalities are fixed and cannot be improved by their own efforts; they use brands to signal their positive qualities to themselves and others.[73] These findings highlight the extraordinary power of brand personalities. Not only do consumers choose brands because they want to underscore some aspect of who they are or who they want to be, but—to some extent—brands also make consumers who they are.

Global Perspectives

Brand Personalities Differ by Country

Brand personality may be critical to developing brand loyalty, but the specific dimensions that describe a brand's personality can differ from country to country. These differences reflect cultural dissimilarities in basic values. For example, Korean and U.S. cultures exhibit different values, which are reflected in the way the two countries view the same brands.[74]

In Western cultures, consumers emphasize emotional independence, privacy, autonomy, and individual needs. Westerners tend to focus on self-reliance, hedonism, and competition. Americans in particular value individualism.[75] In contrast, East Asian cultures tend to value emotional dependence, group harmony, cohesion, and the collective over the individual. Koreans in particular draw on their Confucian heritage, where harmony among humankind is the overarching goal.

Research shows that when Korean and U.S. consumers perceive powerful global brands, such as BMW, Samsung, Nike, Mercedes Benz, Sony, Levi's, and Adidas, they see cultural-specific brand personalities. Koreans perceive these global brands to be more likeable, sophisticated, intelligent, and big than do Americans. U.S. consumers, on the other hand, perceive the same set of brands as more competent, trendy, rugged, and traditional than do Koreans.[74] The implications for global marketers are clear: do not assume that a global brand has a one-size-fits-all personality. Marketers need to make sure that a brand's personality is adapted or customized to the characteristics of each country's culture.

OBJECTIVE ⑤ **Cognitive Factors**

One critical difference between the social sciences (e.g., consumer behavior) and the natural sciences (e.g., biotechnology) is that the former recognizes the importance of **cognitive personality variables**, those personality traits that describe an individual's mental responses to objects. Individual differences in cognition can explain how consumers respond differentially to various marketing activities. Earlier in the chapter, we learned that high self-monitors, individuals who are sensitive and responsive to social cues, constantly change and adapt their behavior to match the particular social situation. Conversely, low self-monitors behave more consistently across various situations. Similarly, **locus of control** describes the extent to which an individual possesses internal or external reinforcement beliefs. Individuals with an external locus of control believe that their outcomes are controlled primarily by fate, luck, or more powerful factors.[76] Consequently, their behaviors seem to vary almost randomly across situations. Individuals with an internal locus of control, however, believe that they are masters of their own destinies and so, are more likely to behave in accordance with their internal states, i.e., opinions, beliefs, and attitudes.[77]

In contrast to multiple trait theory, cognitive approaches often identify one particular cognitive trait relevant to consumers' beliefs, attitudes, and intentions regarding products and services. Traits labeled as "needs" generally reflect consumers' desires or tendencies to engage in specific mental activities. Three of these motivational traits—need for cognition, need for humor, and need for cognitive closure—are discussed next.

Need for Cognition

Just as there are situational differences that enhance consumers' motivations to carefully evaluate persuasive messages, personality differences can also affect consumers' processing motivation in persuasive situations. **Need for cognition** (NFC) measures an individual's natural tendency to engage in and enjoy effortful cognitive activities. Specifically, individuals high in NFC are more intrinsically motivated to engage in effortful cognitive analyses than are those individuals low in NFC.[78] Research shows that consumers who score high in NFC focus primarily on the product-relevant information in an advertisement. Motivated to evaluate the cogency of the message, these consumers are relatively unaffected by irrelevant background appeals, such as celebrity endorsements. On the other hand, consumers who score low in NFC pay attention to ancillary message cues, such as celebrities and attractive people in the ad. Related research reveals that when presented with unfamiliar brands, the attitudes of high NFC individuals are based on evaluation of product attributes, while those low in NFC develop attitudes based on simple peripheral cues.[79]

Need for cognition can also explain consumers' Internet preferences. Research evaluating individual differences in web usage shows that those high in NFC use the Web to search for product information, current events and news, and for general education purposes. In contrast, web users low in NFC are more likely to use the Web for entertainment purposes.[80] In general, those high in NFC, who enjoy thinking and effortful intellectual pursuits (e.g., chess, bridge, crossword puzzles, Sudoku), tend to be more heavily influenced by rational appeals, while those low in NFC—who do not enjoy effortful cognitive exercises and who think carefully only when necessary—are influenced more by emotional appeals.[81]

Need for cognition can provide helpful guidelines for public policy makers, who have embraced the use of marketing activities to improve public health by preventing the spread of HIV infection. A recent study shows that high NFC individuals develop a better understanding of the risks of unsafe sexual conduct when the information is presented in a written (versus comic strip) format. The opposite is true for those low in NFC.[82] Results of another study demonstrated the usefulness of need for cognition in reducing addictive behaviors, such as smoking. As their perceived vulnerability to the negative health effects of smoking increased, smokers more correctly inferred that smoking-cessation gimmicks (e.g., Quest Cigarettes) were no healthier than regular cigarettes, especially when their NFC was high. This finding was consistent with previous studies demonstrating that increased levels of motivation to process a persuasive communication are associated with more critical appraisals of that communication.[83]

Need for Humor

Humor is such a key ingredient in social communication that it is unusual to witness a casual conversation in which jokes and other humorous stimuli are *not* attempted. Similar to the need for cognition, individual differences in an individual's need for humor play an important role in the processing of persuasive communications. **Need for humor** (NFH) represents an individual's tendency to crave, seek out, and enjoy humor, a construct more motivationally driven than sense of humor.[84] The domain of NFH includes amusement, wit, and nonsense. Research suggests that the influence of humorous ad appeals are shaped by the joint interplay of the level of humor present in an ad and an individual's NFH.[85] Specifically, those consumers low in NFH appear indifferent to the level of humor in the ad, while those high in NFH not only form more favorable attitudes towards humorous ads, but are also turned off by understated or weak humor.

More interesting, NFC may act as an "on-off switch" regarding consumers' NFH. People high in NFC are motivated to process issue-relevant ad claims rather than peripheral cues, so their NFH may be switched "off" during message evaluation. As a result, the level of humor in an ad has little effect on their attitudes. In contrast, those low in NFC are not motivated to critically evaluate the message; they are interested in peripheral cues, such as humor. Consequently, their NFH is switched "on." Taken together, consumers who are *low* in NFC and *high* in NFH tend to respond most favorably to humorous ad appeals. Finally, related research indicates that NFH can influence message recall. Individuals with low NFH recall more ad claims if they do not anticipate humor to be present in the communication, i.e., the humor is completely unexpected.[86]

On the basis of humor's prevalence in advertising and the belief in its universal effectiveness, NFH may be useful as a segmentation tool. For example, it may be helpful in identifying audiences who are more likely, under certain conditions, to respond favorably to humorous ads. NFH can differentiate subjects' attitudes under varying conditions of humor content. Thus, if marketers' objectives include attitude change, humor targeted at audiences high in NFH may produce favorable results. As with other "need" traits, it is rarely practical to survey members of target audiences; however, market research may identify media vehicles that draw audiences characterized by high NFH. For example, *National Lampoon* readers, *Saturday Night Live* watchers, and Twitter users may tend to score high in NFH. Advertisers could use this information to determine which product categories or brands tend to be popular with users of these media. For instance, *Saturday Night Live* viewers may also be heavy users of video games. In a similar vein, research firms such as SRI-CBI use values and lifestyle data (VALS) to identify marketing opportunities by segmenting on the basis of key personality traits that motivate consumer behavior. The premise of VALS is that consumers express their personalities through their actions. Accordingly, VALS defines consumer segments on the basis of those personality traits that affect consumer behavior. By including NFH as a key personality variable, VALS might discover that consumers who score high in NFH are more likely to perform karaoke, attend amusement parks, and watch comedy. Thus, NFH may be helpful both in media selection and in targeting audiences for specific products and services.

Need for Cognitive Closure

When making decisions, consumers must frequently make the difficult trade-off between speed and accuracy. Some decisions require immediate action, and consumers must make quick judgments. Other tasks afford consumers the opportunity to think about the decision more carefully and for longer periods of time. A quick decision may serve as only a temporary and partial solution to a consumer's problem. For example, consumers may select a brand based on familiarity or other heuristic choice strategies. Unfortunately, the brand may not satisfy a consumer's future needs. Let's say a consumer wanted a docking station to charge and play her iPod, and she also wanted an alarm clock feature built-in. If this consumer purchased an iHome, she may later discover that the sound reproduction is inferior to such brands as Bose. Accordingly, longer deliberations generally result in better decisions. Research dealing with the **theory of lay epistemology**, the formation and use of everyday knowledge, suggests that individuals differ in the degree to which they make the important trade-off between speed and accuracy.[87] The **need for cognitive closure** (NFCC) describes a consumer's desire for definite knowledge of any kind to reduce confusion or ambiguity. As the need for cognitive closure increases, people consider fewer alternatives, consider smaller amounts of information about each alternative, make snap judgments that have obvious and immediate implications for action, and are insensitive to evidence inconsistent with their judgments. Ironically, they exhibit high levels of confidence in the appropriateness of their judgments, decisions, and actions.

In short, the need for cognitive closure promotes *epistemic seizing* and *freezing*. *Seizing* refers to the tendency to attain closure quickly, even if this means oversimplifying an issue or failing to carefully consider all sides of an issue. Alternatively, *freezing* refers to the tendency to maintain closure as long as possible, even if this means being closed-minded or unwilling to consider other options. People differ in their NFCC—some are strongly motivated to reach conclusions quickly at the risk of overlooking important qualifiers and limiting conditions; others are willing to deliberate carefully for long periods of time at the risk of appearing indecisive or to lack confidence. Situations also differ in the extent to which they increase or decrease NFCC. Time pressure increases the motivation to attain closure quickly. Concerns about accuracy and the long-term consequences of one's actions decrease motivation to attain closure quickly.

Recent research shows that the degree to which price is perceived to predict quality (the price-quality heuristic) is overestimated when consumers' NFCC is high. For people with a heightened NFCC, attaining closure quickly and perpetuating that closure are paramount. For these consumers, selectively focusing on belief-consistent information and ignoring potentially disconfirming evidence promotes closure because it allows one to reconfirm and maintain preexisting beliefs.[88] Research also reveals that when the attributes of a brand under consideration (target brand) cannot be readily compared to a previous brand (referent brand), evaluations for the target brand suffer, particularly if a consumer has a high NFCC.[89] Need for cognitive closure also provides insights into criminal investigations. Recent evidence suggests that criminal investigators with high NFCC are less likely than those low in NFCC to acknowledge observations that are inconsistent with their hypothesis about a given crime.[90]

Chapter Summary

Self-concept is the totality of an individual's thoughts and feelings about him or herself, including role identities, personal qualities, and self-evaluations. Role identities represent the various positions that consumers occupy in society. Personal qualities involve personality traits, or tendencies to behave in a certain way across similar situations. Self-evaluations are constructed when consumers consider the strength of their performances in various roles. The sum of all self-evaluations comprises self-esteem, which is the overall evaluative component of self-concept. The self-concept can be broken down into two dimensions—the actual versus ideal, each with two parts. The actual self-concept represents how consumers perceive themselves, while the actual public-concept embodies others' true perceptions of a consumer. The ideal self-concept describes how consumers would like to see themselves, and the ideal public-concept represents how consumers would like others to see them.

Self-concept is important to marketers because consumers' self-perceptions influence their attitudes toward products and subsequent purchase behavior. If marketers want consumers to recall something about their brands, they should create communications that are consistent with consumers' actual self-concepts. Alternatively, if marketers' goals involve creating positive attitudes or images about their brands, they should communicate information that is congruent with consumers' ideal self-concepts. The relationship between a consumer's self-concept and his or her possessions is called the extended self. Possessions for which we develop a deep affection are known as "loved objects." Loved objects can help consumers resolve internal psychological conflicts.

The term "malleable self" refers to the notion that consumers can hold various self-concepts about themselves. Consumers will employ a particular self-concept, depending on the situation and their level of self-monitoring, which describes the extent to which consumers use situational cues to guide their social behavior. People who change their behavior to meet the expectations of others are known as high self-monitors, while people who act primarily on the basis of their internal beliefs and attitudes are known as low self-monitors.

The process of creating contrived images for others is known as impression management. Impression management involves our appearance, ingratiation, and aligning actions. Consumers control their selection of clothes, grooming, habits, language, and possessions. Ingratiation is the purposeful attempt to gain benefits or favors from others. Aligning activities are attempts to realign our behavior so it comes close to matching norms.

A consumer's personality consists of a set of unique psychological characteristics that influence thoughts, feelings, and behavior regarding products and services. Multiple trait theory holds that individuals' personality traits describe their tendencies to respond in given ways across similar situations. Brands also have personalities, comprised of the human characteristics we associate with them. Brand personalities are derived from the typical user, typical use situation, product associations, and brand characterization.

Personality differences can affect consumers' motivation to respond favorably to marketing activities and brands. Need for cognition (NFC) describes a consumer's tendency to engage in and enjoy effortful cognitive activities. Need for humor (NFH) represents an individual's inclination to crave and engage in humor. Finally, need for cognitive closure (NFCC) explains a consumer's desire for any kind of knowledge that reduces confusion or ambiguity.

Key Terms

accounts
actual public-concept
actual self-concept
aligning activities
appearance management
brand anthropomorphism
brand image
brand personality
brand personification
cognitive personality variables
compulsive buying
disclaimers
extended self

Five-Factor Model
flattery
ideal self-concept
ideal public-concept
impression management
ingratiation
locus of control
loved objects
malleable self
need for cognition
need for cognitive closure
need for humor
opinion conformity

personal qualities
personality
personality traits
role identities
self-conceptions
self-concept
self-esteem
self-evaluation
self-monitoring
self-presentation
self-schemas
theory of lay epistemology
traits

Review and Discussion

1. What is the difference between the actual self-concept and the actual public-concept? How do the ideal self-concept and ideal public-concept differ?

2. When consumers try to recall brand information, are they more likely to reference their actual or ideal selves? When they evaluate brands, which self-concept is activated? Explain.

3. How do loved objects help consumers resolve internal (personality) conflicts?

4. How does self-monitoring help explain how consumers use their malleable self?

5. Review the three tactics of impression management. When students conjure up excuses for late assignments, what are the best tactics?

6. Review the Five-Factor Model of personality. Explain how it might be used to account for consumer complaining, compulsive shopping, and binge drinking.

7. As the marketplace becomes more crowded with brands, do you think brand personality will be more or less important to consumers? Explain.

8. Select one of your favorite brands and describe its brand personality based on the model provided in Figure 12.5. Be sure to include descriptions of the brand's typical users, typical use situations, product associations, celebrity endorser's personality traits, and brand characterizations.

9. Explain how brand characters such as Tony the Tiger, Captain Morgan, and the Budweiser Clydesdales can be useful in global marketing.

10. Review the cognitive variables, NFC, NFH, and NFCC. How can they be used to help marketers identify suitable target markets?

Short Application Exercises

1. On 15 numbered lines, write down 15 different things about yourself. Write the answers in the order that they occur to you. Do this prior to reading the next sentence. Now label each of the 15 descriptions about yourself as either:

   a. Role Identities—personal relationships, ethnic/religious groups, professional/ hobby groups

   b. Personal Qualities—abilities, attitudes, emotions, interests, motives, opinions, and traits

   c. Extended self—tangible objects that refer to your body or your possessions.

   Which of the three categories of your self-concept is most prevalent?

2. Consider the Ethics Box describing Unilever's "Real Beauty" and "Body Language" campaigns for Dove. From the viewpoint of a marketer, develop a list describing positive and negative aspects of such a campaign. Make the same list from the viewpoint of the consumer. Compare and contrast your responses.

3. Identify brands that have become a part of your "extended self" in five of the following ten categories:

- body
- personal space
- consumable goods
- durable goods
- home and property
- significant others
- children
- friends
- mementos
- pets

For example, Boflex or Lean Cuisine may help consumers view their bodies as their extended self. Golf lessons for a golf professional's daughter may allow the pro to see his daughter as an extension of himself.

4. Conduct a mini-experiment with 15 friends. First, ask each of them to indicate, on a seven-point scale, the importance of the brand name versus the warranty for a laptop. Then, administer the self-monitoring scale to each. Evaluate whether low or high self-monitors found brand name to be more important.

Managerial Application

Imagine you work in the marketing department of a major athletic shoe firm. Your supervisor wants to understand how consumers view the top competitors in terms of brand personality. Use the five dimensions of brand personality discussed in the text as a framework (see Figure 12.4).

Your Challenge:

1. Conduct a mini-experiment regarding brand personality. Ask 20 friends to write down the first several words that come to mind when they hear the brand names Nike, Adidas, and Reebok.

2. From these descriptions, summarize each of the three brands' personalities.

3. Describe the possible differences in target markets based on your research.

4. Select one particular brand and design a magazine ad that reflects what you learned from your research.

5. Explain which magazine would be an appropriate media vehicle for your ad.

End Notes

1 Patton, P. (2011, October 13). Newest Small Cars Trade on Both Looks and Personality. *The New York Times* [Online]. Available: http://www.nytimes.com/2011/10/14/automobiles/newest-small-cars-trade-on-both-looks-and-personality.html?_r=2

2 Bowman, Z. (2011, April 20). Kia Hamsters Win Nielsen's Top Auto Award for Second Year in a Row. *Autoblog* [Online]. Available: http://www.autoblog.com/2011/04/20/kia-hampsters-win-nielsens-top-auto-ad-award-for-second-year-in/#continued.

3 Rosenberg, M. (1979). *Conceiving the Self.* New York: Basic Books, Inc.

4 Gordon, C. (1968). Self-Conceptions: Configurations of Content. In C. Gordon and K. J. Gergen (Eds.), *The Self in Social Interaction, I: Classic and Contemporary Perspectives* (pp. 115–136). New York: Wiley.

5 Michener, H. A., and DeLamater, J. D. (1994). *Social Psychology* (3rd ed.). Fort Worth, TX: Harcourt Brace & Company.

6 Richins, M. L. (1991). Social Comparison and the Idealized Images of Advertising, *Journal of Consumer Research, 19,* 303–316; Richins, M. L. (1995). Materialism, Desire, and Discontent. Contributions of Idealized Advertising Images and Social Comparison. In R. P. Hill (Ed.), *Marketing and Consumer Research in the Public Interest* (pp. 109–132). London: Sage Publications.

7 Lockwood, P., and Kuna, Z. (1997). Superstars and Me: Predicting the Impact of Role Models on the Self. *Journal of Personality and Social Psychology, 73,* 91–103.

8 Kiran, K., Zinkhan, G. M. and Lum, A. B. (1997). Brand Personality and Self-Concept: A Replication and Extension. *AMA Summer 1997 Conference,* 165–171.

9 Sirgy, M. J. (1980). Self-Concept in Relation to Product Preferences and Purchase Intentions. In V. V. Bellur (Ed.), *Developments in Marketing Science, 3,* 350–355. Marquette, MI: Academy of Marketing Science; Sirgy, M. J. (1982). Self-Concept in Consumer Behavior: A Critical Review. *Journal of Consumer Research, 9,* 287–300.

10 Sirgy, M. J. (1987). The Moderating Role of Response Mode in Consumer Self-Esteem/Self-Consistency Effects. *AMA Winter Educator's Conference,* 5–55.

11 Zinkhan, G. M., and Hong, J. W. (1991). Self Concept and Advertising Effectiveness: A Conceptual Model of Congruency, Conspicuousness, and Response Mode. *Advances in Consumer Research, 18,* 348–354.

12 Swaminathan, V., Stilley, K. M., and Ahluwalia, R. (2009). When Brand Personality Matters: The Moderating Role of Attachment Styles, *Journal of Consumer Research, 35,* 985–1001.

13 Burns, Robert (2006, October 9). Army Launching "Army Strong" Campaign. *Boston.com* [Online]. Available: http://www.boston.com/news/nation/washington/articles/2006/10/09/army_launching_army_strong_ad_campaign/.

14 U.S. The Official Homepage of the United States Army (2011, May 24). Army Builds on 'Army Strong' Campaign with New Advertising. WWW.ARMY.MIL [Online]. Available: http://www.army.mil/article/57012

15 Rochelle, C. (2001, January 10). Army Retires "Be All You Can Be" Jingle. *CNN.com* [Online]. Available: http://archives.cnn.com/2001/US/01/10/new.army/index .html.

16 Belk, R. W. (1988). Possessions and the Extended Self. *Journal of Consumer Research, 15,* 139–168.

17 James, W. (1890). *The Principles of Psychology* (Vol. 1). New York: Henry Holt.

18 McClelland, D. (1951). *Personality.* New York: Holt, Rinehart, & Winston.

19 Ellis, L. (1985). On the Rudiments of Possessions and Property. *Social Science Information, 24,* 113–143.

20 Rosenblatt, P. C., Walsh, R, P., and Jackson, D. Q. (1976). Grief and Mourning in Cross-Cultural Perspective. New Haven, CT: Human Relations Area Files.

21 McLeod, B. (1984). In the Wake of Disaster. *Psychology Today, 18,* 54–57.

22 Niederland, W. G., and Sholevar, B. (1981). The Creative Process—A Psychoanalytic Discussion. *The Arts in Psychotherapy, 8,* 71–101.

23 Howard, Theresa (2005, August 28). Dove Ads Enlist All Shapes, Styles, and Sizes. *USAToday.com* [Online]. Available: http://www.usatoday.com/money/advertising/adtrack/2005-08-28-track-dove_x.htm.

24 Howard, Theresa (2006, November 11). Dove Ad Gets Serious for Super Bowl. *USAToday.com* [Online]. Available: http://www.usatoday.com/money/industries/retail/2006-01-11-dove-usat_x.htm.

25 Gibson, M. (2010, June 29). Dove's "Real Beauty" Campaign: Seeking Models Only? *Time Newsfeed* [Online]. Available: http://newsfeed.time.com/2010/06/29/doves-real-beauty-campaign-seeking-models-only/.

26 Clegg, Alicia (2005, April 18). Dove Gets Real. *Brandchannel.com* [Online]. Available: http://www.brandchannel.com/features_effect.asp?pf_id=259#more.

27 Chapman, M. (2011, March 30). Dove Ditches "Real Beauty" in Favour of "Body Language." *MarketingWeek* [Online]. Available: http://www.marketingweek.co.uk/sectors/fmcg/dove-ditches-%E2%80%98real-beauty%E2%80%99-in-favour-of-body-language/3025003.article.

28 Sherry, J. F., and McGrath, M. A. (1989). Unpacking the Holiday Presence: A Comparative Ethnography of Two Gift Stores. In E. C. Hirschman (Ed.), *Interpretive Consumer Research* (pp. 148–167). Provo, UT: Association for Consumer Research.

29 Ahuvia, A. C. (2005). Beyond the Extended Self: Loved Objects and Consumers' Identity Narratives. *Journal of Consumer Research, 32,* 171–184.

30 Snyder, M. (1974). The Self-Monitoring of Expressive Behavior. *Journal of Personality and Social Psychology, 30,* 526–537.

31 Snyder, M., and Tanke, E. D. (1976). Behavior and Attitude: Some People Are More Consistent Than Others. *Journal of Personality, 44,* 501–517.

32 Graeff, T. R. (1996). Image Congruence Effects on Product Evaluations: The Role of Self-Monitoring and Public/Private Consumption. *Psychology & Marketing, 13,* 481–499.

33 Becherer, R. C., and Richard, L. M. (1978). Self-Monitoring as a Moderating Variable in Consumer Behavior. *Journal of Consumer Research, 5,* 159–162.

34 Mischel, W. (1968). *Personality and Assessment.* New York: John Wiley & Sons.

35 Markus, H., and Kunda, Z. (1986). Stability and Malleability of the Self-Concept. *Journal of Personality and Social Psychology, 51,* 858–866.

36 Aaker, J. (1999). The Malleable Self: The Role of Self-Expression in Persuasion. *Journal of Marketing Research, 36,* 45–47.

37 Snyder, M. (1987). *Public Appearances, Private Realities: The Psychology of Self-monitoring.* New York: W. H. Freeman.

38 Tetlock, P., and Manstead, A. S. (1985). Impression Management versus Intrapsychic Explanations in Social Psychology: A Useful Dichotomy? *Psychological Review, 92,* 59–77.

39 Stone, G. P. (1962). Appearances and the Self. In A. Rose (Ed.), *Human Behavior and Social Processes* (pp. 86–118). Boston: Houghton Mifflin.

40 Von Baeyer, C. L., Sherk, D. L., and Zanna, M. P. (1981). Impression Management in the Job Interview: When the Female Applicant Meets the Male (Chauvinist) Interviewer. *Personality and Social Psychology Bulletin, 7,* 45–51.

41 Schlenker, B. R., and Leary, M. (1982). Audiences' Reactions to Self-Enhancing, Self-Denigrating, and Accurate Self-Presentations. *Journal of Experimental Social Psychology, 18,* 89–104.

42 Baumeister, R. F., Hutton, D. G., and Tice, D. M. (1989). Cognitive Processes during Deliberate Self-Presentations: How Self-Presenters Alter and Misinterpret the Behavior of Their Interaction Partners. *Journal of Experimental Social Psychology, 25,* 59–78; Frey, D. (1978). Reactions to Success and Failure in Public and Private Conditions. *Journal of Experimental Social Psychology,14,* 172–179.

43 Harlow, R. E., and Cantor, N. (1994). Social Pursuit of Academics: Side Effects and Spillover of Strategic Reassurance Seeking. *Journal of Personality and Social Psychology, 66,* 386–397.

44 Jones, E. E., and Wortman, C. (1973). *Ingratiation: An Attributional Approach.* Morristown, NJ: General Learning Press.

45 Tice, D. M., Butler, J. L., Muraven, M. B., and Stillwell, A. M. (1995). When Modesty Prevails: Differential Favorability of Self-Presentation to Friends and Strangers. *Journal of Personality and Social Psychology, 69,* 1120–1138.

46 Schlenker, B. R. (1975). Self-Presentation: Managing the Impression of Consistency When Reality Interferes with Self-Enhancement. *Journal of Personality and Social Psychology, 32,* 1030–1037.

47 Byrne, D. (1971). *The Attraction Paradigm.* New York: Academic Press.

48 Cline, T. W., Mertens, D. P., Vowels, N. S., and Davies, A. (2009). All Ingratiation Is Not Equal: A Two Dimensional Model of Consumer Ingratiation, *Society for Consumer Psychology 2009 Winter Conference.*

49 Hunter, C. H. (1984). Aligning Actions: Types and Social Distribution. *Symbolic Interactions, 7,* 155–164.

50 Hewitt, J. P., and Stokes, R. (1975). Disclaimers. *American Sociological Review, 40,* 1–11.

51 Riordan, C. A., Marlin, N. A., and Kellogg, R. T. (1983). The Effectiveness of Accounts Following Transgression. *Social Psychology Quarterly, 46*, 213–219.

52 Blumstein, P. W. (1974). The Honoring of Accounts. *American Sociological Review, 39*, 551–566.

53 Referred to as the "father of psychoanalysis," Sigmund Freud (1856–1939) popularized such notions as the unconscious, defense mechanisms, dream symbolism, psychosexual development, and Freudian slips. Freud maintained that a person's personality is developed based on a fundamental, internal conflict between physical gratification and appropriate social behavior. Freud's work is preserved in the 24-volume *The Standard Edition of the Complete Psychological Works of Sigmund Freud.* (2001). London: Hogarth Press.

54 Horney, K. (1950). *Neurosis and Human Growth.* New York: Norton; Jung, C. G. (1959). The Archetypes and the Collective Unconscious. In H. Read, M. Fordham, and G. Adler (Eds.), *Collected Works* (Vol. 9, part 1). Princeton, NJ: Princeton University Press.

55 Cattell, R. B. (1957). *Personality and Motivation: Structure and Measurement.* New York: Harcourt, Brace & World.

56 Goldberg, L. R. (1992). The Development of Markers for the Big Five-Factor Structure. *Psychological Assessment, 4*, 26–42.

57 Wiggins, J. S. (1996). *The Five-Factor Model of Personality.* New York: Guilford Press.

58 Mowen, J. C. (1999). Understanding Compulsive Buying among College Students: A Hierarchical Approach, *Journal of Consumer Psychology, 8*, 407–430.

59 Faber, R. J., and O'Guinn, T. C. (1988). Compulsive Consumption and Credit Abuse. *Journal of Consumer Policy, 11*, 97–109.

60 Harris, E. G., and Mowen, J. C. (2001). The Influence of Cardinal-, Central-, and Surface-level Personality Traits on Consumers' Bargaining and Complaint Behaviors. *Psychology & Marketing, 18*, 1155–1185.

61 Schoen, H., and Schumann, S. (2007). Personality Traits, Partisan Attitudes, and Voting Behavior: Evidence from Germany. *Political Psychology, 28*, 471–498.

62 Hopwood, C. J., Morey, L. C., Skodol, A. E., Stout, R. L., Yen, S., Ansell, E. B., Grilo, C. M., and McGlashan, T. H. (2007). Five-Factor Model Personality Traits Associated with Alcohol-Related Diagnoses in a Clinical Sample. *Journal of Studies on Alcohol & Drugs 68*, 455–460.

63 Aaker, J. L. (1997). Dimensions of Brand Personality. *Journal of Marketing Research, 35*, 347–356.

64 Park, B. (1986). A Method for Studying the Development of Impressions of Real People. *Journal of Personality and Social Psychology, 51*, 907–917.

65 McCracken, G. (1989). Who Is the Celebrity Endorser? Cultural Foundations of the Endorsement Process. *Journal of Consumer Research, 16*, 310–321.

66 Batra, R., Lehmann, D. R., and Singh, D. (1993). The Brand Personality Component of Brand Goodwill: Some Antecedents and Consequences. In D. A. Aaker and A.

Biel (Eds.), *Brand Equity and Advertising* (pp. 83–96). Hillsdale, NJ: Lawrence Erlbaum Associates.

67 Keller, K. (1993). Conceptualizing, Measuring, and Managing Customer-based Brand Equity. *Journal of Marketing, 57*, 1–22.

68 Gecko-Mania Sweeps Country. [Online]. Available: http://www.geico.com/about/background /geicoWordSponsor.htm. Retrieved July 27, 2007.

69 M&M Characters Are US Favourites. [Online]. Available: http://www.bandt.com.au/news/89/0c027889.asp. Retrieved September 23, 2004.

70 *Forbes,* June 17, 1996.

71 Ogilvy, D. (1983). *Confessions of an Advertising Man.* New York: Dell.

72 Fennis, B. M., Pruyn, A. T., and Maasland, M. (2005). Revisiting the Malleable Self: Brand Effects on Consumer Self-Perceptions of Personality. *Advances in Consumer Research, 32*, 371–377.

73 Park, J. K, and John, D. R. (2010). Got to Get You into My Life: Do Brand Personalities Rub Off on Consumers? *Journal of Consumer Research, 37*, 655–669.

74 Sung, Y. and Tinkham, S. F. (2005). Brand Personality Structures in the United States and Korea: Common and Culture-Specific Factors, *Journal of Consumer Psychology, 15* (4), 334–350.

75 Triandis, H. C. (1995). *Individualism and Collectivism,* Boulder, CO: Westview.

76 Rotter, J. B. (1966). Generalized Expectancies for Internal versus External Control of Reinforcement. *Psychological Monographs, 80*, (1, Whole No. 609).

77 Sherman, S. J. (1973). Internal-External Control and Its Relationship to Attitude Change under Different Social Influence Techniques. *Journal of Personality and Social Psychology, 26*, 23–29.

78 Cacioppo, J. T., and Petty, R. E. (1982). The Need for Cognition. *Journal of Personality and Social Psychology, 42*, 116–131.

79 Haugtvedt, C. P., Petty, R. E., and Cacioppo, J. T. (1992). Need for Cognition and Advertising: Understanding the Role of Personality Variables in Consumer Behavior. *Journal of Consumer Psychology, 1*, 239–260.

80 Tuten, T. L., and Bosnjak, M. (2001). Understanding Differences in Web Usage: The Role of Need for Cognition and the Five-Factor Model of Personality. *Social Behavior and Personality, 29*, 391–398.

81 Venkatraman, M. P., Marlino, D., Kardes, F., and Sklar, K. B. (1990). The Interactive Effects of Message Appeal and Individual Differences on Information Processing and Persuasion. *Psychology & Marketing, 7*, 85–96.

82 Carnaghi, A., Cadinu, M., Castelli, L., Kiesner, J., and Bragantini, C. (2007). The Best Way to Tell You to Use a Condom: The Interplay between Message Format and Individuals' Level of Need for Cognition. *AIDS Care, 19*, 432–440.

83 Cacioppo, J. T., Petty, R., Feinstein, J., and Jarvis, B. (1996). Dispositional Differences in Cognitive Motivation: The Life and Times of Individuals Varying in Need for Cognition. *Psychological Bulletin*, *119*, 197–253.

84 Cline, T. W., Machleit, K., and Kellaris, J. J. (1999). Is There a Need for Levity? In K.A. Machleit and M. Campbell (Eds.), *Proceedings of the Society for Consumer Psychology 1998 Winter Conference*. Austin, TX: American Psychological Association.

85 Cline, T. W., Altsech, M. B., and Kellaris, J. J. (2003). When Does Humor Enhance or Inhibit Ad Responses? The Moderating Role of Need for Humor, *Journal of Advertising*, *32*, 31–46.

86 Kellaris, J. J., and Cline, T. W. (2007). Humor and Ad Memorability: On the Contributions of Humor Expectancy, Relevancy, and Need for Humor. *Psychology & Marketing*, *24*, 497–509.

87 Kruglanski, Q. W., and Webster, D. M. (1996). Motivated Closing of the Mind: "Seizing" and "Freezing." *Psychological Review*, *103*, 263–283.

88 Cronley, M. L., Posavac, S. S., Meyer, T., Kardes, F. R., and Kellaris, J. J. (2005). A Selective Hypothesis Testing Perspective on Price-Quality Inference and Inference-based Choice. *Journal of Consumer Psychology*, *15*, 159–169.

89 Zhang, S., Kardes, F., and Cronley, M. (2002). Comparative Advertising: Effects of Structural Alignability on Target Brand Evaluations. *Journal of Consumer Psychology*, *12*, 303–311.

90 Ask, K., and Granhag, P. A. (2005). Motivational Sources of Confirmation Bias in Criminal Investigations: The Need for Cognitive Closure. *Journal of Investigative Psychology and Offender Profiling*, *2*, 43–63.

MARKETING METRICS

Measuring Loved Objects

Imagine that you work for a marketing research firm. Your firm is trying to determine which categories of product are most likely to achieve "loved" status. With this information, you will be able to advise clients who are marketing "loved objects" on how to build highly emotional campaigns and personalities for their brands that tug on the heartstrings of potential consumers. The following data represent responses from 20 randomly selected consumers, ten women and ten men (column 2). Columns 3–6 provide consumers' responses to the following statement, "I love my _____," on a five-point Likert Scale, where 5 = strongly agree, and 1 = strongly disagree.

Response Data (DT8-1.xls)

(1) Customer Number	(2) Gender 0=M, 1=F	(3) Automobile (1–7 Scale)	(4) Pet (1–7 Scale)	(5) House (1–7 Scale)	(6) Cell Phone (1–7 Scale)
1	0	1	2	3	2
2	0	3	4	1	3
3	0	4	3	3	1
4	0	1	2	2	3
5	0	3	2	4	1
6	0	4	4	3	2
7	0	2	1	3	4
8	0	5	3	4	1
9	0	1	4	3	5
10	0	5	2	2	3
11	1	3	4	3	2
12	1	4	5	2	4
13	1	3	4	4	1
14	1	5	4	3	1
15	1	3	3	2	3
16	1	1	5	4	2
17	1	4	4	3	2
18	1	3	4	3	5
19	1	5	5	2	4
20	1	3	5	2	1

Your Task:

Use the Excel file (DT8-1.xls) to execute the following analyses:

1. Compute means (statistical averages) for columns 3–6. Does one product category stand out as having achieved "loved status"? Does any category fall short? Use the following Excel formula: =Average(range).

2. A standard deviation depicts the variation or "spread" inherent in a data set. Higher standard deviations indicate that there is disagreement among the respondents, whereas lower standard deviations indicate more agreement. Compute the standard deviations for Columns 3–6. Does one product category exhibit more variation?

3. It may be useful to see if women and men indicate higher levels of "loved status" for various product categories. Conduct a two-sample (independent) *t-test* to determine whether men and women differ in their views toward automobiles. Find the data analysis tab and click "t-Test: Two Sample Assuming Unequal Variances." For variable range 1, use B2:B11. For variable range 2, use B12:B21. Use 0 for the hypothesized mean difference, put the output in G2, and click OK. The first three rows in the second column of output show the statistics for men, whereas the first three rows in the third column of output show the statistics for women.

   • Who likes their automobiles more, men or women?

   • Is there a difference in the variance between men and women? What does this imply?

   • Look at the two-tailed p-value for the test: $P(T<=t)$ two tail. $1-$(p-value) provides the level of confidence in concluding that there are statistically significant differences between men and women with regard to the loved status of their cars. How would you interpret the findings?

4. Compare how people feel about their pets versus how they feel about their cell phones. This requires a paired (or matched) *t-test* because we are pairing responses to two questions rather than comparing the responses to one question between two groups. Find the data analysis tab and click "t-Test: Paired Two Sample for Means." For variable range 1, use C1:C21. For variable range 2, use E1:E21. Use 0 for the hypothesized mean difference, put the output in G15, and click OK.

   • Look at the two-tailed p-value for the test: $P(T \leq t)$ two tail. $1-$(p-value) provides the level of confidence in concluding that there are statistically significant differences between how the entire sample feels about pets versus cell phones. How would you interpret the findings?

SOCIAL INFLUENCE AND BEHAVIORAL COMPLIANCE

OBJECTIVES *After studying this chapter, you will be able to …*

1. Define behavioral compliance

2. Explain the automaticity principle

3. Explain the commitment and consistency principle

4. Explain the reciprocity principle

5. Explain the scarcity principle

6. Explain the social validation principle

7. Explain the liking principle

8. Explain the authority principle

The Power of Influence

Sarah recently graduated from college and landed a new job requiring some travel to and from work. She decided to shop for a new car. Sarah was leaning towards a mid-sized hybrid SUV with all-wheel drive. After several hours of comparing models and prices on the Internet, she was ready to visit a dealership.

After browsing a car lot with several brands of hybrids, an unassuming salesperson approached her and said, "I'm here to help you find the right automobile for *your* needs." The salesperson was not pushy at all. In fact, he seemed genuinely curious about her life. "Where do you live? Tell me about your new job. What are your hobbies?" As it turns out, the salesperson seemed remarkably similar to Sarah. He had graduated from the same high school as she, enjoyed the same hobbies, listened to the same music, and rooted for the same sports teams.

Sarah was initially overwhelmed with all the possible options available in different hybrid models such as engine size, gas mileage, safety features, and so on. The salesperson indicated that he could simplify the decision. He asked Sarah a series of questions about her driving habits. After a few calculations, the salesperson recommended the Ford Escape Hybrid. The base model happened to be on sale this weekend for only $29,999, or $2,000 off the original price. In fact, The Ford Escape Hybrid was listed as a "best buy" in a leading consumer magazine. "Thousands of satisfied customers have already chosen it; they can't all be wrong," claimed the salesperson. Sarah took a test drive and liked the car. "Another customer was looking at this vehicle today," he said cautiously. "If I were you, I'd purchase it while it's still available."

Sarah had become committed to the Ford Escape Hybrid, and she seized the opportunity to buy the last remaining unit. She waited patiently for the salesperson to return with the paperwork. Upon returning, the salesperson told Sarah, "This particular vehicle includes a number of important upgrades, such as rearview camera system and optional Active Park Assist to aid in parallel parking. They are not included in the base price—but the difference is only an additional $2,999. You're going to love the automatic parking feature." The salesperson went on, "I assume that you would like the three-year, Easy-Care warranty?" "It covers on-site service with no trip charge, all non-technical service calls, and common repairs due to normal use. That's an additional cost of only $1,999, but it practically pays for itself in two years," the salesperson noted. Sarah wasn't expecting an expensive warranty fee, so she declined this particular add-on. "I understand," the salesperson remarked sympathetically. "How about the one-year Easy-Care for only $999? It will save you some much time and stress." Sarah quickly accepted this more reasonable deal and drove off in her new hybrid, thanks in large part to a well-trained salesperson who understands the principles of social influence.

OBJECTIVE # Defining Compliance

The car salesperson is not the only influence agent in the marketplace. Fund-raisers, politicians, con artists, bosses, parents, friends, family members, and even professors use a variety of techniques to get consumers to say "yes." The wording of their requests is crucial—a request worded one way may be effective, but if the same request is worded just a little differently, it may be completely ineffective. Timing is also important, as the window of opportunity when people may be susceptible to a request is narrow. Consumer psychologists use the term **verbal compliance** to describe a situation where someone says "yes" to a specific request. The term **behavioral compliance** describes a situation where someone actually carries out that request. Researcher Robert Cialdini has conducted many pioneering scientific investigations of behavioral compliance techniques and has uncovered numerous principles about their effectiveness. You can be sure that con artists and others who like to persuade us wish that Professor Cialdini had kept his findings to himself.[1] This chapter discusses some findings uncovered by Cialdini and other researchers and offers a glimpse of the interesting experiments that generated the principles. Specifically, seven key principles of behavioral influence are explained: automaticity, commitment and consistency, reciprocity, scarcity, social validation, liking, and authority. Knowing these principles helps consumers become more influential with people. Perhaps even more important, understanding how these principles work helps consumers stay on guard against unwanted influence.

OBJECTIVE # The Automaticity Principle

People often use simple heuristics when evaluating the requests of others, sometimes automatically. The **automaticity principle** is the cornerstone of all influence techniques. As the name suggests, this principle asserts that people often think mindlessly and as a result, behave automatically, without fully evaluating the consequences of a request. Harvard University psychologist Ellen Langer[2] finds that people typically spend a large portion of their day in a mindless state. Routine, habitual behaviors (like answering a text message or responding to "good morning") are performed over and over with relatively little conscious thought because people don't have the time or resources to think carefully about everything they do. Only a few important behaviors receive careful consideration; others are carried out mindlessly.

Suppose a student is about to use the photocopier in the school library and another student approaches her and says, "Excuse me, I have five pages. May I use the copy machine?" Such a small request typically involves little thought, and many people simply agree without considering the consequences. After all, five pages isn't much. Moreover, people are more likely to comply with a small request if you give them a real reason to comply. In fact, this is precisely what happened in a classic field experiment conducted by Langer and her colleagues.[3] (A field experiment is an experimental study conducted in the real world, as opposed to a laboratory setting.) When the request was basic (i.e., no additional information was provided), compliance was 60%. This is called the control group. In contrast, when the request included real information (e.g., "Excuse me, I have five pages. May I use the photocopier *because I'm in a rush*?"), compliance rates increased to 94%. The most interesting results, however, occurred when the word *because* was used without any real information (known as placebic information). The request, "Excuse me, I have five pages. May I use the photocopier *because* I have to make copies?" generated compliance of 93%, statistically equivalent to compliance for the real request. How could this happen? Clearly, placebic information is less compelling than real information. According to the **because heuristic**, however, people tend to process small requests mindlessly. So, merely hearing the word *because* may be enough to trigger compliance. With mindless processing, people don't evaluate the specific reasons for a request. If they hear the word "because," they simply move forward with compliance. "Because" is a signal—a green light for carrying out the request. But that's not the entire story. When the request was changed from small (5 copies) to large (25 copies) the results also changed. People don't automatically agree to everything. Relatively larger requests tend to encourage more purposeful thinking, which reduces the effect of the because heuristic. This is exactly what happened in Langer's study. When the request was, "Excuse me, I have 25 pages. May I use the photocopier?" compliance rates dropped to 24%. Furthermore, the because heuristic did not increase compliance in this large request condition; it remained at 24%. In contrast, when real information was given with the large request, compliance increased from 24% to 42%. These findings suggest that when people have a substantial request, providing real information is the best strategy. In contrast, if a request is relatively small, people may respond favorably simply by hearing the magic word "because." There's no need to come up with elaborate excuses. Figure 13.1 provides a summary of this interesting study.

The because heuristic involves the use of only one cue or piece of information—the word "because." Other, potentially more relevant pieces of information tend to be neglected. Although the rationale provided *after* the word "because" should be important, people often ignore it as a result of mindless thinking. They respond automatically.

FIGURE 13.1 | Mindless Compliance Experiment

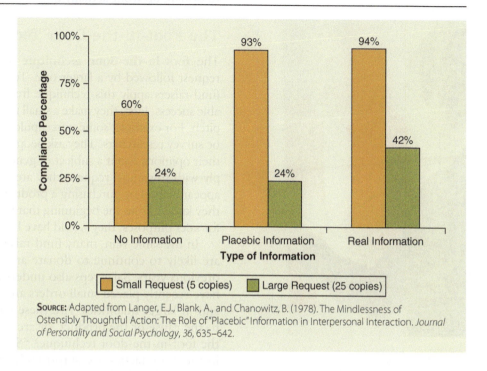

Source: Adapted from Langer, E.J., Blank, A., and Chanowitz, B. (1978). The Mindlessness of Ostensibly Thoughtful Action: The Role of "Placebic" Information in Interpersonal Interaction. *Journal of Personality and Social Psychology, 36*, 635–642.

OBJECTIVE ③

The Commitment and Consistency Principle

Pressure to maintain consistency is surprisingly powerful. People are expected to exhibit beliefs, attitudes, and behaviors that are stable and coherent. Inconsistencies often invite interpretations of personality flaws or, in extreme cases, mental illness.[4] This principle is known as the **commitment and consistency principle**. When people identify an inconsistency in their pattern of beliefs, they often change one or more beliefs to balance the system. People also attempt to keep their relationships and attitudes consistent. Similarly, when people initially say "yes" to a request or offer, they are likely to continue to say "yes" to subsequent requests regarding the same topic or task. After complying with an initial small request, people tend to comply with larger requests. And after initially saying "yes" to a deal, people tend to stick with their initial commitment—even if the deal changes.

The influence of commitment and consistency extends to fund-raising drives. An interesting study shows that consumers' own self-prophecy can increase their donations.[5] Self-prophecy is founded on two psychological effects. First, asking people to make predictions about socially influenced behaviors can cause people to respond as they think they should. Second, when later asked to perform those same behaviors, people tend to remain consistent with their predictions. In this particular study, when asked to predict whether they would donate to their university fund drive, 49% of the people predicted they would

Foot-in-the-door tactics often involve asking consumers for their opinions, followed by a sales pitch.

do so. In contrast, only 30% of the group that was simply asked to donate up front actually did so.

The Foot-in-the-Door Technique

The **foot-in-the-door technique** involves a making a small request followed by a larger one. Telemarketers, sales reps, and fund-raisers apply this technique frequently and with considerable success. First, they make a small request. Then comes the real pitch. For example, some unscrupulous telemarketers pretend to be survey researchers. They ask people if they are willing to share their opinions about a subject of general interest. If people comply with this initial request, they are more likely to continue to appear helpful by purchasing a product or service. However, had they known from the beginning that the phone call was primarily for sales purposes, they would have been more resistant.

In the same vein, many fund-raisers know that past donors are likely to continue to donate and at greater levels than in previous years. Sales reps also understand that customers who have recently placed small orders are likely to continue to buy and in larger quantities. Are these customers genuinely loyal to the cause or the product, or are they simply falling prey to the foot-in-the-door technique? "Start small and build" foot-in-the-door tactics are surprisingly simple to recognize and dangerously effective.[6]

In another classic field experiment, people went door-to-door asking California residents to post a large, ugly sign on their front lawns.[7] The sign read, "Drive Carefully." Not surprisingly, only 17% of the residents agreed to this target request. The results changed dramatically, however, when the foot-in-the-door technique was applied. When people were first asked to carry out a small favor (posting a small "Be a Safe Driver" sign in their yards), 76% complied with the larger, target request and posted the bigger, uglier sign. These results are even more interesting when you realize that the large request was made nearly two weeks after the small request and that two different people made the requests. In contrast, if the small favor dealt with a *topic* that was unrelated to the large request (e.g., posting a small "Keep California Beautiful" sign instead of a "Drive Carefully" sign) or if the initial, small *task* was different from the larger request (e.g., sign a petition instead of posting a small sign), compliance for the larger, target request decreased significantly from 76% to 48%. These results demonstrate a critical lesson. The foot-in-the-door technique is not as effective if the task or topic of the initial, small request is unrelated to the larger, target request. In both cases, people feel less connected to the original request and correspondingly their need to behave consistently attenuates.

The most widely accepted psychological explanation for the foot-in-the-door technique is based on self-perception theory.[8] **Self-perception theory** suggests that complying with a small request leads people to label themselves as helpful, good citizens or as reasonable people. Once people have labeled themselves as such, they have a strong desire to maintain this self-perception, and they are likely to continue complying. Figure 13.2 is a bar graph depicting the findings of research on foot-in-the-door technique.

FIGURE **13.2** | Foot-in-the-Door Technique

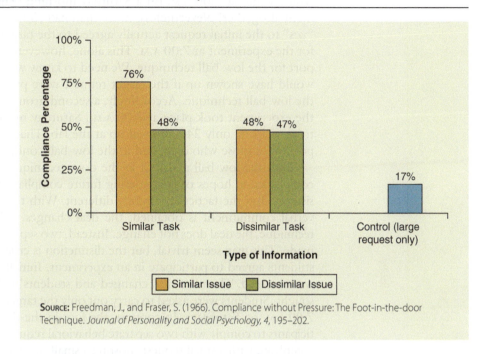

Source: Freedman, J., and Fraser, S. (1966). Compliance without Pressure: The Foot-in-the-door Technique. *Journal of Personality and Social Psychology, 4,* 195–202.

The foot-in-the-door technique is surprisingly easy to apply. Complying with small requests like, "Will you do me a small favor?," "Would you like to test drive this vehicle?," "Would you like to try on this suit?," "Try a sample of this perfume," and "Sign up for a free 30-day trial membership for Internet anti-malware protection" is all that is necessary to establish an initial commitment. Once the foot is in the door, consumers too often comply with the larger, more substantial request that follows.

The Low-Ball Technique

Car salespersons are notorious for their use of the **low-ball technique**. They try to get an initial commitment, and then they change the deal. First, the salesperson offers a consumer an attractive deal. Next, the consumer completes half a dozen forms and falls in love with the car. But after the consumer is committed, the deal changes. The consumer learns that the car is actually more expensive than originally thought. Perhaps the salesperson made a mistake, or the cost of an expensive option was not included. Maybe the salesperson's boss did not approve the sale. Sometimes the deal changes at the last possible moment, even when a consumer is signing the financial agreement. Whatever the case, once consumers commit to a deal, they tend to stick with it, even when it is no longer as attractive.

Professor Cialdini first learned about the low-ball technique while pretending to be a sales trainee at a Chevrolet dealership. After experiencing the technique first-hand, he returned to his psychology lab and began conducting a series of experiments.[9] Both experiments involved college students. In the first study, students were approached on their way to classes and asked if they would be willing to participate in an experiment. This is a reasonable request. Experiments can be fun, and so most students said, "Yes." But then the deal changed. After agreeing to participate, students were told that the experiment would begin at 7:00 A.M. on a Saturday morning. That's a different arrangement altogether! Nevertheless, more than half (56%) of the students who said "yes" to the initial request actually agreed to the target request and showed up for the experiment at 7:00 A.M. This alone, however, doesn't demonstrate support for the low-ball technique. We need to know what proportion of students would have shown up if the target request were presented up front, without the low-ball technique. Accordingly, a second group of students was told that the experiment took place at 7:00 A.M., Saturday morning. Of those agreeing to participate, only 24% showed up at the lab. That's fewer than half the proportion of those who complied in the low-ball condition.

Both the low-ball and foot-in-the door techniques involve obtaining initial compliance in hopes of engendering future compliance through mindless consistency. But the tactics are slightly different. With the low-ball technique, after verbal commitment is obtained, the deal changes. With the foot-in-the-door technique, the deal does not change. Instead, two separate behavioral requests are made. This may seem trivial, but the distinction is crucial. In the low-ball study, students agreed to participate in an experiment. Initially, only verbal compliance was obtained. Then the deal changed and students' behavioral compliance was sought. Students were asked to carry out only the target request (e.g., show up at 7:00 A.M. on Saturday). In contrast, the foot-in-the-door experiment asked participants to comply with two separate behavioral requests. After first agreeing and complying with a small request (posting a small sign), they were asked to comply with the second, target request (posting a larger sign). The low-ball technique is convincing. But so is the foot-in-the-door technique. Which is more influential? Professor Cialdini matched the two techniques, head-to-head, in a second study.

In this field experiment, students were approached in their dorms. In the low-ball condition, students were first asked if they would be willing to help with the United Way—a request requiring verbal compliance only. After obtaining the crucial "yes," the deal changed and students were then told that they needed to go to the dormitory's front desk to get the door posters. This was the target request. In the foot-in-the-door condition, students were first asked to display a small window poster that was given to them—a small behavioral request. If they complied with this small request, they were asked to go to the dormitory's front desk to get the door posters, the same target request as in the low-ball condition. In the control group, students were simply asked, up front, to go to the dormitory's front desk to get the door posters. The low-ball technique was the winner. Only 10% of the students complied with the target request in the foot-in-the-door condition, but 60% complied when the low-ball technique was employed. Interestingly, 20% complied in the control condition. Figure 13.3 provides a summary of the results.

Why is the low-ball technique so effective? Research shows that it works through the principle of commitment and consistency. **Commitment theory** suggests that the purpose of obtaining an initial commitment is to impart resistance to change. People don't like to change their minds. It suggests internal contradiction that creates psychological disharmony. The low-ball technique works by first gaining closure and commitment to an idea or deal. When people become committed to a deal, they feel compelled to behave in such a way that maintains their consistency. Thus, they sustain their commitment, even after

FIGURE 13.3 | Low-Ball versus Foot-in-the-Door

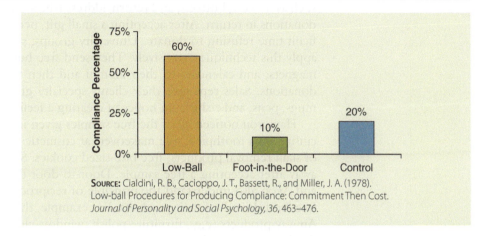

SOURCE: Cialdini, R. B., Cacioppo, J. T., Bassett, R., and Miller, J. A. (1978). Low-ball Procedures for Producing Compliance: Commitment Then Cost. *Journal of Personality and Social Psychology, 36,* 463–476.

the deal changes. Let's return briefly to the opening vignette in this chapter. The car salesperson applied the low-ball technique when he told Sarah that the only model she liked included upgrades of $2,999. He knew that after hours evaluating various cars and settling on a particular brand, Sarah was committed.

It is important to recognize that car salespeople and experimenters are not the only ones who use the low-ball technique. People get low-balled every day. The low-ball technique is particularly effective when the initial agreement is a no-brainer—quick and easy. Obtaining public commitment is also crucial. People are especially resistant to change when others hear them agree to a deal. People don't want to appear wishy-washy in front of others. Finally, research shows that the low-ball technique is most powerful when people believe that they agreed to the initial request by their own free will. So, the next time someone asks, "Would you do me a favor?" the correct answer is, "It depends. Tell me what the favor is *first*."

The **bait-and-switch** tactic is a special case of the low-ball technique. Sometimes known as the *lure procedure*,[10] this approach "lures" customers by advertising a low-priced product or service. When customers discover that the product is not available, a salesperson encourages them to purchase a substitute that, of course, costs more. Bait-and-switch is considered fraud if the supplier is not capable of actually selling the advertised product. However, if the seller is able to sell the advertised product, but simply chooses to aggressively promote a competing product, no fraud exists. The bait-and-switch tactic operates under the same principle as the low-ball technique. Customers become committed to the low-priced "bait." When the good deal is taken away, customers feel uncomfortable and seek to reduce this discomfort by accepting the "switch," so long as the new offer is a reasonable substitute.

OBJECTIVE **4**

The Reciprocity Principle

When someone does you a favor, you feel obligated to return it in kind. This is the premise of the **reciprocity principle**. It is not just a principle of social etiquette; it's also a surprisingly powerful influence technique. The problem is that people are often tricked into returning much larger favors than they receive. For example, nonprofit organizations often give people small gifts—such as flowers, buttons, and return address labels—and then ask for charitable donations in return. After accepting a small gift, people have a surprisingly difficult time refusing to donate. University groups, such as alumni associations, apply this technique extensively. They send free bumper stickers, refrigerator magnets, and calendars to their alumni and then follow up with appeals for donations. Sales reps give their clients specialty gifts or *swag*, such as coffee mugs, pens, and t-shirts, in hopes of creating a feeling of reciprocity.

Have you noticed all of the free samples given in shopping malls? Japanese cuisine on a toothpick, free makeovers at cosmetic boutiques, demonstrations of stain removal products, free bite-sized cookies. Sometimes it's hard to walk away after accepting a free sample. Door-to-door distributors such as Amway and Avon also understand the principle of reciprocity. Their salespeople offer free "test drives" of their products. For example, the BUG consists of a bag of Amway products (e.g., furniture polish, window cleaner, detergent, shampoo, deodorizer, pesticide). Amway salespersons leave the BUG with clients for a few days and ask them to try the products for free. After accepting the BUG bait, people are more likely to purchase items from Amway.

A free sample invokes the reciprocity principle, where the recipient of the sample oftentimes feels obligated to make a purchase in return.

Sheldon Lewis / Alamy

Infomercial sponsors are particularly skilled at applying reciprocity. Proactiv Solutions, Boflex Extreme, Total Gym 1500, One-Touch Can Opener, Magic Bullet Blender, Hip-Hop Abs, and Core Secrets all offer "no-obligation" deals, which operate similarly to free samples. Even children's magazines, such as *Highlights*®, offer evaluation samples to induce trials for their brands. Of course, after consumers use the products in their homes for several weeks, the likelihood of returning them is low.

The Door-in-the-Face Technique

Invoking the reciprocity principle need not involve free gifts, samples, or test-drives. More subtle approaches are also used. For example, following up a large, unreasonable request with a smaller, more sensible request usually improves behavioral compliance. This is known as the **door-in-the-face technique**. The design is opposite of the foot-in-the-door technique, which involves a small request followed by a large request. Instead, when influence agents make a large request that is rejected, they often follow up with a smaller, more sensible request. The smaller request is a concession, and it often engenders reciprocity. When someone tries to act reasonably with us, we feel compelled to reciprocate and act reasonably in return. The technique is sometimes referred to as "rejection followed by moderation." Salespersons and other influence agents know full well that the initial, unreasonable request will be rejected, and the likelihood of obtaining compliance will increase with the second, more moderate request. For example, salespersons often try to sell expensive three-year service plans and extended warranties. Initially, they use fear tactics to sell the general idea of a warranty. After the expensive plan is rejected, they offer a less expensive, one-year service plan. On the basis of reciprocity, consumers often accept the more reasonable offer. Returning again to the opening story in this chapter, the salesperson offered Sarah an expensive three-year, Easy Care warranty for $1,999. When she rejected it, the salesperson quickly offered a more reasonable, one-year warranty for $999—which Sarah accepted without resistance.

A series of interesting field experiments was designed to test the effectiveness of the door-in-the-face technique.[11] In the first experiment, college students were approached on their way to class and asked to work for two years as unpaid volunteers for the Juvenile Detention Center. Not surprisingly, no one complied. Immediately after rejecting this request, students were asked to volunteer to take a group of juveniles to the zoo for two hours. Fifty percent agreed to this more reasonable target request. But is the door-in-the-face technique more effective than simply making the target request up front? A control condition was included to test this possibility. A separate group of students was simply asked to volunteer to take a group of juveniles to the zoo for two hours. Only 17% agreed. In other words, the door-in-the-face technique was more effective than simply making the target request up front.

Still, it is possible that the 50% who verbally complied did so not because of their feelings of reciprocity but because of a simple contrast effect. After all, two hours of volunteer work looks relatively small when contrasted with two years. A third experimental condition tested this hypothesis. A separate group of students was asked, up front, to choose directly between the two alternatives (volunteer for two years *or* two hours). In this condition, only 25% agreed to take the juveniles to the zoo for two hours (half the rate of the door-in-the face technique). This provides strong evidence that the door-in-the-face technique does not operate through a simple compare and contrast effect. Figure 13.4 provides a graphic of these results.

Although the door-in-the-face technique appears not to operate via contrast, a second study evaluated reciprocity as the underlying mechanism. In this experiment,

FIGURE 13.4 | Door-in-the-Face Technique

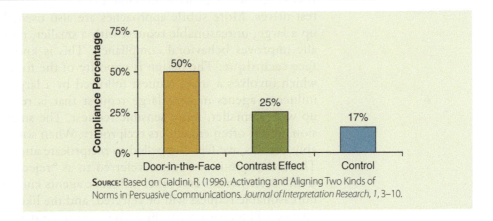

SOURCE: Based on Cialdini, R. (1996). Activating and Aligning Two Kinds of Norms in Persuasive Communications. *Journal of Interpretation Research, 1,* 3–10.

students were asked to serve as unpaid volunteers for a group of low-income children (not juvenile delinquents). After this request was rejected, students in the door-in-the-face group were asked to take the children to the zoo for two hours (the same target request as in the first study). Again, the door-in-the-face technique was effective, as 54% agreed to the target request. A second group of students was also exposed to the door-in-the-face technique, with one critical twist: Two *different* people made the requests. One individual made the initial large request, and a different individual made the second, more reasonable request. Consistent with the reciprocity principle, the two-requestor condition approach was less effective, as only 33% complied. Thus, a concession occurs only when the *same* individual makes both requests. This is intuitively appealing. Reciprocity is about relationships. People feel reciprocity to other people—not to abstract objects or ideas.

Which is more effective, the door-in-the-face technique or the foot-in-the-door technique? You probably know the answer already: "It depends." In a study that directly compared the two techniques, the timing of the requests was varied.[12] In a no-delay condition, the initial and target requests were administered back-to-back, as in the previous studies. In the delay condition, however, seven to ten days separated the requests. The target request was the same for both techniques. Participants were asked to distribute 15 traffic safety pamphlets to their neighbors. In the door-in-the-face condition, this request was preceded by a very large unreasonable request: "Would you keep a record of traffic flow at a busy intersection for two hours?" In the foot-in-the-door condition, the target request was preceded by a very small request: "Would you answer a few short questions about driving safety?" The results of the study clearly indicate that the door-in-the-face technique was more effective than the foot-in-the-door technique when there was no delay in the requests. Conversely, the foot-in-the-door technique outperformed the door-in-the-face technique when the second request was delayed. The illusion of concession is shattered after a period of several days. Consumers' feelings of reciprocity dissipate over time, and thus, the rejection-then-moderation approach is only effective when the requests are close in time. Consistent with the self-perception explanation of the foot-in-the-door technique, the start-small-and-build approach is effective regardless of the timing of the requests. Labeling oneself as helpful and compliant apparently has more long-lasting consequences than does reciprocity. Thus, these two multiple-request techniques operate by different psychological processes. Figure 13.5 provides a summary of the findings.

FIGURE **13.5** | **Door-in-the-Face versus Foot-in-the-Door**

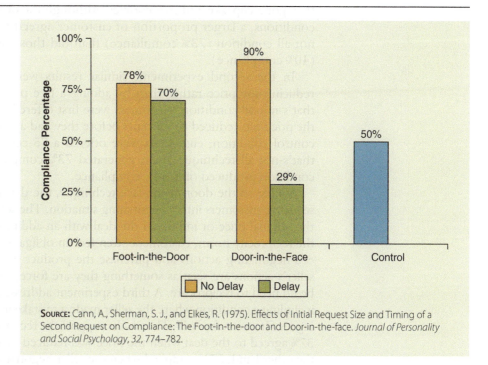

SOURCE: Cann, A., Sherman, S. J., and Elkes, R. (1975). Effects of Initial Request Size and Timing of a Second Request on Compliance: The Foot-in-the-door and Door-in-the-face. *Journal of Personality and Social Psychology, 32,* 774–782.

Firms that sell knives and other household items via infomercials often use the that's-not-all technique.

The That's-Not-All Technique

The Ginsu knife, blue-light specials at Kmart, and vacation packages to Cancun, Mexico, are classic examples of the **that's-not-all technique**. Infomercials and shopping networks are notorious for applying this technique to drowsy viewers at 3:00 A.M. How does it work? Opposite of the low-ball-technique, the that's-not-all technique starts high and builds in a downward fashion. The initial deal is changed into an even better deal *before* the consumer has an opportunity to reject the first offer. Long before the consumer can generate counterarguments, extra gifts, deeper discounts, and more attractive financing are incrementally added to the original offer (e.g., "Today only, the Ginsu Stainless Block Set has been reduced in price from $129.95 to $89.95. But that's not all. Order today and you get a free pair of kitchen shears. And if you order with a credit card right now, we'll make the first payment for you!"). The that's-not-all technique invokes the norm of reciprocity: with each increment, the sponsor appears to be offering a better and better deal, so the customer feels an increasing obligation to comply in response to these concessions. It is all part of a social norm—a general rule of behavior.

Professor Jerry M. Burger conducted a series of field experiments to test the effectiveness and underlying causes of the that's-not-all technique.[13] In the first experiment, customers in the that's-not-all condition were offered a cupcake for 75 cents at a college bake sale, but the deal was sweetened (literally) by adding two free cookies before the customers had a chance to respond. In the control condition, customers were told up front that for 75 cents, they got a cupcake and two cookies. Although the deal was identical for both conditions, a larger proportion of customer agreed to the deal in the that's-not-all condition (73% compliance) than did those in the control condition (40% compliance).

In the second experiment, similar results were obtained—this time by reducing the price rather than by adding a free product to the deal. In the that's-not-all condition, customers were first offered a cupcake for $1.00, but the price was reduced to 75 cents before they had a chance to say "no." In the control condition, customers were offered a 75-cent cupcake up front. The that's-not-all technique again generated 73% compliance, while the control condition produced only 44% compliance.

Similar to the door-in-the-face technique, the that's-not-all tactic works by seducing customers into a negotiating situation. The seller has come down from the original price or improved the deal with an additional product. Abiding by the reciprocity norm, customers often feel an obligation to reciprocate the seller's negotiating actions and purchase the product. On the other hand, if the seller's actions are seen as something they are forced to do, then there should be no need to reciprocate. A third experiment addressed this very hypothesis by including a condition where the seller made a mistake in price rather than reducing it of her own free will. The results support the reciprocity explanation, as only 37% agreed to the deal when the price was reduced as a result of a *mistake*. On the other hand, 57% complied when the seller negotiated the price downward.

The next experiment tested a simple contrast-effect explanation. Is reciprocity really the motivation for complying, or does 75 cents simply compare favorably to $1.00? One group of customers was told that the cupcakes sold for 75 cents; a second group was told that they cost $1.00. Next, both groups were asked how much they would be willing to pay for the cupcakes. The groups estimated similar price points. This indicates that a contrast effect is not driving customers' decisions.

A follow-up experiment compared the that's-not-all-technique against a common bargain technique. Prices were raised beyond the prices in the earlier studies to reduce mindless compliance. In the that's-not-all condition, $1.25 cupcakes were reduced to $1.00 because the students wanted to close down the bake sale. In the bargain condition, customers were told, "These are only a dollar now. We were selling them for $1.25 earlier." Compliance was significantly higher in the that's-not-all condition (55%) than in the bargain condition (25%). This provides evidence that a perceived bargain cannot account for the effectiveness of the that's-not-all technique.

If reciprocity is the underlying motive for both the that's-not-all and the door-in-the-face techniques, which tactic is superior? In the final experiment, these two techniques were matched head-to-head. Recall that the door-in-the-face technique allows customers the opportunity to refuse the initial deal or request and a second, more reasonable offer follows. In contrast, the that's-not-all technique offers a better deal immediately, eliminating the opportunity to refuse the initial offer. In the that's-not-all condition, the price of the cupcakes was reduced from $1.25 to $1.00 as in the previous study. In the door-in-the-face condition, cupcakes were initially offered for $1.25. If customers refused this deal, *then* the price was reduced to $1.00. In the control condition, cupcakes were sold for $1.00 up front. Compliance was highest in the that's-not-all condition, second for door-in-the-face, and lowest in the control condition.

There are two important lessons to learn from Professor Burger's field studies. First, the that's-not-all technique operates through the principle of reciprocity. When salespeople offer better and better deals, customers often feel obligated to reciprocate these acts of concession. So, consumers can avoid unnecessary feelings of reciprocity by focusing only on the final deal—without considering the incremental offers. Second, similar to the because heuristic, the that's-not-all technique is only effective when consumers behave relatively mindlessly. Of course, consumers can avoid the negative consequences of mindless behavior by concentrating on real information—evaluating the substance, not the fluff.

The Multiple-Deescalating-Requests Technique

The door-in-the face technique involves two separate requests—a large request followed by a smaller, more reasonable appeal. The **multiple-deescalating-requests technique** involves more than two requests. However, it differs from the that's-not-all technique in that once a request is refused, additional requests follow—one after the other—until one is finally accepted. In contrast, the that's-not-all technique provides multiple offers without allowing customers to respond until the final deal is presented. Research shows that the multiple-deescalating-requests technique can be effective in the context of university fund-raising. Telemarketers initially request $1,000 donations for their university. If this request is rejected, a request of $750 follows. If this fails, there is an appeal for $500, and so on. This approach yields greater compliance rates and donation amounts compared with a standard request. Moreover, the multiple-deescalating-requests technique is more effective than presenting statistical information about typical donation levels and ranges (a common fund-raising technique). In fact, presenting statistical information is no more effective than the standard request.[14] These results are consistent with the automaticity principle and with research on consumers' tendency to neglect statistical information.

The Even-a-Penny Technique

Influence agents can appear to be reasonable and induce clients to comply through a wide variety of reciprocity-based tactics: free gifts, concessions, or multiple concessions. Another way to appear reasonable is to make extremely small requests. This approach is known as the **even-a-penny technique**, and it involves the legitimization of trivial contributions (e.g., a penny, a dollar, one minute of your time). Research shows that this approach can be effective in increasing compliance rates without decreasing the average amount donated by contributing individuals in fund-raising efforts. One field study tested the effectiveness of the even-a-penny technique by soliciting donations door-to-door for

© Craig Wactor/Shutterstock.com

the American Cancer Society.[15] In the control group, potential donors were given the standard plea, "Would you be willing to help by giving a donation?" In the even-a-penny condition, the solicitor added, "Even a penny will help." The even-a-penny technique generated almost twice the compliance rate (50%) as the control condition (28%). More interesting, the median dollar contributions by individuals were identical. This is a powerful lesson for nonprofit organizations: The even-a-penny technique does not sacrifice dollar contributions for higher compliance rates. Further research shows this technique can increase donations to the American Heart Association[16] and the Reye's Syndrome Foundation. Finally, this reciprocity-based technique appears to be equally effective in both face-to-face and telemarketing contexts.[17]

OBJECTIVE **5**

The Scarcity Principle

"While Supplies Last," "Limited Edition," "Sale Ends Soon," and "One-Time-Offer" all proclaim a sense of urgency to imply scarcity for products and services. Do consumers prefer items that are abundant or rare? According to the **scarcity principle**, people often want what they cannot have. Consumers also want things that may not be available in the future. Stamp collectors covet the rare Curtis Jenny inverted airmail stamp. Only 100 were created in 1918, all on a single sheet created by a printer error. Baseball card collectors dream about the scarce 1909 T206 Honus Wagner tobacco card, also known as the "Holy Grail of baseball cards." Incredibly, this 1-7/16" × 2-5/8" card was once owned by hockey great Wayne Gretzky and recently sold for $2.35 million to an anonymous Los Angeles buyer.[18] The scarcity principle rests on the premise that because valuable objects are rare, it follows that rare objects must be valuable. This backwards logic is known as **affirmation of the consequent**, or confusion of the inverse. In fact, there are lots of scarce items that have little value—obsolete mainframe computers, turntable record players, and manual typewriters, to name a few. Still, consumers associate scarcity with value. Clever marketers create scarcity by limiting production or supply. Some manufacturers, including Harley-Davidson and Porsche, deliberately limit production on expensive models. In the case of Harley-Davidson, some customers are willing to wait more than a year to take title to their new motorcycles. Other marketers influence perceptions of scarcity by limiting distribution. Until July 2000, L.L.Bean resisted expanding its bricks-and-mortar retail stores beyond its single outlet in Freeport, Maine. White House Black Market (WHBM), a high-end women's clothing boutique, does not distribute its products through discount retailers such as Walmart. Firms like WHBM understand that consumers' perceptions of exclusivity are inversely related to distribution intensity and that exclusive (or scarce) products command higher margins. For decades, the DeBeers Company has successfully convinced consumers that diamonds are rare. Diamonds, which are basically compressed carbon, have not been "rare" since their discovery in South Africa in 1867. Today, diamonds are mined in about 25 countries, on every continent except Europe and Antarctica.

Government attempts to limit the availability of a product via prohibition or censorship often backfire because telling us we cannot have a product makes us want it even more. During the Prohibition Era in the United States, alcoholic beverages became scarcer and so, more desirable. Consequently, consumers went to great lengths (even committing crimes) to obtain alcohol. Similarly, telling us *not* to do something makes the behavior more desirable. For example, some research raises questions about the effectiveness of the D.A.R.E. Program (Drug Abuse Resistance Education).[19] Similar criticisms have been raised against programs aimed at reducing teenage smoking and alcohol consumption. In the mind of a teenager, "If everyone is telling us not to do it, it must be *really* good." Censorship can also increase demand.[20] The publication of Salman Rushdie's *The Satanic Verses* in 1988 provoked violent reactions from radical Muslims because it was perceived as irreverently portraying the prophet Muhammad. Rushdie received threats and a fatwa issued by Ayatollah Khomeini, calling for his execution. How did the book sell? It headlined on *The New York Times* bestseller list for more than a year and has produced 14 hardcopy editions since, quite a feat for a modern-day novel that received mixed reviews and was generally regarded as not being an easy read.

Research on the effects of scarcity show that reducing availability increases desirability. Field experiments demonstrate that something as simple as the number of chocolate chip cookies in a jar can exert a surprisingly powerful effect on the desirability of a product.[1] Participants in a field study selected more cookies when there were only two (versus ten) cookies in the jar. This effect was more pronounced when limited product availability was the result of an accident (i.e., the experimenter grabbed the wrong jar). Moreover, desire for the scarce cookies was highest when product availability was reduced because of demand (i.e., the product was chosen frequently by previous participants). Interestingly, these scarcity effects did not occur because of preferences in taste.

It is important to guard against the power of the scarcity effect when marketers inundate us with claims of product shortages or limited time offers. Recall the Xbox 360 shortage during Christmas, 2005? Rumors of retail shortages sent consumers scurrying to eBay to buy the product for as much as $3,000. The bidding wars that ensued only pushed prices higher (the manufacturer's suggested retail price was about $399). Judging by the thousands of Xbox 360 listings on eBay during that holiday season, one might wonder if the shortage was real or simply crafted to benefit the scalpers.

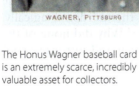

The Honus Wagner baseball card is an extremely scarce, incredibly valuable asset for collectors.

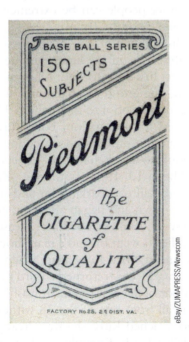

OBJECTIVE ⑥   # The Social Validation Principle

Thousands of satisfied customers can't be wrong, and firms like Procter & Gamble, Toyota, and Verizon Communications spend more than $1 billion in advertising each year reminding us of the popularity of their brands. For decades, McDonald's has proclaimed "over one billion [hamburgers] sold." Public broadcasting stations, charity telethons, and university fund-raisers delight in presenting long lists of names of individuals who have been involved in their causes in the past. Salespeople often provide prospects with their list of clients, emphasizing that some of the names are friends or acquaintances of the prospect. In televised fund-raising drives, dozens of telephones are ringing and volunteers are answering them, supposedly taking the names of eager contributors. Shopping networks show a digital count of the number of units sold along with the time remaining until the product sells out, and eBay displays the cumulative number of bids and times the page has been visited for each auction item. Bartenders, street musicians, and deli-clerks, among others, salt their tip jars to give the impression that many people leave tips—and large ones. Nightclub ushers limit the number of people allowed into the club so that long lines form outside the door, suggesting that the club is extremely popular. Canned laugh tracks are still used on television sitcoms to make the shows seem funnier (even though people claim not to like canned laughter).[21]

What do all these examples have in common? They are applications of the **social validation principle**, also known as "proof in numbers." The social validation principle maintains that the perceived validity (or correctness) of an idea increases as the number of people supporting the idea increases. In fact, the opinions of other people can be extremely informative, especially under conditions of ambiguity or uncertainty.[22]

Presenting a list of supporters or donors to a prospect is known as the **list technique**. Research on the list technique shows that it can significantly increase compliance. In a door-to-door fund-raising campaign for the American Heart Association, one group of prospective donors was shown a long list of names of previous donors prior to the request. The control group received only the standard request for a donation. Forty-three percent donated in the list technique condition, but only 25% donated in the control condition.[23]

People also look to the behavior of others when they decide *not* to do something. On March 13, 1964, Catherine "Kitty" Genovese parked her car by the Long Island Railroad parking lot and began walking home. Winston Mosley chased her down and began attacking her. Injured and terrified, Kitty screamed, "Oh my God! He stabbed me! Please help me!" Mosley fled when nearby apartment lights went on and a man shouted, "Let that girl alone!" But Mosley returned and stabbed Kitty again when no one actually came forward to help. At 3:25 A.M., Mosley returned a third time and stabbed Kitty as she lay inside the front door of her apartment. It wasn't until 3:50 A.M. that the police finally received a call from one of the 38 witnesses to the murder. Tragically, by the time police reached Kitty, she was already dead.[24] Why did none of the witnesses help? What kind of people would simply watch and not intervene?

These questions have been asked over and over again. The truth is, the witnesses' behavior—though disturbing—is normal. Classic research on bystander nonintervention shows that people are less likely to help a person when many other people are present.[25] One explanation for this bystander nonintervention is that people don't think others need help if no one else appears alarmed or concerned. People look for cues from other group members. If no one quickly steps forward to act, then the likelihood of anyone acting decreases and a snowball of pluralistic ignorance ensues. This peculiar inaction among group members is known as the **diffusion of responsibility**. In fact, people are much more likely to help when they perceive themselves to be the only person available to help, i.e., responsibility for helping the person in need cannot be diffused.

Do consumers diffuse their responsibilities in the marketplace? Do they ignore good causes when few people seem to support them (e.g., world hunger)? Do consumers shy away from superior products that lack advertising clout (e.g., blood pressure monitors)? Conversely, do they jump on the bandwagon of brands because we see others buying them (e.g., iPads and smartphones)? Classic research indicates that people observe and model (imitate) the behavior of others.[26] Moreover, the effects of peer pressure and conformity on consumers' perceptions of what is correct can be powerful.[27]

Global Perspectives

Persuasion versus Negotiation: East versus West

According to Don E. Schultz, professor emeritus-in-service at Northwestern University in Evanston, Illinois, Western countries view marketing communication differently than do the Chinese. The West uses marketing communication primarily to persuade— to get people to accept the value of their propositions and agree with their arguments. This is evident in their advertising appeals: proofs, demonstrations, testimonials, and comparisons. Each of these is designed to convince and persuade the audience. In contrast, the Chinese see marketing communication as a tool for negotiating—situations to be considered, bargained for, and haggled over.[28] Each is designed to come to an arrangement on a price or value on which both parties agree and are comfortable.

Professor Schultz argues that in the United States, "we... try to convert others to our way of thinking. We try to convince them to forego present products and services and to switch to our brand of offering. Alternatively, the Chinese are consummate negotiators. They've practiced the skill and art

of negotiation for 50 or so centuries—trading and bartering and sharing value through negotiation during that entire period."

Shultz maintains that marketing has become difficult in the West because we live in a *negotiated* marketplace, and yet Western marketing communication is designed to be *persuasive*. New media forms such as social media, blogs, and interactivity are negotiated, unlike traditional media, such as TV, magazines, or newspapers, which serve as one-way forums for persuasion. Hence, the mismatch: the West is attempting to force persuasion into negotiated media, and it doesn't fit. Ironically, a majority of social media sites such as Facebook, YouTube, LinkedIn, and even Twitter were invented in the United States. Perhaps marketing communication will adapt to the new media in an attempt to bring people together, not just for the purposes of selling, but to create sharing, conversation, and long-term, value-laden, win-win relationships. After all, isn't that the purpose of marketing?[28]

Cultural and Individual Differences

All consumers are not equally susceptible to peer pressure. High self-monitoring individuals (those who are highly sensitive and responsive to social cues) are more susceptible to social influence than are low self-monitors.[29] Individuals from collectivistic (versus individualistic) cultures are also more given to social influence.[30] Members of individualistic cultures tend to define themselves as independent from groups and focus on personal goals, while members of collectivistic cultures define themselves in terms of group membership and emphasize group goals. In general, Western cultures such as North America and Western Europe are individualistic and Eastern cultures such as Japan, South Korea, and China are more collectivistic. Even within a culture, however, people differ. Those with a strong collectivistic (versus individualistic) orientation tend to be more responsive to social influence, regardless of the prevailing culture. In fact, research indicates that individual differences may be more important than cultural differences.[31]

An interesting study tested the effectiveness of social-validation procedures versus commitment and consistency techniques for influencing consumers in the United States and Poland. The United States is considered an individualistic culture, while Poland is considered relatively more collectivistic. Individual differences were also measured using an individualistic/collectivistic personality scale. Students were asked to imagine that they had been approached by a representative from the Coca-Cola Company who wished to ask them some questions about Coca-Cola. In the social-validation condition, students were told that all (or half) their classmates had agreed to participate. In the commitment and consistency conditions, students were told that, in the past, their classmates had always (or never) complied with survey requests. Two important findings emerged. First, the social-validation procedure was more effective with the Polish students, but the commitment and consistency technique worked better with the American students. Second, students' personal orientation (individualistic versus collectivistic) had a stronger impact on their compliance than did the overall cultural orientation.[31]

Injunctive versus Descriptive Norms

Sometimes well-intended communications may actually send the *wrong* message. In 1971, Keep America Beautiful, Inc., created a dramatic public service announcement hoping to convince Americans to stop littering. The first spot aired on Earth Day and featured Iron Eyes Cody, a famous Native American actor, quietly canoeing through a polluted river. As Iron Eyes Cody emerged from the river near a busy highway, a motorist threw a bag of garbage, which splattered at the Indian's feet. The ad ended with a close-up of Iron Eyes' solemn face, and a tear trickles down his cheek (this classic PSA can be viewed online at www.kab.org, on the About Us page). Titled "People Start Pollution, People Can Stop It," the ad became a classic and was partially credited with helping to establish the nascent environmental movement in the United States. But did it send the wrong message?

Despite the drama created by the "Iron Eyes Cody spot," research shows that the ad contains features that may encourage behavior opposite of that supported by the sponsors.[32] Recall that **norms** serve as important behavioral guidelines for a culture. Professor Cialdini's research suggests that Keep America Beautiful may have unwittingly pitted two specific types of social norms against one another—descriptive and injunctive norms. **Descriptive norms** involve perceptions of which behaviors are common or popular, i.e., what is everyone doing? Previous research has demonstrated the powerful influence of descriptive norms. For example, by increasing the number of people looking up from a street corner to a bogus image in the sky, experimenters increased the number of pedestrians who also stopped and looked up.[33] By observing what most other people are doing, people can imitate these common actions and usually make good choices.[34] Have you ever attended a church, synagogue, or mosque that was foreign to you? If so, you understand the importance of descriptive norms. Marketers understand descriptive norms, too. By showing crowded stores, excited customers, and declaring their brands to be "best sellers," marketers are implying that their products are desirable. The proof is in the numbers.

In contrast, **injunctive norms** involve perceptions of which behaviors are accepted or rejected by society. While descriptive norms tell us what *is* done, injunctive norms tell us what *should* be done. Injunctive norms motivate us with social rewards for appropriate behavior and social punishment for inappropriate actions. Both kinds of norms motivate human action because people tend to do what is popular *and* what society approves.[35] As such, the two norms could be potential competitors, descriptive norms pulling consumers in one direction and injunctive norms tugging the other way. Could it be that the "Iron Eyes Cody spot" sends a mixed message to its audience by showing a regrettable but common behavior? By featuring a littered environment, the audience may simply interpret the message as validating their belief that everyone litters. Worse, if the ad focuses attention on the undesirable behavior (e.g., showing someone in the act of littering), then the effect may be to increase that very undesirable behavior. If everybody's doing this, it must be normal. Here, the descriptive norm (what people actually do) may win the battle against the injunctive norm (what people ought to do). Even the voice-over for the ad, "People Start Pollution …" invokes a descriptive norm—everyone pollutes.

Professor Cialdini tested this hypothesis in a field study.[32] Flyers regarding automotive safety week were tucked under the windshield wipers of parking garage patrons. One area was filled with litter; the other was clean. In addition, patrons either witnessed a person drop a large flyer on the floor (littering condition) or witnessed a person walk by (walk-by condition). The results showed that parking patrons were more likely to litter in the littered environment than in the clean environment. More important, patrons who witnessed a person litter in the littered environment also littered more (54%) than did those patrons who saw no littering in the littered environment (32%). Finally, patrons who witnessed a person litter in the clean environment littered less (6%) than did those patrons who saw no littering in the clean environment (14%). This important interaction is depicted in Figure 13.6.

FIGURE 13.6 | **Descriptive versus Injunctive Norms**

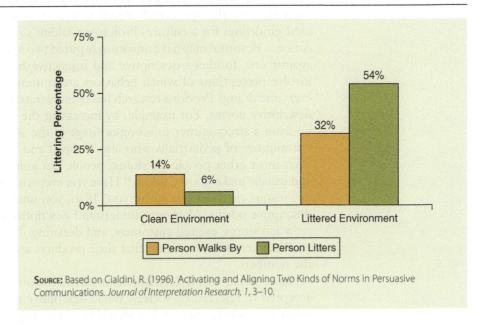

SOURCE: Based on Cialdini, R. (1996). Activating and Aligning Two Kinds of Norms in Persuasive Communications. *Journal of Interpretation Research, 1,* 3–10.

The results of this study are intuitively appealing. The rationale to litter in a dirty garage may involve something like, "Littering won't do much additional damage here; it's already a mess." Moreover, observing someone else litter in a dirty environment increases littering behavior (54%). Here the descriptive norm (everyone litters) overpowers the injunctive norm (littering is wrong). Conversely, witnessing someone litter in a very clean environment may invoke a more powerful injunctive norm, "Why would he litter? This place is clean!" The lesson from this research is important. When communicating that a particular behavior is socially objectionable, advertisers should not portray the undesirable behavior as common. Instead, they should focus their message on the desired outcome. Otherwise, they run the risk of emphasizing the descriptive norm (e.g., lots of people perform the unwanted behavior) over the injunctive norm (e.g., the unwanted behavior is wrong).

Changing behavior is important for many nonprofit organizations and cause-related marketers. Stopping smoking, driving under the influence, and texting while driving all require cessation of a negative behavior. In contrast, getting mammograms, exercising regularly, and eating healthy foods all involve the adoption of a positive behavior. In both cases, marketers who understand descriptive and injunctive norms are better equipped to obtain the desired outcome. In *The Tipping Point*, author Malcolm Gladwell discusses how social phenomena like fashion trends and crime begin, gather momentum, and finally "tip" to become epidemics.[36] He also argues that America's anti-smoking messages during the previous two decades may have backfired. Recent data from the American Lung Association indicate that approximately 20% of college students are regular smokers. But the American Lung Association notes that smoking rates among students fluctuate greatly, and they attribute the most recent decline to higher prices for cigarettes and more regulations barring smoking in public areas and colleges.[37] Gladwell argues, however, that health organizations should stop trying to change attitudes about tobacco. Smoking, *per se*, has never been cool. It's the *smokers* who are cool. From James Dean to Steve McQueen to Sarah Jessica Parker, each embodies rebellion, sexuality, and most of all, sophistication. Though Gladwell makes a case for limiting the nicotine in cigarettes and reducing smoking by understanding its links to depression, he would probably agree that emphasizing injunctive norms (smoking is bad) just fuels teenage interest in smoking. Ad campaigns that portray teenage smokers as delinquent or antisocial simply acknowledge the frequency of the behavior. Besides, teenagers are often drawn to rebellious behavior; it's part of being a teenager. The current anti-smoking campaigns run parallel to the Keep America Beautiful campaign. Both emphasize the common, descriptive norms over the prescriptive, injunctive norms. And the descriptive norms are likely to win; in other words, if everyone is doing it, it must be normal.

Marketing in Action

Back by Popular Neglect

Research in consumer behavior can be helpful to nonprofit organizations looking for solutions to national problems, such as littering. Professor Cialdini's 1996 study demonstrates that previous techniques aimed at stopping littering may actually endorse and increase littering behavior.[32] The 1971 Iron Eyes Cody public service announcement from Keep America Beautiful (KAB) is a perfect example. By showing a littered environment to the audience, with an implicit warning that littering is harmful, the audience actually views a scene validating their belief that everyone litters. KAB didn't know about Cialdini's research in 1971, but they did by 1998.

First aired on April 21 (Earth Day) in 1998, KAB's sequel to the 1971 ad recalls the famous face and tear of Iron Eyes Cody. The ad begins with a scene at an urban bus stop. Prior to climbing on the bus, a young African American woman prepares to litter her gum, a middle-aged Caucasian businessman litters his newspaper, an African American man innocently places his Styrofoam cup on the ground, while a casually dressed white man tosses his cigarette and extinguishes it with his foot. After the litterbugs get on the bus, the ad focuses on the littered environment, where a breeze tosses the trash about. Finally, the camera pans to a large poster of Iron Eyes Cody, which is strategically positioned inside the bus stop shelter. In high drama, a tear rolls down his face—the same tear he cried some 35 years ago. Unfortunately, as with the 1971 ad, the same effects are likely to occur. Once again, the ad features both a littered environment and copious littering behavior, and this time the message is even stronger—people of all races, genders, and socioeconomic backgrounds litter. It's a recipe for misinterpretation and an invitation to litter. The tagline, "Back by

Popular Neglect," refers to environmental neglect. However, it could just as easily refer to KAB's disregard for consumer research. As recently as 2012, KAB continued to emphasize littering as a descriptive norm. A link from KAB's web page, "Littering is Wrong Too," encourages consumers to write in or shoot videos of other people littering. Doesn't this just legitimize the descriptive norm?

So what is the correct approach? According to research, the lowest frequency of littering occurs when people view *one* thoughtless person littering in a *clean* environment. This approach would send the message that *few* people litter, and any individual who does so significantly harms the environment. How about a scene of Iron Eyes Cody wiping away his 42-year-old tear and replacing it with a smile as a sole litterbug changes his course by picking up not only his litter but also a misplaced item near a tidy and conspicuously positioned recycling bin?

KAB isn't the only organization that appears to ignore the recommendations of consumer research. The National Highway Traffic Safety Administration's (NHTSA) seat belt enforcement campaign, "Click It or Ticket," shows various scenes of police officers ticketing motorists who have failed to buckle up. The NHTSA cites the campaign as helping to create 82-percent seat belt usage nationwide. One can't help but wonder how high usage would be if the NHTSA's ads featured a majority of drivers buckling up and avoiding traffic tickets. Similarly, the U.S. Department of Transportation's "Sir, Have you been Drinking Tonight?" campaign presents a series of drunk drivers opening their car doors, while various forms of alcoholic beverages pour out. All of the drivers are arrested. An ad with a series of sober drivers successfully negotiating a check-point while one drunk gets caught seems more in line with Cialdini's research.

OBJECTIVE **7**   # The Liking Principle

The **liking principle** is remarkably simple—we tend to comply with the requests of those whom we like. So, the more an individual likes you, the more power you have over him or her. Your overall social power is proportionate to the number of people who like you. Take Joe Girard, for example. Joe is the famous Chevrolet salesman who won the title "Number One Car Salesman" 12 years in a row and earned more than $200,000 annually.[1] Girard is also listed as the world's greatest car salesman in the *Guinness Book of World Records*. How does he do it? Joe claims people like him because he offers his customers a fair deal. But he also does something else. Each month, Joe sends more than 13,000 greeting cards to his customers. The message inside is always the same three words, "I like you." Let's explore the formula for the liking principle. It rests on four primary factors: familiarity, attractiveness, similarity, and ingratiation.

Familiarity

The *mere exposure effect* suggests that the more familiar we become with an object, the more we like it. This explains why an initially unfamiliar stimulus such as a new song becomes more likable over time. We aren't too sure about the song the first time we hear it. After repeated exposure, however, the tune becomes more familiar; by the third or fourth play, we are singing along. Recent research shows that the mere exposure effect is also applicable to our familiarity with specific people. In a recent study, participants repeatedly viewed photographs of people's faces and then viewed the same photographs again, along with photographs of new (similarly attractive) faces. The familiar faces were rated as more likable and evoked more smiles than did the unfamiliar faces.[38] The lesson is simple: we tend to like familiar people.

Physical Attractiveness

Of all the factors influencing likability, physical attractiveness may be the most intriguing. Research shows that we automatically assume attractive people to be intelligent, kind, and honest.[39] This *halo effect* suggests that we may over-generalize, assuming that one positive trait (e.g., physical attractiveness) implies the presence of many other positive traits. Accordingly, successful marketers closely attend to the latest fashions and try to appear attractive. And they should. Research demonstrates that well-groomed female job candidates can receive more favorable hiring decisions.[40] A recent study shows that attractive men and women are more likely to be hired than less attractive applicants.[41] Another study shows that attractive employees earn approximately 12 to 14% more income than their less attractive colleagues.[42] Similarly, attractive individuals are found to experience superior levels of professional and academic development.[43]

Attractiveness effects don't necessarily end in the workplace. A mesmerizing criminal trial, known as "The Preppy Murder Trial," began during 1986. Robert Chambers was charged with and tried for the second-degree murder of Jennifer Levin, whose semi-clad body was found by a bicyclist near Fifth

Avenue and 83d Street, behind the Metropolitan Museum of Art in New York. Robert Chambers was an attractive young man. Standing 6'4" and weighing 200 pounds, his blue eyes and movie-star proportions won favor with the media. Chambers was described as a handsome "altar boy" with a promising future. In contrast, the media attacked Levin's reputation. Although the jury was deadlocked for nine days, Chambers' legal team ultimately struck a plea bargain—manslaughter. In the end, Chambers was sentenced to serve only 5 to 15 years in prison. He served all 15 years, mostly because of his bad behavior while incarcerated.

The movie-star persona of Robert Chambers may have influenced those involved in "The Preppy Murder Trial," leading to an alleviated sentence.

Does physical attractiveness affect the legal process? An experiment demonstrates that attractive defendants who serve time are less likely to return to jail than their less attractive counterparts.[44] A group of New York City inmates underwent plastic surgery to remove facial disfigurements. A second group received only the typical rehabilitation services, such as counseling and training. The group who received cosmetic surgery was significantly less likely to be re-incarcerated. There's more. Attractive people are more likely to receive help in times of need (from both sexes) than are less attractive people.[45] Finally, physically attractive politicians have been shown to receive more than twice as many votes as their less attractive opponents.[46] Overall, attractive people enjoy significant social advantages in our culture. They are viewed as more intelligent, earn higher incomes, and receive preferential treatment. Given this background, it's not surprising that Hooters of America, Inc. quickly settled a class action lawsuit for more than $3 million in exchange for the right to hire only (attractive) women as waitresses. Men are permitted to work at the Hooters restaurants, but only as cooks, dishwashers, and managers. The company website argues that "Hooters Girls" have the same right to use their natural female sex appeal to earn a living as supermodels. Hooters understands that attractiveness generates liking, and liking generates power.

It also should come as no surprise that in 2010, almost a quarter of a million cosmetic procedures were performed on young people between the ages of 13 and 19, including about 47,000 nose jobs and 9,000 breast augmentations.

This represents nearly a 10% increase in teen cosmetic surgeries since 2002.[47] At a more mundane level, how many men have grown mustaches or beards, and how many women have changed their hair color? How many people wear contact lenses to improve their youthfulness or lose weight in order to improve their body appearance? Perhaps these measures are less extreme than surgery, but they are still just a variation on an important theme—attractiveness.

Similarity

For those people who are happy with (or resigned to) their perfectly normal appearance, the *similarity tactic* can be tapped to influence liking. People tend like others who are similar to themselves in terms of appearance, attitudes, opinions, lifestyle, personality, and social or educational background.[48] Of course, the opposite is also true. We tend to dislike those who are dissimilar to us, and this finding has important implications for understanding stereotyping and prejudice.[49] One classic study from the 1970s shows that people are more likely to help those who dress as they do. An experimenter dressed either conservatively or in "hippie" garb and asked college students for a dime to make a phone call (obviously, the study took place in the pre-cell phone era). When the experimenter was dressed the same as the students, more than two-thirds of the students complied. In contrast, when the experimenter dressed differently than the students, fewer than half met his request.[50] Even trivial similarities can be influential. Recent research demonstrates that an incidental (trivial) association between individuals can have a persuasive influence in a sales context. Consumers who found that they shared the same birthday or birthplace with a service representative reported more favorable attitudes and higher purchases intentions for the salesperson's promotion.[51] Accordingly, salespeople are trained to find out what hobbies and leisure activities potential clients enjoy and to feign similar interests. Car salespeople are even trained to look in the trunks of potential clients' cars for clues. In fact, many sales training programs instruct trainees to "mirror" their client's body posture, mood, and verbal style.[52] Remember how the car salesperson in the opening vignette preferred the same music and sports as the customer? What a coincidence. The *Little Red Book of Selling* specifically instructs salespeople to establish some kind of rapport that includes finding some common ground with a customer.[53] Rapport with customers is usually established by identifying similarities in attitudes, opinions, and experiences. Because similarities can easily be manufactured and masqueraded, consumers should pay special attention to influence agents who claim to be just like them.[1]

Ingratiation

If you suspect that someone is paying you compliments because they want a favor, you're probably right. **Ingratiation** is a tactic commonly used to engender liking. It involves purposefully bringing oneself into the good graces of another person. In fact, we tend to like those who like us, and we are hopelessly addicted to compliments. Research shows that even when consumers realize that they are being flattered, they still like the flatterer. What's more, the ingratiation doesn't have to be accurate to work. Research shows that compliments

Ethics

If a salesperson at Best Buy tells you the battery of the laptop you're considering lasts "about 500 minutes," as opposed to "almost eight hours," you are likely to view his estimate as more precise—so long as you think the salesperson is knowledgeable.[54] Every day, consumers encounter dozens of numerical estimates. When talking with friends, one person might tell you that the average salary for new marketing majors last year was about $36,000 annually. Another friend reports that it was about $3,000 a month. A third friend indicates that the average pay was approximately $692 per week. Which estimate would you find more accurate? Similarly, let's say you wanted to place a custom order for furniture, and you asked the service rep how long it would take until delivery. Would it make a difference if the rep answered, "two months," "eight weeks," or "120 days"? In both examples, the respective expressions of time are identical. However, consumers perceive the speakers' reports as differentially precise and reliable.

A new study shows that the same time expression is perceived as more precise when expressed in finely-tuned units, rather than larger, coarser units. But the advantage of using fine-grained units only occurs when the communicator is assumed to have relevant knowledge and is generally trustworthy.[55] Could marketing and public relations professionals use this knowledge to deceive consumers? Not necessarily. While consumers may infer low precision from large, or coarser units, if the finely-tuned information is perceived to exceed the communicator's knowledge level, it could undermine the credibility of the claim and possibly the trustworthiness of the organization. Returning to the first example, if you believe your friend could really estimate a new marketing major's salary in weekly wages, then he'll be perceived as the most accurate. On the other hand, if you don't think his knowledge warrants that level of precision, he'll lose credibility.

by an evaluator produced the same liking whether the compliments were true or not.[56] Remembering a client's name[57] and asking a person how he or she is doing can also facilitate liking and thus, produce compliance.[58] Ingratiation, however, is not a panacea. It can backfire if the ingratiator goes too far with the flattery, making it exaggerated or inappropriate. This is known as the "ingratiator's dilemma."[59] Thus, ingratiation should be subtle. Some tactics include paying compliments about someone to a third party, agreeing with someone only *after* expressing some initial resistance, and performing useful (versus superfluous) favors, i.e., favors that actually help the target of the ingratiation.[60]

Creating **indirect associations** to a positively evaluated stimulus (such as a popular university, sports team, or brand) can also increase liking for the stimulus. For example, when our team wins, we are more likely to wear hats, hoodies, and T-shirts adorned with the team's logo. This is known as basking in reflected glory, or BIRGing. Although fans don't have much to do with the performance of the team, a victory feels like a personal triumph. On the other hand, when our team loses, it feels like a personal defeat.[61] Simply by wearing NFL gear or drinking from a mug that displays our favorite brand, we increase our likability for that particular organization. If the team or brand performs poorly, however, we tend to disassociate from the brand or cut off reflected failure, also known as CORFing.

People also like to be the first to communicate *good news*—with good reason. The positive feelings created by the good news often transfer to the communicator. **Affect transfer** is a special case of classical conditioning. It occurs when the positive affect (or feelings) created by an unconditioned stimulus becomes associated with a conditioned stimulus. Advertisers are famous for attempting to transfer the positive feelings created by the drama in an ad to the sponsored brand. Conversely, people are reluctant to communicate bad news, because the bad feelings created by unfavorable news can also be indirectly associated with the communicator. The tendency to keep mum about unpleasant messages is called the **MUM effect**.[62] Research demonstrates that the MUM effect is more pronounced when future contact with the message recipient is anticipated, because communicators are concerned about the consequences of their message.[63] In fact, the MUM effect has been around for centuries. Ancient Persian kings used to "kill the messenger" when the news was bad. In summary, the liking principle suggests that how we look and what we say makes a strong impression on others.

OBJECTIVE (8)

The Authority Principle

Why do people comply with the requests of police officers, physicians, priests, and flight attendants? They all share one important characteristic—uniforms. According to the **authority principle**, authority figures use titles, clothes (such as uniforms), or expensive possessions that convey status to impress and influence others. Disobeying authority figures can produce obvious negative consequences, but how far will people go when following the orders of someone in authority? Yale University professor Stanley Milgram attempted to answer this question in one of the most influential and controversial studies in the annals of experimental psychology.[64] Participants were told that they would take part in an experiment intended to measure the effects of punishment on learning. Participants playing the role of "teacher" read questions to other persons who played the role of "learner." The teacher was directed to inflict a series of electric shocks on the learner, increasing the intensity of the shocks with each incorrect response. An impressive array of shock switches with very clear labels (i.e., slight shock, strong shock, intense shock, danger—severe shock, and maximum 450 volts) was positioned directly in front of the teachers. As shock intensity increased, the learner screamed louder and louder, begging to be released from the experiment. However, anytime the teacher hesitated, an authority figure (dressed in a while lab coat) told the teacher that he or she must continue. How many people would administer the shocks, all the way to the maximum 450 volts?

These exact experimental procedures were described to a group of 39 psychiatrists who were asked to predict how many participants would "go all the way" and use the maximum shock on the learner. The psychiatrists predicted that only one person in a thousand, or one tenth of a percent, would pull the maximum-volt switch. The actual results are startling. Sixty-five percent of the participants complied. Fortunately, the learner was just an actor, and no real shock was delivered. Milgram was "shocked" by the results, and so he conducted the study with different people, using newspaper ads to recruit subjects from outside the university. Also, he varied the distance between the learner and the teacher and he moved the location of the laboratory away from the university. Nevertheless, the results were similar. When an authority figure in a lab coat was present, a majority of the participants continued to deliver the highest shock. Milgram's experiments showed no significant difference in compliance rates between women and men,

© istockphoto.com/Karen Mower

Uniforms are not present simply for the sake of fashion; they exude an air of authority necessary to strengthen public compliance.

and other researchers replicated the results in countries beyond the United States.[65] In an attempt to partially explain the Holocaust, Milgram originally hypothesized that Germans may be more blindly obedient to authority than Americans. In the end, however, Milgram concluded that ordinary people, simply doing their jobs, are astonishingly obedient to authority. He warned that blind obedience to authority could happen anywhere, not just in Nazi Germany.

Do consumers blindly comply with authority figures in the marketplace? A physician prescribes a series of complicated medical tests; a technical advisor instructs consumers to purchase new software; an automobile mechanic tells automobile owners that they need new brakes; a beautician recommends supplementary hair products; and a cashier tells shoppers to move to another checkout line. Usually, consumers comply. Waiters escort diners to a table (of the waiter's choice); credit card companies change their lending policies; flight attendants ask customers to switch seats with someone; orthodontists tell parents that their children need braces; even professors change their test dates. And still consumers comply. In fairness, the cost of disobeying can often be greater than the cost of complying. If patients don't submit the complicated (and expensive) medical tests, they may not survive the consequences. Foregoing anti-virus software may result in the loss of valuable data, and so on. Nevertheless, consumers should avoid *mindless* compliance. Two simple questions usually answer the question of whether consumers should comply: What is the influence agent's motive and what are the consequences of *not* complying?

Chapter Summary

People are susceptible to a wide variety of influence techniques. This chapter identifies seven key principles of influence on consumer behavior: automaticity, commitment and consistency, reciprocity, scarcity, social validation, liking, and authority. The automaticity principle recognizes that people often think mindlessly, without fully evaluating the consequences of their compliance. The commitment and consistency principle indicates that people try to maintain consistency in their belief systems. The foot-in-the-door and low-ball techniques take advantage of consumers' tendencies to choose courses of action consistent with past commitments and decisions. The reciprocity principle shows that consumers often feel obligated to return favors—often beyond the value of what they received. The door-in-the-face, that's-not-all, multiple-deescalating-requests, and even-a-penny techniques capitalize on this tendency. The scarcity principle suggests that because valuable objects are rare, consumers often assume that rare objects are valuable. Marketers create perceptions of scarcity for their goods and services by limiting distribution and emphasizing the uniqueness of their brands. The social validation principle rests on the premise that the validity of an idea increases with the number of people supporting it. In the marketplace, consumer popularity begets more popularity. Conversely, diffusion of responsibility occurs when people look for others to react first. Efforts to influence consumers can backfire if descriptive norms overpower injunctive norms. Likability is also a powerful weapon of influence; consequently, similarity, attractiveness, and impression management can be used to increase liking for a person or brand. Finally, most people are compliant with authority figures. Understanding these seven key principles of social influence can help people avoid being unduly compliant.

Key Terms

affect transfer
affirmation of the consequent
authority principle
automaticity principle
bait-and-switch tactics
because heuristic
behavioral compliance
commitment and consistency
  principle
commitment theory

descriptive norms
diffusion of responsibility
door-in-the-face technique
even-a-penny technique
foot-in-the-door technique
indirect associations
ingratiation
injunctive norms
liking principle
list technique

low-ball technique
multiple-deescalating-requests
  technique
MUM effect
reciprocity principle
scarcity principle
self-perception theory
social validation principle
that's-not-all technique
verbal compliance

Review and Discussion

1. Do you think the because heuristic would be more effective when people are busy or in a rush? Explain.

2. Both the door-in-the-face and that's-not-all techniques apply the principle of reciprocity. In fact, they both begin with deals that are eventually improved. Explain the difference between the two techniques.

3. Do you think businesses that give out free samples are mostly applying the reciprocity principle or the foot-in-the door technique? Does it depend on the nature of the sample? Explain.

4. Why do you think Cialdini found the low-ball technique to be more effective than the foot-in-the-door technique? Can you think of circumstances where the foot-in-the-door technique might be superior?

5. The door-in-the-face technique has two important limitations:

   a. The same person must make both requests.

   b. The two requests must be close in time.

   How does the principle of reciprocity explain these limitations?

6. Why do you think Cialdini found the that's-not-all technique to be more effective than the door-in-the-face technique? Are there situations where the reverse might be true?

7. What does the scarcity principle suggest about the legalization of marijuana?

8. Aren't *fads* just a special case of the social validation principle? Why do fads lose their appeal?

9. How does the mere exposure effect work?

10. Drawing on your knowledge of descriptive and injunctive norms, how well do you think abstinence programs that emphasize the high rate of teenage pregnancy will work?

Short Application Exercises

1. Conduct your own mini-experiment using the because heuristic. Test it in the cafeteria or workout room. Compare your findings to those of Langer and colleagues.

2. Make a trip to your nearest bookstore. Observe the behavior at the bargain counter. See if the number of people at the bargain counter increases when two or three stop and browse. How would you explain this behavior?

3. Conduct a mini-experiment comparing the low-ball technique against the door-in-the face technique. Make the target requests identical for both techniques. In the low-ball condition, ask a group of students for a small favor and then change it to the target request after people initially say "yes." In the door-in-the-face condition, ask a different group of students to complete a very large request. When they say "no," ask for the target request. See which technique produces the higher rate of compliance.

4. Watch 60 minutes of network television, uninterrupted. Keep a log of the commercials, tallying the number that use any of the seven principles of influence. Report the findings in a graph or table.

5. Survey 30 adults to find out how often they question their family doctors about a medical prescription. Survey 30 fellow students. Ask them if they have ever contested a traffic ticket. Do your results support the authority principle?

Managerial Application

Re-read the opening vignette in this chapter. The car salesperson attempted to apply five different behavioral compliance techniques discussed in the chapter. Imagine that you are the manager of that auto dealer and you are observing the salesperson's attempts to persuade the customer.

Your Challenge:

1. Evaluate each of the five influence techniques attempted by the salesperson. Which technique do you think was most effective? Which technique was most important in generating revenue for the dealer?

2. What could the auto dealer do to reduce the customer's cognitive dissonance relating to the purchase?

3. How could customers like the one at the auto dealer avoid being persuaded by behavioral compliance techniques?

End Notes

1 Cialdini, R.B. (2007). *Influence: The Psychology of Persuasion.* New York: HarperCollins.

2 Langer, E. J. (1978). Rethinking the Role of Thought in Social Interaction. In J. H. Harvey, W. I. Ickers, and R. F. Kidd (Eds.), *New Directions in Attribution Research* (Vol. 2, pp.35–38). Hillsdale, NJ: Lawrence Erlbaum Associates.

3 Langer, E.J., Blank, A., and Chanowitz, B. (1978). The Mindlessness of Ostensibly Thoughtful Action: The Role of 'Placebic' Information in Interpersonal Interaction. *Journal of Personality and Social Psychology, 36,* 635–642.

4 Dawes, R. M. (1994). *House of Cards: Psychology and Psychotherapy Built on Myth.* New York: Free Press.

5 Obermiller, C. (2004). Improving Telephone Fundraising by Use of Self-Prophecy. X Forum of International Association of Jesuit Business Schools, Bilbao Spain.

6 Cialdini, R.B. (2007). *Influence: The Psychology of Persuasion.* New York: HarperCollins.

7 Freedman, J., and Fraser, S. (1966). Compliance without Pressure: The Foot-in-the-Door Technique. *Journal of Personality and Social Psychology, 4,* 195–202.

8 Bem, D. J. (1972). Self-Perception Theory. In L. Berkowitz (Ed.), *Advances in Experimental Social Psychology, 1,* 199–218.

9 Cialdini, R. B., Cacioppo, J. T., Bassett, R., and Miller, J. A. (1978). Low-ball Procedures for Producing Compliance: Commitment Then Cost. *Journal of Personality and Social Psychology, 36,* 463–476.

10 Gouilloux, F., and Weber, F. (1989). The Lure: A New Compliance Procedure. *Journal of Social Psychology, 129,* 741–749.

11 Cialdini, R. B., Vincent, J. E., Lewis, S. K., Catalan, J., Wheeler, D., and Darby, B. L. (1975). Reciprocal Concessions Procedure for Inducing Compliance: The Door-in-the-Face Technique. *Journal of Personality and Social Psychology, 31,* 206–215.

12 Cann, A., Sherman, S. J., and Elkes, R. (1975). Effects of Initial Request Size and Timing of a Second Request on Compliance: The Foot-in-the-Door and Door-in-the-Face. *Journal of Personality and Social Psychology, 32,* 774–782.

13 Burger, J. M. (1986). Increasing Compliance by Improving the Deal: The That's-not-all Technique. *Journal of Personality and Social Psychology, 51,* 277–283.

14 Comer, J. M., Kardes, F. R., and Sullivan, A. K. (1992). Multiple Deescalating Requests, Statistical Information, and Compliance: A Field Experiment. *Journal of Applied Social Psychology, 22,* 1199–1207.

15 Cialdini, R. B., and Schroeder, D. A. (1976). Increasing Compliance by Legitimizing Paltry Contributions: When Even a Penny Helps. *Journal of Personality and Social Psychology, 34,* 599–604.

16 Reingen, P. H. (1978). On Inducing Compliance with Requests. *Journal of Consumer Research, 5,* 96–102.

17 Brockner, J., Guzzi, B., Kane, J., Levine, E., and Shaplen, K. (1984). Organizing Fundraising: Further Evidence on the Effect of Legitimizing Small Donations. *Journal of Consumer Research, 11,* 611–614.

18 Johnson, A. (2007, February 27). Honus Wagner Card Sells for $2.35 Million. *ABC News* [Online]. Available: http://abcnews.go.com/US/wireStory?id=2907128.

19 Research Triangle Institute (1994). Past and Future Directions of the D.A.R.E. Program: An Evaluation Review. Supported under Award # 91-DD-CX-K053 from the National Institute of Justice, Office of Justice Programs, U.S. Department of Justice.

20 Worchel, S. Arnold, S. E. and Baker, M. (1975). The Effect of Censorship on Attitude Change: The Influence of Censor and Communicator Characteristics. *Journal of Applied Social Psychology, 5,* 222–239.

21 Nosanchuk, T. A., and Lightstone, J. (1974). Canned Laughter and Public and Private Conformity. *Journal of Personality and Social Psychology, 29,* 153–156.

22 Kruglanski, A. W., and Mayseless, O. (1990). Classic and Current Social Comparison Research: Expanding the Perspective. *Psychological Bulletin, 108,* 195–208.

23 Reingen, P. H. (1982). Test of List Procedure for Inducing Compliance with a Request to Donate Money. *Journal of Applied Psychology, 67,* 110–118.

24 Rosenthal, A. M. (1969). *Thirty-eight Witnesses.* New York: Free Press.

25 Latane, B. and Rodin, J. (1969). A Lady in Distress: Inhibiting Effects of Friends and Strangers on Bystander Intervention. *Journal of Experimental Social Psychology, 5,* 189–202.

26 Bandura, A. and Menlove, F. L. (1968). Factors Determining Vicarious Extinction of Avoidance Behavior through Symbolic Modeling. *Journal of Personality and Social Psychology, 8,* 99–108.

27 Asch, S. (1948). The Doctrine of Suggestion, Prestige, and Imitation in Social Psychology. *Psychological Review, 55,* 250–276.

28 Schultz, D. E. (2010). Distance is Measured in More than Miles. *Marketing News, 44* (9), 11.

29 Bearden, W. O. and Roase, R. L. (1990). Attention to Social Comparison Information: An Individual Difference Factor Affecting Consumer Conformity. *Journal of Consumer Research, 16,* 461–471.

30 Han, S. and Shavitt, S. (1994). Persuasion and Culture: Advertising Appeals in Individualistic and Collectivistic Societies. *Journal of Experimental Social Psychology, 30,* 326–350.

31 Cialdini, R. B., Wosinska, W., Barrett, D. W., Butner, J., and Gornik-Durose, M. (1999). Compliance with a Request in Two Cultures: The Differential Influence of Social Proof and Commitment/Consistency on Collectivists and Individualists. *Personality and Social Psychology Bulletin, 25,* 1242–1253.

32 Cialdini, R. (1996). Activating and Aligning Two Kinds of Norms in Persuasive Communications. *Journal of Interpretation Research, 1,* 3–10.

33 Milgram, S., Bickman, L., and Berkowitz, O. (1969). Note on the Drawing Power of Crowds of Different Size. *Journal of Personality and Social Psychology, 13,* 79–82.

34 Cialdini, R. B. (1993). *Influence: Science and Practice.* New York: HarperCollins.

35 Deutsch, M. and Gerard, H. B. (1955). A Study of Normative and Informational Social Influences upon Individual Judgment. *Journal of Abnormal and Social Psychology, 51,* 629–636.

36 Gladwell, M. (2002). *The Tipping Point.* New York: Back Bay Books.

37 Smoking by Students Declines (2008, September 8). *Inside Higher Ed* [Online]. Available: http://www.insidehighered.com/news/2008/09/08/smoking.

38 Harmon-Jones, E., and Allen, J. J. B. (2001). The Role of Affect in the Mere Exposure Effect: Evidence from Psychophysiological and Individual Differences Approaches. *Personality and Social Psychology Bulletin, 27,* 889–898.

39 Eagly A. H., Ashmore, R. D., Makhijani, M. G., and Longo, L. C. (1991). What Is Beautiful is Good, But…: A Meta-Analytic Review of Research on the Physical Attractiveness Stereotype. *Psychological Bulletin, 110,* 109–128.

40 Mack, D. and Rainey, D. (1990). Female Applicants' Grooming and Personnel Selection. *Journal of Social Behavior and Personality, 5,* 399–407.

41 Hosoda, M., Stone-Romero, E., and Coats, G. (2003). The Effects of Physical Attractiveness on Job-Related Outcomes: A Meta-Analysis of Experimental Studies. *Personnel Psychology, 56,* 431–462.

42 Hamermesh, D. S., and Biddle, J. E. (1994). Beauty and the Labor Market. *American Economic Review, 84,* 1174–1194.

43 Dickey-Bryant, L., Lautenschlager, G. J., Mendoza, J. L., and Abrahams, N. (1986). Facial Attractiveness and its Relation to Occupational Success. *Journal of Applied Psychology, 71,* 16–19; Langlois, J. H., Kalakanis, L., Rubenstein, A. J., Larson, A., Hallam, M., and Smoot, M. (2000). Maxims or Myths of Beauty? A Meta-Analytic and Theoretical Review. *Psychological Bulletin, 126,* 390–423.

44 Kurtzburg, R. L., H. Safar, and N. Cavior (1968). Surgical and Social Rehabilitation of Adult Offenders. *Proceedings of the 76th Annual Convention of the American Psychological Association, 3,* 649–650.

45 Benson, P. L., Karabenic, S. A., and Lerner, R. M. (1976). Pretty Pleases: The Effects of Physical Attractiveness, Race, and Sex on Receiving Help. *Journal of Experimental Social Psychology,12,* 409–415.

46 Efran, M. and Patterson, E. (1974). Voters Vote Beautiful: The Effect of Physical Appearance on National Debate. *Canadian Journal of Behavioral Science, 6,* 352–356.

47 American Society of Plastic Surgeons (ASPS), cited in Cox, C. (2011, April 4). Bullied on Facebook, Teen, 13, Gets Nose Job. *ABC News Radio* [Online]. Available: http://abcnewsradioonline.com/health-news/tag/cosmetic-surgery.

48 Byrne, D. (1971). *The Attraction Paradigm.* New York: Academic Press.

49 Rosenbaum, M. E. (1986). The Repulsion Hypothesis: On the Nondevelopment of Relationships. *Journal of Personality and Social Psychology, 51,* 1156–1166.

50 Emswiller, T., Deaux, K., and Willits, J. (1971). Similarity, Sex, and Requests for Small Favors. *Journal of Applied Social Psychology, 1,* 284–291.

51 Jiang, L., Hoegg, J., Dahl, D. W., and Chattopadhyay, A. (2010). The Persuasive Role of Incidental Similarity on Attitudes and Purchase Intentions in a Sales Context, *Journal of Consumer Research, 36,* 778–791.

52 LaFrance, M. (1985). Postural Mirroring and Intergroup Relations. *Personality and Social Psychology Bulletin, 11,* 207–217.

53 Gitomer, J. (2004). *Little Red Book of Selling: 12.5 Principles of Sales Greatness.* Austin, TX: Bard Press.

54 Shea, C. (2011, December 21). This Laptop's Battery Lasts 500 Minutes. *The Wall Street Journal* [Online]. Available: http://blogs.wsj.com/ideas-market/2011/12/21/this-laptops-battery-lasts-500-minutes/.

55 Zhang, Y. C., and Schwarz, N. (2012). How and Why 1 Year Differs from 365 Days: A Conversational Logic Analysis of Inferences from the Granularity of Quantitative Expressions. *Journal of Consume Research, 39,* 248–259.

56 Drachman, D., deCarufel, A., and Insko, C. A. (1978). The Extra Credit Effect in Interpersonal Attraction. *Journal of Experimental Social Psychology, 14,* 458–465.

57 Howard, D. J., Gengler, C., and Jain, A. (1995). What's in a Name? A Complimentary Means of Persuasion. *Journal of Consumer Research, 22,* 200–211.

58 Howard, D. J. (1990). The Influence of Verbal Responses to Common Greetings on Compliance Behavior: The Foot-in-the-Mouth Effect. *Journal of Abnormal and Social Psychology, 20,* 1185–1196.

59 Jones, E. E., & Wortman, C. (1973). *Ingratiation: An Attributional Approach.* Morristown, NJ: General Learning Press.

60 Shari, C. (1997). The Fine Art of Ingratiation. *Industry Week, 246,* 41.

61 Hirt, E. R., Zillmann, D., Erickson, G. A., and Kennedy, C. (1992). Costs and Benefits of Allegiance: Changes in Fans' Self-Ascribed Competencies after Team Victory versus Defeat. *Journal of Personality and Social Psychology, 63,* 724–738.

62 Tesser, A., and Rosen, S. (1975). The Reluctance to Transmit Bad News. In L. Berkowitz (Ed.), *Advances in Experimental Social Psychology* (Vol. 8, pp. 193–232). New York: Academic Press.

63 Kardes, F., and Kimble, C. E. (1984). Strategic Self-Presentation as a Function of Message Valence and the Prospect of Future Interaction. *Representative Research in Social Psychology, 14,* 2–11.

64 Milgram, S. (1963). Behavioral Study of Obedience. *Journal of Abnormal and Social Psychology, 67,* 371–378.

65 Meeus, W. H. J., and Raaijmakers, Q. Q. W. (1986). Administrative Obedience: Carrying Out Orders to Use Psychological-Administrative Violence. *European Journal of Social Psychology, 16,* 311–324.

MARKETING METRICS

The Value of Persuasion

Re-read the opening vignette in this chapter. The car salesperson spent considerable time persuading the customer to purchase an automobile, and he was successful. Imagine that you are the manager of that auto dealer and you would like to evaluate his performance.

Car Salesperson Data (DT13-1.xls)

Commission Rate on Gross Profit	25%
Base Price	$ 30,000
Upgrades	3,000
Easy Care Warranty	1,000
Total Revenue	
Dealer's Cost	(31,000)
Gross Profit	
Commission	-
Net Contribution	-

Your Task:

Use the Excel file (DT13-1.xls) to conduct the following analyses:

1. Round the base price to $30,000, the upgrades to $3,000, and the Easy-Care, one-year warranty to $1,000. What was the total revenue generated by the salesperson?
2. Assume that the dealer's cost for the vehicle was $31,000. What was the gross profit for the dealer (total revenue − dealer cost)?
3. If the salesperson makes a 25% commission on gross profit, what is the net contribution to the dealer (Gross profit − commission)?
4. If Sarah had negotiated the base price from $30,000 to $29,000, what would the salesperson have earned in commission? What would be the net contribution under this scenario?

THE INFLUENCE OF CULTURE AND VALUES

© iStockphoto.com/macroworld

OBJECTIVES   *After studying this chapter, you will be able to…*

1 Define culture, cultural values, and subculture.

2 Describe how cultural meaning moves from society to consumer products and eventually to individual consumers.

3 Explain the differences among the four consumer rituals: exchange,

possession, grooming and divestment.

4 Explain the differences between high- and low-context cultures.

5 Understand the differences among product attributes, benefits, and values.

Culture and Color

Colors considered neutral in Western culture might carry political connotations in the East. Similarly, colors with positive connotation in one country may be viewed negatively in another. For this reason, global marketers will be more successful if they research the meaning of color in specific cultures and use the colors appropriately to reach their target markets.[1]

For example, Orange, the brand name of France Telecom's mobile and Internet subsidiaries, ran a successful ad campaign in the 1990s using the slogan, "The Future's Bright—the Future's Orange." However, the company apparently had to alter its slogan for politically divided Northern Ireland, where people strongly associate the color orange with the Orange Order, also known as the "Protestant Loyalists." Due to interreligious violence between Catholics and Protestants, France Telecom even considered changing its brand name entirely in Ireland. Similarly, when EuroDisney featured purple in its signs, some European Catholic visitors

© Ekler/Shutterstock.com

perceived the signs as morbid because of purple's close associations with the crucifixion.

Cultures often maintain completely different interpretations of the same color. White is the bridal color in Western culture, however, red is the bridal color in China. Red signifies joy in parts of Asia, but it symbolizes mourning in parts of Africa. Black represents death in Western culture, but white is the color of death in India and China. In many Middle Eastern countries, green would be a poor color choice for a product or package because the color is linked to the prophet Mohammad, who wore a green turban. Although no particular color has consistent meanings across every culture, blue is thought to be the "safest" global color because it evokes positive or at least neutral meaning in most countries.

Color is often the first impression a package, logo, or brandmark makes, so it's critical to get it right when conducting business outside of an organization's home country. To help avoid unpleasant surprises, the following online references should be useful:

- *Color Meanings by Culture:* http://www.globalization-group.com/edge/resources /color-meanings-by-culture/
- *Colours in Culture:* http://www.informationisbeautiful.net/visualizations/colours-in -cultures/
- *Visual Color Symbolism Chart by Culture:* http://webdesign.about.com/od /colorcharts/l/bl_colorculture.htm
- *Psychological Effects of Color:* http://www.csustan.edu/OIT/WebServices /SupportResources/PsychOfColor.html

OBJECTIVE (1)   # Culture Defined

Culture is a lot like humor—it's easy to recognize but difficult to define. In fact, countless definitions of culture exist in various disciplines such as anthropology, sociology, and social psychology. Some behavioral scientists define **culture** as the patterns of meaning acquired by members of society expressed in their knowledge, beliefs, art, laws, morals, customs, and habits. Edward B. Tylor, a British anthropologist, introduced this notion of culture in 1871.[2] Although we can see the manifestations of a culture, its meaning only exists in the collective minds of a society. As a result, culture is abstract, fragile, and dynamic. Geert Hofstede, the founder of comparative intercultural research, conducted a comprehensive study on how culture influences values. He defines culture as "the collective programming of the human mind that distinguishes the members of one human group from those of another." In this sense, culture can be thought of as a system of collectively held values.[3] **Cultural values** comprise a collective set of beliefs about what is important, useful, and desirable. Simply put, culture reflects the *personality* of a society. **Subcultures** are smaller groups of a larger culture that share some cultural values with society overall and yet demonstrate unique cultural values and patterns of behavior within the individual subgroup. Subcultures provide opportunities for marketers to segment society into more manageable groups that are likely to respond similarly to products and services based on their similar needs and wants. Geography, gender, age, race, nationality, religion, and social class form important subcultures. This chapter, however, provides a broader focus than a discussion of individual subcultures. Instead, we examine in general how cultural values move from the collective minds of society to individual consumers, with the help of marketing efforts and the fashion system.

The opening vignette of the chapter provides a glimpse of cultural differences regarding the interpretation of color. Perhaps the best lessons learned about international color preferences come directly from real customers. For example, IKEA proactively made color changes to better target California's Latino population. After designers visited the homes of Hispanic staff members, the Swedish furniture retailer realized subdued Scandinavian colors were too understated for Latino tastes. As a consequence, the company added warmer colors to their showrooms.[1]

Consumers who travel to foreign countries often encounter cultural differences. If these differences are extreme, they experience "culture shock," a state of anxiety associated with trying to deal with this new and unfamiliar environment. Cultural differences can also create vast differences in consumer behavior. Consumer behavior is concerned with all consumer activities associated with the purchase, use, and disposal of goods and services, including the consumer's cognitive, affective, and behavioral responses that precede, determine, or follow these activities. Accordingly, this chapter discusses the characteristics of culture that are most likely to influence consumer behavior: language and symbols, customs and rituals, norms, and consumer values. Before discussing these specific aspects of culture, let's look as some theories that offer understanding on how culture evolves in a consumer society.

A Cultural Framework for Consumer Behavior

Anthropologist Grant McCracken provides a framework that describes the mobility of cultural meaning and the instruments that transfer this meaning from society to consumer products, and then from consumer products to individual consumers.[4] Figure 14.1 illustrates this movement of cultural meaning.

FIGURE 14.1 | **The Movement of Cultural Meaning**

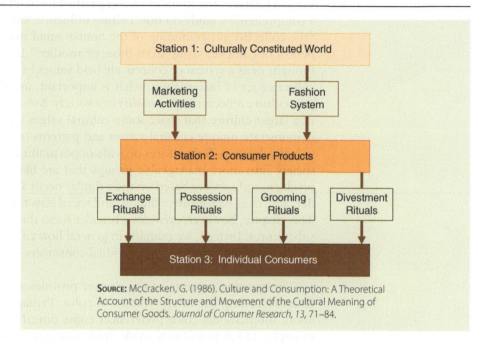

Source: McCracken, G. (1986). Culture and Consumption: A Theoretical Account of the Structure and Movement of the Cultural Meaning of Consumer Goods. *Journal of Consumer Research, 13,* 71–84.

OBJECTIVE ② **Station 1 in Figure 14.1: The Culturally Constituted World**

Consumers' broadest understanding of culture resides in the **culturally constituted world**, where all consumer experiences are shaped by the intangible beliefs and values of society. This is Station 1 in Figure 14.1. It is helpful to think of the culturally constituted world as a place where society's widely shared values are collected and stored. But note that these values are ever-changing. As a warehouse for society's values, the culturally constituted world supplies meaning for consumers via two interrelated concepts: cultural categories and cultural principles. **Cultural categories** help organize a society by dividing the world into specific and distinct segments of time, space, and people. Categories comprising people, such as age, gender, social class, and occupation, are most important to the study of consumer behavior. Cultural categories are the ancestors of market segments, but their purpose is not to identify groups of potential customers. Instead, cultural categories exist to help people understand the world in which they live, and although abstract, their meaning can be substantiated through the visible consumption of goods and services. In short, consumer products provide a tangible explanation for the existence of intangible cultural categories.

For example, in most cultures, women typically use more cosmetic products than do men; families with young children purchase a majority of packaged goods; and the upper class is most likely to own yachts. Here, gender, life cycle, and social class categories help us understand the culturally constituted world by allowing us to examine specific products chosen by distinct subgroups within each category. More subtle differences also exist within each category, such as gender. Recent research demonstrates that young men typically stress functional buying motives, whether shopping online or in conventional stores. In contrast, young women emphasize the social and experiential value of conventional shopping but show similar functional motives as men when shopping online.[5] Thus, a cultural shift from conventional to online shopping requires more attitude change for women, which provides one explanation as to why women are often less satisfied than men with online shopping.[6]

Cultural principles are the *ideas* that help guide the construction of cultural categories. Consumer products also illustrate cultural principles. For example, clothing can communicate "refinement" for the upper class and "rebellion" for the punk culture. Similarly, women's clothing communicates something about the "feminine" nature of women, while men's clothing shows the "masculine" characteristics of men. Here, cultural principles work hand-in-hand with cultural categories. In sum, cultural principles give us the reasons for performing segmentation, and cultural categories provide useful descriptors for these segments. Both can be seen in consumer products.

Station 2 in Figure 14.1: Consumer Products

Cultural meaning is transferred from the culturally constituted world to consumer products. Consumer products represent the second stop in the journey to understanding the movement of cultural meaning. Consumer products serve as Station 2 in Figure 14.1. *Marketing activities* provide one important conduit for this movement. Through deliberate marketing efforts, such as advertising, promotion, distribution, packaging, and pricing, products take on cultural meaning. For example, cellular phone products reflect society's desire for communication that is convenient, global, and remote. Advanced cellular products offer connection to the Internet and access to a consumer's home computer. These innovations depict a specific cultural category or segment (e.g., high-tech consumers), as well as the cultural principle that helped create it (e.g., remote-tasking increases productivity). Because culture is dynamic, however, products continually give up old meanings and take on new ones. SUVs, a specific category of automobile, once communicated outdoor- and sports-related cultural principles. Now, they may also reflect consumer extravagance and

Consumers' clothing can communicate cultural categories such as age, gender, religion, and social class.

excessive fuel consumption. Accordingly, the marketplace offers smaller, more fuel-efficient SUVs. As active participants in the marketing process, consumers are informed about the most current cultural meanings in consumer products through marketing communication. Marketing activities, particularly advertising, provide a pipeline through which cultural meaning moves from the culturally constituted world to consumer products.[4]

Although highly complex and more difficult to observe than marketing activities, the *fashion system* is equally important in transferring cultural meaning from the culturally constituted world to consumer products. The fashion system is not just limited to clothing and body adornment; it includes various forms of social expression such as music, art, architecture, journalism, politics, speech, entertainment, and technology. The fashion system transfers meaning to consumer products in three ways. First, it takes new styles of clothing, music, etc., and associates them with established cultural categories and principles.[7] For example, newer styles of dress (e.g., business casual) may reflect the existing cultural principle productivity, which is linked to the existing cultural category time (work versus leisure). Here, the joint interplay of comfort and productivity are reinterpreted within the context of work time, i.e., comfort increases productivity in the white-collar world. Similarly, new forms of automobiles (e.g., hybrids) highlight a culture's existing desire for environmental stewardship. Stylish hybrid automobiles, a new fashion, join the category fuel-efficient automobiles through the principle "the natural environment is worthy of being preserved." Both category and principle existed earlier, but the changing fashion system revised the cultural meaning surrounding cars and the environment.

Second, the fashion system invents completely new cultural meaning by enlisting opinion leaders who modestly shape and refine existing cultural principles and categories. **Opinion leaders** are individuals who, by virtue of birth, beauty, talent, or accomplishment, are held in high esteem and provide cultural meaning to those of lesser standing.[8] Rain, a South Korean pop singer whose albums have topped the charts in China, Japan, Thailand, Indonesia, and South Korea, has prompted new cultural meaning in music. Nelson Mandela, former president of South Africa, led his nation out of apartheid. By virtue of his character and decency, Mandela remains one of the most compelling moral and political opinion leaders of our time. Actress Angelina Jolie has become an opinion leader regarding humanitarian causes, including eradicating poverty and reversing the spread of HIV/AIDS throughout the developing world. She reportedly raised $10 million for charities by selling pictures of her and partner Brad Pitt's baby, Shiloh, to popular magazines. Warren Buffet is the second richest man in the world, worth over $50 billion. He is also the foremost opinion leader in personal investing. Charles Barkley has followed up his Hall of Fame basketball career with an Emmy Award-winning television career. The consummate entertainer, "Sir Charles" has become a pop culture icon, commanding a diverse

EDWARD PARSONS/AFP/Getty Images

Actress Angelina Jolie has become an opinion leader for humanitarian causes.

audience that may not always agree with him, but respects his ability to talk straight. Never one to dodge controversy, Barkley speaks from the heart. His larger-than-life personality is seeded in his ability to connect with people of all races through a unique combination of humor, honesty, and humility. This enables Barkley to open up uncomfortable but critical dialogues about issues such as racism that impact the day-to-day lives of the members of his community and the world at large.[9] All these opinion leaders invent and deliver new cultural meaning by passing along modest changes in their styles, values, and attitudes to other members of society, who then imitate them.

The third way the fashion system passes on meaning from the culturally constituted world to consumer products is via radical reform. According to Claude Levi-Strauss, Western societies willingly accept—even encourage—radical reform.[10] As a result, Western cultures constantly undergo systematic change. The fashion system serves as an important conduit to capture and move radical and innovative cultural meaning. Who are the people responsible for this radical reform? The people responsible are those at the very fringes of society, such as hippies, punks, and rappers.[11] These radical and innovative groups redefined cultural categories by overturning the established order. For example, hippies protested the Vietnam War and established the recreational drug culture; people in the gay community have reshaped the cultural category gender; and rap artists have influenced such cultural categories as clothing, jewelry, and patterns of speech.

Marketing in Action

Cultural Change via Hip-Hop Fashion

Often, the groups responsible for a radical departure from the culturally constituted conventions of Western societies are those existing at the margins of society.[4] The hip-hop culture, broadly recognized by its rap music, beatboxing, breakdancing, and urban graffiti, created an entirely new clothing fashion. The diffusion of hip-hop fashion into the mainstream illustrates the power that less privileged groups can exercise over the whole of society. Today, hip-hop fashion is a prominent part of popular global fashion for all races and ethnicities. But it didn't start that way. It began with inner city, African-American youth in New York and Los Angeles.

In the early 1980s, hip-hop fashion was novel. Rapper LL Cool J wore brightly colored sweat suits, bomber jackets, and Adidas sneakers with "phats," i.e., oversized shoelaces. Big Daddy Kane wore heavy gold chains, and Salt-N-Pepa donned oversized earrings. Then came the 1990s. Dance rappers like MC Hammer popularized blousy pants, and Lisa "Left Eye" Lopes from TLC helped popularize baseball caps and neon-colored clothing. Wyclef Jean and Lauryn Hill from the Fugees wore dreadlocks, matted ropes of hair that originated

in ancient dynastic Egypt. Polka-dot clothing made a brief but impressionable appearance, thanks to rapper Kwamé, and Starter jackets and Air Jordan sneakers emerged as status symbols. Hip-hop fashion crossed over to high fashion when models began wearing heavy gold jewelry and bomber jackets with thick fur collars. Among the most interesting hip-hop trends of the early 1990s, Treach of *Naughty by Nature* dressed in metallic chain-linked padlocks, in apparent solidarity with "all the brothers who are locked down."[12] This particular trend did not last. Gangsta rap emerged in the mid-1990s with black-ink tattoos, bandanas, and baggy pants without belts. In addition, new street-slang, such as "homeboy," emerged. Interestingly, gangsta rap was influenced to some extent by the gangster styles of the 1930s, shown by a resurgence in the wearing of bowler hats, silk shirts, alligator-skin shoes, and double-breasted suits.

Fashion design houses Polo, Calvin Klein, and Tommy Hilfiger embraced hip-hop fashion in the 1990s. In fact, when Snoop Dogg (who now calls himself Snoop Lion) donned a Hilfiger sweatshirt during an appearance on

Saturday Night Live, this article of clothing then sold out in New York City stores the next day. The late-1990s witnessed the rise of platinum jewelry and aviator warm-up suits, largely inspired by rap star Sean Combs (also known as Puff Daddy and P. Diddy). Do-rags became a hit, supporting the popular African-American hairstyles with cornrows and Caesar low-cuts. Afros also reemerged after 30 years of dormancy. Rappers like Jay Z and The Hot Boys started the "Bling" movement, which featured ostentatious jewelry, including grills, or removable platinum-jeweled teeth covers.

The 2000s ushered in new hip-hop styles, including "prep-hop," featuring polo shirts with popped collars, large, elaborate belt buckles, and fitted caps with straight bills worn sideways. Shorter, tighter t-shirts replaced long t-shirts in an effort to show off decorative belt buckles. More recently, the baggy-pants style appears to be waning. Today, hip-hop fashion has become mainstream. It has moved from the inner cities to the suburbs, even into the boardrooms of McDonald's, Coca-Cola, and Nautica.

The hip-hop style of wearing sagging pants without a belt originated in prisons, where new inmates are immediately stripped of their belts as a safety precaution, i.e., so that the belts cannot be used as weapons or substitutes for a noose. This particular hip-hop trend reemerged in the 2000s, except this time, youth began wearing baggy denim below their waistlines, often exposing their underwear. Some lawmakers at the state and city level took a dim view of this trend. The Virginia State House of Representatives passed House Bill No. 1981 (February 8, 2005), establishing a $50 penalty for any person who exposed his below-waist undergarments in a lewd or indecent manner. On November 23, 2010, Albany, Georgia passed a city ordinance banning pants or skirts that displayed more than three inches below the top of the hips. A first offense fine is $25 and the fine increases up to $250 for subsequent violations.[13] The hip-hop culture adjusted. This time, trendsetters used belts and long t-shirts to avoid the fine; the jeans were still worn below the belt.

Young people of all races and nationalities have embraced the hip-hop culture—its music, clothing, street-slang, tattoos, jewelry, movies, and magazines. Hip-hop artists are "meaning suppliers" for culture. Like the hippies and punks who preceded them, hip-hop artists utilize the fashion system to overturn the established cultural order and inspire new cultural principles and categories. They will not be the last innovative group to effect cultural change.

OBJECTIVE ## Station 3 in Figure 14.1: Consumers

All high-involvement consumer products (e.g., clothing, body adornment, transportation, architecture, music, food) express the beliefs and values present in the culturally constituted world. This meaning continues its journey from consumer products into the day-to-day life of consumers. Consumers represent Station 3 in Figure 14.1. The instruments that transfer meaning to consumers are known as **rituals**. Rituals are symbolic actions that occur in a fixed sequence and are repeated over time.[14] Consumers use four rituals to affirm or revise cultural meaning: exchange, possession, grooming, and divestment. Each represents a different stage by which cultural meaning moves from product to consumer.[4]

Exchange rituals involve one person or a group of people purchasing and presenting consumer products to another. This movement of products from giver to receiver allows the giver to transfer deliberated cultural properties to the receiver. A son who receives books in exchange for good performance in school is also made the recipient of a specific concept about himself as intellectually curious. An engaged daughter who receives a down payment on a new home in lieu of an expensive wedding celebration may come to see herself as practically minded. Western gift exchange rituals—particularly at birthdays and Christmas—provide powerful opportunities for the giver to pass on cultural meanings to the receiver.

Unfulfilled requests can be equally important in passing on cultural meaning. A child's request for and his parents' subsequent refusal to give him toy guns and soldiers signals something about cultural attitudes toward warfare. Similarly, presenting substitute gifts conveys important cultural meaning.

Children who receive *Nancy Drew* computer games as substitutes for *World of Warcraft* games or *Civilization* instead of *Sims* may decode messages about acceptable forms of fantasy. Giving a child a mobile phone that does not include text messaging options may emphasize the serious nature of the mobile communications, i.e., the phone is primarily for safety rather than for socializing. Substituting a trip to Cedar Point in Ohio for Disney World could highlight a family's scarcity of time or money. Recent research suggests that sharing music files from iTunes represents a special case of gift giving.[15] Sharing music and movies provides rich insight into the cultural values being passed to the receiver. What kind of message is being sent along with the "gift" of Beethoven? How about 50 Cent? The Rolling Stones?

Gift-wrapping can also express important cultural meaning. In Japan, for example, the economic value of the gift is subordinate to its symbolic meaning. Consequently, the wrapping paper and adornments are paramount. Many Japanese view giving gifts to friends and family as a reciprocal obligation, known as *kosai*. They perform ritualized activities when giving gifts to both personal and professional acquaintances, all of which can be very stressful. Consistent with the Japanese cultural principle of "saving face," gifts are rarely opened in the presence of the giver, just in case the receiver responds unfavorably to the contents inside the elaborate packaging.[16]

Possession rituals occur when consumers discuss, compare, reflect upon, and display their belongings. "Claiming" takes place when consumers adopt into their existing personalities the specific qualities of a product assigned to it by marketing activities.[4] For example, marketing teaches us that motorcycles represent freedom, power, and rugged individuality. Thus, discussing one's motorcycle may transfer the cultural principle, freedom, from the product to a consumer's personality. Friends who compare the features of their minivans may be emphasizing the nurturing dimension of their personalities—or simply underscoring their pragmatism. Sorting and organizing one's photographs (in either traditional or digital scrapbooks) reinforces existing cultural principles and categories. Photos of vacations offer some insight into as well as depict the category and time of the cultural principle surrounding leisure. Photographs of the consumer at various stages of her life illustrate the category, age, and the principles associated with age-relevant behaviors. Through possession rituals, consumers draw on the ability of consumer products to discriminate between cultural categories and principles. "He's a BMW guy," really means that he's a yuppie (young urban professional). "She's a Target girl," suggests a practical but chic personality. Rolex and Kmart signal class categories and the principles associated with upper versus lower class. Work boots and hard hats represent more than protection; they are symbolic of blue-collar occupations. Trips to Cancun, Mexico, paint a different picture than do excursions to Barcelona, Spain. Interestingly, possession rituals can be equally instructive when consumers fail to embrace the cultural properties of their possessions. "I sold the motorcycle. It wasn't me," provides insight into a consumer's value system. "I no longer shop at Target because they don't carry the brands that I like," similarly reflects a consumer's attitude regarding brands and shopping. Possession rituals help complete the second stage of cultural movement from products to consumers. Consumers extract the meaningful properties of consumer products and adopt or reject them as part of their lives.

Many consumer products do not last indefinitely. Accordingly, **grooming rituals** allow consumers to extract cultural meaning from perishable possessions through repeated use. Products such as shampoo, cosmetics, and clothes facilitate daily grooming rituals. The ritual of "going out" is an example of a more elaborate grooming ritual. Women sometimes describe applying cosmetics as "putting on their faces," while men sometimes behave as though they are preparing for an athletic event when they get dressed in the morning. Pep talks, changing and re-changing clothes, painstakingly styling one's hair, and meticulous shaving all demonstrate consumers' desire to cultivate consumer products and absorb the products' meanings into their personality. "Because you're worth it" (L'Oréal), "Create a storm," (Monsoon), "Gentlemen prefer Hanes," "Because life is not a spectator sport" (Reebok), and "Every kiss begins with Kay" (Kay Jewelers) embody marketing-created meanings that can be transferred from the product to the consumer via grooming rituals. In sum, grooming rituals help draw cultural meaning out of products and invest them in the consumer.[17]

Consumers use **divestment rituals** for two purposes. For previously-owned items such as cars or homes, consumers engage in elaborate cleaning and redecorating rituals to help erase meanings associated with the previous owner. This allows the new owner to free up the cultural meaning of the product and re-associate it with him or herself. Second, when consumers sell or otherwise dispense with a product, they attempt to erase the meaning that they invested in the item. Prior to selling a beloved automobile, consumers remove all personal artifacts, sometimes even the floor mats, and prepare the car for its new owner. Nevertheless, consumers may feel awkward seeing the new owner with his or her old possession. If the products provided cultural meaning for consumers, they may feel strange about someone else driving their cars,

When selling personal belongings, consumers oftentimes feel that some of the item's cultural significance also transfers to the new owner.

© iStockphoto.com/AnthonyRosenberg

wearing their jackets, playing with their golf clubs, sitting on their lawn furniture, or riding their bicycles. Divestment rituals clearly suggest that consumers *believe* cultural meaning can be transferred from products to people.

All four personal rituals help the transfer of cultural meaning from consumer products to consumers. Exchange rituals allow one consumer to impart desirable meaning to another, while possession rituals help reinforce the relationship between a product and its owner. Grooming rituals provide an opportunity to continually extract meaning from perishable goods, and divestment rituals empty products of their meaning before they assume new ownership.

Cultural meaning, which began in the collective minds of society (the culturally constituted world), is transferred to consumer products by deliberate marketing activities and the fashion system. Cultural meanings "get into" consumer products through marketing activities because ads and promotions make clear reference to existing cultural symbols. Similarly, opinion leaders and reference groups provide meaning to products by the associations that consumers hold regarding those groups. Then, consumers extract cultural values from the products they purchase by employing rituals. Through their brand choices, consumers express and build their identities. In the end, cultural meaning—beliefs about what is important, useful, and desirable—resides at all three stations simultaneously: the culturally constituted world, consumer products, and consumers. Next, we explore how consumers learn about their cultures.

Enculturation and Acculturation

Anthropologists refer to learning about one's own culture as **enculturation**. McCracken's cultural framework includes *cultural agents,* who help with this process. Cultural agents gather meaning in one station and help transfer it to the next. Marketing and fashion agents help give meaning to their products. Specifically, marketing agents such as product designers and advertisers decide which product benefits—such as convenience, style, durability, and economy—reside in the culturally constituted world and then promote these benefits to the most responsive consumer markets. Some cultures, such as the United States, appear time-impoverished and respond favorably to any innovation that saves time. In contrast, Latin American cultures rarely feel pressured by time.

Fashion agents such as architects and artists, clothing creators, and automobile designers use the fashion system to inject their creations with cultural meaning. Media agents such as journalists, reporters, and experts observe cultural innovation and decide what is "hot" and what is "not." Other cultural agents such as parents, peers, and teachers impart their cultural values to consumers. Often, these values are reflected in consumers' rituals and help transfer meaning from consumer products to consumers. Thus, cultural agents exist at and between every station in the model (see Figure 14.1).

The process of **acculturation** occurs when people in one culture adapt to meanings in another culture.[18] Acculturation has become increasingly important as a result of global immigration, which can profoundly influence a nation through language and other cultural differences. According to the United Nations, about 200 million people live outside their home country, and approximately 800 million international tourists travel outside their country of origin. After leaving their home country, many immigrants and travelers go through a complex set of emotions when learning the attitudes, behaviors, and values of their new country.[19] **Cultural brands**, a set of products and services from emerging economies such as ethnic food, music, movies, entertainment, and media, serve as a means of expression and represent symbols of a particular culture's identity.[20] Cultural brands may represent a specific product (e.g., Guinness beer from Ireland, BBC television and radio from Great Britain) or an entire category of products (e.g., tequila from Mexico). Recent research shows that consumers living in a new country may have an inflated view of cultural brands from their home county. Specifically, Latinos in the Dallas–Fort Worth area maintain a more glorified view of Spanish-language television broadcast brands—Televisa and TV Azteca—than do residents in Mexico due to feelings of nostalgia for the home country. This suggests that brands introduced across borders are not simply viewed as global brands, and marketers should reinforce the cultural roots of these cultural brands when developing a marketing strategy for consumers living outside their home country.[21]

Language

Perhaps the most obvious difference among cultures lies in their verbal communication systems. Consumers who travel to foreign countries understand the challenges of both oral and written communication. In order for people to function as consumers—nonetheless in a society—they must be able to interact with the prevailing language. Language is not merely a collection of words. Language expresses the beliefs and values of a culture. Anthropologist Benjamin Lee Whorf maintained that language actually shapes the worldview of consumers, their behavior toward others, and their manners of acting.[22]

The semantics of the "got milk?" campaign was misunderstood in Mexico.

Linguists divide the study of verbal language into four categories. *Syntax* comprises the rules of sentence formation; *semantics* deals with systems of meaning; *phonology* deals with sound patterns; and *morphology* involves word formation. A fifth category, *nonverbal communications*, includes body language, gestures, and other forms of unspoken communication. Taken together, all five categories comprise the broader field known as *semiotics*. Figure 14.2 provides several examples of linguistic differences between English, Russian, Spanish, and Japanese.

Solid communication linkages must be established between marketers and customers or *translation problems* are likely to occur. Attempts to translate marketing communications from one language to another often fail because of problems with *semantics*, as illustrated by the following examples. During the late 1990s, Nike aired a television commercial for hiking shoes in Kenya using Samburu tribesmen. The camera closed in on the one tribesman who speaks in the native Maa language. As he speaks, the Nike slogan "Just do it" appears on the screen. The Kenyan is really saying, "I don't want these. Give me big shoes." Similarly, the Dairy Association's huge success with the "got milk?" campaign prompted them to expand their advertising to Mexico. Unfortunately, the Spanish translation read

FIGURE 14.2 | Linguistic Differences

Linguistic Category	Examples
Syntax	English has relatively fixed word order, while Russian has relatively free word order. In Spanish, the adjectives follow nouns; in English, adjectives precede nouns.
Semantics	Japanese words communicate nuances of feeling for which other languages lack exact translations. For example, "yes" and "no" can be interpreted with finer distinction in Japanese than in other languages
Phonology	Japanese does not distinguish between "L" and "R" sounds. Rs are "rolled" in Russian. In Spanish, two Ls, one after another, are spoken like a "y."
Morphology	Russian is a highly inflected language, with six different endings for nouns and adjectives.

SOURCE: Keegan, W. and Green M. (2005). *Global Marketing*, 4th ed. Upper Saddle River, NJ: Pearson Prentice Hall.

"Are you lactating?" Each of these translation blunders occurred because of semantics, i.e., finding words with equivalent meanings.

Phonology frequently complicates cross-cultural communication. Mars, Inc., the $18 billion privately owned candy conglomerate, had difficulty making the M&M's name pronounceable in France, where neither ampersands nor the apostrophe "s" plural form exists. Similarly, Whirlpool struggled with a brand name that is nearly impossible to pronounce in Spain, Italy, France, and Germany.[23] The name Coca-Cola in China was first rendered as Ke-ke-ken-la. Unfortunately, Coke did not discover until after thousands of signs had been printed that the phrase means, "bite the wax tadpole" or "female horse stuffed with wax," depending on the dialect. Coke then researched 40,000 Chinese characters and found a close phonetic equivalent, "ko-kou-ko-le," which translates as "happiness in the mouth," a much better choice.

Cultural Translation

Professor and author Jean-Claude Usunier maintains that many problems in translation are **cultural translation** difficulties, i.e., problems related to the spirit of the language. Some words simply have no foreign equivalent because the meaning may not be relevant to a foreign culture. The English word "upset" for example, does not have a French equivalent, because the English meaning of the word suggests something of an inner personal disruption and loss of self-control. The French cannot be "upset" because generally they are not afraid to show their feelings and emotions to others.[24] In contrast, it is well known that in the language of peoples who live near the Arctic Circle, nearly a dozen different terms are used to describe the English word "snow." The following translation blunders illustrate problems with *cultural translations*.

Samarin is a Swedish over-the-counter remedy for upset stomachs. It is similar to Alka-Seltzer. Several years ago, their ads featured comic strips without text; they used three pictures. The first picture showed a man grasping his stomach, obviously ill. In the second picture, the man drank a glass of Samarin. In the final picture, he appeared smiling. Although the ad campaign was a success in Europe, it failed when printed in Arabic-speaking newspapers. Why? Arabic languages are read from right to left!

In 2003, the Hong Kong Tourist Board was unable to change an advertising campaign that was on billboards throughout Hong Kong and in British versions of *Cosmopolitan* and *Condé Nast Traveller*. The slogan was, "Hong Kong: It will take your breath away." Unfortunately, the campaign coincided with the SARS epidemic that resulted in numerous deaths. Shortness of breath is one of the main symptoms of SARS. Figure 14.3 illustrates 10 classic marketing translation *faux pas*; most are rooted in semantic or cultural translation problems.

FIGURE 14.3 | Ten Classic Marketing Translation Faux Pas

1. Colgate's Cue toothpaste sold poorly in France because the term "cue" is slang for derrière.

2. Managers of an American company were startled when they discovered that the brand name of the cooking oil they were marketing in a Latin American country translated into Spanish as "Jackass Oil."

3. A firm marketed shampoo in Brazil under the name "Evitol." The name translates into "dandruff contraceptive."

4. Esso Oil discovered that its name translates into "stalled car" in Japanese.

5. American Motors marketed its car the Matador based on the image of courage and strength. However, in Puerto Rico, the name means "killer" and was not well received, given the hazardous roads throughout the country.

6. In 2002, UK sports manufacturer Umbro had to withdraw its new sneakers named Zyklon from German markets. They discovered that Zyklon was the name of the gas used in Nazi concentration camps. Hoover made the same mistake when they named one of their brands Zykon, which was supposed to translate as "cyclone."

7. Several companies become tangled up with bad translations for products resulting from misusing the word "mist." "Irish Mist" (an alcoholic beverage), "Mist Stick" (a curling iron from Clairol), and "Silver Mist" (a Rolls Royce car) all bombed in Germany because "mist" translates into "dung" or "manure."

8. Kellogg had to rename its Bran Buds cereal in Sweden; the name roughly translated to "burned farmer."

9. PepsiCo advertised in Taiwan using the slogan "Come Alive With Pepsi," which translated into Chinese as "Pepsi brings your ancestors back from the dead."

10. In Italy, a campaign for Schweppes Tonic Water translated the name into "Schweppes Toilet Water."

Body Language

Although familiarity with verbal language is critical to understanding a culture, it is not the only way cultures express their personalities. Derived from the Greek word *kinein*, meaning "to move," *body language* involves the silent movement of body parts, including *facial expressions* such as scowls, smiles, and stares, *gestures* such as hand and arm signals, *postural shifts* such as leaning forward or crossing one's arms, and forms of *touching*, including slapping and caressing. *Interpersonal spacing* is also an important form of nonverbal communication. Different cultures prefer standing relatively close or far away, facing head-on versus to one side. Latin Americans, Arabs, and Africans typically stand within 18 inches when speaking to a business acquaintance. To them, it is a sign of confidence. In contrast, Germans, Nordics, and Asians generally consider at least 36 inches as their personal space.

Like written and spoken language, nonverbal languages are mostly learned rather than innate. Consequently, the meanings of nonverbal expressions such as gestures can vary from culture to culture. One catalogue retailer learned this the hard way by printing the "OK" finger sign on each page of its catalogue. Unfortunately, in many parts of Latin America such as Brazil, this sign is considered an obscene gesture. The catalogues were scrapped and re-designed to better reflect resident body language. Similarly, Mountain Bell Company marketed its telephone services in Saudi Arabia. One of the ads portrayed an executive talking on the phone with his feet propped up on the desk, showing the soles of his shoes. Arab culture considers the display of one's soles to be disrespectful.

In contrast, emotion expressed by the face tends to contain universal meaning. Research demonstrates that most cultures communicate five different emotions by distinct facial expressions: happiness, sadness, fear, surprise, and anger. Happiness is easily detected in the lower face, while sadness and fear are best understood from the eyes.[25] Still, the rules for using these facial expressions may vary from culture to culture. For example, Americans consider direct eye contact while speaking a sign of trust. South Koreans, however, view this as rude and disrespectful. The French maintain that Americans smile too much. In addition to language, both verbal and nonverbal, marketers must understand the social setting of a culture.

OBJECTIVE **4**

High- and Low-Context Cultures

The social setting, or *context*, can affect intercultural communications. Some cultures are *low-context* and emphasize explicit messages. The meanings of such messages are largely independent of the situation and people involved, and the words are relatively precise in meaning. Other cultures are *high-context* and communicate more implicit meanings. The meanings of the words change depending on who is speaking to whom and under what circumstances. Nonverbal messages such as gestures and body language are important in high-context cultures. Figure 14.4 depicts various cultures on this message-context continuum.[26]

Highly explicit messages can be thought of as unambiguous computer commands; they tend to go with low-context cultures. Conversely, highly implicit messages, usually associated with high-context cultures, are more ambiguous. The Swiss are represented at the extreme lower-left portion of the graph. There is a great deal of precision in their verbal communication. This suggests that Swiss speed limits, contracts, and appointment times should be taken literally. In fact, patients pay a fine if they are late for a doctor's visit. The Germans,

---

FIGURE **14.4** | **Cultural Message-Context Continuum**

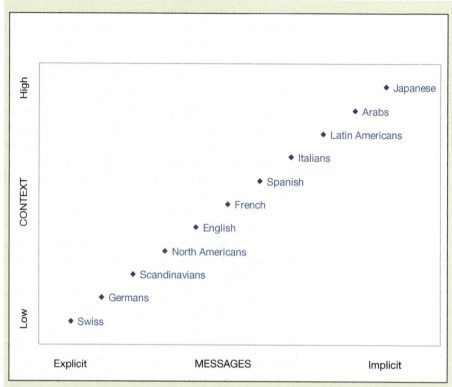

SOURCE: Usunier, J. (1993). *International Marketing: A Cultural Approach.* Englewood Cliffs, NJ: Prentice Hall International (UK) Limited.

Scandinavians, and North Americans also fall in the low-context/explicit message range. In contrast, the Japanese are represented at the upper-right portion of the graph, where context plays a critical role in communication. For example, when a consumer from a Western culture says "no" in negotiating, he or she is usually saying, "I *reject* the deal." The Japanese, however, have at least 14 ways of saying "no." See Figure 14.5.

Eastern and Western cultures also differ in their reactions to surprises, such as unexpected marketing incentives. Some marketers offer customers small gifts in appreciation for their business. Free hats and t-shirts, calendars, and small samples represent a few examples. Nevertheless, East Asians and Westerners do not always react to these incentives in the same way. Faced with the unexpected, East Asians attempt to maintain social harmony and tend to experience less surprise than do Westerners. And in general, less surprise produces less pleasure.[27] East Asian cultures strongly emphasize social harmony. In fact, maintaining balance and harmony in the presence of the unexpected is viewed as one of the highest virtues in Chinese culture. Accordingly, members of East Asian cultures are taught that the private self should be subordinate to the social self.[28] On the other hand, members of Western cultures view themselves as special, value personal achievement, and avoid conformity. These cultural dissimilarities lead to

FIGURE 14.5 | **Fourteen Ways to Say "No" in Japanese**

1. Vague "no."
2. Vague and ambiguous "yes."
3. Silence.
4. Counter-offer.
5. Unrelated response.
6. Physically withdrawing from the conversation.
7. Feigning equivocation or making an excuse.
8. Taking issue with the question.
9. Refusing to acknowledge the question.
10. Conditional "no."
11. Conditional "yes."
12. Delayed response, i.e., "we'll get back to you."
13. Apology.
14. The (rare) equivalent of an English "no."

Source: Usunier. J. (1993). *International Marketing: A Cultural Appraoch.* Englewood Cliffs, NJ: Prentice Hall International (UK) Limited.

different reactions to unexpected marketing incentives. Recent research demonstrates that Westerners are happier than East Asians when their individual efforts (such as games and contests) lead to unexpected rewards. In contrast, East Asians derive more pleasure from unexpected rewards when they attribute the reward to luck or chance, which are signals of good "karma" and universal harmony and are less likely to upset a balance with others.[27]

Arab and Latin American cultures also tend to be high-context and implicit with their messages. Day-to-day consumer behavior in Arab countries differs greatly from that in the West. Consumers are expected to negotiate deals and bargain—even for perishable food products. But cultures do not always fall at the extremes. The Latin-European countries such as Italy, Spain, and France tend to be more intermediate in terms of context and message. Language plays a prominent part in cross-cultural communication, but it is not the only cause of cultural misunderstandings. To communicate effectively, consumers and marketers must possess a common understanding of symbols.[27]

Symbols

Objects created by a culture cannot be communicated solely by their physical characteristics, and consumer products are no exception. Goods and services always contain symbolic elements such as exclusivity, utility, and style. *Symbols* are communication devices that convey meaning through representation. Important marketing symbols include *words* such as brand names, *images* such as brand logos, and *actions* such as body language and gestures. Symbols can be verbal or nonverbal. **Brand jingles** are short, catchy tunes—with or without words—that represent a brand or organization. Marketers understand that music facilitates recall. Children learn much about their world by putting words to songs. Many adults still recall the tune that accompanied the alphabet song. Jingles such as "Mm-Mm-Good" (Campbell's Soup) and "Like a Rock" (Chevy) take advantage of the "stuck song syndrome," or "earworm." Marketing professor and professional musician James Kellaris discovered that although people generally have their own unique earworms, "YMCA," "We Will Rock You," and "The Lion Sleeps Tonight" rank in the top-ten list. According to Kellaris' **theory of cognitive itch**, certain properties of music may be analogous to biochemical agents, such as histamines, which cause an itch on the skin. Exposure to such music may cause a sort of "cognitive itch" in one's mind. The only way to scratch a cognitive itch is to repeat the offending music mentally. But this only exacerbates the itch, trapping the hapless victim in an involuntary cycle of repeated itching and scratching.[29] Thus, advertisers do well to plant their jingles in our heads. But jingles need not contain words to be effective. The Nabisco "ding," the Avon "ding-dong," and the four musical notes representing Intel Inside employ only tones to catch our attention and keep their jingles recycling.

Brand logos take a variety of forms, including colors, shapes, words, and other images. For example, the McDonald's brand includes a *word mark* consisting of the word "McDonald's" written in white lettering across the "golden arches," and superimposed against a red background. The "golden arches" represent a *non-word mark logo*, or *brand symbol*. Many firms use non-word logos to create a distinctive image designed to catch a consumer's eye and trigger positive thoughts about the brand. The AT&T globe, the Mercedes-Benz three-pronged star, Captain Morgan's sea captain, Target's bull's eye, and the Nike swoosh all transcend language with symbolic meaning. What messages do the Hot Wheels flame and pink-scripted *Barbie* symbolize to consumers? What do the Olympic interlocked rings communicate? What does the NBA logo symbolize? Given the substantial investment of creative energy and resources, firms register their brand names, logos, and other brand elements as either *trademarks* or service marks; both provide a form of legal protection for the brand, which is considered intellectual property.

Safeguarding brand logos is an important issue in consumer behavior. On March 16, 2007, AT&T filed suit in the U.S. District Court in Atlanta, demanding that NASCAR allow an AT&T-sponsored car to change its rear quarter to reflect the retirement of the Cingular brand name and the introduction of the AT&T global logo. The car, No. 31, owned by Richard Childress Racing, was driven by Jeff Burton, the third-ranked NASCAR driver.[30] The lawsuit claimed that by not adding the new AT&T logo to the existing Cingular car, NASCAR was doing substantial and irreparable harm to AT&T.

Failure to recognize the cross-cultural implications of symbols can cause problems for marketers and consumers. In Japan, for example, a Western golf ball manufacturing company packaged golf balls in packs of four for convenience. Unfortunately, items packaged in fours are unpopular because the pronunciation of the word "four" in Japanese connotes "death." Nike may have offended Muslims when the "flaming air" logo for its Nike Air sneakers appeared too similar to the Arabic form of God's name, "Allah." Subsequently, Nike pulled more than 38,000 pairs of sneakers from the market. Similarly, a soft drink was introduced into Arab countries with an attractive label featuring six-pointed stars. Some Arab people interpreted this symbol as pro-Israel and refused to buy it. Consequently, another label was printed in ten languages, one of which was Hebrew. Again, it sold poorly. When Pepsodent marketed toothpaste in Southeast Asia, its ad campaign emphasized "teeth whitening." However, some local natives chew betel nuts to blacken their teeth because they find dark teeth attractive. A U.S. telephone company promoted its products and services in Latin America by showing a commercial in which a Latina wife tells her husband to call a friend and explain that they would be late for dinner. The commercial was not received well for two reasons. First, Latina women rarely communicate commands to their husbands. Second, the concept of "lateness" in Latin America is viewed differently than in the United States. Not arriving on time for dinner is *not* considered being "late."

Even within a culture, the meaning of symbols can change over time. Crayola has changed its color names because of the civil rights movement and other social pressures. In 1962, Binney & Smith replaced "flesh" crayons with "peach," in recognition of the global variety of skin tones. In 1999, they changed "Indian Red" to "chestnut." Interestingly, the color was not named after Native Americans, but for a special pigment originating in the country India. By contrast, some symbols are more enduring. For example, Mercedes-Benz understands the importance of their symbol. It has remained relatively unchanged for more than a century.

Norms

Earlier, we described **cultural values** as a collective set of beliefs about what is important, useful, and desirable. From these cultural values flow **norms**, which specify appropriate responses in specific situations. In short, norms are

Global Perspectives

The Mercedes-Benz Brand Logo

Although registered more then a century ago, the Mercedes-Benz brand name initially did not have a logo associated with it. The idea for the three-pointed star logo originated with Paul and Adolf Daimler, the sons of the company's founder. They recalled that their father had once used a star symbol in his family correspondence. Their father, Gottlieb Daimler, was technical director of the Deutz gas engine factory from 1872 until 1881. During this time, Daimler had marked a star on a postcard of Cologne, and Deutz predicted that a star would one day shine over Daimler's own factory, symbolizing its prosperity.

In June, 1909, Gottlieb Daimler registered both a three-pointed and a four-pointed star as trademarks. Although both designs were legally protected, only the three-pointed star was ever used. Beginning in 1910, the three-pointed star appeared as a design feature on the radiators of the

AP Images/David Zalubowski

automobiles. After Daimler's death, his partner, Wilhelm Maybach, enlisted the help of sales-man Emile Jellinek. Following the success of Daimler cars among Jellinek's wealthy acquaintances, Jellinek suggested that Maybach should create a lighter, more powerful car which he named after his elder daughter, Mercedes. After the merger with Benz & Cie., the Mercedes logo was introduced with an addition of the Benz laurel wreath in 1926 to signify the union of the two firms. The brand logo of 2014 looks remarkably similar to the one from 1926.[31]

culture's rules of behavior. **Enacted norms** explicitly and formally prescribe acceptable behaviors. For example, restrooms in the United States provide gender placards, indicating separate facilities for men and women to use. In contrast, the same restrooms can be shared by both sexes in France. **Crescive norms** are implicit and learned only through interacting with other members of a culture. Crescive norms include customs, morés, and conventions. **Customs** are overt behaviors that have been passed down from one generation to the next. Consumer customs may include routine, everyday activities that have been handed down from the past, such as drinking coffee with breakfast and brushing one's teeth at night. They can also be formal and elaborate, such as anniversary celebrations and funerals. Earlier in this book, rituals were described as a series of behaviors in a fixed sequence. Customs are more broadly defined than rituals. It is best to think of a custom as an entire category of behavior (e.g., a wedding) and a ritual as the individual parts (e.g., each of the steps in exchanging vows).

Another form of custom is a **moré** (pronounced "more-ay"), which is a custom with strong moral implications. Morés typically prescribe right and wrong ways of behaving and involve taboos, or forbidden cultural activities involving eating, sex, gender roles, vulgarity, and the like. When consumers violate customs and morés, they are likely to receive strong sanctions from other members of society. For example, in the United States, consumers who "cut in line" at retail stores, restaurants, or amusement parks typically receive strong scoldings from other shoppers and patrons. In extreme cases, aberrant consumers may be removed from the premises. Similarly, in Arab cultures it is forbidden to feature women in advertising. Firms that do so risk serious consumer backlash. By contrast, **conventions** are norms that deal less with right or wrong or tradition, but rather with what is more or less "correct." A list of conventions in Western countries might include how to host a birthday party, how to complement clothes with scarves, how to maintain one's lawn, and how to coordinate a golf outing.

Customs, morés, and norms interact to guide culturally appropriate behavior. For example, a *moré* might tell consumers what gifts are appropriate for a boss or superior. A custom would guide consumers on *when* the gift should be presented, and a convention might suggest *how* to present the gift. In Japan, for example, morés indicate that periodically giving gifts to bosses is appropriate—even expected. The giving of year-end gifts, called *oseibo*, is a Japanese custom. Spending approximately 5,000 yen (about $40) for a store-delivered gift is the convention.

Conducting business in Saudi Arabia can be challenging for Western women. Although the environment is changing, gender separation still exists. It is taboo for women to dine without their husbands. Therefore, public places such as hotels and restaurants provide family rooms where women are served with their husbands. Also, women are forbidden to drive. The norm for women is to dress conservatively—long skirts, elbow-length sleeves or longer, and unrevealing necklines. Finally, it is not customary for Muslim men to shake hands or to engage in conversational body contact with women, but such gestures are common when speaking with other men.

Ethics

On May 2, 1989, 15-year-old Michael Thomas, a ninth grader at Meade Senior High School in Anne Arundel County, Maryland, was strangled by a fellow student who took Thomas' two-week-old Air Jordan basketball shoes and left his barefooted body in the woods near the school. Young Thomas idolized Michael Jordan so much that he paid $115.50 (approximately $250 in today's dollars) to wear the Jordan-endorsed shoes and "be like Mike."

This was not the first crime relating to sneakers, but perhaps the most infamous. This particular story was told in the May 14, 1990 issue of *Sports Illustrated*. Other such crimes have been committed, not only for Air Jordans, but for other brands of athletic shoes, jackets, and caps bearing sports insignia. If you think killing for sneakers

was something that happened only in the 1980s, think again. On February 14, 2004, three 16-year-old teens viciously beat and stabbed Huang Chen to death. The teens had placed a food order with Chen's family's takeout shop. When Chen delivered the order, the three teens murdered him to obtain money for sneakers.

Sociologist Elijah Anderson has argued that crimes among young black males involving apparel can be linked to inequalities in class and race. "The uneducated, inner city kids don't have a sense of opportunity. They feel the system is closed off to them. And yet they're bombarded with the same cultural apparatus [advertising] that the white middle class is. They don't have means to attain the things offered and yet they have the same desire. So they value these 'emblems,' these symbols of supposed success. The golf, the shoes, and the drug dealer's outfit—those things all belie the real situation, but it's a symbolic display that seems to say that things are all right." Professor Anderson argues that advertising fans the flames of this process by presenting

images that appeal to inner-city, black youth, and the shoe companies capitalize on the situation. Anderson stops short of laying all of the blame with marketers. "This is, after all, a free market," he notes.

NBA star Stephon Marbury of the New York Knicks is working on a solution. In September 2006, Marbury announced that he was producing a line of less expensive athletic apparel. In fact, Starbury brand shoes retail for about $15, a far cry from the $150 to $300 for Nike or Adidas shoes. Marbury's hope was to "keep kids a little safer." He reasoned that children wearing low-priced jackets and sports shoes would be less likely to become crime victims. Although Marbury closed his retail stores, he opened Starbury.com to sell his shoes and an expanded product line through a partnership with Amazon.com. Starbury has also announced plans to open dozens of stores and a distributorship in China.[32]

Source: Telander, R. (May 14, 1990). Your sneakers or Your Life. *Sports Illustrated*, 36–49.

Return Potential Model

Because norms are based on a group's cultural values, they not only coordinate the behavior of the culture, they also prescribe behaviors that prolong such values. Norms can also help define and enhance the identity of a culture through the use of distinct clothing, speech dialects, or hairstyles. Perhaps most importantly, norms can provide feedback on how much or how little a behavior is desired. The **return potential model** describes norms on two dimensions. The *behavioral dimension* specifies the amount of behavior regulated by the norm, and the *evaluation dimension* shows the cultural response to that behavior.[33] To illustrate, Figure 14.6 depicts three norms, A, B, and C. Each norm takes a different functional shape based on how much behavior relating to that norm is desired. For example, let's call Norm A "integrity." Approval for Norm A is a positive linear function, i.e., more is always better. So, Norm A is an upward-sloping straight line. Let's define Norm B as "infidelity." Cultural approval for Norm B is a negative linear function. Here, indifference is returned for the lowest level of behavior characterizing infidelity (fidelity is expected), and increasing levels of infidelity bring greater disapproval. So, Norm B is a downward-sloping straight line. Let's call Norm C "sense of humor." Norm C appears as an inverted U-shaped function. Here, cultural disapproval exists for very low levels of behavior relating to humor. In other words, lacking a sense of humor is met with disapproval. Similarly, very high levels of behavior relating to humor are not approved, either. Too many jokes and funny stories may be considered in bad taste. The middle ground is best for Norm C. A moderate level of humor *returns* the greatest approval.

Figure 14.6 also specifies acceptable levels for the three norms at points where the functions lie above the horizontal behavioral line. No level of infidelity (Norm B) is acceptable. Low levels of infidelity are expected, and clearly more is always worse. In contrast, behaviors representing integrity (Norm A) attain acceptance only at moderate or high levels. Sense of humor (Norm C) is like a roller coaster. Too little (slow) is no fun, and too much (fast) is overkill. Moderately low to moderately high levels of behaviors demonstrating sense of humor *return* cultural acceptance. Finally, the return potential model identifies the various levels of *intensity* for each norm by observing the range from the highest point to the lowest point on the *evaluation dimension*. For example, Norms A and C exhibit large distances between high and low points of approval. In contrast, Norm B's range of high and low approval is very small. Thus, one could infer that members of this culture feel more strongly about Norms A and C than they do about Norm B.

FIGURE 14.6 | **Return Potential Curves**

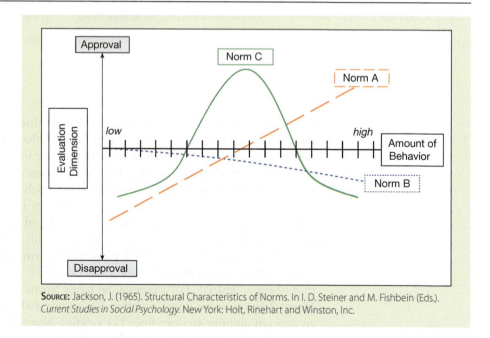

SOURCE: Jackson, J. (1965). Structural Characteristics of Norms. In I. D. Steiner and M. Fishbein (Eds.). *Current Studies in Social Psychology.* New York: Holt, Rinehart and Winston, Inc.

In summary, norms exert tremendous influence on consumer behavior by prescribing which actions are appropriate in specific situations. The return potential model helps explain how much of these actions are desirable and what *return* consumers can expect. The next section further describes how individual consumers adopt cultural values.

Consumer Values

Core Values

Pervasive and enduring cultural values are called *core values*. These important values reflect and shape the collective personality of a culture. Organizational anthropologist Geert Hofstede identified five dimensions of cultural values. Three of the dimensions center on expected social behavior; the fourth describes the search for "truth"; and the final dimension deals with the importance of time.[34] *Power distance* describes the extent to which the less powerful members of a culture tolerate large gaps in power structure. For example, the Hong Kong and French cultures exhibit high power distance—they expect power to be unequally distributed. In contrast, Germans, Austrians, and Scandinavians tend to exhibit low power distance. *Individualism* reflects the degree to which society is partitioned into groups. Individualistic cultures, such as the United States, tend *not* to emphasize group cohesion, while collectivist cultures, such as Japan, emphasize group solidity. *Masculinity* describes the extent to which men are expected to be competitive and ambitious and women are expected to be nurturing and concerned primarily with children and family. Japan exhibits high masculinity, while Spain and Taiwan rank low on this dimension. *Uncertainty avoidance* captures the extent to which a culture is uncomfortable with ambiguous and unstructured situations. Cultures such as Greece and Portugal tend to believe in absolute truth and therefore score high on this dimension. Conversely, Southeast Asia and India tend to behave contemplatively and therefore score low on this dimension. *Long-term orientation (LTO)* represents a culture's search for virtue (versus truth). This dimension measures cultural characteristics such as persistence, social hierarchies, thrift, and a sense of shame. Hong Kong and Taiwan score very high on LTO; Spain and Portugal score low. Differences in cultural core values can explain why some marketing efforts succeed in one culture and fail in another. For example, research shows that North American consumers exhibit more favorable attitudes toward advertising messages that focus on individualistic core values such as self-reliance, self-improvement, and achievement of personal goals. In contrast, South Korean consumers prefer ads that emphasize collectivistic core values including shared goals, family integrity, and group harmony.[35]

An American advertisement that focuses on individualism may not translate successfully into a culture such as that of South Koreans, who prefer ads that showcase group harmony.

At the individual level, core values are central to a consumer's **self-concept**, i.e., his or her awareness and perceptions about him or herself. As such, core values significantly influence consumers' beliefs, attitudes, and behaviors in the marketplace. Understanding consumers' core values helps marketers uncover the basis for the customer-product relationship. Means-end chains help explain how consumers derive core values in the marketplace.

OBJECTIVE ⑤   ## Means-End Chains

Cultural meaning moves from the broader society to consumer goods, and consumers extract meaning from their products and merge these meanings into their own personalities. For example, Red Bull drinkers often differ from Starbucks drinkers, and Corvette owners exhibit personality characteristics that may differ from Cadillac owners. Clearly, consumers do not invite all products to become a part of their self-concept.

A useful approach to understanding how consumers view products is through a means-end chain. A *means-end chain* combines three levels of a consumer's product knowledge—attributes, consequences, and values—to form a sequential network of meaning.[36]

Attributes A means-end chain begins with **attributes**, the basic characteristics of goods and services. Attributes can be *tangible*, such as the processing speed and memory capacity of a computer, the miles per gallon of an automobile, or the fabric of a dress. Attributes can also be *intangible*, such as the style of a house, the design of a jacket, or the comfort of a shoe. Furthermore, attributes are not limited to physical goods. Services such as banks offer tangible products like interest-bearing checking accounts and ATMs and provide intangible attributes like speed of service, friendliness of staff, and convenience of location. Tangible attributes are easily measured. For example, miles per gallon is a numeric value calculated from gas consumption and distance traveled. Similarly, megahertz is the unit of measurement for computer processing speed. Intangible attributes, although largely abstract, can also be measured. Consumers' attitudes toward quality, comfort, and convenience can be measured by survey instruments such as *Likert* (agreement) and rating scales (e.g., 1–10).

Stores such as Whole Foods Market showcase initiatives that make their customers feel environmentally responsible for purchasing products there instead of from competitors.

AP Images/PRNewsfoto/Whole Foods Market

Benefits Consumers rarely evaluate brands solely on the basis of their physical or abstract attributes. Instead, they are interested in what these attributes can do for them. **Benefits** represent the second stage in a means-end chain and embody consumers' perceptions about the outcomes or *consequences* provided by the attributes. Miles per gallon, for example, doesn't mean much as an attribute. It takes on meaning only because it indicates a certain level of economy. Similarly, computer-processing speed is meaningful because it allows for efficient multi-tasking. Benefits can be classified as *functional* or *psychosocial*. *Functional benefits* are tangible outcomes that result from consuming or using a product. For example, the functional benefit of a large engine is greater power and speed, and the functional benefit of consuming 12 ounces of Gatorade is replenishing electrolytes lost during exercise.

In contrast, *psychosocial benefits* include the internal *psychological* and external *social* consequences of using or consuming a product. Often, consumers enhance their self-concepts by purchasing items that make them feel stylish or beautiful. Consumers also derive social benefits from wearing stylish clothes if their peers make positive comments about them publicly. A consumer may benefit psychologically by eating a vegetarian diet and feeling positive about *not* consuming animals.[37] Similarly, a consumer may benefit socially if a colleague champions her vegetarian diet to another colleague.

Values Just as cultural values collectively represent what is important, useful, and desirable, *consumer values* embody consumers' priorities and preferences about their life goals and how products can help them attain these goals. For example, consumers who place a high priority on education may attend graduate school, despite the difficult regimen and foregone income. Consumers who strongly prefer American-made products may purchase only American cars and trucks. In fact, research shows that values relate to a wide variety of consumer behaviors, including automobile purchasing,[38] choice of occupation,[39] and media use.[40] Broadly speaking, values can be classified as instrumental or terminal.[41]

Instrumental values represent preferred modes of behavior. They are actions or "instruments" that provide positive value for consumers. In this sense, instrumental values are mostly transitional, i.e., a means to an end. For example, humor is an instrument for amusement; exercising is an action that provides feelings of vigor; and studying makes students feel responsible and informed. These instrumental values (amusement, exercise, and studying) might also be employed to serve higher-level goals (happiness, health, and wisdom) or **terminal values**, which represent psychological states of being. In this sense, terminal values serve as desirable end points. Figure 14.7 provides a list of related instrumental and terminal values.[42] Whether instrumental or terminal, consumer values represent the final destination of the means-end chain.

FIGURE 14.7 | Instrumental and Terminal Values

Instrumental Values	Terminal Values
Ambitious	The good life
Open-minded	An exciting life
Capable	World peace
Cheerful	Equality
Clean	Freedom
Courageous	Happiness
Forgiving	National security
Helpful	Pleasure
Honest	Salvation
Imaginative	Social recognition
Independent	True friendship
Intellectual	Wisdom
Logical	World beauty
Loving	Family security
Obedient	Mature love
Polite	Self-respect
Responsible	Sense of accomplishment
Self-controlled	Peace of mind

Source: Pollay, R. W. (1983). Measuring the Cultural Values Manifest in Advertising. *Current Issues and Research in Advertising, 6,* 71–92.

Because means-end chains are constructed at the individual level, they are likely to differ greatly among consumers. Also, not every means-end chain leads to an instrumental or terminal value. In fact, a functional benefit may represent the conclusion of a means-end chain. Consider a consumer who is so thirsty that the functional outcome (quenching her thirst) is the only *end* she is seeking. Any *means* (e.g., water, juice, soda) would suffice. In the same vein, a psychosocial benefit can serve as the final end point (e.g., buying a particular hat makes a consumer fit in with his friends). Finally, some products may have missing levels in the means-end chain (e.g., "I don't know why, but this golf ball really flies a great distance") and some products have multiple means-end chains because more than one attribute or benefit is important (e.g., distance and feel are important in a golf ball). Figure 14.8 illustrates a detailed means-end chain and provides examples and explanations for each stage.[43] Tangible attributes (e.g., silk fabric) typically provide functional benefits (e.g., comfort), and intangible attributes (e.g., stylish design) generally lead to psychosocial benefits (e.g., "I feel attractive; others have complimented my choice of style"). Both functional and psychosocial benefits can fulfill instrumental values, and instrumental values (e.g., cheerfulness) can lead to terminal values (e.g., happiness).

FIGURE 14.8 | The Means-End Chain Process

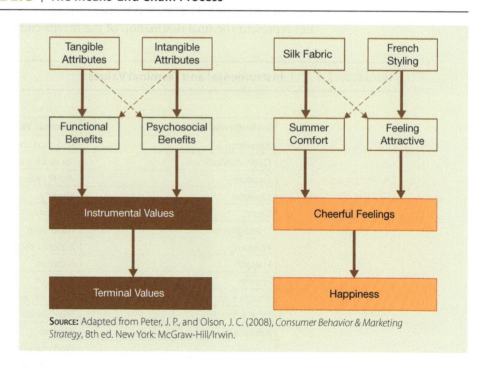

SOURCE: Adapted from Peter, J. P., and Olson, J. C. (2008), *Consumer Behavior & Marketing Strategy*, 8th ed. New York: McGraw-Hill/Irwin.

Rokeach Value Survey

Because instrumental and terminal values can help predict consumer attitudes and behaviors toward brands, researchers have begun to use value models in consumer behavior studies, such as the **Rokeach Value Survey (VALS)**.[41]

This widely used survey instrument is designed to provide insight into global value systems by linking them with consumer beliefs, attitudes, preferences, and behaviors. Some evidence suggests that differences in values across cultures can translate into product- and brand-specific consumer preferences. One interesting study compared adult Brazilians across six terminal value segments using the Rokeach Value Survey.[44] Segment A (13% of the sample) was primarily concerned with world peace, followed by inner harmony and true friendship. Relatively less materialistic in their value system, this group was more likely to be involved in activities such as reading, gardening, and visiting with family members. As consumers, this group was less likely to invest time and money in new products. By comparison, the more self-centered, achievement-oriented pleasure seekers found in Segment B (9% of the sample) were extravagant dressers who value the latest fashions. This segment was more likely to try new products. A third segment (21% of the sample) included relatively younger and more educated individuals who mostly value inner harmony and freedom. This group was motivated to attend artistic and cultural activities and preferred living in large cities. They viewed clothing as more than just bodily protection, but they stopped short of using it as a fashion statement.

The List of Values (LOV)

Similar in purpose to the Rokeach Value Survey, the **List of Values (LOV)** was developed at the University of Michigan Survey Research Center to identify nine consumer value segments and link them to value-related consumer behavior.[45] The nine segments are:

- Security
- Self-respect
- Self-fulfillment
- Accomplishment
- Fun and enjoyment
- Warm relations
- Well-respected
- Belonging
- Excitement[46]

Research demonstrates that the LOV is easier to administer and that it performs as well as VALS in predicting consumer behavior trends.[47] The LOV has been used to show that people who emphasize sense of belonging in their value system tend to be older and more likely to read *Reader's Digest* and *TV Guide* than people who do not endorse this value. People who endorse excitement in their value system are younger and prefer *Rolling Stone* magazine.[48] Finally, LOV has been used to help predict the purchase of several categories of durable goods. For example, consumers who valued security, respect, and sense of belonging showed greater preference for sports, exercise, and luxury products. Those who valued fun and excitement revealed a greater preference for home entertainment products and pets.[49]

Chapter Summary

Culture is often defined as the patterns of meaning acquired by members of society expressed in their knowledge, beliefs, art, laws, morals, customs, and habits. Put simply, culture can be thought of as a system of collectively held values or the *personality* of a society. Cultural values comprise a collective set of beliefs about what is important, useful, and desirable. The meaning of cultural values is mobile within a given society. Cultural meaning begins in the collective minds of society and is transferred to consumer products by marketing efforts and the fashion system. Consumers then adopt cultural values from the products they purchase by employing exchange, possession, grooming, and divestment rituals. Enculturation refers to learning about one's own culture; acculturation occurs when people in one culture adapt to meanings resident in another culture.

Written and spoken language is perhaps the most obvious characteristic of a culture. Many of the problems in translating languages verbally stem from fundamental differences in cultures. Some words and phrases have no translation because the meaning may not exist in a different culture. Nonverbal communication, such as body language and symbols, is also important to cultures. Facial expressions, gestures, postural shift, and touching differ among cultures. A familiar hand signal may have an obscene interpretation in another culture. Different cultures also prefer standing relatively close or far away, depending on their attitudes toward interpersonal spacing. Symbols help convey meaning through representation. Important marketing symbols include brand names and brand logos. Because organizations spend considerable money and effort creating brand symbols, legal protection for these symbols has become paramount.

Norms serve as a culture's rules for behavior. Enacted norms explicitly and formally prescribe acceptable behaviors, while crescive norms are implicit and learned only through experience; these include customs, morés, and conventions. Customs are behaviors that have been passed down from previous generations. A moré is a custom that implies a moral right or wrong way of behaving. Conventions are norms that describe the best or "correct" way of doing something. Because norms differ greatly across cultures, it is important to understand different behavioral expectations prior to traveling or doing business with a foreign culture. The return potential model describes norms on behavioral and evaluation dimensions. Too much or too little behavior, such as humor, can be evaluated either positively or negatively, depending on the cultural norms.

A means-end chain combines three levels of a consumer's knowledge about attributes, consequences, and values to form a chronology of product meaning. Attributes are the fundamental characteristics of features of a product. They can be tangible, such as weight or size, and they can be intangible, such as style or quality. Knowledge about product attributes leads consumers to evaluate the benefits that derive from attributes. Benefits can be functional or psychosocial. Functional benefits provide easily measured outcomes, such as speed and durability, while psychosocial benefits involve the psychological or social consequences of using or consuming a product. Product benefits can provide value satisfaction for consumers. Values are classified as instrumental or terminal. Instrumental values represent actions or modes of behavior, such as being imaginative or honest. Terminal values represent psychological end states, such as happiness or freedom. The Rokeach Value Survey and List of Values (LOV) are survey instruments that help consumer psychologists and marketers predict consumer attitudes and behaviors toward brands.

Key Terms

acculturation
attributes
benefits
brand jingles

brand logos
culture
conventions
crescive norms

cultural categories
cultural principles
cultural translation
cultural values

culturally constituted world
customs
divestment rituals
enacted norms
enculturation
exchange rituals
grooming rituals

instrumental values
List of Values (LOV)
morés
opinion leaders
possession rituals
return potential model
Rokeach Value Survey (VALS)

self-concept
subcultures
terminal values
theory of cognitive itch

Review and Discussion

1. Locate Aesop's fables (you can find them on the Internet). Select your favorite one and explain the cultural value being communicated.

2. Cultural values comprise a collective set of beliefs about what is important, useful, and desirable, i.e., the *personality* of a society. Select a culture or subculture to which you belong and explain this group's cultural values.

3. Identify the three stations in McCracken's theory regarding the mobility of cultural meaning. Explain how marketing activities and the fashion system transfer cultural meaning to consumer goods and how consumers adopt that meaning for themselves via rituals.

4. Think about the last time you sold or gave away an important possession (e.g., car, clothing, collection, etc.). Identify the divestment rituals that you conducted before giving it up.

5. Acculturation is a challenge for nations with diverse populations. Explain why the United States has so much at stake regarding acculturation of its immigrants.

6. Why is body language so important for a high-context culture?

7. Identify a brand jingle that got "stuck in your head." Why was this jingle successful at creating a "cognitive itch"?

8. Select your favorite brand logo. Describe its elements in detail and explain whether the symbols are likely to translate successfully into foreign cultures.

9. Identify one of your family customs and describe it in one phrase. Next, explain the various rituals involved with this custom in one paragraph.

10. Construct a means-end chain for the brand iPod. Identify tangible and intangible attributes, functional and psychosocial benefits, and instrumental and terminal values that derive from this product.

Short Application Exercises

1. If you have traveled to a foreign nation, describe specific characteristics of the culture that created for you the greatest "culture shock." Identify specific differences in cultural values, verbal language, body language, symbols, and norms. If you have not traveled abroad, interview someone who has and ask him or her to identify the cultural differences listed above.

2. Select one specific value from your culturally constituted world (e.g., individuality,

freedom, ambition, responsibility) and trace its movement from society to consumer goods, all the way to consumers. Draw on McCracken's framework for the mobility of cultural meaning. Identify marketing activities and elements of the fashion system that transfer your selected value to consumer products. Select various rituals that subsequently transfer this meaning to individual consumers.

3. Conduct an in-depth interview with a consumer from your parents' generation. Ask

questions about the kinds of gifts they gave their children for their birthdays. Try to identify indirectly the cultural meaning that resides in their exchange rituals.

4. Research the business practice of using "bribes" in Middle Eastern cultures. Explain how this Western concept (bribe) does not take on a pejorative meaning among Arabs.

5. Select a popular slogan from an American product and translate it into a foreign language of your choice. Identify at least three points of confusion regarding the translation. Focus not only on semantics and phonology, but also on cultural translation issues.

Managerial Application

Imagine you work in the marketing research department for a major television network. The network is considering developing a new show targeted at various college subcultures. The network is interested in uncovering core values for this subgroup.

Your Challenge:

1. Use the Return Potential Model as a framework to illustrate the values of (a) politeness, (b) cheerfulness, and (c) conscientiousness in your most important college subculture (e.g., marketing club, drama club, fraternity, sports team, religious group).

2. Interview several members of this subculture regarding the desirability of these three values.

3. Using Figure 14.6 as a framework, draw curves for all three values.

4. Are the functions for politeness, cheerfulness, and conscientiousness simply linear (i.e., is more always better) or do diminishing returns exist?

5. With respect to these three values, how would you advise the network to proceed in designing the show?

End Notes

1 Woote, A. (2011, January 21). Color Meanings Can be Lost and Found in Translation. *Desert News. Times* [Online]. Available: http://www.deseretnews.com /article/705364808/Color-meanings-can-be-lost-and -found-in-translation.html.

2 Tylor, E. B. (1871). *Primitive culture.* New York: Brentano's.

3 Hofstede, G. (2001), *Culture's Consequences,* 2nd ed. Thousand Oaks, CA: Sage Publications.

4 McCracken, G. (1986). Culture and Consumption: A Theoretical Account of the Structure and Movement of the Cultural Meaning of Consumer Goods. *Journal of Consumer Research, 13,* 71–84.

5 Dittmar, H, Long, K., and Meek, R. (2004). Buying on the Internet: Gender Differences in Online and Conventional Buying Motivations. *Sex Roles: A Journal of Research, 50,* 423–444.

6 Rogers, S., and Harris, M. A. (2003). Gender and E-commerce: An Exploratory Study. *Journal of Advertising Research, 43,* 322–329.

7 Barthes, J. (1983). *The Fashion System.* New York: Hill and Wang.

8 McCracken, G. (1985). The Trickle-down Theory Rehabilitated. In M. Solomon (Ed.), *The Psychology of Fashion* (pp. 39–54). Lexington, MA: Lexington Books.

9 McCracken, G. (1985). The Trickle-down Theory Rehabilitated. In M. Solomon (Ed.), *The Psychology of Fashion* (pp. 39–54). Lexington, MA: Lexington Books.

10 Levi-Strauss, C. (1966). *The Savage Mind.* Chicago, IL: University of Chicago Press.

11 Blumberg, P. (1974). The Decline and Fall of the Status Symbol: Some Thoughts on Status in Post-Industrial Society. *Social Problems 21,* 480–498.

12 Pareles, Jon (1993, March 22). Review/Pop: A Party Based on the Grid of Rap. *The New York Times.* [Online]. Available: http://query.nytimes.com/gst/fullpage.html?res =9F0CE4DD103BF931A15750C0A965958260.

13 Skiba, P. (2011, September 27). Saggy Pants Ordinance Brings Cash to Albany. *Albany Herald.* [Online]. Available: http://www.albanyherald.com/news/2011/sep/26/saggy -pants-ordinance-brings-cash-albany/.

14 Rook, D. W. (1985). The Ritual Dimension of Consumer Behavior. *Journal of Consumer Research, 12,* 251–264.

15 Giesler, M., and Pohlmann, M. (2003). The Anthropology of File Sharing: Consuming Napster as a Gift. In P. Keller and D. Rook (Eds.), *Advances in Consumer Research* (Vol. 30). Provo, UT: Association for Consumer Research.

16 Green, R. and Alden, D. (1988). Functional Equivalence in Cross-Cultural Consumer Behavior: Gift Giving in Japan and the United States. *Psychology & Marketing, 5*, 155–168.

17 Rook, D. and Levy, S. (1983). Psychological Themes in Consumer Grooming Rituals. In R. Bagozzi and A. Tybout (Eds.), *Advances in Consumer Research* (Vol. 10, pp. 329–333). Provo, UT: Association for Consumer Research.

18 Faber, R. J., O'Guinn, T. C., and McCarty, J. A. (1987). Ethnicity, Acculturation, and the Importance of Product Attributes. *Psychology & Marketing, Summer*, 121–134.

19 Rudmin, F. W. (2003). Catalogue of Acculturation Constructs: Descriptions of 126 Taxonomies, 1918–2003. In W. J. Lonner, D. L. Dinnel, S. A. Hayes, and D. N. Sattler (Eds.), *Online Readings in Psychology and Culture*, Unit 8, Chapter 8. Bellingham, WA: Center for Cross-Cultural Research, Western Washington University.

20 Holt, D. B. (2004). *How Brands Become Icons: The Principles of Cultural Branding*. Boston: Harvard Business School Press.

21 Guzman, F. and Paswan, A. (2009). Cultural Brands from Emerging Markets: Brand Image across Host and Home Countries. *Journal of International Marketing, 17* (3), 71–86.

22 Carol, J. (1956). *Language, Thought and Reality: Selected Writings of Benjamin Lee Whorf*. Cambridge, MA: MIT Press.

23 Steinmetz, G. and Quintanilla, C. (April 10, 1988). Tough Target: Whirlpool Expected Easy Going in Europe, and It Got a Big Shock. *The Wall Street Journal*, A1, A6.

24 Usunier, J. (1993). *International Marketing: A Cultural Approach*. Englewood Cliffs, NJ: Prentice Hall International (UK) Limited.

25 Ekman, P., and Friesen, W. V. (1975). *Unmasking the Face*. Englewood Cliffs, NJ: Prentice Hall.

26 Hall, E. (1959). *The Silent Language*. New York: Doubleday.

27 Valenzuela, A. Mellers, B., and Strebel, J. (2009). Pleasurable Surprises: A Cross-Cultural Study of Consumer Responses to Unexpected Incentives. *Journal of Consumer Research, 36*, 792–805.

28 Yang-Soo, R. (1981). A Cross-Cultural Comparison of Korean and American Managerial Styles. *Global Economic Review, 10* (2), 45–63.

29 Kellaris, J. (2003). Dissecting Earworms: Further Evidence on the 'Song-stuck-in-your head' Phenomenon, presentation to Society for Consumer Psychology, Feb. 22, 2003.

30 Cuneo, A. (2007, March 16). AT&T Sues NASCAR over Logo: Wants to Rebrand Cingular Car in Nextel-sponsored Racing Series. *Advertising Age*. Available at: http://adage.com/abstract.php?article_id=115626.

31 [Online]. Available: http://www.pakwheels.com/forums/wheels-fan-clubs/69494-history-mercedes-benz-3-pointed-stars and http://www.logoblog.org/mercedes-benz-logo.php.

32 Chao, L. (2010, August 11). Marbury Courts Hoops Fans in China. *The Wall Street Journal*. [Online]. Available: http://online.wsj.com/article/SB1000142405274870343

5104575421191743179492.html?KEYWORDS=starbury#articleTabs%3Darticle.

33 Jackson, J. (1965). Structural Characteristics of Norms. In I. D. Steiner and M. Fishbein (Eds.). *Current Studies in Social Psychology*. New York: Holt, Rinehart and Winston.

34 Hofstede, G., and Bond, M. H. (1988). The Confucius Connection: From Cultural Roots to Economic Growth. *Organizational Dynamics, Spring*, 5.

35 Han, S-P., and Shavitt, S. (1994). Persuasion and Culture: Advertising Appeals in Individualistic and Collectivistic Societies. *Journal of Experimental Social Psychology, 30*, 326–350.

36 Gutman, J., and Reynolds, T. J. (1979). An Investigation of the Levels of Cognitive Abstraction Utilized by Consumers in Product Differentiation. In J. Eighmey (Ed.), *Attitude Research under the Sun* (pp. 125–150). Chicago, IL: American Marketing Association.

37 Alternatively, vegetarianism could serve as a functional benefit for consumers who have improved their health through this diet.

38 Henry, W. (1976). Cultural Values Do Correlate with Consumer Behavior. *Journal of Marketing Research, 13*, 121–127.

39 Rosenberg, M. J. (1957). *Occupations and Values*. Glencoe, IL: The Free Press.

40 Becker, B. W. and Conner, P. E. (1981). Personal Values of the Heavy User of Mass Media. *Journal of Advertising Research, 21*, 37–43.

41 Rokeach, M. J. (1979). *The Nature of Human Values*. New York: Free Press.

42 Pollay, R. W. (1983). Measuring the Cultural Values Manifest in Advertising. *Current Issues and Research in Advertising, 6*, 71–92.

43 Peter, J. P., and Olson, J. C. (2008), *Consumer Behavior & Marketing Strategy*, 8th ed. New York: McGraw-Hill/Irwin.

44 Kamakura, W. A. and Mazzon, J. A. (1991). Value Segmentation: A Model for the Measurement of Values and Value Systems. *Journal of Consumer Research, 18*, 208–218.

45 Kahle, L. R. (1983). *Social Values and Social Change*. New York: Praeger.

46 Kahle, L. R., Beatty, S. E., and Homer, P. (1986). Alternative Measurement Approaches to Consumer Values: The List of Values (LOV) and Values and Life Style (VALS). *The Journal of Consumer Research, 13*, 405–409.

47 Beatty, S. E., Kahle, L. R., Homer, P. and Misra, S. (1985). Alternative Measurement Approaches to Consumer Values: The List of Values and the Rokeach Value Survey. *Psychology & Marketing, 2*, 181–200.

48 Kahle, L. R., & Kennedy, P. (1988). Using the List of Values (LOV) to Understand Consumers. *Journal of Consumer Marketing, 2*, 49–56; Kahle, L., Poulos, B., and Sukhdial, A. Changes in Social Values in the United States during the Past Decade. *Journal of Advertising Research, 28*, 35–41.

49 Corfman, K. P., Lehmann, D. R., and Narayanan, S. (1991). Values, Utility, and Ownership: Modeling the Relationships for Consumer Durables. *Journal of Retailing, 67*, 184–204.

CHAPTER 15

THE INFLUENCE OF DEMOGRAPHY

OBJECTIVES *After studying this chapter, you will be able to…*

1 Understand the importance of population size and demographic transition.

2 Define and understand social class.

3 Explain social structure in the United States.

4 Compare and contrast income versus social class.

5 Understand the importance of social class to consumer behavior.

6 Describe the six age cohorts in the United States.

Marketing to the "Mass Class"

"Mass Luxury," "Mass Prestige," and "Mass Class" caption a relatively new phenomenon in consumer behavior. Consumers are trading up to higher levels of quality and taste. In 2010, more than 45 million U.S. households (about 38%) earned more than $65,000 annually, a group referred to as the "middle-market." In contrast, median household income in 2010 was $49,445 (mean household income was $67,530). Members of the U.S. middle-market are well educated, well traveled, more sophisticated, and generally more adventurous than in the past, and they are happy to spend their discretionary income on high-quality premium-serviced products. They're buying a small taste of the luxury market. While trading up in premium product categories that are emotionally important, the middle-market is trading down to low-cost brands and private labels in categories that are less meaningful. For example, a middle-market household might shop at Costco for household toiletries and at the same time purchase

© iStockphoto.com/macroworld

Sam Adams beer. Businesses now offer a wide variety of new-luxury goods and services, including automobiles, appliances, consumer electronics, shoes, clothes, beer, wine, and spirits. Indeed, new-luxury brands such as Starbucks coffee, Kendall-Jackson wines, and Victoria's Secret lingerie command a premium over traditional brands, but they are priced dramatically below super-premium, old-luxury brands. Bath & Body Works is another good example. They typically offer body lotion at nearly three times the price of Vaseline Intensive Care, and yet B&BW only costs about half as much as Kiehl's Crème de Corps.[1]

Some call this behavior the "ongoing democratization of luxury."[2] And the trend isn't limited to the United States. Firms like Nokia, H&M, Zara, ING Direct, Dell Inc., Gap, Virgin, Microsoft, Nike, EasyJet, and L'Oreal are targeting millions of middle-market consumers all over the world who are seeking luxury at affordable prices. Increasing wealth in developed economies (e.g., South Korea and Hong Kong) encourage entrepreneurs to introduce high quality brands. Economic growth in many developing nations (e.g., Zimbabwe and Botswana) has also generated millions of new consumers who want the same quality brands as the developed world. And worldwide communication channels play on the desires of these new consumers. The following examples demonstrate the eagerness of global firms to embrace the "Mass Class":

- IKEA, the Swedish furniture company, recently opened new mega stores in Russia and China. By 2010, IKEA had a total of 10 new stores in Beijing, Guangdong, and Shanghai's Pudong New District.

- French car manufacturer Renault is building the Logan, also known as the "World Car." Production on the Logan began at Renault's Dacia subsidiary in Romania. Renault hopes to build 200,000 cars a year for Eastern European consumers.

- Two Chinese auto manufacturers, Chery and Geely, have gained a domestic market share of around 10% by undercutting international rivals on price. The Chinese cars cost about RMB 40,000 (US$4800). Geely is planning to increase exports to the Middle East and South America. In 2010, Geely purchased Volvo.

- Indian car maker Tata Motors is appealing to the country's masses with a sporty vehicle priced at US$2000. Tata also owns the Jaguar and Range Rover brands.

Segmentation lies at the very heart of modern marketing. Its premise is simple—all consumers are not alike. It follows that targeting unique groups of consumers seeking similar benefits is good marketing practice. The process of segmentation involves a three-step procedure: (1) define a broad product market, (2) identify a variety of consumer needs within that product market, and (3) organize potential subsets of consumers who share common characteristics and behaviors. This chapter examines consumer characteristics and behaviors relating to demography.

We also provide information on specific groups such as Hispanic and African-American subcultures, Jewish consumers, Generation Y, and working women, and provide key references to help understand these important subgroups on our Cengage Learning website. For example, the U.S. Census Bureau (www.census.gov) provides information regarding the size and trends of all races in the United States, and detailed information on the demographic, economic, and social characteristics of individual cities and counties throughout the country. We encourage our readers to visit our book companion website at www.cengage.com to find more interesting resources for understanding demographics and subcultures.

Demography

Demography refers to the statistical study of human populations. Key population metrics include population size, social class, income, and age. Many professionals, such as marketers, economists, social psychologists, sociologists, and public health officials, are interested in understanding demography. Although marketers rarely begin the segmentation process by arbitrarily selecting a demographic characteristic such as age or income, demography often becomes the launching point for marketing programs once consumer needs are clearly understood.

For example, using the three-step segmentation procedure above, a marketer might first select a broad product category such as time-displaying devices. Second, the marketer identifies a variety of consumer needs relating to the use of time-displaying devices. Asking the question, "who needs these products and why?" is a good starting point for identifying consumer needs. One need might include large, analog displays for children learning to tell time. Another need might be highly decorative time pieces that convey wealth and status. These two needs clearly suggest different strategies for organizing groups of consumers who share common demographic characteristics—age and social class. After identifying consumers who share common demographic characteristics, marketers select appropriate media to develop effective advertising and promotional campaigns. Demographic characteristics are relatively easy and inexpensive to measure, and most secondary data, such as U.S. Census data, are described in terms of demography. We'll begin by examining population changes around the world before moving on to social class, income, and age demographics in the U.S.

OBJECTIVE **1** ## Population Size

The world population recently eclipsed seven billion people (as of October 2011). Professors at the University of Virginia explain the world population through **demographic transition**, a four-step process that occurs as nations develop from pre-industrial to highly developed economies.[3] The idea of demographic transition can be traced to Warren Thompson, an American demographer who identified population shifts during the industrial revolution of the late eighteenth century. Stage 1, the *pre-industrial stage*, depicts a population with

---

TABLE 15.1 | **Demographic Transition**

	Population	Economy	Examples
STAGE 1	Very Slow Growth	Pre-industrial	All countries prior to 1800
STAGE 2	Population Boom	Industrialization in progress	Nigeria, Bangladesh
STAGE 3	Stationary	Industrialized	Brazil, South Africa, U.S.
STAGE 4	Declining	Highly Industrialized	Japan, Germany

Source: Bellow, S. (Spring, 2012). Over Seven Billion Served. *The University of Virginia Magazine*, 26–30.

equally high birth and death rates, and hence a relatively stable population. Stage 1 describes most of human history: life is difficult, and large numbers of children are necessary to support a labor intense, agrarian society. In Stage 2, *the transitional stage*, the onset of industrialization boosts agricultural production. In addition, discoveries in medicine decrease death rates. Birthrates, however, remain high. The early twentieth century describes Stage 2 in much of the world, along with the world population growth of five billion people. During Stage 3, the *industrial stage*, birthrates decline due to increasing affluence and urbanization. Birthrates approach the death rate, and population growth slows to near zero percent. In Stage 4, the *post-industrial stage*, births fall below 2.1 children per woman, which has been defined as the replacement rate necessary to maintain a stable population. Death rates remain low, and the population eventually decreases.

Professor Qian Cia observes that different parts of the world today exhibit different stages of demographic transition. A glance at some major regions of the world support Cia's observations (see Figure 15.1).[3]

FIGURE 15.1 | World Population

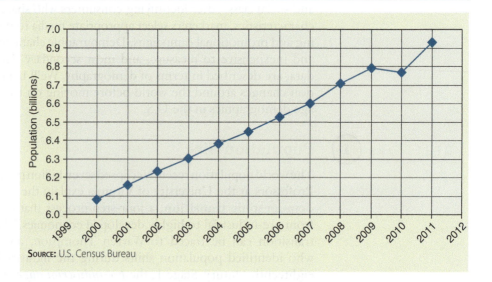

SOURCE: U.S. Census Bureau

The United States The United States is at once growing and aging. The U.S. population tripled during the twentieth century and will exceed 320 million by 2014. Increasing birthrates and immigration accounted for the majority of growth over the past two centuries. During the past decade, however, the U.S. population growth rate has hovered at around only 0.90 percent, never exceeding one percent. Although this growth rate may appear low, other industrialized nations are growing even more slowly. For example, Japan, South Korea, and most of Europe have near zero or even negative growth rates.

The United States is the third most populous nation in the world, yet it is less than one-fourth the size of China (1.35 billion) and less than one-third the size of India (1.22 billion). In contrast, the U.S. produces about $14.7 trillion of the world's $74.5 trillion GDP (2011 purchasing power parity). The U.S.

is responsible for almost 20% of the global economy with fewer than 5% of world's population. This combination makes the U.S. a desirable target market for global marketers.

A current trend in the U.S. population is lower fertility and greater longevity. The result is an increasing proportion of older people. In 2010, approximately 13% of the U.S. population was at least 65 years old. By 2050, this proportion is projected to exceed 20%. Aging is a global trend. The number of people aged 65 and older is expected to reach 1.53 billion (or, 16% of the population) worldwide by the year 2050, three times more than the 516 million in 2010. During the same period, people in the 85-and-older group will increase from 40 million in 2010 to 219 million. Currently, 20% or more of the populations in Germany, Italy, and Japan are 65 years or older. By 2050, approximately one hundred countries will host older populations representing 20% or more of their people, with Europe the world's oldest region. Clearly, the age structure of a population can affect a nation's economy. Highly developed nations with older populations typically demand more health care, assisted living, and travel and financial services.

FIGURE 15.2 | **Projected Proportion of U.S. Population Age 65 and Older**

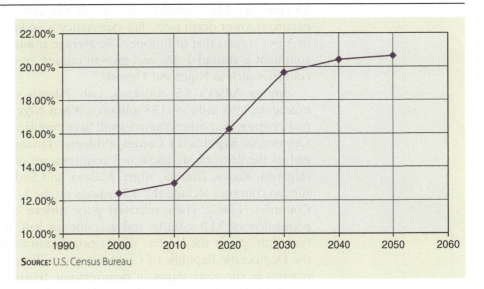

SOURCE: U.S. Census Bureau

South America South America shows vast disparity among wealthy and poor nations. For example, Bolivia and Brazil exist side-by-side; however, they represent different stages of demographic transition.[3] Brazil is the largest nation in South America, with a population of more than 200 million and a growth rate barely over one percent and declining. Brazil's population comprises mostly immigrants and their descendants. The richest economy in South America, Brazil produces the eighth largest GDP in the world ($2.2 trillion in 2011). Characterized by large and well-developed agricultural, mining, manufacturing, and service sectors, Brazil has progressed through the later period of Stage 3 in demographic transition.

Bolivia, on the other hand, is one of the least economically developed nations in Latin America and most likely resides early in Stage 3 of demographic transition. Bolivia's GPD is ranked 92nd in the world at less than $52 billion (as of 2011), behind much smaller nations such as Costa Rica and Slovenia. Although Bolivia's population growth rate is declining slightly, it remains near 2% with a fertility rate of about three children per woman and a median age of 22. In contrast, Brazil's fertility rate is approximately 2.8% with a median age of 30 (the median age in the U.S. is 37).[3]

Professor Hernan Moscoso Boedo links changes in fertility rates to demographic transition. During the first stage, subsistence farmers need children as an inexpensive economic input. In addition, a relatively high fertility rate counteracts high infant mortality. Finally, without the benefit of social security payments, parents need children to take care of their needs as they age. As a nation's economy transitions into Stage 2, however, child labor loses its value and there is less incentive to produce children.[3]

Africa Africa is projected to make significant economic gains over the next decade. Nevertheless, a population boom currently burdens the continent. Africa's population has more than tripled during the second half of the twentieth century, growing from 230 million to over a billion people. Moreover, in many sub-Saharan countries, 40 to 50% of the population is younger than 15 years old. High fertility rates (nearly five children per woman) and comparatively lower death rates (life expectancy is 56 years) helped the population of Africa surpass that of Europe. The average annual growth rate for the entire continent is around 2.3%, and growth rates in excess of three percent exist in countries such as Niger and Uganda.[4]

Among Africa's 55 countries, only Nigeria currently has a population exceeding 100 million (158 million). When Nigeria reaches 390 million at mid-century, four other countries will have populations exceeding 100 million: Democratic Republic of Congo, Ethiopia, Tanzania, and Egypt. Before the end of the century, six additional countries are projected to join this group (Uganda, Kenya, Zambia, Niger, Malawi, and Sudan). Another key group of African countries include the 33 nations on the UN's list of Least Developed Countries (LDC). These relatively poor African countries have a combined population of 510 million and account for half of the continent's population. Ethiopia is the largest, with a population of 83 million, followed by the Democratic Republic of Congo at 66 million. A large portion of Africa remains in the early stages of demographic transition. As death rates begin to fall, birthrates will remain high, which will feed Africa's population boom. Assuming a moderate decline in current fertility levels, Africa's population is expected to double to 2.1 billion by mid-century. At this level, the continent would account for nearly a quarter of the world's population.[1]

Marketing to subsistence economies creates both challenges and opportunities for marketers. Conditions in distribution systems needed to reach consumers in subsistence markets differ greatly from those of highly developed nations. Subsistence consumers often earn less than $2 per day, lack adequate food and education, demonstrate limited literacy, and lack access to transportation. All of this adds up to limited consumption alternatives. When aggregated across the globe, however, subsistence markets demand aggregate purchasing power of more than $5 trillion. A recent study shows that subsistence consumers are members of densely networked social and kinship communities, on which they draw to offset their lack of money, access, and education.[5] One particular marketing approach that works in subsistence markets is referred to as **microenterprises**: small, informal groups that help supply goods and services to rural customers. Some consumers in microenterprises help manage the distribution of products and services while balancing business and family demands. These key players are termed *subsistence consumer-merchants* (SCMs) because of the multiple roles they play. SCMs can sustain relationships in three interdependent areas: (1) vendor, (2) customer, and (3) family. These relationships are managed through buying, selling, and receiving, as well as granting of credit. Marketers who want to work with SCMs should try to understand how they operate their businesses and how they manage these highly interdependent relationships.

Asia Asia hosts six of the most populous nations in the world (China, India, Indonesia, Pakistan, Bangladesh, and Japan). Challenges faced by large populations include the strain they place on resources and infrastructure. Large populations with extreme poverty, unstable governments, and civil unrest impede demographic transition. Countries such as Pakistan and Afghanistan, where political instability delays economic development, still maintain very high birth and death rates. China, on the other hand, has made a deliberate attempt to control its population growth through its one-child law, and its birthrates have declined as a result. China has passed through demographic transition quickly and appears to be at the same stage of development as the U.S.[3] India's fertility rate fell during the late 1990s, and both India and China have demonstrated exceptional economic growth. With more than 2.5 billion people in both countries, per capita wealth has increased in kind.

Marketing strategies to subsistence economies differ greatly from strategies in more developed nations.

Charlotte Thege/Images of Africa Photobank/Alamy

China's economic rise over the last generation has been meteoric. China now boasts the second largest economy in the world with more than $10 trillion GDP (2011 purchasing power parity). Nevertheless, projections of its future power ignore that its fertility rate is 30% below replacement rate, i.e., the birthrate is not sufficient for long-term population stability. The Census Bureau estimates that China's population will peak in 2026, its labor force will shrink, and its over-65 population will more than double over the next 20 years—from 115 million to 240 million. In short, China will age rapidly. Only Japan has aged more quickly. However, Japan had the advantage of growing rich before growing old. By 2030, China will have a slightly higher proportion of elderly people than Western Europe does today. In fact, Western Europe has a higher median age than Florida! That puts this data in perspective.[6]

Like China, other highly developed countries in Asia face population decline. Japan, South Korea, Singapore, and Hong Kong face aging populations and declining birthrates. The Census Bureau projects that Japan's population will decrease by 30 million people over the next 40 years. During the past decade, Japan's death rate exceeded its birthrate. Today, Japan's death rate is approximately ten deaths per 1,000 people per year. By comparison, Japan's birthrate is about seven births per 1,000 people per year. In nations where the death rate exceeds the birthrate, fewer workers will be supporting more retired people.

Europe Europe, once the bastion of kingdoms, will account for only seven percent of the world's population by 2050. Nevertheless, all of Europe is not shrinking. Despite low birthrates, countries such as Great Britain, Ireland, and Spain maintain modest growth. Ireland, for example, has maintained

---

FIGURE 15.3 | **Japan's Birth and Death Rates**

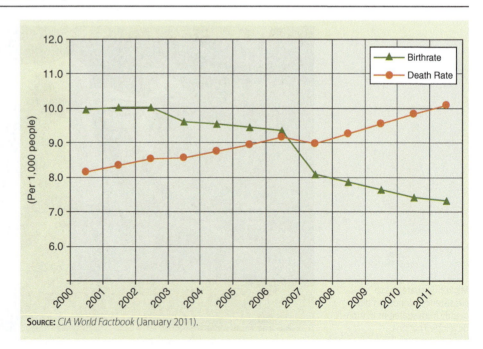

SOURCE: *CIA World Factbook* (January 2011).

Global Perspectives

Marketing to Asia's Low-Income Population

Four billion people across the globe live on about $2,000 a year; most of them live in Asia. Can marketers satisfy the needs of these consumers both ethically and profitably? The late professor C. K. Prahalad reasoned that marketers penalize the poor when they fail to give them access to high-value, mass-marketed products.[7] Nevertheless, a majority of global marketers have focused primarily on the affluent Asia minority. These high-income consumers tend to live in urban areas and share the product preferences of their Western counterparts. Yet low-income Asians have the same aspirations as the wealthy—they want to live the good life, raise their children to be respected by their peers, and signal their achievements through purchasing and using high-value brands. Herein lies a marketing opportunity. As a group, low-income Asians aren't necessarily cost-conscious; they are value-conscious. And they have strong feelings about the roles brands play in their lives. They prefer high-value brands because these brands carry an implied "quality guarantee." For example, Heinz offers Complan Family, a nutritional powdered-milk supplement that has gained strong brand equity among Indian consumers. Heinz markets two-serving packs, which enables mothers who cannot afford large quantities to give it to their children during stressful times as a nutritional boost. For their part, Proctor & Gamble designed and markets a completely new version of Tide that recognizes the washing habits and water conditions of Chinese consumers. This is strikingly divergent from the practices of multinational firms that simply strip down premium brands by offering inferior ingredients and packaging, or just sell smaller sizes.

Michelle Kristula-Green, Global Head of People and Culture for Leo Burnett Worldwide, offers some strategies for marketing to Asia's low-income majority:

- Don't assume that a $2,000-a-year income is poverty. Many of these consumers pay little to no taxes, have no housing or child-care expenses, and buy inexpensive, fresh food. Eighty-four percent of Chinese earning about $2,400 a year have a cell phone.
- Live with the people. Visit their homes, go to their markets, and travel in their mode of transportation.
- Understand that low-income Asians are willing and able to purchase high-value products and services.
- Don't take an existing brand and water-it-down so that it can be sold at a lower price. Design the brand for the specific needs of the market.
- Invest in local distribution systems that employ rural villagers.

What is evident from the points listed above is that significant marketing opportunities exist for the four billion people at the bottom of the economic pyramid. Marketers should think about new product development (contents, packaging, and pricing), new distribution alliances, novel business models, and local support for successfully marketing to the Asian masses.

Is Nestlé's Infant Formula Better than Breastfeeding?

Ethics

In June 2011, Nongovernmental organizations (NGOs) in Laos openly criticized Nestlé for unethical practices regarding its infant formula. The heart of the matter was Nestlé's suggestion that its formula was better than breastfeeding, a claim that both the UN Children's Fund (UNICEF) and the World Health Organization (WHO) dispute. Moreover, Nestlé's assertion doesn't consider the circumstances required to safely prepare the formula for consumption. In many developing countries, infant formula is prepared in unhygienic circumstances due to unsafe water and misinterpreted instructions.

Another issue centers on the use of Nestlé's anthropomorphized (humanlike) bear brand logo, which showed a baby bear breastfeeding from its mother bear. The problem: a coffee creamer that uses the same bear logo was fed to children by mothers who do not speak English or Thai, and the product labels were not translated into local languages in countries such as Pakistan, Bangladesh, and Laos. Following the negative publicity, Nestlé removed the bear logo from its infant formula and insists that they follow local and international regulations in product marketing.[8]

a population growth rate of at least one percent over the past decade, and Spain's growth rate recently increased, from near zero in 2009 to just under 0.6 percent in 2011. On the other hand, the populations of Germany, Bulgaria, and Poland are declining. Similar to highly developed Asian countries, low birthrates and an aging population present problems of population sustainability in Europe. Fewer workers can shrink economies. In the European Union, labor tends to move from country to country for better opportunities.[3] Because the industrial revolution began in Europe, demographic transition occurred there first. Now, much of Europe has reached the fourth stage (contracting).

The population of Russia is also declining. Over the past decade, its population has decreased by more than five percent. According to Professor Katya Makarova, this dramatic decline can be explained primarily by the collapse of the Soviet Union.[3] The most notable feature of Russian decline is the increase in the death rate—particularly among men, resulting in a drop in life expectancy. In fact, the death rate in Russia has been increasing for half a century. Factors such as the collapse of the public health system, alcoholism, drug abuse, suicide, tobacco use, and heart disease have contributed to the increasing death rate.

Marketing in transition economies like Russia can be a challenge. Russia is not a single "country"; it's a huge, sparsely populated region where no one marketing strategy applies. For centuries, Russia has been home to Slavic, Turkic, Finno-Ugric, and many other peoples—a genuine melting pot of cultures.[9] Diverse regional differences in traditions, values, occupations, and buying habits translate into a variety of consumer preferences. That means that what consumers prefer in Moscow may not appeal to buyers in St. Petersburg, and even less so in Siberia. Moreover, Russian markets are so dynamic that successful marketing strategies today may become out of place tomorrow.

Marketing on the basis of population size and growth rates can be complicated. Holding everything else constant, size matters. In China, 1.3 billion

FIGURE 15.4 | **Russian Population**

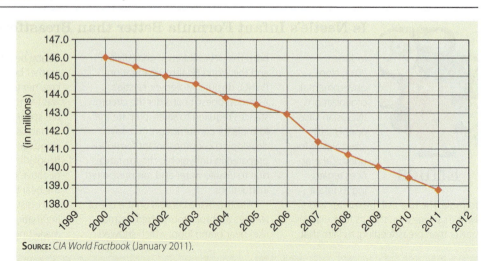

Source: *CIA World Factbook* (January 2011).

consumers offer more potential than 36,000 consumers in Liechtenstein. On the other hand, marketers rarely have the luxury of holding everything else constant. Good market segments must be substantial. For example, Liechtenstein boasts the second highest per capita GDP in the world at $141,000 per person (purchasing power parity). By comparison, the U.S. ranks eleventh in the world at $42,100. Sometimes small, wealthy demographics can be desirable targets. Finally, demographic segments must be measurable, accessible, and actionable. It does a marketer no good to identify Tuvalu consumers only to find limited access to this Polynesian nation in the South Pacific. Similarly, Indian consumers, in general, do not purchase products online. They like to touch and feel the product in order to ensure its quality before actually buying it. Indians tend to obtain information online but make their purchases at traditional stores.[10]

Now that we've examined population changes around the world, let's take a look at a complicated but useful issue in consumer behavior—social class. Social class offers important insights on the marketplace behavior of the nation's consumers. First, we'll define social class. Next, we'll examine class structure, along with various measurements of class hierarchy in the United States. Finally, we'll explain a number of relationships between social class and consumption behavior.

TABLE 15.2 | The Average World Citizen versus the Average U.S. Citizen

	The Average World Citizen	The Average U.S. Citizen
Median Age	28.4	36.9
Life Expectancy	67.0	78.4
Religion	Christian (33.3%)	Christian (79.6%)
Language	Mandarin Chinese (12.4%)	English (82%)
Years in School	11	16
Child Fertility	2.5	2.06
Median Income	$7,000	$27,446

Source: *CIA World Factbook* (2012); U.S. Census Bureau, 2010.

OBJECTIVE **2** ## Social Class

Social class is a construct far easier to use than to define. That's because a consumer's standing in society is determined by a complex set of interacting variables, including family background, income, occupation, and education. Some sociologists view **social structure** as a hierarchical division of homogeneous groups, or "classes," based on a common set of values and lifestyles. Sociologist Max Weber believed that the rankings people attain in society derive from three, distinct domains: (1) prestige or social honor, also called *status*, (2) access and control over valued resources, or *power*, and (3) wealth and property, which he called *class*.[11] Taken together, we define **social class** as the overall *standing* a consumer occupies in society based on characteristics valued by others. Consumers who occupy the same social class are likely to share common lifestyles and preferences based on similarities in one or more of the following factors: family backgrounds, income, ownership of property, occupation, education, and ethnicity. In short, social class can be thought of as groups of people who are approximately equal in *community esteem*.[12] It follows that consumers in the same social class are likely to socialize with one another and share common purchase goals and shopping behaviors.[13] Figure 15.5 depicts the relationship between these factors desired by society, social class, and consumer behavior.

It's fair to note that the factors determining social class are strongly related. One's family background often determines whether a person attends college, trade school, or neither. And level of education is highly correlated with lifetime earnings. Research also demonstrates that the children of the working class tend to be working class, and the children of the upper-class tend to remain upper-class. Finally, whereas social standing predicts consumption patterns (e.g., the very wealthy may send their children to private schools and attend opera), consumption patterns *per se* can signal social standing (e.g., middle class individuals aspiring to achieve a higher social standing may travel abroad and enjoy theatre). These two-way relationships are depicted with bi-directional arrows in Figure 15.5.

FIGURE 15.5 | Social Class

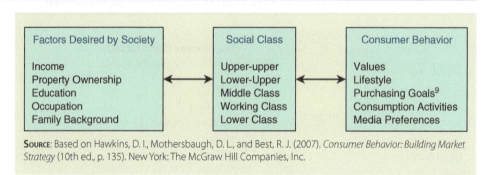

Source: Based on Hawkins, D. I., Mothersbaugh, D. L., and Best, R. J. (2007). *Consumer Behavior: Building Market Strategy* (10th ed., p. 135). New York: The McGraw Hill Companies, Inc.

Social classes are rarely determined by a single characteristic, such as income or education. In fact, income—by itself—can be a very poor predictor of social class. Consider a high school English teacher and an auto mechanic who each earn about $65,000 a year. The teacher and mechanic are likely to have very different views on how life should be lived. This will be manifest in their attitudes, values, avocations, and purchase preferences. The English teacher may enjoy gardening and reading classic novels, whereas the mechanic might prefer bow hunting and classic cars. As a result, the teacher and mechanic will attain a different overall social standing in their communities, based on factors other than income. In a similar vein, education—on its own—doesn't always predict social class. For example, two students who graduate in mechanical engineering from a major university may choose completely different lifestyles. One may open his own contracting business in rural Pennsylvania, while the other might take a corporate job in Houston. These choices will lead to different social classes, based on factors other than their education. Sometimes even two characteristics are insufficient in determining social class. For instance, two graduates of the same law school may take positions as attorneys in the same law firm. One lawyer, however, decides to focus on pro-bono work and consequently earns 50% less than his colleague, who specializes in personal injury cases. These two lawyers' social classes will diverge primarily based on income.

It's also important to consider a person's social class in smaller contexts. Perhaps an accomplished violinist is viewed with esteem by young, aspiring musicians and students, but assumes a lower social position compared to his neighbors who are comprised mostly of physicians. In the broad context of society, however, the violinist's income, occupation, and education will combine to determine how society "ranks" her within the entire class structure.

Social mobility describes the movement of consumers from one social class to another.[11] In the United States, *upward mobility* embodies the American Dream: work hard and move up. And most Americans are optimistic. Poll after poll shows a majority reject the notion that social class is determined by forces beyond their control. In 2009, despite an economy marked by high unemployment, a collapse in the housing market, and a $700 billion bank bailout, 71% still agreed that hard work and personal skill are the greatest predictors of success. In fact, a high degree of social mobility has always defined American culture, from the work of Alexis de Tocqueville to the remarkable story of Barack Obama. But the reality of upward mobility for most Americans is complicated. The recession of the late 2000s came at the end of a period marked by record levels of inequality. Many Americans, lacking true upward mobility, tried to consume their way forward, buying bigger houses or better cars. *Downward mobility* ensued, caused by housing foreclosures, displaced workers, and more under- and part-time employment. As a result, American optimism has been pierced by doubt. In a 2010 poll for *The Economist*, 36% of respondents indicated that they had less opportunity than their parents, compared with 39% who said they had more. Approximately 50% of respondents thought the next generation would have a lower standard of living, more than twice the proportion that indicated living standards would increase.[14] With these considerations in mind, let's explore the social class structure in the United States.

OBJECTIVE ③   ## Social Structure in the United States

Social class is not a perfect measure of a consumer's status or community esteem—it involves a number of interdependent factors. The lines between classes are not clear-cut, and people can move upward and downward over time. But social class is worth investigating because of the insights it offers on the marketplace and the nation's consumers.

The first social structure used by marketers was introduced in the U.S. by sociologist W. Lloyd Warner.[12] He described six, distinct classes of people who were seen as approximately equal in *community esteem* and tended to socialize among themselves and share expectations about life:

- **Upper-upper**
- **Lower-upper**
- **Upper-middle**

- Lower-middle
- Upper-lower
- Lower-lower

Warner's system deviated from the income-only structures and political interest typologies used by other social scientists during the 1940s. Instead, Warner believed that his system of social classification centered on consumers' self-feelings and community respect. Marketers embraced this system when researchers were able to demonstrate that social classes helped explain shopping habits and consumption patterns. In 1957, Joseph Kahl researched communities in the U.S. and described social class as a matter of "style, social networks, and personal prestige."[15] Later, D. Gilbert and J. A. Kahl (1982) combined sociology with political economics to depict the American class structure as a series of "situations" in which people find themselves. These situations comprised occupation, income, general living conditions, and ethnicity.[16] Table 15.3 shows three major groupings of Americans—Upper, Middle, and Lower. The three status divisions seem to fit the contemporaneous thinking of the middle class. They saw people like themselves, people better off, and people not as well off, with income as the major differentiating factor.[13]

TABLE 15.3 | **Gilbert-Kahn Class Structure**

Upper Americans
- *The Capitalist Class* (1%). Their investment decisions influence the national economy. They earn income mostly from assets, enjoy inherited wealth, and maintain prestigious university connections.
- *Upper Middle Class* (14%). Upper-level managers, professionals, and moderately successful business people who are college educated with family income nearly twice the national average.

Middle Americans
- *Middle Class* (33%). Mid-level white-collar and top-level blue-collar workers with education beyond high school. Income slightly above the national average.
- *Working Class* (32%). Mid-level blue-collar and low-level white-collar workers with education and income slightly below the national average.

Marginal Americans
- *Working Poor* (11–12%). Below mainstream America's living standard, but above poverty. Low-paid service workers with some high school education.
- *Underclass* (8–9%). Welfare dependent with standard of living below poverty. Not regularly employed and lacking schooling.

Source: Adapted from Gilbert, D. and Kahl, J. A. (1982). *The American Class Structure: A New Synthesis.* Homewood, IL: The Dorsey Press.

In the 1970s, Richard Coleman and Lee Rainwater described a U.S. class structure based on how people interacted with one another. They believed that people compared themselves to others based primarily on educational credentials and occupation. Income is somewhat downplayed; it's merely a measure of success on the job. The heart and soul of their class system is personal and group prestige, which is partially driven by family history, physical appearance, as well as social aspirations and skills. They used everyday language to describe each class, but also argued that the delineation between classes is clouded by the consumers' aspirations. In other words, some middle-class consumers may behave like upper-middle class in the marketplace and vice versa. They also found a wide range in income within each class.[13] Table 15.4 shows the **Coleman-Rainwater Social Class Hierarchy**.[17]

TABLE 15.4 | Coleman-Rainwater Social Class Structure

Upper Americans
- *Upper-Upper* (0.3%). The world of inherited wealth and aristocratic names. "Old money"
- *Lower Upper* (1.2%). Newer social elite, drawn from corporate leaders and professionals. "New money"
- *Upper-Middle* (12.5%). College graduate managers and professionals interested in private clubs, social causes, and the arts. "Collegiate credentials"

Middle Americans
- *Middle Class* (32%). Average pay white-collar workers and their blue-collar friends, living on the better side of town. "White-collar associations"
- *Working Class* (38%). Average pay blue-collar workers "leading working class lives," regardless of income, education, and occupation

Lower Americans
- *Upper-Lower* (9%). Working, not on welfare with a standard of living just above poverty. Behavior is considered "crude and trashy."
- *Lower-Lower* (7%). On welfare and visibly impoverished, usually out-of-work or working in the "dirtiest jobs." "Bums and criminals."

SOURCE: Adapted from Coleman, R. P. and Rainwater, L. P., with K. A. McClelland (1978). *Social Standing in America: New Dimensions of Class.* New York: Basic Books.

Upper Americans represent a lively mix of many lifestyles, including upper-upper, lower-upper, and upper-middle classes. The top tier, **upper-upper**, or "old money" lives an aristocratic lifestyle. They inherited their money and in the past were often featured in the society pages of newspapers and magazines—they include famous family names such as Roosevelt, Kennedy, Rockefeller, Bush, Mellon, Vanderbilt, Carnegie, DuPont, and Hilton. More recently, the upper-uppers stay out of the public spotlight. They typically live in classic homes, drive luxurious automobiles, and travel the world. Consumers in this highest social class often prefer Ivy League schools, are more likely to seek to enter politics, and enjoy golfing, yachting, and wine tasting. They also frequent exclusive country clubs, resorts, and ranches.

If you're a young member of the upper-upper class in America, you no longer inherit the family fortune as a matter of course. Or if you do, you might not inherit the status that goes with it. Things are expected of you. You must attend a prestigious college. You might be expected to do thrill-seeking, dangerous things, particularly if you're male. Acceptable *ordeals* of danger include sports, aviation, and sailing. You're also expected to contribute something to society—charity work, funding the arts, teaching children, or publishing. These ordeals of the upper class are what tame them and make them a force for positive social good in America. In a sense, they earn their money by developing real virtues. Development of human character is what can make the upper class admirable in the eyes of others, rather than be seen as selfish monsters.[18]

Because their considerable wealth typically has been acquired within their own generation (i.e., not inherited), **lower-uppers** are referred to as "new money" or the **nouveaux riche**. Their income often exceeds that of the upper-uppers, but they are rarely accepted by "old money." Members of the *nouveau riche* often feel discriminated against by the upper-uppers since they "lack the proper pedigree."[19] The behavior of these newcomers is often satirized in American society by implying that they copy the stereotyped, rather than actual, behavior patterns of the upper-uppers. Nevertheless, the importance of the lower-uppers cannot be overstated. Famous entrepreneurs such as the late Steve Jobs (Apple), Meg Whitman (eBay), Oprah Winfrey, Sir Richard Branson (Virgin Mobile), and Sam Walton (Walmart) admirably represent "new money."

Arguably, Bill Gates is the group's most prominent member. Gates' journey was not exactly smooth sailing. A Harvard dropout, Gates founded Microsoft, the software behemoth, with his close friend Paul Allen. Today, Gates is the richest man in the U.S. and the third richest in the world. A lesser-known example of "new money" is Gurbaksh Chahal, an entrepreneur whose start-up businesses, BlueLithium, Yahoo! acquired for $300 million. Gurbaksh, the son of Indian immigrants, is a high school dropout.

Sports stars and other celebrities frequently enter the ranks "new money." Unable to socialize with the upper-uppers, they respond with aggressive **conspicuous consumption**, purchasing publicly consumed luxury goods to demonstrate their newfound wealth. They often buy garish homes, enormous yachts, and posh clothing.

The **upper-middle** class could be labeled as "the professionals." They are college graduates, some with advanced degrees, who have attained upper-class status in their communities through their education and occupation. Physicians, corporate managers, lawyers, college professors, and business owners represent this category. This group pays special attention to prestige brands, and their self-image is one of "spending with good taste." Interesting neighborhoods such as up-and-coming, inner-city areas are appealing to the upper-middles, as are the conventional suburbs or charming rural properties.[20] Upper-middles often dream of more theatre, investment in art, and travel. And they would like some additional "help in the house," "nights on the town," and better schooling for their children. They also aspire to join private clubs for golfing, swimming, and tennis. At the same time, upper-middles have demonstrated volunteerism for good causes and spend much of their spare time on cultural and athletic activities.[13]

Middle Americans comprise two distinct classes: the middle class and the working class.[13] Although these two classes may not differ dramatically by political views or public image, they still represent different social strata with different purchasing attitudes—despite overlapping income levels. The **middle class** is comprised primarily

Celebrities who represent "new money" oftentimes promote expensive brands as symbols of their wealth.

David LEFRANC/Gamma-Rapho/Getty Images

of average-earning, white-collar workers and their blue-collar friends living on the better side of town (e.g., lower-level managers, schoolteachers, and skilled workers such as electricians and factory supervisors). The middle-class household is remarkably diverse. It could include a traditional married couple with children, a single mom head-of-household with one child, a local business owner with no children whose spouse helps run the business, a widow, or a never-married woman. In any case, these middle-class households have no ties to or aspirations to become upper Americans. As a group, they value respectability and conformity, live in modest, suburban homes, and purchase modest furnishings. But they often live paycheck to paycheck, overextending themselves by purchasing liabilities (e.g., boats, computers, big-screen TVs) that they confuse as assets. The middle class has become increasingly concerned about job security due to the shrinking number of modest-paying white- and blue-collar jobs.

The **working-class** Americans have been described as "family folk" who depend heavily on relatives for economic and social support.[13] With below-average education, they typically work in average-paying, blue-collar jobs or low-paying, white-collar positions such as service, sales, and semi-skilled technical fields. Accordingly, this group has been referred to as the "laboring class." Working-class families live in modest homes in marginal neighborhoods or in deteriorating rural areas. With little means to improve their purchasing power, the working class tends to protect what they have and resent upper Americans, particularly those with high levels of formal education. This group sees itself as the unappreciated "backbone" of U.S. industry. Accordingly, they demonstrate a preference for American-made products, carry out more traditional sex-role divisions within the family, and enjoy masculine camaraderie such as camping, fishing, and hunting, as well as the products that support these activities. The working class exhibits a relatively parochial view of the world. Their sports heroes, TV-viewing interests, and vacation spots tend to be local. They prefer brands that are honestly targeted at their working class lifestyles. In general, they prefer bowling to golf, country music to rap, and hamburgers to sushi.

Lower Americans can be separated into two subclasses—the upper-lower class and the lower-lower class. The **upper-lowers** could be labeled the "working poor." Many live *above* the poverty threshold and do not collect welfare benefits. For example, the poverty threshold in 2011 for a household of four people with two children under the age of 18 was $22,811. The lower-lowers have limited high school education and work in unskilled positions. They tend to live in decaying neighborhoods filled with drugs, crime, and gangs. Lack of education, role models, and opportunities often lead to negative purchase behaviors, such as alcohol and cigarettes.[21] Demographically, the working poor resemble Middle Americans. Approximately 67% are white, 18% are black, and almost 12% are Hispanic. Many in this group own property. According to the National Survey, 84% own cars, and a significant number own homes. The primary characteristic of the working poor is their lower level of education. According to the Urban Institute, close to half the household heads of all low-income families have only a high school diploma or GED.[22]

The long work hours, low pay, and family burdens of the upper-lower class create challenges for marketers. Those marketers who have succeeded in reaching this segment pay attention to several important behavioral patterns of the group. They tend to look for value rather than inexpensive products.

They are very sensitive to issues of trust and will talk among family and friends when things go right or wrong. Finally, they tend to be very brand loyal. Some ambitious retailers have attempted to reach lower-income Americans, partially through government incentives and to some extent by taking advantage of the changing character of the upper-lowers. Drugstores, supermarkets, and dollar stores have increased their presence in lower-class neighborhoods. Part of the success of the off-price retailers has been offering an assortment of private-label brands and simple pricing schemes. For example, some dollar stores offer every product for 99 cents or a dollar.[22]

The **lower-lowers** live below the threshold of poverty and rely heavily on government assistance programs. Sociologists often refer to this group as the "underclass." Marketing "sin" products such as cigarettes and beer to the lower-lowers is even more controversial than marketing to the working poor. And yet the same marketing principles that showed success with the upper-lowers can be applied to this group. A long-term commitment to value-laden brands and enough volume might be the recipe.

OBJECTIVE **Income versus Social Class**

Although income is only one component of social class, Americans often equate "class" with income. Figure 15.6 shows the distribution of household income in the United States. Notice the relatively normal distribution across income categories, with roughly five percent of American households in both the top and bottom categories. Also notice the most frequent category, $50,000 to $74,999, captures the average household income ($67,530). That is not to suggest that income is distributed equally in the United States. It should come as no surprise that top earners in America earn significantly more than those in the middle of the distribution. In fact, income inequality is greater in the

FIGURE 15.6 | 2010 U.S. Household Income Distribution

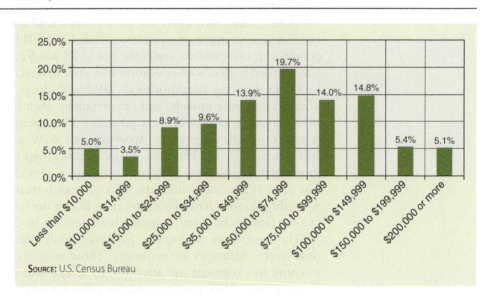

SOURCE: U.S. Census Bureau

U.S. than in most developed nations. America ranks in the bottom third of the list of 90 countries measured for income inequality by Branko Milanovic, an economist with the World Bank.[23] But while America ranks relatively high in income inequality among rich nations, plenty of countries demonstrate greater inequality, particularly in Latin America. Honduras and Guatemala show the most income inequality. Income inequality has also increased in Russia and China. Russia shows slightly less inequality, whereas China has greater income inequality than the U.S.

In some cases, income can be an adequate predictor of whether consumers will have access to certain product categories. After all, income is the gateway to luxury goods such as vacations, boats, and pools. But income alone does not explain what kind of vacations or jewelry consumers prefer. Moreover, what is considered a necessity to the very wealthy may be a luxury to the poor (e.g., automobiles). Coleman points out that a wide range of ages of household heads, single consumers, and dual-income couples can be found in every social class, and that adding income via a second job doesn't necessarily elevate a family into a higher class status.[13] Sometimes the new social elite of the lower-upper class earn more money than the Upper-upper Americans, but they lack the community esteem of "old money." Similarly, high-earning working class people often tend to lead "working class life styles," unconcerned with doing the "proper things" or moving their families to "the better side of town." In summary, we believe the Coleman-Rainwater class structure, which includes income, is generally a better predictor of consumer behavior than income alone. However, we acknowledge the following generalizations about income and social class provided by professor Charles Schaninger[24]

- Social class is better at predicting consumer behavior than is income for low-dollar expenditures that reflect status and lifestyle (e.g., coffee, beer, breakfast cereal, shampoo, and cosmetics).
- Income is an adequate predictor of consumer behavior for high-dollar expenditures that don't reflect lifestyle or values. "Affordability" is key (e.g., tires, televisions, and computers).
- Social class, with income as a special consideration, is the best indicator for understanding moderate to high-dollar expenditures on items that signal status (e.g., automobiles, homes, and jewelry).

OBJECTIVE **5** **Social Class and Consumer Behavior** The origins of social class may date back to primate hierarchies.[25] In fact, most animal species demonstrate dominance-submission ranks (e.g., wolf packs). The very term **pecking order** originates from chicken hierarchies. A pecking order among chickens determines who is the "top hen," who is the "bottom hen," and where the other hens fill in the ranks. Because the beak is used for defense and aggression, birds skilled with their beaks peck more and established dominance over those that pecked less. A dominance hierarchy in animals is thought to reduce the incidence of intense conflicts and determine which animal gets preferential access to resources such as food and mates.[26] Similarly, social class ranks people in terms of their community esteem, which produces more unified social functioning and determines consumers' access to resources such as safety, food, education, housing, and other consumer products.

Research demonstrates that social class can bestow or withhold interpersonal privileges. Unlike externally assigned, or **ascribed status** (gender, race and age, social class), social class conveys **achieved status**, attributed to internal factors such as effort and ability.[27] It follows that people are assumed to be responsible for their own social class—the upper class are credited for their higher standing, and the lower class are blamed for their inferior status. In addition, the upper class are presumed to be more competent, even under ambiguous performance. A classic study involved participants watching the same video of a little girl taking an oral exam. She performed inconsistently across questions. Sometimes she performed well, sometimes poorly. Before viewing the video of her oral exam, however, participants watched another video of the little girl in her social-class setting—either upper class or lower class. In the upper-class background video, the little girl was shown in a large, suburban home and in an attractive playground; in the lower-class background video, she was seen in a deteriorating home and in a neglected playground. Interestingly, the participants rated the little girl's performance on the oral exam much better when they had previously viewed the upper-class background video than the lower-class video. Even when they didn't view the background video, they saw her as brighter, more motivated, sociable, and mature when they were simply given her social class.[28]

It doesn't take long for the upper class to benefit from dispositional attributions, or positive character traits. Elementary school children rate the performance of wealthy children better than poor children.[29] This effect is consistent across cultures in the U.S., Europe, and Asia. In contrast, the upper class are typically thought to be less warm and less trustworthy.[30] In addition to being thought of as competent, studies also show that people think the wealthy have somehow earned their lot in life due to their strong work ethic.[31]

Apparently, the upper class also think highly of themselves. Wealth generates high self-esteem, which increases from childhood through middle age. Moreover, social class is more closely linked to self-esteem for consumers who feel that they have *earned* their high social esteem. For example, people who have achieved educational and occupational success (as opposed to inherited wealth), adults (as opposed to children), professional women, and recent immigrants view social class as integral to their self-esteem.[32]

At a personal level, the upper class tend to engage less with others. Research suggests that, because the wealthy already feel confident, they perform more disengagement cues (e.g., doodling, self-grooming, fiddling) and fewer engagement cues (e.g., nodding, laughing, raising eyebrows). Social class appears to signal consumers' non-verbal expressions of wealth, which are mostly discernible from others.[33] For example, high status consumers tend to demonstrate more relaxed nonverbal communication, such as an open body, calm voice, and stable tone. When engaged, they also express themselves more confidently with posing skills and facial activity and intrude more with direct gazes, closer interpersonal distance, more interruptions, and louder voices.[34] In general, people tend to excessively stereotype the nonverbal communication of the upper class as cold and severe. In contrast, consumers are skillful at detecting the pecking order between two people.[35] What are some of the cues that signal dominance? An open body, literally taking up more space by sitting upright with arms draped over adjacent chairs, and crossing one leg with an ankle on the other knee, are more dominant postures than sitting with hands in lap, with knees together, or slouching.[36]

Nonverbal status cues can also elicit conformity. Curiously, pedestrians will follow high-status jaywalkers into traffic,[37] and the lower class are less likely to honk their horns at high-status vehicles.[38] Finally, higher social status is related to less stress and illness, because the upper class are more likely to experience fewer negative life events and have more resources for coping with those that do occur.[39] It's no surprise that the wealthy represent a prime target for marketers—they possess the resources and motivation to buy products that enhance their lives and help them return to normalcy when things go wrong. In summary, higher status brings privileges such as presumed competence, increased self-esteem, freedom from nonverbal engagement, and pursuing the status quo.[27] Now that we've discussed social class and income, we'll examine another key demographic factor that influences consumer behavior—age.

OBJECTIVE **6**

Age Subcultures

Perhaps no demographic variable suggests such intuitive market segments as age. Age literally defines who we are—how we communicate, how we shop, and even our attitudes toward marketing activities. Age can also define our needs and wants. Babies need small clothing and diapers, adolescents want products that enhance their social skills, and seniors often seek products that help maintain health and fitness. Consumers of various ages seek different solutions to the similar problems, providing rich opportunities for marketers to design and communicate age-relevant products. Consider the need for entertainment. Many children enjoy the vibrant colors and uncomplicated story lines of Disney movies. Teens, however, often prefer entertainment with an "edgier" feel, such as the John Hughes movies of the 1980s (*The Breakfast Club* and *Pretty in Pink*, to name two) and more contemporary movies such as *Mean Girls* and *Juno*.

Marketers often divide consumers into *generations* or **age cohorts**, groups of people who have experienced a common social, political, historical, and economic experience. In other words, people in the same age cohort have experienced similar world conditions, and of course, they are about the same age. Although there is no universally accepted cut-off for age cohorts, we have drawn on *American Demographics'* "Where Generations Divide: A Guide" to provide approximations for six American Generations:[40]

- **The Pre-Depression Generation**—born prior to 1930
- **The Depression Generation**—born between 1930 and 1945
- **The Baby Boomers**—born between 1946 and 1964
- **Generation X**—born between 1965 and 1976
- **Generation Y**—born between 1977 and 1995
- **Generation Z**—born after 1995

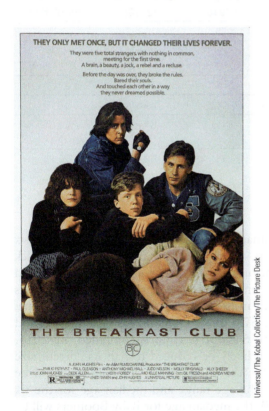

Universal/The Kobal Collection/The Picture Desk

In *The Breakfast Club*, commonalities from age and life cycle help five teens from all walks of life to eventually transcend their differences over the course of a Saturday detention session.

Table 15.5 describes the six primary age cohorts in the U.S., along with key characteristics. Columns 1 and 2 give common names for the cohorts. Column 3 shows the birth years for each cohort, and column 4 gives the size of the cohort birth range. For example, the Depression Generation was born between 1930 and 1945 inclusive, a 16-year birth range. Column 5 provides the ages of the cohort members in 2010 (the most recent census). For example, in 2010, members of Gen X were between 34 and 45 years old. Columns 6 and 7 show the populations for each cohort in 2010 and their percent of the U.S. population, respectively. The Baby Boomers (24.6%) and a majority of their offspring, represented by Gen X (26.2%), comprise more than half of the U.S. population. Adjusting for the birth range, however, the populations are fairly balanced. For example, the baby boomers capture 24.6% of the population; however, their cohort spans 19 years, which is 23.5% of the total cohort range (81), not including the Pre-Depression cohort.

TABLE 15.5 | U.S. Age Cohorts and Characteristics in 2010

1	2	3	4	5	6	7
Cohort Name	AKA	Cohort Birth Dates	Birth Range (years)	Age Range Cohort in 2010	Approximate Population (2010)	Percent of total Population
Pre-Depression	GI Generation	–1929	–	>80	10,338	3.3%
Depression	Silent Generation	1930–1945	16	65–80	29,891	9.6%
Baby Boomers	Me Generation	1946–1964	19	46–64	76,460	24.6%
Generation X	Baby Busters	1965–1976	12	34–45	49,876	16.1%
Generation Y	Millennials; Echo Boom	1977–1995	19	15–33	81,287	26.2%
Generation Z	Echo Bust; Gen I	1996–	15	<15	62,381	20.1%

Source: U.S. Census Bureau, *Current Population Survey*, Annual Social and Economic Supplement, 2010.

Figure 15.7 depicts the approximate population distribution among the six U.S. age cohorts in 2010 for men, women, and total population. A quick glance at this figure reveals two obvious relationships: First, Gen X is squeezed between the Baby Boomers and Gen Y. Second, Gen Y (81.3 million) has surpassed the Baby Boomers (75.5 million) in population, if not in scope. Also noteworthy, women comprise 57% of the combined Pre-Depression and Depression cohorts, compared with 51% of all cohorts combined. By 2015, the Pre-Depression Generation will likely be reduced to half its current size and will all but disappear by 2020 (the youngest of this cohort would be 91 years old). Table 15.6 projects the age range and median age for the six U.S. age cohorts in 2020. By 2020, the median age for Baby Boomers will be 65, about half of the Depression Generation will be older than 80, and most members of Gen Y will be in their thirties. When 2020 arrives, Generation Z will have been around for 25 years, and a new cohort will likely be named.

FIGURE 15.7 | 2010 U.S. Age Cohorts

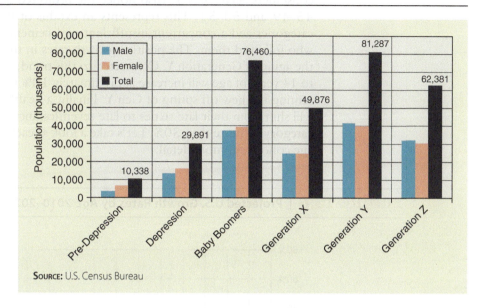

SOURCE: U.S. Census Bureau

TABLE 15.6 | U.S. Age Cohorts and Characteristics in 2020

1	2	3
Cohort Name	Ages of Members in 2020	Median Age In 2020
Pre-Depression	>90	–
Depression	75–90	82.5
Baby Boomers	56–74	65.0
Generation X	44–55	49.5
Generation Y	25–43	34.0
Generation Z	<25	–

SOURCE: U.S. Census Bureau, *Current Population Survey*, Annual Social and Economic Supplement, 2010.

Tracking age cohorts is not the same as observing the number of consumers in a particular age group. The purpose of cohort analysis is to track a specific group of people who were born during a specific time frame because they are likely to share attitudes and preferences based on their shared experiences. When people are born into a cohort, they remain there for life. So, the size of established cohorts can never increase. As cohorts mature, they simply shift into older age categories and eventually die off. This shifting of cohorts, along with birth and death rates, influences the number of consumers in particular age categories at a given time. For example, as the large cohort of Baby Boomers matures, it will dramatically add numbers to the upper-age categories. From 2010 to 2020, the surviving Baby Boomers will have shifted from ages

46–64 to ages 56–74. Figure 15.8 shows a 57% increase in the number of consumers aged 70–74. Also notice the projected decrease in age categories 45–49 and 50–54. This represents an exodus of Baby Boomers from these categories and a concurrent insufficient replacement rate from Generation X, who followed them. The positive growth rates in the 25–39 category shows the aging of Generation Y. Connected to this trend, the number of children up to 14 years of age will increase approximately 10% from 2010 to 2020, representing the new off spring of Gen Y. Finally, a healthy Depression Generation will shift from their late sixties to late seventies, increasing the 75–79-year-old category by more than 30%. Let's take a look at each of the six generations, or age cohorts, in more detail.

FIGURE 15.8 | Projected U.S. Growth Rates by Age 2010–2020

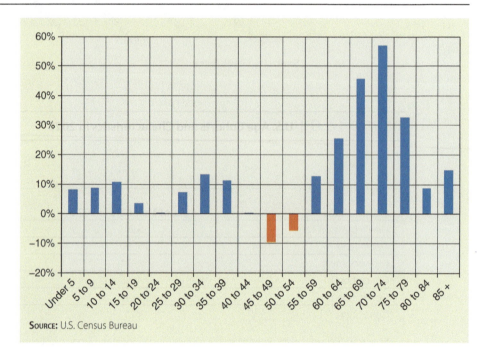

Source: U.S. Census Bureau

The Pre-Depression Generation

Born prior to 1930, the **Pre-Depression Generation**, or the *GI Generation*, came of age during the Depression (1930–1941) and went on to build modern America. In 2010, more than ten million people in this cohort represent about 3.3% of the U.S. population. In 2020, all the surviving members of this group will be more than 90 years old. Before the stock market crash of 1929, about three percent of Americans were unemployed. By 1933, the figure had increased to 25%.[41] No surprise that this generation helped create the U.S. Social Security System. Many gave life to the Baby Boomers. Many of the men and women from this cohort served in World War II (1941–1945). Accordingly, their attitudes and behaviors are largely shaped by frugality and patriotism.[42] This generation turns off the lights when they leave a room, and they keep the heat low. They don't waste food, and they're inclined to fix or repair products rather than throw out and replace worn items. The Pre-Depression Generation has witnessed exciting product developments—from air travel to antibiotics to digital technology. They danced to big band music and still enjoy Sinatra. When the war ended, many obtained free college education on the GI Bill.

Americans now recognize this generation for their unselfish and heroic behavior. Veteran reporter and former *NBC Nightly News* anchor Tom Brokaw, traveled to France to make a documentary marking the fortieth anniversary of D-Day in 1984. Although he was well versed on the historical background of the invasion, he was unprepared for how it would affect him emotionally. Flooded with childhood memories of World War II, Brokaw asked veterans at the ceremony to revisit their past and talk about what happened, which triggered war-torn confessions that inspired Brokaw to write *The Greatest Generation*.[43] In 2010, members of this cohort were at least 80 years old, facing the realities of age-related frailty. As a group, they are conservative thinking and primarily concerned about their health and personal security. Over time, this generation will become increasingly concerned with long-term health care and assisted living. Forward-thinking retailers, banks, and health care providers will find distribution systems that make their goods and services accessible to this aging cohort.

The Depression Generation

Also known as the *Silent Generation*, the **Depression Generation** was born between 1930 and 1945. In 2010, nearly 30 million consumers in this age cohort comprised about ten percent of the American population. In 2010, their median age was about 72; the youngest were entering the traditional retirement years at age 65. The term "silent" may have been unflattering, but it wasn't entirely inaccurate. By today's standards, this group was uninvolved with politics and self-removed from social strife. They transitioned from a childhood marked by economic depression to a post-war adulthood of economic prosperity. For the most part, the Silent Generation grew up during the 1950s—in peace and prosperity. After WWII, many Depression Generation women married GI men and became parents of the Baby Boomers. Because the women of this generation had children earlier than any other twentieth century cohort, they were the first generation of women to go to work in significant numbers.[42] For some, their lives were shaped by the Cold War and the nuclear arms race. In addition, many served in the Korean War. This group is sometimes referred to as the *Swing Generation* because they took part in rapid advances in technology, and as a result, American lifestyles began to change.

Early members of this cohort (born 1930–1939) manifest attitudes and behaviors similar to the Pre-Depression Generation—they work hard and save money. On the other hand, the later part of this group (born 1940–1945) behaves more like older Baby Boomers. They popularized rock-n-roll, enjoyed the first television programs, and sparked the first civil rights and feminist movements in the U.S. This dichotomy within the Depression Generation shows how difficult it can be to draw lines between generations, and that every member of a defined age cohort does not behave identically. Nevertheless, the Depression Generation is generally conservative, tending not to go against the grain. They typically worked for a single employer for much of their careers, married early, saved money, and lived within their means. They also represent the last generation to count on pensions and defined-benefit plans. Life was relatively simple.

The Depression Generation has deep pockets, but they are sometimes overlooked by marketers who are smitten with younger demographics.[44] The youngest segment of this group doesn't like to be called "old," and they are no more brand-loyal than any other age cohort—which means marketers cannot simply assume that they'll continue to purchase the same brands they did as young adults. This group is not particularly enamored with nostalgia. Accordingly, marketers should speak to their current life-styles, not to relics of their past. Consumers in this age group have at least 50 years of exposure to marketing and media. As a result, they prefer straight-sell approaches and dislike advertising hyperbole. This group is comfortable with traditional media, including newspapers, magazines, and television. But online marketing works too, as almost 60% of this generation uses the Internet.[45] Because members of this group have an empty nest, they also have money to spend on their grandchildren, and they frequently shop for children's toys, books, furniture, and clothes. For themselves, they buy leisurely travel, healthy activities, and adult education. Because of their wealth, they also represent prime targets for asset management, legal, and insurance professionals. Some estimates place the value of wealth transfer from this group to their beneficiaries at more than $1 trillion.[46]

Marketers must avoid the pitfall of overlooking the members of the Depression generation.

© Anna Lurye/Shutterstock.com

The Mature Market The **mature market** includes a broader group of consumers aged 55 years and older. In 2010, the mature market consisted of the Pre-Depression and Depression Generation cohorts, along with approximately half of the Baby Boomers. By 2020, the mature market will include all of the Baby Boom Generation. One approach to understanding the mature market is known as **gerontographics**, a segmentation philosophy that maintains mature consumers' receptivity to marketing activities is related more to life changes rather than to chronological age. Some life-changing events are physical, such as the onset of chronic health problems. Others, however, are social and psychological, such as becoming a grandparent or losing a spouse. The gerontographics life-stage model has identified four, distinct groups of mature consumers. Typically, mature consumers move from one group to another—sometimes slowly as a result of scaling back their work, other times abruptly due to illness.[47]

1. *Healthy Indulgers* (18%). These mature consumers have experienced the fewest life-changing events. In general, both spouses are alive and free from chronic health problems, and at least one spouse is working. Middle-aged Baby Boomers comprise a majority of this group. Consequently, Indulgers are most likely to feel and act young. This group enjoys independent living on a reduced scale from their child-rearing years. They typically sell their large, single-family homes and buy townhouses or condos near shopping centers and recreational venues. And they have money to spend on furnishing their new homes with home-security systems, carpeting, furniture, and high-tech gadgets. Because they value convenience and personal service, this group is well suited for moderate-risk investments and personalized banking services. Finally, Indulgers are more likely to take expensive vacations via air and cruise ship.

2. *Healthy Hermits* (36%). This group has experienced life events that have challenged their self-concepts, such as the loss of their spouse. As a result, they become socially withdrawn. To a large extent, this group resents its isolation and the expectations that they should behave like old folks. Because they are less sociable, Hermits respond favorably to conformity in the marketplace, particularly with clothing. They prefer to blend in with a crowd, and like their appearance to match their same-age colleagues. As a group, they prefer well-known brands, and they don't mind paying a little extra for them. Hermits like to remain in the homes where they raised their families. This makes them a good target for do-it-yourself remodeling.

3. *Ailing Outgoers* (29%). Compared to Healthy Hermits, this group is neither healthy nor reclusive. They typically battle chronic health problems, and yet they maintain positive self-concepts, accept their old age, and enjoy getting the most out of life. Outgoers like their independence, which includes dining outside of the home. In general, they respond positively to restaurant and grocery promotions that focus on their health and dietary needs. And they appreciate bargains, as they are not as financially well off as Indulgers. With respect to clothing, Outgoers want to appear socially acceptable. But they value function over form. Clothes that accommodate increasing waistlines do well with this group. Finally, Outgoers represent a prime target for health-care products and services. Due to their upbeat nature, Outgoers

face the aging process from a straightforward perspective, which makes them good targets for long-term medical insurance and health club memberships with senior discounts.

4. *Frail Recluses* (17%). This segment of the mature market has accepted their old age and adjusted their lifestyles accordingly. Their physical deterioration may have limited their mobility, but they have become spiritually stronger. Many Indulgers, Hermits, and Outgoers eventually become Recluses. This group is not entirely capable of handling their health-care needs. As a result, they are good targets for transportation services to hospitals and clinics, as well as home exercise equipment and self-diagnosing medical kits for diabetes, blood pressure, and cholesterol. Finally, Recluses appreciate human-to-human contact when buying and using services such as banking.

Marketing to matures (age 55 and older) creates challenges for marketers because the mature market represents a wide variety of social classes and comprises three, separate age cohorts. Research provides some guidelines when marketing to this large and diverse group:[48]

- Instead of chronological age, consider mobility, marital status, and faith.
- Consider health-status. Many older women suffer from arthritis, and men are assuming more household duties.
- Make packaging easy to open and technology simple to use.
- Use easy-to-see colors such as oranges and reds.
- Feature models and spokespeople who are ten years younger than the target audience.
- Create simple layouts for web pages.
- Use 60-second advertisements (versus 30-second spots) to allow for adequate processing time.
- Advertise in newspapers and magazines. The mature market still reads them.

It seems intuitive that chronological age would affect consumer behavior. Yet many products designed to appeal to older consumers have been rejected by matures. In some cases, older consumers have boycotted products and vendors because of offensive age stereotyping in advertisements.[49] In fact, a long-standing challenge in marketing to older consumers is how to target them with products and promotions (e.g., senior discounts) without stigmatizing them based on their age. Recent research demonstrates that **subjective age**, how old someone *feels*, can be more predictive of consumer behavior than **chronological age**, the number of years a person has lived.[50] Many consumers who are chronologically eligible for age-related promotions are holding on to younger age-based self-concepts. Specifically, matures aged 50–54, who maintain younger subjective ages, are reluctant to use senior citizen discounts to avoid being thought of as "old." In contrast, matures 65 years and older do not mind being labeled as seniors.[51] Unless older consumers feel old (subjective age), they are not likely to respond favorably to products targeted to consumers in their chronological age group. Many of the middle-aged Baby Boomers in the mature market really feel young at heart, and marketers should use spokespersons and celebrities who reflect subjective, not chronological age. Moreover, the promotional labels should be age-neutral. For example, "loyalty discount" works better than "senior discount."[50]

The Baby Boomers

Born immediately after World War II (1946–1964), more than 76 million **Baby Boomers** made up about 25% of the total U.S. population and nearly one-third of the U.S. adult population in 2010. At that time, their ages ranged between 46 and 64, with a median age of 55. Although Generation Y recently began to outnumber the Boomers, the latter continues to generate considerable interest from marketers, in large part due to its spending power. The Boomers may not have the wealth of their GI Generation parents, but they spend more than any other generation. Research also shows that Boomers are just as likely as younger consumers to try new products and switch brands. As an example, Boomers purchased more of Proctor & Gamble's Swiffer Sweepers than any other age cohort.[52] Many Boomers were at the height of their earning power during the most recent recession (2008–2009). Consequently, many in this group are working late into their sixties, beyond the point at which they can receive full social security benefits (age 65). This trend may augment Boomers' discretionary income and further increase their propensity to spend, including helping their children through a stagnant economic climate. Despite general curiosities about the baby boomers, some researchers believe that this group is being taken for granted in the market place. According to the Nielsen Company, less than five percent of advertising dollars are targeted at 35–64 year-olds.[53] This presents an opportunity for marketers to exploit Boomers' generous TV habits (more than 44 hours per week) with uncluttered messages. In addition, nearly 80% of boomers are online, and more than 60% with access to broadband.

Because this cohort spans 19 years, researchers often divide Boomers into two sections—**Leading-Edge Boomers**, born between 1946 and 1955, and **Younger Boomers**, born between 1956 and 1964. Leading-Edge Boomers represent our images of the Vietnam War, Woodstock, and the sixties in general. They came of age when the U.S. economy was robust and booming. Inflation was stable (1–2%), unemployment was low (5–6%), and average salaries increased dramatically (by as much as 20%).[54] In 2010, Leading-Edge Boomers were 55 to 64 years old. This group's parents (the GI Generation) gave them what they didn't have as children, and the Leading-Edge Boomers expected to live better than their parents—forever. They were taught that nothing was impossible for them to achieve. Moreover, they were encouraged to be individualistic, sometimes to a fault. Many became rebels, experimenting with a hippie lifestyle, which included recreational drugs and protesting the Vietnam War. They were responsible for the sexual revolution, along with the advent of the birth control pill. They became the most educated cohort in history, with access to job opportunities unavailable to previous generations.

During their thirties and forties, Leading-Edge Boomers often eschewed delayed gratification, over-extending themselves on large homes, new automobiles, and expensive gadgets. But they were also willing to work like no generation before them in order to support their self-gratifying purchases. By 2015, all Boomers will account for about 40% of U.S. spending, particularly in categories such as consumer electronics, clothing, home furnishings, restaurants, and health care. As many of this group approach retirement, the older Boomers appear to be scaling back their buying and planning to work beyond age 65. Indeed, 60% of Boomers will not be able to maintain their current lifestyles without continuing to work. Some studies indicate that the Boomers' newfound frugality could stall the U.S. economy.[55] Additional research has called for business to prepare for the changing needs of Leading-Edge Boomers.[56] Sixty percent of this group now suffers from chronic health problems, and they will represent more than twice as many single households as their parents. They also demonstrate higher rates of drinking and psychiatric problems than any generation that preceded them. Most Boomers are skeptical of traditional financial services, mistrust financial advisors, and don't feel that doctors take enough time to understand their health problems. Bayer Nutritional Science recognized these characteristics and has developed a line of eye, heart, mind, and joint supplements for older Boomers.

But Boomers are nothing if not resourceful, eager to try new products and services that benefit their lifestyles. A majority of older Boomers watch videos online, 43% participate on a social networking site, and almost all of them use email (93%). Eighty-five percent look for health information online, 76% get their news from the Internet, and almost 70% have purchased products online. They're also catching up with texting; 30% of this group sends instant messages.[45]

Younger Boomers experienced a different world than did older Boomers. Whereas the older Boomers enjoyed Woodstock and a strong economy, the Younger Boomers came of age during the Cold War and lengthy recessions (1973–1975; 1980–1982). Younger Boomers were the first latchkey kids as the number of working women began to increase.[42] More than 50% of women participated in the labor force during the early 1980s (by 2010, the figure approached 60%). This group also endured their parents' divorces at a rate heretofore unmatched in U.S. history. In fact, their parents' marriages lasted only 6.6 years on average.[57] Unlike the older Boomers, the Younger Boomers didn't expect everything to be handed to them; they sensed that life requires uphill battles—both economically and socially. Younger Boomers display a remarkable comfort with technology. More than 80% are online; of that proportion, 70% make travel reservations online, 62% watch videos, 50% maintain social networking sites, 50% download or stream music, and 35% send instant messages.[45]

As a whole, Boomers' shrinking income and high expectations will challenge marketers.[55] They want it all—strong brands with high levels of service at low prices. Still, hustling firms have been successful with this group. Southwest Airlines, for example, combines low prices and strong on-time service. Similarly, Charles Schwab offers more personalized services than do most online brokers and at comparable prices. Internet applications such as Skype's videoconferencing have been a hit with Boomers who want to keep in touch with their children and grandchildren. Brand-conscious Boomers have also embraced the high-value offering of Target and JetBlue. The former offers a wide variety of products for receptive Boomers, along with a clean environment and attractive displays. For their part, JetBlue targets Boomers with flights from New York to Florida, combining low prices and comfortable seating with extra leg room.

Richard B. Levine/Newscom

Boomers demand a high level of services at low prices, and some marketers have been able to deliver on that demand.

Generation X

Squeezed between the Boomers and Millennials, **Generation X**, also known as Xers or Baby Busters, were born between 1965 and 1976. In 2010, this cohort included about 50 million consumers and represented about 16% of the U.S. population. Busters will be in their thirties and forties for most of the current decade. To some Americans, this group carries a reputation as "slackers" or "whiners," because they openly show concern about job loss and financial stability. Gen X created "PC" or "politically correct" language. They are more ethnically diverse than the preceding generations, and they appear to champion their diversity.

As a group, Xers express pessimism about their futures, perhaps with good reason. They tend to blame Boomers for the sagging economy and for draining government programs such as Social Security and Medicare. Generation X grew up watching their parents work like carpenter ants, only to be rewarded with layoffs and downsizing in the workplace. As a result, Xers tends to care less about their careers and more about their quality of life. But this philosophy may be backfiring, as they are considered the most economically stressed of all generations.[52] Crowded in the workforce by Boomers who refuse to retire and Millennials who are desperate for jobs, Xers' income hasn't kept pace with inflation during the past decade. From 2000 to 2008, male income decreased by more than 10%, whereas female income remained constant. As a consequence, Xers' homeownership rates are lower than any other preceding generation, and homeownership stands out as a primary goal for this cohort.

The Baby Busters may be the most college-bound generation in history—but not the most educated.[58] In 1992, the percentage of 18-to-24-year-olds enrolled in college or who had completed one year was 54%, up from 43% a decade earlier. In 1993, however, only 24% of this cohort had earned bachelor's degrees, not much different from the 22% who had earned degrees in 1982. So while Gen X may be eager for diplomas, many have not attained the education necessary for better jobs and higher earnings. It is also noteworthy that women Xers are better educated than men, with 34% of women earning college degrees or higher compared to 32% of men. As a group, Xers are 25% more likely to be self-employed than previous generations.[59] Currently, Busters are approaching their peak earning years, and they spend more on food (particularly out-of-home dining) than any other generation. In addition, they spend more than the average American on housing, clothing, and entertainment.[52] These spending patterns can be linked to child-rearing, as nearly half of Xers have children at home. And Xers value spending time with families. They grew up in an era marked general uncertainty—dual-income parents, divorce, and job uncertainty. This makes Gen X a principal target for family-oriented products and services—everything from movies to toilet tissue. Because they long for the pre-recession days, Xers respond favorably to aspirational appeals in advertising. At the same time, this group spends conservatively and appreciates a savings account, which suggests an opportunity for marketing necessities and practical goods and services. Eighty-six percent of Gen X is online, with 62% on social networking sites. No generation gets more news online than Xers (79%), and they lead in making online travel reservations (67%), participating in online auctions (31%), and donating to charities through the Internet.[45] A majority came of age during the recent era of media fragmentation—cable television, specialized magazines, digital radio, podcasts, and other online media. It comes as no surprise that the Baby Busters watch less television than the Baby Boomers. They also played a

Marketers can oftentimes appeal to Generation Xers' desire to build a solid family life.

major role in the success of technological advances such as Google, YouTube, and Amazon.

Generation Y

Largely created by their Baby Boomer parents, **Generation Y** (also known as the Millennials, or Echo Boom), were born between 1977 and 1995. In 2010, they comprised more than 26% of the U.S. population with more than 81 million consumers. In 2010, Generation Y's age range was between 15 and 33, with a median age of 24. Also noteworthy, Gen Y recently surpassed the Baby Boomer generation (76 million) in size. Like the Boomers, the Echo Boom came of age in relatively peaceful and economically prosperous times, and they generally share their parents' optimism about the future. Raised with a healthy dose of civic-mindedness, Gen Y appears to be committed to good race relations, improving communities, and environmental stewardship.[60] Their living preferences seem to reflect their values, and a majority indicates that they want to live in racially and ethnically diverse neighborhoods. No wonder—this is the most ethnically diverse cohort in history, with only 55% of the population projected to be Caucasian by 2030.

Gen Y received "quality time" from their parents, who emphasized boosting their children's self-esteem. As a result, the Millennials are skilled self-advocates, are comfortable questioning authority, and believe everyone is a "winner."[61] Nevertheless, the Millennials also came of age in an era marked by the AIDS epidemic, gang violence, and global terrorism. In fact, for the older Millennials, the terrorist attacks of September 11, 2001 is the defining event of their generation. Gen Y grew up in a small world—thanks to the Internet. As a result, they are tech-savvy, literally redefining how we communicate and share information. They embrace 24/7 connectedness and multi-tasking on computers, cell phones, and MP3 players and iPods. Comfortable with digital technology, Gen Y expects personal communication with brands and likes to share its opinions about products and services online. Almost a third of this group has rated a product or service online. Gen Y is online (95%), and a correspondingly large percentage gets their news from the Internet (76%).[45]

Unlike their parents (who emptied the nest after college), Gen Y created a phenomenon called **boomerang kids**, children who return home to live indefinitely after graduating from college. Some estimates indicate that about 65% of Gen Y has moved back in with their parents at some point.[62] About 56% of men and 43% of Gen Y adult children lived with their parents in 2004. By 2010, this figure had risen to about 60%. The reason? Unemployment and debt. Although fewer than half of Millennials have reached full-time employment age, they comprise about 45% of the unemployed in the U.S., the highest unemployment rate of any generation.[53] In addition, the average Gen Y college graduate owes more than $20,000 in loans. This debt has contributed to Millennials delaying the formation of their own households and decreased their discretionary spending, two trends marketers must watch carefully. For marketers, boomerang kids represent an interesting opportunity, as the adult children in the household influence their parents' purchases. Parents are turning to their children for advice on everything from automobiles to refinancing, and especially on high-tech products like smartphones, DVRs, and laptops. As a group, Millennials embrace change; in fact, they expect it. This is reflected in their marketplace behavior, as more than 60% of 18- to 24-year-olds like trying new products and brands.[52] One area where Gen Y discriminates is digital media—they rarely listen to podcasts, avoid banner ads, and pay little attention to tweets—63% don't read them and 72% don't send them. In contrast, 42% visit social media sites multiple times per day. But they get information from each other—not from marketers. So, marketers must be patient, authentic, and unobtrusive. Marketers don't successfully sell to Generation Y; Generation Y comes to them through recommendations from their friends, colleagues, and communities.

Because Gen Y is considered an "experience" culture, they don't like to be told what to like or what to do. They want to experience the world for themselves and make their own judgments. Leadership coach Bea Fields recommends reaching the Millennials through the following:[63]

- Social networking sites (e.g., Facebook, Delicious, Digg, Second Life)
- Concerts
- Extreme sporting events
- Movies
- Video games and video game competitions
- Mashups (e.g., Weather Bonk, Where's Tim Hibbard, Y! Mash, Sims on Stage)
- Tattoo parlors (36% have at least one tattoo)

The Gen Y group like to experience life for themselves, without being told what to do.

Photo Yoko Aziz/Alamy Limited

Generation Z

Although there is rarely complete agreement about when one generation ends and another begins, **Generation Z** is commonly thought to include those born during the latter half of the 1990s through the late 2000s, specifically after 1995. In 2010, this cohort consisted of more than 62 million consumers and about 20% of the U.S. population; they were no older than 15 years of age. This group is sometimes called the Echo Bust because they are largely the offspring of the Baby Busters (Generation X).

Also known as *Gen I,* due to their alleged me-centric attitudes, this group is well versed in the social issues of the day. They have already shown interest in socially-conscious activities, such as recycling efforts and community service. They are even more tech-savvy than Gen Y, routinely upgrading software and navigating through any new smartphone app without instruction. And they tend to embrace change, which makes the world less boring to them. Although Gen I shares similarities with Gen Y, members of Gen I possess the following unique characteristics:[64]

- self-esteem-building parents who over-celebrate and reward them for the most trivial accomplishments
- being over-scheduled, well-traveled, and uniquely mature for their ages
- living in non-traditional households and moving to new households with different family structures
- respond to powerful advertising and branding
- perpetual connectedness through smartphones
- a preference for written over verbal communication (e.g., texting)
- having access to media on demand, such as iTunes, videos, and movies
- nonplussed by violence, sex, and other adult content in the media
- highly tolerant, but less conscious of ethnicity, gender, and age than Gen Y

Like the later members of Gen Y, Generation Z wields tremendous influence on daily household spending. Many parents provide Gen I with self-allocated discretionary income (we used to call it an "allowance"). Those of Gen I who are fortunate to receive allowances are expected to make their own purchase decisions regarding clothing, video games, and electronic gadgets. Despite this enormous potential, the teenage market continues to frustrate marketers. Today's teens have access to more information than any other generation, through a plethora of media. This makes them more accessible to marketers, but also more skeptical. Teen skepticism centers primarily on advertising, which implies that teen members of Gen I recognize that advertisers are trying to persuade; hence, they conclude that advertisers must be biased and untruthful.[65] Moreover, because Gen I typically does not respond to lectures from parents (what generation did?); they absorb the views of their peers. It follows that ads targeting teens in Gen I should use teenage spokespersons.[66] Research also demonstrates that advertising using a unique selling proposition (versus straightforward information) featuring a nonconformity message increases teens' brand awareness and stimulates product trial.[67] Marketers can learn a great deal from Gen I.

Marketing in Action

Designer Gum for Generation Z

In the past, chewing gum was simply meant to be chewed. But today's teen market seems to have embraced it as a designer brand, not unlike clothing, shoes, and jewelry. Attempting to reverse declining sales, chewing gum producers advertise unique selling propositions such as "energy-boosting," "biodegradable," "aspartame-free," and even "vegan" gum. The result of these new campaigns? Gum has become hip. According to psychologist Renee White Fraser, "Teenagers want to be spontaneous and iconoclastic. Now, they can choose a gum that delivers that each time they chew."[68]

Chewing gum represents a $2.6 billion domestic industry (nearly the size of the economy of Belize). Like many categories locked in the maturity phase of the product life cycle, overall sales have been declining (4% decrease in 2012). So, new flavors aren't likely to excite Gen Z; they need socially relevant reasons for chewing. The following brands claims seek a connection with the fastidious teen market:

- Kraft introduced its iD brand, which features artistic designs created by young artists on each stick and comes in a magnetic sealing package.
- Wrigley plans to sell its Orbit and 5 Gum brands in pellet-sizes. They will be available in mini-bottles that hold approximately 30 pieces.
- The Rev7 brand claims that it is the first "degradable" and "removable" gum. It is targeted at environmentally conscious teens. Apparently, this gum can decompose into a fine powder with a little water and rubbing action.

- PUR gum is a vegan and aspartame-free product made with natural sweeteners. Their positioning statement is, "the cleanest gum on the market."
- Rockstar Iced Mint Energy gum is positioned as an energy-booster. It contains caffeine and taurine, similar to the brand's energy drinks.
- Stride gum offers Shaun White Whitemint, with Shaun's likeness prominently displayed on the package.

© iStockphoto.com/jfmdesign

Chapter Summary

Demography is the statistical study of human populations. Key population measures discussed in this chapter include population size, social class, income, and generations. Shifts in the world population can be explained through demographic transition, a four-step process that occurs as nations develop from pre-industrial to highly developed economies. Recently, the U.S. accounted for almost 20% of the global economy with less than five percent of world's population. This combination makes the U.S. an attractive target market for global marketers. The least developed African countries account for half of the continent's population. In subsistence markets such as these, one particular marketing approach that works is microenterprises, or small groups that bridge the gap between subsistence consumers and companies. China now boasts the second largest economy in the world with more than $10 trillion GDP (purchasing power parity). The Census Bureau estimates that China's population will peak in 2026; its labor force will shrink, and its over-65 population will more than double over the next 20 years. Europe, on the other hand, will account for only seven percent of the world's population by 2050. Thus, China may become the most important target for global marketers.

Social class is the overall standing a consumer occupies in society. Consumers who occupy the same social class are likely to share common lifestyles and preferences based on similarities in one or more of the following factors: family backgrounds, income, ownership of property, occupation, education, and ethnicity. Social class is not a perfect measure of a consumer's status or community esteem. It involves a number of interdependent factors; the lines between classes are not clear-cut, and people can move upward and downward over time. Sociologist W. Lloyd Warner described six, distinct classes of people who are seen as approximately equal in community esteem: upper-uppers, lower-uppers, upper-middles, lower-middles, upper-lowers, and lower-lowers.

Marketers often divide consumers into generations or age cohorts—groups of people who have experienced common social, political, historical, and economic experiences. Although there is no universally accepted cut-off for age cohorts, the journal *American Demographics* provides approximations for six American Generations: the Pre-Depression Generation (born prior to 1930), the Depression Generation (born between 1930 and 1945 inclusive), the Baby Boomers (born between 1946 and 1964), Generation X (born between 1965 and 1976), Generation Y (born between 1977 and 1995), and Generation Z (born after 1995). Understanding generations isn't easy, but it's worthwhile to marketers. Each generation has its own perspectives because its members were born during a similar period and shared similar experiences. This common ground often translates into shared purchase behaviors.

Key Terms

achieved status
age cohorts
ascribed status
Baby Boomers
boomerang kids
chronological age
Coleman-Rainwater Social Class Hierarchy
conspicuous consumption
demographic transition
demography
Depression Generation
Generation X

Generation Y
Generation Z
gerontographics
Leading-Edge Boomers
Lower Americans
lower-lower
lower-middle
lower-upper
mature market
microenterprises
Middle Americans
middle-class
nouveaux riche

pecking order
Pre-Depression Generation
social class
social mobility
social structure
subjective age
Upper Americans
upper-lower
upper-middle
upper-upper
working-class
Younger Boomers

Review and Discussion

1. Briefly explain *demographic transition,* and how it affects the world economies.

2. Describe some of the problems and opportunities involved in marketing to subsistence economies.

3. In the U.S., the proportion of consumers over the age of 65 is projected to comprise more

than 20% of the population by 2040 (See Figure 15.2). You are likely to be entering your peak earning years during this period. Identify some of the changes you expect to see in the marketplace.

4. Why is income, by itself, insufficient at explaining social class?

5. Evaluate the Coleman-Rainwater Social Class Structure (Table 15.4). Does it match your intuition about the three primary categories of Americans—upper, middle, and lower class? Explain.

6. How do the characteristics of the middle-class differ from the working class? How does this affect their purchase behavior?

7. Explain the difference between *ascribed status* and *achieved status*. Why do you think people give the upper-class credit for being more competent than the lower class?

8. What do you think is more useful for marketers: tracking age cohorts (generations) as they mature or evaluating the changes within a given age group over time? Explain.

9. What are the different characteristics of Leading-Edge Boomers versus Younger Boomers?

10. Chewing gum has become a "designer" product for Generation Z (See the "Marketing in Action" feature in this chapter). Identify several other commodity-type products that might be elevated to "designer status" for this cohort.

Short Application Exercises

1. Demographic transition describes a four-step process that occurs as nations develop from pre-industrial to highly developed economies. Use the CIA World Factbook to compare and contrast the United States, Japan, and China with regards to birth and death rates. What are the implications for consumer behavior? Refer to https://www.cia.gov/library /publications/the-world-factbook/.

2. Research and identify three recent firms who deliberately market to the lower class. What are the business issues involved with marketing to the lower class from the perspective of the marketer? What are the ethical issues from the viewpoint of society?

3. Select three social groups to which you belong (e.g., college major, athletics, arts, church). Consider the social class structure of each group. What variables determine the "pecking order" of members in the group, and where do you stand?

4. Generations Y and Z have been described as "comfortable with change" and racially and ethnically diverse. Identify several marketing opportunities that would make the most of these qualities.

Managerial Application

Sales in the home repairs and improvement market increased about four percent in 2011 to $269 billion. As employment growth accelerates and housing markets improve through 2015, home improvement sales are expected to increase by about six percent annually (according to the Home Improvement Research Institute). Imagine that you are a marketing manager for a home improvement retailer such as Lowes or Home Depot. Your firm is considering separate marketing strategies for various age cohorts and product/service categories.

Your Challenge:

1. Within the category of "lawn care and landscaping," identify several needs for (a) the Depression Generation and (b) Generation X.

2. Within the category of "home improvement," identify several needs for (a) the Pre-Depression Generation and (b) the Younger Baby Boomers.

3. Match the needs in questions 1 and 2 with products and services that will provide unique solutions for the two age cohorts.

4. Design a "problem-solution" advertisement that will communicate directly with one of the cohorts.

End Notes

1 Silverstein, M. J., and Fiske, N. (2003, April). Luxury for the Masses. *Harvard Business Review, 81* (4), 48–57.

2 Mass Class. (2003, Jun/Jul). *Trendwatching.com.* [Online.] Available at: http://www.trendwatching.com/trends /MASS_CLASS.htm.

3 Bellow, S. (2012, Spring). Over Seven Billion Served. *The University of Virginia Magazine,* 26–30.

4 Chamie, J. (2011, June 13). Africa's Demographic Multiplication. *The Globalist.* [Online]. Available: http:// www.theglobalist.com/storyid.aspx?StoryId=9167.

5 Viswanathan, M., Rosa, J. A., and Ruth, J. A. (2010). Exchanges in Marketing Systems: The Case of Subsistence Consumer–Merchants in Chennai, India. *Journal of Marketing 74* (3), 1–17.

6 Shedlock, M. (2012, May 5). China's Population Poised to Crash in Perfect Demographic Storm. *HoweStreet.com* [Online]. Available: http://howestreet.com/2012/05 /chinas-population-poised-to-crash-in-perfect-demographic -storm/.

7 Kristula-Green, M. (2007, August 6). How to Market to Asia's Masses. *Advertising Age, 78* (31), 14–15.

8 Laos: NGS' Flay Nestlé's Infant Formula Strategy (2011, June 23). IRIN. [Online.] Available at: http:// www.irinnews.org/Report/93040/LAOS-NGOs-flay -Nestl%C3%A9-s-infant-formula-strategy.

9 Repiev, A. (October 2008). A Glimpse of Russia's Advertising and Marketing. *A. Repiev School of Advertising & Marketing.* [Online]. Available: http://www.repiev.ru /articles/glimps_en.htm.

10 Indian Television.com's News Releases (2012, May 7). [Online]. Available: http://www.indiantelevision.com /release/y2k12/apr/aprrel22.php#top.

11 Turner, H. J. (1981). *Sociology: Studying the Human System,* 2nd ed. (Santa Monica, CA: Goodyear).

12 Warner, W. L. with Lunt, P. S. (1941). *The Social Life of a Modern Community,* New Haven, CT: Yale University Press.

13 Coleman, R. P. (1983). The Continuing Significance of Social Class to Marketing. *Journal of Consumer Research, 10* (December), 265–280.

14 *The Economist* (2010, April 17). Upper Bound. [Online]. Available: http://www.economist.com/node/15908469.

15 Kahl, J. S. (1957). *The American Class Structure,* New York: Rinehart.

16 Gilbert, D. and J. A. Kahl (1982). *The American Class Structure: A New Synthesis,* Homewood, IL: The Dorsey Press.

17 Coleman, R. P., and L. P. Rainwater, with K. A. McClelland (1978). *Social Standing in America: New Dimensions of Class,* New York: Basic Books.

18 Locklin, S. (2010, August 25). Social Classes: The Upper Class in America. *Alternative Right.* [Online.] Available: http://www.alternativeright.com/main/blogs/zeitgeist

/social-classes-the-upper-class-in-america/. Aldrich, N. W. (1996). *Old Money: The Mythology of Wealth in America.* New York: Allworth Press.

19 Burris, V. (2000). The Myth of Old Money Liberalism: The Politics of the Forbes 400 Richest Americans. *Social Problems, 47* (3): 360–378.

20 Coleman, R. P. (1977). Attitudes toward Neighborhoods: How Americans Want to Live, Cambridge, MA: Joint Center for Urban Studies of Massachusetts Institute of Technology and Harvard University, Working Paper No. 49.

21 Henry, P. (2004). Hope, Hopelessness, and Coping. *Psychology & Marketing,* 375–403.

22 Fattah, H. (2001, April). The Rising Tide. *American Demographics,* 48–53.

23 Luhby, T. (2011, November 8). American Dream Deferred: Global Income Inequality: Where the U.S. Ranks. *CNNMoney.* [Online.] Available: http://money .cnn.com/2011/11/08/news/economy/global_income _inequality/index.htm.

24 Schaninger, C. M. (1981, May). Social Class versus Income Revisited: An Empirical Investigation. *Journal of Marketing Research, 18,* 192–208.

25 Sapolsky, R. M. (2004). Social Status and Health in Humans and Other Animals. *Annual Review of Anthropology, 33,* 393–418.

26 Ruch, F. L., and P. G. Zimbardo (1971). *Psychology and Life,* 8th ed. Glenview, IL: Scott Foresman.

27 Fiske, S. T. (2010). Group-based Status: Opening Doors. In S. T. Fiske, D. T. Gilbert, and G. Lindzey (Eds.). *Handbook of Social Psychology* (pp. 941–982). Hoboken, NJ: Wiley & Sons.

28 Darley, J. M., and Gross, P. H. (1983). A Hypothesis-Confirmation Bias in Labeling Effects. *Journal of Personality and Social Psychology, 44,* 20–33.

29 Woods, T. A., Kurtz-Costes, B., and Rowley, S. J. (2005). The Development of Stereotypes about the Rich and Poor: Age, Race, and Family Income Differences in Beliefs. *Journal of Youth and Adolescence, 34,* 437–445.

30 Cuddy, A. J. C., Fiske, S. T., Kwan, V. S. Y., Glick, P., Demoulin, S., Leyens, J-Ph., Bond, M. H., Croizet, J. C., Ellemer, N., Sleebos, E., Htun, T. T., Yamamoto, M., et al. (2009). Is the Stereotype Content Model Culture-Bound? A Cross-Cultural Comparison Reveals Systematic Similarities and Differences. *British Journal of Social Psychology, 48,* 1–33.

31 Russell, A. M., and Fiske, S. T. (2009, February). Social Class Ambivalence: Polarized Reactions to the Poor. Paper presented to *Society for Personality and Social Psychology,* Tampa, FL.

32 Twenge, J. M., and Campbell, W. K. (2002). Self-Esteem and Socioeconomic Status: A Meta-Analytic Review. *Personality and Social Psychology Review, 6,* 59–71.

33 Kraus, M. W., and Keltner, D. (2009). Signs of Socioeconomic Status: A Thin Slicing Approach. *Psychological Science, 20,* 99–106.

34 Hall, J.A., Coats, E. J., and LeBeau, L. S. (2005). Nonverbal Behavior and the Vertical Dimension of Social Relations: A Meta-Analysis. *Psychological Bulletin, 131,* 898–924.

35 Moors, A., and De Houwer, J. (2005). Automatic Processing of Dominance and Submissiveness. *Experimental Psychology, 52,* 296–302.

36 Tiedens, L. Z., and Fragale, A. R. (2003). Power Moves: Complementarity in Dominant and Submissive Nonverbal Behavior. *Journal of Personality and Social Psychology, 85,* 1049–1061.

37 Lefkowitz, M., Blake, R. R., and Mouton, J. S. (1995). Status Factors in Pedestrian Violation of Traffic Signals. *Journal of Abnormal and Social Psychology, 51,* 704–706.

38 Doob, A. N., and Gross, A. E. (1968). Status of Frustrator as an Inhibitor of Horn-Honking Response. *The Journal of Social Psychology, 76,* 213–218.

39 Alder, N. E., Boyce, T., Chesney, M. A., Cohen, S., Folkman, S., Kahn, R. L., and Syme, S. L. (1994). Socioeconomic Status and Health: The Challenge of the Gradient. *American Psychologist, 49,* 15–24.

40 Crispell, D. (1993, May). Where Generations Divide: A Guide. *American Demographics* (5), 9–11.

41 Washburne, C. K. (1995). *America in the Twentieth Century 1930–1939.* New York: Marshall Cavendish.

42 Timmermann, S. (2007, May). What a Difference a Generation Makes: How Our Life Experiences Shape Our Viewpoints and Behaviors. *Journal of Financial Service Professionals,* 25–28.

43 Amazon.com book review. [Online.] Available at: http://www.amazon.com/The-Greatest-Generation-Tom-Brokaw/dp/0375502025.

44 Gordon, K. T. (2004, August). Young at Heart. *Entrepreneur, 32* (8), 68–69.

45 Zickuhr, K. (2010, December 16). Generations 2010. [Online.] Available at: http://pewinternet.org/~/media/Files/Reports/2010/PIP_Generations_and_Tech10.pdf.

46 Weiss, M. J. (2003, May). Great Expectations. *American Demographics, 25* (4), 26–35.

47 Moschis, G. P. (1996, September). Life States of the Mature Market. *American Demographics, 18* (9), 44–51.

48 Williams, K. D. (2007, September 24). How to Target Older Demos. *Advertising Age, 78* (38), p. 8.

49 Moschis, G. P. (1992). *Marketing to Older Consumers: A Handbook of Information for Strategy Development.* Westport, CT: Quorum Books.

50 Moschis, G. P., and Mathur, A. (2006). Older Consumer Responses to Marketing Stimuli: The Power of Subjective Age. *Journal of Advertising Research, 46* (3), 339–346.

51 Tepper, K. (1994). The Role of Labeling Processes in Elderly Consumers' Response to Age Segmentation Cues. *Journal of Consumer Research, 20* (4), 503–519.

52 Levy, P. (2011, May 15). Segmentation by Generation. *Marketing News 45* (6), 21–23.

53 *American Generations: Who They Are and How They Live* (2010). The Nielsen Co.

54 Layman, R. (Ed.). (1995). American Decades. In *Boomers, Exers, and Other Strangers.* Detroit, MI: Gale Research.

55 Welch, D. (2009, August 3). The Incredible Shrinking Boomer Economy. *BusinessWeek, 4141,* 26–30.

56 Court, D., Farrell, D., and Forsyth, J. E. (2007). *McKinsey Quarterly, 4,* 102–113.

57 Gordon, L., and Gordon, A. (Ed.). (1995). The Columbia Chronicles of American Life: 1910–1992. In Layman, R. (Ed.) *Boomers, Exers, and Other Strangers.* New York: Columbia University Press.

58 Zill, N., and Robinson, J. (1995, April). The Generation X Difference. *American Demographics, 17* (4), 24–33.

59 Reynolds, C. (2004, May). Gen X. *American Demographics,* (26): 8–9.

60 Howe, N., and Strauss, W. (2000). *Millennials Rising.* Vintage Books (vintagebooks.com).

61 The Millennials are Coming. *60 Minutes.* CBS News. (2008, May 23). [Online.] Available at: http://www.cbsnews.com/stories/2007/11/08/60minutes/main3475200.shtml.

62 Returning to the Nest. (2004, February, 29). *Baltimore Sun.*

63 Fields, Bea. Marketing to Gen Y: What You Can't Afford Not to Know. *Startupnation.* [Online.] Available at: http://www.startupnation.com/business-articles/9011/1/marketing-GenY.htm.

64 Gassaway, B. (2011, Winter). What Can We Learn from the Youth Market? *Marketing Research, 23* (4), 11–15.

65 Mangleburg, T. F., and Bristol, T. (1998). Socialization and Adolescents' Skepticism. *Journal of Advertising, 27* (3), 11–21.

66 Keillor, B. D., Parker, R. S., and Schaefer, A. (1996). Influences on Adolescent Brand Preferences in the United States and Mexico. *Journal of Advertising Research, 36* (3), 47–56.

67 Bao, Y., and Shao, A. T. (2002). Nonconformity Advertising to Teens. *Journal of Advertising Research, 42* (3), 56–65.

68 Horovitz, B. (2012, May 8). Gum Goes from Humdrum to Teen Fashion Statement. *USA Today.*

MARKETING METRICS

Generational Differences in Attitudes

Interview 10–15 members from *two* separate age cohorts: (1) Pre-Depression, (2) Depression, (3) Baby Boomers, (4) Generation X, (5) Generation Y, and (6) Generation Z. Ask them to respond to the following statements by circling the answer that answer that best reflects their feelings:

1. "Overall, I am optimistic about the outlook for my financial well-being over the next several years."
   Strongly Agree (5) Agree (4) Neither Agree nor Disagree (3) Disagree (2) Strongly Disagree (1)
2. "I prefer name brands over store brands."
   Strongly Agree (5) Agree (4) Neither Agree nor Disagree (3) Disagree (2) Strongly Disagree (1)
3. "I prefer doing my banking online."
   Strongly Agree (5) Agree (4) Neither Agree nor Disagree (3) Disagree (2) Strongly Disagree (1)

Your Task:

Use the Excel file (DT15-1.xls) as a template for entering your participant's responses. Enter *5* for "strongly agree," *4* for "agree," *3* for "neither agree nor disagree," *2* for "disagree" and *1* for "strongly disagree."

1. After entering the data in the spreadsheet, compare the arithmetic means (averages) for means for columns B–D and F–H. Compare column B to F, C to G, and D to H. Do any of the differences appear large?
2. A standard deviation depicts the variation, or "spread," inherent in a data set. Higher standard deviations indicate that there is disagreement among the respondents, whereas lower standard deviations indicate more agreement. Compare the standard deviations for columns B through D. Do any of these measures appear considerably large or small? Do the same for columns F through H.
3. Test the differences in financial outlook *between* cohorts by conducting a two-sample *t-test*. Find the data analysis tab and click "t-Test: Two Sample Assuming Unequal Variances." Variable range 1 is F3:F17, and variable range 2 is B12:B21. Use 0 for the hypothesized mean difference, put the output in J2, and click "OK." The first three rows in the second column of

463

output show the statistics for Cohort 1, whereas the first three rows in the third column of output show the statistics for Cohort 2.

- Which cohort appears to be more optimistic about their financial outlook?

- Is there a difference in the variance between cohorts? What does this imply?

- Look at the two-tailed *p-value* for the test: P(T≤t) two tail. 1–(p-value) provides the level of confidence in concluding that there are statistically significant differences between the two cohorts with regards to their financial outlook. How would you interpret the findings?

4. Conduct similar *t-tests* for the other two questions. What are your conclusions?

CONTEMPORARY STRATEGIES IN REACHING CONSUMERS

OBJECTIVES   *After studying this chapter, you will be able to…*

1 Define word-of-mouth communication and understand why it is so powerful.

2 Discuss the ways marketers create and promote word-of-mouth through buzz marketing.

3 Explain how consumer generated marketing has become a unique way to push the "buzz button."

4 Discuss how celebrity and athlete endorsers bring unique value to brands and understand how important it is for a marketer to pick the right endorser for a brand.

5 Explain why product placement is an essential tool for marketers today and discuss the various types of product placement.

6 Describe the emerging trend of mobile marketing.

© iStockphoto.com/macroworld

Mercedes-Benz and the QR-Trophy Chase

Car enthusiasts are always on the hunt. They can't resist trying to find those masked, hidden, veiled prototype cars, trying to snap an image and see what the new shape of the car will look like. Once the press gets hold of such an image that the car manufacturers try to keep secret, the pictures usually spread fast, especially in today's digital, connected world. So Mercedes-Benz decided to leverage its car fans' curiosity with the QR-Trophy Chase campaign to promote the manufacturer's new A-class car.

The new prototype car was wrapped in the images of QR Codes. (As we will discuss later in the chapter, a QR Code is a two-dimensional matrix box barcode that can be read by mobile devices, such as a smartphone.) The goal was to find four special QR Codes hidden on the car. The QR Codes were also distributed on the Internet and on the street. People scanned the

codes, hoping to find the four special trophy codes. The person who found the codes would win a trip to the world premiere of the new car.

With no media budget, the car that wasn't even launched yet was all over the Internet, magazines, television, and media, and Mercedes-Benz was able to generate excitement for its new model. Campaigns like the Mercedes-Benz QR-Trophy Chase are designed to get people interested and talking about a brand, and are an alternative type of campaign that companies hope will cut through the clutter of traditional media today.[1]

Consumers are all too familiar with the traditional methods that marketers use to reach and persuade them—advertisements on television and radio, on billboards and signs, in newspapers, from telemarketers, in junk mail, and from face-to-face salespeople. But companies are now turning to alternative means to reach consumers in non-traditional ways. In this chapter, we examine some of the more unique ways marketers reach out to consumers, including word-of-mouth or buzz marketing, consumer generated marketing campaigns, celebrity and athlete endorsers, product placements, and mobile marketing. Why study these alternative promotional methods and media? Many of the consumer behavior concepts we study are usually researched and taught through the lens of conventional marketing practices like mass advertising only. Understanding non-traditional marketing tactics and strategies enhances our understanding of the nuances of consumer behavior theories and practices.

OBJECTIVE ①

Word-of-Mouth: Pushing the Buzz Button

Some say it is the age of clutter. It seems like there are more and more commercials on television—12 minutes per hour during network primetime.[2]

And the costs of those commercials are high. The average cost of a 30–second network television commercial is around $125,000, with prices for the most popular primetime shows reaching over $500,000 per spot.[3] At that kind of investment, companies expect to see results. But the system seems to be at a breaking point. According to media researcher AC Nielsen, network television viewership has been eroding at a rate of about two percent per year, and cable channels now draw larger audiences than network television, resulting in greater fragmentation.[4] In addition, the proportion of time consumers spend with other media, especially the Internet, is growing, as broadband penetration around the world continues to grow. Now armed with digital video recorders (DVRs), video-on-demand channels, and shows that can be streamed over the Internet, consumers are skipping over or fast-forwarding through commercials entirely. Thus, it appears that the effectiveness of traditional television advertising is faltering. So, marketers are turning more attention to non-traditional tactics. One of those tactics is buzz marketing, a technique designed to generate word-of-mouth.

Websites like Hulu.com now stream television shows over the Internet, further fragmenting traditional television viewership.

Courtesy of Hulu.com

Why Is Word-of-Mouth So Powerful?

Some marketers claim that **word-of-mouth** (or "buzz") is the most powerful form of marketing—period. Word-of-mouth is the act of one consumer talking to another about a brand, and it can happen face-to-face and indirectly via phone, mail, or the Internet. Word-of-mouth has been around as long as human communication (consider one pre-historic hunter telling another where the best hunting spots were). While word-of-mouth can be either positive or negative in nature, marketers attempt to generate positive word-of-mouth about their products and services.

So, why is word-of-mouth so powerful? Word-of-mouth is credible and authentic. Word-of-mouth communication is considered believable because consumers talking to one another rarely involve advertising or sales pitches. The underlying assumption is that the friend, neighbor, co-worker, or Facebook friend engaged in word-of-mouth is someone whom you know and trust, and their opinions are honest and true, free from ulterior motives. People want to share the benefits of their own experiences with fellow consumers. In other words, they want to share their product experiences because they have other people's best interests in mind.

Another reason why word-of-mouth is so powerful is that consumers enjoy discussing their product and service experiences. This is especially so if the person feels emotionally charged about the topic and they want to share their story, according to Jonah Berger, author of *Contagious: Why Things Catch On.*[5] Consumers also like being "in the know." It is appealing to have your peers view you as being on the cutting-edge of a new trend, or your information to be interesting. If a consumer sees a terrific new band play at a local club, he immediately texts or emails his closest friends. If the band stinks, the consumer spreads the word, saving his friends from spending money on poor entertainment. According to Berger, word-of-mouth provides people with a form of social currency—we like to share information that makes us look appealing in the eyes of others. Likewise, people really like giving other people practical advice, so the more practical the advice, the more it will spread via word-of-mouth.[6] Figure 16.1 shows how word-of-mouth can spread quickly and magnify, compared to traditional advertising messages.

Finally, thanks to technology, word-of-mouth can spread faster and farther than ever before, through cell phones, email, text messaging, social networking sites, blogs, instant messaging, chat rooms, and message boards. Because of the Internet, the word-of-mouth story can linger for a long time in cyberspace. For example, back in the early 2000s, the Firestone brand of automobile tire went through a massive product recall when some of their tires were blamed for causing automobile accidents. Today, over a decade later, a simple Internet search still yields dozens of postings about that incident. Given the ever-increasing power of this marketing medium, it is not surprising that marketers are now trying to take better control of the word-of-mouth process through buzz marketing.

FIGURE 16.1 | **Traditional Marketing versus Word-of-Mouth**

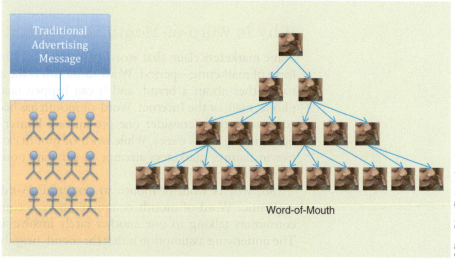

© Olesya Feketa/Shutterstock.com

OBJECTIVE ② **Buzz Marketing**

Word-of-mouth that occurs naturally is called **organic word-of-mouth**. Historically, marketers only *hoped* for positive word-of-mouth, allowing it to generate naturally, as one consumer told another about his or her satisfactory brand experiences. A company might also try to prevent negative word-of-mouth through good service or service recovery following a poor customer experience. In recent years, marketers have become more proactive in trying to deliberately generate and direct word-of-mouth. **Buzz marketing**, also sometimes called **word-of-mouth marketing**, is the execution of marketing tactics specially designed to generate positive word-of-mouth marketing messages and create a virus-like exponential spread of those messages throughout the population of interest. In buzz marketing, the goal is to get key, influential people from the target market to talk about a product, service, or brand experience. These influencers rapidly spread the word, and then the buzz spreads, getting bigger and stronger as it goes.

Variations on buzz marketing are viral marketing, stealth marketing, and community or grassroots marketing. While "buzz," "viral," and "stealth" marketing are sometimes used interchangeably, there are variations among them. Buzz marketing is a general term, encompassing any campaign designed for generating word-of-mouth and helping it spread exponentially.

Viral marketing is a buzz campaign that usually involves the Internet to facilitate the spread of word-of-mouth and spark buzz. We will discuss viral marketing in more depth in the chapter on online marketing. **Stealth marketing** is a buzz marketing campaign that specifically relies on spreading word-of-mouth in a covert or clandestine manner.[7] While the tactics may not differ appreciably in a stealth marketing campaign than in buzz marketing generally, the consumer is supposed to remain unaware that a company is systematically generating buzz.

Who are the key influencers in buzz marketing campaigns? The popular press gives them names like "opinion leaders," "influentials," "alphas," "trend-translators," "hubs," "bees," and "magic people." From the viewpoint of new product development, they are traditionally known as Innovators and Early Adopters. These individuals are the first to try new products and technologies within a given product category. They tend to be opinion leaders that other buyers rely on for product information and recommendations. Malcolm Gladwell, author of *The Tipping Point*, expands on the notion of tapping into these key influencers and the roles they play by identifying individuals he calls Mavens, Connectors, and Salesmen. Mavens (most likely the Innovators and Early Adopters of new products) are product experts in a product category. Connectors are individuals who hook into and span several social groups. Salesmen feed the fire by adding persuasive zeal to the message.[8]

Regardless of what they are called, marketers try to tap into the influence of those who seem to have the ability and willingness to talk about products and brands and generate a buzz. Now, let's examine a few of the specific strategies and techniques companies and marketers use to generate buzz.

Product Pushers

Product pushers are people recruited by a company to get a product prominently seen and talked about in the marketplace. These recruits are usually attractive but approachable and friendly, and are often from the target market's own key influencer set. (This tactic is sometimes referred to as *product seeding.*) A few years ago, Ford Motor Company recruited a few popular opinion leaders in some key college markets and gave them a Ford Focus to drive for six months. In exchange, the brand pushers were supposed to be seen driving the car and handing out Ford promotional materials to anyone who expressed an interest in the car. Also aimed at the college crowd, the Red Bull patrol can often be seen on college campuses during exam time—the company will hire individuals to drive around the campus in a specially decorated car, handing out free cans of the stimulating drink. In addition, throughout the term, college students are hired to carry around spare cans of Red Bull and give them to friends and fellow students who look like they could use an energy boost.

Product pushers get the product seen and talked about in the marketplace.

Frances M. Roberts/Newscom

While brand pushers may really be users of the product they are employed to sample, push, and talk about to fellow members of the target market, they can also be more obvious. For example, beer companies often hire beautiful models to "crash" nightclubs and bars dressed in company logo attire, hand out coupons for free beer, and otherwise generate excitement. Oscar Meyer uses the famous "Weinermobile" to generate excitement and buzz at special events like store openings, where employee hand out free samples and coupons.

A special type of brand pusher has emerged on the Web. Companies like BzzAgent provide a forum for people who want to be involved in buzz campaigns, letting consumers do the legwork. Real people who are real consumers sign up to be agents. They volunteer to try to create buzz for a product in their own communities through grassroots efforts. For example, they may tell their friends about the product, ask their local store to carry the brand, or hand out coupons to people they meet in the street. In exchange, the people who sign up as agents occasionally get previews of new products for free and free samples of the brands they promote. These agents are not under any obligation to push a product if they don't like it. But there are plenty of ordinary people willing to participate. BzzAgent has access to millions of shoppers and has run more than 1,500 buzz campaigns for companies like Kraft, American Express, Sony, and Kellogg's.[9] Vocalpoint and Tremor, two word-of-mouth marketing websites developed by Procter & Gamble, also have large memberships that aim to attract moms with kids and teenagers, respectively.[10]

Stealth Marketing

As stated, stealth marketing is a buzz marketing campaign that specifically relies on spreading word-of-mouth in a covert manner. Also, known as *undercover marketing,* this buzz generating tactic is similar to other buzz generating tactics but tries to operate without consumer knowledge. For example, when gaming company Essential Reality wanted to market a virtual 3-D video game controller glove, it used actors in local restaurants and coffeehouses to engage passersby. There was no hard sell, just a casual conversation about an innovative new product.[11] Interestingly, even Hollywood has been interested in stealth marketing. *The Joneses,* a satire about stealth marketing starring David Duchovny and Demi Moore, focuses on a family that moves into an upscale neighborhood and engages in a large-scale stealth marketing scheme. While stealth marketing has been decried as unethical by the Word of Mouth Marketing Association (WOMMA), this technique continues to be an appealing buzz generating tactic to marketers. Imitation evangelists and stealth celebrity endorsers are two common stealth techniques.

Imitation Evangelists Imitation evangelists are actors put on the payroll for stealth buzz campaigns. Their task is to slip commercial messages and recommendations into everyday conversations under the consumer's nose, with the hope of igniting a natural buzz. They differ from regular brand pushers owing to the stealthy nature of the campaigns. The consumer is never supposed to know that the encounter is not authentic. For example, when Sony Ericsson Mobile Communication Company wanted to promote a new camera-cell phone, they created the "fake tourist" campaign. Young, attractive couples posed as tourists in popular vacation spots around the United States. They asked passersby to snap their photo with the phone. The chance encounter became a moment to generate interest and buzz about the product.

Another popular stealth technique is to use "fake shoppers." On the Internet, these people post on blogs, participate in chat rooms, and post product reviews. The music industry has also planted hip shoppers in music stores to chat about new artists so other shoppers overhear. Likewise, cigarette manufacturers sometimes hire women to give packs of cigarettes to smokers because, they claim, "the pack doesn't fit in my purse."[12] Finally, some alcohol manufacturers hire "leaners." These stealth marketers pose as bar patrons, leaning on the bar, ordering the particular brand, and recommending the drink to others around them.

Stealth Celebrity Endorsers Celebrities are also sometimes part of stealth marketing campaigns. In a standard celebrity endorsement, a celebrity is paid to appear in a commercial. The viewer knows that the celebrity is being compensated for participating in the commercial. What consumers often don't realize is that celebrities are also sometimes compensated with fees or free merchandise to use or talk about products in their everyday lives as well. It is common for clothiers, jewelers, and hair and perfume companies to court celebrities to appear in their products. Alternatively, when actress Kathleen Turner appeared on ABC's *Good Morning America* and talked about an illness she had, she directed people to a website sponsored by a pharmaceutical company. However, she said nothing about the fact that the drug manufacturer had paid her for her public appearances on its behalf.[13] Celebrities who discuss their health ailments in media interviews but fail to disclose their related endorsement deals have been criticized for taking stealth marketing too far.

Experiential Marketing

Most people would agree that we learn from our experiences. A buzz marketing technique based on this idea is **experiential marketing**. This type of marketing creates one-on-one experiences that allow consumers to experience the brand in a sensory way that is usually unique, fun, and entertaining. Experiential marketing campaigns are often built around sight-seeing venues or sporting, entertainment, and charity events. For example, the makers of Ocean Spray Cranberry Juice created "Bog Across America," which involved simulated cranberry bogs inside cities. Employees, dressed in waders, distributed coupons, samples, and recipes to visitors. Vans shoes host a yearly rock concert, called the Warped Tour, where thousands of fans can see bands for a low ticket price and buy Vans merchandise. And ASICS shoes, during the weekend of the New York City Marathon, put up a 60-foot video wall where people could virtually race against U.S. marathoner Ryan Hall.

Proponents of experiential marketing claim that these techniques not only generate word-of-mouth but also strengthen the emotional connections between the brand and consumer.[14] Experiential marketing focuses on creating unique, interactive, emotional, memorable encounters with the brand, and when done correctly it often generates buzz.

Experiential marketing focuses on creating unique, interactive, emotional, and memorable encounters with the brand in order to create buzz.

ZUMA Press, Inc./Alamy

Community Marketing

Another type of buzz generating technique centers on engaging with consumers on a community level. **Community marketing** is organizing and supporting niche communities that share a common interest surrounding a brand. These communities may take place offline or online, and include communities such as fan clubs, user groups and forums, and discussion groups. For example, the Apple Forum is an online discussion forum for Apple brand users where people can share tips and support. The Harley Owners Group (H.O.G.) is a member group for Harley-Davidson motorcycle owners, where riders can participate in local chapter rides or state and national rallies.

Grassroots marketing, a type of community marketing, involves organizing and supporting communities on a personal and local level. Grassroots efforts often rely on volunteers for execution, such as a local volunteer going door-to-door in a neighborhood to raise donations for a charity or pass out flyers in support of a political campaign. The BzzAgent campaigns we described earlier could also represent a form of grassroots marketing.

The next subject, consumer generated marketing, is a non-traditional form of marketing that attempts to combine the advantages of good buzz generating tactics with traditional advertising.

OBJECTIVE **3**

Consumer Generated Marketing

Consumer generated marketing is the creation of advertising or other marketing content by the customer. Here, companies leverage their own customers to generate not only interesting advertisements or other marketing content (e.g., sharing images, posting digital stories and testimonies, "liking" brands in the social media, etc.—see the Marketing in Action Box), but also some resulting good press and buzz too. Often, a company invites participants to create marketing content, often an advertisement, for its brand through some kind of promotion or contest. The content is usually submitted via the company's website. Selected "winners" may have their content appear on the company website or in the broader community, such as on social media websites. Occasionally, the content may cross over to television, radio, magazines, etc. For example, for the last several years Frito-Lay's Doritos brand chips has held a consumer generated advertising campaign. The winning advertisements are shown during the Super Bowl and other television programming.

Why would a company solicit consumer generated advertising and content? The answers are numerous, if not obvious. First, the costs of producing traditional advertising are very high. User-generated content is much cheaper. Second, when customers decide to participate, they have to really think about the brand creatively, generating a new depth of interaction with the brand, something that marketers want. Third, the content created is often quite good. A consumer who loves a brand enough to produce creative work can generate truly inspiring and compelling content. Finally, consumer generated advertising and other content is also a great marketing research tool: what better way is there for marketers to see how people feel about the brand and how the brand is actually positioned in the marketplace? In sum, the goal of consumer generated advertising campaigns is not to create award-winning advertising, although sometimes this happens. Instead, the goal is to allow consumers to express, in their own words, how they feel about the brand. As a result, these authentic, innovative, and entertaining messages offer greater opportunity for generating positive buzz about the brand than do traditional marketing communications. When consumers are engaged in the process, they feel empowered.

Of course, serious risk exists in consumer generated advertising. First, such advertising may not be applicable for all products. It is hard to be passionate about toilet paper and fabric softeners. Products that are new, unique, or edgy, or brands with an iconic brand identity are usually better candidates for this type of campaign. For example, even though ketchup is a commodity-type product, the H. J. Heinz Company has managed to inspire a passion and love for its ketchup brand over the years. To cash in on these feelings, the company ran a consumer generated campaign called, "Top This TV Challenge." The commercials submitted were shown on YouTube.com, and the top 15 ads (selected by the company) were also featured on the company's website. The cyber public then voted for the winners. The top five commercials were shown in national television advertising spots, and the winning commercial won $57,000 (a reference to the number "57," which is part of the Heinz trademark).

Furthermore, with the good ads also come the bad. When an uncontrollable and unqualified public has free rein to submit anything, a company has to spend time and money sifting through all the bad content to find a few advertising gems—and there's no guarantee there will be any worthy of public display. Heinz had no guarantee that any of the advertisements submitted would be any good, but the company was committed to running the five finalists on national television. Thus, Heinz assumed considerable risk in making the promise to air the winning ads no matter what.

Finally, brands with passionate devotees also tend to attract consumers who dislike the brand. While a firm may reject negative content for its website and marketing activities, harmful information can easily find its way onto the Internet and into the press. For example, when the marketers of Chevrolet automobiles decided to hold a contest to see who could produce the best television commercial for its Tahoe SUV (in coordination with the show *The Apprentice*), they didn't necessarily count on Chevy bashers joining the game. The majority of entries to the contest were extremely positive, but a number of negative videos were submitted too, with sharply satirical content talking about global warming, a war for oil, and social injustice. Chevy could have removed the negative content, but the company allowed it to stay, apparently deciding that it was more credible to let everyone who wanted to participate have a say. This strategy paid off. The contest website drove people to the Chevy website, and sales rose.[15] In consumer generated advertising, marketers ask customers what they think and how they define the brand. While this level of customer interaction and brand co-creation may be risky, many marketers realize that controlling the advertising message and trying to force a brand image onto the consumer doesn't necessarily work the way it used to. Consumers want a say.

Consumer generated content is an interesting form of customer engagement that leverages the capabilities of digital communications. Will this new form of marketing stick around or will it lose its appeal as the novelty wears

Marketing in Action

Disney Leverages Consumer Memories

Research shows that nearly half of vacation-goers post photos to social media websites, and 20% share their experiences as they happen in real-time. This includes visitors to Disney amusement parks and resorts who share their experiences with friends and family through photos, videos, and anecdotes, both online and offline. Disney has tried to leverage these guest experiences and the consumer generated content genre with its "Let Memories Begin" campaign.

The campaign incorporates photos and videos submitted by visitors to Disney resorts and amusement parks. Disney visitors can upload content to the Disneyparks website and

the Disney Facebook pages. Disney then uses this content in television and print ads as well as in social media campaigns. For example, Disney incorporated user-generated content into a Twitter and Facebook contest, and winners got to see a show with the cast of Modern Family and its star, Julie Bowen.

In-park marketing is also included. Disney also now uses pictures taken daily by the onsite park photographers (called Disney PhotoPass photographers) and projects the candid shots into the evening sky at Disney World and Disneyland (with the guests' permission, of course). Thus, visitors might see their own faces projected over the park.[16]

---

off? We don't know the answer to that question, but celebrity and athlete endorsers, our next topic, have secured what appears to be a permanent place in the repertoires of marketing managers.

OBJECTIVE **4** # Celebrity and Athlete Endorsers

Consumers often think of brands in terms of the famous people who endorse them. A **celebrity endorser** is an individual who enjoys public recognition and uses this recognition on behalf of a consumer product by appearing in an advertisement or engaging in some other marketing tactic. Celebrity and athlete endorsements are pervasive, and some estimates indicate that more than 20% of all marketing campaigns feature such an endorser; internationally, these numbers may be higher. For example, in China, celebrity endorsements are quite common.

Celebrities have been endorsing brands for more than a century. In 1882, British actress Lily Langtrey, a very close friend of King Edward VII, endorsed Pears Soap. Mark Twain promoted his own brands of flour and cigars. Before he entered politics, former president Ronald Reagan appeared in ads for Chesterfield cigarettes, and actor Sean Connery endorsed Jim Beam bourbon. See Table 16.1 for a sample of celebrity endorsements, both classic and contemporary.

What benefits does Tiger Woods bring to Nike? How does actress Anne Hathaway help jeweler Tiffany? What about Willem Dafoe and Mercedes-Benz? Although research is mixed on the value of celebrity and athlete endorsements, under certain conditions, the use of celebrities can increase message recall and aid in brand recognition.[17] Research also shows that celebrities can provide brands with increased levels of trustworthiness, likeability, and persuasion.[18] One interesting study even demonstrates that investors react positively to the

TABLE 16.1 | Celebrity Endorsements and Brand Personalities

Celebrity	Claim to Fame	Brand name
Zooey Deschanel	Actress/Singer	Apple iPhone
Tina Fey	Actress/Comedian	Garnier
David Beckham	Athlete	Adidas
Natalie Portman	Actress	Christian Dior
Salma Hayek	Actress	Got Milk?
Nicki Minaj	Singer/Performer	Pepsi
Will.i.am	Singer/Performer	Budweiser
Charles Barkley	Athlete/Commentator	Weight Watchers
Tiger Woods	Athlete	Nike
Sofia Vergara	Actress	Cover Girl

announcement of celebrity endorsements.[19] Another study shows that celebrity endorsers can reduce consumers' perceptions of risk involved in technology products, provided that the celebrity is a good fit for the product.[20]

Much of the value of employing celebrities and athletes derives from their attractiveness, which includes both physical attractiveness and likability. And in addition to attractiveness, credibility is crucial to the success of celebrity and athlete endorsements. Credibility is established when the endorser is knowledgeable, which means the endorser has the expertise and skill to evaluate the brand, and also when the endorser is trustworthy, which means the consumer believes the endorser to be sincere and honest about the brand.

Celebrities and athletes are also successful when they can portray themselves as typical brand users in typical use situations. Research suggests that when a consumer sees a celebrity endorsing a product, the consumer makes correspondent inferences. A **correspondent inference** is the assumption that a person's behavior is a reflection of their beliefs and underlying dispositions, rather than the result of some situational variable. So, a celebrity wearing a certain brand of watch leads the consumer to infer that the celebrity actually likes the brand and is a typical user of the brand. This occurs despite the fact that most consumers are aware that celebrities and athletes are paid large sums of money to endorse brands.[21]

Along with correspondent inferences, research also suggests that celebrity and athlete endorsers come with "cultural meanings." These cultural meanings are transferred to the brand. If the endorser and the product are a good "match" so that the transfer of cultural meaning is possible, then the endorser is more effective. Consumers usually develop preconceived images about celebrity and athlete endorsers, resulting in images about the endorser transferring to the brand.[22] Thus, the managerial implication is that the endorser should "fit" the product endorsed.

Beyond the issue of "fit," celebrity endorsement can be risky. Famous stars can overshadow a brand, and celebrity scandals can tarnish a brand's image. Chrysler dropped Celine Dion, believing her sponsorship sold more music than automobiles. Similarly, Pepsi broke off its relationship with Beyoncé over concern that the brand didn't benefit from the promotion as much as she did (it did, however, resume its relationship with Beyoncé in 2012). Firms also drop celebrity endorsers quickly when they are linked to negative publicity. In 2010, Gatorade discontinued its relationship with Tiger Woods after a scandal surrounding his marriage became known. Marketers also vigorously avoid negative political fallout. Sharon Stone was dropped from Christian Dior ads after she stated that an earthquake in China was "bad karma" due to the country's treatment of the Dalai Lama. Michael Vick, the popular quarterback of the Atlanta Falcons, was indicted on federal conspiracy charges for his role in a dog-fighting venture. Vick lost about $37.5 million in earnings, including a lucrative deal with Coca-Cola. And, Michael Phelps, Olympic gold medal winner, was dropped by Kellogg's after photos emerged that showed Phelps smoking marijuana.

Not surprisingly, marketers are adamant about protecting their brand images from the deleterious impact of celebrity and athlete misbehavior. Many firms now include morals clauses in celebrity endorsement contracts that allow the company to terminate a deal should a celebrity behave in an unbecoming manner. See Table 16.2 for a *Forbes Magazine* list of the most powerful celebrities and athletes in terms of earnings, media, Web, and social ratings.

TABLE 16.2 | *Forbes* Most Powerful Celebrities (2012)

Rank	Celebrity	Pay (millions)	Web/Social Rank
1	Jennifer Lopez	$52	13/19
2	Oprah Winfrey	$165	19/18
3	Justin Bieber	$55	9/3
4	Rihanna	$53	5/2
5	Lady Gaga	$52	8/1
6	Britney Spears	$58	15/11
7	Kim Kardashian	$18	6/16
8	Katy Perry	$45	7/4
9	Tom Cruise	$75	32/42
10	Steven Spielberg	$130	46/80
11	Taylor Swift	$57	14/7
12	Tiger Woods	$58	25/45
13	Angelina Jolie	$20	3/83
14	Donald Trump	$63	35/62
15	LeBron James	$53	23/22
16	Beyonce Knowles	$40	12/9
17	Elton John	$80	48/58
18	Simon Cowell	$90	84/79
19	Rush Limbaugh	$69	31/66
20	Tyler Perry	$105	64/30

Source: Pomerantz, D. (2012, May 16). The World's Most Powerful Celebrities. On *Forbes* [Magazine website]. Retrieved from: http://www.forbes.com/celebrities/#p_1_s_a0_All%20Categories_

Finally, athlete endorsers have become major factors in today's media culture, especially with technological advances in broadcast and interactive media. Consumers can now view sporting events on cell phones, for example. See Table 16.3 for the highest paid athletes in the world, based on appearance fees, endorsement income, salaries, bonuses, and prizes, according to *Forbes*.

Athlete endorsers' responsibilities can range from using or wearing specific brands (e.g., Tiger Woods and Nike apparel) to offering actual testimonials on behalf of the brand (e.g., Payton Manning and Sprint). Despite the widespread use of athlete endorsers, their influence on advertising objectives remains controversial, similar to the use of traditional celebrity endorsers. Some research suggests that sports celebrities may not connect to intended target markets.[23] Other research, however, demonstrates that athlete endorsers positively influence adolescents' favorable world-of-mouth and brand loyalty. In other words, not only are athletes important to adolescents making brand choices, but adolescents also talk about the brands to their friends and peers. Regardless of whether athletes *desire* to be role models, research indicates that teenagers *consider* athletes as important role models—regardless of their public behavior.[24]

TABLE 16.3 | *Forbes* Best-Paid Athletes (2012)

Athlete	Sport	$ (millions)
Manny Pacquaio	Boxing	$67
Tiger Woods	Golf	$58
LeBron James	Basketball	$58
Roger Federer	Tennis	$52
Kobe Bryant	Basketball	$50
Phil Mickelson	Golf	$48
David Beckham	Soccer	$46
Peyton Manning	Football	$42
Cristiano Ronaldo	Soccer	$42
Floyd Mayweather	Boxing	$40
Lionell Messi	Soccer	$39
Alex Rodriguez	Baseball	$34
Rafael Nadal	Tennis	$33
Tom Brady	Football	$27
Maria Sharapova	Tennis	$26

Source: *Forbes* Sports' Highest Earners. On *Forbes* [Magazine website]. Retrieved from http://www.therichest.org/nation/forbes-highest-paid-athletes/.

OBJECTIVE **5** ## Product Placement

What Is Product Placement?

What follows is a brief bit of dialogue from an episode of the TV program *Modern Family*. The scene opens; the family is having breakfast and getting ready for the day. The main characters, Claire and Phil, are talking about Phil's birthday. The dialogue proceeds:

Phil: Big Saturday tomorrow.

Claire: That's right. It's somebody's birthday.

Phil: Not just that—the iPad comes out on my actual birthday. It's like Steve Jobs and God got together to say we love you Phil.

Claire: What is so great about that doohickey anyhow?

Phil: Doohickey Elly May? It's a movie theater, a library, and a music store all rolled into one awesome pad...

Knowing this is what Phil really wants for his birthday, zany hijinks ensue throughout the episode as Claire tries to purchase the iPad for Phil's birthday. Finally, the episode ends with Phil getting his iPad, blowing out virtual candles on the screen, and Phil affectionately stroking the product. So goes the famous iPad episode of *Modern Family*. Would the premise of the episode have worked with a generic gift? Probably. But would it have been as funny or memorable? Maybe not, especially because at the time the show aired, the product wasn't yet on the market.

Product placement that is key to advancing the plot is called product integration. It is one of the most powerful forms of product placement.

Product placement is the insertion of branded goods and services within the content of popular media, including television, movies, video games, books, and music. When done correctly, product placement adds a sense of continuity and realism to the context that a generic product cannot. On the flipside, if you have ever watched a television show or movie and felt like you were watching one really long commercial, you've probably been on the receiving end of poor product placement.

Product placement has been around since the beginning of movies and television, but has seen explosive growth as an alternative marketing method over the last few years. One of the earliest documented product placements was in 1951 for Gordon's Gin in the movie *The African Queen*.[25] Katherine Hepburn didn't drink the gin in the film but threw it overboard. Another classic example is from the 1982 film *E.T. the Extra-Terrestrial*, which helped launch Reese's Pieces from Hershey Foods Corporation. In the film, Henry Thomas lures the alien inside his home with the candies. While Hershey paid nothing for the inclusion, the payoff for Reese's Pieces was significant, with sales for the candy skyrocketing within a week of the movie's premier. Interestingly, the producers originally wanted to use M&Ms candy, but the company turned down the placement. More recently, Apple products appeared in the movie *Mission Impossible: Ghost Protocol*. According to some industry experts, the placement was worth over $23 million dollars to Apple, whose products appeared on screen for five minutes.[26]

While product placement is traditionally associated with movies and television, it is now present in all types of media. For example, Lana Del Rey has a song called "Diet Moutain Dew." Other brands often mentioned in popular music include Cadillac, Coca-Cola, Lexus, Versace, Porsche, Gucci, and Cartier. In addition, when product placement makes it into the lyrics of a song, product placement is also likely to be seen in that song's music video. In Lady Gaga's music video for her song "Telephone" there are product placements for Miracle Whip and Virgin Mobile, and the video has been viewed over 200 million times on YouTube.com.

Books are not immune to product placement either. Fay Weldon's book *The Bulgari Connection* featured the famous Bulgari jewelry company, and the bestselling Sookie Stackhouse novels by Charlaine Harris, upon which the HBO show *True Blood* is based, often feature the main character drinking a Coca-Cola. Product placement is even appearing in more and more video games. Just like in movies, video game creators insert real products and brands into their cyber-environments to lend realism and cohesiveness to the game. Going a step farther, *advergaming* is the practice of creating a whole game specifically designed around a product. For example, the makers of Minute Maid juices, working with Skyworks productions, created "Minute Maid Maj Jong," which combines brand messages and gaming.

Why Is Product Placement Growing?

In recent years, product placement has surged as companies search for new ways to reach consumers and the costs of production for traditional advertising have risen. While product placement has become an essential tool for marketers, it is also an important revenue stream for media providers. Below are just some of the benefits of product placement.

Added Realism Product placements link fictional content to real life, making the story more believable. The benefit for the product is that consumers see it perform in real life situations (hopefully in ways that improve the perception of the brand).

Reach and Longevity Product placement is extremely economical when you consider that television shows, movies, books, videos, and songs usually have a long shelf life and typically cost a fraction of traditional broadcast television advertising. A song may be heard by millions of people many times over months or even years. With DVD sales and syndication, movies and television shows can be watched for decades. Viewers still see Will Smith wearing Ray-Ban sunglasses in the movie, *Men in Black* (1997). Year after year, viewers watch

Ralphie almost shoot out his eye with his longed-for Red Ryder BB Gun in *A Christmas Story* (1983). In addition, when a brand is featured within a show, it is definitely seen—but in a broadcast commercial, it can be skipped via the fast-forward button on the DVR.

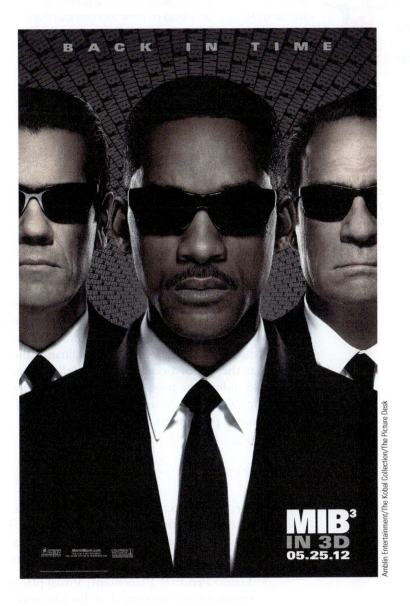

Product placement has reach and longevity.

Indirect Endorsements When an actor is seen in close proximity to a product or is shown using a product in a dramatic scene or situation, an association between the character and/or the celebrity and the brand can be made in the consumer's mind, creating an indirect celebrity endorsement. Strategic product placement with the right characters or actors can convey ideas about the positioning of the brand. Research has shown that when consumers see celebrities endorsing a brand, they typically assume the celebrities like and use the brand "in real life." Recall our earlier discussion of correspondent inferences.

Ethics

Is product placement a form of subliminal advertising? As has been already discussed in this book, *subliminal perception* is the unconscious perception of a stimulus. Many subliminal messages actually fall above the absolute threshold of physical perception, but are still consciously repressed by the viewer. Given this definition, does product placement fall within these boundaries? One can argue that this may be the case.

Many times, a person may not consciously notice a product or brand in the background of a television or movie scene. Even so, the brand may be noticed on some subconscious level. Other times, while the brand is noticed, it may be integrated so seamlessly into the action that viewers may simply not realize they are watching a type of advertisement. In addition, product placements are not overtly disclosed at the time the good or service is featured. Commercial Alert, a consumer advocacy group, has called for full disclosure of product placement arrangements both before and during television programs. In fact, the group claims that product placements are inherently deceptive and subliminal.[27]

On the flipside, product placements don't fall below the absolute threshold of perception; marketers want them to be seen and heard. Also, the appearance of a brand in itself does not call the consumer to action. In other words, there is no overt "sales pitch." The Federal Trade Commission has argued that this lack of overt advertising messages exempts product placement from full disclosure. Also, because some placements are unpaid, consumers cannot know which products are included for the sake of advertising and which are there to enhance the entertainment.

So, while most people would agree that product placement is some form of advertising, is it actually subliminal advertising? You decide.

Cost Reduction Product placement can help reduce the costs of producing media because producers do not have to purchase set items and props, plus it can provide cash to support the creative process. For example, Mark Burnett, creator of CBS's *Survivor*, helps finance the show this way. It was speculated that the James Bond movie *Skyfall* covered a large part of its budget with $45 million in product placement revenue from Heineken. Another Bond film, *Tomorrow Never Dies* (1997), received over $100 million from various product placements.[28]

Types of Product Placement

All product placements are not created equal. They have varying degrees of impact on and interaction with the media. Typically, as the involvement of a brand with the editorial content in question increases, so does the value of its placement within the media. Types of product placement include:

- **Visual Product Placement**: Visual placement entails placing the brand on screen within the setting or background of a program. While this is probably the most common form of product placement in movies, television, and other visual media, it is also the easiest to overlook because there is little or no interaction between the actors and the product, and the product itself may not be integral to the story. Included in this category is a variant on product placement called *advertisement placement*. This occurs when an advertisement for a brand is placed in the media, rather than the brand itself. Examples include a television commercial playing in the background of a scene or an actor driving his car past a billboard in an action sequence.

- **Verbal Product Placement**: Verbal placement is when an actor references or requests a product by name. This type of placement is most common in non-visual media, such as music and books.
- **Brand Interaction**: Brand interaction occurs when the characters actually handle the product or physically interact with it in some way. An actor drinking a popular soft drink in a scene of a television show would be an example of this type of product placement.
- **Brand Integration**: Brand integration occurs when the brand is woven into the thread of the story, becoming part of the plot or context in a fashion similar to the famous Junior Mint scene in an episode of *Seinfeld*, the BMW Z3 scene in a James Bond movie, and the iPad scene in the television show *Modern Family*.
- **Sponsorship and Branded Entertainment**: This type of product placement is the most intensive form of marriage between content and a brand. In this type of placement, the brand is the sponsor of the content, has extensive editorial control of the content, and the editorial content or style typically matches closely the targeted audience of the brand.

Regardless of the type of product placement used, marketers must be creative to obtain the placement. The most straightforward way of placing a brand is for the marketer to pay a fee for the brand to appear in the show or program. According to some industry experts, product placement is a $25 billion dollar industry.[29] Ford and Coca-Cola paid at least $35 million each for their sponsorship/product placement deals with Fox's *American Idol* reality show.[30] This investment has apparently paid off because the sponsors keep coming back year after year. In fact, the famous red Coca-Cola cups that have appeared on the judges' table during the show are reported to be the most widely seen product placement on television, according to an article in *Advertising Age*.[31] Although no industry standards exist regarding product placement cost and use, marketers usually have some "veto power" in decisions about how their brands are used.

Some companies do not like to pay for product placement, preferring instead to provide free merchandise to support the production of the show through a type of barter agreement. In exchange, the producers include the product. More than half of all product placements occur through this exchange method. For example, Apple claims that it does not pay for product placements, but Apple computers, iPhones, and iPods appear frequently in popular television shows, including *CSI: NY*, NBC's *30 Rock,* and HBO's *True Blood*. In addition, Apple-branded products have appeared in more movies in the last decade than practically any other brand, including appearing in one-third of all the top U.S. box office films in the last decade.[32]

Finally, some product placements just appear in some productions, with or without the brand's permission, because the producer or director feels the product enhances the quality of the production. For example, in an episode of HBO's classic show *The Sopranos*, a can of Raid bug killer was used in a violent scene without the permission of SC Johnson Company, the manufacturer. While some companies have tried to block some product placements by suing producers for trademark infringement, there are currently no specific laws that directly prohibit a director or producer from placing a product in a scene or context. Most disputes have been handled on a case-by-case basis. Given the rapid growth of this practice, however, more rigid regulation of product placement may be on the horizon.

While product placement has been around for decades, mobile marketing is an emerging medium for marketing communication that we examine next.

OBJECTIVE **6**

Mobile Marketing

True to its name, **mobile marketing** is any marketing communication directed to a mass audience, targeted group, or individual using a mobile device, such as a mobile phone, tablet, or music device with wireless access. More formally, according to the Mobile Marketing Association, mobile marketing "is a set of practices that enables organizations to communicate and engage with their audience in an interactive and relevant manner through any mobile device or network."

Mobile marketing has been around for around 10–15 years, but only recently have marketers begun to try to leverage this marketing medium. Just within the last few years, the industry has grown from practically nothing to a billion dollar industry in the United States, and a market seven times that large internationally, and it is projected to grow exponentially in the next few years.[33] In the United States, this growth is primarily due to the increase in mobile subscriptions, which now encompasses 88% of the U.S. population; smartphone market penetration, which is now over 60%; and it also includes growth in the mobile applications (i.e., Apps) market.[34] Apple's App Store has reached over 50 billion downloads.[35] Now let's look at some of the common forms of mobile marketing.

Global Perspectives

Mobile Marketing

While mobile marketing is just emerging as a significant marketing medium in the United States, the mobile marketing industry is much more established internationally, particularly in the Asia-Pacific (APAC) region. APAC has close to three billion mobile subscribers, more than three times the number of subscribers in the United States, and mobile marketing is well-established in this region. Unsurprisingly, much of this growth comes from India and China. For instance, industry experts claim that in India, consumers are more easily reached through mobile marketing than through television. In some countries, such as Hong Kong and Singapore, there are more mobile phones than people, with subscriptions at more than 100% of the population.

Consumers in these markets also seem to have a willingness to experiment with new technologies and explore new ways to experience media content. QR-Codes were actually invented in Asia, and in Japan, these codes are commonly found on most products. And, like the United States, consumers are trending toward the adoption of smartphones, which expands the flexibility of delivering mobile content.

In addition to the willingness to embrace mobile marketing on the consumer side, industry experts recognize that Eastern marketers take a more holistic view of mobile marketing, incorporating these tactics more seamlessly into overall multi-channel marketing strategies to improve branding, promotion, and the retail experience. While the United States is making quick progress in the use of mobile marketing, international marketers are ahead of the game.[36]

Types of Mobile Marketing

Application Marketing This type of mobile marketing utilizes smartphone mobile applications technology to engage consumers. For many marketers, especially in the United States, this is the gateway, or first step, into mobile marketing. As stated, the mobile applications market has created billions of customer interactions, and mobile applications are central components of smartphone usage, especially Apple's iPhone.

Leveraging this technology, a company might use established popular applications to market itself, such as applications for Facebook, Twitter, Tumblr, Urbanspoon, Yelp, and Foursquare. For example, Foursquare, a location-based social networking website, and American Express teamed up in a campaign where consumers received a discount on their bill if they checked in at a store using the Foursquare application and then charged a purchase with their American Express credit card.[37]

Alternatively, a company might create its own custom application. Captial One offers an application where users can check credit card balances, access bank accounts, redeem card points, and find ATMs. National grocery chain Kroger offers an application where customers can see weekly discount specials, find stores, and download digital coupons. Time Warner Cable's mobile application lets users watch television live, check listings, and set DVR recordings remotely.

Companies engaging in applications marketing may create their own custom applications or leverage existing applications.

© iStockphoto.com/Gary Arbach

QR-Codes A Quick-Response Code (QR-Code) is a two-dimensional matrix box barcode that can be read by mobile devices, such as a smartphone. These codes can link consumers in real time with product information, reviews, pricing information, coupons, and product websites. For example, Delta Airlines has taken paperless travel to the next step by utilizing QR-Codes for travelers to use an electronic boarding pass. (See this chapter's opening vignette to read how Mercedes-Benz utilized QR-Codes in an interesting way.)

SMS Marketing This type of mobile marketing (SMS stand for *short message service*) uses text messaging technology to reach consumers. At its most basic, SMS campaigns provide a simple way for consumers to interact with companies. For example, when Procter & Gamble wanted to reach moms in the Philippines, it used an SMS campaign. The company sent text messages to parents containing baby care tips and advice. In turn, parents could earn points toward merchandise and enter contests by texting back specially marked codes on Pampers-brand diaper packages. Alternatively, Motorola created a campaign where users could say goodbye to loved ones as they passed through the Hong Kong International Airport. Users could take a photo of themselves and text it to a special number and the photo and message would be displayed on screens in the airport terminal. This campaign leveraged the mobile medium and the environment (the airport) to create a unique customer experience.[38]

Chapter Summary

In today's technology-driven, cluttered environment, companies cannot simply rely on traditional forms of marketing, such as advertising and face-to-face sales. In this chapter, we examined some contemporary strategies and unique ways marketers reach out to today's consumers, including word-of-mouth marketing (also known as buzz marketing), consumer generated advertising campaigns, celebrity and athlete endorsers, product placements, and mobile marketing.

Word-of-mouth or buzz marketing is the execution of marketing tactics especially designed to generate positive word-of-mouth marketing messages and create a virus-like exponential spread of those positive messages throughout the population of interest. Marketers want to create and direct word-of-mouth because consumers see it as credible and authentic and because it is so easy to spread and sustain on the Internet. To help execute buzz marketing campaigns, companies often hire people to push the brand, either online or in person. When these people keep their activities clandestine, they are said to be engaging in stealth marketing. Marketers also engage in experiential and community-based marketing tactics to engage consumers one-on-one and generate positive buzz.

Consumer generated marketing campaigns try to harness the benefits of traditional advertising and buzz marketing by encouraging the creation of advertisements or other media content by consumers themselves. These campaigns have the advantages of engaging the customers in new, meaningful ways, and providing the company with valuable consumer insights.

Another contemporary strategy that has become standard in marketing is the use of celebrity and athlete endorsers. Consumers often think of brands in terms of the famous people who endorse them, and research has shown that celebrity endorsers can have positive persuasive effects. On the flipside, marketers must use care when using celebrity and athlete endorsers. Famous stars can overshadow a brand, and celebrity scandals can tarnish a brand's image.

Product placement is the insertion of branded goods and services within the content of popular media, including television, movies, video games, books, and music. When done correctly, product placement adds a sense of continuity and realism to the story while promoting the brand in subtle but meaningful ways.

Finally, an emerging type of marketing is mobile marketing, which is marketing communication directed to a mass audience, targeted group, or individual using a mobile device, such as a mobile phone, tablet, or music device with wireless access.

Marketers engage consumers in this medium with applications available via smartphone technology, and through QR-Codes and SMS marketing efforts.

Key Terms

brand integration	experiential marketing	stealth marketing
brand interaction	grassroots marketing	verbal product placement
buzz marketing	mobile marketing	viral marketing
celebrity endorser	organic word-of-mouth	visual product placement
community marketing	product placement	word-of-mouth
consumer generated marketing	sponsorship and branded	word-of-mouth marketing
correspondent inference	entertainment	

Review and Discussion

1. Why is word-of-mouth so powerful?
2. Why is buzz marketing also referred to as "viral" marketing?
3. What is the distinction between buzz marketing and stealth marketing?
4. What are some of the potential ethical implications of doing a stealth marketing campaign?
5. What are some of the benefits of a consumer generated advertising campaign? What are the risks?
6. Review the *Forbes Magazine* list of best-paid athletes presented in the text. Do you think they are worth the money they are paid for endorsements? Explain.
7. In what type of media is product placement found?
8. How do product placements add realism to the media in which they are placed?
9. Describe the differences between brand interaction product placement and brand integration product placement. Which is better? Why?
10. Define the three predominant types of mobile marketing.

Short Application Exercises

1. In buzz marketing, identifying and leveraging opinion leaders is very important. Choose a group that might be influenced by an opinion leader and put together a photo collage displaying at least five opinion leaders for that group. The collage should identify who the people are, why they are opinion leaders, and what products or brands each of them would most successfully endorse.
2. Think about one brand for which you would like to create a consumer generated advertisement. What would your ad say about the brand?
3. Find an example of an advertisement using a celebrity endorser. Based on what you learned about in the chapter, is the celebrity endorser effective? Why or why not?
4. Watch one hour of television. Try to identify one example of each type of product placement in the program(s) you watch. Justify your example.

Managerial Application

Imagine that you have been hired by a company to "promote" their product via stealth marketing. You will most likely do this by pretending to be a "regular customer" yourself and by trying to influence other customers to show interest in or purchase the product.

Team up with a partner. Go to a mall or shopping area and choose a product to secretly promote. Choose a consumer or group of consumers as the object of this exercise. Then, using any kind of "stealth technique" you can think of, try to influence the consumer(s) to purchase the product. You can be overt or subtle—it's up to you. Take your time; do not rush. You are successful if the person or group is persuaded in any way to take interest in the product—sampling it, examining it, or purchasing

it. You should try this multiple times and see the various reactions you receive. For example, try it out on different demographic groups (e.g., older versus younger, similar to you versus different, etc.) with various approaches.

Next, develop a set of field notes, describing the experience. In these field notes, describe what you chose to do and the results of the exercise. After you have finished describing what took place, offer some analysis, explanation, and opinion of your actions and the subsequent results. Were you successful? Why or why not? Were your results surprising? Lastly, offer your opinion as to the ethical appropriateness of stealth marketing. Is this form of marketing okay? Should it be restricted or not allowed at all?

End Notes

1 Sources for the article include: Cruz, X. (2012, May 29). Mercedes-Benz: QR code trophies. On CreativeGuerrillaMarketing.com. [Online.] Retrieved from: http://www.creativeguerrillamarketing.com/mobile-marketing-2/mercedes-benz-qr-code-trophies/. Mercedes-Benz: QR code trophies. (2012, May 13). On DigitalBuzz.com. [Video Blog.]. Retrieved from: http://www.digitalbuzzblog.com/mercedes-benz-qr-code-trophies/.

2 Based on one of the authors' anecdotal research.

3 Friedman, W. (2013, March 3). Trad 30-sec Spot Shines. On Mediapost.com. [Online.] Retrieved from: http://www.mediapost.com/publications/article/195725/trad-30-sec-spot-shines-costs-up-5.html#axzz2WybK9nTq. Cultra, S. (2011, December 17). Complete List of 30-second Ad Cost for All Primetime TV Shows: A $200,000 Domain Looks Like a Bargain. On DomainShare.com. [Online.] Retrieved from: http://domainshane.com/complete-list-of-30-second-ad-cost-for-all-primetime-tv-shows-a-200000-domain-looks-like-a-bargain/.

4 Garfield, B. (2005, April 4). The Chaos Scenario. *Advertising Age*, 1, 57–59.

5 Berger, J. (2013). *Contagious: Why Things Catch On*. New York: Simon and Schuster.

6 Berger, J. (2013). *Contagious: Why Things Catch On*. New York: Simon and Schuster.

7 Kaikati, A. M., and Kaikati, J. G. (2004). Stealth Marketing: How to Reach Consumers Surreptitiously. *California Management Review*, 46 (4), 6–22.

8 Gladwell, M. (2000). *The Tipping Point*. New York: Little, Brown and Company.

9 [Company website Information]. Retrieved on 2012, June 4, from: http://about.bzzagent.com/word-of-mouth/about.

10 For information on Vocalpoint and Tremor: www.tremor.com.

11 Leung, R. (2009, February 11). Undercover Marketing Uncovered. CBSnews.com. [Online.] Retrieved from: http://www.cbsnews.com/2100-18560_162-579657.html.

12 Kaikati, A. M., and Kaikati, J. G. (2004). Stealth Marketing: How to Reach Consumers Surreptitiously. *California Management Review*, 46 (4), 6–22.

13 Kaikati, A. M., and Kaikati, J. G. (2004). Stealth Marketing: How to Reach Consumers Surreptitiously. *California Management Review*, 46 (4), 6–22.

14 Building Brands through Experiential Marketing: 11 Awesome Examples. On *More Than Branding* [Blog]. (2011, November 28). Retrieved from: http://morethanbranding.com/2011/11/28/building-brands-through-experiential-marketing-11-awesome-examples/.

15 Rose, F. (2006, December). In a Risky Experiment, Chevrolet Asked Web Users to Make Their Own Video Spots for the Tahoe. A Case Study in Customer Generated Advertising, *Wired*. [Online.], issue 14.12. Retrieved from: http://www.wired.com/wired/archive/14.12/tahoe.html.

16 Sources for the article include: Disney Wants You: Brand Turns to User Generated Content. On Seattlepi.com. [Online.] (n. d.). Retrieved from: http://blog.seattlepi.com/hottopics/2010/09/23/disney-wants-you-brand-turns-to-user-generated-content/. Bly, L. (2010, September 23). Disney Wants Your Theme Park Memories. On *USA Today*. [Online.] Retrieved from: http://travel.

usatoday.com/destinations/dispatches/post/2010/09
/disney-ad-campaign-orlando-disneyland/124946/1.

17 Friedman, H. H. and Friedman, L. (1979). Endorser
Effectiveness by Product Type. *Journal of Advertising
Research*, *19*, 63–71. Petty, R. E., Cacioppo, J. T., and
Schumann, D. (1983). Central and Peripheral Routes
to Advertising Effectiveness: The Moderating Role of
Involvement. *Journal of Consumer Research*, *10*, 135–146.

18 Freiden, J. B. (1984). Advertising Spokesperson Effects:
An Examination of Endorser Type and Gender on Two
Audiences. *Journal of Advertising Research*, *24*, 33–41.

19 Agrawal, J., and Kamakura, W. A. (1995). The Economic
Worth of Celebrity Endorsers: An Event Study Analysis.
Journal of Marketing, *59*, 56–62.

20 Dipayan, B. Abhijit, B., and Das, N. (2006). The
Differential Effects of Celebrity and Expert Endorsements
on Consumer Risk Perceptions. *Journal of Advertising*,
35, 17–31.

21 Cronley, Maria L., Houghton D. C., Goddard, P., and
Kardes, F. R. (1999). Endorsing Products for the Money:
The Role of The Correspondence Bias in Celebrity
Advertising. *Advances in Consumer Research*, *26*, 627–631.

22 Atkin, C., and Block, M. (1983). Effectiveness of Celebrity
Endorsers. *Journal of Advertising Research*, *23*, 57–61.

23 Sukhdial, A. S., Aiken, D., and Kahle, L. (2002). Are You
Old School? A Scale for Measuring Sports Fans' Old-School
Orientation. *Journal of Advertising Research*, *42*, 71–81.

24 Bush, A. J., Martin, C. A., and Bush, V. D. (2004). Sports
Celebrity Influence on Behavioral Intentions of Generation Y.
Journal of Advertising Research, *44*, 108–118.

25 Duffy, J. (2005, March 30). Well Placed. On *BBC News
Magazine*. [Online.] Retrieved from: http://news.bbc
.co.uk/2/hi/uk_news/magazine/4391955.stm.

26 Sauer, A. (2012, February 13). Announcing the 2012
Brandcameo Product Placement Award Winners. On
Brandchannel.com. [Online.] Retrieved from: http://
www.brandchannel.com/home/post/2012/02/13/2012
-Brandcameo-Product-Placement-Awards-021312.aspx#one.

27 Product Placement. [On Public Citizen Commercial Alert
website]. (n. d). Retrieved 2012, June 2, from: http://
www.commercialalert.org/issues/culture/product
-placement.

28 Osterhout, J. E. (2012, November 7). Welcome to the Bond
Marketing… and the Pricey World of Product Placement
in 007 Movies. *New York Daily News*. [Online.] Retrieved
from: http://www.nydailynews.com/entertainment
/tv-movies/bond-market-007-movies-article-1.1197053.
Infographic: The Growing Product Placement Industry. On
MarketingTechBlog.com. [Industry Blog.] (n. d.). Retrieved
on 2012, June 5, from: http://www.marketingtechblog.com
/product-placement-infographic/.

29 Infographic: The Growing Product Placement Industry. On
MarketingTechBlog.com. [Industry Blog.] (n. d.). Retrieved
on 2012, June 5, from: http://www.marketingtechblog
.com/product-placement-infographic/.

30 Ford, Coke and AT&T Return as American Idol Sponsors.
The Hollywood Reporter. [Online.] (2011, Januray, 19).
Retrieved from: http://www.hollywoodreporter.com
/news/ford-coke-att-return-american-73533. Gunelius, S.
(2008, January 18). Ford, Coke and AT&T Pay More
to Sponsor American Idol. On Everyjoe.com. [Online.]
Retrieved from: http://everyjoe.com/work/ford-coke-att
-pay-more-to-sponsor-american-idol/.

31 Atkinson, C. (2007, January 8). "Idol" Juggernaut
Passes $2.5 Bil and Hits the Gas. *Advertising Age*, *78*
(2), 1–29.

32 Sauer, A. (2012, February 13). Announcing the
2012 Brandcameo Product Placement Award Winners.
On Brandchannel.com. Retrieved from: http://www
.brandchannel.com/home/post/2012/02/13/2012
-Brandcameo-Product-Placement-Awards-021312.
aspx#one.

33 Global Mobile Statistics 2012: All Quality Mobile Marketing
Research, Mobile Web Stats, Subscribers, Ad Revenue,
Usage, Trends… On Mobithinking.com. [Online.] (n. d.).
Retrieved on 2012, June 5, from: http://mobithinking.
com/mobile-marketing-tools/latest-mobile-stats.
Birkner, C. (2011, December 30). Looking back means
looking ahead. *Marketing News*. pp. 16–19.

34 Apple's App Store Marks Historic 50 Billionth Download.
[Company website.] (2013, May 16). Retrieved from:
http://www.apple.com/pr/library/2013/05/16Apples
-App-Store-Marks-Historic-50-Billionth-Download.html.
Birkner, C. (2011, December 30). Looking Back Means
Looking Ahead. *Marketing News*. pp. 16–19. Sullivan, E. A.
(2010, April 30). The Tao of Mobile Marketing. *Marketing
News*, pp. 16–20. Wesserman, T. (2013, June 6). Study:
U.S. Smartphone Penetration Now at 61%. [Online.]
Retrieved from: http://mashable.com/2013/06/06
/smartphones-61-percent/.

35 Bonnington, C. (2012, March 5). Apple's App Store
Reaches 25 billion Global Downloads. On Wired.com.
[Online.] Retrieved from: http://www.wired.com
/gadgetlab/2012/03/app-store-25-billion/.

36 Source for the entire article: Sullivan, E. A. (2010, April
30). The Tao of Mobile Marketing. *Marketing News*,
pp. 16–20.

37 Birkner, C. (2011, December 30). Looking Back Means
Looking Ahead. *Marketing News*. pp. 16–19.

38 Sullivan, E. A. (2010, April 30). The Tao of Mobile
Marketing. *Marketing News*, pp. 16–20.

CHAPTER 17

ENGAGING CONSUMERS THROUGH ONLINE MARKETING

OBJECTIVES *After studying this chapter, you will be able to …*

1 Define Internet marketing and identify benefits of this type of marketing.

2 Explain e-tailing and how it differs from bricks-and-mortar retailing.

3 Understand the characteristics of online shopping through websites and e-tailers.

4 Define search engine marketing and explain its two major types.

5 Explain the role of Internet advertising in Internet marketing.

6 Discuss the various types of social media marketing.

7 Understand the implications of reduced search costs for consumer behavior.

Pinterest Has Captured the Imagination of Millions

For Pinterest users, life is about the "board." Maybe the board is about a woman's dream wedding, favorite recipes, interests in fashion, or just a montage of everything interesting. Pinterest is a social photo-sharing website, organized in a pinboard style. Users browse, sort, save, and upload images, known as pins to themed pinboards. Others' boards can also be viewed and favorite content can be re-pinned across boards. And, the "Pin It" icon is becoming commonplace next to the Facebook and Twitter share buttons that now reside on most websites.

Pinterest has captured the imagination of millions of users, the majority of whom in the United States are women. Launched in 2010, the website has been growing at a tremendous rate. Nine months after the initial launch, the site had over nine thousand users, and *Time* magazine listed it as one of the fifty best websites of the year. By 2013,

the site had over forty-eight million unique users, breaking the record of the fastest-growing website by ten million. Today, Pinterest is one of the largest social network services.

How do businesses cash in on Pinterest? Companies take advantage of Pinterest by creating their own themed pinboards, where users can easily search for and see new products displayed for sale, see different uses for products to enhance usage and customer loyalty, and read reviews from other users. Companies also use Pinterest for online referrals, often finding potential customers who show interest in the company. Interestingly, a recent research survey found that Pinterest users are 79% more likely than Facebook users to purchase an item they saw pinned.

For over 11 million users, Pinterest has become a unique way to share visual representations of life. Sharing life is at the heart of social media, and in this chapter we explore how marketers are trying to incorporate this new cultural reality into marketing strategy.[1]

OBJECTIVE ① # The Age of Interactivity and Internet Marketing

As the Pinterest vignette illustrates, the Internet is changing the way firms do business. Companies can communicate with and market to consumers in personal, customized, interactive, and entertaining ways. Further, social digital environments enable marketers to learn more about satisfying consumers' diverse needs and wants more effectively. Search engines such as Google and Yahoo! give consumers access to staggering amounts of information and help people navigate that information effectively. Interactive shopping environments allow consumers to have access to a larger variety of products at reasonable prices. As the number of choice options increases, the potential for making better decisions increases. However, too much information can be overwhelming and confusing. In this chapter, we examine some of the ways in which companies engage consumers in the online environment.

Traditional mass marketing uses tools like television, radio, newspapers, traditional mail, billboards, and magazines to deliver a one-way message to consumers about product benefits. **Internet marketing**, also known as *online marketing*, *web marketing*, and *e-marketing*, is any type of marketing activity that is done via the Internet and/or email. It can include any type of traditional marketing and consumer engagement, such as product design, marketing research, advertising, public relations, buzz marketing, sales, and customer service.

Internet Marketing Provides a Unique Consumer Behavior Environment

At the heart of this type of marketing is interactivity. Internet marketing relies on interactive two-way communications between marketers and consumers with fast response times between communications and high levels of response contingency.[2] This means that one party's response depends on the other party's response, and this helps both parties get the information they need *when* they need it. This creates a unique consumer behavior environment because the consumer has active control over the interaction, rather than being a passive recipient of information. In addition, the marketer can respond quickly to consumer requests (see Figure 17.1).

In addition to the interactive nature of Internet marketing, there are other benefits to engaging consumers through this type of marketing. Companies can approach and engage consumers one-on-one with personal, customized information. This allows the marketer to appeal to an individual's specific interests or behaviors, taking segmentation, targeting, and positioning down to the individual level.

Furthermore, Internet marketing may be less expensive than a traditional mass marketing campaign, on a per contact basis, because it is often reaching the consumer *when* they are interested, such as when they are doing a keyword search on a search engine or seeking out information on a company website. Thus, a company can reach a large Internet audience with a smaller overall budget. In addition, with organic word-of-mouth, online referral, and social

FIGURE 17.1 | **Types of Interactive Internet Marketing**

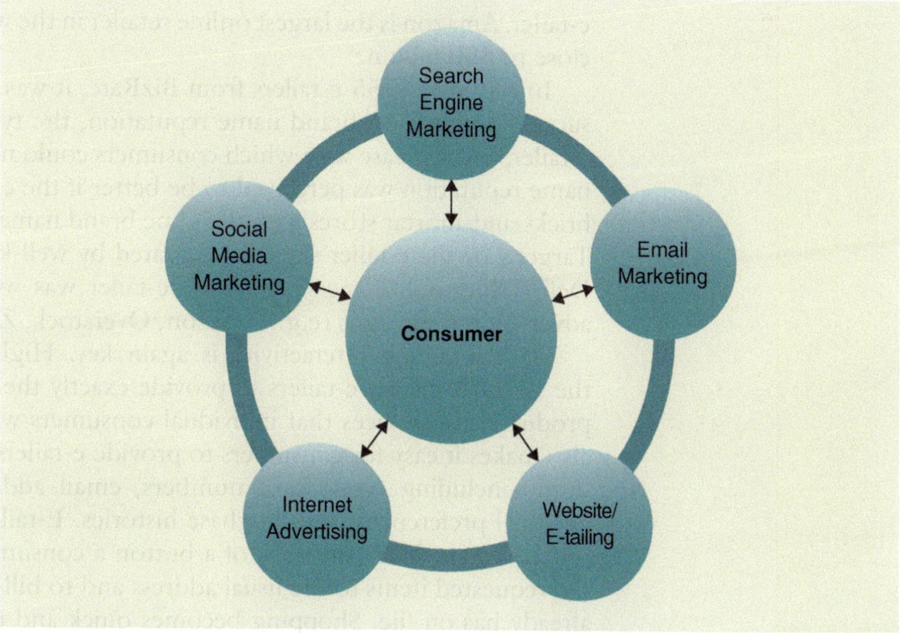

networking, a marketer may even reach consumers at no cost. One Facebook or Twitter post about a brand can reach hundreds or even thousands of people. (Recall the advantages of word-of-mouth discussed in the previous chapter.)

Finally, Internet marketing provides the advantage of easy and quick feedback analytics. Most Internet marketing efforts can be measured, traced, and tracked—often more easily than traditional marketing campaigns—due to the inherent technology in place. For example, a company can easily track the number of times an Internet ad is clicked on or count the number of visitors to a website.

There is a multitude of ways that Internet marketers are engaging consumers today. While we don't have space to discuss every Internet marketing tactic, broad types of Internet marketing include website marketing and e-tailing, search engine marketing, Internet advertising, and social media marketing. First, we will discuss website marketing and e-tailing.

OBJECTIVE ② # Website Marketing and E-tailing

E-tailing (electronic retailing) is a form of commerce where consumers buy products and services directly over the Internet. A company may operate its own proprietary website where all sales are made, or which supplements and complements a physical bricks-and-mortar retail operation. For example, on Target.com customers can purchase merchandise directly, but can also search for store locations, see if a product is available at a local store, and arrange for in-store pickup of merchandise purchased online. When a retailer's website and online retailing efforts seamlessly complement its bricks-and-mortar operation, this is sometimes called *360-degree retailing*. Alternatively, a marketer may also choose to sell products and services through a third-party e-tailer. Amazon is the largest online retailer in the world, with annual revenues close to $50 billion.[3]

In a study of 755 e-tailers from BizRate, it was found that online business success depends on brand name reputation, the type of products sold by the e-tailer, and the ease with which consumers could navigate the website.[4] Brand name reputation was perceived to be better if the e-tailer also had well-known bricks-and-mortar stores with the same brand name (e.g., JCPenney, Walmart, Target), or the e-tailer sites were created by well-known manufacturers (e.g., Dell, Whirlpool, Timex), or if the e-tailer was well-known due to national advertising campaigns (e.g., Amazon, Overstock, Zappos).

With e-tailing, interactivity is again key. High levels of interactivity on the Internet enable e-tailers to provide exactly the type of information about products and services that individual consumers wish to receive. Interactivity also makes it easy for consumers to provide e-tailers with the information they want—including credit card numbers, email addresses, shipping addresses, personal preferences, and purchase histories. E-tailers also try to make repeat purchase easy. With the click of a button a consumer can tell e-tailers to ship the requested items to the usual address and to bill a credit card that he or she already has on file. Shopping becomes quick and easy. A consumer can shop from his or her home or mobile device for products from anywhere in the world without driving to a traditional bricks-and-mortar retail store, struggling to find a parking spot, or waiting in line.

In addition to making shopping easy, the online environment makes shopping fun, at least for some consumers. People are having the most fun when they are in a state of **flow**.[5] Flow is experienced when people perform an activity skillfully with little thought or effort. Golfers and other athletes often talk about being in the "zone," or performing extremely well without thinking. Birdies, touchdowns, and home runs just seem to come naturally, without a great deal of effort. Athletes sometimes say that golf balls, footballs, or baseballs seem to pop right out at them when they're in a state of flow, and targets look huge when they're in the "zone." Similarly, when consumers navigate through a well-designed website, shopping becomes automatic, effortless, and fun.

OBJECTIVE ③

Characteristics of Shopping Through E-tailers

Choice and Customization The biggest difference between online stores (electronic stores on the Internet) and bricks-and-mortar stores (physical stores found in shopping plazas, shopping malls, etc.) is that online stores often offer greater choice and greater information customization and product customization.[6] Online stores have virtually unlimited inventory because they enable consumers to shop for products across stores, across state lines, and even across international borders. Online stores also permit greater customization of sales information because sellers can provide as much information as they wish, including product samples (e.g., music clips, video clips), comments from other customers, and comprehensive comparisons to competitors' offerings. In terms of product customization, in an online ordering situation, sellers can often allow customers to make customized product choices, rather than having to rely on the inventory on-hand in a physical store.

Information Search and Navigation Some types of products are easier to shop for online than others. *Information search costs* refers to how difficult it is to acquire information in terms of time, money, or effort. The scope of information search is greater and information search costs are typically lower in online environments than in offline, bricks-and-mortar environments for many types of products. Specifically, it is easier to obtain information and to evaluate the quality of *search goods*, relative to *experience goods* or *credence goods*.[7] (Recall our discussion of search, experience, and credence goods in the chapter on attitude and judgment formation and change.) The quality of search goods can be examined by simply examining a picture of it. The product might have a particularly effective design or appearance, or the brand name or the price of the product might be enough to convince consumers that the product is of high quality. The quality of experience goods, however, is determined by touching, feeling, or using the product. Sensory attributes like taste, smell, and touch determine the quality of experience goods. The quality of credence goods is even more difficult to judge, because quality depends on years of experience and use. Attributes like reliability and durability determine the quality of credence goods. E-tailers are more successful if they primarily sell search goods, rather than experience goods or credence goods.

Some creative e-tailers, like Lands' End, have tried to make it easier to shop online for experience goods (in this case, clothes) by providing detailed descriptions of experience and credence attributes, and by showing color pictures accompanied by information about stitching and construction

E-tailers try to make it easier to shop for experience goods by providing detailed descriptions and pictures.

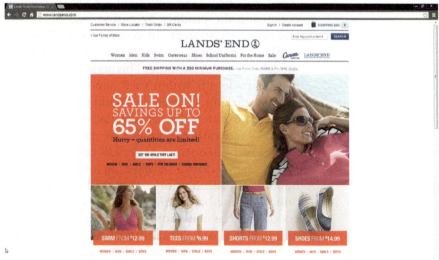

Courtesy of Lands' End

materials. Lands' End also uses a risk-free return policy to build trust and to assure consumers that its products are of high quality.

Navigation ease depends on ease of ordering, ease of payment, delivery methods, security, and the ease with which consumers can contact service representatives. Consumers prefer many different ordering methods (e.g., online, email, phone, fax), many different payment methods (e.g., credit and debit cards, personal check, PayPal), and many different delivery methods (e.g., USPS, UPS, overnight shipping, two-day shipping).

Organization of Information The design of a website also influences whether consumers are more likely to use a *compensatory decision-making strategy* or a *non-compensatory decision-making strategy*. (Recall our discussion of these strategies in the chapter on the decision-making process.) When consumers use a compensatory strategy, they make trade-offs between attributes—this enables a good attribute to compensate for, or at least reduce concerns about, a bad attribute. When consumers use a non-compensatory strategy, they do not make trade-offs across attributes, and a bad attribute usually leads to the rejection of an alternative. Unfortunately, even an alternative that is very good overall can be rejected if that alternative has one bad attribute. Consumers often make better decisions if they use a compensatory strategy rather than a non-compensatory strategy, and consumers are more likely to use a compensatory strategy if a website is organized by options rather than by attributes.[8]

When a website is organized by options, consumers are also likely to click on more options and consider a broader range of alternatives, and this also increases the quality of a decision. Consumers also click on more options when the attributes are negatively correlated, because negatively correlated attributes encourage consumers to attempt to make trade-offs between attributes. For example, e-tailers like Dell provide laptop shoppers with a "customize and buy" option. Consumers click a series of options, beginning with components (processor, memory, hard-drive, graphics card, and display) and ending with accessories (e.g., mouse, keyboard, carrying case). Consumers can easily see the trade-offs between two, negatively correlated attributes such as processing speed and price; a consumer can get a faster computer but will pay more. Thus, organizing the product by customized options encourages trade-offs and a compensatory strategy. In contrast, if Dell organized its laptop offerings by attribute only (e.g., by processor), consumers would be forced to evaluate models across this attribute. This presentation would discourage consumers from making trade-offs within each alternative and encourage non-compensatory decision-making. Consumers would tend to look at each brand in isolation and reject those brands that failed to satisfy a specific criterion.

As noted earlier, e-tailers are more successful if they have bricks-and-mortar or offline stores as well as online stores (e.g., Sears.com and Sears). If an e-tailer does not have an offline store, managers should consider building an alliance or a partnership with an offline store. Research on online–offline brand alliances shows that such alliances encourage consumers to form assimilation effects between online and offline brands.[9] This means that as online brand quality increases, consumers' perceptions of the

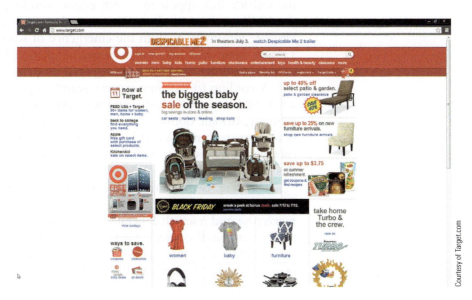

E-tailers are more successful if they have bricks-and-mortar or offline stores as well as online stores.

quality of offline brands also increase, and vice versa. Similarly, if online brand quality decreases, consumers' perceptions of the quality of offline brands decrease, and vice versa. Hence, if an alliance or a partnership is formed, it is important to choose a partner that is well known for selling high-quality brands.

A large part of website marketing and e-tailing is driving business to the site. One major way in which this is done is with search engines, which we will examine next.

Ethics

From fake purses and shoes to imitation drugs, counterfeit products sold over the Internet are a persistent and growing problem. Product counterfeits and piracy cost U.S. businesses over $200 billion a year, and some research suggests that approximately 25% of all products sold on the Internet are counterfeit.

While counterfeit designer purses and watches are costly, counterfeit pharmaceuticals are dangerous. Fake medicines have drastically increased over the last few years, and some research shows that 90% of fake drugs are sold over the Internet at some point in time. These illegal drug sellers often don't have physical addresses, which makes them more difficult to track down. This illegal trade costs pharmaceutical companies millions of dollars each year and potentially endangers the lives of consumers. Some of the most commonly copied drugs include Pfizer's Viagra, Eli Lilly's Cialis, and Adderall. And unfortunately, it has become increasingly difficult to tell real drugs from counterfeits.[10]

OBJECTIVE (4)

Search Engine Marketing (SEM)

Search engine marketing (SEM) is a type of Internet marketing that is designed to promote a website and drive consumers to the site by having the website link appear in search engine results pages. As the Web grew in the 1990s, online search engines started appearing to help people locate and navigate information. With the emergence of search engines such as Google, Yahoo!, Bing, and Ask, search engine marketing has become an integral part of most Internet marketing strategies. Thus, this industry is large and growing. According to industry experts, search engine marketing is close to being a $20 billion yearly industry and is growing over 10% per year. And, not surprisingly, Google dominates this market with the majority of marketers, both in business-to-business and business-to-consumer markets.[11] Yahoo! and Bing (both powered by Microsoft through an alliance) are also very large players in this market.

There are two broad types of search engine marketing, *search engine optimization* (SEO; also known as natural or organic search) and *paid search marketing*, and research generally shows that companies tend to engage more in the former than the latter.[12] Social media marketing and Internet advertising are also closely tied to this type of marketing and are often included in discussions of search engine marketing. We will discuss these topics later in the chapter.

Search engine optimization is the practice of making adjustments, modifications, and rewrites to a website in order to achieve a higher natural ranking in organic search engine results pages. To understand search engine optimization, it is important to understand how search engines work. When a person does a search, let's say in Google, a results page is shown. On this page, there are results that come up naturally or organically that relate to the person's search. This information is generally available on the Web and is accessed by Google to help a person find what they are looking for. There are also search results that appear on the page for which a sponsoring company has paid. Finally, there are also usually paid advertisements that appear on the results page. Search engine optimization influences only organic search results, not paid results. In order to improve search engine optimization, a company might

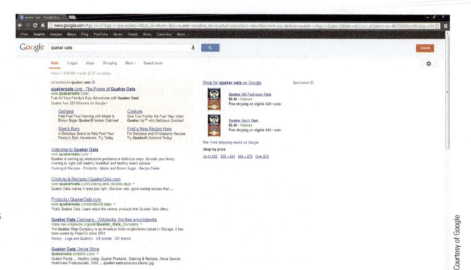

Search engine marketing includes both search engine optimization to improve natural search results and paid inclusion in search results.

give its website a unique, descriptive title, improve description tags within the website, make the website easier to navigate by adding categories, and add images and quality content to the website. All of these factors can influence organic search engine results.

Paid search marketing is where a company will pay to be included in the results page of a search engine. (Specific variations or types of paid search strategies depend on the proprietary search engine and may include *pay-per-click*, *cost-per-click*, *contextual ads*, or *sponsored listings*.) Under a pay search marketing arrangement, a company may pay a fee to be included in the search results page and/or pay to appear near the top of the results list. The company might pay a sponsoring fee for a determined period of time or a flat fee for an *x*-number of appearances in the results list. Alternatively, a company may pay-per-click where the fee is paid when the searcher clicks the link or advertisement and is directed to a website. Similar to an advertisement in a traditional newspaper, these types of search ads often, although not always, appear alongside, but separate from the organic search content. Notably, Google requires that paid search results are labeled and separated from organic search content.

Generally, search engine marketing is beneficial to both marketers and consumers. It allows for more customized and targeted marketing efforts because the marketer can reach consumers with specific information they are seeking, and consumers get information that is highly relevant to them. And, as technology evolves, this customized targeting will continue to refine. For instance, Google now offers behavioral targeting to its AdWords clients, which involves customizing search engine results pages based on a searcher's previous browsing and web activity.

Finally, search engine marketing is tied closely to the emergence of mobile device Internet capabilities. (See the discussion of mobile marketing in the previous chapter on contemporary strategies.) Many search engine marketers see this trend as having a large future impact on the effectiveness of search marketing tactics as consumers can make their searches mobile and even more convenient.

OBJECTIVE ⑤ # Internet Advertising

A natural complement to search engine marketing in driving consumers to a marketer's website is Internet advertising. Internet advertising is one of the oldest forms of Internet marketing. Just as with search engines, in the mid-1990s as the Web really began to grow, **content websites**—websites that function to collect stories, helpful information, commentary, video, and images for people to view (as opposed to e-tailing websites)—began running banner advertisements in order to generate revenue.

As most people know, *banner ads* are the strip-like ads that run across the top of a website page. Back when these types of advertisements were new, websites could charge fees of $30–$100 per 1,000 impressions for these ads. In fact, this lucrative model helped fuel the growth of the Internet boom of the early 2000s.[13] However, marketers eventually realized that most people ignored these advertisements; there were too many of them across the Web, and they weren't effective in driving people to click through to a website. As a result, prices dropped significantly. Today, typical costs for a generic banner ad range from around ten cents to one dollar per thousand impressions, unless the website is extremely popular or serves a very specific niche market. For example, Facebook charges around fifty cents per thousand impressions for a banner ad. Furthermore, the typical click-through rate on banner ads is quite low, with .1% (1 click-through per 1,000) serving as the industry standard. Of course, adding a smart targeting strategy for a banner ad, such as putting a golf shoe ad on a golfing website like PGA.com, can help improve the click-through rate.

In addition to banner ads, several other types of advertising formats are used on the Internet. Here are some examples of the most common types:

- **Skyscraper Ads:** A *skyscraper ad* (also known as a sidebar ad) is like a banner ad but runs vertically down the side of a website page, rather than across the top. These ads actually tend to be more effective than traditional banner ads because they are larger and harder to ignore with scrolling. Skyscraper ads have a click-through rate of about 1% (10 clicks per 1,000 impressions), and thus are also more expensive than regular banner ads.[14]
- **Pop-ups, Pop-Unders, and Floating Ads:** A *pop-up ad* appears in its own window when a website page is opened, obscuring the overall website. A *pop-under ad* appears under the website content and is seen when the user closes a window. A *floating ad* appears when the user loads a website and then it flies over the page. These ads are actually quite effective at grabbing consumers' attention, and often have higher click-through rates than banner ads because they are animated, cover up content, and cannot be ignored. However, these types of ads tend to significantly annoy users because they cover up content and must be moved or closed to proceed. As a result, users often implement ad-blocking software to avoid these types of ads. Thus, the use of these types of ads has decreased over the last few years.
- **Interstitial and Superstitial Ads:** An *interstitial ad* is a full-page or pop-up, graphic, animated, or video ad that appears on the screen before a user proceeds on to the intended web page. They run between website pages as

pages load. A *superstitial ad* is the same except it uses a "polite" delivery system, which means it loads in the background and then plays as the user moves to the next web page.

- **Video and In-stream Ads:** A *video ad* is any type of ad that uses moving video. *In-stream ads* display a television-like video advertisement before, during, or after other video content, as is typical on websites like YouTube.

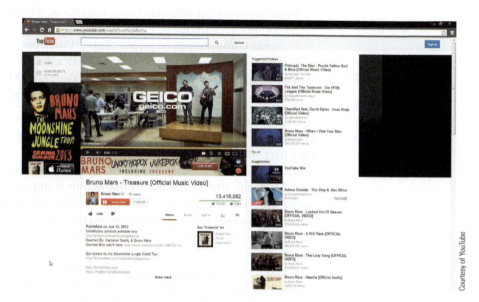

Internet ads can be targeted toward a more direct customer base.

Courtesy of YouTube

Generally, Internet advertising is attractive to marketers because it can be done with a relatively small overall budget. It also transcends geographic and time barriers that restrict traditional mass media advertising. The main benefit to consumers is that a person can control whether they view, read, and/or click on the ads.

Search engine marketing and Internet advertising are well established genres in the Internet marketing areas. Now we will discuss the most diverse and fast-growing area of Internet marketing: social media marketing.

OBJECTIVE **6**

Social Media Marketing

Social media marketing is a type of Internet marketing that uses social media to achieve some marketing goal. This type of marketing is closely tied to word-of-mouth, as the goal of social media marketing is often to attract consumer attention, initiate conversations with consumers, better understand consumer preferences, and generate positive buzz. Before delving into how marketers engage in social media, it is helpful to define what social media is and its scope.

What Is Social Media?

Social media is any online media environment that allows for the creation and exchange of user generated content. At the heart of social media are engagement, sharing, and collaboration among users.

There are many forms of social media, and there really are no "rules" for what classifies as social media. Users who engage in social media might interact with online technologies such as wall-posting, emailing, instant messaging, music-sharing, video-sharing, photo-sharing, pinning, liking, blogging, and crowd sourcing. Generally, the following types of online media are considered classifications or forms of social media:

- Social networking websites (e.g., Facebook, MySpace, LinkedIn)
- Blogs and microblogs (e.g., Gizmodo, Twitter)
- Content communities (e.g., YouTube, Pinterest)
- Collaborative media websites (e.g., Wikipedia, Wikia)
- Virtual gaming worlds (e.g., World of Warcraft, Minecraft)
- Virtual social worlds (e.g., Planet Calypso, Second Life, IMVU[15])

As stated, social media marketing uses social media to achieve marketing goals. This genre of Internet marketing is growing and becoming an important part of marketing strategy. According to a survey done by *Social Media Examiner,* an online social media magazine, over 80% of the marketers surveyed indicate that social media marketing is important to their business, and social media marketing provides the benefits of increased business exposure, increased traffic, and important marketing insights.[16] Also according to the survey, the most popular social media websites used by marketers include Facebook, Twitter, LinkedIn, and YouTube.

Let's examine more closely a few of the ways in which marketers engage consumers through social media. We will look at social networks and social buying websites, blogging and microblogging, and viral marketing on the Internet through content communities.

Social Networks

Social media, and social networking specifically, has a longer history than one might expect, dating back to the late 1970s when university professors at Duke and University of North Carolina exchanged information over an electronic bulletin board called Usenet.[17] Like most of the Web, social networking took off in the 1990s with the launch of Geocities, one of the first social networking websites. AOL's instant messaging system was also launched in 1997. Friendster, an example of today's typical social networking website where friends connect and communicate online, was launched in 2002, followed by MySpace in 2003, and Facebook in 2004. In just a few years, in 2008, Facebook surpassed MySpace as the most popular social networking website on the planet.[18]

So how does a marketer actually use social networking websites to market products and services? That's a difficult question, of course, because it depends on the website itself. Generally, however, companies engage in social networking in the same ways in which individuals do. For example, many companies and brands have Facebook pages, and they work hard to put interesting content on their page in order to attract fans and generate consumers' "liking" their page. Companies also engage users with advertising within the social networking websites. Interestingly, Facebook, which claims to have about 40% of all online banner ads, has click-through rates that are actually well below industry standards at .051%—despite the sites' huge popularity.[19] Nevertheless, advertisers are still attracted to Facebook because of the website's ability to specifically segment and target key audiences. On a site like Facebook, marketers are often more concerned about making sure the right audiences are seeing the ads, and with driving the "likes" and overall activity on the page, rather than on the click-through rate.

Many of the aspects of search engine marketing also apply in social networks and in social media marketing in general because most social media websites have search engine capabilities. For example, on YouTube, marketers can engage in pay-per-view and priority/first-viewing strategies.

When products and companies engage in social networking, people can more naturally interact with the product company, which feels personal to users and which may increase loyalty and positive feelings and attitudes toward the product or company. In addition, social networking allows users to pass on information and comments about products and companies, thus extending the company's reach exponentially.

Social Buying Websites A special type of social network is the social buying (also known as daily deal) websites. These types of websites are becoming increasingly popular. Groupon and LivingSocial are the leaders in this genre

Global Perspectives

Facebook is Bigger Worldwide

We all know Facebook is huge, with nearly a billion users. The social networking website, which was launched out of a Harvard University dorm room in 2004 by Mark Zuckerberg and his fellow students, is now the standard in what social networking means.

But what isn't so well known about Facebook is that about 80% of Facebook users come from outside the United States and Canada. In addition, Facebook has been translated into over 100 different languages and has a presence in over 200 countries. Brazil, India, and Indonesia are top Facebook countries, with over 40 million users in each country. Mexico, the United Kingdom, and Turkey each have over 30 million users. In India, Facebook has become synonymous with the Internet, and has taken over the social networking market previously held by Orkut, a Google-owned Indian social networking website. Interestingly, Facebook is not in China, possibly due

to concerns over governmental restrictions. With the massive penetration Facebook has in global markets, it's not surprising that the social networking site has been credited with playing a central role in political and social uprisings around the world, including uprisings in North Africa, Egypt, Tunisia, and Libya. Facebook's ability to provide instantaneous communication from anywhere by anyone may explain the key role of social media in these world events.[20]

© iStockphoto.com/Hocus Focus Studio

of social media. Some research shows that 60% of all online shoppers subscribe to a daily deal website.[21] Social buying website users tend to be younger, more educated, and more affluent than typical online users, and these websites tend to be more popular with females.[22] Social buying websites draw on the idea of consumers' desires to purchase locally and be budget conscious.

Blogs and Microblogs

Weblogs, or **blogs** for short, are frequently updated web journals that provide information in the form of "posts" about products, services, politics, or just about anything. Similar to an online diary, entries or posts are typically placed in the blog in reverse chronological order (the newest entries appear at the top of the web page) and may include text, pictures, video, and links to other websites. In addition, most blogs are interactive in some way, allowing viewers to make comments or send messages. Historically, blogs were created and maintained by a single entity, although today multi-authored blogs are quite common.

Although blogs have been around nearly as long as the Web has, they became tremendously popular during the 2004 presidential election, when politicians began using blogs for voter outreach and blogs became a legitimate news source. Today, there are over 150 million blogs worldwide covering a wide range of topics. The collective online community of blogs is called the *blogosphere*. Many companies have learned that blogs are useful tools for reaching consumers, often in unique ways. For example, Starbucks uses its blog as an idea-generating website and to highlight its community outreach programs. Customers post ideas for new food and drink items, new packaging, and new store locations. General Electric's blog has entertaining stories about energy, people, and communities.

Marketing in Action

LivingSocial

LivingSocial is an online social buying network. The online source (www.livingsocial.com) helps consumers find local experiences and deals. For example, in Chicago the website might offer a 50% discount on baseball tickets; in Boston there may be an offer for 90% off a haircut. According to the LivingSocial website, "We inspire our members to find, share, and enjoy the best of their neighborhoods by connecting them with handpicked local businesses."

How does LivingSocial offer discounts? It uses the purchasing power of many consumers—in order to receive a discount, a minimum number of people have to sign up for the deal.

Users sign up, pick a deal, and then if it "hits" the minimum number of buyers, you get the deal.

LivingSocial's products include providing members with price deals for local merchants; distinctive travel packages for local, regional, and global travelers; social packages for members to meet one another and socialize; packaged family activities; resource information for take-out delivery from local restaurants; and offers on high-end dining experiences. With millions of customers in more than 22 countries, many consumers have discovered the benefits of LivingSocial.

Many companies have learned that blogs are useful tools for reaching consumers, often in unique ways.

Courtesy of Starbucks

Microblogging A microblog is a special type of blog. **Microblogs** are characterized by shorter posts, sometimes called *microposts*. Twitter is the most famous microblogging social news stream blog today. First started as a way for friends to keep tabs on one another, Twitter has since become a powerful vehicle for marketing. Companies can post up-to-the-minute updates to followers and talk to customers one-on-one.

Viral Marketing on the Internet with Video

Viral marketing involves the Internet in order to facilitate the spread of word-of-mouth and spark buzz. (Recall our previous discussion of buzz marketing.) Marketers can try to spark a "virus" on the Internet in a variety of ways, but one of the most common tactics is the use of video marketing. Videos draw large audiences and spark talk about the brand and the video, thanks to video sharing websites such as YouTube. YouTube uploads about 30,000 hours of footage every day! In addition, research shows that YouTube and other types of video marketing are the fastest-growing form of social media marketing.[23] For example, T-Mobile, as part of their "Life's for Sharing" campaign, placed a viral video link on YouTube called "The T-Mobile Dance," which showed a large group of people doing a seemingly impromptu dance routine in a London train station. At the end of the video, the T-Mobile logo is flashed on the screen; the video also has a link to the T-Mobile website. By midsummer 2013, the video had been viewed more than 38 million times.

If a company wants to use videos to engage in viral marketing, it can create its own content, such as the T-Mobile dance described above, or it can link promotions to content that already exists. YouTube, which is part of Google, has a sophisticated user marketing program that allows customers to select videos and attach pop-up type ads to them or to run video ads before or after content. With this system, marketers can precisely target the type of viewers most likely to view the content.

Social media marketing is a quickly changing and evolving form of Internet marketing. Like all forms of Internet marketing, companies that engage consumers in this way must deal with the reality that the ways in which consumers search for information and shop are different in online environments than in offline environments. Next, we will examine the implications of reduced search costs for information.

OBJECTIVE ⑦ # The Implications of Reduced Search Costs for Information

Typically, consumers find it is easier to acquire information about products and services by using the click of a button on the Internet than by using phone calls and customer visits to several different bricks-and-mortar stores. Of course, so much information is available on the Internet that consumers can also become confused or overwhelmed. Consumers behave as limited information processors and are only able to consider about seven pieces of information at a time.

One way consumers deal with this problem is by eliminating options that do not meet their requirements in the first stage of the decision-making process, and then by evaluating the remaining options more carefully in the second stage of the decision-making process. In an online environment, consumers can leverage technology to make this easier. Consumers have the option of using interactive decision aids (or smart agents or bots) that make it easier to eliminate options in the first stage and to evaluate options in the second stage.[24] A **recommendation agent** is an interactive decision aid that helps consumers to eliminate options by using information about their personal preferences or about their prior purchase histories. Amazon, for example, uses the latter approach. A **comparison matrix** is an interactive decision aid that helps consumers to evaluate options by providing a brand-by-attribute matrix that makes it easy for consumers to compare options. Research shows that both types of interactive decision aids improve the quality of consumers' decisions by helping them to manage large amounts of information more effectively.

Because it is easier to search for information in online environments than in offline environments, as mentioned earlier in the chapter, search costs are lower in online environments. Accordingly, consumers tend to search for more information in online environments. Consumers also search for more information when the purchase decision is important and consequential[25] or when they feel highly uncertain about which product or brand they should purchase.[26]

Prior knowledge also influences information search.[27] Novices, or consumers who are unfamiliar with a particular product category, tend to search for little information, even in online environments, because they don't know how to interpret or how to use this information. For example, if you don't know anything about a complex product like plasma TVs, learning that a particular model has a resolution of 1080p doesn't help you to evaluate this product. Moderately knowledgeable consumers tend to search for a lot more information because they know how to interpret and how to use this information. Surprisingly, experts or highly knowledgeable consumers tend to search for relatively little information because they often feel confident that they already know everything they need to know to make an informed choice. Hence, there's an inverse-U shaped relationship between prior knowledge and search, with the greatest amount of search occurring for moderately knowledgeable consumers.

As has been previously stated, search costs are much higher in offline environments than in online environments. It takes planning, time, physical energy, and mental energy to visit many different offline stores and to compare many different brands on many different attributes. Consequently, consumers often search for relatively little information, even in a single offline store. For example, the typical grocery shopper spends only 12 seconds per decision, and many shoppers (41%) don't even bother to check the price of the products they purchased.[28] Comparing prices takes time and energy, even when brands are located right next to each other on the same shelf.

Conversely, search costs are much lower on the Internet. With the click of a button, consumers can scan the prices and features of hundreds of products quickly and easily by using interactive decision aids such as those provided by Nextag, Bizrate, Shopzilla, and other websites. When it is easy to compare prices for a product carried by many different retailers, cost transparency increases.[29] That is, a seller's costs become more obvious to buyers, and buyers can use this information to determine if a price is fair. Manufacturers and retailers are concerned about cost transparency because it decreases their ability to charge high prices and earn high margins.

Cost transparency can potentially turn brands into commodities, subsequently reducing brand loyalty. Brokerage firms that rely more on an online presence (e.g., E*TRADE) provide nearly the same products and services as traditional brokers for much lower fees. If a product or service is perceived as pretty much the same no matter who offers it, why not buy the least expensive option? Economists refer to this industry structure as perfect or "pure" competition because there is little to differentiate the brands and firms become "price takers," i.e., they must sell at the going rate.

Of course, price information is not the only type of information available on the Internet. The Internet also offers vast amounts of information about product quality and product reliability. The Internet, particularly social media, is dramatically reducing search costs for many different types of information, as we discussed earlier in the chapter.

Research on traditional advertising has shown that price advertising—or advertising that compares prices across brands—increases price sensitivity and encourages consumers to purchase the less expensive brand.[30] However, differentiating advertising—or advertising that compares specific features and benefits across brands—decreases price sensitivity and encourages consumers to purchase the higher quality brand.[31]

Similar results have been found for Internet advertising.[32] In a highly influential experiment, mock web pages were created by systematically varying the design of a web page similar to the real Wine.com web page. Specifically, price comparability (high or low), quality comparability (high or low), and store comparability (high or low) were manipulated independently, and graduate students and university staff were randomly assigned to conditions. In high-price comparability conditions, price information was presented on the first page and a tool that sorted wines by price was also provided. In low-price comparability conditions, consumers had to click on a brand name to find its price and no sorting tool was provided. In high-quality comparability conditions, wines could be sorted by grape (e.g., Chardonnay, Cabernet Sauvignon) and detailed information about quality was provided (e.g., complexity, acidity, body, dryness). In low-quality comparability conditions, consumers had to click on a brand name to obtain information about the grape and the quality of the wine. In high-store comparability conditions, a split screen was used so that consumers could easily compare two stores (e.g., Dionysus and Jubilee). In low-store comparability conditions, consumers could only visit one store at a time.

The results show that price sensitivity is lower when quality comparability is high rather than low. When it is easy to compare brands in terms of quality, the effects of price on choice decrease. Furthermore, when one store offered brands not offered by the other store, store comparability had no effect on price sensitivity. Store comparability influenced price sensitivity only when both stores offered the same brands. The results also demonstrate that consumers enjoyed navigating through the website the most when all three search costs were low. Not surprisingly, consumers also made better decisions when all three search costs were low. These findings suggest that retailers should cooperate with smart agents and strive to reduce search costs for price, quality, and store information because this increases consumer satisfaction, which subsequently increases repeat purchase rates.

In a follow-up experiment, it was shown that using smart agents to reduce search costs for quality information can increase price sensitivity when price and quality are uncorrelated, especially when consumers are highly preoccupied with price.[33] Otherwise, search costs for quality information have opposite effects on price sensitivity and product differentiation, consistent with the results of the previous experiment. Furthermore, the follow-up experiment shows that these results generalize to several different product categories.

The Internet has reduced consumers' information search costs, reduced transaction costs, increased the number of options available, and increased communication among consumers. As a result, the Internet has increased consumer power. At the same time, Internet marketing is allowing companies to engage consumers in new and exciting ways.

Chapter Summary

The Internet is changing the way firms do business. Companies can communicate with and market to consumers in personal, customized, interactive, and entertaining ways. Internet marketing is any type of marketing activity that is done via the Internet and/or email and includes any type of traditional marketing and consumer engagement, such as product design, marketing research, advertising, public relations, buzz marketing, sales, and customer service. With Internet marketing, companies can approach and engage consumers one-on-one with personal, customized information, often in a less expensive manner. In addition, Internet marketing provides the advantage of easy and quick feedback analytics.

E-tailing is a form of commerce where consumers buy products and services directly over the Internet. The most successful websites are owned by companies with reputable brand names. These successful sites sell goods and are easy to evaluate and navigate. The biggest difference between online stores and bricks-and-mortar stores is that online stores often offer greater choice and greater information customization and product customization.

Search engine marketing is a type of Internet marketing that is designed to promote a website and drive consumers to the site by having the website link appear in search engine results pages. Search engines like Yahoo!, Google, and Ask help consumers to navigate through enormous amounts of information stored on the Web. Reduced search costs have increased consumer power and have encouraged companies to adopt more consumer-friendly policies and services. There are two broad types of search engine marketing, search engine optimization and paid search marketing. Search engine optimization is the practice of making adjustments and modifications to a website in order to achieve a higher natural ranking in organic search engine results pages. Paid search marketing is where a company will pay to be included in the results page of a search engine.

A natural complement to search engine marketing in driving consumers to a marketer's website is Internet advertising. Internet advertising is one of the oldest forms of Internet marketing and includes many types of ads, such as banner ads, skyscraper ads, pop-up ads, and video ads.

Social media marketing is a type of Internet marketing that uses social media to achieve some marketing goal. This type of marketing is closely tied to word-of-mouth, as the goal of social media marketing is often to attract consumer attention and generate positive buzz. Social media marketing utilizes the social media environment, which includes social networks, blogs, content and collaborative communities, and virtual worlds. This genre of Internet marketing is growing and becoming an important part of marketing strategy.

When products and companies engage in social networking, people can more naturally interact with the product company in a personal way. In addition, social networking allows users to pass on information and comments about products and companies, thus extending the company's reach exponentially. A special type of social network is the social buying (also known as daily deal) websites.

In addition to social networks, marketers also engage in blogging—web journaling—and video marketing to engage consumers in social media. Social media marketing is a quickly changing and evolving form of Internet marketing. Like all forms of Internet marketing, companies that engage consumers in this way must deal with the reality that the ways in which consumers search for information and shop are different in online environments than in offline environments. While search costs are lower in online environments, in order to deal with the vast amount of information on the Internet, consumers often turn to recommendation agents and comparison matrices to aid in decision making.

Key Terms

blog
comparison matrix
content website
e-tailing
flow

internet marketing
microblog
paid search marketing
recommendation agent
search engine marketing

search engine optimization
social media
social media marketing

Review and Discussion

1. What is Internet marketing and what are the benefits of this type of marketing?

2. What are the key differences between e-tailors and offline shopping environments?

3. What types of products are particularly easy to shop for on the Web? What types of products have you shopped for on the Web?

4. What are the two types of search engine marketing, and what is the distinguishing difference between them?

5. What are the differences between banner ads, skyscraper ads, and floating ads?

6. Describe the six major forms of social media identified in the chapter.

7. How do companies use Facebook to market products?

8. How do most social buying websites (e.g., LivingSocial) work?

9. What is the difference between a blog and microblog?

10. How do search costs influence amount of search?

Short Application Exercises

1. Discuss your most favorite and least favorite web shopping experiences. What were the key factors that contributed to these experiences?

2. Use a search engine to find information for a product that you have never shopped for and that you know little about. Although you know little about this product, could you use the Web to learn a lot relatively quickly?

3. Visit the Facebook page of a favorite company. Does the company do an effective job in enticing you to "like" the page? Why or why not?

4. Investigate whether your school has a blog. If so, what types of content does it have? Is it effective? Why or why not?

Managerial Application

Deanna Brown, President of Scripps Networks Interactive, says, "Being in tune with the consumer palette allows us to think smartly about what people are thinking about on a day-to-day, week-to-week basis." FoodNetwork.com has grown to over 10 million users, and big events like the Super Bowl encourage many consumers to use FoodNetwork.com recipes and products for home entertaining. Walmart is one of FoodNetwork.com's largest clients, and Stephanie Prager, Associate Digital Director for Walmart at MediaVest, says, "There's a challenge we've seen with other cable networks in that they might have a great program on-air, but their site is not as robust."

Your Challenge:

1. Imagine that you are a manager at FoodNetwork.com and you've been asked to analyze your company's website. What are the most positive features of FoodNetwork.com's website?

2. How could you improve FoodNetwork.com's website?

3. Besides Walmart, what other new clients would you pursue and why?

End Notes

1 Sources for this article: What is Pinterest? [Company website]. (n.d.). Retrieved from: http://pinterest.com/about/. McCracken, H. (2011, August 16). The 50 best websites of 2011. On *Timespecials*. Retreived from: http://www.time.com/time/specials/packages/article/0,28804,2087815_2088159_2088155,00.html. Sloan, P. (2011, December 22). Pinterest: Crazy Growth Lands It as Top 10 Social Site. Retrieved from: http://news.cnet.com/8301-1023_3-57347187-93/pinterest-crazy-growth-lands-it-as-top-10-social-site/?tag=mncol;txt. Pinterest Users Nearly Twice as Likely to Purchase than Facebook Users, SteelHouse Survey Shows. On *MarketWatch*.com. (2012, May 30). Retrieved from: http://www.marketwatch.com/story/pinterest-users-nearly-twice-as-likely-to-purchase-than-facebook-users-steelhouse-survey-shows-2012-05-30.

2 Alba, J., Lynch, J., Weitz, B., Janiszewski, C., Lutz, R., Sawyer, A., & Wood, S. (1997). Interactive Home Shopping: Consumer, Retailer, and Manufacturer Incentives to Participate in Electronic Marketplaces. *Journal of Marketing*, 61, 38–53.

3 Amazon.com Inc. On *BloombergBusinessweek*.com. (n. d.) Retrieved from: http://investing.businessweek.com/research/stocks/earnings/earnings.asp?ticker=AMZN:US.

4 Weathers, D., & Makienko, I. (2006). Assessing the Relationships between E-Tail Success and Product and Website Factors. *Journal of Interactive Marketing*, 20, 41–54.

5 Csikszentmihalyi, M. (1990). *Flow:The Psychology of Optimal Experience*. New York: Harper & Row.

6 Bellman, S., Johnson, E. J., Lohse, G. L., & Mandel, N. (2006). Designing Marketplaces of the Artificial with Consumers in Mind: Four Approaches to Understanding Consumer Behavior in Electronic Environments. *Journal of Interactive Marketing*, 20, 21–33.

7 Wright, A., & Lynch, J. G. (1995). Communication Effects of Advertising Versus Direct Experience When Both Search and Experience Attributes Are Present. *Journal of Consumer Research*, 21, 708–718.

8 Fasolo, B., McClelland, G. H., & Lange, K. A. (2005). The Effect of Site Design and Interattribute Correlations on Interactive Web-Based Decisions. In C. P. Haugtvedt, K. A. Machleit, & R. F. Yalch (Eds.), *Online Consumer Psychology: Understanding and Influencing Consumer Behavior in the Virtual World* (pp. 325–342). Mahwah, NJ: Erlbaum.

9 Levin, A. M., Levin, I. P., & Heath, C. E. (2005). Finding the Best Ways to Combine Online and Offline Shopping Features. In C. P. Haugtvedt, K. A. Machleit, & R. F. Yalch (Eds.), *Online Consumer Psychology: Understanding and Influencing Consumer Behavior in the Virtual World* (pp. 401–417). Mahwah, NJ: Erlbaum.

10 Sources for this article include: Internet Led to Global Explosion of Fake Drugs. On *Yahoo*.com. (2012, June 15). Retrieved from: http://ph.omg.yahoo.com/news/internet-led-global-explosion-fake-drugs-092515740.html. Wotherspoon, D., Cheng, M., & Martineau, F. (2009, June 6). Let's Get Real about Eliminating Fake Goods. On *Manufacturing*.net. Retrieved from: http://www.manufacturing.net/articles/2009/06/let%E2%80%99s-get-real-about-eliminating-fake-goods. Zaichowsky, J. L. (2006). *The Psychology Behind Trademark Infringement and Counterfeiting*. Mahwah, NJ: Erlbaum.

11 SEMPO State of Search Marketing Report 2011. On *Econsultancy*.com. (n. d.). Retrieved from: http://econsultancy.com/us/reports/sempo-state-of-search.

12 SEMPO State of Search Marketing Report 2011. On *Econsultancy*.com. (n. d.). Retrieved from: http://econsultancy.com/us/reports/sempo-state-of-search.

13 Brain, M. (n. d.) How Web Advertising Works. On *howstuffworks*.com. Retrieved from: http://computer.howstuffworks.com/web-advertising1.htm.

14 Brain, M. (n. d.) How Web Advertising Works. On *howstuffworks*.com. Retrieved from: http://computer.howstuffworks.com/web-advertising1.htm.

15 Kaplan, A. M., & Haenlein, M. (2010). "Users of the World, Unite! The Challenges and Opportunities of Social Media." *Business Horizons*, 53 (1), 59–68.

16 Stelzner, M. (2012, April). 2012 Social Media Industry Marketing Report. Retrieved from: http://www.socialmediaexaminer.com/social-media-marketing-industry-report-2012/.

17 Kaplan, A. M., & Haenlein, M. (2010). "Users of the World, Unite! The Challenges and Opportunities of Social Media." *Business Horizons*, 53 (1): 59–68.

18 O'Dell, J. (2011, January 24). The History of Social Media. On *Mashable*.com. Retrieved from: http://mashable.com/2011/01/24/the-history-of-social-media-infographic/.

19 VanGrove, J. (2012, February 2). What Facebook isn't Telling You about its Risky Ad Business. On *Venturebeat*.com. Retrieved from: http://venturebeat .com/2012/02/02/facebook-ctr/. Wasserman, T. (2011, January 31). Facebook Ads Perform Half as Well as Regular Banner Ads. On *Mashable*.com. Retrieved from: http://mashable.com/2011/01/31/facebook-half-click -throughs/.

20 Sources for this article: Paul, I. (2012, February 2). Facebook Goes Public: Interesting Facts from IPO Paperwork. In *Today@PC World* Blog. [Blog]. Retrieved from: http://www.pcworld.com/article/249206 /facebook_goes_public_surprising_facts_learned_from_ ipo_paperwork.html. Vadlamani, S. (2012, January 31). India is Now Top Facebook Nation Outside the US. On *Asian Correspondent*.com. Retrieved from: http:// asiancorrespondent.com/74941/indias-now-top-facebook -nation-outside-the-us/. Facebook Statistics by Country. On *Socialbakers*.com. (n.d.). Retrieved from: http://www .socialbakers.com/facebook-statistics/. Beaumond, P. (2011, February 24). The Truth about Facebook, Twitter and the Uprisings in the Arab World. On *Theguardian*.com. Retrieved from: http://www.guardian.co.uk/world/2011 /feb/25/twitter-facebook-uprisings-arab-libya.

21 Freed, L. (2012, March 5). Daily Deal Websites and Emails Bring in New and Existing Customers for Retailers. [Company website]. Retrieved from: http://www.google .com/url?sa=t&rct=j&q=&esrc=s&source=web&cd=1&ved =0CJgBEBYwAA&url=http%3A%2F%2Fwww.foreseeresults .com%2Fresearch-white-papers%2F_downloads%2Fdaily-deal -commentary-2012-foresee.pdf&ei=5QjeT5n_CaPp6gHam c2JCw&usg=AFQjCNG2VYu1UsldbgDbd4XNJeHa-uYJiw &sig2=RFlZtYOyHmwJ4Ppyu544Xw.

22 Deal Me In: Behind the Bargain-Hunting Audiences of Local Deal Sites. On *Nielsen*.com (2011, April 26). Retrieved from: http://blog.nielsen.com/nielsenwire /online_mobile/deal-me-in-behind-the-bargain-hunting -audiences-of-local-deal-sites/.

23 Stelzner, M. (2012, April). 2012 Social Media Industry Marketing Report. Retrieved from: http://www .socialmediaexaminer.com/social-media-marketing-industry -report-2012/.

24 Haubl, G., & Trifts, V. (2005). Consumer Decision Making in Online Shopping Environments: The Effects of Interactive Decision Aids. *Marketing Science, 19*, 4–21. Murray, K. B., & Haubl, G. (2005). Processes of Preference Construction in Agent-Assisted Online Shopping. In C. P. Haugtvedt, K. A. Machleit, & R. F. Yalch (Eds.), *Online Consumer Psychology: Understanding and Influencing Consumer Behavior in the Virtual World* (pp. 265–283). Mahwah, NJ: Erlbaum.

25 Beatty, S. & Smith, S. (1987). External Search Effort: An Investigation across Several Product Categories. *Journal of Consumer Research, 14*, 83–95.

26 Urbany, J. E., Dickson, P. R., & Wilkie, W. L. (1989). Buyer Uncertainty and Information Search. *Journal of Consumer Research, 16*, 208–215.

27 Johnson, E. J., & Russo, J. E. (1984). Product Familiarity and Learning New Information. *Journal of Consumer Research, 11*, 542–550.

28 Dickson, P. R., & Sawyer, A. G. (1990). The Price Knowledge and Search of Supermarket Shoppers. *Journal of Marketing, 54*, 42–53.

29 Sinha, I. (2000). Cost Transparency: The Net's Real Threat to Prices and Brands. *Harvard Business Review*, 43–50.

30 Popkowski-Leszczyc, P. T. L., & Rao, R. C. (1990). An Empirical Analysis of National and Local Advertising Effects on Price Elasticity. *Marketing Letters, 1*, 149–160.

31 Mitra, A., & Lynch, J. G. (1995). Toward a Reconciliation of Market Power and Information Theories of Advertising Effects on Price Elasticity. *Journal of Consumer Research, 21*, 644–659. Mitra, A., & Lynch, J. G. (1996). Advertising Effects on Consumer Welfare: Prices Paid and Liking for Brands Selected. *Marketing Letters, 7*, 19–29.

32 Lynch, J. G., & Ariely, D. (2000). Wine Online: Search Costs Affect Competition on Price, Quality, and Distribution. *Marketing Science, 19*, 83–103.

33 Diehl, K., Kornish, L. J., & Lynch, J. G. (2003). Smart Agents: When Lower Search Costs for Quality Information Increase Price Sensitivity. *Journal of Consumer Research, 30*, 56–71.

Glossary

A

absent-mindedness - poor memory performance that occurs with shallow or superficial processing of information during encoding or retrieval (132)

absolute threshold - the minimum level of stimuli needed for an individual to experience a sensation (101)

accessibility - the ease with which information is retrieved from memory (132)

accounts - *excuses* and *justifications*; the former reduce or deny one's responsibility for inappropriate actions; the latter acknowledge responsibility but rationalize the behavior as appropriate, given the circumstances (337)

acculturation - the process that occurs when people in one culture adapt to meanings in another culture (401)

achieved status - is attributed to internal factors such as effort and ability (442)

acquisition strategies - strategies that focus on attracting new customers (85)

activation - (or *retrieval*) refers to the transfer of information from inactive long-term memory to active short-term memory (134)

actual brands - the set of all brands that exist along with measures of each of their attributes (247)

actual public-concept - embodies others' true perceptions of a consumer (325)

actual self-concept - represents how consumers in fact perceive themselves (325)

adaptation - the process of becoming desensitized to sensual stimuli (103)

adaptive unconscious - when the unconscious mind can be trained to perform routine mental activities (149)

additive-difference heuristic - comparing two brands at a time, one attribute at a time, and subtract the evaluative differences (285)

adjustment function - the function in which hedonic (or pleasure/pain) appeals are useful for changing attitudes (173)

advertising wear-out - when an advertisement is overexposed, it loses the ability to attract attention and interest (103)

affect transfer - a special case of classical conditioning; occurs when the positive affect (or feelings) created by an unconditioned stimulus becomes associated with a conditioned stimulus (383)

affective forecasting - comparing the predictions of forecasters with the evaluations of experiencers; forecasters attempt to predict future reactions to positive or negative events, whereas experiencers rate current reactions to positive or negative events (311)

affirmation of the consequent - the backwards logic or confusion of the inverse (372)

age cohorts - groups of people who have experienced a common social, political, historical, and economic experience (443)

aligning activities - consist of comments that attempt to realign our behavior with norms (336)

anchoring-and-adjustment heuristic - making predictions based on a first impression or an initial judgment (or anchor) and then shift (adjust or fine-tune) this judgment upward or downward depending on the implications of the imagined possibilities (283)

appearance management - the decisions regarding how consumers control their physical appearances and surroundings (334)

applied research - research that examines many of the same variables as basic research, but within a specific context of interest to a marketer (20)

approach - movement toward a desired object our outcome (170)

arousal - a state of physical wakefulness or alertness; also influences consumers' attention (107, 169)

ascribed status - includes externally assigned characteristics such as gender, race, and age (442)

assimilation effect - participants who completed the puzzle with expensive brand names rated the ambiguous automobile as expensive (151)

assimilation effect - a shift in judgment of the target toward the reference point (or standard or point of comparison) (198)

associations - the links that connect related nodes or ideas (134)

associative interference - in which new associations compete with and block old associations (135)

associative network - the complex connection of nodes into a single association (134)

attention - focusing on one or more environmental stimuli while potentially ignoring others (98)

attitude-based choice - overall evaluations and general impressions of brands in the consideration set based on a combination of everything (274)

attitudes - evaluative judgments, or ratings of how good or bad, favorable or unfavorable, or pleasant or unpleasant consumers find a particular person (e.g., salesperson, spokesperson), place (e.g., retail outlet, website, vacation site), thing (e.g., product, package, advertisement), or issue (e.g., political platform, economic theory) (196)

attraction effect - a target brand seems more attractive when it is compared to inferior brands and less attractive when compared to superior brands (270)

attribute loyalty - the strong preference for a specific attribute (83)

attribute-based choices - comparing the specific attributes or features of each brand and selecting the one that performs best on key attributes (274)

attributes - the basic characteristics of goods and services (414)

authority principle - the principle that uses titles, clothes (such as uniforms), or expensive possessions that convey status in order to impress and influence others (384)

automatic information processing - mental processes that occur without awareness or intention, but nevertheless influence judgments, feelings, goals, and behaviors (147)

automaticity principle - the cornerstone of all influence techniques; it asserts that people often think mindlessly and as a result, behave automatically, without fully evaluating the consequences of a request (359)

availability heuristic - making predictions based on how easily they can retrieve information can be retrieved from memory (282)

avoidance - movement away from an undesired object or outcome (170)

B

(brand) entry strategies - strategy for bringing a new product to market (73)

Baby Boomers - generation born in the years immediately after WWII (1946–1964); more than 76 million Boomers made up about 25% of the U.S. population in 2010 and nearly one-third of the adult population (451)

backward conditioning - the conditioned stimulus is presented after the unconditioned stimulus; learning still takes place, but the associations are weaker; higher levels of repetitive advertising are needed for learning to occur (123)

bait-and-switch - a special case of the low-ball technique—sometimes known as the *lure procedure*, this approach "lures" customers by advertising a low-priced product or service; when customers discover that the product is not

available, a salesperson encourages them to purchase a substitute that, of course, costs more (365)

basic research - research that looks for general relationships between variables, regardless of the specific situation (19)

because heuristic - processing small requests mindlessly by people; hearing the word *because* may be enough to trigger compliance (360)

behavioral compliance - a situation where someone actually carries out that request (359)

behavioral science - applies the scientific method, relying on systematic, rigorous procedures to explain, control, and predict consumer behavior (15)

behavioral-based segmentation - groups consumers based on their preference for a particular product attribute or benefit, usage occasion, user status, rate of product usage, and loyalty status (51)

beliefs - non-evaluative judgments or ratings about product attributes and benefits (193)

benefits - represent the second stage in a means-end chain and embody consumers' perceptions about the outcomes or consequences provided by the attributes (414)

blocking - occurs when the first predictive stimulus blocks or prevents learning for other predictive stimuli encountered later (124)

blogs - frequently updated web journals that provide information in the form of "posts" about products, services, politics, or just about anything (16)

boomerang kids - a Gen Y phenomenon representing children who return home to live indefinitely after graduating from college (455)

bounded rationality - the idea that consumers can only make rational decisions within the limits of time and cognitive capability (245)

brand anthropomorphism - assigns both human traits and *form* to non-humans (342)

brand equity - the value that a brand accrues based on the goodwill attached to associations with the brand name (79)

brand extensions - different products with the same brand name (e.g., Coke Classic, Cherry Coke, Vanilla Coke, Coke Zero) (79)

brand integration - occurs when the brand is woven into the thread of the story, becoming part of the plot or context (483)

brand interaction - occurs when the characters talk about the product or brand or actually handle the product, i.e., they physically interact with it (483)

brand jingles - short, catchy tunes—with or without words—that represent a brand or organization (407)

brand laziness - a consumer's natural inertia toward a product or service based on familiarity and convenience, rather than a fundamental commitment to the brand (227)

brand logos - brand logos take a variety of forms, including colors, shapes, words, and other images; used to catch a consumer's eye and trigger positive thoughts about the brand (408)

brand loyalty - the strong preference for a specific brand (83)

brand loyalty - consumers who indicate first and second choices with the same brand name rather than within the same attribute; or intrinsic commitment to a brand based on the benefits or values it provides consumers (229)

brand overload - a condition brought on by the proliferation of bands that offer few distinctive attributes or benefits (242)

brand personality - the set of human characteristics associated with a brand; brand personality comprises the human side of a brand's image (340)

brand personification - giving non-humans human-like traits to brands (342)

brand positivity effect - consumers form unrealistically favorable evaluations of moderately favorable brands when they form singular evaluations, but not when they form comparative evaluations (309)

brand resonance - a consumer's intense and actively loyal relationship with a brand (79)

brand variance - a consumer's awareness of uncertainty as to an individual brand's attributes (249)

buzz marketing - buzz marketing is a general term, encompassing any campaign designed at generating word-of-mouth (469)

C

cancellation - in gambles with different stages, such as a game show in which you need to win in stage one in order to advance to stage two, stage one should cancel out, or be ignored, if it is identical for two different gambling games (295)

cannibalization - occurs when products offered by the same firm are so similar that they compete among themselves, thus creating a case of *over-segmentation* (45)

cannibalization - when sales of one product on the line "eat up" or reduce sales of another product on the same line (82)

causal relationship - a relationship between two variables where the variables are correlated and that one variable influences the other, but not vice versa (28)

causal research - research concerned with identifying and understanding cause-and-effect relationships through experimentation (27)

celebrity endorser - an individual who enjoys public recognition and uses this recognition on behalf of a consumer product by appearing in an advertisement or engaging in some other marketing tactic (475)

central route - when involvement is high, and when the ability to think about a marketing claim is high, consumers are likely to follow the central route to persuasion by focusing on information most central to or important for forming an accurate attitude (206)

channel length - the number of intermediaries (e.g., wholesalers, distributors, and retailers) needed to get the product from the manufacturer to the consumer (87)

choice architecture - the structuring of choice options in a manner that helps people make informed (302)

choice deferral - deciding not to choose anything (275)

chronological age - represents the number of years a person has lived (450)

classical conditioning - a learning theory centered on creating associations between meaningful objects or ideas (or what researches call *stimuli*) to elicit desired responses (122)

closure - the tendency for a person to perceive an incomplete picture as complete, either consciously or unconsciously (111)

cluster frontier - the best possible combination of attributes observed within a cluster (249)

cluster size - the number of brands the consumer places in the cluster (249)

cluster variance - the degree to which brands within a single cluster are dissimiliar from each other (249)

clustering - a process where the consumer simplifies the task of choosing a brand by thinking not of many individual brands, but of a few clusters of brands, each with a key attribute (249)

cognitive capacity - the ability to pay attention to and think about information (99)

cognitive dissonance theory - a theory that suggests consumers shift their attitudes to increase behavior-attitude consistency (179)

cognitive personality variables - the personality traits that describe an individual's mental responses to objects (345)

coleman-Rainwater Social Class Hierarchy - U.S. class structure based on how people interacted with one another; the heart and soul of their class system is personal and group prestige, which is partially driven by family history, and physical appearance, as well as social aspirations and skills (437)

commitment and consistency principle - people are expected to exhibit beliefs, attitudes, and behaviors that are stable and coherent; inconsistencies often invite interpretations of personality flaws or, in extreme cases, mental illness (361)

commitment theory - suggests that the purpose of obtaining an initial commitment is to impart resistance to change (364)

community marketing - organizing and supporting niche communities that share a common interest about a brand (473)

comparative evaluation - comparing two or more products concurrently by the consumers (303)

comparison matrix - an interactive decision aid that helps consumers to evaluate options by providing a style brand-by-attribute matrix that makes it easy for consumers to compare options (506)

comparison-based contrast effect - occurs when information is included in the representation of the reference point or standard of comparison (199)

compatibility principle - the principle in which different measurement techniques highlight different aspects of the choice options (302)

compensatory process - the process by which the consumers select a single brand from among the brands in the considered cluster (249)

comprehension - the ability to interpret and assign meaning to new information by relating it to knowledge already stored in memory (99)

compromise effect - the increased probability of buying a compromise brand; is especially likely to occur when consumers are concerned about making a bad decision (270)

compulsive buying - the drive to consume uncontrollably and to buy in order to avoid problems (338)

conditioned response - response that occurs without the original unconditioned stimulus (123)

conditioned stimulus - a neutral object (123)

confirmation bias - the tendency for consumers to interpret ambiguous evidence as consistent with their current beliefs (84)

conjunctive heuristic - setting a minimum value for all relevant attributes and selecting the first brand that meets this value for each attribute (286)

consideration set - the group of brands that consumers think about buying when they need to make a purchase (268)

conspicuous consumption - involves consumers purchasing publicly consumed luxury goods to demonstrate their newfound wealth (438)

consumer behavior - includes all consumer activities associated with the purchase, use, and disposal of goods and services, including the consumer's emotional, mental,

and behavioral responses that precede, determine, or follow these activities (7)

consumer generated marketing - the creation of advertising or other marketing content by the customer (473)

consumer insight - a deep, profound knowledge of the consumer that comes from integrating traditional marketing research tools with consumer behavior theories (18)

consumer preference heterogeneity - the extent to which tastes and preferences differ among consumers (44)

content websites - a website that functions to collect stories, videos, and images for people to view (as opposed to an e-tailing website) (500)

context effects - occur because the background or context in which an object is judged influences judgments (198)

continuity pricing - offering a lower price for multiple units of a product (87)

continuous reinforcement - when reinforcement occurs every time the desired response occurs (128)

contrast effect - participants who were primed with inexpensive brands rated the moderately priced target (with a clearly visible brand name) as expensive, while participants who were primed with expensive brands rated the target as inexpensive (152)

contrast effect - a shift in judgment of the target away from the reference point (198)

conventions - the norms that deal less with right or wrong or tradition, but rather with what is more or less "correct" (410)

core benefit proposition - relies on a single attribute or benefit that differentiates the brand from competitors' offerings (59)

corrective advertising - advertising that is used in response to misleading advertising; states the previous ad was misleading (131)

correlated - when a statistically testable and significant relationship exists between two variables (27)

correspondent inference - the assumption that a person's behavior is a reflection of their beliefs and underlying dispositions, rather than the result of some situational variable (476)

credence attributes - attributes that can be judged or rated only after *extended* use (194)

crescive norms - implicit and learned only through interacting with other members of a culture (410)

cultural brands - a set of products and services from emerging economies such as ethnic food, music, movies, entertainment, and media; serve as a means of expression and represent symbols of a particular culture's identity (402)

cultural categories - help organize a society by dividing the world into specific and distinct segments of time, space, nature, and people (394)

cultural principles - the *ideas* that help guide the construction of cultural categories (395)

cultural translation - the difficulties and problems related to the spirit of the language (403)

cultural values - a collective set of beliefs about what is important, useful, and desirable (393, 409)

culturally constituted world - the place where all consumer experiences are shaped by the intangible beliefs and values of society (394)

culture - the patterns of meaning acquired by members of society expressed in their knowledge, beliefs, art, laws, morals, customs, and habits (393)

customer delight - goes a step beyond customer perceived value, suggesting customer benefits that not only meet, but also exceed expectations in unanticipated ways (13)

customer perceived value - the estimated net gain customers receive from their sacrifice of time, money, and effort expended to purchase, use, and dispose of a product or service (i.e., benefits versus costs) (13)

customs - the overt behaviors that have been passed down from one generation to the next (410)

D

demographic characteristics - customers' vital population statistics; includes age, gender, income, education, occupation, social class, marital status, household size, family life cycle, and culture or ethnicity (47)

demographic transition - four-step process that occurs as nations develop from pre-industrial to highly developed economies (425)

demography - the statistical study of human populations; key population metrics include population size, social class, income, and age (425)

Depression Generation - generation born between 1930 and 1945; also known as the "silent generation," this group was uninvolved with politics and self-removed from social strife (447)

derived varied behavior - describes situations where consumers' brand switching is either *externally imposed* or *extrinsically motiviated* (230)

descriptive beliefs - beliefs based on direct experience with a product or what we see with our own eyes or hear with our own ears (194)

descriptive norms - involve perceptions of which behaviors are common or popular (i.e., what is everyone doing?) (377)

descriptive research - research undertaken to describe the characteristics of some group or their behaviors, or to make predictions about trends or variables (25)

determinant attributes - characteristics of a product that are most likely to affect the buyer's final choice (232)

devaluation effect - when consumers are extremely hungry, they rate non-food products as less desirable (170)

differentiating advertising - advertising that emphasizes the differences in quality among brands (87)

diffusion of innovation - the rate at which a new product spreads or is adopted across the marketplace (73)

diffusion of responsibility - the peculiar inaction where people look for cues from other group members; if no one quickly steps forward to act, then the likelihood of anyone acting decreases and a snowball of pluralistic ignorance ensues (375)

diminishing sensitivity - the outcomes having weaker effects on people as distance from the reference point increases (297)

disclaimers - verbal assertions, made in advance, to offset the potential negative effects of a behavior (336)

disjunctive heuristic - setting an acceptable value, rather than a minimum value, for all relevant attributes and select the first brand that meets this value on one particular attribute—which is not necessarily the most important attribute (286)

divestment rituals - rituals in which consumers believe cultural meaning can be transferred from products to people (400)

dominate - better choices than alternatives with lower expected values (294)

door-in-the-face technique - following up a large, unreasonable request with a smaller, more sensible request usually improves behavioral compliance (367)

drive - the tension that influences the urgency with which actions are taken to return to the desired goal-state (169)

dual-process model - theoretical framework that describes the two styles of thinking; this model maintains that information processing sometimes occurs quickly and effortlessly, and sometimes occurs slowly and with great effort (147)

dual-process model - these models of attitude formation assume that consumers think a great deal when involvement is high but they don't think much when involvement is low (201)

durability bias - found where people believe they will be happy or sad for a long time following a positive or negative event; the bias tends to be stronger for negative events (311)

duration neglect - occurs when people are asked to indicate their preferences for two events that are similar, but differ in terms of temporal duration (311)

E

ego depletion - when cognitive resources are depleted by one task, leaving fewer for subsequent tasks (177)

ego-defensive function - the function in which authority and fear appeals are useful for changing attitudes (173)

elaboration likelihood model - a high involvement route in which consumers think a lot (i.e., the central route of the elaboration likelihood model and the systematic route of the heuristic/systematic model) (201)

elimination-by-aspects heuristic - rejecting all brands that do not have a key feature consumers want (285)

enacted norms - explicitly and formally prescribe acceptable behaviors (410)

encoding - refers to attention, comprehension, and the transference of information from short-term memory to long-term memory (132)

encoding-specificity principle - memory is context dependent (135)

enculturation - referred to by anthropologists in learning about one's own culture (401)

endowment effect - the tendency to view a product as more valuable if one owns it than if one does not own it (299)

enduring involvement - a consumer's long-term and continuous interest in a brand or product category (241)

entity theorists - consumers that believe the world is rigid or fixed and that change is nearly impossible (81)

e-tailing - type of commerce where consumers purchase products directly over the Internet (493)

evaluative-cognitive consistency - strong attitudes tend to be highly accessible from memory, maintained with high confidence, held with little uncertainty, and highly correlated with beliefs (197)

even-a penny technique - the legitimization of trivial contributions (e.g., a penny, a dollar, one minute of your time) (371)

exchange rituals - rituals that involve one person or a group of people purchasing and presenting consumer products to another (398)

expectancy disconfirmation model - suggests that consumers form expectations about product performance prior to purchasing a brand (257)

expectancy-value models - suggest that attitudes toward a product depend on consumers' subjective evaluation of the product's attributes multiplied by the expectancy that the product possesses each attribute (201)

expected utility theory - the theory in which the alternatives can be ranked from worst to best (294)

experience attributes - attributes that can be judged or rated only by using a product (194)

experiential marketing - creates one-on-one experiences for consumers with the brand that allows consumers to experience the brand in a sensory way, and usually in a unique, fun, and entertaining way (472)

experiments - the manipulation of variables in a controlled setting to determine their relationship to one another (29)

explicit attitudes - attitudes that consumers express consciously (157)

explicit memory - searching for information stored in memory (151)

exploratory research - broad, *qualitative* research done to generate ideas or help further formulate problems for further research (22)

extended self - the relationship between a consumer's self-concepts and his/her possessions (328)

extensive problem solving - requires a deliberate and systematic effort, from consumers, where they generally do not have well-established criteria to evaluate brands or may be unfamiliar with the product category (226)

external search - search which involves personal sources (e.g., friends and relatives), market sources such as advertisements and brochures, public sources, and product trial (i.e., examining or testing the product on a limited basis) (240)

external uncertainty - causing consumer's perceived brand universe to differ from the true brand (247)

extinction - a reduced conditioned response, or the absence of a reward (127)

extinction - the absence of a reward (128)

F

figure-ground principle - from a perception prospective, when a stimulus is salient, it is figural or focal, and everything else fades into the background (109)

five-Factor Model - this multi-factor structure identifies five basic traits that derive primarily from an individual's genetics and early childhood learning: (1) surgency (outgoingness), (2) agreeableness, (3) conscientiousness, (4) emotional stability, (5) intellect (338)

flattery - excessive compliments or praise designed to make someone feel good about her/himself (335)

focus group - consists of 8 to 12 participants, run by a moderator who monitors and guides the group discussion of the research topic at hand (22)

foot-in-the-door technique - making a small request followed by a larger one (362)

forward conditioning - greater learning or conditioning occurs when the conditioned stimulus is presented before the unconditioned stimulus (123)

frames - perspectives that guide the decision-making process (295)

frequency of good and bad features heuristic - consumers form a simple attitude toward each brand alternative by counting the number of good and bad product features and choosing the brand with the greatest difference between good product features and bad product features (286)

G

generation effect - memory performance is enhanced when people generate their own answers to questions rather than simply reading them (133)

Generation X - generation squeezed between the Boomers and Millennials; Gen X, also known as the Baby Busters, were born between 1965 and 1976 (453)

Generation Y - generation that was largely created by their Baby Boomer parents; Millennials, or the Echo Boom, were born between 1977 and 1995 (455)

Generation Z - generation commonly thought to include those born during the latter half of the 1990s through the late 2000s, specifically after 1995 (457)

geo-demographic segmentation - combines geography and demographic segmentation bases; sometimes called *zip-code marketing*, this segmentation strategy relies on the common tendency for people who are similar along demographic dimensions to live in close proximity (48)

geographic based segmentation - strategy where marketers split the market based on physical location of potential customers (47)

gerontographics - a segmentation philosophy that maintains mature consumers' receptivity to marketing activities is related more to life changes rather than to chronological age (449)

goal - once a need is aroused, a state of tension is created that energizes a person to reduce or eliminate the need, returning to a preferred state (169)

grassroots marketing - a type of community marketing, involves organizing and supporting communities on a personal and local level (473)

grooming rituals - rituals that allow consumers to extract cultural meaning from perishable possessions through repeated use (400)

grouping - the tendency to arrange stimuli together to form well-organized units (111)

H

hedonic products - products consumers use to enjoy positive experiences (181)

heuristic processing - mental shortcuts that help consumers simplify their decision-making tasks (277)

heuristic/systematic model - a low involvement route in which consumers think very little (i.e., the peripheral route of the elaboration likelihood model and the heuristic route of the heuristic/systematic model) (201)

heuristics - enables consumers to make decisions quickly and easily (277)

I

ideal public-concept - represents how consumers would like others to see them (325)

ideal self-concept - describes how consumers would like to be (325)

implementation intentions - behavioral intentions to perform specific actions at specific times and places (160)

implicit Association Test (IAT) - a new procedure for measuring sensitive beliefs, including those held without awareness or intention (156)

implicit attitudes - attitudes that consumers express unconsciously (156)

implicit memory - memory used as a tool without awareness or intention (151)

impression management - the process of creating desirable images of ourselves for others (333)

impulse buying - purchases made without prior planning (245)

incremental theorists - consumers that believe the world is malleable or that change is possible (81)

in-depth interview (IDI) - a one-on-one, interview lasting at least one hour, but sometimes considerably longer (22)

indirect associations - occur when consumers personally connect to a product or service through secondary interactions such as wearing a favorite team's apparel or drinking from a university-branded mug (383)

individual consumers - consumers who purchase goods and services to satisfy their own personal needs and wants or to satisfy the needs and wants of others (8)

inferential beliefs - beliefs that go beyond the information given; consumers often draw their own conclusions, or infer beliefs about attributes and benefits based on both direct and indirect experiences (195)

influence or choice heuristics - the choice which affects consumers' decisions directly (e.g., lexicographic, additive-difference, conjunctive, disjunctive, frequency of good-bad features) (277)

information integration theory - type of expectancy-value model that explains how beliefs are combined to influence attitudes (201)

informational beliefs - beliefs based on indirect experience or on what other people tell us (195)

ingratiation - a set of strategic behaviors designed to increase the probability of gaining benefits or favors from another person (334)

ingratiation - a tactic commonly used to engender liking; it involves purposefully bringing oneself into the good graces of another person (382)

injunctive norms - perceptions of which behaviors are accepted or rejected by society (377)

instrumental products - products consumers use to solve a problem (181)

instrumental values - represent preferred modes of behavior; they are actions or "instruments" that provide positive value for consumers (415)

intermediate problem solving - usually involves limited information search and deliberation (266)

internal search - the deliberate retrieval of information which is common with low involvement decisions that comprise much of consumers' day-to-day activities (240)

internal uncertainty - uncertainty about the consumer him/herself—causes a consumer's perceived utility function to differ from his/her true utility function: absolute utility error and relative utility error (247)

interpretivism - an alternative research approach to behavioral science that relies less on scientific and technological methodology (17)

intrinsic variety seeking - the consumer seeking variety for the inherent pleasure of change and the positive stimulation it brings (230)

intuition - knowing or understanding without purposeful thinking (150)

invariance principle - preferences should remain the same no matter how preferences are measured or how decision alternatives are described (295)

involvement - the personal relevance and importance of an issue or situation (200)

J

judgments - the evaluation of information in the decision-making process (193)

just noticeable difference (j. n. d.) - also called the *differential threshold*; the amount of incremental change required for a person to detect a difference between two similar stimuli (101)

K

knowledge function - the function in which information and facts are useful for changing attitudes (173)

L

leading-edge boomers - those born between 1946 and 1955; they represent our images of Vietnam, Woodstock, and the Sixties in general (451)

lexicographic heuristic - comparing all brands on one key attribute, such as price, size, weight, reliability, durability, calories, sugar, etc., and choosing the brand that performs the best on that single attribute, while generally ignoring the other attributes (284)

libertarian paternalism - the idea that people should have free choice; however, choice options should be arranged in a manner to help people make the best choices (301)

liking principle - complying with the requests of those whom we like (380)

List of Values (LOV) - the process developed at the University of Michigan Survey Research Center to identify nine consumer value segments and link them to value-related consumer behavior (417)

list technique - presenting a list of supporters or donors to a prospect (374)

locus of control - the extent to which an individual possesses internal or external reinforcement beliefs (345)

loss aversion - the losses have a bigger impact on people, relative to equivalent gains (297)

loved objects - a special subset of all possessions that comprise the extended self and play a central role in our knowledge of who we are as people (331)

low-ball technique - trying to get an initial commitment, and then changing the deal (363)

lower Americans - can be separated into two subclasses—the upper-lower class and the lower-lower class (439)

lower-lowers - those who live below the threshold of poverty and rely heavily on government assistance programs; sociologists often refer to this group as the "underclass" (440)

lower-uppers - those referred to as "new money" or the nouveaux riche; their income often exceeds that of the upper-uppers, but they are rarely accepted by "old money" (438)

loyaty programs - programs that provide rewards to customers for repeat purchases (86)

M

majority fallacy - when a company focuses exclusively on large average segments, where the majority of customer preferences lie, and neglect smaller, less typical segments (44)

malleable self - a multifaceted self-concept that includes a *good self, bad self, not-me self, desired self, ideal self*, and *ought-to-be self* (333)

market aggregation - the opposite of *market segmentation*; a single-product, one-size-fits-all strategy in which individual differences among consumers are ignored (42)

market mavens - people who search, accumulate, and share product knowledge with others (242)

market segmentation - the process of dividing the large and diverse mass market into subsets of consumers who share common needs, characteristics, or behaviors, then targeting one or more of those segments with a distinct marketing mix (39)

marketing concept - the idea that firms should discover and satisfy customer needs and wants in an efficient and profitable manner, while benefiting the long-term interests of the company's stakeholders (13)

marketing research - a systematic process of planning, collecting, analyzing, and interpreting data and information relevant to marketing problems and consumer behavior (18)

mature market - includes a broader group of consumers 55 years and older; in 2010, the mature market consisted of the Pre-Depression and Depression cohorts, along with approximately half of the Baby Boomers (449)

memory-based choice - consumers' retrieval of brand and information from memory (273)

mere exposure effect - the more familiar an initially neutral product becomes, the more consumers like the product (137)

microblogs - are like blogs, but are characterized by shorter posts, sometimes called *microposts* (505)

microenterprises - small, informal groups that help supply goods and services to rural customers; some consumers in microenterprises help manage the distribution of products and services while balancing business and family demands (429)

middle Americans - comprise two distinct classes: the middle class and the working class (438)

middle class - average earning white-collar workers and their blue-collar friends living on the better side of town (e.g., lower-level managers, schoolteachers, skilled blue-collar workers, and factory supervisors) (438)

miller's Rule - when people are able to consider approximately five to nine (seven plus/minus two) units of information at one time in working memory (106)

mindset priming effect - occurs when the cognitive activity performed during the first session tends to be performed again in the second, even if the products considered during the two sessions are completely different (153)

misattribution - distortion as a result of confusion (136)

mixed choice - the choice where consumers can see some brands but must remember others (273)

mobile marketing - any marketing communication directed to a mass audience, targeted group, or individual using a mobile device, such as a cell phone, tablet, or music device with wireless access (484)

MODE model - Motivation and Opportunity to deliberate are key DEterminants of the processes that influence consumer choice (274)

moré - a custom with strong moral implications; they typically prescribe right and wrong ways of behaving and involve taboos, or forbidden cultural activities involving eating, sex, gender roles, vulgarity, and the like (410)

motivation - a driving force that moves or incites us to act and is the underlying basis of all behavior (168)

motives - internal drives that push people to resolve a problem or reduce a need (236)

multiple-deescalating-requests technique - the technique that involves more than two requests; once a request is refused, additional requests follow—one after the other—until one is finally accepted (371)

MUM effect - the tendency to keep mum about unpleasant messages (384)

N

naïve theory - theories or assumptions about how the world works (155)

need - a fundamental state of felt deprivation (236)

need for cognition - (NFC) measures an individual's natural tendency to engage in and enjoy effortful cognitive activities (345)

need for cognitive closure - (NFCC) describes a consumer's desire for definite knowledge of any kind to reduce confusion or ambiguity (347)

need for humor - (NFH) an individual's tendency to crave, seek out, and enjoy humor; a construct more motivationally driven than sense of humor (346)

needs - desires that arise when a consumer's current state does not match the consumer's preferred state (168)

negative reinforcement - absence of punishment (128)

node - idea or piece of information stored in memory (134)

non-compensatory process - a simple, although error-prone, way to make a decision in which the person does not consider trade-offs (249)

norms - specify appropriate responses in specific situations; serve as important behavioral guidelines for a culture (377, 409)

nouveaux riche - lower-uppers, "new money" (438)

O

ongoing search - a search involving external search activities independent of solving an immediate purchase problem (240)

operant conditioning - the stimulus follows the response rather than precedes it (127)

opinion conformity - expressing insincere agreement on important issues (335)

opinion leaders - the individuals who, by virtue of birth, beauty, talent, or accomplishment, are held in high esteem and provide cultural meaning to those of lesser standing (396)

opportunity - occurs when a consumer's ideal and actual states simultaneously move in opposite directions (239)

opportunity costs - hidden or unseen costs, including non-monetary costs such as the lost time and pleasure associated with choosing one course of action over another (299)

organic word-of-mouth - word-of-mouth that occurs naturally (469)

organizational consumers - consumers who purchase goods and services in order to produce other goods or services, resell them to other organizations or to individual consumers, and to help manage and run their organization (8)

P

paid search marketing - search engine marketing where a company will pay to be included in the results page of a search engine (499)

parity products - brands that possess functionally equivalent attributes, making one brand a satisfactory substitute for most others (232)

partial reinforcement - when reinforcement occurs only some of the times the desired response occurs (128)

part-list cuing - presenting the names of just some brands when consumers are trying to recall as many brands as possible (269)

peak-end effect - causes *duration neglect*; when memory is better for the worst part of a procedure (the peak) and the end, relative to the rest of the procedure (e.g., a painful medical procedure); also occurs because duration is inherently difficult to evaluate (311)

pecking order - ranks people in terms of their community esteem, which produces a more unified social functioning and determines consumers' access to resources such as safety, food, education, housing, and other consumer products (441)

perceived brands - it is prohibitively costly to gather complete and fully accurate information about all existing brands and their attributes; what is in a consumer's head is not the true brand universe (247)

perceived preference - what a consumer believes his/her reaction will be to various brands and their attributes, differs from his/her true preference (247)

perceived product-market - a patterned organization of brands in the consumer's mind (248)

perceived risk - the possibility of negative outcomes (226)

perception - a process of receiving, selecting, and interpreting environmental stimuli involving the five senses (97)

perceptual mapping - measures the way products are positioned in the minds of consumers and shows these perceptions on a graph whose axes are formed by product attributes (61)

performance-based satisfaction - consumers who set and meet lower expectations are typically less satisfied than consumers who set and meet higher expectations (258)

peripheral route - when consumers are unable to think about a marketing claim, they focus on peripheral cues or superficial information that makes it easy to form an opinion without much thought (206)

persistence - the inability to forget what one wants to forget (138)

personal qualities - modes of interpersonal behavior that distinguish people from one another, such as sense of humor or friendliness (323)

personality - a set of unique psychological characteristics that influence how a person responds to his or her environment, including cognitive, affective, and behavioral tendencies (337)

personality traits - consumers' tendencies to respond in a certain way across similar situations (338)

persuasion heuristics - influencing consumers' beliefs and attitudes (277)

persuasion knowledge model - suggests that when consumers suspect ulterior motives on the part of marketers, they attempt to resist the marketers' persuasion attempts (212)

phenomenal absolutism - the erroneous assumption that everyone else perceives the world as we do (98)

pioneering brand advantage - pioneering brands, or the first brands to enter a new market, often enjoy a long-term preference advantage over copycat brands. (72)

positioning - the process of communicating with a target market through the use of marketing mix variables—a specific product, price, distribution channel, and promotional appeal—in such a way as to help consumers differentiate a product from competitors and understand how a particular product best satisfies their needs (41)

positive reinforcement - presence of a reward (128)

possession rituals - rituals that occur when consumers discuss, compare, reflect upon, and display their belongings (399)

pre-depression generation - generation born prior to 1930; also known as the *GI Generation*, this age cohort came of age during the Depression (1930–1941) and went on to build modern America (446)

prediction heuristics - used to form likelihood judgments (e.g., representativeness, availability, simulation, and anchoring-and-adjustment) (277)

pre-exposure effect - occurs when unconditioned stimulus is ineffective because it was previously encountered alone without pairing (124)

preference reversals - a reversal that people prefer option A over option B at one point in time but can prefer option B over option A at another point in time (296)

premium pricing - sometimes called *prestige pricing*, is pricing the brand at the high end of the product category's price range (60)

prepurchase search - once a problem is recognized, consumers often gather information to inform their purchase decisions (240)

prevention focus - concerned with the presence or absence of negative outcomes and with protection and responsibilities (174)

price bundling - the process used by some firms to aggregate losses (300)

price-quality heuristic - consumers' belief that if the price increases, quality also increases (309)

pricing strategies - strategies that manipulate product prices to attract customers (87)

primary data - new data collected specifically for the research purpose at hand (21)

priming effect - a strong association that leads consumers to think about a brand name, and they start thinking about associations to the brand (134)

priming effect - a temporary increase in the ease with which ideas can be retrieved from memory (145)

proactive interference - occurs when information learned earlier blocks memory for information learned later (135)

proactive strategy - when a firm develops many new products and tries to be first in the race to the market (71)

problem solving - a type of decision making that combines high involvement with high levels of information processing (232)

procedural priming effect - occurs when situations are linked to cognitive or motor processes via "if X, then Y" linkages, where X refers to a specific situation and Y refers to a congitive or behavioral activity (153)

product placement - the insertion of branded goods and services within the content of popular media, including television, movies, video games, books, and music (479)

projective techniques - techniques that use seemingly meaningless exercises to uncover consumers' unconscious points of view (23)

promotion focus - concerned with the presence of absence of positive outcomes and with aspirations and accomplishment (174)

psychographics - the measurement of lifestyle, often combined with measures of attitudes, beliefs, and personalities (50)

punishment - decreases the probability of a response (128)

 Q

qualitative research methods - methods used to collect descriptive, non-empirical data that describe an individual consumer's subjective experience with the product or service (18)

quantitative research methods - methods used to collect empirical data (data that are numerical, based on observation, experiment, or experience, rather than on speculation or theory) (16)

 R

reactive strategy - when a firm waits to see what competitors offer and then develops me-too or copycat brands (71)

reciprocity principle - someone does you a favor, so you feel obligated to return it in kind (365)

recommendation agent - an interactive decision aid that helps consumers to eliminate options by using information about their personal preferences or their prior purchase histories (506)

reference dependence - prospect theory that suggests all outcomes are evaluated with respect to a neutral reference point, and that preferences change as reference points change (297)

regulatory focus theory - suggests that consumers regulate or control their behavior by using either a *promotion focus* or *prevention focus* (174)

repositioning - attempts to change the way consumers perceived a brand, either a firm's own brand or a competitor's (60)

representativeness heuristic - predictions based on perceived similarities between a specific target and a general category (279)

retention strategies - strategies that focus on retaining current customers (85)

retrieval - refers to the transference of information from long-term memory to short-term memory (132)

retroactive interference - occurs when information learned later blocks memory for information learned earlier (135)

return potential model - the model that describes norms on two dimensions; the *behavioral dimension* specifies the amount of behavior regulated by the norm, and the *evaluation dimension* shows the cultural response to that behavior (411)

risk aversion - the choice problem in terms of positive outcomes, such as lives saved or money gained; people typically prefer the sure thing (295)

risk seeking - a choice in terms of negative outcomes, such as deaths or money lost, people tend to prefer the risky option (296)

risky decision making - decision making under uncertainty (294)

rituals - the instruments that transfer meaning to consumers; symbolic actions that occur in a fixed sequence and are repeated over time (398)

Rokeach value survey (VALS) - researchers have begun to use value models in consumer behavior studies, because instrumental and terminal values can help predict consumer attitudes and behaviors toward brands (416)

role identities - the numerous *positions* that people occupy in society such as student, friend, son or daughter, and consumer (323)

routine choice - carried out automatically, with little conscious effort; as such, it involves no information search or deliberation (226)

S

sales-cost trade-off - a trade-off that recognizes that, as market segmentation increases, sales increase because a firm's offerings align more closely to consumers' preferences (44)

salient stimuli - stimuli that draw consumers' attention involuntarily (108)

scarcity principle - people often want what they cannot have (372)

scope insensitivity - occurs when people lack distributional knowledge about attributes that are inherently difficult to evaluate (311)

search attributes - attributes that can be judged or rated simply by examining a product without necessarily buying it (194)

search engine marketing (SEM) - a type of Internet marketing that is designed to promote a website and drive consumers to the site by having the website link appear in search engine results pages (498)

secondary data - data that already exist and are readily accessible (21)

selective thinking - interpretation of ambiguous information as supportive and to integrate information so a preferred brand is cast in a favorable light (307)

self-concept - one's awareness and perceptions about him/herself (323, 413)

self-conceptions - any one of self-concepts that include a *good self, bad self, not-me self, desired self, ideal self,* and *ought-to-be self* (333)

self-esteem - the overall evaluative component of a person's self-concept (324)

self-evaluations - when people consider the adequacy of their performances in various role identities (324)

self-monitoring - the extent to which consumers use situational cues to guide their social behavior (332)

self-perception theory - suggests that complying with a small request leads people to label themselves as helpful, good citizens or as reasonable people (362)

self-presentation - involves either *self-enhancement* or *self-deprecation* (334)

self-regulation - self-control or willpower (176)

self-schemas - the cognitive structures that help us make sense of who we are (326)

sensation - the body's first and immediate response to a stimulus (98)

sensory memory - the preliminary, very brief recording of information that happens during sensation in the perceptual process (106)

shaping - reinforcing successive approximations of the desired response; also can be used to encourage current non-users to buy your product (128)

short-term memory - the part of the memory where small bits of information are paid attention to and processed for short periods of time (106)

simulation heuristic - making predictions based on how easily an event or a sequence of events can be imagined or visualized (283)

singular evaluation - a process in which consumers often evaluate products one at a time (303)

situational involvement - a consumer's relatively temporary and context-dependent interest in a product or category (241)

social class - the overall *standing* a consumer occupies in society based on characteristics valued by others (434)

social media - any online media environment that allows for the creation and exchange of user generated content (501)

social media marketing - a type of Internet marketing that uses social media to achieve some marketing goal (501)

social mobility - describes the movement of consumers from one social class to another (435)

social structure - hierarchical division of homogeneous groups or "classes" based on a common set of values and lifestyles, with rankings derived from status, power, and class (433)

social validation principle - the perceived validity (or correctness) of an idea increases as the number of people supporting the idea increases (374)

source of volume - where future purchases of products will come from (85)

spacing effect - the idea that information is better retained when learned in different contexts and over time (136)

sponsorship and branded entertainment - the most intensive form of marriage between content and brand; in this type of placement, the brand is the sole sponsor of the content, has extensive editorial control of the content, and the editorial content or style typically matches closely the targeted audience of the brand (483)

spreading activation - the idea that when people retrieve a particular node, they automatically think about other closely related nodes (134)

stealth marketing - a buzz marketing campaign that specifically relies on spreading word-of-mouth in a covert or clandestine manner (469)

stimulus-based choice - when consumers can directly and physically observe all relevant brands in the consideration set and their brand attributes (273)

stroop task - a color-naming task in which color words are printed in different color ink than the specific color named; for example, using red ink to print the word "green" (177)

subcultures - smaller groups of a larger culture that share some cultural values with society overall and yet demonstrate unique cultural values and patterns of behavior within the individual subgroup (393)

subjective age - represents how old someone feels (450)

subliminal perception - the unconscious awareness of a stimulus (104)

subliminal priming - presenting priming stimuli below the level of conscious awareness (155)

subtraction-based contrast effect - occurs when information is excluded from the representation of the target (199)

suggestibility - misleading questions and suggestions that can lead to memory distortion (137)

survey - a set of structured questions to which a person is asked to respond (26)

systematic processing - the process in which consumers think carefully about decisions, using all relevant information and considering all implications (276)

T

target market - the segment(s) toward which a firm's marketing efforts are directed (41)

terminal values - represent psychological states of being, or desired end points for a set of actions (415)

that's-not-all technique - the technique starts high and builds in a downward fashion, i.e., the initial deal is changed into an even better deal *before* the consumer has an opportunity to reject the first offer (369)

theory of cognitive itch - properties of music may be analogous to biochemical agents, such as histamines, which cause an itch on the skin; exposure to such music may cause a sort of "cognitive itch" in one's mind that can only be scratched by repeating the offending music—but this only exacerbates the itch, trapping the hapless victim in an involuntary cycle of repeated itching and scratching (408)

theory of lay epistemology - the formation and use of everyday knowledge; suggests that individuals differ in the degree to which they make the important trade-off between speed and accuracy (347)

theory of reasoned action - one specific type of expectancy-value model that explains how beliefs are combined to influence attitudes and how social norms or rules and attitudes influence behavior (201)

thin-slice inferences - guesses made regarding a person's personality traits, current feelings, and goals, based on brief observations of that person's behavior (150)

tip-of-the-tongue effect - when people know the answer to a question, but they cannot quite put their finger on it (133)

traits - tendencies to behave a certain way across similar situations (324)

transience - occurs when people forget details over time (132)

transitive - if a consumer prefers A over B, and B over C, then she should prefer A over C (295)

trial pricing - a large price discount on a single unit of a particular brand (87)

true preference - the actual pleasure a consumer will obtain from consuming various brands, i.e., another objective reality (247)

truth effect - as the familiarity of a product claim increases, the more consumers believe the claim (137)

truth effect - as familiarity with a product claim increases, so does the consumer's belief that the claim is true (157)

U

uncertainty-reduction model - gathering and using product information under uncertainty (246)

unconditioned response - a consumer's automatic or unlearned response to a stimulus (123)

unconditioned stimulus - the meaningful object that helps to learn the results in Pavlovian conditioning (123)

upper americans - represent a lively mix of many lifestyles, including upper-upper, lower-upper, and upper-middle classes (437)

upper-lowers - describes the "working poor"; many live *above* the poverty threshold, not on welfare (439)

upper-middle - the class is known as the "professionals"; they are college graduates, some with advanced degrees, who have attained upper- class status in their communities through their education and occupation (438)

upper-upper - describes the top tier of social structure; also known as "old money," this group lives an aristocratic life style (437)

V

valuation effect - an effect produced by consumers when they are extremely hungry, rating as they rate food products as more desirable than when they are not (170)

value-expressive function - the function in which image appeals are useful for changing attitudes (173)

variety seeking - the desire to choose new alternatives over more familiar ones (229)

verbal compliance - a situation where someone says "yes" to a specific request (359)

verbal product placement - is when an actor references or requests a product by name; this type of placement is most common in non-visual media, such as music and books (483)

viral marketing - usually involves the Internet to facilitate the spread of word-of-mouth and spark buzz (469)

visual product placement - placing the brand on screen within the setting or background of a program (482)

vivid stimuli - stimuli that draw attention automatically and involuntarily; but unlike *salient stimuli*, vivid stimuli are attention-drawing across *all* contexts (111)

W

want-got gap - when a *discrepancy* exists between what the consumer wants the situation to be and what the situation really is (234)

wants - n*eed satisfiers* that are shaped by a consumer's personality, experiences, and culture—including marketing (237)

Weber's Law - the greater or stronger the initial stimulus is, the greater is the amount of change required for it to be noticed (102)

word-of-mouth - the act of one consumer talking to another about a brand; and it can happen face-to-face and indirectly via phone, mail, or the Internet (467)

word-of-mouth marketing - the execution of marketing tactics specially designed to generate positive word-of-mouth marketing messages and create a virus-like exponential spread of those messages throughout the population of interest (469)

working-class - described as "family folk" who depend heavily on relatives for economic and social support; also known as the "laboring class," this group has below-average education, and they typically work in average-paying, blue-collar jobs or low-paying, white-collar positions (439)

Y

Young & Rubicam Brand Asset Valuator - an instrument that uses a set of scales to measure differentiation (How unique is the brand?), relevance (How useful is the brand?), esteem (Is the brand the best?), and knowledge (Does the brand have a clear and consistent image?) (79)

Younger Boomers - born between 1956 and 1964; they came of age during the Cold War and lengthy recessions (451)

Z

Zanna and Rempel - M. P. Zanna and J. K. Rempel developed a theory suggesting that attitudes can be based on cognition (beliefs), affect (feelings, moods, and emotions), or behavior (197)

Name Index

Subject Index

Product/Company Index